Dictionary of Insurance Terms

Second Edition

Dictionary of Insurance Terms

Second Edition

Harvey W. Rubin, Ph.D., CLU, CPCU
Professor/Chair of Insurance
Department of Economics and Finance
Louisiana State University
Shreveport, Louisiana

New York • London • Toronto • Sydney

© Copyright 1991, 1987 by Barron's Educational Series, Inc.

All inquiries should be addressed to:
Barron's Educational Series, Inc.
250 Wireless Boulevard
Hauppauge, New York 11788

Library of Congress Catalog Card No. 90-47794

International Standard Book No. 0-8120-4632-3

Library of Congress Cataloging in Publication Data

Rubin, Harvey W.
    Dictionary of insurance terms / Harvey W. Rubin. —2nd ed.
      p. cm.
    ISBN 0-8120-4632-3
    1. Insurance—Dictionaries.   I. Title.
    HG8025.R83   1991
    368'.003—dc20   90-47794
                                        CIP

PRINTED IN THE UNITED STATES OF AMERICA

1234   9770   98765432

CONTENTS

PREFACE

Insurance is a financial instrument—nothing more, nothing less—which plays a critical role in both personal and business financial planning.

On the personal level, the money an individual spends for insurance over a lifetime surpasses all other types of expenditures—including the purchase of a home. Any doubt concerning this statement can be dispelled by adding up the premium payments made yearly for life insurance, health insurance, pension plan, social security, individual retirement account or Keogh Plan, automobile insurance, homeowners or tenants insurance, professional liability insurance, and umbrella liability insurance. Yet, the individual makes these expenditures usually without adequate knowledge of the insurance product purchased.

Essentially the same situation exists in the business world. Contributions paid into various insurance coverages in most instances exceed other business operating expenses. Employee benefit plan contributions alone have been estimated to range between 30–45 cents for each dollar of salary paid to an employee. When added to the cost of other business related insurance expenditures such as workers compensation, buy-sell insurance funded agreements, key person insurance, business property coverage, business liability insurance, and other business specialty insurances coverages, the total cost can be overwhelming. And, astonishingly, the business insurance purchase decision is also frequently made without sufficient basic knowledge of the various insurance products available.

Thus, one function of Barron's *Dictionary of Insurance Terms* is to serve as a reference source for individuals making personal and business insurance planning decisions. The Dictionary provides concise definitions and examples of those terms most likely to confront the insurance consumer on all levels. The insurance field is rapidly changing. More new insurance products have reached the marketplace in the last few years than in all previous years combined. The Dictionary contains definitions and illustrative examples of these ''state of the art'' offerings as well as of the traditional products. Cross references allow the reader to research variations of the terms to be defined and other relevant definitions.

Another reason for the existence of Barron's *Dictionary of Insurance Terms* is to provide a reference source for practitioners who require succinct, technically accurate answers to insurance and risk management terminology questions. Professionals in the field will find the Dictionary to be a readily accessible reference source for virtually all terms that are used in the everyday conduct of business. The spectrum of insurance activities that is covered ranges from the home office underwriting of the risk to the actual marketing and distribution of the insurance product to protect the risk.

The insurance agent may even find the Dictionary to be useful in marketing and servicing insurance products. Many clients have numerous questions concerning the characteristics of the various insurance products on the market, both new and traditional. The Dictonary can be used as a supplement to the sales literature to answer these questions as well as inquiries about servicing. Fast, accurate responses to these questions can sometimes mean the difference between closing and not closing a sale.

ACKNOWLEDGMENTS

The author would like to acknowledge the contributions made by the reviewer, Diane Orvos of the American Council of Life Insurance. Her many in-depth comments have been of great importance to the technical accuracy of the manuscript. Milton Amsel smoothed and sharpened the author's prose and suggested many meaningful changes that have greatly enhanced the final work. Don Reis and Sally Strauss of Barron's have been invaluable in bringing the manuscript to its final form. Gen Nash's highly professional commitment to typing and correcting the author's many errors along the way has made the presentation of the manuscript possible. Finally, the author wishes to thank his wife, Ofie, and son, Jack, for continuing to be an inspiration.

Harvey W. Rubin

HOW TO USE THIS BOOK EFFECTIVELY

Alphabetization: All entries are alphabetized by letter rather than by word, so that multiple-word terms are treated as single words. For example, **AGE SETBACK** follows **AGENT OF RECORD**, and **ALL RISKS** follows **ALLOCATION OF ASSETS.** In some cases (such as **NAIC** acts and regulations), abbreviations appear as entries in the main text, in addition to appearing in the back of the book in the separate listing of Abbreviations and Acronyms. This occurs when the short form, rather than the formal name, predominates in the common usage of the field. For example, **NAIC** is commonly used in speaking of the "National Association of Insurance Commissioners"; thus, the entry is at **NAIC.** Numbers in entry titles and the ampersand are alphabetized as if they were spelled out.

Many words have distinctly different meanings, depending upon the context in which they are used. The various meanings of a term are listed by numerical or functional subheading. Readers must determine the context that is relevant to their purpose.

Abbreviations and Acronyms: A separate list of abbreviations and acronyms follows the Dictionary.

Cross-References: To add to your understanding of a term, related or contrasting terms are sometimes cross-referenced. The cross-referenced term will appear in SMALL CAPITALS either in the body of the entry (or subentry) or at the end. These terms will be printed in SMALL CAPITALS only the first time they appear in the text. Where an entry is fully defined by another term, a reference rather than a definition is provided—for example: **PRODUCER** *see* AGENT.

Italics: Italic type is generally used to highlight the fact that a word or phrase has a special meaning to the trade. Italics are also used for the titles of publications.

Parentheses: Parentheses are used in entry titles for two reasons. The first is to indicate that another term has a meaning identical or very closely related to that of the entry word; for exmaple, **BENEFITS OF BUSINESS LIFE AND HEALTH INSURANCE (KEY PERSON INSURANCE).** The second reason is to indicate that an abbreviation is used with about the same frequency as the term itself; for example, **FEDERAL TRADE COMMISSION (FTC).**

Special Definitions: Organizations and associations that play an active role in the field are included in the Dictionary along with a brief statement of their mission.

A

AAM *see* ASSOCIATE IN AUTOMATION MANAGEMENT (AAM).

ABANDONMENT AND SALVAGE legal status giving an insurance company all rights to an insured's property. The ABANDONMENT CLAUSE is usually found in MARINE INSURANCE and not in other property insurance policies such as the HOMEOWNERS INSURANCE POLICY and the SPECIAL MULTIPERIL INSURANCE (SMP) policy. An insured may wish to abandon the hull of a ship if the cost of protecting it exceeds its value. The insured must notify the insurance company of its intent to abandon property but the company is under no obligation to accept the abandoned property.

ABANDONMENT CLAUSE in marine insurance, clause giving an insured the right to abandon lost or damaged property and still claim full settlement from an insurer (subject to certain restrictions). Two types of losses are provided for under abandonment clauses.
   1. *Actual total loss*: property so badly damaged it is unrepairable or unrecoverable; causes include fire, sinking, windstorm damage, and mysterious disappearance. For example, until the 1980s the *Titanic*, which sank off Newfoundland in 1912, was deemed to be unrecoverable and the Commercial Union Insurance Company had paid its owners for their loss due to sinking. Owners of ships that mysteriously disappeared in the Bermuda Triangle have been able to collect insurance proceeds. Disappearance of pleasure craft due to drug pirates has resulted in indemnification of owners through insurance proceeds.
   2. *Constructive total loss*: property so badly damaged that the cost of its rehabilitation would be more than its restored value. For example, a ship and/or its cargo is damaged to such a degree that the cost of repair would exceed its restored value. The insured can abandon the property if (a) repair costs are greater than 50% of the value of the property after it has been repaired and (b) the insurance company agrees to the insured's intent to abandon.

ABSOLUTE ASSIGNMENT *see* ASSIGNMENT CLAUSE.

ABSOLUTE BENEFICIARY *see* BENEFICIARY; BENEFICIARY CLAUSE.

ABSOLUTE LIABILITY liability without fault; also known as *liability without regard to fault* or *strict liability*. Absolute liability is imposed in various states when actions of an individual or business are deemed contrary to public policy, even though an action may not have been intentional or negligent. For example, in product liability, manufacturers and retailers have been held strictly liable for products that have caused injuries and have been shown to be defective, even though the manufacturer or retailer was not proven to be at fault or negligent. In many states the owner of an animal is held strictly liable for injuries it may cause, even though it does not have a past history of violence.

ABUSIVE TAX SHELTER illegal tax deduction (as determined by the Internal Revenue Service) taken under the auspices of a limited partnership. One abuse of taxes is inflating the value of purchased assets far beyond their fair market value. Once the IRS determines that tax deductions are illegal, participants in the limited partnership are subject to the payment of back taxes, interest due on the back taxes, and penalties.

ACCELERATED DEPRECIATION method in which larger amounts of depreciation are taken in the beginning years of the life of an asset and smaller amounts in later years. The objective is to defer taxes legally, thereby allowing funds to be retained by a business to finance growth.

ACCELERATED OPTION life insurance POLICY PROVISION under which the POLICYHOLDER may apply the accumulated cash value, in the form of a single premium payment, to pay up the policy or to mature the policy as an endowment.

ACCELERATION LIFE INSURANCE policy under which a portion of the DEATH BENEFIT (generally 25%) becomes payable to the insured for a specified medical condition prior to death. The purpose of the accelerated death benefit is to provide funds necessary to finance medical costs to extend the life of the insured. Upon proof of a specified medical condition, the insurance company will pay 25% of the death benefit. When the insured dies, the remainder of the death benefit is paid to the BENEFICIARY, just as under a traditional life insurance policy.

ACCELERATIVE ENDOWMENT life insurance policy option under which the DIVIDENDS which have ACCRUED may be applied to mature the policy as ENDOWMENT INSURANCE.

ACCEPTANCE agreement to an offer, in contract law, thus forming a contract. For insurance contracts, the insurer usually acknowledges willingness to underwrite a risk by issuing a policy in exchange for a premium from an applicant.

ACCIDENT unexpected, unforeseen event not under the control of an insured and resulting in a loss. The insured cannot purposefully cause the loss to happen; the loss must be due to pure chance according to the odds of the laws of probability. For example, under a PERSONAL AUTOMOBILE POLICY (PAP) if an accident occurs, the insured is covered for loss due to his/her negligent act or omissions resulting in bodily injury or property damage to another party.

ACCIDENTAL DEATH AND DISMEMBERMENT INSURANCE form of accident insurance which indemnifies or pays a stated benefit to insured or his/her beneficiary in the event of bodily injury or death due to accidental means (other than natural causes). For example, an insured's arm is severed in an accident. A predetermined schedule of payment is used to compensate the insured for this particular loss. The schedule also lists the sums payable for other parts of the body that may be lost, or for death by accident.

ACCIDENTAL DEATH BENEFIT *see* ACCIDENTAL DEATH CLAUSE; RIDERS, LIFE POLICIES.

ACCIDENTAL DEATH CLAUSE in a life insurance policy, benefit in addition to the death benefit paid to the beneficiary, should death occur due to an accident. In *double indemnity*, twice the face value of the policy will be paid to the beneficiary; in *triple indemnity,* three times the face value is payable. Accidental death caused by war, aviation except as a passenger on a regularly scheduled airline, and illegal activities are generally excluded. Time and age limits are usually applicable, as for example, the insured must die within 90 days of the accident and be age 60 or less.

ACCIDENTAL DEATH INSURANCE coverage in the event of death due to accident, usually in combination with dismemberment insurance. If death is due to accident, payment is made to the insured's beneficiary; if bodily injury is the result of an accident (such as the loss of a limb), the insured receives a specified sum. *See also* ACCIDENTAL DEATH CLAUSE.

ACCIDENTAL MEANS unexpected, unforeseen event not under the control of the insured that results in bodily injury.

ACCIDENT AND HEALTH INSURANCE coverage for accidental injury, accidental death, or sickness; also called *Accident and Sickness Insurance*. Benefits include paid hospital expenses, medical expenses, surgical expenses and income payments. *See also* GROUP HEALTH INSURANCE; HEALTH INSURANCE.

ACCIDENT AND SICKNESS INSURANCE phrase formerly used to describe coverage for *perils* of accident and sickness. For descriptions of current terms, *see also* ACCIDENT AND HEALTH INSURANCE; DISABILITY INSURANCE; GROUP DISABILITY INSURANCE; GROUP HEALTH INSURANCE; HEALTH MAINTENANCE ORGANIZATION (HMO).

ACCIDENT FREQUENCY number of times an accident occurs. Used in predicting losses upon which premiums are based.

ACCIDENT INSURANCE coverage for bodily injury and/or death resulting from accidental means (other than natural causes). For example, an insured is critically injured in an accident. Accident insurance can provide income and/or a death benefit if death ensues.

ACCIDENT PREVENTION *see* ENGINEERING APPROACH; HUMAN APPROACH.

ACCIDENT RATE *see* ACCIDENT FREQUENCY.

ACCIDENT SEVERITY extent of the loss caused by accidents. Used in predicting the dollar amount of losses upon which the premiums are based.

ACCIDENT-YEAR STATISTICS record of losses and premiums received for accident coverage within a 12-month period. These statistics show the percentage of each premium received which is being paid out in claims and enables the establishment of a basic premium reflecting the pure cost of protection. The trend line generated by the record of losses is an important statistical tool for predicting future losses.

ACCOMMODATION LINE agreement by an insurance company to underwrite business submitted by an AGENT or BROKER even though that business is *substandard*. The object is to continue to attract profitable business of that agent.

ACCOUNTANTS LIABILITY INSURANCE *see* ACCOUNTANTS PROFESSIONAL LIABILITY INSURANCE.

ACCOUNTANTS PROFESSIONAL LIABILITY INSURANCE insurance for accountants covering liability lawsuits arising from their professional activities. For example, an investor bases a buying decision on the balance sheet of a company's annual statement. The figures later prove fallacious and not according to GENERALLY ACCEPTABLE ACCOUNTING PRINCIPLES (GAAP). The accountant could be found liable for his professional actions, and would be covered by this policy. However, if the accountant ran over someone or damaged property with a car, this policy would not provide coverage.

ACCOUNT CURRENT financial statement, issued by the INSURANCE COMPANY on a monthly basis to its agents, showing for each agent his or her commissions earned, premiums written, policy cancellations, and any policy endorsements.

ACCOUNTING *see* GENERALLY ACCEPTED ACCOUNTING PRINCIPLES (GAAP).

ACCOUNTS RECEIVABLE INSURANCE coverage when business records are destroyed by an insured peril and the business cannot collect money owed. The policy covers these uncollectible sums plus the expense of record reconstruction and extra collection fees. It does not insure the physical value of the records themselves such as the paper or computer disks and tapes.

ACCOUNTANTS REPORT *see* STATEMENT OF OPINION (ACCOUNTANTS REPORT, AUDITORS REPORT).

ACCREDITED ADVISOR IN INSURANCE (AAI) professional designation earned after the successful completion of three national examinations given by the INSURANCE INSTITUTE OF AMERICA (IIA). Covers such areas of expertise as insurance production (insurance sales, exposure identification, legal liability, personal lines insurance, commercial lines insurance); multiple-lines insurance production; and agency operations and sales management. Program of study is recommended for individuals who have production responsibilities.

ACCRUE to accumulate. For example, under one of the dividend options of a participating life insurance policy, dividends can accumulate at interest by leaving them with the insurance company; cash values of life insurance accumulate at a given rate; employee retirement credits for pension benefits accumulate at a stipulated rate.

ACCRUED BENEFIT COST METHOD actuarial method of crediting retirement benefits earned and the costs associated with these earned retirement benefits. An increment (unit) of benefit is credited for each year of recognized service which an employee has earned. Then the present value of these benefits (including the employee's life expectancy) is calculated and assigned to the year earned. The benefit earned by the employee can take the form of a flat dollar amount or a percentage of compensation. For example, this may work out to 1½% of an employee's compensation being credited to the employee's account for each year of recognized service.

ACCUMULATION BENEFITS accrual or addition to life insurance benefits. *See also* ACCRUE.

ACCUMULATION PERIOD time frame during which an ANNUITANT makes premium payments to an insurance company. The obligations of the company to the annuitant during this period depend on whether a PURE ANNUITY or REFUND ANNUITY is involved. Many factors enter an annuity purchase, but some experts suggest a pure annuity to minimize cost and if there are no dependents. In other circumstances a refund annuity might be considered. *See also* ANNUITY.

ACQUIRED IMMUNODEFICIENCY SYNDROME (AIDS) condition characterized by illnesses indicative of reduced immune responsiveness in otherwise healthy individuals. Viral organisms dubbed HTLVIII (for human T lymphotrophic virus type III) and LAV (for lymphadenopathy-associated virus), respectively, are the putative causative agents of this destruction of bodily defenses. Together, these viral organisms have become known as *human immunodeficiency virus (HIV)*. The HIV infection is the initial event in the course of a disease which culminates in AIDS in some of its victims.

HIV is a member of the class of RNA viruses known as *retroviruses,* identifiable by their use of the enzyme *reverse transcriptase.* This enzyme permits retroviruses to replicate their own genetic information, utilizing mammalian host cell DNA to produce the new viral RNA necessary for the assembly of new organisms. Reverse transcriptase also allows the virus to incorporate its genetic material into that of the host. In this manner the virus may "immortalize" itself by lying dormant within the host genome while remaining capable of producing new viral organisms at a future time.

HIV infection begins with viral penetration of lymphocytes and monocytes, the white blood cells involved in immune defense. The first phase of the infection frequently causes an illness with symptoms similar to those produced by infectious mononucleosis. After days or weeks of mild illness, some patients appear to recover. In the others, the viral destruction of host cells continues unabated with the virus infecting other tissues, including cells in the brain. After a latent phase, which varies with age, degree of immune responsiveness, and the number of viral particles producing the initial infection, the patient begins to manifest signs and symptoms of immune system damage. These late sequelae of HIV infection include unexplained fevers, lymph node enlargement, persistent infections with fungi or viruses, and unexplained weight loss. When these symptoms fulfill specific criteria, they are referred to as the *AIDS-related complex,* or *ARC*. Only the patients who develop the most severe immune system damage, resulting in infections such as *Pneumocystis carinii* pneumonia (PCP) or unusual cancers like Kaposi's sarcoma, are classified as having AIDS.

The direct impact of the AIDS virus is and will be felt by both the property and casualty insurance and the life and health insurance branches.

Property and Casualty Insurance

From a property and casualty insurance perspective, the AIDS issue could impact the liability sections of the homeowners insurance policy, automobile insurance policies (both personal and business), commercial general liability (CGL) policy, and workers compensation policy:

1. HOMEOWNERS INSURANCE POLICY The INSURANCE SERVICES OFFICE (ISO) homeowners insurance policy form has a communicable disease endorsement EXCLUSION. Most property and casualty companies use this form either in total or with minor modification. Since this exclusion to date has not been subject to an adverse ruling by a court of law, it may be that the homeowners policy does not have an AIDS EXPOSURE.

2. AUTOMOBILE INSURANCE policies (both personal and business) An AIDS exposure could result (these policies do not have a communicable disease endorsement exclusion) because of negligent acts and/or omissions of a driver resulting in:

(a) an injured party contracting AIDS through a blood transfusion necessitated by an accident and then bringing suit against the driver, who is found negligent under the TORT LIABILITY system. In a similar circumstance, an injured party's open wound comes into contact with an open wound of another injured party who has AIDS, with an ensuing suit against the negligent driver. Certainly, the wounds would not have come into contact if the accident had not occurred.

(b) the activation of a previously dormant AIDS virus (as discussed above, the virus may "immortalize" itself by lying dormant within the host genome while remaining capable of producing new viral organisms at a future time) in an injured party, with the injured party bringing suit against the driver whose acts and/or omissions are deemed to be negligent by a court of law. Had the catalyst accident not occurred, the AIDS virus would have remained dormant.

3. COMMERCIAL GENERAL LIABILITY (CGL) policy An AIDS exposure may arise because of negligent acts of employees or circumstances occurring on a business' property:

(a) An AIDS exposure could result in the event that an AIDS-infected employee contaminates a product and/or service being provided to a customer or fellow employee, and the customer or fellow employee brings suit against the business. For example, the infected employee may have a cut finger and drops of his or her blood may accidentally become mixed with the food being consumed by a customer or fellow employee. Or the infected employee could intentionally contaminate the food with his or her body fluid as a vengeful act.

(b) An AIDS exposure could result in the event that a sexual assault by an AIDS-infected assailant (regardless of whether or not the assailant is an employee) is incurred by a customer while visiting the premises of the business and the injured customer brings suit against the business. It is the responsibility of the business to render its premises safe for the invited customer. The Connie Francis case is the precedent sexual assault case for this exposure. A similar circumstance could result if an AIDS-infected assailant assaults an employee.

(c) An AIDS exposure could result in the event that a business fails to maintain the confidentiality of an AIDS-infected employee's personnel file and the employee brings suit against the business for the tort acts of libel, slander, and invasion of privacy.

4. WORKERS COMPENSATION policy An AIDS exposure could result if an employee injured at work receives a blood transfusion from a fellow employee who has AIDS. Is the transmission of AIDS in this manner a job-related injury, thus qualifying the injured employee for benefits under workers compensation? Certainly the injured employee would not have required the blood transfusion had the injury not occurred at work.

In another situation, two or more employees may be injured in a common accident, resulting in open wounds of various employees coming into contact. If at least one of the injured employees is a carrier of the AIDS virus, several employees could become infected. The AIDS virus is most likely to be spread as the result of close contact with blood, blood products, or semen from an infected person. Is this scenario not a classic case for a workers compensation claim?

In each of the two preceding examples, assume that the employer was aware of the AIDS condition of the employee(s) prior to the accident and kept this information confidential so as not to invade the privacy of the employee(s). In this instance, could not the newly AIDS-infected employee(s) seek damages for benefits against the employer beyond that provided by workers compensation? Certainly the employer was aware of an inherently potentially dangerous situation in the workplace and took no actions to alleviate the situation or render it harmless. Is not a similar circumstance the basis for the employer tort cases for job-related injuries resulting from exposure to asbestos?

Life and Health Insurance

AIDS-related deaths could have a significant impact on the LIFE INSURANCE and HEALTH INSURANCE industries as these deaths affect the normal claims pattern for GROUP LIFE INSURANCE and INDIVIDUAL LIFE INSURANCE:

1. *Group Life, Medical, and Disability Insurance* If the insurance policy is a true group policy, all applicants must be accepted during the open enrollment period. Thus a person who has AIDS would automatically be insured.

If, however, there are a significant number of claims under the group policy, the insurance company can reflect this adverse experience in next year's premium rates. The insurance company also has the option of not renewing the group's coverage.

There is also a limit on the DEATH BENEFIT available under group policies. For example, employee group life policies limit the coverage per employee to a multiple (usually twice) of the employee's annual salary. This limitation reduces somewhat the ADVERSE SELECTION associated with the AIDS-infected employee opting for higher limits of coverage.

2. *Individual Life, Medical, and Disability Insurance* In underwriting individual coverages (unlike group insurance, where the factors of age, sex, and industry classification only are considered) numerous factors are evaluated, to include age, sex, personal health record, family health, occupation, vocation, hobbies, habits such as chemical abuse, life-style, and so forth. These factors undergo close scrutiny, especially when the higher limits of coverage are applied for. However, after the applicant becomes an INSURED, he or she could contact AIDS, an eventuality which was not included in the PREMIUM rate. Individual life insurance contracts (ordinary policies and even term insurance, which can be renewed and converted at the option of the insured) are contracts for life. Thus, once the insurer accepts the applicant for coverage, the insurer is at the mercy of any future AIDS epidemic.

Some life insurance policies have POLICY PURCHASE OPTIONS (PPO), whereby the insured can automatically increase the limits of coverage when certain events occur, such as every fifth policy anniversary. The AIDS paitent then could automatically increase his or her coverage over various periods of time. Also, for dividend-paying policies the AIDS patient could use the dividends to automatically purchase paid-up additions to his or her policy without having to take a physical or answer any medical-related questions (in essence, this is GUARANTEED INSURABILITY). Once again, the insurer has no control over these events or distributions.

For life insurance policies already in existence, AIDS-related questions were not asked on the APPLICATION. Thus, many companies have huge blocks of business which may be susceptible to the effects of the AIDS epidemic.

ACQUISITION COST expense of soliciting and placing new insurance business on a company's books. It includes agent's commissions, underwriting expenses, medical and credit report fees, and marketing support services. Because of competition, significant efforts are made by insurance companies to lower acquisition costs. Traditional CAPTIVE AGENT companies have often turned to brokerage as additional distribution or sole distribution channels for this reason.

ACTIVE RETENTION *see* SELF INSURANCE.

ACT OF GOD natural occurrence beyond human control or influence. Such acts of nature include hurricanes, earthquakes, and floods.

ACTS performance of a deed or function. Certain acts are prohibited from coverage in insurance. For example, if the insured commits a felony, the insured's beneficiary cannot collect under the accidental death provision of a life insurance policy. Intentional destruction of an insured's property by the insured or someone hired by an insured to destroy the property is a prohibited act under property insurance, and an insurance policy will not indemnify the insured for losses incurred.

ACTUAL CASH VALUE cost of replacing damaged or destroyed property with comparable new property, minus depreciation and obsolescence. For example, a 10-year-old living room sofa will not be replaced at current full value because of a decade of depreciation. The actual cash value clause is common in property insurance contracts. In some instances artistic or antique property may appreciate over time. To receive full coverage such items must be specifically scheduled in a policy.

ACTUAL TOTAL LOSS *see* TOTAL LOSS.

ACTUARIAL *see* ACTUARIAL SCIENCE; ACTUARY.

ACTUARIAL ADJUSTMENT modification in premiums, reserves, and other values to reflect actual loss experience and expenses and expected benefits to be paid.

ACTUARIAL CONSULTANT independent advisor to insurance companies, corporations, Federal, state, and local governments, and labor unions on actuarial matters. These include evaluation of the liabilities of small insurance companies, estimates of pension plan liabilities and the design of such plans, appearance as an expert witness giving testimony concerning lost income due to an accident, and the design of information systems. *See also* ACTUARIAL SCIENCE; ACTUARY.

ACTUARIAL COST METHODS system for calculating the relationship between a pension plan's present cost and its present future benefits. This relationship shows the extent to which a pension plan's benefits are funded. The objective is to identify on a year-by-year basis the cost of benefits accrued for the particular year. To illustrate, a relationship of 1.0 shows that there is 100% funding available for the pension plan's benefits.

ACTUARIAL EQUIVALENT mathematical determination based on the expectation of loss and the benefits to be paid in such an eventuality. The premium charged will vary directly with the probability of loss.

ACTUARIAL GAINS AND LOSSES experience as it relates to the annual costs associated with a pension plan. In calculating premiums due under a pension plan, basic assumptions must be made concerning future loss experience and expenses. Actual loss experience can prove to be better or worse than envisioned. If the experience is better, the result is an *actuarial gain*. If the experience is worse, the result is an *actuarial loss*.

ACTUARIAL RATE rate based on historical loss experience, from which future loss experience is predicted. *See also* ACTUARIAL EQUIVALENT; ACTUARIAL SCIENCE; RATE MAKING.

ACTUARIAL SCIENCE branch of knowledge dealing with the mathematics of insurance, including probabilities. It is used in ensuring that risks are carefully evaluated, that adequate premiums are charged for risks underwritten, and that adequate provision is made for future payments of benefits.

ACTUARY mathematician in the insurance field. Actuaries conduct various statistical studies; construct MORBIDITY and MORTALITY TABLES; calculate premiums, reserves and dividends for participating policies; develop products; construct annual reports in compliance with numerous regulatory requirements; and in many companies oversee the general financial function. The successful actuary has a strong general business background as well as mathematical ability. Professional actuarial associations provide actuarial qualification examinations.

ACTUARY, ENROLLED individual who has met professional standards of the Internal Revenue Service and the Department of Labor for signing the actuarial reports required by the Employee Retirement Security Act of 1974—Title II. An enrolled actuary may certify annually that benefit cost and funding requirements of a pension plan have been calculated according to accepted actuarial principles as a best estimate of expected experience of the pension plan.

ACV *see* ACTUAL CASH VALUE.

ADDITIONAL DEATH BENEFIT extra layer of life insurance coverage. This term is often applied to double indemnity. For example, some life insurance policies provide a death benefit of a multiple of the face value if the insured dies between certain ages when dependent children may still be living at home. *See also* ACCIDENTAL DEATH CLAUSE.

ADDITIONAL DEPOSIT PRIVILEGE clause in some CURRENT ASSUMPTION WHOLE LIFE INSURANCE policies such as UNIVERSAL LIFE INSURANCE which allows unscheduled premiums to be paid at any time prior to the policy's maturity date, provided there is no outstanding loan. If there is a loan, additional deposits will be first applied against the loan. Most policies have a minimum that will be accepted as an additional deposit, such as $1000.

ADDITIONAL INSURED individual added to a life insurance policy other than the insured named in the policy. For example, an insured father can have a dependent son and daughter added to the policy as additional insureds. In many instances, adding an additional insured to an existing policy is less expensive than purchasing a separate policy for that insured.

In property and liability insurance: another person, firm or other entity enjoying the same protection as the named insured.

ADDITIONAL INTEREST *see* ADDITIONAL INSURED.

ADDITIONAL LIVING EXPENSE INSURANCE coverage under a *Homeowners, Condominium, and Renters* policy, which reimburses costs of residing in a temporary location until the insured's home can be made whole again. It usually provides living expenses of from 10–20% of the structural coverage on the home.

ADDITIONAL LIVING EXPENSE LOSS *see* ADDITIONAL LIVING EXPENSE INSURANCE.

ADEQUACY *see* RATE MAKING.

ADEQUACY, LIFE INSURANCE *see* HUMAN LIFE VALUE APPROACH (EVOIL); NEEDS APPROACH.

ADHESION INSURANCE CONTRACT agreement prepared by an insurance company and offered to prospective insureds on a take-it-or-leave-it basis. If the contracts are misinterpreted by insureds, courts have ruled in their favor since the insureds had no input into the contract. All insurance contracts have been deemed by courts to be contracts of adhesion.

ADJACENT that which adjoins. Most property insurance policies such as the HOMEOWNERS INSURANCE POLICY provide structural coverage on an adjacent building on the same basis as the primary building.

ADJOINING *see* ADJACENT.

ADJUSTABLE LIFE INSURANCE coverage under which the face value, premiums, and plan of insurance can be changed at the discretion of the *policyowner* in the following manner, without additional policies being issued:
1. *face value* can be increased or decreased (to increase coverage, the insured must furnish evidence of insurability). The resultant size of the cash value will depend on the amount of face value and premium.
2. *premiums* and length of time they are to be paid can be increased or decreased. Unscheduled premiums can be paid on a lump sum basis. Premiums paid on an adjusted basis can either lengthen or shorten the time the protection element will be in force, as well as lengthen or shorten the period for making premium payments. For example, assume that John, who is 28, buys a $100,000 adjustable term life policy to age 65 with an annual premium of $1250. As his career prospers, he finds at age 32 that he can double the annual

premium payment to $2500. This increase may change the original term amount to a fully paid-up life policy at age 65. With time, John might experience economic hardship and have to decrease his annual payment by two thirds. This could result in changing the paid-up-at-65 policy back to a term policy to age 65. Thus, at any time the policy can be either *ordinary life* or *term. See also* UNIVERSAL LIFE INSURANCE.

ADJUSTABLE PREMIUM premium that can vary up or down. Some life insurance policies permit the company to change the premiums after the policy is in force, depending on mortality experience, expenses, and investment returns. If profits are sufficient, premiums can be reduced; if not, they can be raised to specific maximums.

ADJUSTED NET WORTH value of an insurance company or other company that consists of capital and surplus and an estimated value for business on the company's books.

ADJUSTED UNDERWRITING PROFIT *see* UNDERWRITING GAIN (LOSS).

ADJUSTER individual employed by a property and casualty insurance company to settle on its behalf claims brought by insureds. The adjuster evaluates the merits of each claim and makes recommendations to the insurance company. *See also* INDEPENDENT ADJUSTER.

ADJUSTER, AVERAGE *see* AVERAGE ADJUSTER.

ADJUSTER, INDEPENDENT *see* INDEPENDENT ADJUSTER.

ADJUSTER, PUBLIC *see* PUBLIC ADJUSTER.

ADJUSTER, STAFF employee of an insurance company who assesses insurance coverage for property claimed to be damaged and determines the insurance proceeds that might be payable for the claim. A *fee adjuster* works for himself and does claims adjustments on a fee basis.

ADJUSTMENT BUREAU company organized with the business objective of providing claims adjustment services to insurance companies that do not have an internal claims department. *See also* ADJUSTER, STAFF.

ADJUSTMENT INCOME income payable to a surviving spouse or other beneficiary upon the death of the primary wage earner to bridge the gap until the beneficiary is self-sufficient. For example, income can be provided for a limited period of time until a widow can regain emotional stability, receive career guidance, as well as training, to establish a permanent career if necessary. The need for adjustment income is a significant consideration in deciding how much life insurance to purchase.

ADMINISTERING AGENCY employer using a self-administered insurance plan; or an insurer that administers a group employee benefit plan. In an employer administered plan, the employer maintains all required administrative records based on demographic and other information from the employer's monthly reports.

ADMINISTRATION performance of management functions associated with administering an EMPLOYEE BENEFIT INSURANCE PLAN, to include actuarial services, booklet and contract plan designing, billing, accounting, and establishing evidence of insurability for the plan participants. *See also* ADMINISTERING AGENCY; ADMINISTRATIVE CHARGE; ADMINISTRATIVE SERVICES ONLY (ASO).

ADMINISTRATION BOND coverage that guarantees that the executor or administrator of an estate will conduct his or her duties according to the provisions of the will and the legal requirements of the jurisdiction. If dishonest acts by the executor or administrator result in financial loss to the estate, the bond will act as an INDEMNITOR to the estate. This bond is posted by the executor or administrator of the estate.

ADMINISTRATIVE CHARGE billing by an ADMINISTERING AGENCY for expenses associated with administering a group employee benefit plan.

ADMINISTRATIVE LAW law created by government regulatory agencies, such as the office of the COMMISSIONER OF INSURANCE, through decisions, orders, regulations, and rules. For example, RATE MAKING hearings conducted by the insurance commissioner are common. Based on the findings of the hearings, rate increases may or may not be granted.

ADMINISTRATIVE SERVICES ONLY (ASO) services provided in an employee benefit plan such as a PENSION PLAN. An employer provides the clerical staff to operate the plan, in effect acting as custodian. The trustee provides direction for investment of the plan's funds, usually in a self-directed investment account. Trustee plans are gaining in popularity as both the employer and employees seek more control over pension funds investments. In a self-insured property or liability plan the group may have an ASO contract with an insurance company or a third-party administrator to handle claims processing and administration.

ADMINISTRATOR court-appointed person to manage the estate of a deceased individual who declared no EXECUTOR or EXECUTRIX. This person so appointed acts in a FIDUCIARY capacity with regard to that estate.

ADMIRALTY LIABILITY maritime acts resulting in a LIABILITY circumstance falling under COMMON LAW and statutory law. *See also* JONES ACT (MERCHANT MARINE ACT).

ADMIRALTY PROCEEDING conducting of maritime suits involving OCEAN MARINE INSURANCE policy claims before an admiralty court.

ADMITTED ASSETS assets permitted by state law to be included in an insurance company's ANNUAL STATEMENT. These assets are an important factor when regulators measure insurance company solvency. They include mortgages, stocks, bonds, and real estate. Historically, a large part of admitted assets consisted of long term mortgages, but with the advent of CURRENT ASSUMPTION WHOLE LIFE INSURANCE policies, short term financial instruments can be used to make up a large part of admitted assets.

ADMITTED COMPANY life insurance company or property and casualty insurance company licensed by a particular state to conduct business there. The company is subject to the state insurance code governing such aspects as company reserves and advertising. If an insurance company is not licensed by a given state or if its license is terminated, the company can no longer conduct insurance business in that state.

ADVANCED FUNDED PENSION PLAN retirement plan in which money is currently allocated to fund an employee's pension. *See also* ALLOCATED FUNDING INSTRUMENT; UNALLOCATED FUNDING INSTRUMENT.

ADVANCED LIFE UNDERWRITING process of analyzing complex personal and business cases according to tax and estate planning requirements to determine life insurance needs. The family life agent or underwriter normally does not become involved in complex business or personal cases, but draws on the expertise of the advanced life underwriter when needed.

ADVANCE FUNDING payment of premiums before their due date. In pension plans, premium payments are allocated to the payment of future benefits prior to benefits becoming payable. *See also* ADVANCED FUNDED PENSION PLAN.

ADVANCE PAYMENTS payments made to the insured by the insurance company before the settlement date. For example, a claim is scheduled to be settled on June 1, 1987, but the insurance company pays the claimant prior to that date.

ADVANCE PREMIUM premium paid before the due date. For example, a premium is due on July 1, 1987, but the insured actually makes the premium payment on January 1, 1987, receiving a premium discount.

ADVERSE SELECTION process in life insurance by which an applicant who is uninsurable, or is a greater than average risk, seeks to obtain a policy from a company at a standard premium rate. Life insurance companies carefully screen applicants for this reason, since their premiums are based on policyholders in average good health and in nonhazardous occupations.

ADVERTISERS LIABILITY INSURANCE coverage for an advertiser's negligent acts and/or omissions in advertising (both oral and written) that may result in a civil suit for libel, slander, defamation of character, or copyright infringement.

ADVERTISING, INSURANCE COMPANY highly visible form of marketing communication with the public with these objectives: (1) encourage agents and brokers to sell insurance company products, (2) predispose customers to be receptive to sales calls, (3) enhance an insurance company's public image, (4) support introduction of new products, and (5) influence public and legislative opinions on issues of importance to the insurance industry. *Product advertising* describes particular products and why they would be beneficial. *Institutional advertising* describes the financial strength and the stability of a company. Depending on target market and size, company advertising may be national, local, or cooperative (a joint venture using both company and agency dollars).

ADVISORY COMMITTEE group that advises on employee benefit plans as to amount of benefits to be paid, how benefits are to be financed, and how employees are to qualify for benefits (VESTING *requirements*). An advisory committee only suggests; it does not have line authority.

AFFILIATED COMPANIES associated insurers that are under common stock ownership or interlocking directorates. Such an arrangement makes it easier to exchange insurance products for sale to the consumer, reduces duplication of efforts, and lowers product research and development costs.

AFFIRMATIVE WARRANTY *see* WARRANTY.

AGE CHANGE date, in insurance, on which a person becomes one year older. Depending on the insurance company, premiums in life and health insurance manuals are figured to the age-nearest-birthday or age-last-birthday.

AGE LIMITS maximum age of an applicant or insured beyond which an insurance company will not initially underwrite a risk or continue to insure it. For example, under some forms of RENEWABLE TERM LIFE INSURANCE, coverage will not be renewed beyond age 60.

AGENCY individuals under common management whose goal is to sell and service insurance. Office may be managed by a GENERAL AGENT or *branch manager. See also* CAPTIVE INSURANCE COMPANY; INDEPENDENT AGENCY SYSTEM.

AGENCY AGREEMENT *see* AGENCY CONTRACT.

AGENCY BY ESTOPPEL *see* ESTOPPEL.

AGENCY BY RATIFICATION confirmation by an insurance company of the acts of its AGENT, regardless of whether or not these acts were committed within the limit of authority granted the agent by the company. By so ratifying the agent's acts, the company becomes responsible for consequences arising from these acts. For example, if the insurance company, with full knowledge of the agent's misdeeds in soliciting the application and the premium from the PROSPECT, accepts the premium for the policy from the agent, this acceptance constitutes ratification of the act of the agent.

AGENCY CONTRACT (AGENCY AGREEMENT) rules of conduct and commissions paid to agents. For example, under the rules of conduct agents may be required to submit all of their business to only that agency. The contract also lists commission schedules.

AGENCY MANAGER individual in charge of an insurance company agency. The manager is an employee of the company and is usually compensated on a salary-and-bonus basis, the latter relating to premium volume production of all the agents in the agency. He or she is responsible for hiring and training agents.

AGENCY PLANT insurance company's total number of agents.

AGENCY SYSTEM *see* AGENT; INDEPENDENT AGENCY SYSTEM.

AGENT individual who sells and services insurance policies in either of two classifications:
  1. *Independent agent* represents at least two insurance companies and (at least in theory) services clients by searching the market for the most advantageous price for the most coverage. The agent's commission is a percentage of each premium paid and includes a fee for servicing the insured's policy. *See also* AMERICAN AGENCY SYSTEM.
  2. *Direct writer* represents only one company and sells only its policies. This agent is paid on a commission basis in much the same manner as the independent agent.

AGENT COMMISSION *see* COMMISSION.

AGENT, GENERAL *see* GENERAL AGENT (GA).

AGENT, INDEPENDENT *see* INDEPENDENT AGENT.

AGENT LICENSE *see* LICENSING OF AGENTS AND BROKERS.

AGENT OF RECORD individual who has a contractual agreement with a policyowner. The agent of record has a legal right to commissions from the insurance policy.

AGENT, POLICYWRITING agent with the authority from an insurance company to prepare and to place into business an insurance policy.

AGENT, RECORDING *see* AGENT OF RECORD.

AGENT'S AUTHORITY authority derived from an agent's contract with an insurance company. *See also* APPARENT AGENCY (AUTHORITY).

AGENT'S BALANCE statement showing the amount of money owed the agent by the insurance company, according to the contract he or she has with the insurance company.

AGENT, SPECIAL *see* SPECIAL AGENT.

AGENT'S QUALIFICATION LAWS legislation establishing the minimum education and experience level required by the state as a prerequisite for a person to become a licensed AGENT. *See also* LICENSE; LICENSING OF AGENTS AND BROKERS.

AGENT, STATE *see* STATE AGENT.

AGE SETBACK subtraction of a number of years from a standard table of life insurance rates under the assumption that a particular group—women—outlive men and presumably will be paying premiums for **a** longer time. For example, a 38-year-old woman may pay the same premiums as a 35-year-old man. Age setback is a women's rights issue, with at least one state having legislated that men and women the same age must be charged the same rates for the life insurance they buy.

AGGREGATE ANNUAL DEDUCTIBLE deductible that applies for the year. For example, a business pays for the first $40,000 of losses incurred during the year and the insurance company pays for all losses above that amount up to the LIMIT OF RECOVERY stated in the policy.

AGGREGATE EXCESS CONTRACT policy in which an insurer agrees to pay property or liability losses (generally 80–100%) in excess of a specific amount paid on all losses during a POLICY YEAR.

AGGREGATE EXCESS OF LOSS RETENTION *see* EXCESS OF LOSS REINSURANCE; STOP LOSS REINSURANCE.

AGGREGATE INDEMNITY total limit of coverage under all policies applicable to the covered loss for which an insured can be indemnified. For example, if two health insurance policies are in force on the same person, the total limit of coverage is that provided by the *primary* policy in combination with the *secondary* policy. *See also* AGGREGATE LIMIT PRIMARY INSURANCE AMOUNT; SECONDARY PLAN.

AGGREGATE LEVEL COST METHOD actuarial method of calculating benefits and their costs for all the employees as a group rather than for each individual employee. The costs of the benefits are measured in the form of a percentage of the total payroll for the employee group.

AGGREGATE LIMIT maximum dollar amount of coverage in force under a health insurance policy, a property damage policy, or a liability policy. This maximum can be on an occurrence basis, or for the life of the policy. The following are examples.
1. *Health insurance.* The insured was billed $107,000 for a serious illness, but the aggregate limit of the policy was $100,000 for the life of the policy, so the most that the insured could be reimbursed is $100,000. The insured would have to pay $7000. Any medical expenses arising from future illness would now have to be paid by the insured.
2. *Liability insurance.* The insured is at fault in an automobile accident (single occurrence) causing injury to four individuals of $100,000, $150,000, $85,000 and $115,000, respectively, a total of $450,000. The aggregate limit of the policy is $400,000. The insured would have to pay the remaining $50,000.

AGGREGATE PRODUCTS LIABILITY LIMIT maximum sum of money which the insurance company will pay, during the time interval that the PRODUCT LIABILITY INSURANCE coverage is in effect, for all product liability-related claims arising which are covered under the policy.

AGREED AMOUNT CLAUSE in PROPERTY INSURANCE, a stipulated agreement between the insurance company and the insured that the amount of insurance coverage under the policy is sufficient to be in compliance with the COINSURANCE requirement.

AGREED AMOUNT FORM *see* AGREED AMOUNT CLAUSE.

AGREEMENT *see* INSURING AGREEMENT.

AGRICULTURAL EQUIPMENT INSURANCE property damage coverage for mobile agricultural equipment and machinery, including harness, saddles, blankets, and liveries. Perils insured are fire, lightning, vandalism, malicious mischief, and removal. Additional perils can be added at extra charge. Excluded from coverage are crops, aircraft, watercraft, feed, hay, and grass. (Crops, aircraft, and watercraft can be covered under other types of insurance policies.)

AIA *see* AMERICAN INSURANCE ASSOCIATION (AIA).

AIAF *see* ASSOCIATE IN INSURANCE ACCOUNTING AND FINANCE (AIAF).

AIC *see* ASSOCIATE IN CLAIMS (AIC).

AIM *see* ASSOCIATE IN MANAGEMENT (AIM).

AIR CARGO INSURANCE coverage for an air carrier's legal liability for damage, destruction, or other loss of a customer's property while being shipped. Coverage is on an ALL RISKS basis subject to specific perils excluded in the policy. Air cargo insurance is a form of MARINE INSURANCE, which at one time only covered goods in transit over waterways. Today, goods in transit can be insured regardless of the means of transportation.

AIRCRAFT HULL INSURANCE coverage on an ALL RISKS basis whether the airplane is on the ground or in the air; also called *hull aircraft insurance*. Exclusions, although none are standard, include illegal use of an aircraft; using an aircraft for purposes other than that described in the policy; wear and tear; piloting the aircraft by someone not named in the policy; operating an aircraft outside stipulated geographical boundaries; and damage or destruction of an aircraft resulting from war, riots, strikes, and civil commotions, mechanical breakdown loss, structural failure loss, and conversion. The hull value includes instruments, radios, autopilots, wings, engines, and other equipment attached to or carried on the plane as described in the policy.

AIRCRAFT LIABILITY INSURANCE coverage for the insured in the event that the insured's negligent acts and/or omissions result in losses in connection with the use, ownership, or maintenance of aircraft. Liability coverage can be provided for bodily injury and/or property damage to passengers and also to individuals who are not passengers. MEDICAL PAYMENTS INSURANCE may be included on an optional basis. *See also* AVIATION INSURANCE.

AIRPORT LIABILITY COVERAGE insurance for owners and operators of private, municipal, or commercial airports, as well as fixed-base operators, against claims resulting from injuries to members of the general public or physical damage to the property of members of the general public, provided that these individuals are on the premises of the airport or its related facilities. The policy may include any or all of the following coverages: (1) PREMISES AND OPERATIONS LIABILITY INSURANCE; (2) PERSONAL INJURY; (3) PREMISES MEDICAL PAYMENTS INSURANCE; and (4) contractual. The policy can be tailored to meet the particular requirements of the INSURED.

ALCM *see* ASSOCIATE IN LOSS CONTROL MANAGEMENT (ALCM).

ALCOHOLIC BEVERAGE CONTROL LAWS *see* DRAM SHOP LAW.

ALCOHOLIC BEVERAGE LIABILITY INSURANCE *see* DRAM SHOP LIABILITY INSURANCE.

ALEATORY CONTRACT contract that may or may not provide more in benefits than premiums paid. For example, with only one premium payment on a property policy an insured can receive hundreds of thousands of dollars should the protected entity be destroyed. On the other hand, an insurance company can collect more in premiums than it ever pays out in benefits, as in a fire insurance policy under which the protected property is either damaged or destroyed. Most insurance contracts are aleatory in nature.

ALIEN INSURER insurance company formed according to the legal requirements of a foreign country. In order for an alien insurer to be able to carry on general operations and sell its products in a particular state in the U.S., it must conform to that state's rules and regulations governing insurance companies.

ALLIANCE OF AMERICAN INSURERS (AAI) membership organization, based in Chicago, Illinois, consisting principally of property and casualty insurance companies. Its objectives are to influence the public and the legislators on matters concerning the property and casualty insurance industry, to publish materials, and to conduct research and various educational programs for member companies.

ALLIED LINES property insurance closely associated with fire insurance and usually purchased in conjunction with a *Standard Fire Policy*. Allied lines include DATA PROCESSING INSURANCE, DEMOLITION INSURANCE, EARTHQUAKE INSURANCE, INCREASED COST OF CONSTRUCTION CLAUSE, RADIOACTIVE CONTAMINATION INSURANCE, SPRINKLER LEAKAGE INSURANCE, STANDING TIMBER INSURANCE, VANDALISM AND MALICIOUS MISCHIEF INSURANCE, WATER DAMAGE INSURANCE.

ALL LINES INSURANCE combination of coverages from property, liability, health, and life insurance into a single insurance policy from one insurance company. *See also* MULTIPLE LINE INSURANCE.

ALLOCATED BENEFITS payments in a DEFINED BENEFIT PLAN. Benefits are allocated to the pension plan participants as premiums are received by the insurance company. Since the benefits purchased are paid up, the employee is guaranteed a pension at retirement, even if the firm goes out of business.

ALLOCATED FUNDING INSTRUMENT insurance or annuity contract used in pension plans to purchase increments of retirement benefits through contributions for each employee paid into a fund. Benefits are guaranteed to employees at retirement; the insurance company is legally obligated to pay all benefits for which it has received premiums. Pension plans, in which no funds are available to purchase benefits prior to retirement involve UNALLOCATED FUNDING INSTRUMENTS (benefits were not purchased at the time premium payments were made).

ALLOCATION OF PLAN ASSETS *see* ALLOCATION OF PLAN ASSETS ON TERMINATION.

ALLOCATION OF PLAN ASSETS ON TERMINATION distribution of assets if a pension plan is terminated. The allocation is made by either (1) refunding all of an employee's contributions, plus interest, or (2) establishment of classes of employees and their beneficiaries according to entitlement to benefits.

ALLOWED ASSETS *see* ADMITTED ASSETS.

ALL RISK INSURANCE *see* ALL RISKS.

ALL RISKS insurance that covers each and every loss except for those specifically excluded. If the insurance company does not specifically exclude a particular loss, it is automatically covered. This is the broadest type of property policy that can be purchased. For example, if an insurance policy does not specifically exclude losses from wind damage, or from a meteor falling on the insured's house, the insured is covered for such losses. *See also* NAMED PERIL POLICY; SPECIFIED PERIL INSURANCE.

ALTERNATIVE MINIMUM COST METHOD means of funding permitted under the EMPLOYEE RETIREMENT INCOME SECURITY ACT OF 1974 (ERISA). The administrator of a pension plan can comply with required minimum funding standards by electing an alternative cost method under which the normal cost is the lesser of the normal cost (1) according to the actuarial cost method of the plan, or (2) according to the accrued benefit cost method without benefit projections.

ALTERNATIVE MINIMUM TAX *see* CORPORATE ALTERNATIVE MINIMUM TAX: IMPLICATIONS FOR CORPORATE-OWNED LIFE INSURANCE.

AMBIGUITY language in the insurance policy that can be considered unclear or subject to different interpretations. Under these circumstances, the courts have generally ruled in favor of insured individuals and against insurance companies since insurance policies are deemed to be contracts of adhesion, and also that insurance companies have sufficient legal talent at their disposal to make policy language clear.

AMENDMENT provisions added to an original insurance policy which alter or modify benefits and coverages of the contract. For example, a HOMEOWNERS INSURANCE POLICY can be endorsed to cover a secondary dwelling; perils can be added for coverage. *See also* ENDORSEMENT; RIDER.

AMERICAN ACADEMY OF ACTUARIES professional association that sets standards of performance for those engaged in actuarial functions. Members are entitled to use the professional designation MAAA (Member, American Academy of Actuaries). The U.S. Department of Labor and the Internal Revenue Service requires that documents filed with these governmental agencies be signed by a member of the American Academy of Actuaries attesting to the validity of actuarial calculations concerning benefits to be paid and their funding. The Academy is located in Chicago, Illinois.

AMERICAN AGENCY SYSTEM marketing of insurance through independent agents; also called *independent agency system*. Independent agents usually represent several insurance companies and try to insure the risk according to availability of coverage and most favorable price. Independent agents are paid a commission in the form of a percentage of the premiums generated by the policy sold. They own all the records of the policies sold and have the right to solicit renewals. They are not restricted to maintaining business with just one company and can transfer the business upon renewal to another company.

AMERICAN COLLEGE (Formerly the American College of Life Underwriters) accrediting body for the CLU (Chartered Life Underwriter) and the ChFC (Chartered Financial Consultant) designations. Provides undergraduate, graduate and continuing education in life insurance and financial services courses on both a residence and correspondence basis. Courses include life insurance, pensions, economics, finance, investments, business evaluations, tax planning and estate planning. The College, which also confers the Master of Science in Financial Services degree, is located in Bryn Mawr, Pennsylvania.

AMERICAN COUNCIL OF LIFE INSURANCE association of life insurance companies focusing on legislation and public relations which may affect the life insurance business on Federal, state, and local levels. Membership is composed of both stock and mutual life insurance companies. The Council lobbies to voice the views of the life insurance business in order to influence public opinion and legislation. It also acts as a control source of information on the life insurance business for the public. Located in Washington, D.C.

AMERICAN EXPERIENCE TABLE chart published in 1868 by Sheppard Homans, an actuary with the Mutual Life Insurance Company of New York, based on insured lives from 1843 to 1858. Historically, it was widely used for life insurance premium and reserve calculations. It was replaced by the C.S.O. Table. *See also* COMMISSIONERS STANDARD ORDINARY MORTALITY TABLE (CSO).

AMERICAN INSTITUTE FOR PROPERTY AND LIABILITY UNDERWRITERS accrediting body for the CPCU (Chartered Property and Casualty Underwriter) designation. The Institute provides undergraduate and continuing education in property and casualty insurance courses on a correspondence basis. Courses include risk management and insurance, commercial property risk management and insurance, commercial liability risk management and insurance, personal risk management and insurance, insurance company operations, legal environment of insurance, management, accounting, finance and economics. Located in Malvern, Pennsylvania.

AMERICAN INSURANCE ASSOCIATION (AIA) membership organization of property and liability insurance companies. The Association promotes the economic, legislative, and public standing of its members through its attention to accounting procedures, catastrophe and pollution problems, auto insurance reform, and other activities. Located in New York City, New York.

AMERICAN LIFE CONVENTION *see* AMERICAN COUNCIL OF LIFE INSURANCE.

AMERICAN LLOYD'S *see* LLOYD'S ASSOCIATION.

AMERICAN MUTUAL INSURANCE ALLIANCE *see* ALLIANCE OF AMERICAN INSURERS (AAI).

AMERICAN RISK AND INSURANCE ASSOCIATION membership organization of companies, academics, and individuals in the insurance business whose interest is to further education and research in insurance and risk management. The association publishes *The Journal of Risk and Insurance,* which is devoted to scholarly articles on insurance, risk management, and allied fields of study.

AMIM *see* ASSOCIATE IN MARINE INSURANCE MANAGEMENT (AMIM).

AMORTIZATION the systematic liquidation of a sum owed. A payment is charged at specific time intervals which will reduce the outstanding debt to zero at the end of a given period of time.

AMORTIZATION SCHEDULE method of paying a sum due whose value has been discounted, according to a predetermined schedule. Each periodic payment includes part of the principal and interest due thereon.

AMORTIZED VALUE *see* AMORTIZATION; AMORTIZATION SCHEDULE.

AMOUNT AT RISK
1. difference between the face value of a permanent life insurance policy and its accrued cash value. The pure cost of protection is based on this difference. For example, if the face value of a life insurance policy is $100,000 and the cash value is $80,000 then the net amount at risk is $20,000. From the Internal Revenue Service perspective, a corridor of protection or net amount of risk must be apparent in a life insurance policy if the policy is to retain its tax advantaged treatment.
2. in property and liability insurance, the lesser of the policy limit or the maximum possible loss to the insured.

AMOUNT FOR WHICH LOSS SETTLED *see* LOSS SETTLEMENT AMOUNT.

AMOUNT SUBJECT *see* MAXIMUM PROBABLE LOSS (MPL).

AMT *see* CORPORATE ALTERNATIVE MINIMUM TAX: IMPLICATIONS FOR CORPORATE-OWNED LIFE INSURANCE.

ANALYSIS *see* ANALYSIS OF PROPERTY AND CASUALTY POLICY; RISK CLASSIFICATION.

ANALYSIS OF PROPERTY AND CASUALTY POLICY determination of (1) property covered, property excluded; (2) perils covered, perils excluded; (3) location covered, location excluded; (4) time period the policy is in force; (5) persons covered, persons excluded; (6) policy limits; and (7) coinsurance requirements

ANALYTIC SYSTEM *see* DEAN ANALYTIC SCHEDULE.

ANCILLARY BENEFITS health insurance coverage for miscellaneous medical expenses associated with a hospital stay. Benefits provided in individual and group health insurance include ambulance service to and from a hospital, drugs, blood, surgical dressings, operating room, medicines, bandages, X-rays, diagnostic tests, and anesthetics. Ancillary benefits are expressed as a multiplier of the daily hospital benefits (10, 15, or 20 times).

ANIMAL HEALTH INSURANCE *see* LIVESTOCK MORTALITY (LIFE) INSURANCE; LIVESTOCK TRANSIT INSURANCE.

ANIMAL LIFE INSURANCE *see* LIVESTOCK INSURANCE.

ANNIVERSARY *see* POLICY ANNIVERSARY.

ANNUAL AGGREGATE LIMIT predetermined dollar amount up to which an insurance policy will cover an insured each year, regardless of the number of claims submitted or defense costs associated with these claims. For example, if the policy limit was established at $1,000,000, the insurance company would pay only up to $1,000,000 regardless of the number of claims during a particular year.

ANNUAL CONVENTION BLANK *see* ANNUAL STATEMENT.

ANNUAL EXPECTED DOLLAR LOSS over a long period of time, the AVERAGE loss an individual, individuals, or an organization can expect to incur from a particular EXPOSURE.

ANNUAL INSURANCE POLICY *see* ANNUAL POLICY.

ANNUAL POLICY contract remaining in force for up to 12 months unless canceled earlier. After 12 months the policy can either be renewed or not renewed by the insurance company or the insured. The policy need not be paid for on an annual basis.

ANNUAL REPORT statement of the financial condition of the insurance company, as well as significant events during the year in which the company has been involved and/or which have affected the company. This statement is furnished to the stockholders (if a STOCK INSURANCE COMPANY) or POLICYHOLDERS (if a MUTUAL INSURANCE COMPANY).

ANNUAL STATEMENT report that an insurance company must file annually with the State Insurance Commissioner in each state in which it does business. The Statement shows the current status of reserves, expenses, assets, total liabilities, investment portfolio, and employees earning over $40,000 per year. It provides information needed to assure that an insurance company has adequate reserves, and that assets are available to meet all benefit payments for which the company has received premiums. The form used is agreed upon by the National Association of Insurance Commissioners (NAIC). This form is also known as *Annual Convention Blank*.

ANNUITANT person who receives an income benefit from an ANNUITY for life or for a specified period.

ANNUITY contract sold by insurance companies that pays a monthly (or quarterly, semiannual, or annual) income benefit for the life of a person (the *annuitant*), for the lives of two or more persons, or for a specified period of time. The annuitant can never outlive the income from the annuity. While the basic purpose of life insurance is to provide an income for a beneficiary at the death of the insured, the annuity is intended to provide an income for life for the annuitant. There are variations in both the way that payments are made by a buyer during the *accumulation period,* and in the way payments are made to the annuitant during the *liquidation period.*

An annuity may be bought by means of installments, with benefits scheduled to begin at a specified age such as 65; or, it may be bought by means of a single lump sum, with benefits scheduled to begin immediately or at a later date. No physical examination is required. For variations in methods of payment, *see* CASH REFUND ANNUITY; FIXED DOLLAR ANNUITY; INSTALLMENT REFUND ANNUITY; JOINT-LIFE AND SURVIVORSHIP ANNUITY; JOINT LIFE ANNUITY; LIFE ANNUITY CERTAIN; PURE ANNUITY; VARIABLE DOLLAR ANNUITY.

ANNUITY ANALYSIS includes rate of return, how long the annuity's interest rate is guaranteed, loads (front, middle and back), financial ranking of the insurance company offering the annuity, the monthly income factor per $1000 of cash value on deposit. For example, for the last item, if the monthly income factor is $6.18 per $1000 of cash value on deposit and the size of the cash value on account is $100,000, a male annuitant would receive a monthly income benefit of $618 at age 65.

ANNUITY, CASH REFUND *see* CASH REFUND ANNUITY.

ANNUITY, CD product which guarantees the initial interest rate for funds on deposit for the length of the maturity, whether it is for a period of 1, 3, 5, 10 or 15 years. At maturity, the POLICYHOLDER has two choices: (1) withdraw the funds without having to pay a SURRENDER CHARGE (it is important to note that taxes must be paid on the interest earned and there is a 10% penalty on the earnings if the policyholder is less than age 59½); or (2) roll the funds over into another annuity for a limited number of years or a product of longer duration. In contrast to certificates of deposit (CDs), interest earned through this ANNUITY accumulates on a tax-deferred basis. This type of annuity provides liquidity, preserves principal, and stipulates a fixed rate of return.

ANNUITY CERTAIN *see* LIFE ANNUITY CERTAIN.

ANNUITY CONSIDERATION single payment or periodic payments which are made to purchase an annuity.

ANNUITY DUE annuity under which payments are made in the beginning of each period (month, quarter, or year).

ANNUITY FORMS *see* ANNUITY, ANNUITY DUE; LIFE ANNUITY CERTAIN; CASH REFUND ANNUITY; INTALLMENT REFUND ANNUITY; VARIABLE DOLLAR ANNUITY.

ANNUITY, INSTALLMENT REFUND *see* INSTALLMENT REFUND ANNUITY.

ANNUITY, JOINT LIFE *see* JOINT LIFE ANNUITY.

ANNUITY TABLES chart showing for a group of people (1) the number living at the beginning of a designated year and (2) the number dying during that year. Yearly probabilities are used in calculating premium payments for future income payments to annuitants.

ANNUITY, TAX DEFERRED *see* TAX DEFERRED ANNUITY.

ANTICOERCION LAW section of the "Unfair Trade Practices Code" of most states which declares the use of coercion to be in violation of the state code. *See also* UNFAIR TRADE PRACTICE.

ANTIFREEZE provision of the 1987 TAX ACT which excludes life insurance owned by a third party or an irrevocable trust from FEDERAL ESTATE TAXES. Life insurance, as well as the deceased's personal residence, was exempted because neither is considered to be an "enterprise" as defined by the Internal Revenue Service (IRS). The IRS defines an enterprise as "any arrangement, relationship, or activity that has significant business or investment aspects."

ANTIREBATE LAW statute that makes it illegal in most states for an agent to rebate (return) any portion of his COMMISSION as an inducement for an applicant to purchase insurance from him.

ANTISELECTION *see* ADVERSE SELECTION.

APP *see* APPLICATION.

APPARENT AGENCY (AUTHORITY) situation wherein the agent's conduct causes a client or prospective insured reasonably to believe that the agent has the authority to sell an insurance policy and contract on behalf of the insurance company. For example, if an agent continues to use insurance company documents, such as its application forms, rate manuals, stationery, and emblems on the door, the client has every reason to believe that the agent does in fact continue to represent the insurance company.

APPARENT AUTHORITY *see* APPARENT AGENCY (AUTHORITY).

APPEAL BOND guarantee of payment of the original judgment of a court. When a judgment is appealed, a bond is usually required to guarantee that if the appeal is unsuccessful, funds would be available to pay the original judgment as well as costs of the appeal. This serves to discourage an individual from appealing merely to stall for time or for frivolous reasons.

APPLETON RULE regulation named after a former Superintendent of Insurance of New York State, and instituted in the early 1900s. It requires every insurer admitted to New York to comply with the New York Insurance Code and even in other states where that insurer does business. This rule has had a nationwide impact on the insurance industry. New York State is known for its leadership role in insurance regulation. Thus, if an insurance company is admitted to conduct business in New York, it is a sign that it has met exacting requirements.

APPLICATION written statements on a form by a prospective insured about himself, including assets and other personal information. These statements and additional information, such as a medical report, are used by an insurance company to decide whether or not to insure the risk. Falsification or nondisclosure of information may give the insurance company grounds for rescinding a policy that has been issued. Statements in the application are also used to decide on an applicant's underwriting classification and premium rates.

APPOINTMENT OF TRUSTEES FOR TERMINATED PLAN plan initiated by the PENSION BENEFIT GUARANTY CORPORATION (PBGC) upon the involuntary termination of a pension plan. With the concurrence of the United States District Court, the PBGC appoints a trustee(s) to administer the terminated plan. The trustee(s) safeguards the remaining assets of the pension plan, protects the assets from being further depleted, limits further increases in liabilities, and in general acts as protector of the benefits for the pension plan's participants.

APPORTIONMENT division of a loss among insurance policies in the proportion that each policy bears to the total coverage applicable to the loss. For example, assume Policies A, B, C, and D have $50,000, $60,000, $70,000 and $80,000 of insurance in force, respectively: a total of $260,000 of coverage. Under the apportionment clause found in many property insurance policies, Policy A's percentage of any loss is 19.23%, Policy B's is 21.43%, Policy C's is 26.92%, and Policy D's is 30.77%.

APPRAISAL valuation of property for damage resulting from an insured peril or for establishing the base amount of insurance coverage to be purchased. If an insured and an insurance company cannot agree on the amount of an insurer's liability for a property loss, the policy may specify that, upon written request, the dispute is submitted to appraisal. Usually, each party selects an appraiser and the two appraisers select a disinterested umpire. Disagreements by the appraisers go to the umpire, whose decisions typically are binding.

APPROVAL acceptance of an application for an insurance policy by the insurance company, indicated by the signature of an officer of the company on the policy. The officer, who must have signature authority, is usually the president or the secretary of the company. The agent who sells the policy normally does not have signature authority to approve the policy.

APPROVED ROOF roof used in construction that is composed of fire-resistive materials such as slate as approved by the UNDERWRITERS LABORATORIES INC. (UL).

APPURTENANT STRUCTURES coverage for additional buildings on the same property as the principal insured building. Most property insurance contracts such as the HOMEOWNERS INSURANCE POLICY cover appurtenant structures. For example, under the Homeowners policy a separate garage on an insured's premise would be covered up to 10% of the home's structure amount.

ARBITRATION *see* ARBITRATION CLAUSE.

ARBITRATION CLAUSE provision in a property insurance policy to the effect that in the event the insured and insurer cannot agree on the amount of a claim settlement, each appoints an appraiser. The appraisers select a disinterested umpire. When at least two of the three, appraisers and umpire, agree on the settlement amount, it is binding on both the insured and the insurer.

ARIA *see* AMERICAN RISK AND INSURANCE ASSOCIATION.

ARM *see* ASSOCIATE IN RISK MANAGEMENT (ARM).

ARMORED CAR AND MESSENGER INSURANCE coverage during the transfer of securities and monies, precious metals, and other specified types of valuables by armored guard services. Policies are specifically designed to fit an insured's requirements. Standard coverage is available on an ALL RISKS basis, excluding perils of war, nuclear disaster, and dishonest acts of shipper and/or consignee.

ARMSTRONG INVESTIGATION inquiry conducted by a committee of the legislature of the State of New York in 1905 which looked at abuses of life insurance companies operating in the state. This study led to stricter supervision by New York and other state insurance departments. For example, many of the policies sold at that time contained language that made the receipt of benefits very difficult to obtain. As a result of the investigation, standard provisions were introduced into life insurance policies. While actual language is not dictated word for word by state regulatory authorities, a policy must provide minimum benefits (such as nonforfeiture provisions) expressed in acceptable language.

ARP *see* ASSOCIATE IN RESEARCH AND PLANNING (ARP).

ARSON actual or attempted malicious and deliberate burning of a physical asset owned by another party. Coverage against arson is provided under property insurance, but only if the insured has not committed the arson. The property insurance business has long worked to discourage arson and to prosecute arsonists.

ASO *see* ADMINISTRATIVE SERVICES ONLY.

ASSAILING THIEVES individuals other than the crew of a ship who forcefully steal the ship and/or its cargo. This event is an INSURED PERIL under OCEAN MARINE INSURANCE.

ASSAULT threatening act, physical and/or verbal, which causes a person to reasonably fear for life or safety. For example, if a boxing champion said he was going to hit someone, this would probably cause a reasonably prudent person to fear serious bodily injury. An insured's liability for assault is excluded from all standard liability policies such as the SPECIAL MULTIPERIL INSURANCE (SMP) and the HOMEOWNERS INSURANCE POLICY.

ASSESSABLE INSURANCE coverage in which an initial premium is charged, with the stipulation that an additional premium can be charged later if the loss experience of the insurance company warrants it; that is, if losses exceed premium income. *See also* ASSESSMENT COMPANY.

ASSESSABLE MUTUAL assessment mutual company that operates on a statewide basis or in more than one state. Assessable or assessment mutuals operate by taking a cash deposit, or premium, from members in exchange for insurance protection. If the company's losses and expenses exceed these deposits, the company can assess members for additional monies to cover losses. These companies are commonly used by a group of local farmers or merchants in a small geographical area. Some states have specific laws governing these mutuals. For example, they might be limited to a certain type of business or have a maximum dollar limit for each risk.

ASSESSED VALUE monetary worth of real or personal property as a basis for its taxation. This value, established by a government agency, is rarely used as a means to determine indemnification of an insured for property damage or destruction. *See also* INDEMNITY; REPLACEMENT COST LESS PHYSICAL DEPRECIATION AND OBSOLESCENCE.

ASSESSMENT COMPANY insurance company which has the authority to assess or charge its policyholders for losses that the company is incurring. This company is sometimes called *stipulated premium company* or *assessment association*. These companies were relatively common in the 1800s and early 1900s but have since become rare. Most insurance companies cannot assess policyholders for losses. *See also* ASSESSMENT INSURANCE; ASSESSMENT PERIOD.

ASSESSMENT INSURANCE contract under which an assessment insurance company can charge policyowners additional sums if the company's loss experience is worse than had been loaded for in the premium. This insurance is sometimes called *stipulated premium* and *natural premium* insurance. *See also* ASSESSMENT COMPANY; ASSESSMENT PERIOD.

ASSESSMENT PERIOD time during which an assessment life insurance company has the right to assess policyholders if losses are worse than anticipated in the premium charged. *See also* ASSESSMENT COMPANY; ASSESSMENT INSURANCE.

ASSESSMENT PLAN *see* ASSESSMENT COMPANY; ASSESSMENT INSURANCE; ASSESSMENT PERIOD.

ASSET entity with exchange or commercial value, such as the book value of property owned by an insurance company as listed on its balance sheet.

ASSETS AND VALUATION actuarial evaluation of the assets of a pension plan according to the fair market value of the assets.

ASSET SHARE VALUE policyholder's equity share of the life insurance company's assets. The share is based on the policyholder's contribution to assets (the company's gross premiums minus cost of insurance, expenses and dividends for the classification to which the policy belongs). This computation is derived from the actual experience of the insurance company instead of the assumptions initially used in calculating premiums and reserves. The actual experience may or may not deviate significantly from the expected experience.

ASSET SUFFICIENCY OR INSUFFICIENCY computation of the ASSET SHARE VALUE, *surrender value*, and *reserve* and the comparison of the three computations in order to judge the adequacy and equity of the tentative GROSS PREMIUM scale to be utilized.

ASSET VALUATION excess or deficit of gross premium above the pure cost of insurance and expenses. The result becomes the valuation of the asset share of the policyholder at the end of a given year. The valuation of the asset share reflects the policyowner's share of the asset of the insurance company.

ASSIGNED CLAIMS *see* AUTOMOBILE ASSIGNED RISK INSURANCE PLAN.

ASSIGNED RISK *see* AUTOMOBILE ASSIGNED RISK INSURANCE PLAN.

ASSIGNED RISK PLAN *see* AUTOMOBILE ASSIGNED RISK INSURANCE PLAN.

ASSIGNEE *see* COLLATERAL CREDITOR (ASSIGNEE).

ASSIGNMENT transfer of rights under an insurance policy to another person or business. For example, to secure a debt, it is not uncommon for the policyowner to transfer to the creditor his rights to borrow on the cash value. Life insurance policies are freely assignable to secure loans and notes (property and casualty insurance policies are not). Creditors such as banks often have printed assignment forms on hand at the time of making loans.

ASSIGNMENT CLAUSE, LIFE INSURANCE feature in a life insurance policy allowing a policyowner to freely assign (give, sell) a policy to another or institution. For example, in order to secure a loan, a bank asks to be assigned the policy. If the insured dies before repayment of the loan, the bank would receive a portion of the death benefit that equals the outstanding loan, the remainder of the death benefit being payable to the insured's beneficiary. The fact that life insurance is freely assignable makes it a useful financial instrument through which to secure a loan. The insurance company does not guarantee the validity of the assignment.

ASSOCIATE IN AUTOMATION MANAGEMENT (AAM) professional designation earned after the successful completion of three national examinations given by the INSURANCE INSTITUTE OF AMERICA (IIA). Covers such areas of expertise as essentials of automation (how computers work, automation terminology, and software); automation in insurance; and managing automated activities. Program of study is recommended for individuals involved in automated activities within the insurance organization.

ASSOCIATE IN CLAIMS (AIC) professional designation earned after the successful completion of four national examinations given by the INSURANCE INSTITUTE OF AMERICA (IIA). Covers such areas of expertise as the claims person and the public, principles of property, liability claims adjusting, property insurance adjusting, and liability insurance adjusting. Program of study is recommended for experienced adjusters, claims supervisors, and examiners who have in-depth knowledge of the claims area but have not undertaken formal study of the claims principles.

ASSOCIATE IN INSURANCE ACCOUNTING AND FINANCE (AIAF) professional designation earned after the successful completion of four national examinations given by the INSURANCE INSTITUTE OF AMERICA (IIA). Covers such areas of expertise as insurance company operations (marketing, underwriting, rate making, claims adjusting, reinsurance, and loss control); statutory accounting for property and liability insurers; insurance information systems; and insurance company finance. Program of study is recommended for individuals involved in the accounting, statistical, and financial areas of an insurance company.

ASSOCIATE IN LOSS CONTROL MANAGEMENT (ALCM) professional designation earned after the successful completion of five national examinations given by the INSURANCE INSTITUTE OF AMERICA (IIA). Covers such areas of expertise as accident prevention, property protection, industrial and environmental hygiene, principles of risk management and insurance, insurance company operations, and management. Program of study is recommended for individuals involved in the area of loss control.

ASSOCIATE IN MANAGEMENT (AIM) professional designation earned after the successful completion of four national examinations given by the INSURANCE INSTITUTE OF AMERICA (IIA). Covers such areas of expertise as the process of management, management and human resources, and managerial decision making. Program of study is recommended for individuals who perform management functions within an insurance organization.

ASSOCIATE IN MARINE INSURANCE MANAGEMENT (AMIM) professional designation earned after the successful completion of six national examinations given by the INSURANCE INSTITUTE OF AMERICA (IIA). Covers such areas of expertise as ocean marine insurance, inland marine insurance, principles of risk management and insurance, insurance company operations, legal environment of insurance, and management. Program of study is recommended for individuals involved in the areas of ocean marine and inland marine insurance.

ASSOCIATE IN PREMIUM AUDITING (APA) professional designation earned after the successful completion of six national examinations given by the INSURANCE INSTITUTE OF AMERICA (IIA). Covers such areas of expertise as premium auditing applications, principles of premium auditing, principles of risk management and insurance, commercial property risk management and insurance, commercial liability risk management and insurance, and accounting and finance. Program of study is recommended for individuals involved in the area of premium auditing for an insurance company.

ASSOCIATE IN RESEARCH AND PLANNING (ARP) professional designation earned after the successful completion of six national examinations given by the INSURANCE INSTITUTE OF AMERICA (IIA). Covers such areas of expertise as business research methods, strategic planning for insurers, principles of risk management and insurance, insurance company operations, economics, and ethics. Program of study is recommended for individuals involved in the areas of corporate planning, research, product development, and forecasting for an insurance company.

ASSOCIATE IN RISK MANAGEMENT (ARM) professional designation earned after the successful completion of three national examinations given by the INSURANCE INSTITUTE OF AMERICA (IIA). Covers such areas of expertise as essentials of risk management (identification and measurement of loss exposures, and analyzing various techniques to deal with the exposure); essentials of risk control; and essentials of risk financing (risk retention and commercial insurance). Program of study is recommended for individuals involved in the areas of risk management for noninsurance companies, as well as insurance producers who want to provide risk management counseling to their clients.

ASSOCIATE IN UNDERWRITING (AU) professional designation earned after the successful completion of four national examinations given by the INSURANCE INSTITUTE OF AMERICA (IIA). Covers such areas of expertise as principles of property and liability underwriting, personal lines underwriting, commercial liability underwriting, and commercial property and multiple lines underwriting. Program of study is recommended for individuals who have experience as underwriters or producers.

ASSOCIATION *see* POOL; SYNDICATE.

ASSOCIATION CAPTIVE insurance company established by a trade group or other association to provide selected types of PRIMARY INSURANCE and/or LIABILITY INSURANCE for members of the association and access to REINSURANCE markets. For example, the American Newspaper Publishers Association has established an association captive to provide LIBEL INSURANCE for member newspapers, and the American Bankers Association sponsors a captive that provides DIRECTORS AND OFFICERS LIABILITY INSURANCE for member banks.

ASSOCIATION GROUP bona fide organization that purchases insurance on a group basis on behalf of members. However, a group cannot be formed for the purpose of purchasing insurance since adverse selection would take place. Group selling permits economies of scale to operate, so that the cost of insurance to a member is appreciably less than an individual policy. The insurance company/agent is able to benefit through individual sales to the group's members. *See also* ADVERSE SELECTION.

ASSOCIATION GROUP INSURANCE *see* ASSOCIATION GROUP.

ASSUME to accept by a REINSURER, part or all of a RISK transferred to it by a primary INSURER or another reinsurer. *See also* CEDE; REINSURANCE.

ASSUMED LIABILITY *see* CONTRACTUAL LIABILITY.

ASSUMED LOSS RATIO projected percentage of the EARNED PREMIUMS which will be required by the insurance company to pay for the INCURRED LOSSES plus the LOSS ADJUSTMENT EXPENSE.

ASSUMPTION acceptance by a REINSURER of part or all of a RISK which has been transferred to it by a primary INSURER or another reinsurer. *See also* CEDE; REINSURANCE.

ASSUMPTION CERTIFICATE *see* CUT-THROUGH ENDORSEMENT (ASSUMPTION OF RISK).

ASSUMPTION OF RISK technique of risk management (better known as *retention* or SELF INSURANCE) under which an individual or business firm assumes expected losses that are not catastrophic losses through the purchase of insurance. For example, a business firm assumes the risk of its employees being absent because of minor illness, but buys disability insurance to cover absences due to extended illness. Also refers to (1) situations where insureds place themselves in situations that they realize pose a danger, and (2) the acceptance of risks by an insurance company.

ASSUMPTION OF RISK RULE *see* ASSUMPTION OF RISK.

ASSUMPTION REINSURANCE form of insurance whereby the buyer (REINSURER) assumes the entire obligation of the CEDENT company, effected through the transfer of the policies from the cedent to the books of the reinsurer. Several thousand policies are transferred annually among insurance companies. Generally, life, health, and investment-type policies such as annuities are the policies most likely to be transferred since they are of longer duration and in many instances cannot be cancelled by the insurance company.

ASSUMPTIONS circumstances taken for granted. For example, in calculating annuity values, a particular interest rate is assumed. This assumption is critical to CURRENT ASSUMPTION WHOLE LIFE INSURANCE policies since projections of future cash values ultimately being realized are determined by the validity of the underlying assumptions.

ASSURANCE *see* INSURANCE.

ASSURED *see* INSURED.

ASSURER *see* INSURER.

ATOMIC ENERGY COMMISSION *see* NUCLEAR REGULATORY COMMISSION.

ATOMIC ENERGY REINSURANCE *see* MUTUAL ATOMIC ENERGY REINSURANCE POOL.

ATTACHMENT addition to a basic insurance policy to further explain coverages, add or exclude perils and locations covered, and add or delete positions covered. For example, an endorsement to the *Standard Fire Policy* might add coverage for vandalism and malicious mischief. This form has largely been replaced by an ENDORSEMENT or RIDER.

ATTACHMENT POINT critical point in the total amount of claims paid above which the EXCESS INSURANCE policy pays a percentage (generally 80–100%) of the claims for any POLICY YEAR EXPERIENCE.

ATTAINED AGE insured's age at a particular point in time. For example, many TERM LIFE INSURANCE policies allow an insured to convert to permanent insurance without a physical examination at the insured's then attained age. Upon conversion, the premium usually rises substantially to reflect the insured's age and diminished life expectancy. Since later in life rates become prohibitive, many insureds do not make an attained age conversion. *See also* ORIGINAL AGE.

ATTAINED AGE CONVERSION *see* ATTAINED AGE

ATTORNEY-IN-FACT *see* RECIPROCAL EXCHANGE.

ATTORNEYS PROFESSIONAL LIABILITY INSURANCE *see* LAWYERS LIABILITY INSURANCE.

ATTRACTIVE NUISANCE property which is inherently dangerous and particularly enticing to children. For example, a swimming pool has a strong attraction to children and could lead to a liability judgment against the pool's owner. The owner must take all necessary steps to prevent accidents, such as building an adequate fence around the pool.

AU *see* ASSOCIATE IN UNDERWRITING.

AUDIT in WORKERS COMPENSATION INSURANCE policies and several business property and liability policies, review of the payroll of a business firm in order to determine the premium for coverage. Premiums in Workers Compensation are based on units of payroll.

AUDITORS REPORT *see* STATEMENT OF OPINION (ACCOUNTANTS REPORT, AUDITORS REPORT).

AUTHORITY TO TERMINATE PLAN means of ending a pension plan only for reasons of business necessity, following IRS regulations.

If the IRS determines that the plan was terminated for other reasons, employee and employer contributions become taxable. Reasons acceptable to the IRS include bankruptcy, insolvency, and the inability of a business to continue to make its contributions because of adverse financial conditions.

AUTHORIZATION maximum amount of insurance coverage that an underwriter will write on a particular class of property or risk exposure.

AUTHORIZED INSURER insurance company that is *licensed* by a state to market and service particular *lines of insurance* in that state.

AUTOMATIC BUILDERS RISK FORM *see* BUILDERS RISKS FORMS.

AUTOMATIC COVERAGE policy that comes into existence or adjusts the amount of coverage to provide protection for newly acquired or increasing values of an insured's real or personal property.

AUTOMATIC INCREASE IN INSURANCE ENDORSEMENT *see* INFLATION ENDORSEMENT.

AUTOMATIC NONPROPORTIONAL REINSURANCE automatic protection for an INSURER against losses that exceed a predetermined loss limit. This reinsurance may be subdivided into three primary types: EXCESS OF LOSS, CATASTROPHE LOSS, and *stop loss*. *See also* REINSURANCE.

AUTOMATIC PREMIUM LOAN PROVISION life insurance policy clause. If at the end of the GRACE PERIOD the premium due has not been paid, a policy loan will automatically be made from the policy's cash value to pay the premium. The primary purpose is to prevent unintentional lapse of the policy. Funds in the cash value must at least be equal to the loan amount plus one year's interest. Many experts recommend this provision because under some circumstances the premium may go unpaid because of illness, vacations, or inadvertence.

AUTOMATIC PROPORTIONAL REINSURANCE form of coverage in which an insurer automatically reinsures individual risks with its reinsurer. The insurer must transfer (cede) the risks to its reinsurer and its reinsurer must accept this transfer (cession). Losses and premiums are shared; the reinsurer shares them in the same proportion as it does that total policy limits of the risks. The insurer receives from the reinsurer a transfer commission reflecting the so-called equity in the unearned premium reserve of the insurer. This provides for acquisition expenses, premium taxes, and the insurer's cost of servicing the business. Automatic proportional reinsurance may be subdivided into two primary types: *quota share* and *surplus*. *See also* REINSURANCE.

AUTOMATIC REINSTATEMENT CLAUSE provision in a property or liability policy stating that after a loss has been paid, the total original limits of the policy are once again in effect. For example, assume a loss of $40,000 has been paid under a $100,000 property damage coverage HOMEOWNERS INSURANCE POLICY. After payment of the loss, the original $100,000 is reinstated.

AUTOMATIC REINSURANCE automatic reinsuring of individual risks by an insurer with a reinsurer. The insurer must transfer the risks to its reinsurer and its reinsurer must accept this transfer. *See also* REINSURANCE.

AUTOMATIC SPRINKLER CLAUSE *see* SPRINKLER LEAKAGE INSURANCE; SPRINKLER LEAKAGE LEGAL LIABILITY INSURANCE.

AUTOMATIC SPRINKLER SYSTEM *see* SPRINKLER LEAKAGE INSURANCE; SPRINKLER LEAKAGE LEGAL LIABILITY INSURANCE.

AUTOMOBILE ASSIGNED RISK INSURANCE PLAN coverage in which individuals who cannot obtain conventional automobile liability insurance, usually because of adverse driving records, are placed in a residual insurance market. Insurance companies are assigned to write insurance for them, at higher prices, in proportion to the premiums written in a particular state. These plans protect motorists who suffer injury or property damage through the negligence of bad drivers who otherwise would not have insurance.

AUTOMOBILE, BOAT, AND AIRCRAFT INSURANCE coverage for motorized vehicles, each of which requires separate policies for property damage and liability exposures. Motorized vehicles are not covered under a HOMEOWNERS INSURANCE POLICY for property damage and/or bodily injury liability situations when operated away from an insured's premises.

AUTOMOBILE COLLISION *see* COLLISION INSURANCE.

AUTOMOBILE COMPREHENSIVE *see* COMPREHENSIVE INSURANCE.

AUTOMOBILE FLEET *see* FLEET POLICY.

AUTOMOBILE INSURANCE *see* BUSINESS AUTOMOBILE POLICY (BAP); PERSONAL AUTOMOBILE POLICY (PAP).

AUTOMOBILE INSURANCE PLAN *see* AUTOMOBILE ASSIGNED RISK INSURANCE PLAN.

AUTOMOBILE LIABILITY INSURANCE coverage if an insured is legally liable for bodily injury or property damage caused by an automobile. The PERSONAL AUTOMOBILE POLICY (PAP) and the BUSINESS

AUTOMOBILE POLICY (BAP) cover the judgment awarded (up to the limits of the policy) and the court cost and legal defense fees. Experts advise against driving an automobile without automobile liability insurance as a matter of common sense, and because state laws require such a policy or evidence of financial responsibility. Passengers in automobiles should assure themselves that drivers are covered by this insurance.

AUTOMOBILE PHYSICAL DAMAGE INSURANCE coverage in the event an insured's automobile is damaged, destroyed, or lost through fire, theft, vandalism, malicious mischief, collision, or windstorm. There are two kinds of property damage coverage—*collision insurance* and COMPREHENSIVE INSURANCE. *See also* BUSINESS AUTOMOBILE POLICY (BAP); PERSONAL AUTOMOBILE POLICY (PAP).

AUTOMOBILE REINSURANCE FACILITY *see* AUTOMOBILE AS-SIGNED RISK INSURANCE PLAN.

AUTOMOBILE SHARED MARKET *see* AUTOMOBILE ASSIGNED RISK INSURANCE PLAN.

AUTOMOBILE THEFT *see* COMPREHENSIVE INSURANCE.

AVERAGE arithmetic mean; the sum of a series of numbers divided by the number of numbers comprising the sum. For example, given the following series of numbers: 1, 4, 5, 6, 8, 9 and 10, the arithmetic mean, or average,

$$= \frac{1 + 4 + 5 + 6 + 8 + 9 + 10}{7}$$

$$= 6.143$$

The arithmetic mean is the EXPECTED LOSS which the insurance company prepares itself to pay, as reflected in the BASIC PREMIUM.

AVERAGE ADJUSTER individual employed by an OCEAN MARINE INSURANCE company to settle on its behalf ocean marine-related claims brought by its insureds. The adjuster evaluates the merits of each claim and makes recommendations to the insurance company.

AVERAGE CLAUSE *see* COINSURANCE; PRO RATA DISTRIBUTION CLAUSE.

AVERAGE, GENERAL *see* GENERAL AVERAGE.

AVERAGE INDEXED MONTHLY EARNINGS (AIME) method of calculating the PRIMARY INSURANCE AMOUNT (PIA) for Social Security benefits. Employees' covered monthly earnings are adjusted to reflect changes in the national average annual earnings. Benefits should rise in proportion to increases in national average annual earnings.

AVERAGE LOSS CLAUSE *see* PRO RATA DISTRIBUTION CLAUSE.

AVERAGE MONTHLY EARNINGS (AME) *see* AVERAGE MONTHLY WAGE (AMW).

AVERAGE MONTHLY WAGE (AMW) figure used in calculating a worker's PRIMARY INSURANCE AMOUNT (PIA) to determine Social Security benefits in the following manner:
1. calculate the number of years between the worker's twenty-first birthday and the year prior to the worker reaching age 62 (a maximum of 40 years).
2. exclude the five lowest years of earnings, thereby selecting the 35 highest years (420 months) of earnings.
3. divide the total of the 35 highest years of earnings by 420 months to calculate the Average Monthly Wage.

   A Social Security Administration table shows the PIA for the Average Monthly Wage calculated in Step 3. The PIA is then increased to reflect the COST-OF-LIVING ADJUSTMENT (COLA) to determine the actual benefit.

AVERAGE NET COST *see* INTEREST ADJUSTED COST.

AVERAGE, PARTICULAR *see* PARTICULAR AVERAGE.

AVERAGE RATE applicable rate, in property insurance, of each location multiplied by the value of the real and/or personal property at that location, all of which is divided by the total value of all real and/or personal property at all locations multiplied by their respective rates.

AVERAGE SEMIPRIVATE RATE in HEALTH INSURANCE, the applicable average rate charged for a semiprivate room in the geographical area in which the charge is incurred.

AVERAGE WEEKLY WAGE wage rate used as the basis for calculating benefits under WORKERS COMPENSATION INSURANCE. *See also* WORKERS COMPENSATION BENEFITS.

AVIATION ACCIDENT INSURANCE life insurance policy (individual or employee group basis) providing protection for a passenger on a regularly scheduled airline. *See also* AVIATION TRIP LIFE INSURANCE.

AVIATION EXCLUSION common exclusion in life and ACCIDENTAL DEATH INSURANCE (double indemnity) policies, indicating that coverage does not apply unless an insured is a passenger on a regularly scheduled airline. For example, if an insured is killed while a passenger in a private plane crash, the aviation exclusion would apply, and the insured's beneficiary would not receive a death payment.

AVIATION HAZARD additional HAZARD associated with aeronautics other than that of being a passenger on a regularly scheduled airline. An extra premium is charged, and/or there are usually exclusions applied to certain benefits associated with this hazard. For example, pilots of small private planes are subject to this hazard.

AVIATION INSURANCE combination of PROPERTY INSURANCE on the hull of an airplane and LIABILITY INSURANCE in the following manner.
1. *property coverage*—provided on an ALL RISKS basis or on a specified perils basis for the hull, autopilots, instruments, radios, and any other equipment in the airplane as described in the policy.
2. *liability coverage*—provided in the event that the insured's negligent acts and/or omissions result in bodily injury and/or property damage to passengers and individuals who are not passengers.

AVIATION TRIP LIFE INSURANCE term life insurance, usually purchased at an airport by an airplane passenger. It provides a death payment to the passenger's beneficiary in the event of a fatal accident on one or more specified flights. The term of coverage is from the time that the passenger enters the airplane until the time that he leaves. Ground transportation to and from the airport may also be covered. With the advent of hijacking and terrorism, this coverage is becoming more widely purchased.

AVOIDANCE technique of risk management. It ensures that an individual or business does not incur any liability relating to a given activity by avoiding the activity in question. For example, a business which does not own computer equipment cannot incur financial loss due to the destruction of the computer by fire. However, in the real world, the risk control technique of avoidance is rarely practical. A more realistic approach is self-insurance or commercial insurance.

B

BACK LOAD expenses taken out when benefits are paid. For example, a specific dollar amount is subtracted from a monthly income payment for company expenses.

BAGGAGE INSURANCE *see* TOURIST BAGGAGE INSURANCE.

BAIL BOND monetary guarantee that an individual released from jail will be present in court at the appointed time. If the individual is not present in court at that time, the monetary value of the bond is forfeited to the court (jumping bail). *Personal automobile policies* commonly cover fees for an insured's bail bond.

BAILEE individual who has temporary rightful possession of another's property. The bailee often furnishes a receipt in exchange for the bailor's property. For example, a dry cleaner has temporary custody of a suit to be cleaned and must exercise proper care to safeguard it against physical loss. If the property is damaged, the bailee's insurance policy often becomes the primary coverage and must indemnify the loss.

BAILEE'S CUSTOMERS INSURANCE coverage for legal liability resulting from damage or destruction of the bailor's property while under the bailee's temporary care, custody, and control. Includes property on or in transit to and from the bailee's premises. Perils covered include fire, lightning, theft, burglary, robbery, windstorm, explosion, collision, flood, sprinkler leakage, earthquake, strike, and damage or destruction in the course of transportation by a common carrier. The insurance is in effect when the bailee issues a receipt to the bailor for the item. Coverage excludes property belonging to the insured bailee and loss due to vermin and insects. For example, a suit to be cleaned is under the temporary control of the bailee (cleaner). The bailor (owner) expects the suit to be returned in good condition. If the suit is stolen from the cleaner, the insurance would cover the loss.

BAILMENT transfer of property from a bailor to a bailee; for example, transferring a suit to be cleaned from the bailor (owner) to the bailee (cleaners). *See also* BAILEE; BAILOR.

BAILOR individual who retains title to property which is being transferred on a temporary basis to the care, custody, and/or control of another. *See also* BAILEE.

BAIL-OUT PROVISION clause found in an ANNUITY contract which enables the owner of that contract to withdraw his or her money without surrender penalties, if the annual interest rate is lowered below a certain predetermined minimum.

BALANCE SHEET accounting statement showing the financial condition of a company at a particular date. Listed on the statement are the company's assets and liabilities, and capital and surplus.

BALANCE SHEET RESERVES amount expressed as a liability on the insurance company's balance sheet for benefits owed to policyowners. These reserves must be maintained according to strict actuarial formulas as they serve to guarantee that all benefit payments for which the insurance company has received premiums will be made.

BANK BURGLARY AND ROBBERY INSURANCE coverage on the bank's premises for burglary of monies, securities and other properties from within the bank's safe(s); robbery of monies and securities; loss of monies and securities as the result of vandalism or malicious mischief; general damage due to vandalism and malicious mischief resulting from burglary and/or robbery.

BANKERS BLANKET BOND coverage for a bank in the event of loss due to dishonest acts of its employees or individuals external to the bank. For example, if a teller goes to Mexico with the bank's money, the bank would be indemnified for its loss.

BANKING ACT OF 1933 *see* GLASS-STEAGALL ACT.

BANK LOAN PLAN *see* FINANCED INSURANCE (MINIMUM DEPOSIT INSURANCE); FINANCED PREMIUM.

BARRATRY violation of duty in marine insurance, such as acts of the master and crew of a ship which result in damage to the vessel including purposefully running it aground, diverting it from its true course of travel, stealing of its cargo, and abandoning the vessel.

BASELINE DATA statistics (such as health data from physical examination of employees or other insureds) used as a benchmark from which deviations and comparisons of expected losses, as well as future actual losses, are measured.

BASE PREMIUM a CEDING COMPANY'S premium to which the *reinsurance premium* factor is used to produce the reinsurance premium.

BASIC BENEFITS, BASIC HOSPITAL PLAN minimum payments provided under a health insurance policy. *See also* GROUP HEALTH INSURANCE; HEALTH INSURANCE.

BASIC LIMIT minimum amount of coverage for which a company will write a LIABILITY INSURANCE policy.

BASIC LIMITS OF LIABILITY required minimum amounts of coverage that an insurance company will underwrite. For example, for auto liability coverage the minimum that many companies will write is $25,000. Most liability suits are not below this range.

BASIC PREMIUM premium applied in WORKERS COMPENSATION INSURANCE and in life insurance. In the latter, it is the portion of a premium which is loaded to reflect an insured's expectation of loss, administrative expenses associated with putting the policy on the company's books, and the agent's commission.

BASIC RATE *see* MANUAL RATE.

BASIC TIME FRAME time period, for a life insurance policy, in which losses occur. This period must be determined to project the FREQUENCY and *severity* of future loss experience.

BASIS POINT unit used to measure movements in interest rates. It is the equivalent to one one-hundredth of 1%. One hundred basis points equals 1%.

BATTERY unlawful application of force to another's person; physical striking of another without permission.

BENCH ERROR mistake made during the manufacturing process of a product which results in an inherit defect in the product. This mistake is covered under PRODUCTS AND COMPLETED OPERATIONS INSURANCE.

BENEFICIARY designation by the owner of a life insurance policy indicating to whom the proceeds are to be paid upon the insured's death or when an endowment matures. Anyone can be named a beneficiary (relative, non-relative, pet, charity, corporation, trustee, partnership). A *primary beneficiary* is the first-named beneficiary, who must survive the death of the insured in order to collect the proceeds. A *contingent* or *secondary beneficiary* will receive the proceeds if the primary beneficiary does not survive the insured. A *revocable beneficiary* (primary or secondary) can be changed by the policyowner at any time. An *irrevocable beneficiary* (primary or secondary) can be changed by the policyowner only with the written permission of that beneficiary. Naming an irrevocable beneficiary removes the policy from the estate of the insured, who thereby gives up incidences of ownership for estate tax purposes.

If a beneficiary is convicted of murdering the insured, the beneficiary cannot collect the death benefit. The insured's estate would receive the benefit.

BENEFICIARY CLAUSE provision in a life insurance policy that permits the policyowner to name anyone as primary and secondary beneficiaries. The policyowner may change the beneficiaries at any time by simply writing the insurance company and sending the policy for endorsement if that is requested. *See also* BENEFICIARY.

BENEFICIARY OF TRUST person for whom the trust was created and who receives the benefits thereof. In many instances a trust is established to prevent the careless exhaustion of an estate. For example, the establishment of a trust for the benefit of a child seeks to guarantee that the parent's estate will not be carelessly diminished.

BENEFIT monetary sum paid or payable to a recipient for which the insurance company has received the premiums.

BENEFIT FORMULA procedure in employee benefit plans to calculate life insurance and retirement benefits to which an employee is entitled. *See also* DEFINED BENEFIT PLAN; DEFINED CONTRIBUTION PENSION (MONEY PURCHASE PLAN); GROUP LIFE INSURANCE.

BENEFIT PERIOD in HEALTH INSURANCE, the number of days for which benefits are paid to the NAMED INSURED and his or her dependents. For example, the number of days that benefits are calculated for a calendar year consist of the days beginning on January 1 and ending on December 31 of each year.

BENEFITS OF BUSINESS LIFE AND HEALTH INSURANCE (KEY PERSON INSURANCE) life insurance and long-term disability income insurance on major employees, with benefits payable to the business. Key person insurance has these advantages: (1) enhances the ability of the business to continue operations; (2) fosters smooth sale of a going business between an estate and a purchaser by providing funds to buy out the interest of a deceased key person; (3) encourages key employees to stay on the job; (4) attracts new key employees; (5) provides funds for expenses of hiring and training of a replacement key employee; (6) provides a line of credit (A permanent life insurance policy has cash values which are available for loans at advantageous rates.); (7) policy proceeds, which are income free, are payable even if the key person is no longer in the employ of the business at the time of death; however, the business must continue to make the premium payments after the key person leaves the employment.); (8) a life insurance policy can be surrendered for its cash value or sold to the insured key person; thus, the business will usually at least receive the return of premiums; (9) long-term disability income insurance on a key person also provides funds for salary continuation to the disabled key person. (For temporary disability, the business might prefer to self insure because the expense of premiums for this coverage is generally excessive when compared with the potential income benefits.)

BETTERMENT INSURANCE *see* IMPROVEMENTS AND BETTERMENTS INSURANCE.

BI *see* BODILY INJURY; BUSINESS INTERRUPTION.

BID BOND bond required of a contractor submitting the lowest bid on a project. If the contractor then refuses to undertake the project, the bid bond assures that the developer will be paid the difference between the lowest bid and next lowest bid. The bid bond encourages contractors to make serious bids and live up to their obligations.

BILATERAL CONTRACT contract under which there is an exchange of a promise for a promise. An INSURANCE POLICY is deemed to be a UNILATERAL CONTRACT.

BILL OF LADING document used in the transportation of goods which must be presented when a claim is made for a loss incurred. This document establishes the fact that the goods were under the care, custody, or control of the shipper at the time the loss occurred.

BINDER temporary insurance contract providing coverage until a permanent policy is issued. In property and casualty insurance, some agents have authority to bind the insurance company to cover until a policy can be issued. For example, the purchaser of an automobile can call the agent, who can then bind the insurance company to temporary coverage.

BINDING AUTHORITY *see* BINDER.

BINDING RECEIPT evidence of a temporary contract obliging a property insurance company to provide coverage as long as the premium accompanies the application. A property insurance agent can *bind* a company to cover a specific risk. Some agents are authorized to give an *oral binder*, which is generally followed with a written binder. For life and health insurance, *see also* CONDITIONAL RECEIPT.

BINOMIAL DISTRIBUTION statistical function that displays the probability of determining a stated number of successes in a series of trials in which the probability of success is the same in each trial. In insurance, the binomial distribution is used to analyze certain future events. Some chance events have only two possible outcomes; the probability of occurrence $p = 1 - q$ and the probability of nonoccurrence $q = 1 - p$. (Note that $p + q = 1$; that is to say, the probability of success plus the probability of failure is always equal to 1.) The probability of exactly *x outcomes (x successes)* in *n independent repetitions* is given by the function

$$f(x) = \binom{n}{x} p^x q^{n-x}$$

where: $x = 0, 1, 2, \ldots, n$

For example, if a fair coin is tossed in the air a total of six times, the *probability* of getting exactly five heads is:

$$f(5) = \binom{6}{5} \left(\frac{1}{2}\right)^5 \left(\frac{1}{2}\right) = \frac{6}{64}$$

BIRTH RATE number of people born as a percentage of the total population in any given period of time.

BLANKET BOND coverage for an employer in the event of dishonesty of any employee. *See also* FIDELITY BOND.

BLANKET CONTRACT policy covering an insured's property at several different locations. This coverage is used by business firms which have several locations and may move property from location to location.

BLANKET COVERAGE *see* BLANKET BOND; BLANKET CONTRACT; BLANKET CRIME POLICY; BLANKET INSURANCE; BLANKET MEDICAL EXPENSE INSURANCE; BLANKET POSITION BOND.

BLANKET CRIME ENDORSEMENT *see* BLANKET CRIME POLICY.

BLANKET CRIME POLICY coverage usually provided as part of the SPECIAL MULTIPERIL INSURANCE (SMP) policy through the attachment of the *Blanket Crime Endorsement*. Perils covered include dishonesty of a business's employees; loss of money both while inside as well as outside a business's premises; lost money orders; forgery due to the acts of a depositor, and counterfeit paper currency. Since this crime policy is so comprehensive it is said to provide the insured with a *blanket of coverage*.

BLANKET FIDELITY BOND *see* BLANKET BOND.

BLANKET FORM *see* BLANKET INSURANCE.

BLANKET HONESTY BOND *see* COMMERCIAL BLANKET BOND.

BLANKET INSURANCE single policy on the insured's property for (1) two or more different kinds of property in the same location; (2) same kind of property in two or more locations; (3) two or more different kinds of property in two or more different locations. Blanket coverage is ideal for such businesses as chain stores, all of whose property is covered with no specific limit on each particular property regardless of its location (thereby enabling the business to shift merchandise from store to store). This insurance can (but need not) be written on an ALL RISKS basis subject to exclusions of war, nuclear disaster, and wear and tear.

BLANKET LIMIT maximum amount of insurance coverage that an insurance company will underwrite in a particular geographic area.

BLANKET MEDICAL EXPENSE INSURANCE health insurance policy providing coverage for an insured's medical expenses except those that are specifically excluded. This may be the most advantageous medical expense policy for an insured because unless a specific medical expense is excluded it is automatically covered.

BLANKET POSITION BOND covers all employees of a business on a blanket basis with the maximum limit of coverage applied separately to each employee guilty of a crime. *See also* COMMERCIAL BLANKET BOND, FIDELITY BOND.

BLANKET RATE premium charged (and applied on a uniform basis) for property insurance covering properties at multiple locations. This rate is used under a BLANKET INSURANCE policy instead of using a specific rate for each location or type of property.

BLOCK POLICY coverage on an ALL RISKS basis for goods in transit, bailment, and while on the premises of others. *See also* JEWELERS BLOCK INSURANCE POLICY.

BLUE CROSS independent, nonprofit, membership hospital plan. Benefits provided include coverage for hospitalization expenses subject to certain restrictions: for example, semiprivate room only. A member hospital agrees to a predetermined schedule for specified medical services. The hospital sends the bills directly to the Blue Cross plan for reimbursement. Also covered are outpatient services, and supplementary or extended care such as nursing home care, as described in the contract.

BLUE SHIELD independent, nonprofit, membership medical-surgical plan. Benefits cover expenses associated with medical and surgical procedures. The physician and/or surgeon bills the Blue Shield Plan directly rather than the patient, who is responsible for any difference between the scheduled rates and the doctor's fees.

BOARD INSURER *see* BUREAU INSURER.

BOBTAIL LIABILITY INSURANCE coverage of a common carrier for liability on trucks that have delivered their cargo and are on the way back to the terminal. The company that hires the truck assumes liability while the truck is loaded, but after delivery, that firm's liability ends.

The carrier can be protected by bobtail liability coverage for the return trip.

BODILY INJURY physical damage to one's person. The purpose of liability (casualty) insurance is to cover bodily injury to a third party resulting from the negligent or intentional acts and omissions of an insured.

BODILY INJURY LIABILITY INSURANCE *see* LIABILITY INSURANCE.

BOILER AND MACHINERY INSURANCE covers losses resulting from the malfunction of boilers and machinery. Most property insurance policies exclude these losses, which is why a separate boiler and machinery policy or a SPECIAL MULTIPERIL INSURANCE (SMP) policy is needed. The insurance covers business property, other property involved, and legal fees if any.

BOND form of suretyship. For example, fidelity bonds reimburse an employer for financial loss resulting from dishonest acts of employees. *See also* BLANKET POSITION BOND; COMMERCIAL BLANKET BOND; CONTRACT BOND; FIDELITY BOND; INDIVIDUAL FIDELITY BOND; JUDICIAL BOND; NAME SCHEDULE BOND.

BOND, CONTRACT *see* CONTRACT BOND.

BOND, COURT *see* JUDICIAL BOND.

BOND, FIDELITY *see* FIDELITY BOND.

BOND (FINANCIAL) corporate or government security that pays interest and obligates the corporation or government agency to pay that interest at the end of specific time intervals, and to pay the principal at maturity of the security.

BOND, FORGERY *see* DEPOSITORS FORGERY INSURANCE.

BOND, MAINTENANCE *see* MAINTENANCE BOND.

BOND, PERFORMANCE *see* CONTRACT BOND.

BOND, PERMIT *see* PERMIT BOND.

BOND, PUBLIC OFFICIAL *see* PUBLIC OFFICIAL BOND.

BOND, SURETY *see* SURETY BOND.

BOOK OF BUSINESS total amount of insurance on an insurer's books at a particular time. *See also* NET RETAINED LINES.

BOOK VALUE cost of the assets listed on the accounting records of the company. These assets include the following: real estate (to include any adjustments for depreciation), transportation equipment (to include any adjustments for depreciation), policy loans (limited to the unpaid principal balance plus any unamortized premiums minus any accrued discounts), mortgage loans (limited to the unpaid principal balance plus any unamortized premiums minus any accrued discounts), cash, and joint ventures. Not listed at book value are securities.

BOOK VALUE PER COMMON SHARE value of a share of common stock, derived by dividing the total common stockholders' equity at the end of a period of time by the total number of shares outstanding at the end of the same period of time.

BOOT property or money received as additional consideration in regard to a tax-free exchange of property. If the POLICYHOLDER receives money in an otherwise nontaxable life insurance policy exchange, the money received will be taxable income to the policyholder. Likewise, if the loan on an old policy is cancelled by the insurer when that policy is exchanged for a new policy, the loan amount so cancelled becomes taxable income to the policyholder. *See also* MINIMUM DEPOSIT RESCUE; TAX-FREE EXCHANGE OF INSURANCE PRODUCTS.

BORDEREAU form of reinsurance that shows loss history and premium history with respect to specific risks. The CEDING COMPANY provides its *reinsurer* with that information. This information is used by the *reinsurance company* in establishing the reinsurance premium rates. *See also* REINSURANCE.

BORDERLINE RISK prospective insurance applicant who has questionable UNDERWRITING characteristics.

BORROWING AUTHORITY OF PENSION BENEFIT GUARANTY CORPORATION (PBGC) authorization to borrow from the U.S. Treasury by the issuance of notes to the Treasury. The Secretary of the Treasury must approve the notes and their interest rates. The PBGC must be self supporting through the premium it charges for various plans and thus its notes carry the same obligations of any notes, in that they are expected to be repaid.

BOSTON PLAN agreement named after the city of Boston under which insurance companies insure real property in lower socioeconomic neighborhoods if property owners correct any hazards found upon inspection.

BOTH-TO-BLAME CLAUSE in OCEAN MARINE INSURANCE, provision stipulating that upon the collision of two or more ships, when all ships are at fault, all owners and shippers having monetary interests in the voyage of the ships involved must share in all losses in proportion to the monetary values of their interests prior to the occurrence of the collision. This clause supercedes all other provisions for the allocation of losses among owners and shippers in ocean marine policies.

BOTTOMRY method of transferring pure risks that is perhaps the seed of the modern day insurance policy. Ancient Greece held to the concept that a loan on a ship was canceled if the ship failed to return to its port. This concept was adopted by Lloyd's of London in the 1600s when insuring England's merchants for goods shipped to the colonies. The formation of property and casualty insurance companies worldwide began by insuring the transport of merchandise over bodies of water.

BPPCF *see* BUSINESS AND PERSONAL PROPERTY COVERAGE FROM (BPPCF).

BRANCH MANAGER *see* AGENCY MANAGER.

BRANCH OFFICE local business headquarters of an insurance company that markets and services its products and lines of insurance. *See also* MANAGER.

BREACH OF CONTRACT failure of a party (not having a legal excuse) to perform in accordance with a promise made. An INSURANCE POLICY consists of legally enforceable promises made by the INSURANCE COMPANY (INSURER) only. No such promises are made by the INSURED. This is the reason why the insurance policy is a UNILATERAL CONTRACT.

BREAK IN SERVICE feature of pension plans whereby an employee whose service has been interrupted can have that period credited toward retirement.

BRIDGE INSURANCE coverage for damage or destruction to an insured bridge. Insures on an ALL RISKS basis subject to exclusions of war, wear and tear, inherent defect, and nuclear damages. Coverage is purchased by state and local governing bodies to limit exposures to the expense of an immediate tax increase to rebuild a damaged or destroyed bridge.

BRIDGE INSURANCE FOR BRIDGES UNDER CONSTRUCTION provides coverage during the construction of a bridge in the event of fire, lightning, collision, flood, rising water, windstorm, ice, explosion, and earthquake. This coverage is essential, since the value of destroyed labor and materials could bankrupt a contractor without insurance protection.

BROAD FORM INSURANCE coverage for numerous perils such as that found in the BROAD FORM PERSONAL THEFT INSURANCE.

BROAD FORM PERSONAL THEFT INSURANCE coverage on an ALL RISKS basis for loss due to theft or mysterious disappearance of personal property; damage to premises and property within resulting from theft; and vandalism and malicious mischief to the interior of the premises as well as to other property of an insured which is away from the insured's premises. Sub-limits are in effect on specialty property which is particularly susceptible to theft, such as money, securities, paintings, coins, and jewelry. This insurance is most often found in Part I Coverage C of the HOMEOWNERS INSURANCE POLICY and is expressed as a percentage of the home's structure.

BROAD FORM PROPERTY DAMAGE ENDORSEMENT attachment to a general liability policy thereby eliminating the exclusion of property under the care, custody, and/or control of an insured. Without this endorsement there would be no coverage under the GENERAL LIABILITY INSURANCE policy in the event of damage or destruction of property under the care, custody, and control of the insured.

BROAD FORM STOREKEEPERS INSURANCE coverage usually provided as part of the STOREKEEPERS BURGLARY AND ROBBERY INSURANCE in the event merchandise, fixtures, equipment, and furniture are lost due to theft and burglary.

BROKER insurance salesperson who searches the marketplace in the interest of clients, not insurance companies. *See also* AGENT, BROKERAGE DEPARTMENT.

BROKERAGE insurance coverage sold by a BROKER as contrasted with insurance coverage sold by an AGENT. *See also* BROKERAGE FEE.

BROKERAGE BUSINESS insurance coverage placed by a BROKER with an insurance company. *See also* BROKERAGE DEPARTMENT.

BROKERAGE DEPARTMENT section of an insurance company which sells through brokers. Some brokerage departments are self-contained in that they have their own underwriting and marketing staffs. Brokerage departments have come into their own in recent times as even captive agent insurance companies have sought additional distribution channels which may be less expensive than the captive agent field force. *See also* BROKER; CAPTIVE AGENT.

BROKERAGE FEE commission paid to a broker for selling an insurance company's products. This fee may or may not include an expense allowance depending on the amount of business the broker places with the company.

BROKER-AGENT independent insurance salesperson who represents particular insurers but may also function as a broker by searching the entire insurance market to place an applicant's coverage to maximize protection and minimize cost. This person is licensed as an agent and broker.

BROKER OF RECORD *see* AGENT OF RECORD.

BUILD to construct.

BUILDERS RISK COVERAGE FORM *see* BUILDERS RISKS FORMS.

BUILDERS RISK HULL INSURANCE property coverage for a builder of ships until possession passes to the owners. Protects against pre-launch and post-launch perils. Coverage can be purchased on an ALL RISKS basis subject to the exclusions of war, nuclear disaster, and inherent defects. The builder buys either insurance that covers the startup value of the property, to be adjusted upward to reflect additional construction (*Reporting Form*); or insurance to cover the completed value of the property (*Completed Form*).

BUILDERS RISK INSURANCE *see* BUILDERS RISKS FORMS.

BUILDERS RISKS FORMS types of contracts that insure building contractors for damage to property under construction. The *completed value form* requires a 100% coinsurance because insurance carried must equal the completed value of the structure. The *reporting form* allows coverage to be carried according to the stage of completion of the structure. Perils insured against are fire, lightning, vandalism, malicious mischief, riot and civil commotion, smoke, sprinkler leakage, water damage, windstorm, and hail.

BUILDING AND PERSONAL PROPERTY COVERAGE FORM *see* BUSINESS AND PERSONAL PROPERTY COVERAGE FORM (BPPCF).

BUMBERSHOOT POLICY liability insurance coverage, primarily for shipyards for ocean marine risks, provided in much the same manner as UMBRELLA LIABILITY INSURANCE for nonmarine risks. Coverages may be provided in addition to liability include PROTECTION AND INDEMNITY INSURANCE (P&I), LONGSHOREMEN AND HARBOR WORKERS ACT LIABILITY, collision, and salvage expenses.

BUREAU INSURER insurance company that is a member of a RATING BUREAU. The insurer usually joins such an organization when its statistical experience in a given *line of insurance* is not sufficient for it to accurately predict loss experience for that line.

BUREAU OF LABOR STATISTICS *see* LABOR STATISTICS, BUREAU OF.

BUREAU RATE *see* RATING BUREAU.

BURGLARY forced entry into premises. Coverage is provided under various property insurance contracts such as HOMEOWNERS and SPECIAL MULTIPERIL INSURANCE (SMP).

BURGLARY INSURANCE coverage against loss as the result of a burglary. Found as part of the SPECIAL MULTIPERIL INSURANCE (SMP) policy and the MERCANTILE OPEN STOCK BURGLARY INSURANCE policy. Covers loss of merchandise, furniture, equipment, fixtures due to force and violence to the exterior of a business's premises in order to gain entry, and damage to the premises of the business as the result of the burglary. There is a coinsurance requirement which ranges from 40 to 80%.

BURGLARY/THEFT INSURANCE *see* BURGLARY INSURANCE.

BURIAL INSURANCE small face amount life insurance policy. *See also* FUNERAL INSURANCE.

BURNING COST RATIO (PURE LOSS COST) ratio of excess losses to premium income. Excess losses are those that a reinsurer is responsible for if its coverage is in effect during the period under consideration. The premium income used for EXCESS OF LOSS and CATASTROPHE LOSS reinsurance is the gross premium less the expense of reinsurance. The premium income used for STOP LOSS REINSURANCE is the earned premium income. The excess losses are defined as the incurred losses in excess of the cedent's retention up to the limits specified in the reinsurance contract. *See also* REINSURANCE.

BURNING RATIO
  1. actual fire losses divided by the total value of the property exposed to the PERIL of fire.
  2. actual losses resulting from fire divided by the total fire amount of IN-FORCE BUSINESS.
     See also BURNING COST RATIO (PURE LOSS COST).

BUSINESS in insurance, volume of premiums written. Also describes commercial activities with the profit motive as the goal of the organization. Commercial insurance companies are organized with the profit motive as the normal business objective.

BUSINESS AND PERSONAL PROPERTY COVERAGE FORM (BPPCF) provision for coverage for buildings and personal property within the SIMPLIFIED COMMERCIAL LINES PORTFOLIO POLICY (SCLP). The buildings and personal property coverage may be classified in three ways:
  1. *Owned buildings*—these buildings are listed and described in the DECLARATIONS SECTION of the policy. Also covered is anything which has become a permanent part of the buildings, to include additions, fixtures, extensions, and machinery and equipment.
  2. *Owned business personal property*—property covered is the business personal property which is owned by the insured and is common in the occupancy usage by the insured.

3. *Nonowned business personal property*—properties covered are improvements and betterments (alterations made by the insured to a building which he or she is leasing and which cannot be removed upon the termination of the lease), and personal property of someone other than the insured which is under the care, custody, or control of the insured.

Extensions of coverage are available under the BPPCF to include:

1. *outdoor property*—trees, shrubs, and plants; signs; radio and television antennas; and fences. There is an overall limit of $1,000 and a sublimit of $250 for each tree, shrub, or plant.

2. *valuable papers and records*—cost of replacing or restoring information lost because of the damage or destruction of valuable papers and records. There is a $1,000 limit of coverage.

3. *personal effects and property of others*—personal effects of the named insured, employees, and others which are under the care, custody, or control of the insured.

4. *business personal property on location at premises newly acquired*—10% of the owned business personal property coverage is applicable, subject to $100,000 limit for each building. Thirty days after the acquisition of property, coverage terminates.

5. *newly acquired buildings or additions*—25% of the owned building coverage is applicable, subject to $250,000 limit for each building. Within 30 days, newly acquired buildings or additions must be reported by the insured.

6. *off-premises property*—property on a temporary location (other than a vehicle) not owned, leased, or operated by the insured.

PERILS insured against are available under three forms:

1. *basic form*—includes fire, lightning, windstorm, hail, explosion, vandalism, smoke, sprinkler leakage, riot or civil commotion, sinkhole collapse, volcano.

2. *broad form*—includes perils found under the basic form plus falling objects causing exterior damage which results in interior damage; weight of ice, sleet, and snow; accidental discharge of water or steam from a system or appliance containing steam or water, but not including an automatic sprinkler system; and breakage of glass; subject to a $500 maximum limit.

3. *special cause-of-loss form*—includes all direct accidental losses except those specifically excluded in the policy (such as flood, war, wear and tear, and earth movement).

ENDORSEMENTS can be added to the BPPCF to include:

1. *perils extension*—adds earthquake, volcanic eruption, and radioactive contamination.

2. *limits of recovery extension*—increase maximum dollar amounts of coverage for trees, shrubs, and plants; radio and television antennas; and outdoor signs.

   3. *replacement cost endorsement*—changes basis of recovery under the
   BPPCF to a REPLACEMENT COST LESS PHYSICAL DEPRECIATION AND
   OBSOLESENCE from an ACTUAL CASH VALUE basis.

BUSINESS AUTOMOBILE POLICY (BAP) coverage for automobiles
used by a business when a liability judgment arises out of the use of
the automobile, or the automobile is subject to damage or destruction.
The business can select coverage for any auto in use, whether business,
personal, or hired. The policy is organized as follows:

   Parts I, II, and III—define terms used in the policy, such as auto,
accident, insured bodily injury, property damage, territorial limits of
coverage.

   Part IV LIABILITY INSURANCE—in a liability judgment against the
insured business and/or individual, the insurance company will pay the
monetary damages up to the limit of the policy. Negligent acts and/or
omissions of the insured business and/or individual must arise out of
the ownership and operation of a covered auto, subject to specific exclusions.

   Part V *physical damage insurance*—in the event of damage to an
auto, the insurance company will pay under one of two categories:
COMPREHENSIVE INSURANCE—damage resulting from fire, explosion,
theft, vandalism, malicious mischief, windstorm, hail, earthquake, or
flood; or *collision insurance*—damage resulting from colliding with another object or the overturning of the insured auto.

   Part VI CONDITION—stipulate what the policyholder must do in the
event of a loss, such as give notice to the insurance company; submit
proof of the loss; submit to inspection of damaged property by the
company; cooperate with the company in the event of a liability suit.

BUSINESS CONTINUATION INSURANCE *see* BUSINESS LIFE AND
HEALTH INSURANCE.

BUSINESS CRIME INSURANCE protection for the assets of a business
(including merchandise for sale, real property, money and securities) in
the event of robbery, burglary, larceny, forgery and embezzlement.
Coverage is provided in package policies such as SPECIAL MULTIPERIL
INSURANCE (SMP) policy Section III, and the BUSINESSOWNERS POLICY
(BOP) Section III. Or coverage can be written under separate policies
such as: BANK BURGLARY AND ROBBERY INSURANCE, COMBINATION SAFE
DEPOSITORY INSURANCE, MERCANTILE OPEN-STOCK, BURGLARY
INSURANCE, MERCANTILE ROBBERY INSURANCE, MERCANTILE SAFE
BURGLARY INSURANCE, MONEY AND SECURITIES BROAD FORM POLICY,
OFFICE BURGLARY AND ROBBERY INSURANCE, PAYMASTER ROBBERY
INSURANCE, STOREKEEPERS BURGLARY AND ROBBERY INSURANCE.

BUSINESS HEALTH INSURANCE *see* BUSINESS LIFE AND HEALTH
INSURANCE.

BUSINESS INSURANCE coverage designed to protect against loss exposures of business firms, as opposed to those of individuals. *See also* BUSINESS AUTOMOBILE POLICY (BAP); BUSINESS CRIME INSURANCE; BUSINESS INTERRUPTION INSURANCE; BUSINESS LIFE AND HEALTH INSURANCE; BUSINESSOWNERS POLICY; BUY AND SELL AGREEMENT; CLOSE CORPORATION PLAN; PARTNERSHIP LIFE AND HEALTH INSURANCE; SOLE PROPRIETOR LIFE AND HEALTH INSURANCE.

BUSINESS INTERRUPTION break in commercial activities due to the occurrence of a peril. Coverage against business interruption by various named perils can be obtained through insurance. *See also* BUSINESS INTERRUPTION INSURANCE.

BUSINESS INTERRUPTION INSURANCE indemnification for the loss of profits and the continuing fixed expenses. Business interruption insurance is available in these forms: CONTINGENT BUSINESS INTERRUPTION FORM, EXTRA EXPENSE FORM, GROSS EARNINGS FORM, PROFITS AND COMMISSIONS FORM, AND TUITION FORM.

BUSINESS LIABILITY INSURANCE coverage for liability exposure resulting from the activities of a business; includes: (1) DIRECT LIABILITY—acts of the business resulting in damage or destruction of another party's property or bodily injury to that party; (2) CONTINGENT LIABILITY—although the business may not have direct liability, it may incur a secondary or contingent liability, for example through the employment of an independent contractor; (3) MEDICAL PAYMENTS TO OTHERS INSURANCE—acts of the business resulting in injury to another party, with the insurance company paying the medical expenses to that party (up to the policy limits) without regard to legal liability of the insured business. The policy has three principal sections:
1. DECLARATIONS SECTION lists the insured, policy limits, premium, time period of coverage, kind of policy, and endorsements, if any.
2. INSURING AGREEMENTS states that if any of the insured perils result in damage or destruction of another party's property or injury to that party, the company will pay (up to the limits of the policy) sums which the business becomes legally obligated to pay. (a) *Time Period of the Loss*—policy can be written either on a *claims occurrence* basis or a *claims made* basis; (b) BODILY INJURY—damage or destruction of a body to include sickness, disease, and/or resulting death (most liability insurance policies provide coverage for this definition); (c) PERSONAL INJURY—defamation of character, libel and slander, false arrest, malicious prosecution, and invasion of privacy (many liability policies can be endorsed to provide these coverages); (d) *Property Damages*—damage or destruction of real and personal property and the loss of use of this property; (e) DEFENSE COSTS—costs of defending the insured business to include investigation, defense, and the settlement of claims which are paid in addition to the

limits of coverage under the policy; and (f) *Policy Limits*—the maximum that the insurance company is obligated to pay on behalf of the insured business.

3. EXCLUSIONS to avoid duplications of coverage in other policies and/or to eliminate certain kinds of coverage, including: property under the care, custody and control of the insured business; liability arising out of contractual obligations between the insured business and another party; liability associated with recall of the insured business's products; liability associated with the insured business's pollution and contamination exposure; and liability that may arise out of conflict with state liquor regulations.

4. *Conditions* stipulate that (a) the insured, after an accident, must behave so as not to increase the severity of bodily injury and/or property damage that has just occurred; (b) the insurance company has the right to inspect the insured business's premises as well as its operations; and (c) if there is more than one policy covering a claim, each policy will pay an equal share of the loss.

BUSINESS LIFE AND HEALTH INSURANCE coverage providing funds for maintenance of a business as closely to normal as possible in the event of a loss of a key person, owner, or partner. *See also* BENEFITS OF BUSINESS LIFE AND HEALTH INSURANCE; BUY-AND-SELL AGREEMENT; CLOSE CORPORATION PLAN; PARTNERSHIP LIFE AND HEALTH INSURANCE.

BUSINESS LIFE INSURANCE *see* BUSINESS LIFE AND HEALTH INSURANCE.

BUSINESS OVERHEAD EXPENSE INSURANCE *see* BUSINESS INTERRUPTION INSURANCE.

BUSINESSOWNERS POLICY (BOP) combination property, liability, and business interruption policy. It is usually written to cover expenses of small and medium size businesses resulting from (1) damage or destruction of business's property or (2) when actions or nonactions of the business's representatives result in bodily injury or property damage to another individual(s). Businesses that qualify under this heading include office buildings three stories or under not to exceed 100,000 square feet; apartment buildings six stories or under not to exceed 60 dwelling units; any other buildings not to exceed 7500 square feet for mercantile space, occupied principally as an apartment, office, or engaging in trade or commerce. Properties that cannot be insured under this policy include banks, condominiums, bars, restaurants, automobiles, recreational vehicles, contractor functions, and manufacturing operations. *See also* BUSINESSOWNERS POLICY—SECTION I: PROPERTY COVERAGES; BUSINESSOWNERS POLICY—SECTION II: LIABILITY COVERAGES.

BUSINESSOWNERS POLICY—SECTION I: PROPERTY COV-ERAGES contract that details coverage for business property losses in three specific areas:

1. *Coverage A (Building).* All buildings on the site are covered with no coinsurance requirement and on a replacement cost basis to include: the buildings themselves; the owner's personal property used to maintain the building(s) and provided to tenants; permanent fixtures, equipment and machinery; improvements and betterments by tenants; removal of debris; and outdoor furniture and fixtures.

2. *Coverage B (Personal Property of the Business).* All personal property used in the business on the premises, as well as personal property of others under the care, custody and control of the owner of the building used to operate the business; and limited coverage for items temporarily away from the premises of the business as well as for property purchased and placed at a new business location.

3. *Coverage C (Loss of Income).* Reimbursement for loss of income because of inability to collect business rent; interruption of normal business functions; and extra expenses associated with resuming normal business activities as the result of the damage or destruction of business property by an insured peril. (Optionally, under Section I, coverage can be extended to insure against burglary, robbery, theft, employee dishonesty, and boiler and machinery explosion. Earthquake damage can be covered through an endorsement.)

BUSINESSOWNERS POLICY—SECTION II: LIABILITY COV-ERAGES coverage that protects a business, up to the policy limits, if actions or non-actions of the insured result in a legally enforceable claim for bodily injury, property damage, or personal injury. Included are coverages for: (1) nonowned automobiles used by the business in its normal operations (owned automobiles are excluded); (2) host liquor liability where the business is having a social gathering. For example, liability at an office party would be covered, since this social function is incidental to normal business activity (excluded would be operation of a liquor store on the premises of the business); (3) fire and explosion legal liability, where the insured is renting business space in a building. If a fire or explosion from business operations is proven to be of negligent origin, the insurer of the owner of the building has subrogation rights against the business; (4) products, for which completed operations coverage is provided. Excluded from Section II coverages are professional liability, owned automobiles of the business, operation of airplanes and other aircraft, Workers Compensation, liquor liability (other than that served as a host at business social functions), and off-premises operation of boats.

BUSINESS PROPERTY AND LIABILITY INSURANCE PACKAGE protection of the property of the business that is damaged or destroyed by perils such as fire, smoke, and vandalism; and/or if the actions (or nonactions) of the business' representatives result in bodily injury or property damage to other individuals. Many insurance policies provide such coverages, but the two most often used are the SPECIAL MULTIPERIL INSURANCE (SMP) policy and the BUSINESSOWNERS POLICY (BOP).

BUSINESS RISK EXCLUSION omissions from coverage found in *products liability insurance*. The policy does not provide coverage if the business manufactures a product that does not meet the level of performance as advertised, represented, or warranted. For example, an automobile antifreeze is advertised as being able to withstand temperatures as low as 30° below zero. An engine block containing the fluid freezes at a temperature of 10° above zero. In this instance a products liability policy would not provide coverage for the insured business.

BUY-AND-SELL AGREEMENT approach used for sole proprietorships, partnerships, and close corporations in which the business interests of a deceased or disabled proprietor, partner or shareholder are sold according to a predetermined formula to the remaining member(s) of the business. For example, a partnership has three principals. Upon the death of one, the two survivors have agreed to purchase, and the deceased partner's estate has agreed to sell, the interest of that partner according to a predetermined formula for valuing the partnership to the survivors. Funds for buying out the deceased partner's interest are usually provided by life insurance policies, with each partner purchasing a policy on the other partners. Each is the owner and beneficiary of the policies purchased on the other partners.

When a sole proprietor dies, usually a key employee is the buyer/successor. The sole proprietorship, partnership, and close corporation under the entity plan can buy and own life insurance policies on the proprietor, partner or shareholder and achieve the same result as when an individual buys and owns the policies.

BUY-BACK DEDUCTIBLE DEDUCTIBLE eliminated through the payment of an additional premium, resulting in FIRST-DOLLAR COVERAGE under the policy.

BYPASS TRUST type of TRUST used to remove assets from a surviving spouse's estate, thereby excluding such assets from FEDERAL ESTATE TAX upon the death of the surviving spouse. This type of trust allows for a lifetime benefit to be available to both spouses while living, as well as to a single surviving spouse. A bypass trust permits a maximum of $1.2 million transfer to heirs of the spouses on a tax-free basis under the unified gift and estate tax credits.

C

CAFETERIA BENEFIT PLAN arrangement under which employees may choose their own employee benefit structure. For example, one employee may wish to emphasize health care and thus would select a more comprehensive health insurance plan for the allocation of the premiums, while another employee may wish to emphasize retirement and thus allocate more of the premiums to the purchase of pension benefits.

CALCULABLE CHANGE OF LOSS *see* PROBABILITY.

CALENDAR YEAR EXPERIENCE paid loss experience for the period of time from January 1 to December 31 of a specified year (not necessarily the current year).

CALENDAR YEAR STATISTICS *see* CALENDAR YEAR EXPERIENCE.

CAMERA AND MUSICAL INSTRUMENTS DEALERS INSUR-ANCE coverage on an ALL RISKS basis for the insured's own property as well as property of others under the insured firm's care, custody, and control. Exclusions are WEAR AND TEAR, MYSTERIOUS DISAPPEARANCE, earthquake, flood, theft from an unlocked and unattended vehicle, loss of market, and delay. For example, if a dealer's personal flute is damaged by fire, or if a customer's camera is stolen, the dealer would be covered for both occurrences up to the limits of the policy.

CANADIAN INSTITUTE OF ACTUARIES membership organization representing professional actuaries in all insurance fields in Canada including life and health, casualty, consulting and fraternal actuaries. A member must reside in Canada and belong to an approved actuarial organization, including the SOCIETY OF ACTUARIES (SA).

CANCEL termination of a policy. Contract may be terminated by an insured or insurer as stated in the policy. If the insurance company cancels a policy, any unearned premiums must be returned. If an insured cancels the policy, an amount less than the unearned premiums is returned, reflecting the insurance company's administration costs of placing the policy on its books. Usually this term is applied only in property and disability insurance.

CANCELLABLE *see* CANCEL; CANCELLATION PROVISION CLAUSE.

CANCELLATION *see* CANCELLATION PROVISION CLAUSE.

CANCELLATION, PRO RATA *see* PRO RATA CANCELLATION.

CANCELLATION PROVISION CLAUSE provision permitting an insured or an insurance company to cancel a property and casualty or a health insurance policy (circumstances vary; *see also* COMMERCIAL HEALTH INSURANCE) at any time before its expiration data. The insured must send written notice to the insurance company, which then refunds the excess of the premium paid above the customary short rates for the expired term. If the insurance company cancels, it sends written notice to the insured of cancellation and refunds the unearned portion of the premium.

CANCELLATION, SHORT RATE *see* SHORT RATE CANCELLATION.

CAP *see* COINSURANCE.

CAPACITY maximum that an insurance company can underwrite. The limits of coverage that a property and casualty company can underwrite are determined by its retained earnings and invested capital. REINSURANCE is a method of increasing the insurance company's capacity, in that a portion of the unearned premium reserve maintenance requirement can be relieved. Commissions earned are ceded, underwriting results are stabilized, and financing of the expansion of the insurer's capacity can take place.

CAPACITY OF PARTIES legal capability of those involved in mutual assent of making a contract, including an insurance contract. Those who have been deemed to be incompetent to make a valid contract include intoxicated and insane persons, and enemy aliens. Minors can enter into a contract, but it is voidable at the option of the minor. For example, if an agent sells an insurance policy to a minor, and the insurance company agrees to underwrite it, the policy can be voided at any time the minor wishes both before and after the minor reaches the age of majority. The insurance company cannot void the contract.

CAPITAL equity of shareholders of a stock insurance company. The company's capital and SURPLUS are measured by the difference between its assets minus its liabilities. This value protects the interests of the company's policyowners in the event it develops financial problems; the policyowners' benefits are thus protected by the insurance company's capital. Shareholders' interest is second to that of policyowners.

CAPITAL GAINS excess of the sales price of an asset over its book value. Listed as part of the *Annual Report* in the summary of the surplus account and/or in the Summary of Operations.

CAPTIVE AGENT representative of a single insurer or fleet of insurers who is obliged to submit business only to that company, or at the very minimum, give that company first refusal rights on a sale. In exchange, that insurer usually provides its captive agents with an allowance for office expenses as well as an extensive list of employee benefits such as pensions, life insurance, health insurance, and credit unions.

CAPTIVE INSURANCE COMPANY company formed to insure the risks of its parent corporation. Reasons for forming a captive insurance company include:

1. Instances when insurance cannot be purchased from commercial insurance companies for a business risk. In many instances companies within an industry form a joint captive insurance company for that reason.
2. Premiums paid to a captive insurance company are deductible as a business expense for tax purposes according to the Internal Revenue Service. However, sums set aside in a self insurance program are not deductible as a business expense.
3. Insurance can be obtained through the international reinsurance market at a more favorable premium, with higher limits of coverage.
4. Investment returns can be obtained directly on its invested capital.

However, competent personnel to manage and staff the company could be excessively expensive; and further, a catastrophic occurrence or series of occurrences could bankrupt the company.

CAPTIVE INSURANCE COMPANIES ASSOCIATION (CICA) trade association located in New York, NY, and consisting of approximately 200 CAPTIVE INSURANCE COMPANIES. The objective of the association is to further the common interests of its members.

CARE, CUSTODY, AND CONTROL phrase in most liability insurance policies which eliminates from coverage damage or destruction to property under the care, custody, and control of an insured. Such coverage is excluded from liability policies because the insured either has some ownership interest in such property (better covered through property not liability insurance) or is a bailor of the property (and can better cover this bailment exposure through an appropriate bailee policy).

CARGO INSURANCE shipper's policies covering one cargo exposure or all cargo exposures by sea on ALL RISKS basis. Exclusions include war, nuclear disaster, wear and tear, dampness, mold, losses due to delay of shipment, and loss of market for the cargo. *One Cargo Exposure (Single Risk Cargo Policy)* covers a single shipment of goods and/or a single trip. *All Cargo Exposure (Open Cargo Policy)* covers all shipments of goods and/or all trips generally used by most shippers which require automatic coverage for all of its shipments, subject to 30 days' notice of cancellation.

CARGO LIABILITY INSURANCE *see* CARGO INSURANCE.

CARGO MARINE INSURANCE *see* CARGO INSURANCE.

CARPENTER PLAN (SPREAD LOSS COVER, SPREAD LOSS REINSURANCE) form of excess of loss reinsurance under which each year's REINSURANCE premium is determined by the amount of the *cedent's* excess losses for a given period of time, usually three or five years. Upon renewal, the first year's initial rate is based on the total of three or five years of previous experience, a form of RETROSPECTIVE RATING. The Carpenter Plan is particularly relevant to economic conditions in the way it handles the factor of inflation.

CARRIER insurance company which actually underwrites and issues the insurance policy. The term is used because the insurance company assumes or carries the risk for policyowners. The agent usually has a *primary carrier* (the insurance company to which most of the business is submitted) and *secondary carriers* (to which lesser amounts are submitted). The primary carrier provides the agent with commission schedules, expense allowance, and the availability of markets for the agent's business.

CAS *see* CASUALTY ACTUARIAL SOCIETY (CAS).

CASH FLOW PLANS method of payment of an insurance premium which allows an insured to regulate the amount and frequency of the premium payments in accordance with cash flow over a stipulated period of time. This enables the insured to maintain control over the funds for a longer period of time and thus reap benefits from their earnings.

CASH OUT OF VESTED BENEFITS money withdrawn by an employee from benefits owned. When an employee exercises this right, future benefits purchased by the employer on behalf of the employee are usually forfeited.

CASH REFUND ANNUITY (LUMP SUM REFUND ANNUITY) if the annuitant dies before receiving total income at least equal to the premiums paid, the beneficiary receives the difference in a lump sum. If the annuitant lives after the income paid equals the premiums paid, the insurance company continues to make income payments to the annuitant for life. *See also* ANNUITY.

CASH SURRENDER VALUE money the policyowner is entitled to receive from the insurance company upon surrendering a life insurance policy with cash value. The sum is the cash value stated in the policy minus a surrender charge and any outstanding loans and interest thereon.

CASH VALUE *see* CASH SURRENDER VALUE.

CASH VALUE LIFE INSURANCE policy which generates a savings element. Cash values are critical to a permanent life insurance policy. The size of a cash value buildup differs substantially from company to company. In many instances there is no correlation between the size of the cash value and premiums paid; in some cases there is an inverse relationship. Everything which the policyowner wishes to do with this policy while living is determined by the size of the cash value. For example, at some future time, a policyowner may wish to convert the cash value to a monthly retirement income. Its size will depend on (1) the amount of the cash value and (2) the attained age of the policy owner. *See also* ANNUITY; NONFORFEITURE BENEFIT (OPTION).

CASH WITHDRAWALS removal of money from an individual life insurance policy or an employee benefit plan. A cash withdrawal from a life insurance policy reduces the death benefit by the amount of the withdrawal plus interest thereon. When a cash withdrawal is made from an employee benefit such as a pension plan, the employee usually forfeits all benefits purchased on the employee's behalf by the employer. *See also* CASH VALUE LIFE INSURANCE.

CASUALTY liability or loss resulting from an ACCIDENT. Such liability or losses are covered under such policies as the following: BUSINESS AUTOMOBILE POLICY (BAP), BUSINESS PROPERTY AND LIABILITY INSURANCE PACKAGE, BUSINESSOWNERS POLICY (BOP), CASUALTY INSURANCE, COMMERCIAL GENERAL LIABILITY FORM (CGL), CONDOMINIUM INSURANCE, HOMEOWNERS INSURANCE POLICY, PERSONAL AUTOMOBILE POLICY (PAP), SIMPLIFIED COMMERCIAL LINES PORTFOLIO POLICY (SCLP), TENANTS INSURANCE, AND WORKERS COMPENSATION INSURANCE.

CASUALTY ACTUARIAL SOCIETY (CAS) accrediting body for the ACAS (Associate of the Casualty Actuarial Society) designation and the FCAS (Fellow of the Casualty Actuarial Society) designation. To earn these designations, members take a series of examinations on actuarial mathematics and related topics as they apply to the property and casualty insurance field. Passing the examinations denotes a sound background in mathematics as well as knowledge of business such as finance and economics. Located in New York City, New York.

CASUALTY CATASTROPHE casualty losses of high severity. *See also* CASUALTY INSURANCE.

CASUALTY INSURANCE coverage primarily for the liability of an individual or organization which results from negligent acts and omissions, thereby causing bodily injury and/or property damage to a third party. However, the term is an elastic one that traditionally has included such property insurance as AVIATION INSURANCE, BOILER AND MACHINERY INSURANCE and *glass and crime insurance*. *See also* BUSINESS LIABILITY INSURANCE.

CATASTROPHE EXCESS REINSURANCE *see* EXCESS OF LOSS REINSURANCE.

CATASTROPHE HAZARD circumstance under which there is a significant deviation of the actual aggregate losses from the expected aggregate losses. For example, a hurricane is a hazard that is catastrophic in nature, since whole units or blocks of businesses may be threatened. Catastrophic hazards often cannot or will not be insured by commercial insurance companies either because the hazard is too great or because the actuarial premium is prohibitive. Where a void exists in the marketplace, a government agency may subsidize the coverage with such programs as FEDERAL FLOOD INSURANCE and SERVICEMEN'S GROUP LIFE INSURANCE (SGLI).

CATASTROPHE INSURANCE *see* COMPREHENSIVE HEALTH INSURANCE; GROUP HEALTH INSURANCE; MAJOR MEDICAL INSURANCE.

CATASTROPHE LOSS high severity loss which does not lend itself to accurate prediction and thus should be transferred by the individual or business to an insurance company. *See also* EXPECTED LOSS; SELF INSURANCE.

CATASTROPHE REINSURANCE *see* AUTOMATIC NONPROPORTIONAL REINSURANCE; AUTOMATIC PROPORTIONAL REINSURANCE; AUTOMATIC REINSURANCE; EXCESS OF LOSS REINSURANCE; FACULTATIVE REINSURANCE; NONPROPORTIONAL REINSURANCE; PROPORTIONAL REINSURANCE; QUOTA SHARE REINSURANCE; STOP LOSS REINSURANCE; SURPLUS REINSURANCE.

CATASTROPHIC COVERAGE ACT *see* MEDICARE CATASTROPHIC COVERAGE ACT.

CATASTROPHIC HEALTH INSURANCE *see* MEDICARE CATASTROPHIC COVERAGE ACT.

CAVEAT EMPTOR Latin expression meaning "let the buyer beware." The purchaser buys a product or service at his or her own risk. This principle has been modified significantly as it relates to an INSURANCE POLICY. *See also* ADHESION INSURANCE CONTRACT; FREE EXAMINATION "FREE LOOK" PERIOD.

CCC *see* CARE, CUSTODY, AND CONTROL.

CD ANNUITY *see* ANNUITY, CD.

CEDE to transfer a risk from an insurance company to a reinsurance company.

CEDENT *see* CEDING COMPANY.

CEDING COMPANY insurance company which transfers a risk to a reinsurance company.

CENTRAL GUARANTEE FUND fund from which losses are paid for the insolvent members of LLOYD'S OF LONDON. Each year, members of Lloyd's of London contribute a percentage of their premium volume to this fund to act as a reserve for losses which insolvent members are unable to pay. *See also* GUARANTY FUND (INSOLVENCY FUND).

CENTRAL LIMIT THEOREM statistical approach stating that if a series of samples is taken from a stable population, the distribution of the means (averages) of these samples will form a normal distribution whose mean approaches the population as the samples become larger.

CENTRAL LOSS FUND *see* GUARANTY FUND (INSOLVENCY FUND).

CERTAIN ANNUITY *see* LIFE CERTAIN ANNUITY.

CERTIFICATE *see* CERTIFICATE OF INSURANCE.

CERTIFICATE OF AUTHORITY written statement by an insurance company attesting to the powers it has vested in an agent.

CERTIFICATE OF INSURANCE document in life and health insurance issued to a member of a group insurance plan showing participation in insurance coverage. In property and liability insurance, evidence of the existence and terms of a particular policy.

CERTIFIED EMPLOYEE BENEFIT SPECIALIST (CEBS) professional designation conferred by the International Foundation of Employee Benefit Plans and the Wharton School of the University of Pennsylvania. In addition to professional business experience in employee benefits, recipients must pass national examinations in pensions, Social Security, other retirement related plans, health insurance, economics, finance, labor relations, group insurance, and other employee benefit related plans. This program responds to the information requirements of individuals responsible for the operation of an employee benefit plan department in large and medium size businesses. (It has been estimated that for every dollar of salary an additional 40 cents is paid to cover employee benefits.)

CERTIFIED FINANCIAL PLANNER (CFP) professional designation conferred by the College For Financial Planning. In addition to professional business experience in financial planning, recipients must pass national examinations in insurance, investments, taxation, employee benefit plans, and estate planning. This program responds to the growing need for help with personal financial planning.

CESSION *see* CEDE.

CESTUI QUE VIE person by whose life the duration of an insurance policy, estate, trust, or gift is measured. This person is generally referred as the INSURED in an insurance policy.

CHANCE OF LOSS *see* PROBABILITY.

CHANGE IN CONDITIONS *see* DIFFERENCE IN CONDITIONS INSURANCE.

CHANGE OF BENEFICIARY PROVISION element of a life insurance policy permitting the policyowner to change a beneficiary as frequently as desired unless the beneficiary has been designated as irrevocable. Here the written permission of that beneficiary must be obtained in order to make a change.

CHARITABLE AND GOVERNMENT IMMUNITY principle that no liability exposure can result from the performance of proprietary functions.

CHARTERED FINANCIAL CONSULTANT (ChFC) professional designation awarded by The American College. In addition to professional business experience in financial planning, recipients are required to pass national examinations in insurance, investments, taxation, employee benefit plans, estate planning, accounting, and management. This program responds to the growing need for help in personal financial planning.

CHARTERED LIFE UNDERWRITER (CLU) professional designation conferred by The American College. In addition to professional business experience in insurance planning and related areas, recipients must pass national examinations in insurance, investments, taxation, employee benefit plans, estate planning, accounting, management and economics. This program responds to a need by individuals for technically proficient help in planning their life insurance.

CHARTERED PROPERTY AND CASUALTY UNDERWRITER (CPCU) professional designation earned after the successful completion of 10 national examinations given by the American Institute for Property and Liability Underwriters. Covers such areas of expertise as insurance, risk management, economics, finance, management, accounting, and law. Three years of work experience are also required in the insurance business or a related area.

CHRONOLOGICAL STABILIZATION PLAN *see* RETROSPECTIVE RATING.

CICA *see* CAPTIVE INSURANCE COMPANIES ASSOCIATION (CICA).

CIVIL ACTION remedy imposed by a court of law, usually in the form of a monetary award, as compensation to the insured party for the CIVIL WRONG incurred. A civil action is initiated by the injured party (the plaintiff) against the party causing the damages (the defendant). The STATUTE OF LIMITATIONS applies to these actions. *See also* CIVIL DAMAGES.

CIVIL DAMAGES sums payable to the winning plaintiff by the losing defendant in a court of law; can take any or all of these forms: *general, punitive,* and *special.*

CIVIL LIABILITY negligent acts and/or omissions, other than breach of contract, normally independent of moral obligations for which a remedy can be provided in a court of law. For example, a person injured in someone's home can bring suit under civil liability law.

CIVIL WRONG an act or violation that consists of two wrongs:
1. TORT—negligent act or omission by one or more parties against the person or property or another party or parties. LIABILITY INSURANCE is designated to cover an insured for unintentional tort.
2. Breach or violation of the provisions of a CONTRACT. *See also* CIVIL LIABILITY.

CLAIM request by an insured for indemnification by an insurance company for loss incurred from an insured peril.

CLAIM ADJUSTER *see* ADJUSTER.

CLAIM AGAINST EMPLOYERS NET WORTH claim by the PENSION BENEFIT GUARANTY CORPORATION (PBGC) against an employer for reimbursement of the PBGC's loss (for a terminated plan) up to 30% of the net worth of the employer. If this amount is not paid, the PBGC may place a lien on all of the assets of the employer.

CLAIMANT one who submits a claim.

CLAIM EXPENSE cost incurred in adjusting a claim. Claim-adjustment expenses include such items as attorneys' fees and investigation expenses (e.g., witness interviews). The claim settlement dollar amount awarded to the injured party is not considered a claim expense item.

CLAIM, OBLIGATION TO PAY clause in liability insurance policies stating that the insurance company has a legally enforceable obligation to pay all claims and defend all suits (even if groundless) up to the policy limits on behalf of the insured for which the insured becomes legally obligated to pay.

CLAIM PROVISION clause in an insurance policy which describes the administration and submission of claims procedure.

CLAIM REPORT report furnished by the ADJUSTER to the INSURANCE COMPANY (INSURER) which documents the amount of payment the insurer is legally obligated to pay to or on behalf of the INSURED under the terms of the POLICY. This report includes the following items:

1. Is there an INSURABLE INTEREST—did the person who submitted the claim have expectation of a monetary loss?
2. Is there a coverable cause of loss—was the source of the loss an INSURED PERIL?
3. Is the property covered—was the damaged or destroyed property insured?
4. What is the location of the loss—was the occurrence of the insured peril within the geographical scope of the policy?
5. What is the date of the loss—did the loss occur while the policy was in effect?
6. What are the applicable EXCLUSIONS—was the loss caused by a peril specifically excluded by the policy?
7. What are the applicable CONDITION(S) and WARRANTY(S)—were the condition(s) and warranty(s) under the policy complied with by the insured?
8. What is the SALVAGE value of the damaged property—is there a portion of the damaged property which can be salvaged and how does the value of the salvageable property affect the total dollar amount of the loss?
9. What is the status of any OTHER INSURANCE in force—are there any other insurance policies in force carried by the CLAIMANT covering the loss?
10. What is the status of SUBROGATION—are there any third parties responsible for a covered loss against which the insurer can take legal action?
11. Was there any MISREPRESENTATION (FALSE PRETENSE) and CONCEALMENT involved—did the insured falsify or withhold material facts from the insurer?
12. What is the status of the availability of documentation—are there photographs available of the damaged or destroyed insured property? Does the insured have receipts or other pertinent records relating to the damaged or destroyed insured property?

CLAIMS AND LOSS CONTROL *see* ENGINEERING APPROACH; HUMAN APPROACH.

CLAIMS MADE *see* CLAIMS MADE BASIS LIABILITY COVERAGE.

CLAIMS MADE BASIS LIABILITY COVERAGE method of determining whether or not coverage is available for a specific claim. If a claim is made during the time period when a liability policy is in effect, an insurance company is responsible for its payment, up to the limits of the policy, regardless of when the event causing the claim occurred.

Experts often advise that it is extremely important, when purchasing a property and casualty policy, to determine if claims are paid on a claims made basis or a *claims occurrence* basis.

CLAIMS MADE FORM *see* CLAIMS MADE BASIS LIABILITY COVERAGE.

CLAIMS OCCURRENCE BASIS LIABILITY COVERAGE method of determining whether or not coverage is available for a specific claim. If a claim arises out of an event during the period when a policy is in force, the insurance company is responsible for its payment, up to the limits of the policy, regardless of when the business submits the claim. Experts often suggest that it is extremely important, when purchasing a property and casualty insurance policy, to determine if claims are paid on a *claims made* basis or on a claims occurrence basis.

CLAIMS OCCURRENCE FORM *see* CLAIMS OCCURRENCE BASIS LIABILITY COVERAGE.

CLAIMS REPRESENTATIVE *see* ADJUSTER.

CLAIMS RESERVE monetary fund established to pay for claims that the insurance company is aware of (claims incurred or future claims) but that the insurance company has not yet settled. This reserve is critical since it is an accurate indication of a company's liabilities. This reserve does not take into account INCURRED BUT NOT REPORTED LOSSES (IBNR).

CLASS group of insureds with the same characteristics, established for rate-making purposes. For example, all wood-frame houses within 200 feet of a fire plug in the same geographical area would have similar probabilities of incurring a total loss. *See also* RATE MAKING.

CLASSIFICATION *see* CLASS.

CLASSIFIED INSURANCE *see* SUBSTANDARD HEALTH INSURANCE; SUBSTANDARD LIFE INSURANCE.

CLASS PREMIUM RATE *see* CLASS RATE

CLASS RATE rate applied to risks with similar characteristics or to a specified class of risk.

CLAUSE in an insurance policy, sentences and paragraphs describing various coverages, exclusions, duties of the insured, locations covered, and conditions which suspend or terminate coverage.

CLAUSES ADDED TO A LIFE INSURANCE POLICY provisions, usually requiring an additional premium, which are appended to an insurance contract. These include WAIVER OF PREMIUM (WP), DISABILITY

INCOME (DI), ACCIDENTAL DEATH CLAUSE, *policy purchase option (PPO)*. The young family with children may wish to consider these clauses since the breadwinner is seven to nine times more likely to become disabled than to die at young ages.

CLEANUP FUND component of necessary coverage determined by the "needs approach" to life insurance for a family. It is intended to cover last-minute expenses as well as those that surface after the death of an insured, such as burial costs, probate charges, and medical bills.

CLEAR-SPACE CLAUSE in PROPERTY INSURANCE policies, a clause which requires that a particular insured property be a specified distance from like insured or noninsured property. For example, stored dynamite should be at least 100 yards from an insured building.

CLIFF VESTING *see* TEN YEAR VESTING (CLIFF VESTING).

CLIFFORD TRUST up to 1986, arrangement to provide a personal trust while the settlor is still alive. The income is paid to named children, who enjoy lower income taxes. After 10 years and a day, the property reverts to the original owner. The Internal Revenue Service had ruled that the income from the property in trust is not income to the original owner. The Clifford Trust was eliminated under the TAX REFORM ACT OF 1986.

CLOSE CORPORATION PLAN prior arrangement for surviving stockholders to purchase shares of a deceased stockholder according to a predetermined formula for setting the value of the corporation. Often, the best source for its funding is a life insurance policy in either of these forms: (1) *Individual Stock Purchase Plan (Cross Purchase Plan)*, much like the *partnership cross purchase* plan. Each stockholder buys, owns, and pays the premium for insurance equal to his/her share of the agreed purchase price for the stock of the other stockholders. (2) *Corporation Stock Purchase Plan (Stock Redemption Plan)*, similar to the *partnership entity plan* is a better choice if the number of stockholders is large. The corporation purchases and pays the premiums on the amount of insurance needed to purchase the decreased stockholder's interest at the price set by the predetermined formula. These premiums are not tax deductible as a business expense, but the death benefits are not subject to income tax. Life insurance owned by the corporation is listed as an asset on the corporation's balance sheet. Ownership of life insurance on the stockholders thus increases the corporation's net worth, and if permanent insurance is purchased, its cash value would be available for loans in the event of business emergencies.

CLU *see* CHARTERED LIFE UNDERWRITER (CLU).

CODING placement of verbal descriptive information into numerical form for the purposes of analysis.

COINSURANCE in PROPERTY INSURANCE, when the insurance policy contains this clause, coinsurance defines the amount of each loss that the company pays according to the following relationship:

$$\frac{\text{Amount of Insurance Carried}}{\text{Amount of Insurance Required}} \times \begin{array}{c}\text{Amount}\\\text{of Loss}\end{array} = \begin{array}{c}\text{Insurance Company}\\\text{Payment}\end{array}$$

Where:

Amount of Insurance Required = Value of Property Insured × Coinsurance Clause Percentage Amount of Insurance Required

Example:

Value of building = $100,000
Coinsurance Clause Percentage Amount of Insurance Required = 80%
Amount of Fire Damage to the Building = $60,000
Amount of Insurance Carried = $75,000

The insurance company would be required to pay $56,250 of the $60,000 loss:

$$\frac{\$75,000}{\$100,000 \times 80\%} \times \$60,000 = \$56,250$$

Note that the indemnification of the insured for a property loss can never exceed (1) the dollar amount of the actual loss; (2) the dollar limits of the insurance policy; (3) the dollar amount determined by the coinsurance relationship. The lesser of the above three amounts will always apply.

In commercial health insurance, when the insured and the insurer share in a specific ratio of the covered medical expenses, coinsurance is the insured's share of covered losses. For example, in some policies the insurer pays 75–80% of the covered medical expenses and the insured pays the remainder. In other policies, after the insured pays a *deductible* amount, the insurer pays 75–80% of the covered medical expenses above the deductible and the insured pays the remainder until a maximum dollar amount is reached (for example, $5,000). The insurer pays 100% of covered medical expenses over this dollar amount up to the limits of the policy.

COINSURANCE CLAUSE *see* COINSURANCE.

COINSURANCE FORMULA *see* COINSURANCE.

COINSURANCE LIMIT in a MERCANTILE OPEN-STOCK BURGLARY INSURANCE policy, the dollar amount of coverage as required by the

COINSURANCE clause. This dollar amount is the MAXIMUM PROBABLE LOSS (MPL) of merchandise that the insurer estimates could result from a single burglary. The indemnification of the insured merchant cannot exceed the lesser of this coinsurance limit or the COINSURANCE PERCENTAGE of the total dollar value of the merchandise which has been insured.

COINSURANCE PENALTY reduction in the amount that the insured receives from the insurer, after having incurred a property loss, because the insurer failed to carry the amount of coverage required by the COINSURANCE clause. *See also* COINSURANCE REQUIREMENT.

COINSURANCE PERCENTAGE in many PROPERTY INSURANCE policies, a requirement that the insured carry insurance as a percentage of the total monetary value of the insured property. If this percentage is not carried, the insured is subject to the COINSURANCE PENALTY. *See also* COINSURANCE; COINSURANCE REQUIREMENT.

COINSURANCE REQUIREMENT amount of insurance that the insured must carry in order to be indemnified for the total dollar amount of the actual loss. If this requirement is met by the insured, the COINSURANCE PENALTY will not go into effect. The amount of insurance required is usually expressed as a percentage of the value of the property insured at the time the loss is incurred; however, the amount may also be expressed as a flat dollar amount. *See also* COINSURANCE; COINSURANCE PERCENTAGE.

COINSURER party which shares in the loss under an insurance policy or policies. *See also* COINSURANCE; COINSURANCE LIMIT; COINSURANCE PENALTY; COINSURANCE PERCENTAGE; COINSURANCE REQUIREMENT.

COLD CALL (COLD CANVASSING) call on a prospective insurance buyer without a prior appointment. Many salespeople find this exercise the most threatening in their career development. Some observers attribute the substantial failure rate among new agents to their repugnance to cold calls.

COLD CANVASSING *see* COLD CALL (COLD CANVASSING).

COLLATERAL ASSIGNMENT designation of a policy's death benefit or its cash surrender value to a creditor as security for a loan. If the loan is not repaid, the creditor receives the policy proceeds up to the balance of the outstanding loan, and the beneficiary receives the remainder. Because life insurance is freely assignable it is readily acceptable to lending institutions as security. Also, the lender is certain to receive the money should death strike the borrower before the loan can be repaid.

COLLATERAL BORROWER individual who assigns rights to a benefit. For example, a life insurance policy may be assigned as security for
a loan made by the borrower. The policy protects the COLLATERAL
CREDITOR (ASSIGNEE) if the borrower does not pay the loan when due.
If a loan remains unpaid at the death of an insured, the loan balance is
subtracted from the death benefit and paid to the creditor, with the
balance going to the insured's beneficiary. On the other hand, if the
insured (the borrower) does not pay the loan when due, the creditor can
withdraw the amount due from the cash value of the policy. When a
loan is repaid, the assignment ends and the policyowner is again vested
with all rights to the policy.

COLLATERAL CREDITOR (ASSIGNEE) individual to whom rights
to a benefit are assigned. A life insurance policy is assigned by the
COLLATERAL BORROWER (assignor) to the collateral creditor (assignee)
as security for a loan. *See also* COLLATERAL BORROWER.

COLLATERAL SOURCE RULE judicial rule of evidence under which
no reduction in damages awarded by a court is allowed for bodily injury,
sickness, illness, or accident merely because the plaintiff has other
financial sources paying benefits such as HEALTH INSURANCE and
DISABILITY INCOME INSURANCE.

COLLECTION BOOK record a debit (or other) agent makes for premiums collected, time period for which the policy is paid, and the week
of collection or date the premium was paid. In essence, the debit agent,
through the collection book, becomes a bookkeeper as well as a salesperson, since at the end of each week the agent has to balance the debit
book, which in some instances is time consuming. *See also* DEBIT
AGENT.

COLLECTION COMMISSION commission paid to an agent as a percentage of the premiums he or she collects on DEBT INSURANCE (HOME
SERVICE INSURANCE, INDUSTRIAL INSURANCE).

COLLECTION FEE fee paid to an agent as compensation for his or her
collecting premiums for DEBIT INSURANCE (HOME SERVICE INSURANCE,
INDUSTRIAL INSURANCE).

COLLECTION EXPENSE INSURANCE *see* ACCOUNTS RECEIVABLE
INSURANCE.

COLLECTIVE MERCHANDISING OF INSURANCE *see* MASS MER-
CHANDISING.

COLLEGE RETIREMENT EQUITIES FUND (CREF) entity maintained by the Teachers Insurance Annuity Association. The fund essen-

tially serves college faculties and staff, who pay premiums through salary deductions toward a tax-sheltered retirement variable annuity.

COLLISION physical contact of an automobile with another inanimate object resulting in damage to the insured car. Insurance coverage is available to provide protection against this occurrence. *See also* PERSONAL AUTOMOBILE POLICY (PAP).

COLLISION DAMAGE WAIVER special property damage coverage purchased by an individual renting an automobile under which the rental company waives any right to recover property damage to the automobile from that individual, regardless of who is at fault. A significant fee is paid by the individual to the rental company for this waiver for coverage that may already be provided by a PERSONAL AUTOMOBILE POLICY (PAP).

COLLISION INSURANCE in automobile insurance, coverage providing protection in the event of physical damage to the insured's own automobile (other than that covered under COMPREHENSIVE INSURANCE) resulting from COLLISION with another inanimate object. *See also* PERSONAL AUTOMOBILE POLICY (PAP).

COLLUSION agreement between two or more individuals to commit fraud. For example, an insured hires someone to burn down this house in order to collect the insurance proceeds.

COMBINATION AGENT representative of an insurance company who sells ordinary and industrial life insurance policies. In an effort to move their field forces into the ordinary life business, many industrial companies have systematically trained their agents to sell ordinary life policies.

COMBINATION POLICY (PLAN)
1. a contract in life insurance that includes elements of whole life and term insurance.
2. in pensions, a combined life insurance policy and a side (auxiliary) fund to enhance the amount of a future pension.
3. in automobile insurance, different coverages using policies of two or more insurance companies (rare).

COMBINATION SAFE DEPOSITORY INSURANCE covers property damage and theft coverage in two areas not subject to a coinsurance requirement or a deductible.
Coverage A. If the bank becomes liable for loss to a customer's property while that property is: (1) on the bank's premises in safe deposit boxes in the vault; or (2) being deposited into or taken out of the safe deposit boxes.

Coverage B. Loss to the bank customer's property due to burglary or robbery, whether actual or attempted, even if the bank is not held liable.

COMBINED RATIO in insurance, combination of the LOSS RATIO and the EXPENSE RATIO:

1. Loss Ratio $= \dfrac{\text{Incurred Losses + Loss Adjustment Expense}}{\text{Earned Premiums}}$

2. Expenses Ratio $= \dfrac{\text{Incurred Expenses}}{\text{Written Premiums}}$

The combined ratio is important to an insurance company since it indicates whether or not the company is earning a profit on the business it is writing, *not* taking into account investment returns on the premiums received. The property and casualty insurance business sometimes goes through cycles. During the 1980s, for instance, it was not unusual to have a combined ratio of over 120%. Obviously, the difference has to be made up from the company's surplus, which in some instances even put the major companies under severe financial strain.

COMBINED SINGLE LIMIT bodily injury liability and property damage liability expressed as a single sum of coverage.

COMMENCEMENT OF COVERAGE date at which insurance protection begins.

COMMERCIAL BLANKET BOND coverage of the employer for all employees on a *blanket* basis, with the maximum limit of coverage applied to any one loss without regard for the number of employees involved. Both *commercial* and *position blanket bonds* work the same way if only one employee causes the loss, or if the guilty employee(s) cannot be identified. For example, five identifiable employees as a team steal $50,000. A $10,000 BLANKET POSITION BOND would cover the loss in full. A $50,000 commercial blanket bond would be required to repay the insured business for the same loss.

COMMERCIAL CREDIT INSURANCE coverage for an insured firm if its business debtors fail to pay their obligations. The insured firm can be a manufacturer or a service organization but it cannot sell its products or service on a retail level to be covered under commercial credit insurance. Under this form of insurance, the insured firm assumes the expected loss up to the retention amount and the insurance company pays the excess losses above that amount, up to the limits of the credit insurance policy.

COMMERCIAL FORGERY POLICY coverage for an insured who unknowingly accepts forged checks. Coverage can be found under the

SPECIAL MULTIPERIL INSURANCE (SMP) policy (SECTION III CRIME COVERAGE INSURING AGREEMENT 5—DEPOSITORS FORGERY).

COMMERCIAL FORMS insurance policies covering various business risks.

COMMERCIAL GENERAL LIABILITY FORM (CGL) liability coverage section of a SIMPLIFIED COMMERCIAL LINES PORTFOLIO POLICY (SCLP). Provides for separate limits of coverage for general liability, fire legal liability, products and completed operations liability, advertising and personal liability, and medical payments. An AGGREGATE LIMIT of liability is in force for the general liability, fire legal liability, advertising and personal liability, and medical payments claims. When total claims for all of these areas exceed a given annual aggregate limit of liability, the policy limits are said to be exhausted and no more claims for that year will be paid under the policy. There is also an aggregate limit of liability in force for products and completed operations liability claims. This form has replaced the COMPREHENSIVE GENERAL LIABILITY INSURANCE (CGL) form.

COMMERCIAL HEALTH INSURANCE coverage that provides two types of benefits, DISABILITY INCOME (DI) and *medical expenses*. Sold by insurance companies whose business objective is the profit motive (as distinct from Blue Cross/Blue Shield) it can be classified by its RENEWAL PROVISION, and types of *benefits provided*.
   1. *Renewal Provisions:* (a) Optionally renewable. The insurance company has the option to renew the policy at the end of the term period, (one year, six months, three months or one month). If the company renews the policy, it has the option to adjust the premium up or down; limit the types of perils insured against; and limit some or all of the benefits. (b) Nonrenewable for stated reasons only. When the insured reaches a certain age or when all similar policies are not renewed, the policy is said to be nonrenewable for the reasons stated. (c) Noncancellable. The insurance company must renew the policy and cannot change any of the provisions of the policy nor raise the premium while the policy is in force. (d) Guaranteed renewable. The company must renew the policy but the company has the option to adopt a new rate structure for the future renewal premiums.
   2. *Benefits Provided:* (a) Disability income for total and partial disability subject to a maximum dollar amount and maximum length of time. Limitations include: pre-existing injury or condition; elimination period beginning with the first day of disability during which no benefits are paid; probationary period during which no benefits are paid for a sickness contracted or beginning during the first 15, 20, 25, or 30 days that the policy is in force; a recurrent disability such that before the current disability will be deemed to be a new disability, the insured must have returned to full time continuous

employment for at least six months. (b) Medical Expense Benefits for hospital charges for room, board, nursing, use of the operating room, physicians and surgeons fees; and miscellaneous medical expenses for laboratory tests, drugs, medicines, X-rays, anesthetics, artificial limbs, therapeutics, and ambulance service to and from the hospital.

COMMERCIAL INSURANCE insurance sold by privately formed insurance companies with the objective of making a profit.

COMMERCIAL INSURANCE COMPANY privately formed insurance company whose objective is to make a profit.

COMMERCIAL LINES insurance coverages for businesses, commercial institutions, and professional organizations, as contrasted with PERSONAL INSURANCE. *See also* BUSINESS AUTOMOBILE POLICY (BAP); BUSINESS CRIME INSURANCE; BUSINESS INTERRUPTION INSURANCE; BUSINESS LIFE AND HEALTH INSURANCE; BUSINESSOWNERS POLICY (BOP); BUY-AND-SELL AGREEMENT; CLOSE CORPORATION PLAN; COMMERCIAL GENERAL LIABILITY FORM (CGL); PARTNERSHIP LIFE AND HEALTH INSURANCE; SIMPLIFIED COMMERCIAL LINES PORTFOLIO POLICY (SCLP); SOLE PROPRIETOR LIFE AND HEALTH INSURANCE.

COMMERCIAL PACKAGE POLICY (CRP) insurance policy which is COMMERCIAL LINES in orientation and is composed of two or more of the following coverages: COMMERCIAL PROPERTY, BUSINESS CRIME, BUSINESS AUTOMOBILE, BOILER AND MACHINERY, and COMMERCIAL GENERAL LIABILITY (CGL).

COMMERCIAL POLICY *see* COMMERCIAL HEALTH INSURANCE.

COMMERCIAL PROPERTY POLICY coverage for business risks including goods in transit, fire, burglary, and theft. A common example is the SPECIAL MULTIPERIL INSURANCE (SMP) policy.

COMMINGLED TRUST FUND pooling of assets of two or more pension funds under common portfolio management.

COMMISSION fee paid to an insurance salesperson as a percentage of the premium generated by a sold insurance policy.

COMMISSIONER OF INSURANCE (INSURANCE COMMISSIONER, SUPERINTENDENT OF INSURANCE) top state regulator of the insurance business who is either elected to office or appointed by a state to safeguard the interests of policyowners.

COMMISSIONERS STANDARD INDUSTRIAL MORTALITY TABLE (CSI) table used in calculating various nonforfeiture values for industrial life insurance policies. These tables give the minimum values that must be generated to the policyowner. The insured's life expectancy, according to the Commissioners Standard Industrial Mortality Table, is shorter than the life expectancy given in ordinary life tables such as the COMMISSIONERS STANDARD ORDINARY MORTALITY TABLE (CSO). Thus the Industrial Mortality Table's premiums are relatively higher than those based on the CSO Table. This is because the life expectancy of purchasers of industrial policies tends on average to be less than that of people who buy ordinary life policies.

COMMISSIONERS STANDARD ORDINARY MORTALITY TABLE (CSO) table used in calculating minimum nonforfeiture values and policy reserves for ordinary life insurance policies. These tables, which give minimum values that must be guaranteed to policyowners as approved by the NATIONAL ASSOCIATION OF INSURANCE COMMISSIONERS (NAIC), depict the number of people dying each year out of the original population, not as individuals, but in age groups.

COMMISSIONERS VALUES specific values of securities computed annually by the NATIONAL ASSOCIATION OF INSURANCE COMMISSIONERS (NAIC) as guidelines and procedures for insurance companies in listing of their securities in their annual statements. Values are the same for all insurers. This gives insurance commissioners a basis for valuing securities and ensuring that a company has sufficient assets to back up the reserve requirements.

COMMON CARRIER transportation firm that must carry any customer's goods if the customer is willing to pay. Common carriers include trucking companies, bus lines, and airlines. *See also* INLAND MARINE INSURANCE.

COMMON DISASTER CLAUSE (SURVIVORSHIP CLAUSE) wording in life insurance policies to determine the order of deaths when the insured and the beneficiary die in the same accident. For example, if the insured is deemed to have died first, the proceeds are payable to a named contingent beneficiary. Otherwise, the proceeds are payable to the insured's estate and are subject to probate and other legal fees.

COMMON LAW legal system in the U.S., Great Britain, and other countries. Inherited from England, it is based on case decisions acting as the precedent, not on written law. *See also* STATUTORY LIABILITY.

COMMON LAW DEFENSES arguments composed of ASSUMPTION OF RISK, CONTRIBUTORY NEGLIGENCE, and FELLOW SERVANT RULE.

COMMON POLICY DECLARATIONS *see* DECLARATION; DECLARATIONS SECTION.

COMMON STOCK INVESTMENTS allocation of monetary resources to equities.

COMMON TRUST FUND *see* COMMINGLED TRUST FUND.

COMMUNITY PROPERTY all property acquired after marriage, deemed to be the result of the joint efforts of both spouses (regardless of whether or not only one spouse has earned income). Each spouse is entitled to one half of the property. Community property states are Arizona, California, Hawaii, Idaho, Louisiana, New Mexico, Oklahoma, Texas, and Washington.

COMMUTATION selection of a lump sum benefit option in exchange for a series of installment benefit payments.

COMMUTATION RIGHT privilege of a beneficiary to take unpaid income payments under a settlement option of an annuity or life insurance policy in the form of a lump sum. For example, if a beneficiary had a series of 20 income payments remaining, the present value of these payments can be commuted to a single lump sum payment.

COMMUTE *see* COMMUTATION RIGHT.

COMMUTED VALUE *see* COMMUTATION RIGHT.

COMPANY ORGANIZATION *see* INSURANCE COMPANY ORGANIZATION.

COMPARATIVE NEGLIGENCE in some states, principle of tort law providing that in the event of an accident each party's negligence is based on that party's contribution to the accident. For example, if in an auto accident both parties fail to obey the yield sign, their negligence would be equal, and neither would collect legal damages from the other.

COMPENSATING BALANCES PLAN premium paid by an insured business to an insurance company from which the company subtracts charges for the cost of putting a policy on its books, premium taxes, and profit. The remainder of the premium is deposited in the insured business's bank account from which the insured business can make withdrawals.

COMPENSATORY DAMAGES *see* LIABILITY, CIVIL DAMAGES AWARDED.

COMPETENCE capacity of parties to an insurance contract to understand the meanings of their action in order for the contract to be valid.

COMPETITIVE STATE FUND *see* MONOPOLISTIC STATE FUND.

COMPLETED OPERATIONS INSURANCE coverage for a contractor's liability for injuries or property damage suffered by third parties as the result of the contractor completing an operation. The contractor must take reasonable care in rendering a project safe and free from all reasonable hazards. *See also* COMPREHENSIVE GENERAL LIABILITY INSURANCE (CGL).

COMPLETION BOND protection for a mortgagee guaranteeing that the mortgagor will complete construction. The mortgagee (such as a Savings and Loan Association) lends money to the mortgagor (the owner of the project) in order to pay the contractor who is actually physically building the project. Upon completion, the project then serves to secure the loan. Should the project not be completed, the mortgagee is protected through the completion bond.

COMPOUND INTEREST accumulation of interest yearly or more frequently, including interest paid on interest.

COMPREHENSIVE AUTOMOBILE LIABILITY INSURANCE *see* AUTOMOBILE LIABILITY INSURANCE; COMPREHENSIVE INSURANCE.

COMPREHENSIVE "3-D" POLICY *see* DISHONESTY, DISAPPEARANCE, AND DESTRUCTION POLICY ("3-D" POLICY).

COMPREHENSIVE CRIME ENDORSEMENT attachment to a SPECIAL MULTIPERIL INSURANCE (SMP) policy to cover counterfeit currency, depositor's forgery, employee dishonesty, and the loss of money, money orders, and securities by the insured business. *See also* SPECIAL MULTIPERIL INSURANCE (SMP) for a description of actual coverages available.

COMPREHENSIVE GENERAL LIABILITY INSURANCE (CGL) coverage against all liability exposures of a business unless specifically excluded. Coverage includes products, completed operations, premises and operations, elevators, and independent contractors.

Products coverage insures when a liability suit is brought against the manufacturer and/or distributor of a product because of someone incurring bodily injury or property damage through use of the product. (The manufacturer of the product must use all reasonable means to make certain that the product is free from any inherent defect.)

Completed operations coverage for bodily injury or property damage incurred because of a defect in a completed project of the insured.

Premises and operations coverage for bodily injury incurred on the premises of the insured, and/or as the result of the insured's business operations.

Elevator coverage for bodily injury incurred in an elevator or escalator on the insured's premises.

Independent contractors coverage for bodily injury incurred as the result of negligent acts and omissions of an independent contractor employed by the insured.

COMPREHENSIVE GLASS INSURANCE coverage on an ALL RISKS basis for glass breakage, subject to exclusions of war and fire. Thus, if a vandal throws a brick through a window of an insured's establishment, the coverage would apply.

COMPREHENSIVE HEALTH INSURANCE complete coverage for hospital and physician charges subject to deductibles and coinsurance. This coverage combines basic medical expense policy and major medical policy. *See also* GROUP HEALTH INSURANCE; HEALTH MAINTENANCE ORGANIZATION (HMO).

COMPREHENSIVE INSURANCE coverage in automobile insurance providing protection in the event of physical damage (other than COLLISION) or theft of the insured car. For example, fire damage to an insured car would be covered under the comprehensive section of the PERSONAL AUTOMOBILE POLICY (PAP).

COMPREHENSIVE LIABILITY INSURANCE policy providing businesses with coverage for negligence based civil liability in: (1) Bodily injury and property damage liability, on an occurrence basis, resulting from the ownership, use, and/or maintenance of the premises, completed operations and products. (2) Bodily injury and property damage liability for operation of an elevator. (3) Medical expenses resulting from bodily injury incurred by a member of the general public through the use of the premises or involvement in the operations. Medical expense reimbursement of the business is without regard to fault of the business.

COMPREHENSIVE MAJOR MEDICAL INSURANCE *see* GROUP HEALTH INSURANCE; HEALTH INSURANCE; HEALTH MAINTENANCE ORGANIZATION (HMO).

COMPREHENSIVE PERSONAL LIABILITY INSURANCE coverage such as HOMEOWNERS INSURANCE POLICY—SECTION II on an ALL RISKS basis for personal acts and omissions by the insured and residents of the insured's household. Included are sports activities, pet activities, and miscellaneous events such as someone tripping in an insured's cemetery plot.

COMPREHENSIVE POLICY combination of several coverages to protect the insured. For example, the COMPREHENSIVE HEALTH INSURANCE policy combines the *basic hospital plan* with MAJOR MEDICAL INSURANCE to cover medical expenses (room, board, surgical and physician expenses) and miscellaneous expenses (surgical dressings, drugs, ambulance services, blood, and operating room). Many policies have a maximum lifetime limit of $1 million for the insured and for each member of the insured's family who is a dependent resident of the insured's household. The COMPREHENSIVE PERSONAL LIABILITY INSURANCE policy covers the insured for just about any negligent act or omission which results in property damage or bodily injury to another party, subject to the exclusions of automotive liability and professional liability. The SPECIAL MULTIPERIL INSURANCE (SMP) policy provides the businessowner with comprehensive property damage coverage on an ALL RISKS basis.

COMPULSORY AUTOMOBILE LIABILITY INSURANCE *see* COMPULSORY INSURANCE.

COMPULSORY INSURANCE coverage required by the laws of a particular state. For example, many states stipulate minimum amounts of automobile liability insurance which must be carried. *See also* FINANCIAL RESPONSIBILITY LAW.

COMPULSORY RETIREMENT AGE mandatory age of retirement.

CONCEALMENT intention to withhold or secrete information. If an insured withholds information on a material fact, about which the insurance company has no knowledge, the company has grounds to void the contract. For example, the insured neglects to tell the company that, within a week of the policy issue date, the manufacture of gunpowder in the insured business's building will commence. If an explosion related to the gunpowder then occurs in the building the company has legal grounds for not paying for the property damage.

CONCURRENCY circumstance in which at least two insurance policies provide identical coverage for the same risk. *See also* DOUBLE RECOVERY.

CONCURRENT INSURANCE *see* CONCURRENCY.

CONDITION action(s) that the insured must take, or continue to take, for the insurance policy to remain in force and the insurance company to process a claim. For example, insured must pay the premiums when due, notify the insurance company as soon as possible in the case of an accident, and cooperate with the company in defense of the insured in case of a liability suit.

CONDITIONAL terms specifying obligations of an insured to keep a policy in force. For example, an insured must pay the premiums due; in life insurance, if death occurs, the beneficiary or the insured's estate must submit proof of death; if there is a property loss, the insured must submit proof of loss.

CONDITIONAL BINDING RECEIPT *see* BINDING RECEIPT; CONDITIONAL RECEIPT.

CONDITIONAL INSURANCE *see* CONDITIONAL SALES FLOATER.

CONDITIONAL RECEIPT evidence of a temporary contract obliging a life or health insurance company to provide coverage as long as a premium accompanies an acceptable application. This give the company time to process the application and to issue or refuse a policy, as the case may be. If the applicant were to die before a policy is issued, the company will pay the death benefit if the policy would have been issued. For example, Mr. A applies for $100,000 of life insurance but is killed by an automobile before the policy is issued. The company finds that it would have issued the policy, and therefore pays $100,000 to the beneficiary. *See also* BINDING RECEIPT.

CONDITIONAL RENEWABLE HEALTH INSURANCE automatic right of an insured to renew a policy until a given date or age except under stated conditions. It is extremely important for the purchaser to review the conditions for renewal in order to make sure of their acceptability.

CONDITIONAL SALES FLOATER coverage for the seller of property on an installment or conditional sales contract if it is damaged or destroyed. For example, a television set is sold on an installment basis but is destroyed by a customer. The seller would be indemnified for the loss.

CONDITIONAL VESTING *see* VESTING, CONDITIONAL.

CONDITIONS FOR QUALIFICATION rights and duties of an insured as a prerequisite for collecting benefits. For example, in the event of property damage, the insured may be required to submit proof of loss to the insurance company.

CONDOMINIUM INSURANCE coverage under the *Homeowners Form-4 (HO-4)* for the insured's personal property and loss of use against fire and/or lightning; vandalism and/or malicious mischief; windstorm and/or hail; explosion, riot and/or civil commotion; vehicles; aircraft; smoke; falling objects; weight of ice, sleet, and/or snow; volcanic eruption; damage from artificially generated electricity; freezing of plumbing, heating, air conditioning or sprinkler system or household appliances; accidental tearing apart, cracking, burning, or bulging of a steam or hot water heating system, air conditioning system, or an automatic fire protective sprinkler system.

CONFIDENCE LEVEL percentage of confidence in a finding. For example, if an insurance company's total LOSS RESERVES should be

$10,000,000 in order to attain an 80% confidence level that enough money will be available to pay anticipated claims, then, in 8 times out of 10, after all claims have been settled the total claims paid out will be less than $10,000,000. Conversely, in 2 times out of 10 the total claims paid out will be greater than $10,000,000. In another example, a 70% confidence level of one's house burning would mean that the house would burn approximately once every 3.33 years $[1 \div (1 - 0.70) = 3.33]$.

CONFINING CONDITION term describing illness, sickness, or disability incurred by the insured such that the insured is restricted to his or her home, a hospital, or a nursing home. Many HEALTH INSURANCE policies provide benefits only if the insured is restricted in such a manner.

CONFUSION OF GOODS peril that occurs when personal property of two or more people is mixed to such an extent that any one owner can no longer identify his or her property.

CONSEQUENTIAL LOSS value of loss resulting from loss of use of property. For example, a fire damages the structure of business premises and the business loses customer income until it can reopen. The loss in income—the consequential loss—can be covered under BUSINESS INTERRUPTION INSURANCE. Basic property insurance policies, such as the *Fire Policy*, do not cover the consequential or indirect loss.

CONSERVATION effort to keep life insurance policies from *lapsing*. Many life insurance companies have conservation officers who contact lapsing *policyowners* explaining the benefits of keeping their policies in force. Often, the AGENT OF RECORD is notified of policies in danger or in process of lapsing so that the agent may also contact the policyowner.

CONSERVATOR court-appointed or COMMISSIONER OF INSURANCE-appointed custodian to manage the affairs of an insurance company whose management is deemed unable to manage that company in a proper fashion. Usually such a company faces INSOLVENCY prior to the appointment of the conservator.

CONSIDERATION
1. under contract law, anything of value exchanged for a promise or for performance that is needed to make an instrument binding on the contracting parties.
2. adherence to all provisions of an insurance policy by an insured; for example, the insured agrees to make all premium payments when due in order to maintain a policy in full force.
3. payment for an annuity. *See also* INSURANCE CONTRACT, LIFE; INSURANCE CONTRACT, PROPERTY AND CASUALTY.

CONSIGNMENT INSURANCE coverage for items that are on consignment, including exhibits, goods up for auction, and goods awaiting someone's approval. The stipulation for coverage is that these items cannot be under the care, custody, and control of the owner.

CONSTRUCTION BOND *see* BID BOND; COMPLETION BOND; LABOR AND MATERIAL BOND; MAINTENANCE BOND; SURETY BOND.

CONSTRUCTION INSURANCE property coverage for damage or destruction of structures in the course of construction. For example, the standing frame of a house destroyed by fire would be covered. *See also* BUILDER'S RISK PROPERTY INSURANCE.

CONSTRUCTIVE TOTAL LOSS partial loss of such significance that the cost of restoring damaged property would exceed its value after restoration. For example, an automobile is so badly damaged by fire that fixing it would cost more than the restored vehicle would be worth.

CONSULTANT in insurance, independent advisor who specializes in pension and profit sharing plans. Usually a licensed insurance agent.

CONSUMER CREDIT PROTECTION ACT 1968 Federal legislation which makes it mandatory for lenders to disclose to credit applicants the annual interest percentage rate (APR) and any finance charge.

CONSUMER PROTECTION ACT *see* CONSUMER CREDIT PROTECTION ACT.

CONTENTS
1. in PERSONAL PROPERTY insurance, coverage is for personal property items which are movable, that is, not attached to the building's structure (the home), such as television sets, radios, clothes, household goods. Not included under the coverage are animals, automobiles, and boats.
2. in COMMERCIAL PROPERTY insurance, coverage is for the business's personal property items which are movable, that is, not attached to the building's structure such as inventory, machinery, equipment, furniture and fixtures. Not included under the coverage are animals, automobiles, boats, and crops.

CONTENTS RATE premium rate charged on the property within a building, but not on the building structure.

CONTESTABLE CLAUSE *see* INCONTESTABLE CLAUSE.

CONTINGENCIES unexpected claims occurring above the expected claims for which a CONTINGENCY RESERVE is maintained.

CONTINGENCY event which may or may not occur in a given time period. For example, whether a specific person will die, or a particular house will burn this year is a contingency.

CONTINGENCY RESERVE percentage of total surplus retained, in insurance company operations, that serves as a reserve to cover unexpected losses as well as to cover the short fall if the earned surplus in a particular year is not adequate to maintain a company's announced dividend scale for participating policies.

CONTINGENCY SURPLUS *see* CONTINGENCY RESERVE.

CONTINGENT ANNUITANT *see* BENEFICIARY.

CONTINGENT ANNUITY contract providing income payments beginning when the named contingency occurs. For example, upon the death of one spouse (the contingency), a surviving spouse will begin to receive monthly income payments.

CONTINGENT BENEFICIARY *see* BENEFICIARY.

CONTINGENT BUSINESS INTERRUPTION FORM coverage for loss in the net earnings of a business if a supplier business, subcontractor, key customer, or manufacturer doing business with the insured business cannot continue to operate because of damage or destruction. For example, a specialty hot dog stand noted for its great buns cannot sell its product if the bakery supplier of hot dog buns burns down. In instances where a business is heavily dependent on its suppliers or subcontractors, interruption of the flow of material from the supplier usually results in a substantial loss to the business.

CONTINGENT BUSINESS INTERRUPTION INSURANCE *see* CONTINGENT BUSINESS INTERRUPTION FORM.

CONTINGENT LIABILITY (VICARIOUS LIABILITY) liability incurred by a business for acts other than those of its own employees. This particular situation may arise when an independent contractor is hired. The business can be held liable for negligent acts of the contractor to the extent that its representatives give directions or exercise control over the contractor's employees.

CONTINGENT LIABILITY INSURANCE coverage for contingent liability exposure. *See* CONTINGENT LIABILITY.

CONTINGENT TRANSIT INSURANCE coverage if an insured cannot collect on property damage or destruction losses from the hired transporter. For example, a truck transporting furniture of the insured is involved in an accident and the furniture is damaged. The truck owner refuses to compensate the insured for damages; the recourse of the insured is to collect from the insurance company.

CONTRACT in insurance, agreement between an insurer and an insured under which the insurer has a legally enforceable obligation to make all benefit payments for which it has received premiums.

CONTRACT BOND a guarantee of the performance of a contractor. In general, contract bonds are used to guarantee that the contractor will perform according to the specifications of the construction contract. If the contractor fails to perform according to contract, the insurance company is responsible to the insured for payment, up to the limit of the bond, which is usually for an amount equal to the cost of the construction project. The insurance company then has recourse against the contractor for reimbursement. *See also* BID BOND; PAYMENT BOND; PERFORMANCE BOND.

CONTRACT CARRIER transportation firm that carries only select customers' goods and is not obligated to carry any particular customer's goods even if that customer is willing to pay. Contrast with COMMON CARRIER.

CONTRACT HOLDER in insurance, individual with rightful possession of an insurance policy, usually the *policyowner*.

CONTRACT INCEPTION AND TIME OF LOSS *see* CLAIMS MADE BASIS; CLAIMS OCCURRENCE BASIS LIABILITY COVERAGE.

CONTRACT OF ADHESION *see* ADHESION INSURANCE CONTRACT.

CONTRACT OF INDEMNITY property and liability insurance contracts that restore the insured to his/her original financial condition after suffering a loss. The insured cannot profit by the loss; otherwise an unscrupulous homeowner, for example, could buy several fire insurance policies, set fire to the house, and collect on all the policies.

CONTRACT OF INSURANCE *see* CONTRACT; HEALTH INSURANCE CONTRACT; INSURANCE CONTRACT, GENERAL; INSURANCE CONTRACT, LIFE; INSURANCE CONTRACT, PROPERTY AND CASUALTY.

CONTRACT OF UTMOST GOOD FAITH *see* UBERRIMAE FIDEI CONTRACT.

CONTRACTORS EQUIPMENT FLOATER form of marine insurance that covers mobile equipment of a contractor, including road building machinery, steam shovels, hoists, and derricks used on the job by builders of structures, roads, bridges, dams, tunnels and mines. Coverage is provided on a specified peril or an ALL RISKS basis, subject to exclusions of wear and tear, work, and nuclear disaster.

CONTRACTORS EQUIPMENT INSURANCE *see* CONTRACTORS EQUIPMENT FLOATER.

CONTRACTUAL LIABILITY liability incurred by a party through entering into a written contract. *See also* CIVIL LIABILITY; CIVIL WRONG.

CONTRIBUTE-TO-LOSS STATUTE law in some states which permits an insurance company to deny payment of a claim resulting from an insured loss because of breach of warranty or misrepresentation, provided that the breach of warranty or misrepresentation made a material contribution to the loss.

CONTRIBUTING INSURANCE *see* CONTRIBUTION.

CONTRIBUTING PROPERTIES COVERAGE *see* CONTINGENT BUSINESS INTERRUPTION FORM.

CONTRIBUTING PROPERTY BUSINESS INTERRUPTION form that covers an insured business in the event that a manufacturer's operations are interrupted or suspended, thereby resulting in a monetary loss because a supplier of the insured has had his facility damaged or destroyed by an insured peril. *See also* CONTINGENT BUSINESS INTERRUPTION INSURANCE.

CONTRIBUTION principle of equity in property, casualty, and health insurance. When two or more policies apply to the loss, each policy pays its part of the loss, unless its terms provide otherwise. For example, if two policies each insure a risk for $100,000 and there is a $50,000 loss, then each policy (depending on coinsurance requirements) will pay $25,000. In employee benefits, payment made by an employee.

CONTRIBUTION CLAUSE clause, generally found in BUSINESS INTERRUPTION INSURANCE, that establishes the same indemnification basis as the COINSURANCE clause.

CONTRIBUTORY employee benefit plans under which both the employee and the employer pay part of the premium. Contribution ratios vary. For example, an employer contributes two dollars for every dollar contributed by the employee up to 6% of the employee's salary.

CONTRIBUTORY NEGLIGENCE principle of law recognizing that injured persons may have contributed to their own injury. For example, by not observing the "Don't Walk" sign at a crosswalk, pedestrians may cause accidents in which they are injured.

CONVENTION BLANK *see* ANNUAL STATEMENT.

CONVENTION VALUES monetary sums attached to an insurance company's assets, as listed on the ANNUAL STATEMENT.

CONVENTION EXAMINATION audit of the *convention blank* (NAIC Statement Blank) every third year as to (1) all of the financial activities of a company; (2) company claim practices; and (3) general policyowner relations.

CONVERSION
1. tort against another person's property, designed to detain or dispose of it in a wrongful manner. For example, wrongful selling of another person's automobile without permission would qualify as an act of conversion.
2. in group life and health insurance, a provision that allows a certificate holder to convert group coverage to an individual policy under specified conditions.

CONVERSION FACTOR FOR EMPLOYEE CONTRIBUTIONS inverse of the actuarial present value of a life annuity, taking the employee's life expectancy into account, to commence income payments at the NORMAL RETIREMENT AGE of the employee. It is used in a DEFINED BENEFIT PLAN to determine the amount of accrued benefits that result from the employee's contributions.

CONVERSION PRIVILEGE right of a certificate holder to convert group life or group health insurance to an individual policy without a physical examination to furnish evidence of insurability. Usually this must be done within 31 days of termination of employment. Under group life insurance, conversion is made at the employee's attained age rate, which can be prohibitively costly in later years. Many term life insurance policies can be converted to a whole life policy at the insured's attained age, with no physical examination required.

CONVERTIBLE *see* CONVERTIBLE TERM LIFE INSURANCE.

CONVERTIBLE TERM LIFE INSURANCE coverage that can be converted into permanent insurance regardless of an insured's physical condition and without a medical examination. The individual cannot be denied coverage or charged an additional premium for any health problems.

COOPERATIVE INSURANCE *see* SOCIAL INSURANCE.

COOPERATIVE INSURER mutual insurance association which issues insurance to its members on a nonprofit basis. Examples of such associations include fraternal societies, unions, and employee membership groups.

COORDINATION OF BENEFITS arrangement in health insurance to discourage multiple payment for the same claim under two or more policies. When two or more group health insurance plans cover the insured and dependents, one plan becomes the *primary* plan and the other plan(s) the *secondary* plan(s). For example, two working spouses have health insurance at their respective places of employment. If one spouse becomes ill, his/her policy at work would become the primary plan. Medical expenses not covered under the primary plan would be covered under the secondary plan of the other spouse. *See also* COINSURANCE.

COPAYMENT partial payment of medical service expenses required in group health insurance, in addition to the membership fee. For example, for each visit of a physician a member may be required to pay $5, regardless of the expense of the services rendered. Or, for each prescription for drugs and medicines, the member may have to pay a flat $2 regardless of the actual cost.

CORPORATE ALTERNATIVE MINIMUM TAX: IMPLICATIONS FOR CORPORATE-OWNED LIFE INSURANCE tax that exhibits direct impact on the book income preference. Beginning with the year 1990, the book income preference became equal to 75% of the excess of current adjusted earnings of the alternative minimum taxable income (AMTI). Book income preferences are affected by corporate-owned life insurance in the following situations:

1. If the insured dies, the excess of the life insurance policy's DEATH BENEFIT over the CASH SURRENDER VALUE becomes book income to the corporation.

2. If the insurance policy's annual premium exceeds the increase in the cash surrender value for a particular year, the result is a decline in the book income and thus a decline in the corporation's exposure to the alternative minimum tax (AMT).

3. Conversely, if the insurance policy's cash surrender value exceeds the increase in the annual premium for a particular year, the result is an increase in the book income and thus an increase in the corporation's exposure to the alternative minimum tax.

Generally, if the corporation in any given year has taxable income, corporate-owned life insurance results in an alternative minimum tax liability if a significant death benefit is paid to the corporation upon the death of the insured. The result is that the alternative minimum tax will cause a reduction in the net death benefit from the life insurance policy paid to the corporation.

CORPORATION STOCK PURCHASE PLAN *see* CLOSE CORPORATION PLAN.

CORRIDOR DEDUCTIBLE type of major medical deductible amount which acts as a corridor between benefits under a basic health insurance plan and benefits under a major medical insurance plan. After benefits are paid under the basic plan, a fixed dollar per-loss deductible amount often is required of the insured (benefits paid under the basic plan do not apply towards this deductible) before major medical benefits are paid.

COST *see* PREMIUM, PURE PREMIUM RATING METHOD.

COST-BENEFIT ANALYSIS comparison of the cost of a solution and the economic benefits that would accrue if the solution is put into effect. This analysis is a prerequisite to the installation of an employee benefit plan. Questions to be answered include: (1) will the cost result in greater loyalty of employees? (2) will the cost result in greater productivity; and (3) will the benefits encourage employees to participate in their cost?

COST CONTAINMENT PROVISION in many HEALTH INSURANCE and DENTAL INSURANCE policies, stipulation that, if the estimated cost of a recommended plan of treatment exceeds a specified sum, the insured must submit the plan of treatment to the insurance company for review and predetermination of benefits before service begins. Usually, however, predetermination of benefits is not necessary for emergency treatment.

COST OF INSURANCE value or cost of the actual net protection, in life insurance, in any year (face amount less reserve) according to the yearly renewal term rate used by an insurance company. *See also* INTEREST ADJUSTED COST.

COST-OF-LIVING ADJUSTMENT (COLA) automatic adjustment applied to Social Security retirement payments when the consumer price index increases at a rate of at least 3%, the first quarter of one year to the first quarter of the next year. *See also* RIDERS, LIFE POLICIES.

COST-OF-LIVING INCREASE *see* COST-OF-LIVING ADJUSTMENT (COLA); COST-OF-LIVING RIDER.

COST-OF-LIVING PLAN plan providing benefits that are adjusted according to variations in a specified index of prices. For example, some pension plans adjust retirement benefits yearly according to the rise in the Consumer Price Index (CPI).

COST-OF-LIVING RIDER usually term insurance for one year added to a basic life insurance policy. In effect, this increases or decreases the face amount of the basic policy to reflect cost-of-living changes as measured by the Consumer Price Index (CPI). This rider can also be used in conjunction with a disability income policy in which the income benefit is adjusted to reflect fluctuations in the CPI.

COST OF LOSS *see* EXPECTED LOSS.

COST OF PROTECTION *see* COST OF INSURANCE; PREMIUM; PURE PREMIUM RATING METHOD.

COST OF RISK (COR) quantitative measurement of the total costs (losses, risk control costs, risk financing costs, and administration costs) associated with the RISK MANAGEMENT function, as compared to a business's sales, assets, and number of employees. The purpose of such a comparison is to determine whether the total costs of the risk management function are increasing, decreasing, or remaining constant as a function of the business's economic activity. After the quantitative measurement has been derived, a comparison can be made between the COR of that business and the CORs of its peer groups. In addition, COR will allow the business to focus on the areas of operation that will have the greatest long-term effects on its total risk management function costs.

COST PLUS insured plan under which the insurance company agrees to provide the insured with a series of benefits on a benefits-paid basis plus administrative services on a stipulated-fee basis. This plan enables the POLICYHOLDER to control more of its own cash flow than it can under traditional insurance plans. While this plan is similar to the ADMINISTRATIVE SERVICES ONLY (ASO) plan, it is dissimilar in that it is an insured plan.

COTTON INSURANCE coverage for property damage by a covered peril to insured cotton during the time period from its weighing in at the gin until its delivery to the buyer. Written either on a *specified peril* basis or on an ALL RISKS basis. The purpose of cotton insurance is much the same as the purchase of insurance by a merchant to protect business inventory prior to its sale, since in many instances the primary asset is the inventory.

COUNTERSIGNATURE licensed AGENT'S signature on an insurance policy.

COUNTERSIGNATURE LAW state law which requires that an insurance policy issued by an insurance company in a particular state be signed by an AGENT of the company holding a LICENSE in that state.

COUPON POLICY *nonparticipating life insurance* (also called a *guaranteed dividend* or *guaranteed investment policy*) sold by a stock life insurance company, usually as a 20-payment policy with coupons attached. The *policyowner* can cash in each coupon (which is actually one of a series of pure endowments) for a stipulated sum at the time of paying the annual premium.

COURT BOND *see* JUDICIAL BOND.

COURTESY INTEREST husband's interest in his wife's property upon her death. A husband has an INSURABLE INTEREST in that property and can purchase a property and casualty insurance policy to cover the EXPOSURES on it. *See also* DOWER INTEREST.

COVER to place insurance in force on an individual, individuals, or an organization. *See also* CONTRACT; COVERAGE, INDIVIDUAL; COVERAGE, LOCATION; COVERAGE OF HAZARD; COVERAGE, PERIL; COVERAGE, PROPERTY; COVERED EXPENSES.

COVERAGE protection under an insurance policy. In property insurance, coverage lists perils insured against, properties covered, locations covered, individuals insured, and the limits of indemnification. In life insurance, living and death benefits.

COVERAGE, INDIVIDUAL *see* INDIVIDUAL INSURANCE.

COVERAGE, LOCATION *see* PROPERTY INSURANCE, COVERAGE.

COVERAGE OF HAZARD *see* HAZARD INCREASE RESULTING IN SUSPENSION OR EXCLUSION OF COVERAGE.

COVERAGE PART section of the INSURANCE POLICY which lists all of the provisions that are applicable to the insurance coverage provided under that section. This section is attached to the policy JACKET (which lists the provisions common to all the insurance coverages) to form the insurance policy.

COVERAGE, PERIL *see* ALL RISKS; PROPERTY INSURANCE, COVERAGE.

COVERAGE, PROPERTY *see* PROPERTY INSURANCE, COVERAGE.

COVERED *see* COVERAGE.

COVERED EXPENSES
1. in health insurance, reimbursement for an insured's medically related expenses, including room and board, surgery, medicines, anesthetics, ambulance service to and from a hospital, operating room expenses, X-ray, and fluoroscope.
2. in business interruption insurance, reimbursement of an insured for loss if a business cannot operate, including payroll expense and taxes.
3. in extra expense insurance, reimbursement of an insured for extra expenditures made to keep a business operating even under emergency conditions.

COVERED EXPENSES, PRO RATA DISTRIBUTION CLAUSE *see* DOUBLE RECOVERY; PRO RATA DISTRIBUTION CLAUSE.

COVERED LOCATION, PROPERTY INSURANCE *see* PROPERTY INSURANCE, COVERAGE.

COVERED LOSSES *see* LOSS.

COVERED PERSON, PROPERTY INSURANCE *see* PROPERTY INSURANCE, COVERAGE.

COVER NOTE document issued to the INSURED by an AGENT or BROKER as evidence that the insurance is in force. This instrument is sometimes used instead of a BINDER.

CPCU *see* CHARTERED PROPERTY AND CASUALTY UNDERWRITER (CPCU).

CPL *see* COMPREHENSIVE GENERAL LIABILITY INSURANCE (CGL).

CREDIBILITY OF LOSS EXPERIENCE *see* LOSS DEVELOPMENT.

CREDIT CARD FORGERY *see* CREDIT CARD INSURANCE.

CREDIT CARD INSURANCE coverage under a HOMEOWNERS INSURANCE POLICY in the event that a credit card is fraudulently used or altered. Fraud includes theft and the unauthorized use of a credit card.

CREDIT HEALTH INSURANCE coverage issued to a creditor on the life of a debtor so that if the debtor becomes disabled, the insurance policy pays the balance of the debt to the creditor.

CREDIT INSURANCE *see* CREDIT HEALTH INSURANCE; CREDIT LIFE INSURANCE (CREDITOR LIFE INSURANCE).

CREDIT INVESTIGATION *see* RETAIL CREDIT REPORT.

CREDIT LIFE INSURANCE (CREDITOR LIFE INSURANCE) insurance issued to a creditor (lender) to cover the life of a debtor (borrower) for an outstanding loan. If the debtor dies prior to repayment of the debt, the policy will pay off the balance of the amount outstanding. Credit life insurance is sold on a group or individual basis, and usually is purchased to cover small loans of short duration. When issued under a group policy, a certificate is issued to the debtor, the master policy being issued by the creditor. The face value of a credit life insurance policy decreases in proportion to the reduction in the loan amount until both equal zero.

CREDITOR LIFE INSURANCE *see* CREDIT LIFE INSURANCE (CREDITOR LIFE INSURANCE).

CREDITOR RIGHTS IN LIFE INSURANCE *see* LIFE INSURANCE, CREDITOR RIGHTS.

CREDIT, PENSION PLAN value of benefit or contribution allocated to an employee under a pension plan; method of determining benefits due a retired employee. Each private pension plan establishes rules for awarding credits to employees, taking into account age, amount of time with the employer, number of days worked per year, breaks in service, maximum salary, and position in the company. For an employee who joined a firm before the plan was put in place, the company computes *past service credit*, crediting work done prior to establishment of the plan. Ultimately, credits determine the level of pension income the employee receives upon retiring.

CREDIT REPORT *see* RETAIL CREDIT REPORT.

CRIME INSURANCE coverage for the perils of burglary, theft, and robbery. *See also* BURGLARY INSURANCE; BUSINESS INSURANCE; HOMEOWNERS INSURANCE POLICY; PERSONAL AUTOMOBILE POLICY (PAP); SIMPLIFIED COMMERCIAL LINES PORTFOLIO POLICY (SCLP); SPECIAL MULTIPERIL INSURANCE (SMP).

CRIMINAL LIABILITY crime against the state for which an officer of the state can bring legal action. Society is harmed by an individual breaking the laws of the state. Usually there is no statue of limitations for criminal liability. Property and casualty insurance is not designed to provide coverage for the criminal acts of an insured individual.

CROP INSURANCE coverage for crops in the event of loss or damage by insured perils including hail, fire, and lightning. Prior to the passage of the Federal Crop Insurance Act in 1938 it was virtually impossible to obtain insurance protection against crop damage. Today coverage is available from the Federal Crop Insurance Corporation as well as from private sources. Exclusions from coverage include the perils of war and nuclear disaster.

CROSS LIABILITY LIABILITY incurred by one INSURED as the result of his or her damaging another insured when both insureds are covered under the same LIABILITY INSURANCE policy. Each insured must be treated as a separate entity under a cross-liability clause in a liability insurance policy.

CROSS PURCHASE PLAN *see* PARTNERSHIP LIFE AND HEALTH INSURANCE.

CRUDE DEATH RATE total deaths as a percentage of total population for a stipulated period of time.

CRUMMEY TRUST unfunded trust that acts as the owner of a life insurance policy. The trust receives a donor's cash payments on a periodic basis, from which the beneficiary of the trust has a specified period in which to make a cash withdrawal. If this is not done, the cash paid by the donor is used to pay the premiums due on the life insurance policy. Under this circumstance the IRS deems that a gift of present value interest by the donor has been made. It is important that a gift of present value interest be established because such a gift in trust will enable the donor to contribute up to $10,000 ($20,000 if two donors such as husband and wife contribute) in premium payments and enjoy the gift tax exclusion. When the donor dies, the life insurance policy in trust is effectively removed from the donor's estate.

CSL *see* COMBINED SINGLE LIMIT.

CSO TABLE *see* COMMISSIONERS STANDARD ORDINARY MORTALITY TABLE (CSO).

CUMULATIVE LIABILITY
Reinsurance: total of the limits of liability of all reinsurance policies that a reinsurer has outstanding on a single risk. The total of all such limits includes all *ceding* contracts from all insurers representing all lines of coverage for the single risk.
Liability insurance: total of the limits of liability of all policies that an insurer has outstanding on a single risk. Examples are the HOMEOWNERS INSURANCE POLICY, PERSONAL AUTOMOBILE POLICY (PAP), and *personal umbrella liability policy*.

CUMULATIVE TRAUMA injury that continues after a wound from physical or psychic entry. (The latter is a wound that makes a lasting impression on the mind, especially upon the subconscious mind; for example, a three-year-old child could be traumatized by seeing father abuse mother.) Trauma results in other injuries of a continuing nature and is usually covered under health insurance policies.

CUMULATIVE TREND METHOD approach to derive trend lines that can be applied to rating insured losses. Other methods require substantial preliminary operations to solve systems of equations of several unknowns. The cumulative method reduces the probability of mistakes because a relatively simple computation is required to prepare a set of data for the BURNING COST RATIO.

CURE *see* REST CURE.

CURRENT ASSUMPTIONS basis for calculating life insurance premiums and benefits using current interest and mortality rates, rather than historic rates. Current assumptions are critical to interest-sensitive products such as *Universal Life*. When interest rates are high, benefits projections (such as cash values) are high. When interest rates are low, these projections are not as alluring. The thesis of current-assumption life insurance products is that policyowner earnings should reflect current market conditions.

CURRENT ASSUMPTION WHOLE LIFE INSURANCE variation of ORDINARY LIFE INSURANCE under which current mortality experience and investment earnings are credited to the insurance policy either through the cash value account and/or the premium structure (in a stock company) or the dividend structure (in a mutual company). Regardless of whether a company is stock or mutual, the policy has these characteristics:

1. premiums are subject to change based on the experience (mortality, expenses, investment) of the company. The *policyowner* does not exercise any control over the changes.
2. a policyowner can use the cash value to make loans just as with traditional ordinary life insurance.
3. a minimum amount of cash value is guaranteed, just as with traditional ordinary life insurance.
4. the death benefit does not fluctuate.

CURRENT DISBURSEMENT payment of premiums and benefits as they come due. In pension plans, known as the "pay as you go basis." The plan depends on new employees coming into the work force so that their contributions can help pay for the benefits of the retiring employees. If the company is not experiencing growth and is in fact part of a matured or even a dying industry, there may not be enough on hand to pay benefits of retiring employees.

CURRENTLY INSURED STATUS Social Security provision under which the family of a deceased insured worker can receive survivor benefits even if the worker was not *fully insured*.

CUSTODIAL ACCOUNT account established to manage the assets of a minor. This account is under the auspices of a custodian (either an individual or an institution). The GIFT TAX exclusion would apply on any annual gifts to a minor.

CUSTODIAL CARE assistance provided to a person in performing the basic daily necessities of life, such as dressing, eating, using a toilet, walking, bathing, and getting in and out of bed. This type of care does not require hospitalization for the treatment of a disease, illness, accident, or injury. Its cost may or may not be covered by health insurance.

CUSTOMARY AND REASONABLE CHARGE term referring to the most common charge, in HEALTH INSURANCE, for a service.

CUT-THROUGH ENDORSEMENT (ASSUMPTION OF RISK) guarantee by a reinsurance company that payment for losses incurred by a third party will be made even though that third party has no contractual arrangement with the reinsurance company.

D

DAILY FORM (REPORT) shortened report showing pertinent insurance policy information, copies of which are distributed in the insurance company's HOME OFFICE and BRANCH OFFICES, as well as to AGENTS and BROKERS.

DAMAGES sum the insurance company is legally obligated to pay an insured for losses incurred.

DAMAGE TO PROPERTY OF OTHERS *see* HOMEOWNERS INSURANCE POLICY—SECTION II (LIABILITY COVERAGE).

D&O *see* DIRECTORS AND OFFICERS LIABILITY INSURANCE.

DATA PROCESSING INSURANCE coverage on data processing equipment, data processing media (such as magnetic tapes, disks), and extra expense involved in returning to usual business conditions. The data processing equipment is usually written as ALL RISKS on a specifically scheduled basis. The data processing media is usually written on an ALL RISKS basis. No COINSURANCE is required for the data processing media and the extra expense coverage.

DATE OF ISSUE date when an insurance company issues a policy. This date may be different from the date the insurance becomes effective.

DATE OF PLAN TERMINATION stipulation of the exact time when the PENSION BENEFIT GUARANTY CORPORATION assumes the legal liabilities for an insured pension plan which is being terminated. *See also* PENSION BENEFIT GUARANTY CORPORATION (PBGC).

DDD *see* DIRECTORS AND OFFICERS LIABILITY INSURANCE.

DEALERS INSURANCE coverage on an ALL RISKS basis, subject to listed exclusions, for personal property of the insured dealer that is used in normal business activities. Goods that have been sold on an installment basis contract upon leaving the care, custody, and control of the insured dealer; furniture and fixtures used in the business activities of the insured dealer; money; securities; and items that are in the process of being manufactured are generally excluded from coverage.

DEAN ANALYTIC SCHEDULE rating method for commercial fire insurance according to a predetermined schedule. Published by A. F. Dean in 1902, this method was the first comprehensive qualitative analysis procedure to take into consideration the numerous physical factors impacting the fire exposure. No longer widely used, since most companies have developed their own schedules or use schedules advocated by the INSURANCE SERVICES OFFICE (ISO).

DEATH termination of life. A death certificate is required by a life insurance company for a beneficiary to receive the death payment.

DEATH BENEFIT amount payable, as stated in a life insurance policy, upon the death of the insured. This is the face value of the policy plus any riders, less any outstanding loans and the interest accrued thereon.

DEATH BENEFIT ONLY LIFE INSURANCE PLAN *see* KEY EMPLOYEES, INSURANCE PLANS FOR.

DEATH PLANNING estimate of the funds necessary to maintain the lifestyle of a family after the death of the wage earner. *See also* HUMAN LIFE VALUE APPROACH (ECONOMIC VALUE OF AN INDIVIDUAL LIFE).

DEATH RATE *see* MORTALITY RATE.

DEBIT in insurance, DEBIT AGENT'S list of total premiums to be collected. This also applies to the geographical area in which an agent collects the premiums.

DEBIT AGENT (HOME SERVICE AGENT) insurance company representative who sells debit life insurance (industrial life insurance). This agent is usually more of a collector of small premium payments on a weekly, bi-weekly, or monthly basis than a salesperson.

DEBIT INSURANCE (HOME SERVICE INSURANCE, INDUS-TRIAL INSURANCE) life insurance on which a premium is collected on a weekly, bi-weekly, or monthly basis, usually at the home of a policyholder. The face value of the policy is usually $1000 or less. *See also* DEBIT; DEBIT AGENT.

DEBIT LIFE INSURANCE *see* DEBIT INSURANCE.

DEBIT SYSTEM *see* DEBIT INSURANCE.

DEBRIS REMOVAL CLAUSE in property insurance, contract section providing for reimbursement for removal of debris resulting from an insured peril. The amount of reimbursement under the HOMEOWNERS INSURANCE POLICY ranges from 5-10% of the face value.

DECEPTIVE PRACTICE CONCEALMENT of the actual fact. For example, an insurance agent tells a prospective insured that a policy provides a particular benefit when in actual fact this benefit is not in the written language of the policy. *See also* TWISTING.

DECLARATION statement that the insured makes (declares) about loss exposures in an application for a policy. For example, in a personal automobile policy the applicant states his/her name, address, occupation, type of automobile, expected mileage per year, etc. Based on this information, the insurance company decides which underwriting classification in which to place the risk; applicable premium rate; maximum limits of coverage; and any special conditions to govern the insured's behavior that is to be attached to the policy.

DECLARATIONS SECTION in property and casualty insurance, contract section containing such information as name, description, and location of insured property, name and address of the insured, period a policy is in force, premiums payable, and amount of coverage.

DECLINATION rejection by an insurance company of an application for a policy.

DECREASING TERM LIFE INSURANCE coverage in which the face amount of a life insurance policy declines by a stipulated amount over a period of time. For example, the initial face amount of a $100,000 decreasing term policy decreases by $10,000 each year, until after 10 years the face value equals zero. The premium does not decrease.

DEDUCTIBILITY OF EMPLOYER CONTRIBUTIONS contributions (under qualified employee benefit plans, such as pensions and health insurance) made by an employer on behalf of employees, deducted as a business expense for tax purposes. Employer contributions are not considered current taxable income to the employee. Thus, significant tax advantages are available to both an employer and an employee.

DEDUCTIBLE amount of loss that insured pays in a claim; includes the following types:
1. *Absolute dollar amount.* Amount the insured must pay before the company will pay, up to the limits of the policy. The higher the absolute dollar amount, the lower the premium.
2. *Time period amount (Elimination period/Waiting period).* Length of time the insured must wait before any benefit payments are made by the insurance company. In disability income policies it is common to have a waiting period of 30 days during which no income benefits are paid to the insured. The longer this time period, the lower the premium.

    The consumer would be well advised to select the highest deductible (by dollar amount and/or time period) that he/she can afford. First dollar coverages are very costly. A high deductible allows the insured to self-insure expected losses—those of high frequency and low severity.

DEDUCTIBLE, AGGREGATE ANNUAL *see* AGGREGATE ANNUAL DEDUCTIBLE.

DEDUCTIBLE, BUY-BACK *see* BUY-BACK DEDUCTIBLE.

DEDUCTIBLE CLAUSE provision in insurance policies which states the DEDUCTIBLE. *See also* COINSURANCE; LOSS SETTLEMENT AMOUNT; SETTLEMENT OPTIONS, PROPERTY AND CASUALTY INSURANCE.

DEDUCTIBLE, CORRIDOR *see* CORRIDOR DEDUCTIBLE.

DEDUCTIBLE, DISAPPEARING *see* DISAPPEARING DEDUCTIBLE.

DEDUCTIBLE, FRANCHISE *see* FRANCHISE DEDUCTIBLE.

DEDUCTIBLE, PERCENTAGE-OF-LOSS *see* PERCENTAGE-OF-LOSS DEDUCTIBLE.

DEDUCTIBLE, PERIOD *see* DISABILITY INCOME INSURANCE (ELIMINATION PERIOD).

DEDUCTIBLE, SPLIT *see* SPLIT DEDUCTIBLE.

DEFAMATION OF CHARACTER oral or written statement that results in injuring the good name or reputation of another, causing that individual to be held in disrepute.

DEFENDANT BOND type of COURT BOND filed on behalf of the defendant and used to release assets to him or her which have been attached pending a court decision. *See also* APPEAL BOND; BAIL BOND; INJUNCTION BOND; JUDICIAL BOND.

DEFENSE AGAINST UNINTENTIONAL TORT *see* TORT, DEFENSE AGAINST UNINTENTIONAL.

DEFENSE CLAUSE *see* DEMOLITION CLAUSE.

DEFENSE COSTS expense of defending a lawsuit. To mount a legal defense against civil or criminal liability, a defendant faces expenses for lawyers, investigation, fact gathering, bonds, and court costs. Of critical importance in purchasing liability insurance is not only the limits of coverage under the policy but also the obligation of the insurance company to defend the insured against suits, even if a suit is without foundation. Because legal defense costs can be extremely high, the consumer should consider liability insurance that pays all defense costs in addition to the policy limits.

DEFENSE OF SUIT AGAINST INSURED clause in a liability insurance policy under which an insurance company agrees to defend an insured even if a lawsuit is without foundation. The costs of defending the insured are covered, in addition to the limits of coverage under the policy. For example, if the limits of coverage under a policy is $1,000,000 and defense costs are $120,00, the $120,000 costs are in addition to the $1,000,000 of coverage. This is critical, since defense costs can be quite high.

DEFENSE RESEARCH INSTITUTE (DRI) organization of trial attorneys who specialize in the representation of defendants who become subject to TORT actions. Generally, these tort actions involve bodily injury or personal injury claims against the defendant.

DEFERRED ANNUITY annuity that can be paid either with a single premium or a series of installments. For example, an annuitant pays a single premium of $100,000 on June 1 of the current year and is scheduled to receive a monthly income of $1300 at a specified later date. Or, the annuitant pays $50 a month to the insurance company, starting June 1, 1968, and ending June 1, 1987, and begins receiving a monthly income of $1300, beginning July 1, 1987. *See also* ANNUITY.

DEFERRED BENEFITS AND PAYMENTS *see* DEFERRED CONTRIBUTION PLAN; DEFERRED RETIREMENT CREDIT.

DEFERRED COMPENSATION PLAN means of supplementing an executive's retirement benefits by deferring a portion of his or her current earnings. Deferring income in this manner encourages the loyalty of executives. To qualify for a tax advantage, the IRS requires a written agreement between an executive and the employer stating the specified period of deferral of income. An election by an executive to defer income must be irrevocable and must be made prior to performing the service for which income deferral is sought.

DEFERRED CONTRIBUTION PLAN arrangement in which an unused deduction (credit carryover) to a profit sharing plan can be added to an employer's future contribution on a tax deductible basis. It occurs when the employer's contribution to a profit sharing plan is less than the annual 15% of employee compensation allowed by the Federal Tax Code.

DEFERRED GROUP ANNUITY retirement income payments for an employee that begin after a stipulated future time period, and continue for life. (A beneficiary of a deceased annuitant may receive further income, depending on whether the contract is a PURE ANNUITY or REFUND ANNUITY). Each year, contributions are used to buy a paid-up single premium deferred annuity. These increments, added together, provide income payments at retirement.

DEFERRED PREMIUM life insurance premium which is not currently due. Future payments are made on a frequency basis other than annual.

DEFERRED PROFIT-SHARING portion of company profits allocated by an employer, in good years, to an employee's trust. Contributions on behalf of each employee are expressed as a percentage of salary with 5% being common practice. If the profit sharing plan is a *qualified* plan according to the IRS, employer contributions are tax deductible as a business expense. These contributions are not currently taxable to the employee; benefits are taxed at the time of distribution.

DEFERRED RETIREMENT retirement taken after the normal retirement age. For example, if the normal retirement age is 65 or 70 an employee may continue to work beyond those ages. Normally the election of deferred retirement does not increase the monthly retirement income when the employee actually retires.

DEFERRED RETIREMENT CREDIT former arrangement under which retirement benefits payable to an employee who continued to work beyond NORMAL RETIREMENT AGE were frozen, and not increased in recognition of added work time. This was eliminated by the Federal *Omnibus Budget Reconciliation Act of 1986.*

DEFERRED VESTING *see* VESTING, DEFERRED.

DEFICIENCY RESERVE addition to reserves of a life insurance company required by various states because the VALUATION PREMIUM is greater than the GROSS PREMIUM. Without a deficiency reserve, the normal reserve by itself would be less than the actual reserve required.

DEFINED BENEFIT PLAN retirement plan under which benefits are fixed in advance by formula, and contributions vary. The defined benefit plan can be expressed in either of two ways:
1. *Fixed Dollars:* (a) *Unit benefit* approach—a *discrete* unit of benefit is credited for each year of service recognized by the employer. The unit is either a flat dollar amount or (more often) a percentage of compensation—usually 1½-2½%. Total years of service are multiplied by this percentage. For example, if total years of service is 30 and the percentage is 1½, 45% would be applied to either the career average earnings or final average earnings (highest three of five consecutive years of earnings). If the average of the highest five consecutive years of earnings is $100,000, the yearly retirement benefit would be $45,000. (b) *Level Percentage of Compensation*— After a minimum number of years of service (usually 20) and a minimum age (usually 50), all employees will receive the same percentage of earnings as a retirement benefit, regardless of income, position in the company, or years of service. For example, each employee who is at least 50 years of age, with at least 20 years of service receives 20% of compensation. This plan is more common than the flat amount approach described below. (c) *Flat Amount*— After having attained a minimum number of years of service (usually

20) and a minimum age (usually 50), all employees will receive the same absolute dollar amount as a retirement benefit, regardless of income, position in the company, or years of service. For example, each employee who is at least 50 years of age, with at least 20 years of service receives $8000 a year in retirement benefits.

2. *Variable Dollars:* (a) Cost-of-Living Plan—benefits are modified according to changes in a predetermined price index—usually, the Consumer Price Index (CPI). For example, when the CPI increases by at least 3% benefits are increased by that percentage. (b) Equity Annuity Plan—premiums are paid into a variable annuity plan to purchase accumulation units. At retirement, the accumulation units are converted to *retirement* units whose values fluctuate according to the common stock portfolio in which the premiums were invested.

DEFINED CONTRIBUTION PENSION PLAN (MONEY PURCHASE PLAN) retirement plan under which contributions are fixed in advance by formula, and benefits vary. These plans are often used by organizations that must know what the cost of employee benefits will be in the years ahead. For example, nonprofit organizations such as charities need to project future pension expenses that will not rise above a preset limit. This enables budgets to be established that provide guidelines for their solicitation of funds.

DEFINITE LOSS *see* REQUIREMENTS OF INSURABLE RISK.

DEGREE OF CARE minimum of care owed by one party for the physical safety of another. Liability suits are brought because of negligent acts and omissions resulting from failures to exercise due care.

DEGREE OF RISK amount of uncertainty in a given situation. Probability that actual experience will be different from what is expected.

DELAY CLAUSE in CASH VALUE LIFE INSURANCE policies, provision which allows the insurance company to refuse the POLICYHOLDER a loan on the cash value for a period of time, usually up to 6 months, from the request date. The only exception is for premium payments due on the policy.

DELAYED PAYMENT CLAUSE life insurance policy provision stating that after the death of an insured, the proceeds from a policy are not immediately paid to the primary beneficiary; instead, they are delayed for a specified time period. This usually occurs in *common disaster* situations.

DELIVERY physical handing of an insurance policy to the insured. Sales training emphasizes the importance of delivery of a policy by the agent. This develops a caring attitude on the part of the agent and reinforces the insured's belief that he or she made the right decision in purchasing the policy.

DEMOLITION CLAUSE in PROPERTY INSURANCE policies, provision which excludes the insurance company's liability for indemnification of the insured for the insured's expenses incurred in the demolition of undamaged property.

DEMOLITION INSURANCE coverage that will indemnify the insured for the expenses, up to the limits of the policy, if a building is damaged by a peril such as fire, and zoning requirements and/or building codes mandate that the building be demolished.

DEMURRAGE compensation payable to the owner of a ship detained for reasons beyond his or her control who incurs a loss of earnings because of the delay. Detainment can be caused by a delay in the loading or unloading of the ship.

DEMUTUALIZATION (STOCKING A MUTUAL) conversion of form of ownership from a MUTUAL INSURANCE COMPANY to a STOCK INSURANCE COMPANY. Interest in demutualization of life insurance companies surged in the early 1980s among many large mutual companies because they felt they needed new sources of capital to compete in the financial services revolution.

DENTAL INSURANCE coverage for dental services under a group or individual policy.

DEPARTMENT STORE INSURANCE FLOATER coverage for items of property being delivered to a customer. The means of transportation covered include such common carriers as aircraft, railroads, trucks, express carrier and other variations, as well as the department store's trucks and other delivery vehicles. Coverage can be purchased on an ALL RISKS basis subject to excluded perils such as war and nuclear disaster. Coverage applies on a *blanket* basis meaning that all locations of points of delivery are covered.

DEPENDENT a person who relies on another for economic support. For insurance purposes, the following may be included: (1) the insured's legal spouse; (2) any unmarried children younger than a specified age who are dependent upon the insured for support (age requirements vary from plan to plan); (3) unmarried children between specified years of age who are dependent upon the insured for support, and who are fulltime students in an educational institution (age requirements vary).

A dependent child cannot be covered under more than one insured employee's plan. For example, if the husband and wife are both insured employees of different companies, coordination of benefits would determine which plan is *primary* and which plan is *secondary*. In some states, the father's plan is primary; in other states, the *birthday rule* would be used: the parent with the earlier birthday would have the primary plan.

DEPENDENT ADMINISTRATION COVERAGE *see* DEPENDENT; DEPENDENT COVERAGE.

DEPENDENT CARE ASSISTANCE PLANS (DCAP) fringe benefit provided by the employer to its employees as sanctioned under the 1981 Economic Recovery Tax Act. Under Internal Revenue Code Section 129, this benefit is nontaxable to the employee and the costs incurred by the employer are considered tax deductible as a necessary business expense. The dependent under DCAP is defined as a dependent child under age 15, a dependent elderly relative, or a dependent mentally and/or physically handicapped individual. DCAP can be implemented through a salary reduction program under which the employee can choose to reduce his or her salary up to a maximum of $5,000 annually for dependent care-related expenses. A current EMPLOYEE BENEFIT INSURANCE PLAN can be amended to include DCAP, thereby making the benefit available to all employees. DCAP permits the employee to select the type of dependent care program that he or she prefers.

DEPENDENT COVERAGE coverage under life and health insurance policies for dependents of a named insured to include a spouse and unmarried children under a specified age. Under some life insurance policies an insured's spouse and dependent children, unmarried and under age 21, can be added at favorable rates. Health insurance policies cover the same dependent individuals at a far cheaper rate than the cost of separate policies for them.

DEPOSIT ADMINISTRATION GROUP ANNUITY *see* PENSION PLAN FUNDING: GROUP DEPOSIT ADMINISTRATION ANNUITY.

DEPOSIT ADMINISTRATION PLAN unallocated funding instrument for pension plans under which premiums are placed on deposit, and are not currently allocated to the purchase of benefits for the employee. At retirement, an immediate retirement annuity is purchased for the employee. The amount of monthly income depends on the investment results of the funds left on deposit. Many insurance companies guarantee a minimum rate of return on funds left on deposit.

DEPOSITORS FORGERY INSURANCE coverage provided for individuals or businesses for loss due to forgery or alteration of such financial instruments as notes, checks, drafts, and promissory notes.

DEPOSIT PREMIUM premium required by an insurance company for plans subject to premium adjustment. The initial provisional premium is paid to put a commercial property or liability insurance policy into force. The final premium is determined at the end of the policy period, based on an insured's actual exposures and loss experience.

DEPOSIT TERM LIFE INSURANCE policy in which a premium (the deposit) is paid in the first policy year, in addition to the regular term insurance premiums required. The deposit is left to accumulate at interest for a specific number of years, e.g., 10. Thereafter, the *policyowner* can receive the deposit plus interest or may renew the policy without the INSURED having to furnish EVIDENCE OF INSURABILITY. This procedure can be repeated every 10 years, in some instances up to age 100. A deposit term policy can be converted to ORDINARY LIFE, or DECREASING TERM LIFE INSURANCE without evidence of insurability. However, if the policyowner cancels the policy prior to the initial 10 years, the deposit and any interest is forfeited. If the insured dies before the policy is converted, the deposit plus the interest is added to the death benefit.

DEPRECIATION actual or accounting recognition of the decrease in the value of a hard asset (property) over a period of time, according to a predetermined schedule such as *straight line depreciation.*

DEPRECIATION INSURANCE *see* REPLACEMENT COST LESS PHYSICAL DEPRECIATION AND OBSOLESCENCE.

DEVIATED RATE rates used by a property and casualty insurance company which are different from that suggested by a RATING BUREAU. An insurance company may use deviated rates because it feels they are more indicative of the company's experience.

DEVIATION *see* DEVIATED RATE.

DIAGNOSIS RELATED GROUP method of determining reimbursement from medical insurance according to diagnosis on a prospective basis. It originated with the MEDICARE program.

DIC *see* DIFFERENCE IN CONDITIONS INSURANCE.

DIFFERENCE IN CONDITIONS INSURANCE coverage for a physical structure, machinery, inventory, and merchandise within the structure in the event of earthquakes, flood collapses, and subsidence strikes. Even though coverage is on an ALL RISKS basis, important perils are excluded such as fire, vandalism, sprinkler leakage, employee dishonesty, boiler and machinery losses, and mysterious disappearance, since it is assumed that the insured business already has coverage for these perils under a business property insurance policy.

DIP-DOWN CLAUSE provision in an UMBRELLA LIABILITY INSURANCE policy under which the policy will pay those losses which come within the retention limits of the primary policy, but the primary policy cannot pay because its aggregate limits have no further capacity.

DIRECT COVER AUTOMATIC NONPROPORTIONAL REINSURANCE treaty or AUTOMATIC PROPORTIONAL REINSURANCE treaty which provides coverage for losses upon which claims are made while the treaty is in force, without regard to when these losses actually occurred. *See also* CLAIMS MADE BASIS LIABILITY COVERAGE; CLAIMS OCCURRENCE BASIS LIABILITY COVERAGE.

DIRECT LIABILITY legal obligation of an individual or business because of negligent acts or omissions resulting in bodily injury and/or property damage or destruction to another party. There are no intervening circumstances.

DIRECT LOSS property loss in which the insured peril is the *proximate cause* (an unbroken chain of events) of the damage or destruction. Most basic property insurance policies (such as the *Standard Fire Policy*) insure against only direct loss and not INDIRECT LOSS or CONSEQUENTIAL LOSS. For example, a fire within the wall structure of a house causes the drapes to catch fire, which in turn fans flames onto the furniture— a direct loss. An indirect loss would be inconvenience of the inhabitants, who would not be able to sleep in their home, thus causing a drop in their efficiency at work.

DIRECTORS AND OFFICERS LIABILITY INSURANCE coverage when a director or officer of a company commits a negligent act or omission, or misstatement or misleading statement, and a successful libel suit is brought against the company as a result. Usually a large deductible is required. The policy provides coverage for directors' and officers' liability exposure if they are sued as individuals. Coverage is also provided for the costs of defense such as legal fees and other court costs.

DIRECT RECOGNITION immediate taking-into-account of present interest rates, mortality experience, and expenses in premiums currently charged. This is critical to the formulation of CURRENT ASSUMPTION WHOLE LIFE INSURANCE products. *See also* UNIVERSAL LIFE INSURANCE.

DIRECT RESPONSE MARKETING (DIRECT SELLING SYSTEM) method of selling insurance directly to insureds through a company's own employees, through the mail, or at airport booths. The company uses this method of distribution rather than independent or captive agents for effectiveness and efficiency.

DIRECT SELLING *see* DIRECT RESPONSE MARKETING (DIRECT SELLING SYSTEM).

DIRECT SELLING SYSTEM *see* DIRECT RESPONSE MARKETING (DIRECT SELLING SYSTEM).

DIRECT WRITER
1. property insurer that distributes its products through a *direct selling system*. Traditionally, insurers often were known as direct writers if they used either a direct selling system or an *exclusive agency system* for distribution. Increasingly, the term applies only to those using a direct selling system.
2. reinsurer that deals directly with a CEDING COMPANY, without using a REINSURANCE BROKER.

DIRECT WRITING AGENT *see* CAPTIVE AGENT.

DIRECT WRITTEN PREMIUM total premiums received by a PROPERTY AND LIABILITY insurance company without any adjustments for the ceding of any portion of these premiums to the REINSURER.

DISABILITY physiological or psychological condition which prevents an insured from performing normal job functions.

DISABILITY BENEFIT income paid under a disability policy that is not covered under WORKERS COMPENSATION BENEFITS. It is usually expressed as a percentage of the insured's income prior to the disability, but there may be a limit on the amount and duration of benefits. The most advantageous policy pays a monthly disability income benefit for as long as the insured is unable to perform suitable job functions determined by experience, education, and training.

DISABILITY BENEFIT, COMMERCIAL HEALTH INSURANCE *see* DISABILITY BENEFIT.

DISABILITY BUY-OUT INSURANCE buy-sell agreements found in partnerships, sole proprietorships, and close corporations. Either the business entity or the surviving members of the business agree to buy out the interest of a disabled member according to a predetermined formula funded through insurance. Disability buy-out insurance can be more important to a business than death buy-out insurance because the chances of becoming disabled are 7 to 10 times greater than death, depending on the age of the individual. The mechanisms available for the disability buy-out are the same as those found under BUSINESS LIFE AND HEALTH INSURANCE. *See also* PARTNERSHIP LIFE AND HEALTH INSURANCE.

DISABILITY INCOME (DI) life insurance payment issued after the insured has been disabled for at least six months. One percent of the face value of the policy is paid the insured as a monthly income benefit and premiums are waived for the duration of the disability. A DISABILITY

INCOME RIDER can be attached to an ordinary life insurance policy to provide this disability income benefit at extra charge. The insured can have a WAVIER OF PREMIUM benefit without a disability income benefit, but cannot have the disability income benefit without the waiver of premiums benefit.

DISABILITY INCOME INSURANCE health insurance that provides income payments to the insured wage earner when income is interrupted or terminated because of illness, sickness or accident. Definitions under this insurance include:

1. *Total and Partial Disability*—reduction in benefits if the insured is found to be partially disabled instead of totally disabled.

2. *Amount of Benefits*—many policies stipulate that all sources of disability income cannot exceed 50 to 80% of the insured's earnings prior to the disability, subject to a maximum absolute dollar amount.

3. *Duration of Benefits*—length of time benefits will be paid. Some policies will pay benefits for one or two years, whereupon the insured must agree to be retrained for other work. Other policies pay benefits, as long as the insured is unable to do the job for which he/she is suited by training, education, and experience (often up to age 65, when retirement programs take over). Some policies pay lifetime benefits.

4. ELIMINATION PERIOD (*Waiting Period*)—period beginning with the first day of disability, during which no payments are made to the insured. The longer this period, the lower the premiums.

5. *Physician's Care*—the insured must be regularly attended by a legally qualified physician because it is necessary to assess changes in severity of disability.

6. PREEXISTING CONDITION—if an insured has a pre-existing injury, sickness or illness, most policies will not pay income benefits either for the duration of the policy or until a period of time (usually from six months to one year) has elapsed.

7. *Recurrent Disability*—most policies will not pay income benefits to an insured who is experiencing a recurrent disability unless the recurrent disability is deemed a new disability. Some more progressive policies define a recurrent disability as a new disability if there has been a break of at least six months between the first disability and the current disability, and the insured has returned to work during that break.

8. RESIDUAL DISABILITY—many policies pay for the unused portion of the total disability period, limited to age 65.

DISABILITY INCOME RIDER addition to a life insurance policy stating that when an insured becomes disabled for at least six months, premiums due are waived. Depending on the rider, the insured may begin to receive a monthly income, (usually 1% of the face value of the policy) or, only the premium may be waived. The length of time that income payments will continue depends on the definition of disability in the policy. During the time that premiums are waived, the life insurance policy stays in force, so that if the insured dies, the beneficiary receives the face value of the policy. Cash values continue to build, and if the policy is participating, dividends continue to be paid. *See also* DISABILITY INCOME (DI); DISABILITY INCOME INSURANCE.

DISABILITY INSURANCE *see* DISABILITY BENEFIT; DISABILITY BUY-OUT INSURANCE; DISABILITY INCOME (DI); DISABILITY INCOME INSURANCE; DISABILITY INCOME RIDER; PARTNERSHIP LIFE AND HEALTH INSURANCE.

DISABILITY INSURANCE, CONDITIONS *see* DISABILITY BENEFIT; DISABILITY INCOME INSURANCE.

DISABILITY, LONG TERM *see* LONG-TERM DISABILITY INCOME INSURANCE.

DISABILITY OF PARTNER BUY AND SELL INSURANCE *see* PARTNERSHIP LIFE AND HEALTH INSURANCE.

DISABILITY, PERMANENT PARTIAL *see* DISABILITY INCOME INSURANCE; PERMANENT PARTIAL DISABILITY.

DISABILITY, PERMANENT TOTAL *see* DISABILITY INCOME INSURANCE; PERMANENT TOTAL DISABILITY.

DISABILITY, SHORT-TERM *see* DISABILITY INCOME INSURANCE.

DISABILITY, TEMPORARY PARTIAL *see* DISABILITY INCOME INSURANCE; TEMPORARY DISABILITY BENEFITS.

DISABILITY, TEMPORARY TOTAL *see* DISABILITY INCOME INSURANCE; TEMPORARY DISABILITY BENEFITS.

DISAPPEARING DEDUCTIBLE in property insurance, amount that an insured does not have to pay when a loss exceeds a predetermined sum; here the insurance company pays more than 100% of the loss, so that the deductible amount specified in a contract "vanishes." For example, if a deductible amount is $100, an insurance company may pay 125% of the losses exceeding $100, 150% of the losses exceeding $200, and if the losses exceed $300 the company pays the total amount of the loss (so that the insured does not assume any deductible for losses over $300). In another application an insured pays 125% of all losses over $100, the deductible disappears for any loss of $500 or more. *See also* DEDUCTIBLE.

DISASTER CLAUSE *see* COMMON DISASTER CLAUSE (SURVIVORSHIP CLAUSE).

DISCONTINUANCE termination of coverage in insurance.

DISCONTINUANCE OF CONTRIBUTIONS termination of premium payments by an employer on behalf of an employee to an employee benefit plan. *See also* GROUP DISABILITY INSURANCE; GROUP HEALTH INSURANCE; GROUP LIFE INSURANCE; GROUP PAID-UP LIFE INSURANCE; GROUP PERMANENT LIFE INSURANCE; GROUP TERM LIFE INSURANCE; PENSION PLAN; PENSION PLAN FUNDING INSTRUMENTS.

DISCONTINUANCE OF PLAN termination of a plan. Under Federal tax law, a plan can only be terminated for reasons of business necessity. Otherwise, prior employer tax deductible contributions under the plan are disallowed.

DISCOVERY PERIOD clause in a BOND that permits a principal who was formerly insured by the bond to report a loss to the surety company that occurred while the bond was in force. The period of time for reporting after the bond terminates is usually limited to one year.

DISCRETIONARY AUTHORITY legal power of the Commissioner of Internal Revenue to approve any classification of employees that does not discriminate in favor of a prohibited group. Such approval is necessary before a retirement plan can be a *qualified pension plan* and thus subject to tax benefits.

DISCRIMINATION failure of an insurance company to offer similar insurance coverages at comparable premium rates to all individuals or groups with the same UNDERWRITING characteristics. Such discriminatory practices are prohibited by state and federal law.

DISEASE illness or sickness such as cancer, poliomyelitis, leukemia, diphtheria, smallpox, scarlet fever, tentanus, spinal meningitis, encephalitis, tularemia, hydrophobia, and sickle cell anemia, all of which are covered in health insurance policies as specified.

DISHONESTY, DISAPPEARANCE, AND DESTRUCTION POLICY ("3-D" POLICY) COMBINATION POLICY PLAN of *fidelity insurance* and *crime insurance* under five standard agreements:
1. *Insuring Agreement I*—dishonesty of employees on either a COMMERCIAL BLANKET BOND or BLANKET POSITION BOND basis.
2. *Insuring Agreement II*—coverage inside an insured's premises or a bank premises if money and securities are lost due to dishonesty, disappearance, or destruction.
3. *Insuring Agreement III*—coverage of money and securities being transported by an insured's messenger outside an insured's premises if they are lost due to dishonesty, disappearance, or destruction.
4. *Insuring Agreement IV*—coverage if an insured accepts counterfeit U.S. or Canadian paper currency or money orders of no value.

5. *Insuring Agreement V*—coverage for depositor forgery if an insured's own commercial paper is forged or altered. Additional coverages can be added through endorsement, including check forgery, paymaster robbery, *broad form* payroll robbery coverage both inside and outside an insured's premises, broad form payroll robbery coverage inside premises only, burglary and theft of merchandise, forgery of warehouse receipts, wrongful obstruction of securities or lessees from safe deposit boxes, burglary of office equipment, theft of office equipment, paymaster robbery inside premises only, and forgery in use of credit cards.

DISMEMBERMENT BENEFIT income paid under health insurance for loss of use of various parts of the body due to an accident. A schedule of benefits available in a policy lists payments for each part of the body that is dismembered.

DISMEMBERMENT INSURANCE *see* ACCIDENTAL DEATH AND DISMEMBERMENT INSURANCE.

DISTRIBUTION BY LIVING HAND *see* ESTATE PLANNING; ESTATE PLANNING DISTRIBUTION.

DISTRIBUTION CLAUSE *see* PRO RATA DISTRIBUTION CLAUSE.

DISTRIBUTION OF PROPERTY AT DEATH OF OWNER *see* ESTATE PLANNING; ESTATE PLANNING DISTRIBUTION.

DIVIDED COVER insurance coverage purchased on the same item from two or more insurance companies.

DIVIDEND sum returned to a policyowner by an insurance company under a participating policy. Dividends are not deemed as taxable distributions, as the Internal Revenue Service interprets them as a refund of a portion of the premium paid. There are several ways in which the policyowner may use dividends. *See also* DIVIDEND OPTION.

DIVIDEND ACCUMULATION option under a participating life insurance policy in which dividends are left on deposit with the company to accumulate at a specified interest rate. If this option is chosen it is important to determine the interest rate. Interest on dividends left on deposit is taxable.

DIVIDEND ADDITION option in a participating policy under which dividends are used to purchase fully paid-up units of whole life insurance. This option deserves careful consideration by young families since it allows the purchase of extra life insurance without having to take a physical examination. Paid-up additions generate dividends and cash values which in turn will generate additional dividends and cash values.

DIVIDEND OPTION methods of handling policyholder dividends. In a participating life insurance policy, dividends are paid to the policyowner according to which of the following options is selected: (1) applied to reduce premiums; (2) paid in cash; (3) purchase increments of paid-up life insurance; (4) left on deposit with the insurance company to accumulate at interest; or (5) purchase extended term life insurance for one year in the amount a dividend can buy (Fifth Dividend Option). Some health and property insurance policies have dividend options.

DIVISIBLE CONTRACT CLAUSE in PROPERTY INSURANCE contracts, provision which states that the violation of one or more contract condition(s) at a particular location which is insured will not void coverage at other insured locations.

DIVISIBLE SURPLUS proportion of an insurance company's total surplus at the end of each year's operation that is distributed to policyowners of participating life insurance policies.

DOC *see* DRIVE OTHER CAR INSURANCE.

DOCTRINE OF LAST CLEAR CHANCE *see* LAST CLEAR CHANCE.

DOMESTIC INSURER insurance company incorporated according to the laws of the state in which a risk is located and the policy issued. The insurance company is *domiciled* in that state.

DOMICILE state in which an insurance company has its principal legal residence; where an individual resides in a fixed permanent home.

DOMINO THEORY OF ACCIDENT CAUSATION theory developed in 1931 by *H. W. Heinrich*; states that an accident is only one of a series of factors, each of which depends on a previous factor in the following manner:
1. accident causes an injury.
2. individual's negligent act or omission, or a faulty machine, causes an accident.
3. personal shortcomings cause negligent acts or omissions.
4. hereditary and environment cause personal shortcomings. *See also* HEINRICH, H. W.

DOUBLE INDEMNITY *see* ACCIDENTAL DEATH CLAUSE.

DOUBLE-PROTECTION POLICY life insurance contract which combines TERM LIFE INSURANCE with WHOLE LIFE INSURANCE. The term portion of the contract expires after a stipulated time period. If the insured dies during this stipulated period, both the term portion and the whole life portion of the contract will pay. If the insured dies after the stipulated time period, only the whole life portion of the contract will pay.

DOUBLE RECOVERY payments in excess of the value of the loss—a prohibited practice. When an insured has more than one policy covering a risk, the full value cannot be collected from each policy if a loss occurs. The most that can be collected is each policy's pro rata share of the loss. For example, a home is insured under two policies of $100,000 each. If there is a fire loss of $100,000, the most that can be collected from each policy is $50,000.

DOWER INTEREST wife's interest in her husband's property upon his death. The wife has an *insurable interest* in that property and can purchase a property and casualty insurance policy to cover the EXPOSURES faced by it. *See also* COURTESY INTEREST.

DRAM SHOP LAW liquor liability legislation in 20 states under which a dispenser of alcoholic beverages is held responsible for bodily injury and/or property damage caused by its customers to a third party. Insurance coverage is available, but at a high premium rate. *See also* DRAM SHOP LIABILITY INSURANCE; LIQUOR LIABILITY LAWS.

DRAM SHOP LIABILITY INSURANCE coverage for dispensers of alcoholic beverages against suits arising out of bodily injury and/or property damage caused by its customers to a third party. Establishments covered include bars, restaurants, hotels, motels, or wherever the alcoholic beverages are dispensed. These establishments are excluded from coverage under GENERAL LIABILITY INSURANCE.

DREAD DISEASE INSURANCE health insurance coverage only for a specified catastrophic disease such as cancer. It is important to ascertain the waiting period required, maximum benefits and maximum length of time they are payable, and the exact definition of the disease covered. Individual and group health insurance usually cover all diseases, including dread diseases.

DRIVE OTHER CAR INSURANCE (DOC) endorsement to an automobile insurance policy which protects an insured in either or both of two circumstances when driving a nonowned car:
   1. *business endorsement*—if the insured's negligent acts or omissions result in bodily injury or property damage to a third party while the insured is driving a nonowned car for business activities.
   2. *personal endorsement*—if the insured's negligent acts or omissions result in bodily injury or property damage to a third party while the insured is driving a nonowned car for nonbusiness activities.

DRIVING WHILE INTOXICATED (DWI) term for operating an automobile while under the influence of alcoholic beverages so as to be unable to drive safely. An insurance company can suspend auto coverage under a PERSONAL AUTOMOBILE POLICY (PAP).

DROP DOWN in REINSURANCE contracts, clause which requires the REINSURER to provide coverage if an underlying carrier is unable to fulfill its obligations under the policy CEDED to the reinsurer.

DRUGGISTS LIABILITY INSURANCE coverage in the event that, while practicing the profession of druggist, an act or omission is committed resulting in bodily injury, personal injury and/or property damage to a customer. Also covered is liability arising through the use of products on and off of the business's premises. For example, a child is born after a druggist negligently places sugar tablets in a container for a customer instead of birth control pills. The druggist may have to provide funds necessary to sustain the child until the age of majority.

DUAL CAPACITY DOCTRINE rule of law under which a defendant who has two or more relationships with a plaintiff may be liable under any of these relationships. For example, an employer may be liable in two ways to an employee who incurs bodily injury on the job as the result of using a product or service produced by that employer: first, as the employer of the injured employee and second, as the producer of the product or service which caused injury to the employee. The injured employee may then either collect benefits for job related injuries under *workers compensation* or sue the employer as the producer of the defective product or service. For example, if an employee injures an arm at work while operating a machine with a defective blade which the employer manufactures, the employee can receive benefits under workers compensation or sue the employer as the manufacturer of the defective blade.

DUAL LIFE STOCK COMPANY stock life insurance company which sells PARTICIPATING INSURANCE and NONPARTICIPATING INSURANCE.

DUPLICATION OF BENEFITS coverage in health insurance by two or more policies for the same insured loss. In such a circumstance, each policy pays its proportionate share of the loss, or one policy becomes *primary* and the other policy *secondary. See also* COORDINATION OF BENEFITS.

DUPLICATION OF EXPOSURE UNITS *see* SEGREGATION OF EXPOSURE UNITS.

DURATION OF BENEFITS *see* DISABILITY INCOME INSURANCE.

DUTIES OF AN INSURED IN THE EVENT OF LOSS UNDER PROPERTY AND CASUALTY POLICY *see* PROPERTY AND CASUALTY INSURANCE PROVISIONS.

DUTIES OF INSURED *see* INSURANCE CONTRACT, LIFE; INSURANCE CONTRACT, PROPERTY AND CASUALTY.

DWELLING, BUILDINGS, AND CONTENTS INSURANCE (DB&C)
coverage when residential property does not qualify according to the
minimum requirements of a homeowner's policy, or because of a requirement for the insured to select several different kinds of coverage
and limits on this protection. DB&C insurance coverages can be selected
from the following forms and attached to the Standard Fire Policy:

1. *Basic/Regular/General Form*—Coverage for property damage to a
   building used as a dwelling, as well as its contents. (Contents coverage is not restricted to the building or dwelling; coverage can be
   applied to contents of buildings such as hotels, that do not qualify
   as dwellings under the DB&C). The property coverage for the building includes items attached to the building such as equipment and
   fixtures, built-ins, furnace, air conditioner, hot water heater, and
   lighting fixtures. An optional extension of the dwelling coverage of
   up to 10% can be applied to private structures on the premises such
   as a garage. Contents coverage on household and personal goods
   within the dwelling can be extended to off-premises household and
   personal contents for up to 10%. Perils insured for both dwelling
   and contents are fire, lightning, and removal of the property from
   the premises to further protect it from damage from the perils. For
   an additional charge, vandalism and malicious mischief can also be
   insured against.
2. *Broad Form*—Includes the basic coverages plus the additional perils
   of burglary; falling objects; weight of snow and/or ice; accidental
   discharge, leakage, or overflow of water or steam from an air conditioning, heating, and/or plumbing mechanism, and/or household
   appliance; glass breakage, damage resulting from water or freezing
   of plumbing and/or heating mechanisms; and structural problems
   leading to the collapse of the building. Damage from insured perils
   resulting in additional living expenses is also provided.
3. *Special Form*—Coverage on an ALL RISKS basis for only the structure
   of a dwelling, with no coverage for its contents.

DWELLING COVERAGE *see* DWELLING, BUILDINGS, AND CONTENTS
INSURANCE (DB&C).

DWELLING FORM *see* DWELLING, BUILDINGS, AND CONTENTS
INSURANCE (DB&C).

DWELLING INSURANCE POLICY PROGRAM coverage for a
dwelling's structure; appurtenant structures on the premises; personal
contents and household items within the dwelling; and 10% of the coverage applicable to such personal contents and household items away
from the premises, for example at a hotel. Additional living expenses
are covered because of the damage of an insured peril to the dwelling
and/or its contents, and loss of rental value of the dwelling and/or its
contents.

DYNAMIC changing state of the economy associated with changes in human wants and desires such that losses or gains occur. Dynamic changes are not insurable.

DYNAMIC RISK *see* DYNAMIC.

DYNAMO CLAUSE *see* ELECTRICAL EXEMPTION CLAUSE.

E

E&O *see* ERRORS AND OMISSIONS LIABILITY INSURANCE

EARLY RETIREMENT term in pensions; leaving a job before normal retirement age, subject to minimum requirements of age and years of service. There usually is a reduction in the monthly retirement benefit.

EARNED PREMIUM portion of a premium paid by an insured which has been allocated to the insurance company's loss experience, expenses, and profit year to date.

EARNED SURPLUS *see* RETAINED EARNINGS.

EARNINGS INSURANCE *see* GROSS EARNINGS FORM.

EARTHQUAKE INSURANCE coverage that can be purchased as an endorsement to many property policies such as the *Standard Fire Policy* or as a separate policy. Coverage is for direct damage resulting from earthquake or volcanic eruption. If there is a lapse of at least 72 hours between earthquake shocks, then each loss by a given earthquake is subject to a new claim. Excluded are losses resulting from fire, explosion, flood or tidal wave.

EASEMENT right of one party to use land owned by another party. For example, an electric utility can obtain an easement through court action to place its power lines across someone's property, even if the owner is unwilling to give permission.

ECONOMIC BENEFIT *see* SPLIT DOLLAR LIFE INSURANCE.

ECONOMIC LOSS total estimated cost incurred by a person or persons, a family, or a business resulting from the death or disability of a wage earner (KEY EMPLOYEE), damage or destruction of property, and/or a liability suit (negligent acts or omissions by a person result in property damage or bodily injury to a THIRD PARTY). Factors included in the total cost are loss of earnings, medical expenses, funeral expenses, property damage restoration expenses, and legal expenses. *See also* ECONOMIC OR USE VALUE; HUMAN LIFE VALUE APPROACH (ECONOMIC VALUE OF AN INDIVIDUAL LIFE) (EVOIL); SPLIT DOLLAR LIFE INSURANCE.

ECONOMIC OR USE VALUE property valued according to its earnings potential. However, property insurance contracts generally indemnify an insured on a REPLACEMENT COST LESS PHYSICAL DEPRECIATION AND OBSOLESCENCE BASIS.

ECONOMIC VALUE OF AN INDIVIDUAL LIFE (EVOIL) *see* HUMAN LIFE VALUE APPROACH (ECONOMIC VALUE OF AN INDIVIDUAL LIFE) (EVOIL).

EDUCATIONAL FUND factor considered in determining amount of life insurance to purchase in order that funds will be available to pay for a child's education expenses in the event of the premature death of the wage earner. *See also* NEEDS APPROACH.

EEL *see* EMERGENCY EXPOSURE LIMIT (EEL).

EFFECTIVE DATE date at which an insurance policy goes into force. *See also* DATE OF ISSUE.

EFFECTIVE TIME *see* DATE OF ISSUE; EFFECTIVE DATE.

ELECTRICAL (ELECTRICAL APPARATUS) EXEMPTION CLAUSE common element in property insurance which excludes electrical damage or destruction of an appliance unless the damage is caused by a resultant fire.

ELEMENTS OF AN INSURANCE CONTRACT *see* ANALYSIS OF PROPERTY AND CASUALTY POLICY; INSURANCE CONTRACT, GENERAL; INSURANCE CONTRACT, HEALTH; INSURANCE CONTRACT, LIFE; INSURANCE CONTRACT, PROPERTY AND CASUALTY.

ELEVATOR COLLISION INSURANCE liability coverage for damage or destruction of a structure, elevator, and/or personal property due to the collision of an elevator.

ELEVATOR LIABILITY INSURANCE coverage for suits brought by a plaintiff as the result of bodily injury incurred while using an elevator on the insured's premises.

ELIGIBILITY PERIOD length of time in life and health insurance in which an employee can apply for and pay the first premium without having to show evidence of insurability (take a physical examination). The period is usually the first 30 days of employment. After expiration of the eligibility period, an employee may have to take a physical or provide medical history information to qualify for coverage. If the employee does not pass the physical, coverage can be denied under a group plan or the employee can be charged a much higher premium rate than the group rate. This is why it is extremely important for a new employee to apply for group life and health insurance during the eligibility period.

ELIGIBILITY REQUIREMENTS conditions found in employee benefit plans such as pensions, under which minimum requirements, such as 20 years of service, must be met by an employee to qualify for benefits.

ELIGIBLE EXPENSES *see* GROUP HEALTH INSURANCE.

ELIMINATION PERIOD form of deductible usually found in disability income insurance; for example, no benefits may be payable for a length of time beginning with the first day of illness. Subsequently, benefits are usually paid only for costs incurred after the end of the elimination period. The longer the elimination period in a policy, the lower the premium.

EMBEZZLEMENT theft of another's property by a person entrusted with that property. Coverage can be found under various bonding arrangements. *See also* FIDELITY BOND.

EMERGENCY EXPOSURE LIMIT (EEL) maximum amount of a toxic agent to which an individual can be exposed for a very brief (emergency) period of time and still maintain physical safety. *See also* THRESHOLD LEVEL.

EMERGENCY FUND factor considered in determining amount of life insurance to purchase in order that funds will be available to pay the emergency expenses following the death of a family member. *See also* NEEDS APPROACH.

EMPIRICAL CONSIDERATION LOADING to the BURNING COST RATIO for a reinsurer's expenses, profit, and to build a reserve to meet unusually large claims.

EMPIRICAL PROBABILITY mathematical relationship resulting from experimentation. For example, the PROBABILITY DISTRIBUTION for the possible number of heads from four tosses of a fair coin having both a head and a tail can be calculated from experimentation and observation by allowing for the accumulation of empirical data.

EMPIRICAL RATE CALCULATION adjustment of the BURNING COST RATIO for the increase in number and size of losses (losses likely in excess of that used in the unadjusted burning cost rate), INCURRED BUT NOT REPORTED LOSSES (IBNR), inflation, expenses, profits, and contingencies.

EMPLOYEE AS AN INSURED *see* BUSINESS LIABILITY INSURANCE; BUSINESSOWNERS POLICY (BOP).

EMPLOYEE BENEFIT INSURANCE PLAN provision by an employer for the economic and social welfare of employees. Generally include: (1) pension plans for retirement; (2) group life insurance for death; (3) group health insurance for illness and accident; (4) group disability income insurance for loss of income due to illness and accident; and (5) accidental death and dismemberment. Dental insurance, eyeglass insurance, and legal expense insurance may be included. These plans are established for the reasons of morale, to reduce turnover, and for tax benefits (contributions are usually deductible as business expenses to employers and not currently taxable income to employees).

EMPLOYEE CONTRIBUTIONS workers' premiums in a contributory employee benefit plan.

EMPLOYEE DEATH BENEFITS *see* EMPLOYEE BENEFIT INSURANCE PLAN.

EMPLOYEE DISHONESTY *see* FIDELITY BOND.

EMPLOYEE HEALTH BENEFITS *see* EMPLOYEE BENEFIT INSURANCE PLAN.

EMPLOYEE RETIREMENT INCOME SECURITY ACT OF 1974 (ERISA) law that established rules and regulations to govern private pension plans, including vesting requirements, funding mechanisms, and general plan design and descriptions. For example, three ways of vesting were established: full vesting after 10 years of service (Cliff Vesting); FIVE TO FIFTEEN YEAR RULE (at least 25% of benefits vest at end of 5 years of service, 5% each year during the next 5 years, and 10% each year during the next 5 years); and Rule of 45 (when employee's age and years of service add up to 45), 50% of the benefits must be vested with 10% additional vesting each year thereafter.

Under the TAX REFORM ACT OF 1986, vesting requirements were changed to 100% vesting after 5 years of service or 20% vesting after 3 years of service, 40% at the end of 4 years of service, 60% at the end of 5 years of service, 80% at the end of 6 years of service and 100% at the end of 7 years of service. (These vesting requirements are effective as of January 1, 1989.)

EMPLOYEE STOCK OWNERSHIP PLAN (ESOP), TRUST (ESOP) type of benefit in which an employee obtains shares of stock in the company, the amount normally determined by the employee's level of compensation. ESOP acts as a leverage tool through which the business is able to obtain a source of capital. The procedure is for a lender (usually a bank) to lend money to the ESOP. The ESOP then takes the borrowed money to buy stock from the company's treasury. In the meantime, the ESOP has signed a note with the lender for the borrowed funds with the stock pledged as collateral for the loan, and the business has guaranteed repayment if the ESOP fails to do so. The stock held in the ESOP is allocated to each employee as the business pays its contributions into the ESOP. The ESOP uses the company's contributions to repay the loan and the interest thereon. The contributions per employee that the company makes into the ESOP are tax deductible, and they are not taxable to the employee until the benefits are received.

EMPLOYER CREDITS credits, in a pension plan, that an employer is required to make against future contributions (other than a cash basis as required by the IRS). Such credits may arise when an employee leaves an employer prior to being fully *vested*, works beyond normal retirement age.

EMPLOYERS CONTINGENT ESCROWING OF ASSETS LIABILITY *see* EMPLOYERS CONTINGENT NET WORTH LIABILITY DETERMINATION.

EMPLOYERS CONTINGENT INSURANCE COVERAGE LIABILITY coverage mandated by the EMPLOYEE RETIREMENT INCOME SECURITY ACT OF 1974 (ERISA) under which employers are required to purchase insurance to cover their contingent liability for unfunded employee pension benefits in the event a pension plan is terminated. This requirement is enforced by the PENSION BENEFIT GUARANTY CORPORATION (PBGC).

EMPLOYERS CONTINGENT LIABILITY *see* EMPLOYERS CONTINGENT INSURANCE COVERAGE LIABILITY; EMPLOYERS CONTINGENT LIEN AGAINST ASSETS LIABILITY.

EMPLOYERS CONTINGENT LIEN AGAINST ASSETS LIABILITY claim (lien) of the PENSION BENEFIT GUARANTY CORPORATION (PBGC) against an employer's assets upon termination of a pension plan for the amount of an employee's unfunded benefits.

EMPLOYERS CONTINGENT NET WORTH LIABILITY DETERMINATION requirement upon termination of a pension plan; an employer must reimburse the PENSION BENEFIT GUARANTY CORPORATION (PBGC) for any loss that the PBGC incurs as the result of paying employee benefits that were the responsibility of the employer. The law requires reimbursement of up to 30% of the plan's net worth without regard to any contingent liability. This net worth is increased by escrowing or transferring any assets by the employer in contemplation of the plan's termination.

EMPLOYERS INSURANCE *see* BUSINESS AUTOMOBILE POLICY (BAP); BUSINESS CRIME INSURANCE; BUSINESS INTERRUPTION INSURANCE; BUSINESS LIFE AND HEALTH INSURANCE; BUSINESS PROPERTY AND LIABILITY INSURANCE PACKAGE; BUSINESSOWNERS POLICY (BOP).

EMPLOYERS LEGAL OBLIGATION TO FUND pension plan format. After deciding how much to contribute, the employer can suspend, reduce, or discontinue contributions during the first 10 years only for reasons of business necessity; otherwise the employer will face a substantial IRS tax penalty. If a plan is terminated or if contributions to the plan are discontinued, the employer is only liable for benefit payments for which contributions were previously made.

EMPLOYERS LIABILITY COVERAGE *see* WORKERS COMPENSA-TION, COVERAGE B.

EMPLOYERS NET WORTH *see* EMPLOYERS CONTINGENT NET WORTH LIABILITY DETERMINATION.

EMPLOYERS NONOWNERSHIP LIABILITY INSURANCE coverage for the employer in the event of a TORT committed by an employee in the use of his or her own car while conducting business on behalf of the employer.

ENCUMBRANCE claim, such as a worker's lien, to property under the care, custody, and control of another. This situation occurs when a worker is not paid for labor provided. For example, a carpenter unable to collect payment for installing wood finishings seeks an encumbrance on the owner's property.

ENDORSEMENT written agreement attached to a policy to add or subtract insurance coverages. Once attached, the endorsement takes precedence over the original provisions of the policy. For example, under a homeowners policy an inflation guard endorsement is used so that property damage limits are increased automatically to reflect an increase in the cost of construction in the community. Vandalism and malicious mischief can be added to the *Standard Fire Policy* through an endorsement.

ENDOWMENT INSURANCE life insurance under when an insured receives the face value of a policy if the individual survives the endowment period. If the insured does not survive, a beneficiary receives the face value of the policy. An endowment policy is the most expensive type of life insurance.

ENERGY-RELEASE THEORY (OF ACCIDENT CAUSATION) method, developed in 1970 by Dr. William Haddon, Jr., of classifying and preventing damage caused by accidents. The thesis is that accidents are caused by the transfer of energy with such force that bodily injury and property damage result. According to Dr. Haddon, strategies can interrupt or suppress the chain of accident-causing events. These strategies revolve around (1) control and prevention of buildup of energy that is inherently injurious; (2) creation of an environment that is not conducive to injurious buildup of energy; and (3) production of counteractive measures to injurious buildup of energy.

ENGINEERING APPROACH approach in loss prevention placing emphasis on physical features of the workplace as a potential cause of injuries. For example, if a product is inherently dangerous in design or during manufacture, an insurance company may assign an engineer to analyze the situation and recommend changes which could improve safety and lower insurance premiums.

ENROLLED ACTUARY *see* ACTUARY, ENROLLED.

ENROLLMENT CARD document used to sign up employees for plans such as salary savings, life insurance, or other employee benefits.

ENTIRE CONTRACT CLAUSE feature of life and health insurance policies which stipulates that the policy represents the whole agreement between the insurance company and the insured, and that there are no other outstanding agreements.

ENTITY PLAN *see* PARTNERSHIP LIFE AND HEALTH INSURANCE.

EQUIPMENT DEALERS INSURANCE coverage on ALL RISKS basis for such items as binders, reapers, harvesters, plows, tractors, pneumatic tools and compressors, bulldozers, and road scrapers. Excluded from coverage are wear and tear, loss due to delay, loss of market, consequential loss such as loss of income because of damage to the equipment, and mechanical breakdown. Property excluded includes aircraft, water craft, motor vehicles, and property sold on an installment contract basis after it has left the care, custody, and control of the insured dealer.

EQUIPMENT FLOATERS INSURANCE coverage for property that moves from location to location from the perils of fire, lightning, explosion, windstorm, earthquake, collapse of bridges, flood, collision under one of the following forms: AGRICULTURAL EQUIPMENT INSURANCE, CONTRACTORS EQUIPMENT FLOATER; LIVESTOCK INSURANCE, PHYSICIANS AND SURGEONS EQUIPMENT INSURANCE.

EQUITIES representation of ownership rights such as stocks.

EQUITY fairness (as an objective of insurance pricing). Premium rates are set according to expectation of loss among a classification of policyowners. The premise is that all insureds with the same characteristics should have the same expectation of loss and should be listed under the same underwriting classification. For example, in life insurance, individuals with a good personal health history, family health history, a job with no special hazards, and who are of good character should be classified as standard risks and thereby pay standard rates.

EQUITY AMONG POLICYOWNERS grouping of applicants for life insurance according to expected mortality, so as to produce an underwriting classification in which the spread between health of the worst and best applicant is not so great as to skew the distribution curve.

EQUITY ANNUITIES *see* VARIABLE DOLLAR ANNUITY.

EQUITY, POLICYOWNERS *see* POLICYOWNERS EQUITY.

ERRORS AND OMISSIONS LIABILITY INSURANCE policies generally available to the various professions that require protection for negligent acts and/or omissions resulting in bodily injury, personal injury, and/or property damage liability to a client. For example, insurance agents are constantly exposed to the claim that inadequate or improper coverage was recommended, resulting in the client suffering a loss of indemnification. If sustained, the agent (or the carrier) would have to make good the claim of the client without the adequate insurance coverage.

ESTATE PLANNING procedure for accumulating, conserving, and distributing personal wealth. In essence, estate planning focuses on enhancement of the value of an estate and its conservation. At the death of an owner, estate planning seeks to transfer the estate to the heir(s) with a minimum loss in taxes and other expenses. Depending on the size and nature of an estate, the expertise of one or more of these specialists may be useful: lawyer, accountant, life insurance agent, banker, or a qualified financial or estate planner.

ESTATE PLANNING, DEATH PLANNING *see* ESTATE PLANNING; ESTATE PLANNING DISTRIBUTION.

ESTATE PLANNING DISTRIBUTION plan that involves distribution of property by living hand and distribution of property after the death of its owner. Distribution by living hand can take the form of an outright gift, a grant of limited property interest, or a gift in trust. Distribution at death can be accomplished through a will; or if there is no will, as directed by state law. Common terms include:
Beneficiary of Trust person who receives the benefits of the trust.
Life Estate property that can be used in any manner that pleases the donee during his/her life. Upon the death of the donee, the property reverts to the donor or the donor's estate.
Living Trust property distributed by living individuals.
Personal Trust one in which an owner of property gives it to another person to safeguard, hold, and use for the benefit of a third party.
Power of Appointment owner of a property grants the right to another person to decide who should receive title to the property.
Tenancy donee has the right to use property and to receive income it generates for a limited time, whereupon the property reverts to the owner.
Testamentary Trust property disposed at the death of the trustor, who has previously described what property is to be placed in the trust, how it is to be managed, and who is to be the trustee. The trustor can change the provisions of the trust by a will. But at the death of the trustor, the testamentary trust becomes irrevocable.

Trustee person to whom a trustor transfers property. The trustee is obligated to safeguard, manage, and use the property in accordance with the terms and conditions of the trust.

Trustor individual who puts his/her thoughts in writing concerning the terms of the trust and the process of transferring the property to the trustee.

ESTATE PLANNING, LIFE PLANNING *see* ESTATE PLANNING; ESTATE PLANNING DISTRIBUTION.

ESTATE TAX *see* FEDERAL ESTATE TAX.

ESTIMATED PREMIUM method of premium payment under which a temporary premium is charged based on projected loss experience. At the end of the year this premium is adjusted to reflect the actual loss experience. *See also* RETROSPECTIVE RATING.

ESTOPPEL stop or bar, such that one party makes a statement upon which a second party has every reason to rely, thereby preventing the first party from denying the validity of that statement. For example, the misleading actions of an agent of the insurance company result in the insured being estopped from having to perform according to the provisions of the contract.

EVIDENCE CLAUSE clause requiring an insured to cooperate with an insurance company by producing all evidence requested in settlement of a claim. The company may have difficulty settling a claim without the proper examination and documentation of evidence.

EVIDENCE OF INSURABILITY documentation of physical fitness by an applicant for insurance. Usually this takes the form of a medical examination. Group plans (life, health, disability) require such evidence if the 30-day eligibility period expires before the employee has applied for coverage. *See also* ELIGIBILITY PERIOD.

EXAMINATION *see* CONVENTION EXAMINATION; MEDICAL EXAMINATION.

EXAMINED BUSINESS life or health insurance policy written on an applicant who has passed a MEDICAL EXAMINATION and signed the APPLICATION but has not paid the premium due.

EXAMINER
Life and Health: physician appointed by an insurance company to examine applicants for insurance. *See also* EXAMINED BUSINESS.
Regulatory: representative of the COMMISSIONER OF INSURANCE who conducts an audit of the insurance company's records. *See also* CONVENTION EXAMINATION.

EXCEPTED PERIOD *see* PROBATIONARY PERIOD.

EXCEPTION *see* EXCLUSIONS; EXCLUSIONS, BUSINESS LIABILITY INSURANCE; EXCLUSIONS FROM MEDICAL BENEFITS EXEMPTION; EXCLUSIONS, HOMEOWNERS INSURANCE; EXCLUSIONS, PROPERTY AND CASUALTY INSURANCE.

EXCESS INSURANCE property, liability, or health coverage above the primary amount of insurance. For example, the primary coverage is $100,000 and the excess insurance is $1 million. After the losses exceed $100,000 the excess insurance will pay for the losses up to a total of $1 million.

EXCESS INTEREST amount credited to the cash value of an insured's life insurance policy above the minimum interest rate it guarantees. This payment is of extreme importance to a policyowner since it will directly affect the size of the cash value. *See also* CASH VALUE LIFE INSURANCE.

EXCESS INTEREST WHOLE LIFE INSURANCE type of insurance under which it is assumed that the interest earned will exceed the interest rate guaranteed. Excess interest is credited to the policyowner in the following manner:
1. in a mutual company—paid to policyowners through the policy dividend structure.
2. in a stock company—paid to policyowners through their cash values or future premiums due. *See also* CURRENT ASSUMPTION WHOLE LIFE INSURANCE.

EXCESS LIMIT in a LIABILITY INSURANCE policy, limit above the minimum amount of coverage for which the policy can be written according to company or legal restrictions. *See also* EXCESS INSURANCE.

EXCESS LINE BROKER (SURPLUS LINE BROKER) insurance salesperson who is licensed to place coverage with an insurance company that is not licensed to do business in the state of domicile of the broker. The excess line coverage must be unavailable from a company licensed in the broker's state.

EXCESS LOSS COVER *see* EXCESS OF LOSS REINSURANCE.

EXCESS (NONPROPORTIONAL) REINSURANCE *see* EXCESS OF LOSS REINSURANCE.

EXCESS OF LOSS REINSURANCE method whereby an insurer pays the amount of each claim for each risk up to a limit determined in advance and the reinsurer pays the amount of the claim above that limit up to a specific sum. For example, assume that an insurer issues automobile liability policies of $150,000 on any one risk and retains the first $50,000 of any risk. The insurer purchases excess loss reinsurance for $100,000 in excess of $50,000 on any one risk. The insurer pays the first $50,000 of all losses and the reinsurer pays any excess amount up to a maximum of $100,000.

EXCESS PER RISK REINSURANCE *see* EXCESS OF LOSS REINSURANCE.

EXCESS POLICY policy that pays benefits only when coverage under other applicable insurance policies has become exhausted. For example, the *personal umbrella liability* policy pays after the liability limits in the homeowners insurance policy have been exceeded.

EXCESS-SURPLUS LINES *see* SURPLUS LINES (EXCESS-SURPLUS LINES).

EXCLUDED PERIL *see* EXCLUSIONS; EXCLUSIONS, BUSINESS LIABILITY INSURANCE; EXCLUSIONS FROM MEDICAL BENEFITS EXEMPTION; EXCLUSIONS, HOMEOWNERS INSURANCE; EXCLUSIONS, MEDICAL BENE-FITS; EXCLUSIONS, PROPERTY AND CASUALTY INSURANCE.

EXCLUDED PERIOD *see* PROBATIONARY PERIOD.

EXCLUDED PROPERTY *see* EXCLUSIONS, BUSINESS LIABILITY INSURANCE; EXCLUSIONS, PROPERTY AND CASUALTY INSURANCE.

EXCLUSION RATIO *see* TAX DEFERRED ANNUITY.

EXCLUSIONS provision in an insurance policy that indicates what is denied coverage. For example, common exclusions are: hazards deemed so catastrophic in nature that they are uninsurable, such as war; wear and tear, since they are expected through the use of a product; property covered by other insurance, in order to eliminate duplication that would profit the insured; liability arising out of contracts; and liability arising out of Workers Compensation laws. Exclusions are also listed in a BOILER AND MACHINERY INSURANCE policy, BUSINESS AUTOMOBILE POLICY; BUSINESS INTERRUPTION INSURANCE, HOMEOWNERS INSURANCE POLICY. *Liability Policy*, and SPECIAL MULTIPERIL INSURANCE (SMP) policy.

EXCLUSIONS, BUSINESS LIABILITY INSURANCE provision used to avoid duplication of coverage in other policies; to eliminate coverage for property under the care, custody and control of an insured business; as well as to avoid liability arising out of contractual obligations between the insured business and another party; liability associated with recall of the insured business's products; liability associated with the insured business's pollution and contamination exposure; and liability that may arise if the insured business is found to be in conflict with state liquor regulations.

EXCLUSIONS FROM MEDICAL BENEFITS EXEMPTION found under the "Exceptions and Exclusions Section for All Medical Benefits" in many health insurance policies which exclude:

1. complications arising from elective, nontherapeutic voluntary abortion.
2. necessary cosmetic surgery for the immediate repair of a nonoccupational disease, illness, accident, or injury.
3. custom built orthopedic shoes, wedges, or arch supports.
4. speech therapy ordered by a physician to restore partial or complete loss of speech resulting from stroke, cancer, radiation laryngitis, or cerebral palsy.
5. services, supplies, or treatment in connection with or related to endogenous obesity or obesity resulting from external causes which the physician certifies is associated with a serious or life-threatening disorder.

EXCLUSIONS FROM MEDICAL BENEFITS GROUP HEALTH INSURANCE *see* EXCLUSIONS, MEDICAL BENEFITS; EXCLUSIONS FROM MEDICAL BENEFITS EXEMPTION.

EXCLUSIONS, HOMEOWNERS INSURANCE provision that excludes from coverage under *Form No. 3*: flood damage, except if the flood causes a fire, explosion, or theft; water damage from the back up of sewers; earthquake, except if the earthquake causes a fire explosion, theft, or glass breakage; war; nuclear exposure (hazard); wear and tear; vandalism and malicious mischief, or glass breakage if the house has been vacant for more than 30 consecutive days before the day of the loss.

EXCLUSIONS, MEDICAL BENEFITS limiting provision. Exclusions listed in group health plans include: benefits under Workers Compensation; certain dental procedures; convalescent or rest cures; medical expenses resulting from the insured person and/or covered dependents committing a felony or misdemeanor; cosmetic surgery, unless required immediately because of non-occupational disease, illness, accident, injury, or congenital anomaly in an insured newborn infant; expenses incurred by a member of a HEALTH MAINTENANCE ORGANIZATION (HMO) or other prepaid medical plan; expenses associated with intentional self-inflicted injuries or attempt at suicide; unreasonable charges for services or supplies; convenience items such as telephone and television.

EXCLUSIONS OF POLICY *see* EXCLUSION.

EXCLUSIONS, PROPERTY AND CASUALTY INSURANCE denial of coverage for various perils (such as war, flood); hazards (storing dynamite in the home thereby increasing the chance of loss); property (such as pets); and locations. These are excluded because they are uninsurable by nature in that the loss frequency and severity do not lend themselves to accurate predictions, the premium rates chargeable would be prohibitive, and in some instances coverages are found in other policies.

EXCLUSIVE AGENCY SYSTEM *see* CAPTIVE AGENT.

EXCULPATORY PROVISION clause in legal contracts that excuses a given party to the contract from liability for unintentional negligent acts and/or omissions.

EXECUTOR fiduciary named in a will to settle an estate of a deceased person. The executor must act as a reasonably prudent man in safeguarding that property in his care, custody, and control. Insurance coverages are available for executors. *See also* FIDELITY BOND.

EXECUTRIX woman executor. *See also* EXECUTOR.

EXEMPLARY DAMAGES *see* LIABILITY, CIVIL DAMAGES AWARDED.

EXEMPTION size of estate passing free from estate and gift of taxes. The exempted amount as of January 1, 1987 is $600,000.

EX GRATIA PAYMENT "from favor" payment by an insurance company to an insured even though the company has no legal liability. The company makes such a payment for goodwill purposes.

EXHIBITION INSURANCE coverage provided on an ALL RISKS basis for an exhibitor whose product while being displayed at a public exhibition is damaged or destroyed by a peril which is not specifically excluded in the policy.

EXPECTATION OF LIFE *see* LIFE EXPECTANCY.

EXPECTATION OF LOSS *see* EXPECTED LOSS.

EXPECTED EXPENSE RATIO relationship between expected incurred insurance-related costs (not including claims) and expected written premiums. *See also* EXPENSE RATIO; MANUAL RATE; RATE MAKING.

EXPECTED EXPENSES anticipated insurance-related costs, not including claims-related costs.

EXPECTED LOSS probability of loss upon which a basic premium rate is calculated.

EXPECTED LOSS RATIO proportion of a premium allocated to pay losses which is equivalent to $(1.00 - \text{EXPENSE RATIO})$.

EXPECTED MORBIDITY expectation of illness or injury. The probability of such occurrence is shown by a MORBIDITY TABLE, which is important in determining the premiums for health insurance policies.

EXPECTED MORTALITY expectation of death. The probability of its occurrence is shown by a MORTALITY TABLE, which is important in determining the premiums for life insurance policies.

EXPECTED VALUE sum of money to be received by an insured in the event a given loss occurs.

EXPEDITED FUNDS AVAILABILITY ACT legislation passed in 1988 by the U.S. Congress to facilitate movement of checks through the collection system. As the result of this Act, the Federal Reserve has established rules for the endorsement of checks stipulating that the endorsement must be within an area of $1\frac{1}{2}$ inches from the left edge of the back of the check and no additional marks or notations can be made on the back of the check beyond this $1\frac{1}{2}$ inch boundary.

EXPEDITING EXPENSES payment by an insurance company to a damaged or destroyed business to hasten its return to normal business operations. For example, if a kitchen of a restaurant is damaged by fire, the insurance company may be willing to pay overtime wages to enable the restaurant to return to normal operations as soon as possible.

EXPENSE cost of doing business, not including pure *expectation of loss*. *See also* EXPENSE LOADING.

EXPENSE ALLOWANCE payment to an insurance agent in addition to commissions. Expense allowances, which differ from company to company, vary with the amount of business agents place with that company and the need of the company to attract future business.

EXPENSE INCURRED *see* INCURRED EXPENSE.

EXPENSE LIMITATION ceiling on expense reimbursement allowance, as stated in New York insurance law, which an insurance company licensed in New York State can give its agents. This is one reason why a company that is admitted (licensed) in all states but New York may have a sister company doing business only in New York State. If an insurance company is not admitted in New York State, it can allocate greater expense allowances and commissions to agents, thereby attracting more of their business.

EXPENSE LOADING amount added to the basic premium (expectation of loss) to cover an insurance company's expenses. These expenses include agent commissions, premium taxes, costs of putting a policy on the books, marketing support costs, and contingencies. CURRENT ASSUMPTIONS products, in order to be competitive, must emphasize low expense loadings. Companies which sell these products make special efforts to control expenses.

EXPENSE RATIO formula used by insurance companies to relate income and expenses:

$$\text{Expense Ratio} = \frac{\text{Incurred Insurance - Related Expenses}}{\text{Written Premiums}}$$

This ratio is of critical importance to the insurance company since it reflects the percentage of the premiums income that goes for expenses; that is, how much it costs the company to acquire the premiums, a key element in today's competitive marketplace.

EXPENSE REIMBURSEMENT ALLOWANCE *see* EXPENSE ALLOWANCE.

EXPENSE RESERVE insurance company's liability for incurred but unpaid expenses. *See also* INCURRED BUT NOT REPORTED LOSSES (IBNR).

EXPENSES OF REPLACEMENT *see* VALUABLE PAPERS (RECORDS) INSURANCE.

EXPERIENCE record of losses, whether or not insured. This record is used in predicting future losses and in developing premium rates based on *expectation of insured losses*.

EXPERIENCE ACCOUNT loss experience of a given insured.

EXPERIENCED MORBIDITY actual morbidity experience of an insured group as compared to the EXPECTED MORBIDITY for that group.

EXPERIENCED MORTALITY actual mortality experience of an insured group as compared to the EXPECTED MORTALITY for that group.

EXPERIENCE MODIFICATION adjustment of premiums resulting from the use of EXPERIENCE RATINGS. Experience rating plans take the form of *retrospective plans* or *prospective plans*. Under retrospective plans, premiums are modified after the fact. That is, once the policy period ends, premiums are adjusted to reflect actual loss experience of an insured. In contrast, under prospective plans, an insured's past experience (usually for the immediate preceding three years) is used to determine the premium for the current year of coverage.

EXPERIENCE, POLICY YEAR *see* POLICY YEAR EXPERIENCE.

EXPERIENCE RATING statistical procedure used to calculate a premium rate based on the loss experience of an insured group. Applied in group insurance it is the opposite of manual rates. Here the premiums paid are related to actual claims and expense experience expected for that specific group. In PROSPECTIVE RATING, the past three years loss experience of the insured is the basis for the premium calculation for the current year of coverage. In RETROSPECTIVE RATING, the current premium rate for the current period of time is modified at the close of that period to reflect actual loss experience. The premium actually paid then can be adjusted, subject to a pre-agreed minimum and maximum rate.

EXPERIENCE REFUND return of a percentage of premium paid by a business firm if its loss record is better than the amount loaded into the basic premium. *See also* EXPERIENCE MODIFICATION.

EXPIRATION termination date of coverage as indicated on the insurance policy. *See also* EXPIRATION FILE.

EXPIRATION CARD *see* EXPIRATION FILE.

EXPIRATION FILE agents records showing when clients' policies expire.

EXPIRATION NOTICE written notice to an insured showing date of termination of an insurance policy.

EXPIRY point in time when a TERM LIFE INSURANCE policy terminates its coverage.

EXPLOSION, COLLAPSE, AND UNDERGROUND EXCLUSION inherent danger resulting from certain construction procedures that are excluded from general business liability policies. Coverage for this exclusion can be acquired at an extra premium through an ENDORSEMENT to the various business liability policies.

EXPLOSION INSURANCE *see* EXTENDED COVERAGE ENDORSEMENT.

EXPORT-IMPORT BANK partnership between an agency of the U.S. government and the Foreign Credit Insurance Association (50 commercial insurance companies, both stock and mutual). Insures that businesses are indemnified for losses resulting from uncollectible accounts for goods sold in foreign markets. Additional perils covered are war, insurrection, confiscation and/or currency devaluation. This coverage encourages the American businesses to sell their products in foreign markets.

EXPOSURE possibility of loss. The most cost efficient way to purchase insurance is to insure an unexpected loss with a low probability of occurrence. Insuring a loss with a high probability of occurrence means swapping dollars with an insurance company, since the premium charged would reflect the expected probability of loss. Expense and profit loadings would also be added by the insurer. *See also* SELF INSURANCE.

EXPRESSED WARRANTY *see* WARRANTY.

EXPROPRIATION INSURANCE coverage against foreign country expropriation underwritten by the OVERSEAS PRIVATE INVESTMENT CORPORATION (OPIC) for U.S. owned companies investing in given developing countries.

EXTENDED COVERAGE ENDORSEMENT extension of coverage available under the *Standard Fire Policy*. The standard policy only covers the perils of fire and lightning. The endorsement covers riot, riot attending a strike, civil commotion, smoke, aircraft and vehicle damage, windstorm, hail, and explosion.

EXTENDED TERM INSURANCE nonforfeiture option which uses the cash value of an ordinary life policy as a single premium to purchase term life insurance in the amount of the original policy. The length of the term policy depends on (1) the size of the cash value and (2) the attained age of the insured.

EXTORTION INSURANCE coverage in the event of threats to injure an insured or damage or destroy his property.

EXTRA EXPENSE INSURANCE form that covers exposures associated with efforts to operate a business that is damaged by a peril such as fire. For example, a special electrical generator may have to be purchased in the event of a long-range loss of electricity if the business is to continue to operate.

EXTRA PERCENTAGE TABLES form of substandard ratings which shows additions to standard premiums to reflect physical impairments of applicants for life or health insurance. The additions reflect the greater probability of mortality or morbidity. *See also* SUBSTANDARD HEALTH INSURANCE; SUBSTANDARD LIFE INSURANCE.

EXTRA PREMIUM addition to reflect exposures with a greater probability of loss than standard exposures. For example, insuring a munitions factory obviously requires a premium greater than that required for insuring an accounting office.

EXTRATERRITORIALITY provision in WORKERS COMPENSATION INSURANCE under which an employee who incurs an injury in another state, and elects to come under the law of his home state, will retain coverage under the workers compensation policy.

F

401 (k) PLAN *see* SECTION 401 (K) PLAN (SALARY REDUCTION PLAN).

403 (b) PLAN *see* SECTION 403 (B) PLAN.

FACE first page of an insurance policy.

FACE AMOUNT (FACE OF POLICY) sum of insurance provided by a policy at death or maturity.

FACE OF POLICY *see* FACE AMOUNT (FACE OF POLICY).

FACILITY OF PAYMENT CLAUSE element usually found in industrial life insurance policies under which the insurance company upon the death of the insured under certain conditions is allowed to choose the beneficiary if the beneficiary named in the policy is a minor or deceased. For example, the funeral home may receive a death benefit if the beneficiary is not alive.

FACTORY INSURANCE ASSOCIATION (FIA) association of stock property insurance companies, formed to provide engineering services for member companies. These companies generally insure highly protected risks (risks characterized by a high degree of care taken for safety and potential loss reduction).

FACTORY MUTUAL organization of a group of insurers composed of mutual property and casualty insurance companies, a subsidiary stock insurance company, and a subsidiary safety engineering company. Their objective is to provide insurance and safety engineering services for large manufacturing companies, substantial housing projects, public institutions, and educational institutions. Coverage includes the perils of fire, explosion, windstorm, riot, civil commotion, sprinkler leakage, malicious mischief, damage to vehicles, and damage to aircraft. Field offices staffed by salaried personnel deal directly with insureds; there is no agency field force.

FACTUAL EXPECTATION strong expectation of an occurrence resulting in a monetary interest which gives rise to an insurable interest. For example, a daughter has a strong expectation of wearing her mother's wedding gown and thus has an insurable interest in the gown even though the gown is still the property of her mother.

FACULTATIVE OBLIGATORY TREATY hybrid between FACULTATIVE REINSURANCE and *treaty reinsurance* where the CEDING COMPANY may elect to assign certain risks that the reinsurer is obligated to accept.

FACULTATIVE REINSURANCE individual risk offered by an insurer for acceptance or rejection by a reinsurer. Both parties are free to act in their own best interests regardless of any prior contractual arrangements. With proportional facultative reinsurance, the reinsurer assumes a proportional share of premiums and losses. On a nonproportional basis, the reinsurer is liable only for losses which exceed the insurer's retention level; premiums vary with loss expectation.

FAILURE MODE AND EFFECT ANALYSIS analytical procedure to predict the failure rate of a system still in the design stage.

FAILURE TO PERFORM EXCLUSION coverage which is excluded under COMMERCIAL GENERAL LIABILITY INSURANCE (COMPREHENSIVE GENERAL LIABILITY INSURANCE) for the loss of use of undamaged tangible real or personal property as the result of failure of the performance of a product or service as warranted or represented by the insured.

FAIR ACCESS TO INSURANCE REQUIREMENTS (FAIR) PLAN insurance that grew out of the urban demonstrations and riots of the 1960s. Because of the deteriorated social and economic circumstances in these areas, it became impossible for many business owners and homeowners to purchase property insurance. As a result, the Federal government established the FAIR plans based on the stop loss reinsurance method. If a business owner or homeowner cannot purchase property insurance through conventional means, application can be made through an agent who represents an insurance company participating in the FAIR plan. If the property is acceptable to the company, insurance will be provided. If the property is deficient, improvements are suggested, and upon compliance the policy is issued.

FAIR CREDIT REPORTING ACT federal legislation giving an insurance applicant the right to contact a reporting organization doing a credit check and be advised of information contained in the applicant's file showing the reason for rejection for insurance.

FAIR PLAN *see* FAIR ACCESS TO INSURANCE REQUIREMENTS (FAIR) PLAN.

FALLEN BUILDING CLAUSE section in some property insurance contracts which eliminates further coverage for buildings after they have collapsed from causes other than fire or explosion. For example, fire coverage would not be applicable to buildings that collapse because of inherent defects.

FALSE IMPRISONMENT tort of wrongful physical confinement of an individual. This is not restricted to physical confinement but includes any unjustified limitation of another's freedom of movement. If an individual is intimidated into responding to an order, the courts have interpreted this as false imprisonment.

FALSE PRETENSE *see* MISREPRESENTATION (FALSE PRETENSE).

FAMILY CONSIDERATIONS factors influencing the amount of life insurance to purchase, such as marketable skills of spouse, age of children, savings, investments, number of future working years expectancy, amount of bills and notes outstanding, and funds necessary to maintain the family's customary life style should the wage earner die. *See also* LIFE INSURANCE.

FAMILY COVERAGE insurance coverage for the NAMED INSURED and his or her eligible dependents.

FAMILY EXPENSE INSURANCE type of health insurance under which an insured's coverage extends to all family members if they are residents of the insured's household. Insures all medical expenses (except those excluded), among them room and board, surgical and physician costs, drugs and medicines, blood, ambulance service to and from the hospital, X-rays, and floor nursing. *See also* INSURANCE.

FAMILY HISTORY background information used in life and health insurance underwriting to ascertain the probability of hereditary disease. The purpose is to determine if the disease is of such a nature that the life expectancy of an applicant will be adversely affected and if so to what degree?

FAMILY INCOME POLICY contract combining whole life and decreasing term insurance. A monthly income is paid to a beneficiary if an insured dies during a specific period. At the end of that period, the full face amount of the policy is also paid to the beneficiary. It is designed to provide income for a household while the children are still young. If an insured dies after the specified period, only the face amount of the policy is paid. For example, the face value of a family income policy is $100,000 and the specified period is 20 years. If the insured dies 10 years into the specified period, the beneficiary receives a monthly income of 1% of the face amount ($1000) for the remaining 10 years. At the end of the 10 years, the beneficiary also receives $100,000. If the insured dies after the 20 year specified period, the beneficiary receives $100,000, which is the face amount. *See also* FAMILY INCOME RIDER; FAMILY MAINTENANCE POLICY.

FAMILY INCOME RIDER attachment of decreasing term life insurance to an ordinary life policy to provide monthly income to a beneficiary if death occurs during a specified period. If the insured dies after the specified period, only the face value is paid to the beneficiary since the decreasing term insurance has expired. *See also* FAMILY INCOME POLICY.

FAMILY MAINTENANCE POLICY combination of whole life and level term that provides income to a beneficiary for a selected period of time (e.g., 20 years) if an insured dies during that period. At the end of the income paying period the beneficiary also receives the entire face amount of the policy. If an insured dies after the end of the selected period, the beneficiary receives only the face value of the policy. The remainder of the benefits are the same as under the FAMILY INCOME POLICY. *See also* FAMILY INCOME RIDER.

FAMILY POLICY contract providing whole life insurance on the father and term insurance on the mother and all children, including newborns after reaching a stated age, usually 15 days. Children, upon reaching the age of majority, have the right to convert their insurance to a permanent policy up to the amount of term coverage without having to show evidence of insurability (take a physical examination). The premium is the same regardless of the number of children covered.

FAMILY PROTECTION ENDORSEMENT *see* UNINSURED MOTORIST COVERAGE; UNDERINSURED MOTORIST ENDORSEMENT.

FAMILY SUPPORT ACT OF 1988 legislation that changed the tax treatment concerning child-care expenses so that an employee who has incurred child-care expenses greater than $4,800 and who is participating in a company-sponsored dependent care assistance program is required to choose between the company plan and the child-care credit. The tax benefit gained by the employee from the child-care credit is reduced dollar for dollar to the extent that the company plan is used to cover child-care expenses.

FARMERS COMPREHENSIVE PERSONAL LIABILITY INSURANCE provides the same coverage as a COMPREHENSIVE PERSONAL LIABILITY INSURANCE policy, plus coverage to exposures which are peculiar to farms, such as farm business operations, farm employees engaged in farm business activities, and liability arising out of selling farm products.

FARMOWNERS AND RANCHOWNERS INSURANCE package coverage for a dwelling and its contents, barns, stables, and other land structures as well as liability coverage. By means of a number of special forms which follow the format of the HOMEOWNERS INSURANCE POLICY, this insurance protects a number of named perils and liabilities.

FASB 87 *see* FINANCIAL ACCOUNTING STANDARDS BOARD (FASB) 87.

FAULT TREE ANALYSIS diagram of cause and effect relationships, showing the possible outcomes if a particular course of action is taken or continued. This method of analysis, which is founded in the testing of aerospace materials, has increasingly been applied to safety engineering accident cause and prevention.

FAULTY INSTALLATION coverage in the event of property damage or destruction resulting from wrongful installation of equipment.

FAYOL, HENRI French industrialist whose thesis is that all business activities revolve around six areas: *technical* (production), *commercial* (buying and selling), *financing* (capital employment), *accounting* (financial record keeping), *managerial* (planning, organizing, directing, coordinating, controlling), and *security* (protection of property against loss and the physical safety of individuals). Fayol's view of security has become the RISK MANAGEMENT of modern business.

FCAS *see* FELLOW, CASUALTY ACTUARIAL SOCIETY (FCAS).

FC&S *see* FREE-OF-CAPTURE-AND-SEIZURE CLAUSE.

FCIC *see* FEDERAL CROP INSURANCE.

FDIC *see* FEDERAL DEPOSIT INSURANCE CORPORATION (FDIC).

FEDERAL CRIME INSURANCE protection under the auspices of the Federal government where such insurance cannot be purchased by a homeowner, business owner, or tenant at affordable community rates. A homeowner or tenant's personal property is covered for burglary and/or robbery, and premises for damage due to burglary and robbery. A business owner's fixtures, furniture, equipment, merchandise, money and securities due are covered for burglary and/or robbery. *See also* FEDERAL INSURANCE ADMINISTRATION.

FEDERAL CROP INSURANCE protection against natural disasters which may strike crops. Coverage on ALL RISKS basis began in 1948 under the auspices of the U.S. Department of Agriculture. Premiums reflect actual losses incurred by farmers. The objective is to level out farmers' income that otherwise would be adversely affected by natural disasters striking their crops. *See also* FEDERAL INSURANCE ADMINISTRATION.

FEDERAL DEPOSIT INSURANCE CORPORATION (FDIC) agency formed as the result of bank failures in the 1930s to insure the deposits of customers of member banks. The FDIC, an agency of the Federal government, is self supporting in that it receives fees from the member banks at the rate of .5% of the bank's deposits and the income from reserves that have been invested. Each account is insured up to $100,000.

FEDERAL EMPLOYEES GROUP LIFE INSURANCE (FEGLI) plan administered through a primary private life insurer and reinsured through other private life insurers, providing a death benefit equal to: (1) one year's salary for active employees at least age 45 until they reach age 65; and (2) two years' salary for active employees age 35 and under. The death benefit is graduated for Federal employees age 36 through 44. After retirement, the full death benefit remains in force until the retired employee reaches age 65, whereupon the death benefit is reduced by 2% per month until it levels off at 25% of the employee preretirement annual salary. The Federal government pays approximately one-third of the monthly premium and the employee pays the remainder.

FEDERAL EMPLOYERS LIABILITY ACT (FELA) Federal law comparable to state workers compensation statutes setting out liability of railroads for work-related injuries or death of their employees. Railroad employees are not covered by *workers compensation* laws. Under normal tort law, the injured party must prove he or she did nothing to contribute to the negligence or the risk. But under the terms of the Federal act, railroad employees must only show that negligence on the part of the employer contributed to the injury. Therefore, this law gives railroads responsibility for on-the-job injuries to employees. But the railroads are not protected by the theory that workers compensation should be the only responsibility of employers for their employees, or by the prescribed schedule of benefits.

FEDERAL ESTATE TAX Federal government tax imposed on the estate of a decedent according to the value of that estate. The first step in the computation of the federal estate tax owed is to determine the value of the decedent's gross estate. This determination can be made by adding the following values of assets owned by the decedent at the time of death:

1. property owned outright
2. gratuitous lifetime transfers but with the stipulation that the decedent retained the income or control over the income.
3. gratuitous lifetime transfers subject to the recipient's surviving the decedent.
4. gratuitous lifetime transfers subject to the decedent's retaining the right to revoke, amend, or alter the gift.
5. annuities purchased by the decedent which are payable for the lifetime of the named survivor as well as the annuitant.
6. property jointly held in such a manner that another party receives the decedent's interest in that property at the decedent's death because of that party's survivorship.
7. life insurance in which the decedent retained incidents of ownership.
8. life insurance which was payable to the decedent's estate.

The second step in the computation of the federal estate tax owed is to subtract allowable deductions (including bequests to charities, bequests to the surviving spouse, funeral expenses, and other administration expenses) from the gross estate. This results in the taxable estate. Adjustable taxable gifts are then added to the taxable estate, resulting in the computational tax base. From the table below, the appropriate tax rate is then applied to the computational tax base, resulting in the tentative (certain credits may still be subtracted) federal estate tax.

If Computational
   Tax Base

Is More Than:	and	Equal to or Less Than:	Tentative Tax Is:	
$ 0	$	10,000	18%	
10,000		20,000	$1,800 + 20% of excess over	$10,000
20,000		40,000	$3,800 + 22% of excess over	$20,000
40,000		60,000	$8,200 + 24% of excess over	$40,000
60,000		80,000	$13,000 + 26% of excess over	$60,000
80,000		100,000	$18,200 + 28% of excess over	$80,000
100,000		150,000	$23,800 + 30% of excess over	$100,000
150,000		250,000	$38,800 + 32% of excess over	$150,000
250,000		500,000	$70,800 + 34% of excess over	$250,000
500,000		750,000	$155,800 + 37% of excess over	$50,000
750,000		1,000,000	$248,300 + 39% of excess over	$750,000
1,000,000		1,250,000	$345,800 + 41% of excess over	$1,000,000
1,250,000		1,500,000	$448,300 + 43% of excess over	$1,250,000
1,500,000		2,000,000	$555,800 + 45% of excess over	$1,500,000
2,000,000		2,500,000	$780,800 + 49% of excess over	$2,000,000
2,500,000		No limit	$1,025,800 + 50% of excess over	$2,500,000

Note that the above tax schedule is applicable to the taxable estate only after the adjustment for settlement costs, administrative expenses, and the unified estate and gift tax credit.

It is important to note that there is an unlimited marital deduction (the estate of the decedent passes to the spouse free of federal estate taxes) and that all federal estate taxes are eliminated on estates having a computational tax base of $600,000 or less. To conform with the unlimited marital deduction in estates, tax-free gifts between spouses are allowed in unlimited amounts.

FEDERAL FLOOD INSURANCE coverage made available to residents of a community on a subsidized and nonsubsidized premium rate basis once the governing body of the community qualifies that community for coverage under the National Flood Insurance Act. Residents include business and nonbusiness operations with coverage written on structures and their contents. Coverage is purchased through licensed agents. Prior to passage of the Housing and Urban Development Act of 1968 of which the National Flood Insurance Act is a part, it was virtually impossible to obtain flood insurance coverage on an industrial building, residential building, retailing building, or a single family dwelling.

FEDERAL GOVERNMENT INSURANCE (FTC) *see* FEDERAL CRIME INSURANCE; FEDERAL CROP INSURANCE; FEDERAL DEPOSIT INSURANCE

CORPORATION (FDIC); FEDERAL FLOOD INSURANCE; FEDERAL SAVINGS AND LOAN INSURANCE CORPORATION (FSLIC); SOCIAL INSURANCE.

FEDERAL INSURANCE ADMINISTRATION government agency whose function is to administer the *Federal Flood Insurance Program*, the *Federal Crime Insurance Program*, and the FAIR ACCESS TO INSURANCE REQUIREMENT (FAIR) PLAN.

FEDERAL INSURANCE CONTRIBUTIONS ACT (FICA) tax charged to finance the OLD AGE, SURVIVORS, DISABILITY, AND HEALTH INSURANCE (OASDHI) plan. Both employer and employee share in the cost, making contributions on an equal basis. The employer pays the tax on its payroll, and the employee pays the tax on wages earned. The total contribution (employer and employee payments) tax rate is 15.3% in 1990 for the covered wages.

FEDERAL NUCLEAR REGULATORY COMMISSION *see* NUCLEAR REGULATORY COMMISSION.

FEDERAL OFFICIALS BOND coverage for the Federal government in the event of loss due to dishonest acts of Federal government employees.

FEDERAL SAVINGS AND LOAN INSURANCE CORPORATION (FSLIC) agency of the Federal government formed as the result of bankruptcies of savings and loan associations during the 1930s. Insures deposits of customers up to $100,000 for each account. In 1986, 1987, 1988, 1989, and 1990, when numerous savings and loan associations failed or nearly failed, FSLIC backed up their deposits and prevented runs.

FEDERAL TAXATION *see* ANNUITY; TAX FREE INCOME; TAXATION, INSURANCE COMPANIES; TAXATION, INTEREST ON DIVIDENDS; TAXATION, PARTICIPATING DIVIDENDS; TAXATION, PROCEEDS; TAX BENEFITS OF LIFE INSURANCE.

FEDERAL TRADE COMMISSION (FTC) government agency, under the MCCARRAN-FERGUSON ACT (PUBLIC LAW 15), that has no authority over insurance matters to the extent the states regulate insurance to the satisfaction of Congress. However, this does not prevent the FTC from conducting investigations into the insurance industry. For example, in 1970 the Congress charged the FTC with the responsibility of enforcing the FAIR CREDIT REPORTING ACT, which requires an insurance company to notify an insurance applicant of an impending INSPECTION REPORT and to release information so collected to the applicant upon request. If the report results in the applicant's rejection for insurance, he must be notified of the adverse report and his right to its contents. Perhaps the best known FTC investigation involved its study, ''Life Insurance

Cost Disclosure,'' that was extremely critical of industry cost disclosure practices.

FEE SIMPLE ESTATE form of common law ownership of real property that permits disposition of property by its holder in any manner desired. Both the holder and the holder's heirs have use of property in perpetuity and have an insurable interest in the property.

FELLOW, CASUALTY ACTUARIAL SOCIETY (FCAS) designation earned by passing 10 national examinations on subjects including mathematics of property and casualty insurance, actuarial science, insurance, accounting, and finance. Examinations and course materials are prepared and administered by the Casualty Actuarial Society.

FELLOW, LIFE MANAGEMENT INSTITUTE (FLMI) professional management designation earned by passing 10 national examinations on life and health insurance subjects including insurance, finance, marketing, law, information systems, accounting, management, and employee benefits. Examinations and course materials are prepared and administered by the Life Office Management Association.

FELLOW SERVANT RULE formerly an employer's defense under which an injured employee had to bring a cause for action against the fellow employee causing the injury, not the employer. Workers Compensation laws have nullified the rule for job-related injuries. *See also* WORKERS COMPENSATION, COVERAGE B.

FELLOW, SOCIETY OF ACTUARIES (FSA) designation earned by passing 10 national examinations on subjects including mathematics of life and health insurance, actuarial science, insurance, accounting, finance, and employee benefits. Examinations and course materials are prepared and administered by the Society of Actuaries.

FIA *see* FEDERAL INSURANCE ADMINISTRATION.

FICTITIOUS GROUP assembly of people formed only for obtaining GROUP INSURANCE. Such a group is uninsurable and violates underwriting principles concerning group insurance.

FIDELITY AND SURETY CATASTROPHE INSURANCE mechanism used by a fidelity and surety insurance company to spread its liability through REINSURANCE by issuing a *surplus treaty* as a first layer of coverage, thereby enabling a *cedent* to limit its liability on the business written while at the same time utilizing the flexibility that the surplus method offers. The reinsurance *catastrophe cover* provides a second layer of coverage. Reinsurance covers are used by the insurance company to:

1. avoid accumulation of liability on individual principles. Warehouse bonds are an example of such accumulations because they are required in great number and they result in large aggregate amounts.
2. achieve a balance among the various types of bonds that the insurer assumes.
3. reduce violent fluctuations in experiencing high loss ratios on many classes of bonds.

FIDELITY BOND coverage that guarantees that the insurance company will pay the insured business or individual for money or other property lost because of dishonest acts of its bonded employees, either named or by positions. The bond covers all dishonest acts, such as larceny, theft, embezzlement, forgery, misappropriation, wrongful abstraction, or willful misapplication, whether employees act alone or as a team. Businesses often bond their employees not only because the insurance will pay for the losses, but also because the bonding company may prevent losses by uncovering dishonesty in the work history of a new employee. Since a fidelity bond makes up only a part of protection against theft, other crime insurance is mandatory. Employee dishonesty insurance is usually bought through an individual Fidelity Bond, BLANKET POSITION BOND, COMMERCIAL BLANKET BOND, or a NAME SCHEDULE BOND.

FIDELITY EXCLUSION provision of liability insurance which excludes coverage for dishonest acts of an insured.

FIDUCIARY holding of property, or otherwise acting on behalf of another in trust. The fiduciary must exercise due care in safeguarding property left under personal care, custody, and control. Insurance coverage is available for this exposure. *See also* JUDICIAL BOND.

FIDUCIARY ASPECT OF INSURANCE status in which an insurance company holds funds of its insureds (the payment of premiums) in trust, and through an INSURING AGREEMENT promises to make all benefit payments for which it has received premiums.

FIDUCIARY BOND *see* JUDICIAL BOND.

FIELD FORCE agents, managers, and office personnel serving in the branches of an insurance company.

FILE-AND-USE RATING LAWS use of new rate structures by an insurance company without first obtaining approval of a State Insurance Department.

FILE AND USE STATE *see* RATING BUREAU.

FINAL AVERAGE method of calculating retirement benefits under pension plans, by averaging the highest three or five years of earnings (usually the final five years).

FINAL EXPENSE FUND amount of life insurance required to purchase burial, probate, medical, and other costs associated with death.

FINAL INSURANCE (MINIMUM DEPOSIT INSURANCE) premiums paid out of funds borrowed from the cash value of a life insurance policy.

FINANCED INSURANCE *see* FINAL INSURANCE (MINIMUM DEPOSIT INSURANCE).

FINANCED PREMIUM premiums paid with funds that are not borrowed from life insurance. It is important to ascertain the finance charges and the costs/benefits of such a transaction.

FINANCIAL ACCOUNTING STANDARDS BOARD (FASB) 87 new pension-accounting rule created by the Financial Accounting Standards Board. The objective of this rule is to clarify pension accounting so that investors, employers, and employees will know what the assets and liabilities of a particular pension plan are. The rule requires that a company disclose all relevant figures concerning its pension plan on the face of the company's income statement. Previously, the company could bury these figures in the footnotes of the income statement. Also, under the new disclosure requirement, the expected liabilities of the pension plan must be recalculated annually, assuming market interest rates. Thus, a company's pension liabilities each year will rise or fall according to the market interest rate, thereby affecting the company's income statement and balance sheet.

FINANCIAL CONSIDERATIONS investment and savings position of an insured used in determining the amount of life insurance to purchase. The amount of investment and savings is subtracted from the total insurance requirement.

FINANCIAL INSTITUTIONS REFORM, RECOVERY, AND ENFORCEMENT ACT OF 1989 (FIRREA) legislation designed to provide the structural reform necessary to strengthen the thrift industry after the bailout of the insolvent Federal Savings and Loan Insurance Corporation (FSLIC) in 1989. The Act is designed to accomplish the following through regulatory reform: to establish a stable system for affordable housing financing; to place the FSLIC insurance funds on a sound financial basis; to manage and resolve failed savings associations and, if necessary, to provide the funds required to deal expeditiously with failed savings associations; to improve the supervision of savings associations; and to strengthen the enforcement powers of federal regulators of savings associations. If the preceding aims are accomplished, the federal regulators will have the necessary power and capital to terminate insolvent savings associations in an effective and efficient manner before the crisis stage is reached.

FINANCIAL PLANNING analysis of current financial conditions of an individual or business to include all sources of present income, expenditures, and net worth; projection of this financial condition into the future; establishment of a budget within which the participants must operate; use of various financial instruments (stocks, bonds, insurance, mutual funds) to guarantee financial independence; and plan for orderly transfer of wealth to a selected individual(s) or business(es).

FINANCIAL REINSURANCE transaction of REINSURANCE under which there is a limit on the total liability of the REINSURER and future investment income is a recognized component of the underwriting process. This financial instrument incorporates the time value of money into the CEDING process such that the CEDENT can reinsure its liabilities at a premium rate less than the true rate for the liabilities transferred (difference in the two rates to be made up by the investment income generated during the years the reinsurance contract remains in force). Financial reinsurance can be used effectively in several situations:
1. *surplus relief* (QUOTA SHARE REINSURANCE)—CEDING COMPANY transfers a percentage of its book of business to the reinsurer (the reinsurer will limit its total liability under any one contract).
2. *portfolio transfers*—ceding company transfers reserves on known losses to the reinsurer in exchange for premiums equal to the present value of the future claims experience.
3. *retrospective aggregates*—ceding company transfers reserves on known losses as well as INCURRED BUT NOT REPORTED LOSSES (IBNR).
4. *prospective aggregates*—ceding company pays a premium on a PROSPECTIVE RATING basis to the reinsurer. In exchange, the reinsurer is obligated to pay future losses incurred by the cedent. If these future losses are less than expected, the cedent will receive the UNDERWRITING GAIN. Any gains from investments and fees will be retained by the reinsurer. Through this mechanism, in essence, the cedent gains current capacity for writing additional business by borrowing against income to be received in the future.
5. *catastrophe protection*—coverage against shock losses is provided by spreading the payment of such losses over several years.

FINANCIAL REPORTING recording and presentation of financial statements, such as the ANNUAL STATEMENT, by the insurance company. Financial reporting statements are used by the State Insurance Commissioner in regulating the adequacy of company reserves for benefit liabilities, assets availability, and worth.

FINANCIAL RESPONSIBILITY CLAUSE provision in automobile insurance, such as the PERSONAL AUTOMOBILE POLICY (PAP), stating that a particular policy furnishes adequate coverage, the minimum of which is at least equal to that required by the financial responsibility laws in the state in which the insured is driving.

FINANCIAL RESPONSIBILITY LAW law requiring the operator of an automobile to show financial ability to pay for automobile-related losses. In many states evidence usually takes the form of a minimum amount of automobile liability insurance.

FINANCIAL STATEMENT balance sheet and profit and loss statement of an insurance company. This statement is used by State Insurance Commissioners to regulate an insurance company according to reserve requirements, assets, and other liabilities.

FINANCIAL STRUCTURE *see* ANNUAL STATEMENT, FINANCIAL STATEMENT.

FINANCING securement of funds from outside sources such as by borrowing or by attracting equity control. Use of leverage to improve the profitability of a business. Achievement of an investment return on the borrowed funds at a higher rate than the interest being paid for the use of the funds.

FINE ART DEALERS INSURANCE coverage for works of art, antiques and similar articles of value on ALL RISKS basis, subject to exclusion of wear and tear, war, breakage, repairing, infidelity of the insured's employees, and mysterious disappearance. Fine Arts Insurance Policies are written on a scheduled basis with damaged or destroyed items being indemnified on a valued basis. The same type of coverage for fine arts is available through a *Fine Arts Endorsement* for a SPECIAL MULTI-PERIL INSURANCE (SMP) policy.

FINE ARTS AND ANTIQUES INSURANCE coverage for paintings, pictures, etchings, tapestries, art glass windows, antique furniture, coin collections and stamp collections owned by individuals and businesses. These works are not covered if owned by dealers or auction firms. Protection is on an ALL RISKS basis subject to exclusions of damage from ordinary breakage, wear and tear, war, and nuclear disaster. Each item must be specifically listed and valued in the policy.

FIRE intense combustion resulting in a flame or glow. In order for the fire PERIL to be covered under PROPERTY INSURANCE, the fire must be a HOSTILE FIRE, not a FRIENDLY FIRE.

FIRE CATASTROPHE REINSURANCE means used by a *direct fire underwriter* to protect against accumulation for a fire account, as well as against extremely large fire account liability. For example, heavy liabilities under individual risks can be analyzed by the initial fire underwriter to determine the number of separate fire risks involved. The reinsurance method applied to the risks is a QUOTA SHARE or *surplus* share treaty with the use of a FACULTATIVE REINSURANCE cover if necessary. Under this method, the reinsurer assumes the liability of a proportionate share of the risks in exchange for a proportionate share of the premiums. An extremely large number of losses under individual risks caused by a single event, commonly referred to as a conflagration hazard, arises when different risks may be affected by one fire. An example would be widespread damage to many adjacent private houses. While the loss for each retained individual risk would be small, the aggregate would be so large that it would affect the stability of the fire insurance company. Catastrophe reinsurance would protect any SURPLUS REINSURANCE and EXCESS OF LOSS REINSURANCE up to a stated amount.

FIRE DEPARTMENT SERVICE CLAUSE in PROPERTY INSURANCE policies, provision which states that the INSURED will receive INDEMNITY for expenses incurred as a result of acts by the fire department taken to save or reduce damage to the insured's property. For example, if the insured has a house outside the fire district, the fire department might charge a fee for responding to a fire call.

FIRE DIVISION separation of a building into distinct separate parts by FIRE WALL or open air spaces between buildings to minimize the probability of a fire spreading horizontally or vertically.

FIRE DOOR partition of noncombustible material in a wall of similar material, designed when closed to slow the spread of fire from one side of the wall to the other. The NATIONAL FIRE PROTECTION ASSOCIATION rates the doors according to the number of hours they can be expected to withstand fire before burning through.

FIRE EXTINGUISHER instrument that uses noncombustible substances such as carbon dioxide to deprive a fire of oxygen, thereby extinguishing it.

FIRE INSURANCE—STANDARD FIRE POLICY policy known as the 165-line policy because of the standard form used in most states. The policy is not complete, and additional forms and endorsements are added so that it can cover numerous direct and indirect risks. The Standard Fire Policy is *Section I*—property coverage of most package policies such as the HOMEOWNERS and SPECIAL MULTI-PERIL. It provides the foundation for property insurance coverages regardless of the form in which they appear. The Standard Fire Policy has four sections:
1. DECLARATIONS—description and location of property, insured amount, name of insured.

2. INSURING AGREEMENTS—premium amount, obligations of the insured, actions the insured must take in the event of loss and resultant claim.
3. *Conditions*—describes that which suspends or restricts the coverage, such as an increase in the hazard with the knowledge of the insured.
4. EXCLUSIONS—perils not covered under the policy, such as enemy attack including action taken by military force in resisting actual or immediately impending enemy attack.

Forms that can be added to a Standard Fire Policy include *Dwelling Buildings and Contents Basic Form; Dwelling, Buildings and Contents Broad Form*; GENERAL PROPERTY FORM. Since the Standard Fire Policy insures only against fire and lightning, the EXTENDED COVERAGE ENDORSEMENT can cover the additional perils of windstorm, hail, riot, civil commotion, vehicle and aircraft damage to the insured property, explosion, and smoke damage. A VANDALISM AND MALICIOUS MISCHIEF ENDORSEMENT can also be added.

FIRE LEGAL LIABILITY INSURANCE coverage for property loss liability as the result of negligent acts and/or omissions of the insured which allows a spreading fire to damage others' property. Negligent acts and omissions can result in fire legal liability. For example, an insured through negligence allows a fire to spread to a neighbor's property. The neighbor then brings suit against the insured for negligence. In another example, a tenant occupying another party's property through negligence causes serious fire damage to the property.

FIRE LOAD amount of combustible matter present which can act as a fuel to feed a HOSTILE FIRE.

FIRE MAP detail showing distribution of property coverages written by an insurance company. Illustrates a potential danger of concentration of insured risks.

FIRE MARK historic insignia representing evidence of coverage placed on property insured by a particular insurance company. If the property on fire did not have the company's fire mark, its private fire department would not fight the fire.

FIRE MARK SOCIETY sales honor group of property and casualty insurance agents created by the National Association of Professional Insurance Agents.

FIREPROOF use of engineering approved fire resistive construction materials exclusively within a structure. *See also* FIRE RESISTIVE CONSTRUCTION.

FIRE PROTECTION *see* FIRE RESISTIVE CONSTRUCTION; FIRE WALL; FIREPROOF.

FIRE RESISTIVE CONSTRUCTION use of engineering-approved masonry or fire resistive materials for exterior walls, floors, and roofs to reduce the severity of a potential fire and lower premium rates.

FIRE WALL structure separating parts of a building in order to contain the spread of fire. Fire walls reduce the severity of a potential fire and lower premium rates.

FIRST-DOLLAR COVERAGE insurance policy under which payment is made for a loss not subject to any DEDUCTIBLE or under which payment is made up to the limits of the policy and then an EXCESS INSURANCE policy takes effect. For example, a HOMEOWNERS INSURANCE POLICY—SECTION II (LIABILITY COVERAGE) would pay up to its limits for an insured loss, whereupon an UMBRELLA LIABILITY INSURANCE policy would go into effect.

FIRST LOSS RETENTION (DEDUCTIBLE) *see* EXCESS OF LOSS REINSURANCE.

FIRST PARTY INSURANCE coverage for the insured's personal and real property and the insured's own person. Contrast with THIRD PARTY.

FIRST SURPLUS REINSURANCE *see* SURPLUS LINES; SURPLUS REINSURANCE.

FIRST SURPLUS TREATY *see* SURPLUS REINSURANCE.

FIRST YEAR COMMISSION percentage of first year's premium paid to compensate an insurance agent. This is known as the "*First Years*" to show how much new business the agent is generating, compared with *renewal commissions* generated by previous business.

FIVE PERCENT RULE coinsurance requirement such that if a loss is less than $10,000, and also less than 5% of the total of insurance to cover a loss, then the insurance company will not require that the property not damaged by the peril be inventoried or appraised.

FIVE PERCENT WAIVER CLAUSE *see* FIVE PERCENT RULE.

FIVE TO FIFTEEN YEAR RULE VESTING provision of the EMPLOYEE

RETIREMENT INCOME SECURITY ACT OF 1974 (ERISA) under which vesting must accrue at not less than the following rates:

Years of Service	Vesting
0 to less than 5	0
at least 5	25%
6 to 10	5% increase per year
11 to 15	10% increase per year

At the end of 15 years, 100% vesting has been achieved. The TAX REFORM ACT OF 1986 eliminates this option of vesting beginning January 1, 1989.

FIXED-AMOUNT SETTLEMENT OPTION choice of beneficiary in which the death benefit of a life insurance policy is retained by the company to be paid as a series of installments of fixed dollar amounts per installment until the death benefit and interest are exhausted. Any excess interest earned above the minimum guaranteed is applied to extend the time period for making the payments. This option emphasizes dollar amount per installment as opposed to length of time installments are to be paid. *See also* LIFE INSURANCE; OPTIONAL MODES OF SETTLEMENT.

FIXED ANNUITY *see* FIXED DOLLAR ANNUITY.

FIXED BENEFITS payment to a beneficiary that does not vary; for example, a fixed monthly retirement income benefit of $800 paid to a retired employee.

FIXED DOLLAR ANNUITY ANNUITY that guarantees that a specific sum of money wil be paid in the future, usually as monthly income, to an annuitant. For example, a $1000-a-month income benefit will be paid as long as the annuitant lives; the dollar amount will not fluctuate regardless of adverse changes in the insurance company's mortality experience, investment return, and expenses.

FIXED-PERIOD OPTION SETTLEMENT beneficiary's choice, in a life insurance policy or annuity, for receiving income payments for a given period of time. The number of payments are fixed by the payee; the benefit amount is determined by the death proceeds. For example, an income benefit of $1000 per month is paid for a period of 48 months whereupon all income payments cease.

FIXED PREMIUM payment for coverage that remains throughout the same premium-paying period.

FLAT AMOUNT *see* DEFINED BENEFIT PLAN.

FLAT CANCELLATION cancellation of an insurance policy on the date that policy becomes effective. This type of cancellation does not require any fees to be paid to the insurance company.

FLAT COMMISSION compensation to an agent in the same absolute dollar amount, regardless of the type of insurance policy sold. Contrast with GRADED COMMISSION.

FLAT DEDUCTIBLE *see* DEDUCTIBLE.

FLAT EXTRA PREMIUM certain fixed payment made in addition to the regularly scheduled premium.

FLAT MATERNITY BENEFIT stated fixed payment for maternity costs regardless of the actual costs.

FLAT RATE (FLAT SCHEDULE) rate not subsequently adjusted. The rate stays in effect regardless of an insured's subsequent loss record.

FLAT SCHEDULE *see* FLAT RATE (FLAT SCHEDULE).

FLEET OF COMPANIES several insurance companies under common ownership and often common management.

FLEET POLICY numerous automotive vehicles covered under a common insurance policy.

FLEXIBLE BENEFIT PLAN employee benefit plan which allows the employee to choose among several different benefits offered by the employer. In essence, the employee is provided with the opportunity to make a trade-off by trading one benefit for another which best meets the employee's needs at a particular point in time. Contributions paid into the plan, whether on a CONTRIBUTORY or NONCONTRIBUTORY basis, can be allocated to satisfy the needs of a particular employee rather than those of the employees as a whole. The result should be a balance between the employee's primary needs and the benefit/cost constraints. Among the personal choices which the employee can make are health care plans (choices in types and amount of coverages), WELLNESS PROGRAM plans, child-care benefits, and LONG-TERM CARE (LTC) PLANS.

FLEXIBLE FUNDING arrangement whereby the insured pays the insurance company a relatively small monthly premium payment. In exchange for this premium payment, the insurance company processes and pays claims from a fund owned and maintained by the insured. Should the claims exceed a stipulated limit, the insurance company pays the excess amount of claims.

FLEXIBLE PREMIUM one in which the amount and frequency of payment may fluctuate. *See also* FLEXIBLE PREMIUM ANNUITY; FLEXIBLE

PREMIUM LIFE INSURANCE; FLEXIBLE PREMIUM VARIABLE LIFE; UNIVERSAL LIFE INSURANCE; UNIVERSAL VARIABLE LIFE INSURANCE.

FLEXIBLE PREMIUM ANNUITY annuity with no fixed schedule for payment of premiums. For example, premiums can be paid for 10 straight months, then not paid for the next 10 months, then paid every other month, or any combination thereof.

FLEXIBLE PREMIUM LIFE INSURANCE policy which has an initial premium with flexible premiums thereafter. Within limits, a policyowner can select both the future amount and frequency of premiums, or can stop and start premium payments at his or her discretion. Lump sum premium payments can be deposited, subject only to Federal tax code restrictions.

FLEXIBLE PREMIUM VARIABLE LIFE insurance that combines features of FLEXIBLE PREMIUM LIFE INSURANCE and UNIVERSAL LIFE INSURANCE into one policy in the following manner:
1. *Premiums*—after the required minimum initial premium payment, premiums are flexible. The policyowner can select both their future amount and frequency, with certain restrictions that depend on the design of the policy. The policyowner can stop and start the premiums at his or her discretion, and a lump sum premium can be made at any time subject only to Federal tax restrictions.
2. *Variable*—the death benefit may increase or decrease subject to the performance of an investment account of equities in which the premiums are placed. However, a minimum death benefit is guaranteed—the initial face value of the policy. Cash values fluctuate according to the performance of this investment account.

FLMI *see* FELLOW, LIFE MANAGEMENT INSTITUTE (FLMI).

FLOAT funds set aside by an insurance company to pay INCURRED LOSSES which have not yet been paid.

FLOATER coverage for property which moves from location to location either on a scheduled or unscheduled basis. If the floater covers scheduled property, coverage is listed for each item. If a floater covers unscheduled property, all property is covered for the same limits of insurance. *See also* PERSONAL ARTICLES INSURANCE; PERSONAL PROPERTY FLOATER.

FLOOD INSURANCE *see* FEDERAL FLOOD INSURANCE.

FLOOR PLAN INSURANCE coverage for a lender who has accepted property on the floor of a merchant as security for a loan. If the merchandise is damaged or destroyed the lender is indemnified. The policy is on an ALL RISKS basis.

FLOW-THROUGH COST (NO LOAD INSURANCE) net cost of insurance with no markup to cover an intermediary's profit or expenses. An intermediary, such as a broker, sells an insurance product net; that is, there is no loading for his own cost of soliciting business or his profit margin.

FOLLOWING FORM written form which has precisely the same terms as the other PROPERTY INSURANCE policies covering a particular property.

FOREIGN CREDIT INSURANCE ASSOCIATION *see* EXPORT-IMPORT BANK.

FOREIGN INSURER insurance company whose domicile is in a state other than the one in which the company is writing business.

FORFEITURE relinquishment of rights in an insurance policy or pension plan. For example, by withdrawing contributions to a pension plan, an employee forfeits future retirement benefits under that plan.

FORFEITURE OF VESTED BENEFITS relinquishment of rights to benefits when an employee withdraws previous contributions to a plan. An employee who had not withdrawn these contributions would have been entitled to full benefits at normal retirement age, or to a reduced benefit at early retirement, whether or not he or she is in the service of the employer at that time.

FORGERY BOND *see* DEPOSITORS FORGERY INSURANCE.

FORM attachment to an insurance policy to complete its coverage. For example, the *Standard Fire Policy* must have certain forms attached for it to provide the coverage desired.

FORM NO. 1 (BASIC OR STANDARD), HOMEOWNERS INSURANCE POLICY *see* HOMEOWNERS INSURANCE POLICY—SECTION I (PROPERTY COVERAGE).

FORM NO. 2 (BROAD), HOMEOWNERS INSURANCE POLICY *see* HOMEOWNERS INSURANCE POLICY—SECTION I (PROPERTY COVERAGE).

FORM NO. 3 (SPECIAL), HOMEOWNERS INSURANCE POLICY *see* HOMEOWNERS INSURANCE POLICY—SECTION I (PROPERTY COVERAGE).

FORM NO. 4 (CONTENTS BROAD FORM), HOMEOWNERS INSURANCE POLICY *see* HOMEOWNERS INSURANCE POLICY—SECTION I (PROPERTY COVERAGE).

FORM NO. 6 (CONDOMINIUM UNIT OWNER'S FORM), HOME-OWNERS INSURANCE POLICY *see* HOMEOWNERS INSURANCE POLICY—SECTION I (PROPERTY COVERAGE).

FORM 5500 form that reports the status and activity of retirement plans to the Internal Revenue Service (IRS). The IRS uses this form to determine whether a retirement plan is in compliance with all requirements. Form 5500 must be filed with the IRS by the last day of the seventh month following the plan's year-end.

FORTUITOUS EVENT *see* FORTUITOUS LOSS.

FORTUITOUS LOSS loss occurring by accident or chance, not by anyone's intention. Insurance policies provide coverage against losses which occur only on a chance basis, where the insured cannot control the loss; thus the insured should not be able to burn down his/her own home and collect. Insurance is not provided against a certainty such as wear and tear. Life insurance will not pay a death benefit if the insured commits suicide within the first two years that the policy is in force. Even though death is a certainty, the insured cannot buy a policy with the intention of suicide within the first two years.

FORTY-FIVE YEAR RULE one of three ways vesting must occur in a pension plan under the EMPLOYEE RETIREMENT INCOME SECURITY ACT OF 1974 (ERISA). An employee is entitled to 50% of his or her benefits after 10 years of employment, or when the total years of service (at least 5) and the employee's age equal 45, whichever is the earlier achieved. After that, the employee is credited with 10% for each year of service for the next 5 years, whereupon 100% vesting is achieved. Under the TAX REFORM ACT OF 1986, this vesting rule will no longer be in effect for plan years after December 31, 1988. *See also* VESTING.

FPA *see* FREE OF PARTICULAR AVERAGE (FPA).

FRACTIONAL PREMIUM annual premium expressed on a proportionate basis such as monthly, quarterly, or semiannually.

FRANCHISE DEDUCTIBLE stipulation that no claim will be paid until a loss exceeds a flat dollar amount or a given percentage of the amount of insurance in force. After the loss exceeds this dollar amount or percentage amount, the insurance company pays 100% of the claim loss.

FRANCHISE INSURANCE (WHOLESALE INSURANCE) coverage for small groups that cannot meet the underwriting standards of *true group* insurance. Even though the franchise insurance covers an entire group, individual policies are written on each insured person, each having the right to different coverage than other members. Usually sold to employer groups.

FRATERNAL LIFE INSURANCE group coverage for members of a fraternal association, usually on a nonprofit basis.

FRAUD dishonest act. Coverage for loss by fraud (not liability for committing fraud) is provided under the various bonds and crime insurance policies. *See also* FIDELITY BOND.

FRAUDULENT CLAIM demand without foundation, such as a claim submitted to an insurance company by an insured who caused a loss, or for a loss that never occurred.

FRAUDULENT MISREPRESENTATION dishonest statement to induce an insurance company to write coverage on an applicant. If the company knew the truth it would not accept the applicant. Fraudulent misrepresentation gives a property and casualty company grounds to terminate a policy at any time. A life insurance company, on the other hand, can terminate a policy on the grounds of fraudulent misrepresentation only during its first two years; after that, the INCONTESTABLE CLAUSE takes effect.

FREE EXAMINATION "FREE LOOK" PERIOD right, in most states, of an insured to have 10 days in which to examine an insurance policy, and if not satisfied, to return it to the company for a full refund of the initial premium.

FREE LOOK PERIOD *see* FREE EXAMINATION "FREE LOOK" PERIOD.

FREE-OF-CAPTURE-AND-SEIZURE CLAUSE exclusion of coverage in marine insurance if damage or destruction of property results from war, capture, or seizure.

FREE OF PARTICULAR AVERAGE (FPA) marine insurance contract clause which limits an insurance company's liability. The company agrees to pay only losses which exceed a percentage or flat dollar amount; partial (below this percentage or amount) losses are not paid. In essence, the principle is like the DEDUCTIBLE feature of other policies.

FREE TRADE ZONE geographical area in which commerce can be conducted without tariffs being applied. The concept was adopted in insurance through the use of a REINSURANCE FACILITY for buying and selling of insurance coverages without a premium tax being applied.

FREEZING OF SUPPLEMENTAL LIABILITY procedure whereby there is no amortization of the employer's liability for the supplemental cost of an employee's future benefits to be paid at retirement. *See also* INDIVIDUAL LEVEL COST METHOD WITH SUPPLEMENTAL LIABILITY.

FREIGHT INSURANCE coverage for goods during shipment on a common carrier. *See also* CARGO INSURANCE.

FREQUENCY number of times a loss occurs.

FREQUENCY AND DISTRIBUTION OF LOSSES number of times losses occur, and their severity. These statistics measure expectation of loss, and are critical in establishing a basic premium or the pure cost of protection which is based on expectation of loss.

FRIENDLY FIRE kindling intentionally set in a fireplace, stove, furnace, or other containment which has not spread beyond it. Property insurance does not protect against damage from a friendly fire. For example, smoke damage to the inside of a fireplace is not covered because the fire is in its normal habitat; to insure it would be insuring against a certainty. Insurance is designed to provide coverage against the fortuitous loss. *See also* HOSTILE FIRE.

FRONTING (FRONTING COMPANY) procedure under which the CEDING COMPANY (the primary or fronting company) cedes the risk it has underwritten to its *reinsurer* with the ceding company retaining none or a very small portion of that risk for its own account. *See also* REINSURANCE.

FRONTING COMPANY *see* FRONTING (FRONTING COMPANY).

FRONT LOADING expenses added to the beginning of a premium payment period. For example, an annuity with a 10% front load would include $10 of expenses for each $100 premium paid.

FROZEN KEOGH PLAN plan to which contributions are not being made, but which has not been formally terminated. The freezing of a KEOGH PLAN (HR-10) may occur in the following circumstances:
1. self-employed person stops contributing to the plan.
2. personal corporation is dissolved and stops contributing to the plan even though the employee of the personal corporation may continue in the same occupation.
3. self-employed person under the original plan may form a partnership or incorporate, necessitating the freezing of the original plan and the establishment of a new plan.
   Owners of a frozen plan must make sure the plan continues to conform to current regulations and continue to file annually FORM 5500. Annual administrative costs may be saved by terminating the frozen plan and rolling over its assets into a currently active qualified plan.

FSA *see* FELLOW, SOCIETY OF ACTUARIES (FSA).

FSLIC *see* FEDERAL SAVINGS AND LOAN CORPORATION (FSLIC).

FTZ *see* FREE TRADE ZONE.

FULL COVERAGE all insured losses paid in full.

FULL PRELIMINARY TERM RESERVE PLAN method of valuing a reserve under which a life insurance policy, from an actuarial point of view, combines one-year term insurance and a one-year deferred plan. Here the net premium is sufficient only to pay first-year death claims. For example, a 10-pay life insurance policy issued at age 30 would be viewed actuarially, for full preliminary term reserve plan purposes, as one-year term insurance at age 30 plus a nine-pay policy issued at age 30 but deferred to age 31.

FULL PRELIMINARY TERM RESERVE VALUATION mathematical combination of one-year term insurance and one-year deferred permanent insurance such that no reserve has to be set up for the first year the policy is in force and allowance is made for adjustment in future reserves to reflect this one-year lag.

FULL REPORTING CLAUSE provision in commercial property coverage under which an insured must report the value of an insured property at periodic intervals in order to preserve coverage up to values reported. In essence, this clause requires the insured to maintain total insurance to the value of the property, or 100% coinsurance. If the insured maintains less than the 100% requirement and a loss takes place, only a portion of that loss will be paid. *See also* COINSURANCE.

FULL VALUATION RESERVE method of valuing a reserve under which no reserve is established for a life insurance policy at the end of the first policy year, but reserves are established at the end of the second policy year. This approach enables the company to have more funds available during the first policy year to pay the expenses associated with selling the policy. *See also* FULL PRELIMINARY TERM RESERVE PLAN.

FULL VESTING entitlement to pension benefits without a reduction, even though an employee is no longer in the service of an employer at retirement. For example, under the TEN YEAR VESTING rule, an employee who has worked 10 years for an employer is automatically credited with future retirement benefits. *See also* VESTING, CONDITIONAL.

FULLY INSURED STATUS provision in Social Security: to receive retirement monthly income, a participant must have earned income on which Social Security taxes were paid for at least 10 years or 40 quarters.

FULLY PAID POLICY limited pay whole life policy under which all premium payments have been made. For example, a 20 pay policy is completely paid for after 20 payments; no future premiums have to be made and the policy remains in full force for the life of the insured.

FUNDAMENTAL basic requirements of an employee benefit insurance plan such as minimum age and years of service with an employer.

FUNDED PENSION PLAN plan in which funds are currently allocated to purchase retirement benefits. An employee is thus assured of receiving retirement payments even if the employer is no longer in business at the time the employee retires. *See also* ALLOCATED FUNDING INSTRUMENT.

FUNDED RETIREMENT PLAN *see* FUNDED PENSION PLAN.

FUNDING allocation of funds in a retirement plan. *See also* ALLOCATED FUNDING INSTRUMENT.

FUNDING STANDARD ACCOUNT approach in pension plan funding under which a separate account is maintained for comparing actual contributions to the plan with the minimum contributions required to meet future employee benefit liabilities. This account acts as a reservoir in that it can store excess contributions above the minimum required. It also allows excess contributions to accumulate at interest and then applies these accrued contributions to reduce the minimum required future contributions.

FUNDS PAID IN ADVANCE TO COVER EXPENSES *see* RAIN INSURANCE.

FUNERAL INSURANCE modest life insurance coverage to pay burial expenses upon the death of an insured.

FUR AND JEWELRY FLOATER coverage on an ALL RISKS basis for loss or damage to fur and jewelry at any location. Furs and jewelry must be scheduled in order to be covered.

FURRIER'S BLOCK INSURANCE coverage for furs owned by a furrier, or a customer's furs in the care, custody, and control of the furrier. Coverage is on an ALL RISKS basis except those specifically excluded: wear and tear; war, delay; loss of market; flood; earthquake; loss or damage while furs are being worn by the insured or his/her representatives; loss resulting from infidelity of any person under the care, custody, and control of the insured; damage or destruction of the furs after it leaves the care, custody, and control of the insured which has been sold under an installment contract; and mysterious disappearance.

FURRIERS CUSTOMERS POLICY coverage on an ALL RISKS basis for fur garments belonging to customers of a furrier. *See also* FURRIERS BLOCK INSURANCE.

FURS INSURANCE coverage on fur coats as well as other clothes which have fur trim. Protection is provided at any location on an ALL RISKS basis subject to the exclusions of wear and tear, war, and nuclear disaster. Each item must be specifically listed in the policy.

FUTURE SERVICE BENEFITS retirement payments to be credited for future years of service with an employer.

FUTURES TIED TO REINSURANCE futures contracts based on automobile and health REINSURANCE policies to be traded on the Commodity Future Exchange of the Chicago Board of Trade. The purpose is to allow insurance companies in the United States and abroad to use these futures contracts to hedge against losses on automobile and health policies that the companies underwrite. At the expiration point of the 3-month-long futures contract, certificates of reinsurance (showing evidence of the existence and terms of a particular policy or policies) are issued to the remaining contract holders. After all the claims have been paid, the reinsurance certificates are redeemed for an amount equal to the net earned premium. *See also* FINANCIAL REINSURANCE; AUTOMATIC NONPROPORTIONAL REINSURANCE; AUTOMATIC PROPORTIONAL REINSURANCE; AUTOMATIC REINSURANCE; EXCESS OF LOSS REINSURANCE; FACULTATIVE REINSURANCE; NONPROPORTIONAL REINSURANCE; PROPORTIONAL REINSURANCE; QUOTA SHARE REINSURANCE; STOP LOSS REINSURANCE; SURPLUS REINSURANCE.

G

GAMBLING INSURANCE *see* WAGERING AND INSURANCE.

GARAGE INSURANCE coverage for bodily injury, property damage or destruction, for which the insured garage and/or its representatives become legally liable resulting from the operation of the garage. For example, negligent repair to a customer's automobile brakes cause them to fail, thereby injuring the driver. The garage faces a liability suit for perhaps three types of damages: special, general, and punitive.

GENERAL ADJUSTMENT BUREAU (GAB) national agency supported by property insurance companies. The bureau is used by companies which do not have their own claims adjusters.

GENERAL AGENCY SYSTEM means of distribution that uses general agents rather than branch offices to sell life and health insurance. *See also* GENERAL AGENT (GA).

GENERAL AGENT (GA) individual responsible for insurance agency operation in a particular area, including sale of life and health insurance, servicing policies already sold, recruiting and training agents, and providing administrative support. General agents are compensated on a commission basis and usually pay all expenses of administering their agencies.

GENERAL AGENTS AND MANAGERS CONFERENCE (GAMC) association of general agents and managers affiliated with the NATIONAL ASSOCIATION FOR LIFE UNDERWRITING (NALU). Their objective is to seek solutions to common managerial problems. GAMC provides a forum for exchange of ideas and gives awards for outstanding performance by members.

GENERAL AVERAGE expenses and damages incurred as the result of damage to a ship and its cargo and/or of taking direct action to prevent initial or further damage to the ship and its cargo. These expenses and damages are paid by those with an interest in the ship and its cargo in proportion to their values exposed to the common danger. Contrast with PARTICULAR AVERAGE.

GENERAL CHARACTERISTICS attributes of a particular employee benefit plan. For example, a general characteristic of group life insurance is that the whole group is underwritten, not individual members.

GENERAL CONSIDERATIONS *see* GENERAL CHARACTERISTICS.

GENERAL DAMAGES *see* LIABILITY, CIVIL DAMAGES AWARDED.

GENERAL LIABILITY INSURANCE coverage for an insured when negligent acts and/or omissions result in bodily injury and/or property damage on the premises of a business, when someone is injured as the result of using the product manufactured or distributed by a business, or when someone is injured in the general operation of a business.

GENERALLY ACCEPTED ACCOUNTING PRINCIPLES (GAAP) type of accounting method, in life insurance, designed to match revenues and expenses of an insurer according to principles designed by the *Financial Accounting Standards Board* and the *Audit Guide for Stock Life Insurance Companies* published by the American Institute of CPAs. For example, under GAAP, acquisition expenses (costs of placing insurance on a company's books such as administrative expenses and agent commissions) are recognized in the same proportion that premium income is recognized over the premium paying period, with losses subtracted from premium and investment income as they occur.

GENERAL OPERATING EXPENSE costs incurred by an insurance company other than agent commissions and taxes; that is, mainly the administrative expense of running a company.

GENERAL PROPERTY FORM attachment to a property business insurance policy providing coverage for a business structure and any additions and/or extensions; merchandise and other stock and inventory within the structure (not including animals, pets, watercraft, outdoor trees, shrubs, and plants, outdoor signs, fences, and swimming pools); personal property of the insured while in the insured structure and within 100 feet of the premises; and personal property of a third party under the safekeeping of the insured in the insured structure and within 100 feet of the premises. The General Property Form Provides coverage in three ways:
1. *Specific*—an amount of insurance is provided on a specified piece of property.
2. *Schedule*—an amount of insurance is provided on several specified pieces of property listed in the policy.
3. *Blanket*—an amount of insurance is provided on several different kinds of property, several different locations, or a combination of several different kinds of property at several different locations.

GEOGRAPHICAL LIMITATION *see* TERRITORIAL LIMITS.

GIFT transfer of property without payment.

GIFT IN TRUST value or property given by an individual to a *trustee* who holds and administers it for the benefit of the donee (recipient of the gift). For example, a father entrusts a life insurance policy with all ownership rights to a trustee. The trustee owns the policy, collects the proceeds, and administers the proceeds for the benefit of the donee son. *See also* ESTATE PLANNING DISTRIBUTION.

GIFT OUTRIGHT value or property given by an individual directly to a donee (recipient of the gift), for example, when a father gives a life insurance policy with all ownership rights to his son. *See also* ESTATE PLANNING DISTRIBUTION.

GIFT TAX tax, under Federal and State laws, on transfer of property made without payment or other value in exchange.

GLASS INSURANCE *see* COMPREHENSIVE GLASS INSURANCE.

GLASS-STEAGALL ACT (BANKING ACT OF 1933) legislation excluding commercial banks that are members of the Federal Reserve System from most types of investment banking activities. The coauthor of the Act, Senator Carter Glass of Virginia, believed that commercial banks should restrict their activities to involvement in short-term loans to coincide with the nature of their primary classification of liabilities, demand deposits. Today, many in the banking field view these constraints as particularly burdensome because of increased competition from other financial institutions for customers' savings and investment dollars.

GOLFERS EQUIPMENT INSURANCE coverage for golf clubs and golf equipment on an ALL RISKS basis subject to exclusions of wear and tear, war, and nuclear disaster. Location of coverage is a clubhouse locker or any other building used in golf activities. For example, if a golfer's clubs were in the locker in the clubhouse and they were stolen, the golfer would be indemnified. There is usually no coinsurance requirement and coverage is provided on a replacement cost basis.

GOOD SAMARITAN COVERAGE *see* HOMEOWNERS INSURANCE POLICY—SECTION II (LIABILITY COVERAGE).

GOOD STUDENT DISCOUNT reduction in automobile insurance rate for a student with a good academic record. Some statistical studies suggest that good students have fewer automobile accidents.

GOODWILL monetary value of the reputation of a business. Goodwill is an intangible asset and thus may be difficult to measure.

GOVERNMENT INSURANCE coverage under the auspices of a Federal or state agency which can be either mandatory or elective. *See also* SOCIAL INSURANCE.

GOVERNMENT LIFE INSURANCE coverage for present and past U.S. uniformed services members under one of these programs:

1. *United States Government Life Insurance (USGLI)*—established in 1919 to provide RENEWABLE TERM LIFE INSURANCE up to $10,000. This program is no longer available.
2. *National Service Life Insurance (NSLI)*—established in 1940 to take the place of USGLI; terminated in 1950. Today NSLI exists for amounts ranging from $1000 to $10,000 under five year renewable term and permanent forms of life insurance. The latter policies have the same *nonforfeiture benefits* and OPTIONAL MODES OF SETTLEMENT as COMMERCIAL FORMS of life insurance.
3. SERVICEMEN'S GROUP LIFE INSURANCE (SGLI)—established in 1965 to cover active members of the U.S. uniformed forces; purchased through *commercial insurance companies* on a group basis at a government subsidized rate. Each service person pays a premium which reflects nonmilitary mortality expectation and administrative expenses. The Federal government subsidizes the premium by paying for any extra mortality and administrative expenses associated with the military exposure. Upon discharge, a SGLI policy can be converted, regardless of physical condition, to a five-year nonrenewable Veterans Group Life Policy (VGLI), and then can be converted (after five years)—again regardless of health—to an individual life policy with any of the participating commercial life insurance companies.
4. VETERANS GROUP LIFE INSURANCE (VGLI)—nonrenewable convertible 5-year term insurance to which SGLI is converted at the time a service person is discharged. It has no cash or loan value, disability benefits, paid-up benefits, or extended term benefits. It can be converted to an individual policy with a participating company.

GRACE PERIOD period after the date the premium is due during which the premium can be paid with no interest charged, the policy remaining in force. This period is for 30 or 31 days. If the insured dies during this period, the beneficiary would receive the full face amount of the policy minus the premium owed. Thus the use of the grace period allows the financial technique of leveraging.

GRADED *see* GRADED COMMISSION; GRADED DEATH BENEFIT; GRADED PREMIUM, WHOLE LIFE INSURANCE.

GRADED COMMISSION compensation that varies with the class and type insurance sold. Many insurance companies offer varying commissions according to the volume of business an agent places with the company.

GRADED DEATH BENEFIT death payment that increases with the age of an insured. Graded benefits may increase gradually and then level off, or may increase sharply before becoming level. This type of coverage is most common in juvenile life insurance.

GRADED POLICY insurance for which premiums are charged according to the size of the FACE AMOUNT of the policy, so that the greater the face amount, the lower the cost per $1,000 unit of insurance.

GRADED PREMIUM, WHOLE LIFE INSURANCE coverage under which initial premiums are less than normal for the first few years, then gradually increase for the next several years until they become level for the duration of the policy.

GRADUATED LIFE TABLE MORTALITY TABLE which reflects irregularities from age to age due to chance fluctuations in the sequence of the rates of mortality. The rates of death as reflected by the mortality table in its most idealized form (the ''perfect world'' approach) should proceed smoothly from age bracket to subsequent age bracket. Irregularities may result from:
1. statistical fluctuations due to an insufficiently large data base.
2. use of statistics that are not homogeneous.
3. statistics of one particular mortality study not representing other mortality studies.
4. mortality statistics for later policy years too scanty to yield reliable information, and too heavily weighted towards the earlier policy years.

GRADUATED MORTALITY TABLE *see* GRADUATED LIFE TABLE.

GRANT OF LIMITED PROPERTY INTEREST *see* ESTATE PLANNING DISTRIBUTION.

GRANTOR individual who creates a TRUST and generally places his or her assets in it.

GRANTOR-RETAINED INCOME TRUST (GRIT) irrevocable TRUST into which the GRANTOR places assets and retains the income from or the use of these assets for a stipulated period of time. At the termination of this time period, the principal (assets) of the trust is transferred to the grantor's noncharitable BENEFICIARY. The noncharitable beneficiary may include individual(s) such as a grandchild, niece, nephew, son, or daughter. Should the grantor survive the stipulated period of time, he or she will incur substantial savings in estate and gift taxes. In order for these savings in taxes to occur, the following requirements must be met by the grantor:
1. income to the grantor must be the sale result of the income generated by assets held in the trust.
2. any income generated by the assets held in the trust can be paid only to the grantor of the trust.
3. neither the grantor nor the spouse of the grantor can act as a trustee of the trust.

4. any income retained by the grantor must be for a period of time not to exceed 10 years.

Should the grantor die before the stipulated period of time the trust expires, the value of the assets of the trust are included in the grantor's estate for FEDERAL ESTATE TAX purposes, even though the assets are not physically transferred to the estate of the grantor. *See also* SUPERGRIT.

GROSS *see* GROSS EARNINGS FORM; GROSS INCOME; GROSS PREMIUM.

GROSS EARNINGS FORM coverage for loss in the gross earnings of the business (minus expenses that cease while the business is inoperative) as the result of the interruption of normal business activities caused by damage to the premises by an insured peril. Noncontinuing expenses include light, gas, and advertising for which there is no contractual obligation. Coverage can be obtained on either a 50, 60, 70, or 80% coinsurance basis. Selection of the coinsurance percentage is dependent upon the length of time business is expected not to operate in the worst of circumstances.

GROSS INCOME total income before adjustment for deduction as applied to tax calculation for both the individual and the firm.

GROSS LINE total limit on the amount of coverage an INSURER will underwrite on an individual RISK. The amount underwritten includes the amount to be CEDED through a REINSURANCE agreement.

GROSS NEGLIGENCE reckless action without regard to life, limb, and/ or property, for example, driving 100 miles per hour on a road or highway.

GROSS PREMIUM
General: net premium, plus operating and miscellaneous expenses, and agent's commissions.
Life insurance: premium before dividends are subtracted.

GROUP ANNUITY contract providing a monthly income benefit to members of a group of employees. A group annuity has the same characteristics as an individual annuity, except that it is underwritten on a group basis. *See also* ANNUITY.

GROUP CERTIFICATE summary certificate of benefits issued to an employee in lieu of a policy. The master contract remains with the employer. For example, in group life insurance, an employee receives only a summary certificate of benefits, while the master contract remains with the employer.

GROUP CONTRACT *see* GROUP INSURANCE.

GROUP CREDIT INSURANCE coverage issued to a creditor on the lives of debtors for outstanding loans. If a debtor dies before repayment, the policy pays the remainder of the loan to the creditor. The contract covers an entire group of debtors, rather than each debtor separately.

GROUP CREDITOR INSURANCE *see* CREDIT LIFE INSURANCE (CREDITOR LIFE INSURANCE); GROUP CREDIT INSURANCE.

GROUP DEFERRED ANNUITY contract for retirements benefits in which an entire group of employees is underwritten, as opposed to a single annuity for each employee. Each premium pays for an increment of a paid-up annuity; thus a group deferred annuity is a series of single premium paid-up annuities. It may be considered an ALLOCATED FUNDING INSTRUMENT for purchasing retirement benefits. Single premium paid-up annuities that have already been purchased guarantee that an employee will receive retirement income whether or not the employer remains in business at the time he retires.

GROUP DEPOSIT ADMINISTRATION ANNUITY *see* PENSION PLAN FUNDING: GROUP DEPOSIT ADMINISTRATION ANNUITY.

GROUP DISABILITY INSURANCE coverage of an employee group whose members receive a monthly disability income benefit, subject to a maximum amount, if illness or accident prevents a member from performing the normal functions of his job. Benefits are usually limited to a stated length of time, and the maximum monthly income benefit is usually no more than 50-60% of earnings prior to the disability, or a flat dollar amount, whichever is less.

GROUP HEALTH INSURANCE coverage underwritten on members of a natural group, such as employees of a particular business, union, association, or employer group. Each employee is entitled to benefits for hospital room and board, surgeon and physician fees, and miscellaneous medical expenses. There is a DEDUCTIBLE and a COINSURANCE requirement each employee must pay. Characteristics of group health insurance include:
1. TRUE GROUP PLAN—one in which all employees must be accepted for coverage regardless of physical condition. (For example, coverage cannot be denied because of a pre-existing condition such as cancer.) Usually an employee must apply and pay the first premium within the first 30 days of employment or he/she forfeits the right to automatic coverage (a form of GUARANTEED INSURABILITY). Individuals are covered under a MASTER CONTRACT, each receiving a certificate denoting coverage.
2. *Schedule of Benefits*—describes what the insured and his/her covered dependent(s) is entitled to in the event of disease, illness, or injury. After the insured or the covered dependent has satisfied the DEDUCTIBLE (defined as the first portion of all of the eligible expenses which

occur during a calendar year of coverage), the insurance company pays a given percentage (usually 80%) until a total sum (*stop loss*), usually $5000, is reached for the calendar year. After the total sum has been reached, the insurance company pays 100% of the total eligible expenses until the end of the calendar year subject to a maximum lifetime amount. *See also* DEPENDENT.

3. *Eligible Expenses*—include hospital bills, surgery, doctor's services, private nursing, medicines, and X-rays. Payment allowed for these and other expenses are spelled out in the policy. For example, the hospital's daily charge for room and board is subject to a specified maximum.

4. *Exclusions from Provisions of Medical Benefits*—many exclusions occur in group health plans, including benefits under Workers Compensation; certain mouth conditions; convalescent or rest cures; expenses incurred by a member of a HEALTH MAINTENANCE ORGANIZATION (HMO) or other prepaid medical plan; expenses associated with intentional self-inflicted injuries or attempt at suicide.

5. COORDINATION OF BENEFITS—when there are two or more group health insurance plans covering the insured one plan becomes the *Primary Plan* and the other plan(s) becomes the *Secondary Plan(s)*. *The Primary Plan* is required to pay benefits due the insured and/or covered dependents before any other plan pays benefits. When a claim is made, the primary plan must pay the claim without regard to the benefits provided under any other plan. The secondary plan pays the difference between the total claim amount and the amount which the primary plan has paid, up to total allowable expenses.

GROUP IMMEDIATE PARTICIPATION GUARANTEED ANNU-ITY *see* PENSION PLAN FUNDING; GROUP IMMEDIATE PARTICIPATION GUARANTEED (IPG) CONTRACT ANNUITY.

GROUP INSURANCE single policy under which individuals in a natural group (such as employees of a business firm) and their dependents are covered. *See also* GROUP ANNUITY; GROUP CERTIFICATE; GROUP CREDIT INSURANCE; GROUP DEFERRED ANNUITY; GROUP DISABILITY INSURANCE; GROUP HEALTH INSURANCE; GROUP LIFE INSURANCE; GROUP PAID-UP LIFE INSURANCE; GROUP PERMANENT LIFE INSURANCE; GROUP TERM LIFE INSURANCE; PENSION PLAN FUNDING; GROUP DEPOSIT ADMINISTRATION ANNUITY.

GROUP LIFE INSURANCE basic employee benefit under which an employer buys a master policy and issues certificates to employees denoting participation in the plan. Group life is also available through unions and associations. It is usually issued as yearly renewable term insurance although some plans provide permanent insurance. Employers may pay all the cost, or share it with employees. Characteristics include:

1. *Group Underwriting*—an entire group of employees is underwritten, unlike individual life insurance whereunder only the individual is underwritten.

2. *Guaranteed Issue*—every employee must be accepted; an employee cannot be denied coverage because of a pre-existing illness, sickness, or injury.

3. *Conversion at Termination of Employment*—regardless of whether termination is because of severance, disability, or retirement, the employee has the automatic right to convert to an individual life policy without evidence of insurability or taking a physical examination. Conversion must be within 30 days of termination. The premium upon conversion is based on the employee's age at the time (ATTAINED AGE).

4. DISABILITY BENEFIT—available in many policies to an employee less than 60 years of age who can no longer work because of the disability. The benefit takes the form of waiver of premium, and the employee is covered for as long as the disability continues. The beneficiary will receive the death benefit even though the employee may not have been in the service of the employer for a long time.

5. DEATH BENEFIT Structure or Schedule—is usually based on an employee's earnings. The benefit is a multiple of the employee's earnings, normally 1 to $2\frac{1}{2}$ times the employee's yearly earnings. In many companies if the employee dies while on company business, 6 times the yearly earnings are paid as a death benefit. For example, a $50,000 a year employee dies in an accident while traveling on company time; the beneficiary would receive $300,000. But if the same employee died in his sleep at home, the beneficiary would receive $100,000 (assuming that the normal death benefit is twice annual earnings).

GROUP OF COMPANIES *see* FLEET OF COMPANIES.

GROUP PAID-UP LIFE INSURANCE combination of two basic plans: (1) accumulating units of paid-up permanent life insurance, and (2) decreasing units of group term life insurance. The premium paid each month consists of the (a) employee's contribution and (b) employer's contribution. The employee's portion purchases increments of paid-up insurance and the employer's portion purchases group decreasing term. The employer's contribution is tax deductible as a business expense and these contributions are not taxable income to the employee. (However, if the employer purchases increments of paid-up units of permanent insurance, these contributions are taxable income to the employee on a current basis.) Paid-up units purchased by an employee are vested and thus can be taken as a paid-up life benefit regardless of the reason for termination of employment. The paid-up benefit will always remain in force; no further premium payments are required.

GROUP PERMANENT *see* GROUP PERMANENT LIFE INSURANCE.

GROUP PERMANENT LIFE INSURANCE coverage following the same structure as *group term*, the significant difference being that premiums go toward the purchase of permanent insurance instead of term insurance. The employee has a vested interest in the increments of paid-up insurance purchased. Because of the tax consequences to the employee, group permanent insurance usually is applied to fund retirement plans such as pensions instead of providing life insurance coverage. If the employer purchased permanent insurance on the employee's behalf, the contributions would become taxable income to the employee on a current basis. Group life insurance is *experience rated*, in that the loss experience of the entire group determines the premium rate applied to each employee.

GROUP TERM LIFE INSURANCE one-year coverage that is renewable at the end of each year. Since the group plan is subject to EXPERIENCE RATING, the premium rate upon renewal is based on such factors as the loss record (death) of the group and range of employee ages. All employees are insured with term life insurance. Realistically, coverage is temporary because on termination of employment, the employee usually does not convert group term to individual permanent insurance because the conversion is at a higher attained age rate. *See also* ATTAINED AGE.

GROWTH OF ASSETS rate of increase in asset value.

GUARANTEED COST PREMIUM premium charged for an insurance policy whose coverage does not vary according to the insured loss experience. The premium is calculated either on a specified rating basis or on a prospective basis (fixed or adjustable).

GUARANTEED INSURABILITY right of an insured to make additional purchases of life insurance without having to take a physical examination or show other evidence of insurability. Additions can be bought at (1) stated times; (2) upon specified policy anniversaries such as every fifth year of a policy up to a maximum age (usually 40 or 45); or (3) upon the birth of a child. Many young families should consider adding this option, since a likely time to add to a life insurance portfolio is when family obligations increase. *See also* RIDERS, LIFE POLICIES.

GUARANTEED INVESTMENT CONTRACT (GIC) institutional investment sold by life insurance companies that guarantees principal and offers withdrawal flexibility. This conservative investment, which can be used with a corporate qualified plan, became one of the most popular choices in such *salary reduction plans* as the 401 (k) plan. Many of these plans offered employees three choices for depositing their pre-tax retirement dollars: a stock fund, a bond fund and a GIC. By 1987, about 40% of employees had elected GIC investments.

GUARANTEED ISSUE the right to purchase insurance without physical examination; the present and past physical condition of the applicant are not considered.

GUARANTEED PURCHASE OPTION *see* GUARANTEED INSURABILITY.

GUARANTEED RENEWABLE CONTRACT (LIFE OR HEALTH) insurance policy renewable at the option of the insured for a specified number of years or to a stated age. The insurance company cannot refuse to renew the policy and cannot change any of its provisions except the PREMIUM RATE. If the insurance company changes the premium it must do so for the entire policyholder classification, not just for one or a few members. *See* GUARANTEED INSURABILITY.

GUARANTEED RENEWABLE HEALTH INSURANCE *see* COMMERCIAL HEALTH INSURANCE.

GUARANTEES, LACK OF *see* UNALLOCATED FUNDING INSTRUMENT.

GUARANTOR term in surety coverage. Through the issue of a surety bond, a surety company is in effect the guarantor. *See also* SURETY BOND.

GUARANTY FUND (INSOLVENCY FUND) aggregate sums, in certain states, to pay claims of insolvent insurance companies. These funds are maintained by contributions of companies operating in a particular state in proportion to their business written in the state. A guaranty fund insures the integrity of the insurance business.

GUERTIN LAWS standard State Valuation and Nonforfeiture Law approved by the NATIONAL ASSOCIATION OF INSURANCE COMMISSIONERS (NAIC) in 1942. This law is named for Alfred N. Guertin, the actuary who headed the NAIC committee which studied the need for a new mortality table to be used in calculating life insurance nonforfeiture values. In essence, application of this law guarantees that an insured is entitled to all benefits for which the life insurance company has received premiums. The insured cannot be made to forfeit his equity built up in a life insurance product. *See also* NONFORFEITURE BENEFITS (OPTION).

GUEST LAW legal right of a passenger in an automobile involved in an accident to bring a liability suit against the driver. It is deemed that a special standard of care is owed by an automobile driver towards the passenger. This law bars suits only for ordinary—not gross or criminal—negligence. In many states such actions by a passenger are prohibited; in other states, intentional misconduct of the driver must be shown.

GUIDING PRINCIPLES title of a published set of rules, adhered to by member companies of major property and liability associations, which stipulate how losses should be adjusted when the same loss is covered by more than one insurance company. Particular emphasis is placed on how the cost of the losses should be apportioned among the companies under various situations.

H

HABITS behavior or character standing of an individual in a community. Some personal habits are considered in underwriting an insurance application.

HAIL INSURANCE coverage against hail damage to crops. Coverage is on a proportionate basis; that is, in the event of loss, a farmer will recover an amount based on the ratio of the damaged part of a crop to the entire crop.

HANGARKEEPERS LEGAL LIABILITY INSURANCE coverage for the owner of an airplane in circumstances where use of his premises as an aircraft hangar results in bodily injury or property damage to a third party. Excluded from coverage is property under the care, custody, and control of the insured. Another application of this policy covers the operator of a hangar for liability from damage to an aircraft that the owner has placed under his care, custody, and control for storage or repair.

HARDSHIP existence of a financial need which permits in-service withdrawals of funds from a SECTION 401 (k) PLAN or a SECTION 403 (b) PLAN to pay tuition for postsecondary education for a participant or his or her spouse, children, or other dependents.

HAZARD circumstance that increases the likelihood or probable severity of a loss. For example, the storing of explosives in a home basement is a hazard that increases the probability of an explosion.

HAZARD INCREASE RESULTING IN SUSPENSION OR EXCLUSION OF COVERAGE provision commonly found in fire insurance contracts. If the insured knows that a hazard is increased, most property contracts permit the insurance company to suspend or terminate coverage. For example, manufacture of drugs in the home would give the insurance company the right to invoke this clause if it could show that the manufacturing process increases the probability of fire. *See also* LOSSES PAID.

HAZARD, MORAL *see* MORAL HAZARD.

HAZARD, MORALE *see* MORALE HAZARD.

HAZARD, PHYSICAL *see* HAZARD; INCREASED HAZARD.

HEAD OFFICE *see* HOME OFFICE.

HEALTH INSURANCE three basic plans are available to cover the costs of health care: COMMERCIAL HEALTH INSURANCE, *private noncommercial* (BLUE CROSS/BLUE SHIELD), and SOCIAL INSURANCE (*Social Security*). *See also* MEDICAID; MEDICARE; AND WORKERS COMPENSATION INSURANCE.

HEALTH INSURANCE ASSOCIATION OF AMERICA (HIAA) organization that seeks to educate the public on the benefits of private health insurance coverage. Its membership consists of private companies that sell health insurance. The HIAA publishes materials and lobbies Federal and state legislatures in an effort to support its objective. Based in Washington, D.C.

HEALTH INSURANCE CONTRACT policy that pays benefits to an insured who becomes ill or injured, provided that documentation is offered to confirm the illness or injury. *See also* DISABILITY INSURANCE; GROUP DISABILITY INSURANCE; GROUP HEALTH INSURANCE; HEALTH INSURANCE; HEALTH MAINTENANCE ORGANIZATION (HMO); SURGICAL EXPENSE INSURANCE.

HEALTH INSURANCE RENEWABILITY *see* HEALTH INSURANCE.

HEALTH MAINTENANCE ORGANIZATION (HMO) prepaid group health insurance plan which entitles members to services of participating physicians, hospitals, and clinics. Emphasis is on preventive medicine. Members of the HMO pay a flat periodic fee (usually deducted from each paycheck) for these medical services:
1. *HMO Managing Physician*—a new member can select an HMO physician, who is then responsible for providing all of his/her health care needs. If necessary, the managing physician makes arrangements for the member to see a specialist.
2. *HMO Copayment*—a member may be required to pay an amount in addition to required periodic payments, for example, a $5 flat fee for each visit regardless of how expensive the services may be. Or, for each prescription, to pay a flat amount of $2 regardless of the actual cost.
3. *HMO Hospital Services*—include, among others, room and board, operating room, laboratory tests, radiation, medications, and physical therapy.
4. *HMO Physicians and Surgeons Services in Hospital*—include surgeons and related medical specialists, with no copayment.
5. *HMO Outpatient Hospital Care*—members receive the same services that are provided under Inpatient Hospital Services, as authorized by the managing physician; there is no copayment.
6. *HMO Outpatient Health Services Provided at HMO Facility*—include physician services, preventive health services, diagnosis and treatment services, skilled nursing facility services, mental health

and/or alcohol and drug abuse services, dental care under specific circumstances, and emergency services in and out of the HMO area. A copayment may be required.

HMO exclusions include custodial care, experimental procedures, conveniences not medically related such as television, radio, and telephones, and cosmetic care except for medically necessary reconstruction.

HEINRICH, H. W. executive of Travelers Insurance Company who developed the DOMINO THEORY OF ACCIDENT CAUSATION by studying over 75,000 industrial accidents and concluding that most accidents would be preventable if only the acquired behavior of individuals could be changed. Heinrich held that extensive programs should be conducted by industrial companies to convince employees to act safely.

HIGHLY PROTECTED RISK exposures where action has been taken to reduce the frequency and severity of loss, such as adding sprinkler systems in public buildings. These actions may result in a significant reduction in the fire insurance premium.

HOBBIES OR AVOCATIONS activities of interest in underwriting an application for life insurance to determine the rate classification (premium) for the applicant. For example, a sky diver is at greater personal risk than average, and accordingly is charged a much higher premium for life insurance.

HOLD-HARMLESS AGREEMENTS assumption of liability through contractual agreement by one party, thereby eliminating liability on the part of another party. An example is a railroad sidetrack agreement with a manufacturing company under which the manufacturer is held harmless for damage to railroad equipment and tracks.

HOME OFFICE central (main) office of an insurance company whose facilities usually include actuarial, claims, investment, legal, underwriting, agency, and marketing departments.

HOME OFFICE LIFE UNDERWRITERS ASSOCIATION (HOLUA) organization of home office underwriters of life insurance companies. HOLUA offers educational material and national examinations for home office life underwriters, the individuals who evaluate applications for insurance, decide if an applicant meets the requirements of the company for issuing insurance, and determine the rate classification into which the applicant should be placed.

HOME OFFICE UNDERWRITER *see* UNDERWRITER LAY; UNDERWRITING; UNDERWRITING CYCLE; UNDERWRITING GAIN (OR LOSS).

HOMEOWNERS INSURANCE POLICY package policy that combines (1) coverage against the insured's property being destroyed or damaged by various perils, and (2) coverage for liability exposure of the insured.

Homeowners policies cover both individuals as well as property. In addition to the insured, those covered include his/her spouse, their relatives, and any others under 21 who are residents of the insured's household.

HOMEOWNERS INSURANCE POLICY—SECTION I (PROPERTY COVERAGE) section providing protection in four areas:

1. *Coverage A (Home)*—the structure of the home (basic contract amount). Other property coverages in Section I are expressed as a percentage of Coverage A.
2. *Coverage B (Garage or Appurtenant Private Structures)*—structures not attached to or part of the home, covered up to 10% of the basic home structure.
3. *Coverage C (Contents or Personal Property)*—coverage of 40 to 50% (depending on the form selected) of the structural coverage of the home for the contents or personal property in the home; coverage of up to 10% applies to contents away from the home. For example, a home whose value is $100,000 would have coverage on the contents of $50,000 (assuming 50 percent contents coverage); away from home contents coverage would be up to $5000.
4. *Coverage D (Additional Living Expenses)*—coverage if the home is damaged or destroyed and the insured must seek temporary lodging. Reimbursement is 10 to 20% of the structural coverage of the home, depending on the form selected.

   All four property coverages A, B, C, and D are offered through one of the following forms:
1. *Form No. 1 (Basic or Standard)*—coverage for fire, lightning, windstorm, hail, explosion, smoke, theft, vandalism, malicious mischief, riot, civil commotion, glass breakage, vehicles, and aircraft.
2. *Form No. 2 (Broad)*—coverage for a broader spectrum of perils than under Form No. 1.
3. *Form No. 3 (Special)*—provides that Coverage A (*Home*), Coverage B (*Garage or Appurtenant Private Structures*) and Coverage C (*Contents or Personal Property*) are insured on an ALL RISKS basis. This form is sometimes called "landlords and tenants insurance" since the building and garage or appurtenant private structure and contents are covered on an all risks basis. There are a number of exclusions under Form No. 3.
4. *Form No. 4 (Contents Broad Form)*—coverage only for the contents of a dwelling (Coverage C) and additional living expense (Coverage D) as the result of the perils listed in Form No. 2. This form is called the "renters form" since it does not cover damage to the structure of an apartment building, its garages or appurtenants.

5. *Form No. 6 (Condominium Unit Owners Form)*—provides the same coverage as Form No. 4 but extends coverage for damage to additions and/or alterations that the unit owner may have made inside the unit. Coverage goes into effect as an excess amount above that insurance (if any) that the condominium association may have.

Numerous endorsements can be added to each one of the above forms to increase the limits of coverage and the properties insured. For example, specified property such as jewelry, furs, silverware and guns can be added through a *valuable personal articles endorsement*. Also, an inflation guard endorsement (reflecting increases in the cost of construction) can be added to Coverage A, which automatically increases Coverages B, C, and D since they are expressed as a percentage of Coverage A.

The insured is obligated to take certain actions following a loss, including: notifying the company or agent immediately; if the loss is due to theft, notifying the police immediately; if credit cards are stolen, notifying the credit card company immediately; and protecting the property from further damage.

There is usually an 80% coinsurance requirement which means that the insured must carry insurance on a replacement cost basis of at least 80%. For example, a home is worth $200,000, and a fire does $50,000 damage. If the insured carries $150,000 of insurance, only $46,875 would be covered according to the following formula:

$$\frac{\text{Amount of Insurance Carried}}{\substack{\text{80\% Insurance to Value} \\ \text{Replacement Cost Basis}}} \times \text{Loss} = \text{Insured Reimbursement}$$

$$\frac{\$150,000}{\$160,000} \times \$50,000 = \$46,875$$

If however the insured had carried an 80% insurance to a value of $160,000, then the total loss of $50,000 would have been to the following formula:

$$\frac{\$160,000}{\$160,000} \times \$50,000 = \$50,000$$

HOMEOWNERS INSURANCE POLICY—SECTION II (LIABILITY COVERAGE) section providing protection under three coverages:

1. *Coverage E (Personal Liability)*—coverage in the event a suit is brought against the insured because of bodily injury and/or property damage resulting from the acts or non-acts of the insured. Also covers the insured's spouse, relatives of either, and others under age 21 under the insured's care. Just about any personal act is insured. For example, if the insured lives in Shreveport, Louisiana and hits someone with a tennis ball in a game in Hong Kong, the insured is covered against a possible lawsuit. The insurance company must also pay for the costs of defending the insured even if a suit has no reasonable basis. Defense costs are separate and in addition to the limits of liability in the policy. For example, if the limits of the policy are $100,000 and the defense costs are $200,000 the insurance company could have to pay a total of $300,000 on behalf of the insured. Once the insurance company pays the $100,000 limit in the policy, the insurance company's obligation to defend the insured any further ends. The basic liability limits are $100,000—the minimum amount stipulated in the policy. (For a relatively few dollars these limits can be increased substantially.)

2. *Coverage F (Medical Payments to Others)*—coverage for reimbursement of reasonable medical expenses incurred (a) by the insured (and individuals as defined in Coverage E, above); and (b) for injuries sustained by a third party either on or off of the insured's premises as a result of the activities of the insured and others covered. This is called "Good Samaritan Coverage" because by providing emergency medical expenses of an injured third party, the insured does not admit liability, nor does the injured third party relinquish his/her right to bring suit against the insured by accepting the medical aid.

3. *Coverage G (Damage to Property of Others)*—as with Coverage F, the insured is reimbursed for expenses incurred up to $250 regardless of legal liability for damage to the property of a third party. The insured and covered residents of the household make payment out of a feeling of moral responsibility for the damage to the property which may have the result of a liability suit not being brought.

HOME SERVICE AGENT *see* DEBIT AGENT (HOME SERVICE AGENT).

HOME SERVICE INDUSTRIAL INSURANCE *see* INDUSTRIAL LIFE INSURANCE.

HOME SERVICE LIFE INSURANCE *see* DEBIT INSURANCE (HOME SERVICE INSURANCE, INDUSTRIAL INSURANCE).

HOME SERVICE ORDINARY life insurance in which the *debit system* is used to collect premiums on a monthly basis. *See also* DEBIT INSURANCE (HOME SERVICE INSURANCE, INDUSTRIAL INSURANCE); ORDINARY LIFE INSURANCE.

HOMESTEAD RIGHT use of a home, and the land and buildings surrounding that home, free from the claim of creditors. This right gives rise to an INSURABLE INTEREST.

HOMOGENEITY *see* INSURABLE RISK.

HOMOGENEOUS EXPOSURES elements within a group under study that have the same characteristic(s), have the same EXPECTATION OF LOSS, are very much alike with respect to the variable under consideration, and do not show significant differences through any given time periods. Homogeneity of exposure units is extremely important to the accuracy of the prediction of future losses based on historical loss experience. For example, if an ACTUARY is going to predict the number of wood-frame houses likely to suffer a fire loss, the sample upon which the prediction is based should consist of wood-frame houses, not brick-frame houses.

HOSPICE facility which provides short periods of stay for a terminally ill person in a homelike setting for either direct care or respite. A "terminally ill" person has a life expectancy of six months or less. A hospice provides continuous care. Some health insurance plans pay benefits in full up to a maximum without a deductible for charges incurred for a terminally ill person while in a hospice care program Also provided is bereavement benefits up to a maximum (usually $200) per family unit.

HOSPITAL EXPENSE INSURANCE *see* GROUP HEALTH INSURANCE; HEALTH INSURANCE; HEALTH MAINTENANCE ORGANIZATION (HMO).

HOSPITAL INDEMNITY INSURANCE *see* GROUP HEALTH INSURANCE; HEALTH INSURANCE; HEALTH MAINTENANCE ORGANIZATION (HMO).

HOSPITALIZATION INSURANCE *see* GROUP HEALTH INSURANCE; HEALTH INSURANCE; HEALTH MAINTENANCE ORGANIZATION (HMO).

HOSPITAL LIABILITY INSURANCE form of insurance covering (1) liability arising out of the provision or nonprovision of hospital services so as to have an action brought against the hospital for malpractice, error, or mistake; (2) injuring of a patient by another patient; (3) food and other items resulting in injury to the patients; (4) injury to a person treated in an ambulance; and (5) costs to defend the hospital even if the suit is groundless.

HOSPITAL MEDICAL INSURANCE *see* GROUP HEALTH INSURANCE; HEALTH INSURANCE; HEALTH MAINTENANCE ORGANIZATION (HMO).

HOSPITAL SERVICES, HMO *see* HEALTH MAINTENANCE ORGANIZATION (HMO).

HOSPITAL, SURGICAL, AND MEDICAL EXPENSE INSURANCE *see* GROUP HEALTH INSURANCE; HEALTH INSURANCE; HEALTH MAINTENANCE ORGANIZATION (HMO).

HOSTILE FIRE unfriendly fire not confined to its normal habitat. For example, fire in the fireplace leaps onto the sofa. Property contracts protect against damage from a hostile fire, not from damage from fire in the fireplace, its normal habitat. The insurance is designed to cover FORTUITOUS LOSS, which the hostile fire is. *See also* FRIENDLY FIRE.

HOST LIABILITY exposure created by an individual acting as a host serving alcoholic beverages at no charge to persons already intoxicated, resulting in these intoxicated individuals causing property damage and/ or bodily injury to third parties. *See also* DRAM SHOP LAW.

HOST LIQUOR LIABILITY *see* HOST LIABILITY.

HOW LONG A POLICY WILL BE IN FORCE duration of a policy. Property and casualty coverages are usually written for one year, although a personal automobile policy can be for six months. Life insurance can be written on (1) a term basis (1 year, 5 years, 20 years, to age 65), (2) whole of life basis, or (3) any combination of the two. Health insurance can be written on a multiple time period basis.

HR-10 PLAN *see* KEOGH PLAN (HR-10).

HULL MARINE INSURANCE coverage of the hull of a ship and its tackle, passenger fittings, equipment, stores, boats and ordnance. Coverage is provided under the following types of policies: BUILDERS RISK HULL INSURANCE; NAVIGATION RISK INSURANCE, and PORT RISK INSURANCE.

HUMAN APPROACH technique of loss control and reduction of losses in insurance. Supporters of this method believe that the safety attitudes of individuals determine the safety precautions they take. The human approach seeks to convince people to *want* to be safe in order to reduce loss frequency and severity. For example, campaigns encouraging the use of seat belts help promote a safety-conscious society.

HUMAN FACTORS ENGINEERING *see* HUMAN APPROACH.

HUMAN LIFE VALUE APPROACH (ECONOMIC VALUE OF AN INDIVIDUAL LIFE) (EVOIL) quantitative measure to determine the amount of life insurance required to replace lost future earnings of a wage earner. Three steps are used in arriving at the needed sum
1. Determine average yearly earned income devoted to a family in the future by the wage earner (AEIDF).
2. Determine future number of years wage earner is planning to work (n).
3. Determine the interest rate (i) (discount factor) to be used in calculating the present value of the average yearly earned income devoted to family.

The calculation uses this equation:

$$\text{EVOIL} = \sum_{n=1}^{m} \text{AEIDF} \, (1 + i)^{-n}$$

where m = last year at work before normal retirement
$\quad\quad\;\; n$ = first remaining year of life

HURRICANE INSURANCE part of windstorm coverage, usually one of a group of property coverages which covers all kinds of winds such as storms and tornadoes. *See also* STORM INSURANCE (WINDSTORM INSURANCE).

I

IBNR *see* INCURRED BUT NOT REPORTED LOSS (IBNR).

IDENTIFICATION first step in the risk management process. The objective is to determine the sources of losses. For example, the profit and loss statement of a business firm not only shows the sources of its earnings but identifies exposures that these sources face from various perils, such as worker injuries, ill-designed products and hazardous manufacturing conditions.

IMMEDIATE ANNUITY ANNUITY that begins payments after a single premium is paid. For example, the annuitant pays a single premium of $100,000 on June 1 of the current year and begins receiving a monthly income of $1200 for life starting July 1.

IMMEDIATE PARTICIPATION GUARANTEE PLAN (IPG) *see* PENSION PLAN FUNDING: GROUP IMMEDIATE PARTICIPATION GUARANTEED (IPA) CONTRACT ANNUITY.

IMMEDIATE VESTING entitlement of an employee to benefits immediately upon entering a retirement plan. As benefits are earned, they are credited to the employee's account. These "portable" future benefits can be withdrawn by individuals leaving the service of the employer.

IMPAIRED RISK (SUBSTANDARD RISK) in life and health insurance, person whose physical condition is less than standard or who has a hazardous occupation or hobby. For example, an applicant with a history of strokes is regarded as an impaired risk. Some substandard insurance companies specialize in insuring substandard risks, applying an additional premium (surcharge) to reflect the higher probability of loss from a particular impairment.

IMPAIRMENT OF CAPITAL situation where a stock insurer must invade its capital account in order to meet its obligations. Most states do not allow insurers to do this and quickly rescind their right to do business.

IMPLIED AUTHORITY *see* APPARENT AGENCY (AUTHORITY).

IMPREST ACCOUNT fund established to pay specified losses, usually the low *severity* property losses. This type of account is an excellent device in conjunction with a SELF-INSURANCE plan in which the fund is infused with new money as it goes to zero after paying property losses.

IMPROVEMENTS AND BETTERMENTS INSURANCE tenant's modifications of leased space to fit his particular needs. Up to 10% of contents coverage inside the structure may be applied to insure against damage or destruction of improvements or betterments made by a tenant who does not carry coverage on the structure itself. For example, under the HOMEOWNERS INSURANCE POLICY, if the contents of an apartment are insured for $25,000, then $2500 would apply to cabinets that the tenant built into the kitchen.

IN-AREA EMERGENCY SERVICES provision of HEALTH MAINTENANCE ORGANIZATION (HMO) coverage. A member who is critically injured within the geographical service area of the HMO can use the nearest hospital for emergency care, rather than a more distant HMO-authorized hospital.

INCENDIARISM act of starting a fire; arson. Arson is a covered peril under a PROPERTY INSURANCE contract, provided that the owner of the property is not responsible for the arson.

INCEPTION DATE *see* EFFECTIVE DATE.

INCHMAREE CLAUSE provision of MARINE INSURANCE. It protects property damaged or destroyed as the result of the negligent acts of the crew. The name is derived from a steamer in which a pump was damaged by its crew's negligence.

INCIDENCE RATE *see* FREQUENCY AND DISTRIBUTION OF LOSSES.

INCIDENTAL CONTRACT secondary (not primary) reason for forming a contract. In group insurance, the group must be formed and maintained for reasons other than obtaining insurance. If the group were formed primarily to obtain insurance, ADVERSE SELECTION would take place.

INCIDENTAL MALPRACTICE medical malpractice that is the legal responsibility of a person or organization not in the medical profession or business. It is usually covered under a PROFESSIONAL LIABILITY INSURANCE policy.

INCIDENTS OF OWNERSHIP policyowner rights under a life insurance policy, including the right to name a new beneficiary at any time and to surrender the policy for its cash value.

INCOME all sources of cash flow, usually stated on an annual basis.

INCOME AVERAGING income averaged over a specified period of years. For example, to calculate benefits in a pension plan, it is common to average the highest three years or five years of earnings.

INCOME CONTINUATION INSURANCE *see* PARTNERSHIP LIFE AND HEALTH INSURANCE.

INCOME (PERSONAL) INSURANCE *see* DISABILITY INCOME INSURANCE.

INCOME POLICY proceeds from a life insurance policy paid on a monthly basis instead of in a lump sum.

INCOME REIMBURSEMENT INSURANCE *see* INCOME REPLACEMENT.

INCOME REPLACEMENT benefit in disability income insurance whereby an injured or ill wage earner receives a monthly income payment to replace a percentage of his lost earnings. *See also* DISABILITY INCOME INSURANCE (Amount of Benefits).

INCOME-SHIFTING STRATEGIES ownership of tax-free or tax-deferred investments by a child or for a child, given that these investments will not reach maturity before the child attains at least age 14. The objective is to shift investment producing current income from high-tax-bracket adults to low-tax-bracket children. Possible means of achieving this objective would be the utilization of the following investment instruments:
1. *Municipal bonds*—interest earned is not subject to federal or state taxes.
2. *Savings bonds* (U.S. EE savings bonds that have a maturity date after the child attains age 14)—these bonds guarantee payment of 85% of the average interest rate of U.S. Treasury notes and bonds subject to a minimum guarantee rate of 6%. These bonds must be held for at least 5 years for the full interest rate to apply.
3. PERMANENT LIFE INSURANCE—earnings accumulate on a tax-deferred basis with the possibility of avoiding taxes on the accrued earnings if the policy remains in force until the insured's death.
4. DEFERRED ANNUITY—this instrument offers the same tax-deferred treatment as life insurance.
5. *Growth equities*—taxes need not be paid on "paper gains;" taxes on gains are paid only after stock is sold.
6. *Custodial account*—parent retains control of the asset owned by the child until the child reaches the age of majority. The first $1,000 of income in the account is taxed at the child's rate (if child is less than age 14) and any additional income is taxed at the parent's rate. When the child reaches age 14, all income in the account becomes taxable at the child's rate.

INCONTESTABLE CLAUSE section in a life insurance policy stating that after the policy is in force two years, the company cannot void it because of misrepresentation or concealment by the insured in obtaining the policy. For example, when asked on the application if there is a history of diabetes in the family, the applicant writes no, knowing that both her father and mother have diabetes. This does not void the policy after two years. However, if the age of the applicant had been understated, say to obtain a lower premium, the company will recalculate the benefit according to the correct age.

INCORPORATION INTO FUNDING AGREEMENT factors taken into account concerning the instrument used in funding a pension plan. For example, an allocated funding instrument guarantees that benefits will be paid for all premium payments received. This should eliminate concerns of employees about the availability of funds to pay their benefits at retirement.

INCORPOREAL INTERESTS right to insurable interest in property such as the right of a secured creditor in the property pledged as security.

INCREASED COST ENDORSEMENT coverage for extra expenses associated with the reconstruction of a damaged or destroyed building where zoning requirements mandate more costly construction material. This endorsement is attached to property policies.

INCREASED COST OF CONSTRUCTION CLAUSE coverage if state or municipal law requires that a damaged or destroyed building must be rebuilt at an increased cost to comply with building code provisions that were not in effect when the building was originally constructed.

INCREASED HAZARD state that increases the probability of a loss. For example, storage of flammable material next to a furnace in one's home increases the hazard with the knowledge of an insured, and is grounds for suspension of a policy by an insurance company.

INCREASING LIFE INSURANCE term or whole life policy with a face value that increases over time.

INCURRED BUT NOT REPORTED LOSSES (IBNR) insured losses that have occurred but have not been reported to a PRIMARY INSURANCE company. These types of claims have a tremendous effect on a REINSURANCE treaty, which may be showing a healthy profit when in reality it is losing money. Hence, under this false security, the reinsurer will continue operating under a rating plan that is totally inadequate for the losses. This explains why a provision for incurred but not reported losses should be made in a rating plan. Also, the reinsurer must establish an adequate reserve for IBNR claims to make a correct analysis of its business. If such a reserve is not established, overly optimistic evaluation of the real loss may not be revealed for several years. A method of deriving the reserve for IBNR claims is to calculate a percentage of the *Claims Paid and Outstanding*.

INCURRED EXPENSES expenses that have or may not yet have been paid by an insurance company.

INCURRED LOSSES losses which have occurred within a stipulated time period whether paid or not.

INCURRED LOSS RATIO proportion of losses incurred to premiums earned. This ratio indicates the amount of a premium dollar which is being consumed by losses.

INDEMNIFY *see* INDEMNITY.

INDEMNITEE recipient of an indemnity.

INDEMNITOR provider of an indemnity payment.

INDEMNITY compensation for loss. In a property and casualty contract, the objective is to restore an insured to the same financial position after the loss that he/she was in prior to the loss. But the insured should not be able to profit by damage or destruction of property, nor should the insured be in a worse financial position after a loss.

In life insurance the situation is totally different. By the payment of a single premium, the beneficiary of an insured can be placed in a much better financial position at the death of an insured than he/she was in prior to the death. However, the payment of a predetermined amount upon the insured's death does not make a life insurance policy a contract of indemnity.

In hospital indemnity and other health insurance plans, COORDINATION OF BENEFITS is designed so that the insured cannot profit from an illness. *See also* COORDINATION OF BENEFITS.

INDEMNITY AGREEMENT policy provision designed to restore an insured to his or her original financial position after a loss. The insured should neither profit nor be put at a monetary disadvantage by incurring the loss. *See also* INSURANCE CONTRACT, GENERAL; INSURANCE CONTRACT, LIFE; INSURANCE CONTRACT, PROPERTY AND CASUALTY.

INDEMNITY BOND coverage for loss of an obligee in the event that the principal fails to perform according to standards agreed upon between the obligee and the principal.

INDEPENDENT ADJUSTER independent contractor who adjusts claims for different insurance companies. Such services are used by insurance companies whose financial resources or volume of claims do not warrant employing their own in-house adjusters.

INDEPENDENT AGENCY SYSTEM means of selling and servicing property and casualty insurance through agents who represent different companies. The agents own the records of the policies they sell. *See also* INDEPENDENT AGENT.

INDEPENDENT AGENT contractor who represents different insurance companies and who searches the market for the best place for a client's business. The independent agent, who owns the records of policies sold, is not controlled by any one company, pays agency's expenses out of the commissions earned, and is responsible for maintaining employee benefits.

INDEPENDENT CONTRACTORS INSURANCE *see* OWNERS AND CONTRACTORS PROTECTIVE LIABILITY INSURANCE.

INDEPENDENT INSURANCE AGENTS OF AMERICA (IIAA) association of independent agents whose objective is to further the interests of these agents through education, lobbying, and professional ethics.

INDEPENDENT INSURER insurance company that is not a member of a rating bureau or is not under common ownership or management with other companies. The insurance company is said to *stand alone*. *See also* INDEPENDENT AGENT; INDEPENDENT AGENCY SYSTEM.

INDETERMINATE PREMIUM LIFE INSURANCE *nonparticipating life insurance* under which the first few annual premiums are smaller than would be the case under a traditional nonparticipating policy. While the maximum amount of these initial premiums is guaranteed, future premiums can be increased, but not beyond a guaranteed maximum. Adjustments to premiums reflect the insurance company's anticipated mortality experience, investment return, and expenses. If these three elements are more profitable than had been loaded for in the initial premiums, future premiums will be reduced; if less profitable, they will be increased but not greater than the guaranteed maximum. *See also* ADJUSTABLE LIFE INSURANCE.

INDEXED LIFE INSURANCE policy with a face value that varies according to a prescribed index of prices; otherwise benefits provided are similar to ordinary whole life. The death benefit is based on the particular index used, such as the Consumer Price Index (CPI). The policyowner has the choice of having the index applied either automatically or on an elective basis. With an *automatic index* increase, the premium remains level since it has already been loaded to reflect the automatic increase. If the policy allows for an *optional index increase*, an extra premium is charged when this option is exercised by the policyowner. Regardless of which index is selected—automatic or optional—the increased death benefit does not require another physical examination or other evidence of insurability.

INDEXED LIFE POLICIES *see* INDEXED LIFE INSURANCE.

INDIRECT LOSS loss that is not a direct result of a peril. For example, damage to property of a business firm would be a direct loss, but the loss of business earnings because of a fire on its premises would be an indirect loss.

INDIVIDUAL BALANCE SHEET statement showing assets and liabilities of an individual.

INDIVIDUAL CONTRACT PENSION PLAN *see* PENSION PLAN FUNDING: INDIVIDUAL CONTRACT PENSION PLAN.

INDIVIDUAL FIDELITY BOND bond that reimburses a business for loss caused by the dishonest act of an employee. Since crime insurance policies exclude coverage of dishonest acts of employees, it is necessary to have a fidelity bond for this protection. Fidelity bonds cover mercantile business and financial institutions. *See also* FIDELITY BOND.

INDIVIDUAL INCOME STATEMENT report showing sources of income and expenses of an individual.

INDIVIDUAL INSURANCE single policy under which one individual is insured. *See also* ANNUITY; BROAD FORM PERSONAL THEFT INSURANCE; COMPREHENSIVE PERSONAL LIABILITY INSURANCE; DISABILITY INCOME INSURANCE; FAMILY INCOME POLICY; FAMILY INCOME RIDER; FAMILY MAINTENANCE POLICY; FAMILY POLICY; FARMERS COMPREHENSIVE PERSONAL LIABILITY INSURANCE; HEALTH INSURANCE; HOMEOWNERS INSURANCE POLICY; INDIVIDUAL LIFE INSURANCE; LIFE AND HEALTH INSURANCE, PERSONAL AND FAMILY EXPOSURES; PERSONAL AUTOMOBILE POLICY (PAP).

INDIVIDUAL LEVEL COST METHOD means, in pension plans, by which a projection is made of benefits credited to each employee's account at retirement age. Costs are then allocated on a level basis over a specified future period of time. This cost method can be classified according to whether there is or is not a supplemental liability. *See also* INDIVIDUAL LEVEL COST METHOD WITH SUPPLEMENTAL LIABILITY; INDIVIDUAL LEVEL COST METHOD WITHOUT SUPPLEMENTAL LIABILITY.

INDIVIDUAL LEVEL COST METHOD WITHOUT SUPPLEMENTAL LIABILITY means of projecting the costs of pension plans on a level basis over a specified future period of time. The actuarial value of each employee's future benefits to be paid at retirement is determined (including past service benefits to be credited, if any) and their costs are spread equally over the remaining work experience of the employee. The equation states that the present value of future benefits equals the present value of future costs.

INDIVIDUAL LEVEL COST METHOD WITH SUPPLEMENTAL LIABILITY means of projecting the costs of pension plans on a level basis over a specified future period of time. The actuarial value of each employee's future benefits to be paid at retirement is determined (beginning with the first day an employee could have joined the pension plan, had it been in effect at that time—thereby creating a supplemental liability), and their costs are spread equally over the remaining work experience of the employee.

INDIVIDUAL LIFE INSURANCE coverage of a single life, in contrast to group life insurance, which covers many lives. *See also* ENDOWMENT INSURANCE; LIFE INSURANCE; ORDINARY LIFE INSURANCE; TERM LIFE INSURANCE.

INDIVIDUAL POLICY PENSION TRUST *see* PENSION PLAN FUNDING, INDIVIDUAL CONTRACT PENSION PLAN.

INDIVIDUAL RETIREMENT ACCOUNT (IRA) fund under the TAX REFORM ACT OF 1986 into which any individual employee can contribute up to $2000. However, income level and eligibility for an employee pension plan determine whether or not the employee's contribution or a percentage is tax deductible. The following are the circumstances of contribution to an IRA and the tax consequences under the current law:

Income		Covered by Employee Pension Plan	Tax Consequences of $2000
Individual	*Family*	*(Either or both spouses)*	*Contribution*
No restrictions on income	No restrictions on income	No	Totally deductible
$25,000 or less	$40,000 or less	Yes	Totally deductible
Between $25,000 and $35,000	Between $40,000 and $50,000	Yes	Partially deductible
Greater than $35,000	Above $50,000	Yes	No deduction

Note that relevant employee pension plans include *401 (k), 403 (b), Keogh*, and DEFINED BENEFIT PLAN. (There is no requirement for the employee to have benefits vested.) IRA earnings remain tax deferred. Withdrawals prior to age $59\frac{1}{2}$ are subject to a 10% penalty except for disability or death.

INDIVIDUAL RETIREMENT ACCOUNT PLUS (IRA PLUS) proposal, endorsed by President Bush and Secretary of the Treasury Nicholas Brady, which expands in a significant manner the number of individuals who could take advantage of the effect of tax-deferred compounding of savings for retirement. The plan would be available to everyone since there are no income caps, to include employees who are covered under an employer's qualified pension plan. A spouse without an earned income could also establish such an account. Contributions to this account would be made with after-tax dollars. All principal would compound on a tax-free basis, so that no taxes would be due upon distribution. As the plan is currently designed, a participant could withdraw without penalty up to 25% of his or her account to purchase a first home, to meet catastrophic medical bills, or to pay for college expenses. Contrast with INDIVIDUAL RETIREMENT ACCOUNT (IRA).

INDIVIDUAL RISK PREMIUM MODIFICATION PLAN in group insurance, adjustment of premiums, because of reduced expenses due to economy of scale. Group life premiums are subject to negotiation and modification because of administrative savings in dealing with large numbers of people. In contrast, a single person cannot negotiate his premium rate because each policy is handled individually.

INDIVIDUAL STOCK PURCHASE PLAN *see* CLOSE CORPORATION PLAN.

INDUCEMENT TO ESTABLISHMENT OF PENSION PLANS circumstances that encourage the organization of pension plans by employers. For example, employer contributions are tax deductible as business expenses and not currently taxable income to employees. Pensions also help attract employees, maintain employee loyalty, and help improve the image of a business firm in its community.

INDUSTRIAL LIFE INSURANCE modest amounts of coverage sold on a DEBIT basis. The face amount is usually less than $1000. *See also* DEBIT INSURANCE (HOME SERVICE INSURANCE, INDUSTRIAL INSURANCE).

INDUSTRIAL PROPERTY POLICY PROGRAM predecessor of SPECIAL MULTIPERIL INSURANCE (SMP) policy, which covered property of manufacturing installations, in at least two different locations, including machinery and equipment, and optionally, improvements and betterments.

INFIDELITY EXCLUSION *see* FIDELITY EXCLUSION.

INFLATION ENDORSEMENT attachment to a property insurance policy which automatically adjusts its coverage according to the construction cost index in a community. This endorsement is necessary in a property contract to maintain adequate coverage. Otherwise, it is advisable for a policyowner, at time of renewal, to adjust the limits of coverage to reflect the increased cost of construction and the market value of the property.

INFLATION FACTOR adjustment in property insurance to reflect increased construction costs. *See also* INFLATION ENDORSEMENT.

INFLATION GUARD ENDORSEMENT *see* INFLATION ENDORSEMENT.

IN-FORCE BUSINESS aggregate amount of insurance policies that are paid-up (or are being paid) which a life or health insurance company has on its books. The size of a life or health insurance company is often measured by its in-force business. In a life insurance company, the measure is expressed as a face amount of the insurer's portfolio. In a health insurance company, the measure is expressed as premium volume.

INHERENT EXPLOSION CLAUSE provision of a property insurance policy which covers conditions usually present in a particular location. For example, there is an inherent risk of explosion in a flour mill.

INHERENT VICE EXCLUSION provision of a property policy which excludes construction that it is likely to suffer a loss. For example, the roofing material used may not be able to withstand a wind force of more than 15 miles per hour.

INITIAL PREMIUM premium paid at the time a policy goes into effect. With some policies, such as group health insurance, premiums are subject to adjustment at the end of the policy period to reflect loss experience. If the loss experience is good (that is, if the losses are smaller than anticipated in the premium loading), a significant premium reduction can be made at the end of the policy period, with a refund going to the policyowner. *See also* PREMIUM.

INJUNCTION BOND type of judicial bond under which a plaintiff is held liable for damages in the event of a false injunction. The objective of this bond is to protect the party who has been wrongly accused by a plaintiff and suffers financial loss.

INJURIES AND DISEASES COVERED list of injuries and diseases covered in a health insurance policy. Consumers are well advised to read and understand the definitions of injuries and diseases in a health insurance policy. *See also* HEALTH INSURANCE.

INJURY INDEPENDENT OF ALL OTHER MEANS injury covered in a health insurance policy that is isolated from any previous injury.

INLAND MARINE transit over land.

INLAND MARINE EXPOSURE *see* INLAND MARINE INSURANCE (TRANSPORTATION INSURANCE): BUSINESS RISKS.

INLAND MARINE INSURANCE BUREAU rate-making division of INSURANCE SERVICES OFFICES (ISO) for inland marine insurance coverages of member companies.

INLAND MARINE INSURANCE (TRANSPORTATION INSURANCE): BUSINESS RISKS coverage for (1) property damage or destruction of an insured's property and (2) liability exposure of an insured for damage or destruction of someone else's property under his/her care, custody, or control. The insured (shipper) needs this insurance because the carrier (who can also be the insured and purchase inland marine insurance) may be found not at fault for damage to a property; or the carrier may not have any insurance or adequate insurance.

Perils covered include fire, lightning, windstorm, flood, earthquake, landslide, theft, collision, derailment, overturn of the transporting vehicle, and collapse of bridges. Specialty coverages include: ACCOUNTS RECEIVABLE INSURANCE; AIR CARGO INSURANCE; ARMORED CAR AND MESSENGER INSURANCE; CONSIGNMENT INSURANCE; CONTINGENT TRANSIT INSURANCE; COTTON INSURANCE; DEPARTMENT STORE INSURANCE FLOATER; EQUIPMENT FLOATERS INSURANCE; INSTALLATION INSURANCE; INSTALLMENT INSURANCE; INSTRUMENTALITIES OF TRANSPORTATION INSURANCE; MOTOR TRUCK CARGO INSURANCE; PARCEL POST INSURANCE; RAILROAD ROLLING STOCK INSURANCE; REGISTERED MAIL AND EXPRESS MAIL INSURANCE; STOCK PROCESSING INSURANCE; TRIP TRANSIT INSURANCE; VALUABLE PAPERS (RECORDS) INSURANCE.

INLAND MARINE UNDERWRITERS ASSOCIATION organization of inland marine insurance underwriters.

INNKEEPERS LIABILITY liability arising out of the operation of a motel or hotel as it pertains to the physical safety of guests and their property.

INNKEEPERS LIABILITY INSURANCE coverage for negligent acts or omissions of an operator of a motel or hotel resulting in bodily injury to guests and damage or destruction of a guest's property.

IN-PATIENT resident patient of a medical installation. Previously, health insurance benefits were limited to in-patient care. Today health insurance policies provide an extensive list of out-patient benefits. *See also* GROUP HEALTH INSURANCE; HEALTH MAINTENANCE ORGANIZATION (HMO); OUTPATIENT.

INSECT EXCLUSION exclusion in property insurance eliminating coverage for damage or destruction of property due to insects.

INSOLVENCY bankruptcy. If an insured business firm becomes bankrupt the circumstance does not relieve an insurance company of its obligations under an insurance contract.

INSOLVENCY CLAUSE provision of a reinsurance contract which states that the reinsurance company remains liable for its predetermined share of a claim submitted by an insured, even though the primary insurance company is no longer in business.

INSOLVENCY FUND *see* GUARANTY FUND (INSOLVENCY FUND).

INSPECTION in *property* or *liability* insurance, right retained by the company to inspect the insured premises as well as its operations in order to detect inherent structural defects and other hidden hazards. Inspections also help reduce loss frequency and severity through recommended safety engineering loss prevention and reduction procedures. In WORKERS COMPENSATION INSURANCE, the insurance company must inspect the business's payroll record since premiums are based on the business's gross payroll. In LIFE INSURANCE, the company may obtain verification of statements by an applicant and other information.

INSPECTION RECEIPT form provided for an INSPECTION REPORT.

INSPECTION REPORT statement prepared by an *inspection bureau* for a life or health insurance company which summarizes information about an applicant for a policy, including financial standing, morals, physical condition, habits, and other information. This report is used by a company underwriter in evaluating an application for insurance; that is, whether the company should classify an individual as a standard risk at standard insurance rates, as a substandard risk (charged an extra rate) or as uninsurable.

INSTALLATION INSURANCE property coverage on a dealer's interest in equipment while it is being installed. Labor and material are protected against such perils as fire, lightning, and windstorm. For example, if an elevator was installed and it was damaged or destroyed before the buyer can take possession, the contractor would lose the cost of labor and materials if there was no installation insurance.

INSTALLMENT REFUND *see* INSTALLMENT REFUND ANNUITY.

INSTALLMENT REFUND ANNUITY ANNUITY contract. If the annuitant dies before receiving income at least equal to the premiums paid, a beneficiary receives the difference in installments. If the annuitant lives after the income paid equals the premiums paid, the insurance company continues to make income payments to the annuitant for life.

INSTALLMENT SALES FLOATER *see* CONDITIONAL SALES FLOATER.

INSTALLMENT SETTLEMENT life insurance policy DEATH BENEFIT or cash value paid out in a series of installments, rather than in a lump sum. *See also* FIXED-AMOUNT SETTLEMENT OPTION; FIXED-PERIOD OPTION SETTLEMENT; LIFE INCOME; LIFE INCOME WITH PERIOD CERTAIN.

INSTITUTE OF ACTUARIES *see* CANADIAN INSTITUTE OF ACTUARIES.

INSTRUMENTALITIES OF TRANSPORTATION INSURANCE coverage for entities (other than motorized vehicles) used in the transportation of property, including BRIDGE INSURANCE; BRIDGE INSURANCE FOR BRIDGES UNDER CONSTRUCTION; PIERS, WHARVES, DOCKS AND SLIPS INSURANCE; RADIO AND TELEVISION TRANSMITTING EQUIPMENT; TRANSMISSION LINES, PIPE LINES; TRAFFIC LIGHTS INSURANCE; TUNNEL INSURANCE.

INSURABILITY circumstance in which an insurance company can issue life or health insurance to an applicant based on standards set by the company.

INSURABLE INTEREST expectation of a monetary loss that can be covered by insurance. Insurable interest varies according to the type of policy. These relationships give rise to insurable interest: (1) owner of the property; (2) vendor (to the extent of the unpaid balance due on the property sold to the vendee); (3) vendee; (4) bailee (to the extent of the value of the property under his/her temporary care, custody, and control); (5) bailor; (6) life estates; (7) fee simple estates; (8) mortgagee (to the extent of the unpaid balance due on the loan to which the property is pledged as security); and (9) mortgagor. *See also* INSURABLE INTEREST: LIFE INSURANCE; INSURABLE INTEREST: PROPERTY AND CASUALTY INSURANCE.

INSURABLE INTEREST: LIFE INSURANCE
1. each individual has an unlimited insurable interest in his/her own life, and therefore can select anyone as a beneficiary.
2. parent and child, husband and wife, brother and sister have an insurable interest in each other because of blood or marriage.
3. creditor-debtor relationships give rise to an insurable interest. The creditor can be the beneficiary for the amount of the outstanding loan, with the face value decreasing in proportion to the decline in the outstanding loan amount.
4. business relationships give rise to an insurable interest. An employee may insure the life of an employer, and an employer may insure the life of an employee. *See also* BENEFITS OF BUSINESS LIFE AND HEALTH INSURANCE (KEY PERSON INSURANCE); KEY EMPLOYEE (KEY MAN); PARTNERSHIP LIFE AND HEALTH INSURANCE.

Insurable interest must exist at the inception of the contract, not necessarily at the time of loss. For example, because a woman has an insurable interest in the life of her fiance she purchases an insurance policy on his life. Even if the relationship is terminated, as long as she continues to pay the premiums she will be able to collect the death benefit under the policy.

INSURABLE INTEREST: PROPERTY AND CASUALTY INSURANCE

1. owner of property has an insurable interest because of the expectation of monetary loss if that property is damaged or destroyed.
2. creditor of an insured has an insurable interest in property pledged as security.

Insurable interest has to exist both at the inception of the contract and at the time of a loss. For example, an insured can purchase a homeowners policy because of insurable interest in a home. Upon selling it, the insured no longer has an insurable interest because there is no expectation of a monetary loss should the home burn down.

INSURABLE RISK condition in which an applicant has met an insurance company's standards. Requirements include a loss that is (1) definable; (2) fortuitous; (3) one of a large number of homogeneous exposures; and (4) carries a premium reasonable in relation to a potential loss.

INSURABLE VALUE *see* INSURABLE RISK.

INSURANCE mechanism for contractually shifting burdens of a number of PURE RISKS by pooling them.

INSURANCE AGENT representative of an insurance company in soliciting and servicing policyholders. An agent's knowledge concerning an insurance transaction is said to be the knowledge of the insurance company as well. Wrongful acts of the agent are the responsibility of the company; these bind the company to the customer. Notice given by an insured to the agent is the same as notice to the company. *See also* AGENT; CAPTIVE AGENT; INDEPENDENT AGENT.

INSURANCE AGENTS AND BROKERS LIABILITY INSURANCE coverage for acts or omissions committed by an agent or broker resulting in adequate insurance in the event of a liability suit or property damage to a client.

INSURANCE AND SOCIETY phrase referring to constructive relationship, in which insurance provides society with benefits such as security, savings, encouragement of investment, and reduction in prices of goods to consumers.

INSURANCE BROKER representative of an insured, not of an insurance company. Acts of a broker are not the responsibility of the company, and notice given by an insured to a broker is not the same as notice to the company. The broker searches the insurance marketplace for a company in which to place the insured's business for the most coverage at the best price. The broker is not restricted to placing business with any one company.

INSURANCE CARRIER *see* INSURANCE COMPANY (INSURER); INSURER.

INSURANCE COMMISSIONER *see* COMMISSIONER OF INSURANCE (INSURANCE COMMISSIONER, SUPERINTENDENT OF INSURANCE).

INSURANCE COMPANY, CHOOSING AN consideration should be given to a company's capacity to underwrite a particular risk, as indicated by its financial standing, claims philosophy, price structure, agent representation, loss prevention and reduction services, and risk analysis expertise. Information can be gained in several ways:
1. *Reputation*—a prospective insured can fairly easily learn something about an insurance company through business and professional associates (lawyer, accountant, banker), through conversations with others in the same field, and by discussions with agents and brokers.
2. *Financial capacity*—larger businesses and public libraries often have up-to-date reference books, such as *Best's Insurance Reports* (available in *Life-Health* and *Property-Casualty* editions) giving detailed analyses of hundreds of companies.
3. *State Insurance Department*—information about specific insurance companies may be available from the Insurance Departments located in state capitals.

INSURANCE COMPANY DEPARTMENT *see* INSURANCE COMPANY ORGANIZATION.

INSURANCE COMPANY FLEET *see* FLEET OF COMPANIES.

INSURANCE COMPANY (INSURER) organization which underwrites insurance policies. There are two principal types of insurance companies: *mutual* and *stock*. A mutual company is owned by its policyowners, who elect a board of directors that is responsible for its operation. A stock company is owned by its stockholders. In a mutual company, profits take the form of *policy dividends*, or refunds of part of premiums paid, which are distributed to policyowners. Profits in a stock company take the form of stockholders dividends, which are distributed to stockholders.

INSURANCE COMPANY ORGANIZATION structure. In general, company functions are delegated to several departments: *actuarial*, AGENCY, *claims and loss control*, INVESTMENTS, *legal*, MARKETING, and UNDERWRITING.

INSURANCE CONTRACT *see* HEALTH INSURANCE CONTRACT; INSURANCE CONTRACT, GENERAL; INSURANCE CONTRACT, LIFE; INSURANCE CONTRACT, PROPERTY AND CASUALTY.

INSURANCE CONTRACT, GENERAL legally binding unilateral agreement between an insured and an insurance company to indemnify the buyer of a contract under specified circumstances. In exchange for premium payment(s) the company covers stipulated perils. *See also* ADHESION INSURANCE CONTRACT; ALEATORY CONTRACT; APPLICATION; CAPACITY OF PARTIES; CONDITIONAL; CONSIDERATION; ENDORSEMENTS; INDEMNITY; INSURABLE INTEREST; LEGAL PURPOSE; MUTUAL ASSENT; UTMOST GOOD FAITH.

INSURANCE CONTRACT, HEALTH *see* HEALTH INSURANCE CONTRACT.

INSURANCE CONTRACT, LIFE *see* BENEFICIARY; CLAUSES ADDED TO A LIFE INSURANCE POLICY; NON-FORFEITURE PROVISION; POLICY LOAN; REPRESENTATIONS; STANDARD PROVISIONS, LIFE INSURANCE; SUICIDE CLAUSE; VALUED POLICY; WAR EXCLUSION CLAUSE.

INSURANCE CONTRACT, PROPERTY AND CASUALTY *see* CONCEALMENT; DEDUCTIBLE; DOUBLE RECOVERY; ESTOPPEL; INDEMNITY; INSURANCE TO VALUE; LARGE LOSS PRINCIPLE; MISREPRESENTATION (FALSE PRETENSE); PERSONAL CONTRACT; SMALL LOSS PRINCIPLE; STANDARD PROVISIONS; LIFE INSURANCE; SUBROGATION CLAUSE; WAIVER; WARRANTY.

INSURANCE CRIME PREVENTION INSTITUTE organization of over 300 property and casualty insurance companies whose mission is to investigate fraudulent claims and bring to justice those making such claims.

INSURANCE DEPARTMENT authority that administers state laws regulating insurance and licenses insurance companies and their agents.

INSURANCE EXAMINER employee of a state insurance department who audits statements of insurance companies to determine their continued solvency.

INSURANCE EXCHANGE *see* NEW YORK INSURANCE EXCHANGE.

INSURANCE FIELDS *see* SOCIAL INSURANCE.

INSURANCE FORM attachment to a property and casualty policy that makes it operative. For example, the *Standard Fire Policy* remains inoperative until a form such as the *Buildings and Contents Form* is attached.

INSURANCE GUARANTY ACT law, in several states, establishing a fund to guarantee benefits under policies issued by insurance companies which become insolvent.

INSURANCE INFORMATION INSTITUTE organization having as its objective the education of the general public concerning items of national concern of member property and casualty insurance companies.

INSURANCE INSTITUTE FOR HIGHWAY SAFETY organization located in Washington, D.C., whose membership consists of automobile insurers.

INSURANCE INSTITUTE OF AMERICA (IIA) organization that develops and publishes educational material and administers national examinations in supervisory management, general insurance, claims, management, risk management, underwriting, loss control management, accredited adviser in insurance, premium auditing, research and planning, and accounting and finance.

INSURANCE PLANS COVERED *see* BUSINESS INSURANCE; GROUP INSURANCE; INDIVIDUAL INSURANCE.

INSURANCE PLANS FOR KEY EMPLOYEES *see* KEY EMPLOYEES, INSURANCE PLANS FOR.

INSURANCE POLICY written contract between an insured and an insurance company stating the obligations and responsibilities of each party. *See also* INSURANCE CONTRACT, LIFE; INSURANCE CONTRACT, PROPERTY AND CASUALTY.

INSURANCE POOL *see* POOL.

INSURANCE RATE amount charged to an insured that reflects expectation of loss for a covered risk; and insurance company expenses and profit. *See also* PREMIUM; PURE PREMIUM RATING METHOD.

INSURANCE REGULATION *see* STATE SUPERVISION AND REGULATION.

INSURANCE REGULATORY INFORMATION SYSTEM (IRIS) financial analysis method established by the NATIONAL ASSOCIATION OF INSURANCE COMMISSIONERS (NAIC) to detect problems of property and casualty insurance companies and life and health insurance companies according to these audit ratios:
Property and casualty insurance companies: (1) current year increase or decrease in net written premiums to net written premiums in previous year; (2) net written premiums to adjusted policyowners' surplus; (3) loss ratio for two years; (4) expense ratio for two years; (5) net investment income to average invested assets; (6) liabilities to liquid assets;

(7) unpaid premiums to surplus; and (8) previous year adjusted surplus to current year adjusted surplus.

(Other property and casualty audit ratios concern measurement of the adequacy of a company's *reserve*.)

Life and health insurance companies: (1) yield on investments; (2) nonadmitted assets to assets; (3) net gain to total income; (4) investments in affiliates to capital and surplus; (5) expenses (including agents commissions) to premiums; (6) exchange in capital and surplus; and (7) surplus increase or decrease.

INSURANCE RISK coverage for exposures that exhibit a possibility of financial loss.

INSURANCE SERVICES OFFICE (ISO) organization that calculates rates and develops insurance policies for its property and casualty member companies. The suggested rates are used by smaller companies where the loss experience lacks actuarial accuracy. Its rates are also used by larger companies, which modify them to fit their own loss experience.

INSURANCE SOLICITOR *see* SOLICITOR.

INSURANCE TO VALUE in property coverage, ratio of the amount of insurance to the value of an insured property. This ratio, multiplied by the amount of the loss, determines the indemnification payment. *See also* COINSURANCE.

INSURED party covered by an insurance policy. In life insurance policies there is one designated insured, the person so named; or a policy can be issued to numerous insureds on a group basis. The insured persons in property and casualty policies may also include residents of the insured's household, such as a spouse, relatives of either, and other individuals under their care, custody, and control if under age 21.

INSURED, NAMED *see* NAMED INSURED.

INSURED PERIL source of loss which is covered under an insurance policy, such as a fire, and explosion, among others.

INSURED PREMISES real property (structure(s) attached to the land) that is occupied and/or is under the care, custody, or control of an individual, individuals, or an organization for which an insurance policy provides coverage. Within the insurance policy, the premises will be listed in the DECLARATIONS SECTION and/or further defined in the policy.

INSURED'S OBLIGATION AFTER LOSS *see* PROPERTY AND CASUALTY INSURANCE PROVISIONS.

INSURER company offering protection through the sale of an insurance policy to an insured. *See also* INSURANCE COMPANY (INSURER).

INSURER FINANCES: LIFE AND HEALTH, PROPERTY AND CASUALTY management of premium inflow and benefit outflow. *See also* ASSETS AND VALUATION; FULL PRELIMINARY TERM RESERVE PLAN; INVESTMENTS AND REGULATION PROSPECTIVE RESERVE; REINSURANCE RESERVE; RETAINED EARNINGS; UNDERWRITING GAIN (LOSS).

INSURING AGREEMENT section describing coverages under a policy. Elsewhere in the policy other sections may restrict or exclude coverages. *See also* INSURING AGREEMENT, PROPERTY AND CASUALTY POLICY.

INSURING AGREEMENT, AUTOMOBILE POLICIES *see* INSURING AGREEMENT, PROPERTY AND CASUALTY POLICY.

INSURING AGREEMENT, FIRE *see* INSURING AGREEMENT, PROPERTY AND CASUALTY POLICY.

INSURING AGREEMENT, LIABILITY *see* INSURING AGREEMENT, PROPERTY AND CASUALTY POLICY.

INSURING AGREEMENT, PROPERTY AND CASUALTY POLICY section of a policy specifying: (1) *parties to the contract* (the insurance company and the person or business to be insured); (2) terms of the policy—when it goes into force, and when it ends; (3) premiums and their due date; (4) limits of insurance; (5) types and location of property to be insured; (6) CONSIDERATION; (7) perils (what the policy protects against); and (8) assignment (and under what conditions the policy can be assigned).

INSURING AGREEMENT, WORKERS COMPENSATION AND EMPLOYERS LIABILITY *see* INSURING AGREEMENT, PROPERTY AND CASUALTY POLICY.

INSURING CLAUSE essential part of an insurance policy. It names the individual(s) covered, property and locations covered, perils covered, the time a policy goes into force, and its termination date. *See also* INSURING AGREEMENT, PROPERTY AND CASUALTY POLICY.

INTANGIBLE PERSONAL PROPERTY that which cannot be touched; having no meaning to the senses. It is represented by incorporeal rights in property (that which is evidence or represents value, for example, a copyright).

INTEGRATED DEDUCTIBLE deductible amount between a basic health insurance plan and major medical insurance.

INTEGRATION PERCENTAGE *see* INTEGRATION WITH SOCIAL SECURITY.

INTEGRATION WITH SOCIAL SECURITY method of reducing an employee pension according to IRS procedures:
1. *Offset method*—restricted to a DEFINED BENEFIT PLAN under which a mandatory percentage of the monthly Social Security benefit payable to a retired employee is subtracted from the monthly retirement benefit payable to the employee under a business firm's qualified retirement plan.
2. *Integration method*—used with a defined benefit plan or a *defined contribution plan* under which a basic level of compensation is established for a retired employee so that (a) for compensation above this level, the employee receives a greater retirement benefit; or (b) for compensation below this level, the employee receives a smaller retirement benefit.

INTENTIONAL TORT deliberate act or omission, including trespass, assault and battery, invasion of privacy, libel, and slander. An intentional tort is a branch of civil liability. Liability insurance can be purchased to cover libel and slander but not the other intentional torts.

INTERCOMPANY ARBITRATION settlement of a dispute that arises when two or more insurers cover a single loss and there is a question concerning the amount each is responsible to pay. The companies are bound by the arbitration decision.

INTERCOMPANY DATA information generated by the MEDICAL INFORMATION BUREAU (MIB) and made available to member companies concerning medical information of applicants for life and health insurance. Member companies are required to report to the MIB physical impairments of an applicant as uncovered through the underwriting process.

INTEREST money paid by one party for the use of another party's funds.

INTEREST ADJUSTED COST procedure for calculating the cost of life insurance, taking into account the TIME VALUE OF MONEY (investment return on sums placed in premium dollars had these sums been invested elsewhere). There are several ways to calculate interest adjusted cost based on time value of money. *See also* LINTON YIELD METHOD; NET PAYMENTS INDEX; SURRENDER COST INDEX.

INTEREST ASSUMPTION minimum rate of return, in life insurance, guaranteed to a policyowner in calculating benefits for a life insurance policy. It is also used by an insurance company as the minimum rate of return it expects on its investments in calculating reserves.

INTEREST FREE LOANS means of borrowing at no charge by a policyowner under UNIVERSAL LIFE INSURANCE policies.

INTEREST OPTION use of a life insurance policy dividend by the owner of a participating policy. Here the policy dividend is left with the insurance company to accumulate at a guaranteed minimum interest rate. Also, an interest option is a choice a beneficiary can make by leaving death proceeds with the insurance company to accumulate at interest. Interest earned under either option is subject to Federal and state income taxes.

INTEREST POLICIES *see* CURRENT ASSUMPTION WHOLE LIFE INSURANCE; INTEREST SENSITIVE POLICIES; UNIVERSAL LIFE INSURANCE; UNIVERSAL VARIABLE LIFE INSURANCE.

INTEREST RATES, GUARANTEED/EXCESS circumstances in life insurance in which, although a minimum rate is guaranteed, a policyowner may earn additional (excess) interest, depending on the company's investment return. *See also* CURRENT ASSUMPTION.

INTEREST SENSITIVE POLICIES a newer generation of life insurance policies that are credited with interest currently being earned by insurance companies on these policies.

INTERINSURANCE COMPANY CLAIMS those claims that arise when two or more property and casualty insurance companies have coverage on a loss. Which company then owes which portion of the claim must be determined. *See also* INTERCOMPANY ARBITRATION.

INTERINSURANCE EXCHANGE *see* RECIPROCAL EXCHANGE.

INTERINSURANCE CLAIM SERVICE ORGANIZATION type of organization of property and casualty insurance companies whose objective is to share information on fraudulent claims, handle claims in an expeditious manner, and disseminate public information concerning safeguarding of property. Some interinsurer organizations are the AMERICAN INSURANCE ASSOCIATION (AIA) Index Bureau, INSURANCE CRIME PREVENTION INSTITUTE, NATIONAL ASSOCIATION OF INDEPENDENT INSURANCE ADJUSTERS (NAII), and NATIONAL AUTOMOBILE THEFT BUREAU.

INTERIOR ROBBERY POLICY coverage for the inside of an insured premises of a business firm if it experiences a loss of money, securities, personal property, and damage or destruction of real or personal property due to robbery, whether successful or attempted.

INTERMEDIARY reinsurance broker for a primary company (*the reinsured*). This broker is paid commissions by the reinsurance company, just as an agent is paid commissions by an insurance company for selling its policies.

INTERMEDIATE DISABILITY *see* DISABILITY INCOME INSURANCE; TEMPORARY DISABILITY BENEFITS.

INTERNAL REVENUE CODE Federal statute defining the Federal tax code, covering such topics as credits against tax; business related credits; computing credit for investment in certain depreciable property; computation of taxable income; definition of gross income, adjusted gross income, and taxable income; itemized deductions; pensions, profit-sharing, and stock bonus plans; taxation of estates and trusts; taxation of life insurance companies, capital gains and losses; and other areas.

INTERNAL REVENUE CODE: SECTION 303 STOCK REDEMPTION PLAN portion of the Federal tax code outlining the procedure by which a corporation cancels or redeems its shares with funds paid out of earnings or profits, thus making the distribution a taxable dividend.

INTERNAL REVENUE CODE: SECTION 501 (c) portion of the Federal tax code that determines which organizations are exempt from Federal income taxation. These are generally nonprofit corporations, funds, and foundations for education, religious, charitable, or scientific purposes; civic leagues for general social welfare; fraternal beneficial societies, orders, or associations; and others.

INTERNATIONAL EMPLOYEE BENEFIT NETWORK agreement among insurance companies through which a multinational employer is permitted to purchase employee benefits coverages for two or more of its overseas subsidiaries under a single master policy. This working arrangement (network) may be composed of several overseas independent insurance companies, may consist of a cooperative agreement between a U.S. insurance company and an overseas insurance company, or may be administered by an insurance company which has several subsidiary companies overseas. Employee benefits provided through these multinational networks include life, health, pensions, disability income, and accidental death. Such a network pools the loss experiences of a particular employer's overseas subsidiaries. If the pooled loss experience is better than that expected through the premium charged, a dividend is paid to the employer. However, if the loss experience is worse than that expected through the premium charged, three courses of action are available: (1) the adverse loss experience is charged to the employer's account with any negative balance shifted to the following loss-experience year; (2) the adverse loss experience is absorbed by the insurance companies in the network, and any negative balance is *not* shifted to the following loss-experience year; (3) the adverse loss experience is charged to the employer's account with any negative balance shifted to the following loss-experience year, and a contingency fund is established with annual contributions against which future adverse loss experiences can be charged. The pooling effect allows the employer's adverse loss experience in one country to be offset by better than expected loss experience in another country.

INTERNATIONAL INSURANCE SEMINARS, INC. (IIS) annual meetings of insurance practitioners and academicians from throughout the world interested in exchanging ideas concerning the theory and applications of insurance. The meeting is held in a different part of the world each year.

INTERPLEADER legal procedure through which a court determines the rightful claimant (of two or more claimants making the same claim) against a third party. Insurance companies use interpleader if claims are made by different parties. For example, upon the death of an insured two or more individuals (such as the widow and a former wife), may contest the beneficiary's rights. The insurance company will deposit the policy proceeds with the court until it decides on the ownership.

INTERSTATE COMMERCE COMMISSION ENDORSEMENT certificate of insurance required by law under the auspices of the Interstate Commerce Commission. The endorsement is attached to all INLAND MARINE policies issued to interstate motor carriers. The insurance company covers all damage or destruction on an ALL RISKS basis to property being transported.

INTERSTATE COMMERCE COMMISSION (ICC) Federal agency that regulates commerce across state lines. The ICC does not oversee insurance, which is subject to regulation by the states according to Public Law 15, McCarran-Ferguson Act. However, insurance companies must comply with many Federal laws and regulations.

INTER-VIVO TRUST trust that is established by people still alive. *See also* ESTATE PLANNING; ESTATE PLANNING DISTRIBUTION.

INTESTACY *see* INTESTATE.

INTESTATE death without a will having been drawn. Under this circumstance, the court follows state law in deciding how the estate of the deceased is to be distributed. *See also* ESTATE PLANNING; ESTATE PLANNING DISTRIBUTION.

INTESTATE DISTRIBUTION *see* ESTATE PLANNING DISTRIBUTION.

IN-TRUST (ON-CONSIGNMENT) POLICIES insurance that follows an insured property. *See also* CONSIGNMENT INSURANCE.

INVERTED YIELD CURVE curve that results when yields on short-term treasury issues exceed those on long-term government debt. A widely accepted theory holds that when short-term and intermediate-term issues are higher than those on long-term issues a recession is imminent and investors expect rates to decline further.

INVESTMENT AND VALUATION OF ASSETS *see* INVESTMENTS AND REGULATION.

INVESTMENT EARNINGS OF INSURANCE COMPANY investment income. Insurance companies invest part of their premiums that are not immediately needed for claims and administrative expenses. These earnings are critical to an insurance company. A property and casualty company depends on investment earnings to balance underwriting losses. A life company depends on the investment earnings to help build policy cash values.

INVESTMENT INCOME earnings by an insurance company from dividends on its equity portfolio, rent from real estate and other property it owns, and interest on its bond holdings.

INVESTMENTS money expended with the object of profit. The goal of an insurance company is to invest in assets with a rate of return greater than that to be paid out as benefits under its policies. Traditionally, life insurance companies have invested in long term financial instruments such as mortgages. Today, under CURRENT ASSUMPTION life insurance policies, investments are in short term financial instruments. Property and casualty insurance companies, because of the nature of their policies, favor short term financial instruments as investments.

INVESTMENTS AND REGULATION
Life insurance:
1. *Bonds*—most state regulations permit life insurance company investments in debentures, mortgage bonds, and blue chip corporate bonds.
2. *Stocks*—(a) *preferred stock* investment is limited to 20% of the total stock of any one company, not exceeding 2% of a company's admitted assets; (b) *common stock* investment is limited to the lesser amount of 1% of the ADMITTED ASSETS or the *policyowner's surplus*.
3. *Mortgage*—investment is unlimited in first mortgages on residential, commercial, and industrial real estate.
4. *Real Estate*—investment is limited to 10% of admitted assets.

Valuation of the assets in a typical state is accomplished in the following manner: (1) stocks or bonds in default (principal or interest) cannot be valued at greater than market value; (2) bonds not in default valued according to their purchase price adjusted to equal par at maturity; (3) preferred and common stocks of firms in good financial condition are valued according to purchase price; (4) preferred and common stocks in companies not in good financial condition are valued at market price; and (5) real estate, mortgages, and policy loans are valued at book value.

Property and casualty insurance:

1. DOMESTIC INSURERS and FOREIGN INSURERS must invest according to the minimum capitalization requirement in Federal, state, or municipal bonds.

2. Company funds in excess of minimum capitalization and reserve requirements can be invested in Federal, state, or municipal bonds as well as stocks or real estate. The insurance company is limited in its investment in any one firm up to no more than 10% of its admitted assets; its real estate investment can be no more than 10% of its admitted assets.

INVESTMENT YEAR METHOD OF ALLOCATING INVEST-MENT INCOME procedure in which investment income is paired with each life insurance policy according to the time frame in which the premiums for that particular policy are received.

INVITEE person who is expressly, or by implication, asked to visit property in the possession, care, or control of another person. The inviter has the obligation to render his property safe for the visit of the invitee. Liability insurance is designed to protect an insured in the event that his negligent acts or omissions result in bodily injury to the invitee.

IRA *see* INDIVIDUAL RETIREMENT ACCOUNT.

IRREVOCABLE something that cannot be changed. In life insurance, a beneficiary who has been named as irrevocable, cannot be changed without his or her formal (written) permission.

IRREVOCABLE BENEFICIARY *see* BENEFICIARY CLAUSE.

IRREVOCABLE LIVING TRUST TRUST in which rights to make any changes therein are surrendered permanently by the GRANTOR. The grantor uses this type of trust to transfer assets and any potential depreciation out of his or her estate in order to avoid FEDERAL ESTATE TAX on the second estate distributions to heirs, as well as to avoid PROBATE expenses. The primary disadvantage of this type of trust is that the grantor surrenders all control over the assets and the right to change the terms of the trust. *See also* ESTATE PLANNING DISTRIBUTION; REVOCABLE LIVING TRUST.

IRREVOCABLE TRUST trust that cannot be revoked by the creator. *See also* ESTATE PLANNING DISTRIBUTION.

ISO *see* INSURANCE SERVICES OFFICE.

ISSUED BUSINESS policies that have been sold to and paid for by an insured, but not yet delivered to the insured.

J

JACKET outer covering containing an insurance policy; in many instances it lists provisions common to several types of policies.

JEWELER'S BLOCK INSURANCE POLICY type of INLAND MARINE INSURANCE which provides coverage for jewels, watches, gold, silver, platinum, pearls, precious and semiprecious stones. Property can be owned by the insured jeweler; or can be customer's property in care, custody, and control of the jeweler. Coverage is on an ALL RISKS basis except specifically excluded perils such as wear and tear; war; delay; loss of market; flood; earthquake; loss or damage while jewelry is being worn by the insured or his/her representatives; loss resulting from the infidelity of any person under the care, custody, and control of the insured; damage or destruction of jewelry after it leaves the insured under an installment contract; mysterious disappearance; and shipments of jewelry not sent registered first class mail.

JEWELRY FLOATER *see* PERSONAL JEWELRY INSURANCE.

JEWELRY INSURANCE *see* PERSONAL JEWELRY INSURANCE.

JOB RELATED INJURIES, DEATH incidents covered under WORKERS COMPENSATION BENEFITS.

JOINT AND SURVIVOR OPTION settlement choice under a life insurance policy whereby a beneficiary may elect to have the death proceeds paid in the form of a joint and survivor annuity. *See also* JOINT LIFE AND SURVIVORSHIP ANNUITY.

JOINT ANNUITY *see* JOINT LIFE ANNUITY.

JOINT CONTROL estate under the legal and administrative guidance of both the *surety* and the *fiduciary*. Any actions on the part of the estate requires the signatures of both in order to reduce the chances of fraud.

JOINT INSURANCE *see* JOINT LIFE AND SURVIVOR INSURANCE; JOINT LIFE AND SURVIVORSHIP ANNUITY; JOINT LIFE ANNUITY; JOINT LIFE INSURANCE.

JOINT LIFE AND SURVIVOR INSURANCE coverage for two or more persons with the death benefit payable at the death of the last of those insured. Premiums are significantly lower under joint life and survivor insurance than for policies that insure only one person, since the probability of having to pay a death claim is lower.

JOINT LIFE AND SURVIVORSHIP ANNUITY ANNUITY that continues income payments as long as one annuitant, out of two or more annuitants, remains alive. For example, a married couple would receive an income for as long as both spouses are alive. Thereafter, payments would continue as long as the surviving spouse is alive, usually for a smaller amount. This type of annuity is ideal for a husband and wife in that it guarantees the surviving spouse an income for life. Even with a LIFE ANNUITY CERTAIN or other type of refund annuity it is possible for a surviving spouse to outlive the money that has been funding the annuity. *See also* ANNUITY.

JOINT LIFE ANNUITY retirement plan in which income payments continue until the death of the first of two or more annuitants. This type of annuity is not appropriate for a husband and wife since at the death of the first spouse income payments cease. The monthly benefit is greater than with other annuities since income payments cease at the first death. *See also* ANNUITY.

JOINT LIFE INSURANCE coverage of two or more persons with the death benefit payable at the first death. Premiums are significantly higher than for policies that insure one person, since the probability of having to pay a death claim is higher.

JOINT LOSS APPORTIONMENT *see* APPORTIONMENT.

JOINT PROTECTION *see* JOINT-LIFE AND SURVIVORSHIP ANNUITY; JOINT LIFE INSURANCE.

JOINT TENANCY *see* JOINT TENANTS.

JOINT TENANTS property owned by two or more parties in such a way that at the death of one, the survivors retain complete ownership of the property.

JOINT UNDERWRITER ASSOCIATION combination of several insurance companies to provide the capacity to underwrite a particular type or size of exposure. For example, liability coverage for a drug company's vaccine has been instituted as the result of several insurance companies working together to provide the required capacity due to the extra hazard.

JOINT VENTURE agreement of two or more insurance companies to provide a product or service.

JONES ACT (MERCHANT MARINE ACT) Federal law passed in 1920 which allows any seaman incurring bodily injury as the result of the performance of one or more functions of the job to bring a suit for damages against the employer. The employer's exposures under the Act consist of negligence, unseaworthiness of the vessel, and disability income for the injured man or woman.

JOURNAL OF RISK AND INSURANCE academic publication of the AMERICAN RISK AND INSURANCE ASSOCIATION in which articles deal with aspects of risk, insurance, and allied fields of study.

JUDGMENT decision by a court of law.

JUDGMENT BY DEFAULT decision in the absence of a plaintiff or defendant at the specified court time.

JUDGMENT RATING underwriting phrase denoting the best judgment, based on the experience of an underwriter, in classifying a particular risk.

JUDICIAL BOND type of SURETY BOND that is either a *fiduciary* or *court bond*.
  1. *Fiduciary Bond*—guarantees that individuals in a position of trust will safeguard assets belonging to others placed under their control. For example, guardians appointed by a court who are authorized to pay expenses of the minor and administrators of estates who take care of a deceased's assets may require fiduciary bond.
  2. *Court Bond*—guarantees concerning ligation such as: (1) APPEAL BOND, which guarantees that a judgment will be paid if an appeal is lost in a higher court; (b) *Plaintiff's Replevin Bond*, which guarantees that damages will be paid if the replevin action is wrongfully brought; (c) *Removal Bond*, which guarantees that damages will be paid if improper removal actions are taken.

JUMPING JUVENILE POLICY (JUVENILE ESTATE BUILDER) life insurance coverage on a child in which the initial face amount of the life insurance policy increases when the child reaches the age of majority, with no corresponding increase in premium.

JUVENILE ESTATE BUILDER *see* JUMPING JUVENILE POLICY (JUVENILE ESTATE BUILDER).

JUVENILE INSURANCE life insurance on the life of a child.

K

KEETON-O'CONNELL AUTOMOBILE INSURANCE PLAN early type of no-fault automobile insurance developed by two law professors, Robert Keeton and Jeffrey O'Connell. Its basic premise is that for many accidents it is impossible to place the blame as required by the tort legal system. In this approach, each individual would be able to collect from his or her own insurance company without having to prove fault on the part of anyone.

KENNEY RATIO proposal by Roger Kenney, an insurance journalist, that in order to maintain the solvency of a property and casualty insurance company, insurance premiums written should not exceed more than twice the company's surplus and capital. This historical measure is used by regulators to determine a property and casualty company's capacity to make claim payments while maintaining its solvency.

KEOGH PLAN (HR-10) act first passed in 1962 which permits the self-employed individual to establish his or her own retirement plan. This individual can make nondeductible voluntary contributions and tax-deductible contributions subject to a maximum limit of 25% of earned income up to 30,000 for a defined contribution plan after the reduction for the contribution to the Keogh Plan. This is an equivalent rate of 20% of earned income prior to the contribution to the Keogh Plan.

KEY EMPLOYEE INSURANCE *see* BENEFITS OF BUSINESS LIFE AND HEALTH INSURANCE (KEY PERSON INSURANCE); KEY EMPLOYEE (KEY PERSON).

KEY EMPLOYEE (KEY PERSON) individual who possesses a unique ability essential to the continued success of a business firm. For example, this individual might have the technical knowledge necessary for research and development of products that keep the company at the cutting edge of its field. The death or disability of this key individual could severely handicap the company. *See also* BENEFITS OF BUSINESS LIFE AND HEALTH INSURANCE (KEY PERSON INSURANCE).

KEY EMPLOYEES, INSURANCE PLANS FOR typical NONQUALIFIED PLANS of life insurance for key employees include:
1. PERMANENT LIFE INSURANCE—dividends generated by the policy are used to pay the income tax of the key employee that results from the premiums paid by the employer on the permanent insurance policy. For federal tax purposes the employer-paid premiums are taxed as additional earned income for the employee. Under the better permanent policies, after the policy has been in force a few years

the dividends should exceed the taxable premium income to the employee. The advantages of permanent insurance to the key employee include life insurance coverage for life, increasing cash values, increasing dividends, selection of beneficiary, and ownership of policy.

2. TERM LIFE INSURANCE—premiums paid by the employer are considered federal taxable income to the employee. Employee selects beneficiary and owns policy. Policy probably will not remain in force after retirement because the premiums continue to increase in cost and become prohibitive.

3. SPLIT DOLLAR LIFE INSURANCE—permanent life insurance is purchased on the life of the employee. Premium payments are split between the employee and the employer. The employer has an equity interest in the cash value of the policy to the extent of the premium payment he or she has paid in. The employee has an equity interest in the cash value of the policy to the extent that the cash value exceeds the premiums paid in by the employer. Under the better permanent policies, the cash values will accumulate to a substantial sum, whereupon the employer can withdraw from the cash value an amount equal to his or her premium paid in. At this point the split dollar plan is said to terminate and the employee has sole possession of the policy. The cash values remaining should be sufficient so that no further premium payments are required by the employee to keep the policy in force.

4. SALARY CONTINUATION PLAN—employer usually purchases permanent life insurance on the life of the employee, is the beneficiary of the policy, and owns the policy. If the employee dies before receiving all promised supplemental pension benefits, the employer will pay the remaining supplemental pension benefits to the beneficiary of the deceased employee. Funds for payments are provided from the life insurance proceeds.

5. *Death Benefit Only Life Insurance Plan*—employer usually purchases permanent life insurance on the life of the employee, is the beneficiary of the policy, and owns the policy. Premiums paid by the employer are not considered federal taxable income to the employee. Upon the death of the employee, the employer will use the life insurance proceeds to pay death benefits for several years to the employee's beneficiary. The employer receives the life insurance proceeds tax free; however, the death payments to the employee's beneficiary are federal taxable income to that beneficiary. This plan can also be utilized to supplement the employee's pension plan at retirement.

KEYNESIAN ECONOMICS theory, named after the British economist John Maynard Keynes, that deals with current consumption at the expense of saving. This theory has important implications for life insurance products and annuities since their purchase requires foregoing a portion of current consumption in favor of savings and future financial security. *See also* ANNUITY; SAVINGS ELEMENT, LIFE INSURANCE.

KEY PERSON INSURANCE *see* BENEFITS OF BUSINESS LIFE AND HEALTH INSURANCE (KEY PERSON INSURANCE).

KEY PERSON LIFE AND HEALTH INSURANCE *see* BENEFITS OF BUSINESS LIFE AND HEALTH INSURANCE (KEY PERSON INSURANCE); BUSINESS LIFE AND HEALTH INSURANCE.

KIDNAP INSURANCE coverage in the event an employee is kidnapped from an insured business's premises and forced to return to aid a criminal in a theft.

KIDNAP-RANSOM INSURANCE *see* RANSOM INSURANCE.

KNOCK-FOR-KNOCK AGREEMENT arrangement between two or more insurance companies under which the parties to the agreement waive their SUBROGATION rights against the other. Most such agreements are no longer in use. *See also* INTERCOMPANY ARBITRATION.

L

LABOR AND MATERIAL BOND coverage to indemnify an owner for whom work was done if the completed work is not free of worker's liens for labor and material.

LABOR MANAGEMENT RELATIONS ACT OF 1947 *see* TAFT-HARTLEY ACT.

LABOR STATISTICS, BUREAU OF Federal agency which collects and analyzes numerous U.S. demographics used by government and industry. Insurance companies use the demographics to predict areas of high demand for their products, to perform market segmentation studies, and to position distribution systems.

LAG time which has elapsed between when claims actually occurred and when the claims are actually paid.

LAND OWNERSHIP, USE AND POSSESSION OF liability exposure, in insurance, associated with three classifications of individuals that may come upon an insured property:
1. TRESPASSER—individual enters without permission. Generally the insured has no legal obligation to render his land safe for the trespasser, but the insured cannot create a death trap.
2. LICENSEE—individual enters with permission but there is no mutual profit motive involved. Generally, the insured's only obligation to the licensee is to warn of any hidden dangers of which the insured is aware.
3. INVITEE—individual expressly or by implication is invited to enter property; there is a mutual profit motive. Generally, the insured must use reasonable care to render his property safe for the invitee's visit.

LAPSE
1. in property and casualty insurance, termination of a policy because of failure to pay a renewal premium.
2. in life insurance, termination of a policy because of failure to pay a premium and lack of sufficient cash value to make a premium loan.

LAPSED POLICY *see* LAPSE.

LAPSE RATIO percentage of a life insurance company's policies in force at the beginning of the year that are no longer in force at the end of the year. This ratio is critical because it indicates the rate at which policies are going off the books and the resultant loss of earnings to the company.

LARGE LOSS PRINCIPLE transfer of high severity risks through the insurance contract to protect against catastrophic occurrences. While insurance is generally not the most cost-effective means of recovery of minor losses, an insured cannot predict catastrophes and thus set aside enough money to cover losses on a mathematical basis or to self-insure. Actuarial tables are based on the large loss principle: the larger the number of exposures, the more closely losses will match the probability of loss. In essence, a large number of insureds, each paying a modest sum into an insurance plan, can protect against the relatively few catastrophes that will strike some of their numbers.

LAST CLEAR CHANCE common law rule of negligence which imposes liability on an individual who had one last opportunity to avoid an accident but did not take it. An example is a driver who could have avoided hitting another automobile by applying his brakes but did not do so. One reason for not avoiding—or even causing—an accident is a desire to collect insurance proceeds.

LAW OF LARGE NUMBERS mathematical premise stating that the greater the number of exposures (1) the more accurate the prediction; (2) the less the deviation of the actual losses from the expected losses ($X - \bar{x}$ approaches zero); and (3) the greater the credibility of the prediction (credibility approaches one). This law forms the basis for the statistical expectation of loss upon which premium rates for insurance policies are calculated. Out of a large group of policyholders the insurance company can fairly accurately predict the number of policyholders who will suffer a loss, not by name but by number. Life insurance premiums are loaded for the expected loss plus modest deviations. For example, if a life insurance company expects ($\bar{x}$) 10,000 of its policyholders to die in a particular year and that number or fewer actually die (X), there is no cause for concern on the part of the company's actuaries. However, if the life insurance company expects ($\bar{x}$) 10,000 of its policyholders to die in a particular year and more than that number dies (X) there is much cause for concern by actuaries.

LAWYERS (ATTORNEYS PROFESSIONAL) LIABILITY INSUR-ANCE coverage if a lawyer's professional act (or omission) results in the client inflicting bodily injury or property damage to another party, or if personal injury and/or property damage is incurred by a client, who brings an action for injuries and/or damages suffered. The policy also provides for defense costs, legal fees, and court costs of the defendant, even if the suit is without foundation.

LAYERING combination of several policies with each adding an additional layer or limit of coverage above the limits of the policy which comes before it. For example, Policy A adds $100,000, then Policy B adds $200,000 and then Policy C adds $300,000, for a total of

$600,000. In some instances a business firm cannot obtain the total coverage it requires from a single insurance company. Thus, the business may have to buy several policies from different companies in order to acquire the total needed.

LAY UNDERWRITER home office underwriter who evaluates risk based on probability, statistics, and medical knowledge.

LEAD INSURER insurance company that puts together a consortium of insurance and reinsurance companies to provide an adequate financial base with sufficient underwriting capacity to insure large risks. Usually the lead insurer will take a large percentage of the risk for its own account.

LEASE use of another party's property in exchange for rental payment. *See also* LEASEHOLD INSURANCE; LEASEHOLD PROFIT INTEREST; LEASEHOLD VALUE INTEREST.

LEASEHOLD *see* LEASE.

LEASEHOLD INSURANCE coverage for a tenant with a favorable lease (enabling the lessee to rent premises for less than the market value). If the lease is canceled by the *lessor* because an insured peril (such as fire) strikes, the lessee is indemnified for the loss incurred. The premise is that the lessee will have to forgo earnings derived from having an advantageous lease, and should be indemnified for this incurred loss.

LEASEHOLD PROFIT INTEREST difference between the rent received by a lessee for the subletting property, and the rent the lessee pays the lessor.

LEASEHOLD VALUE INTEREST difference between the rent paid by a lessee as fixed by a lease prior to destruction of property, and the rent received by the lessor after that property has been restored.

LEDGER COST *see* LIFE INSURANCE COST.

LEGAL *see* LEGAL PURPOSE; LEGAL RESERVE; LIABILITY, LEGAL.

LEGAL EXPENSE INSURANCE prepaid legal insurance coverage plan sold on a group basis. Entitles a group member to a schedule of benefits, at a stipulated premium, for adoptions, probates, divorces and other legal services. This emerging employee benefit has had wide acceptance in some localities but limited acceptance elsewhere. After scheduled benefits have been exhausted, subsequent legal fees are usually based on the attorney's customary rate. For example, a prepaid legal insurance plan may provide only three legal consultations a year.

LEGAL LIABILITY *see* LIABILITY, LEGAL.

LEGAL PURPOSE principle stating that an agreement to be entered into must be in line with public policy; that is, it cannot break any laws. The courts will not enforce an agreement based on illegal activities. For example, a contract for murder cannot be enforced in a court of law should the would-be murderer's efforts fail.

LEGAL RESERVE minimum that a life insurance company must maintain as a reserve for policies sold, as required by state insurance laws. Legal reserves are listed as liabilities on the insurance company's balance sheet.

LEGAL RESERVE LIFE INSURANCE COMPANY company in which reserves are determined by state law as sufficient to pay policyholder benefits when due. Reserves are listed as liabilities on the balance sheet of a life insurance company since they represent claims by policyholders against the company's assets. State insurance departments supervise the adequacy of a life insurance company's reserves.

LEMON AID INSURANCE property and casualty coverage that indemnifies automobile dealers if a dissatisfied customer demands a refund within the period of time allowed under the Uniform Commercial Code. This insurance is not widely sold today because of the increase in recalls of vehicles for inherent defects.

LENDER ESTATE V. COMMISSIONER legal decision wherein proceeds of a life insurance policy on which the decedent's corporation paid the preimums within 3 years of his or her death are not includable in the decedent's gross estate, as affirmed by the Tenth Circuit Court of Appeals.

LENDERS HOLDER-IN-DUE-COURSE INSURANCE coverage that indemnifies a third party lender if a customer refuses to repay a loan made on a faulty product, and the dealer who arranged the loan refuses to correct the fault. This coverage has gained new importance as more customers are refusing to repay loans on products with inherent defects.

LEVEL uniformity. *See also* COMMERCIAL HEALTH INSURANCE, LEVEL COMMISSION; LEVEL PREMIUM INSURANCE; LEVEL TERM INSURANCE.

LEVEL COMMISSION compensation in which an insurance agent's fee for the sale of a policy is the same year after year. Most life insurance companies pay a high first year commission and lower commissions in later years. This commission structure is controversial since critics feel that it is heavily weighted towards selling a product at the expense of subsequent service.

LEVEL PERCENTAGE OF COMPENSATION *see* DEFINED BENEFIT PLAN.

LEVEL PREMIUM premium that remains unchanged over time, regardless of any change in the nature of the risk.

LEVEL PREMIUM INSURANCE coverage in which premiums do not increase or decrease for as long as the policy remains in force. In the early years of a policy, the premiums are greater than is necessary to pay mortality costs. The excess is used to build the cash value and to provide for the increasing mortality costs later in the life of the policy.

LEVEL PREMIUM RENEWABLE TERM HEALTH INSURANCE *see* COMMERCIAL HEALTH INSURANCE.

LEVEL TERM INSURANCE coverage in which the face amount of a policy remains uniform, neither increasing nor decreasing for as long as the policy is in force.

LIABILITIES: LIFE INSURANCE COMPANIES future benefits to be paid to the policyholders and beneficiaries, assigned surpluses, and miscellaneous debts. These primary liabilities take the form of reserves, which must be listed on the company's balance sheet as part of the liabilities section. The valuation of a company's reserves, which guarantee that funds will be available to meet its liabilities, is strictly regulated by the state insurance departments. Life insurance company liabilities also include cash surrender values of its policies and annuities.

LIABILITY legal obligation to perform or not perform specified act(s): In insurance the concern is with the circumstance in which (1) one party's property is damaged or destroyed, or (2) that party incurs bodily injury as the result of the negligent acts or omissions of another party. Liability insurance is designed to provide coverage for either exposure on a business or personal basis. *See also* BUSINESS LIABILITY INSURANCE; COMPREHENSIVE PERSONAL LIABILITY INSURANCE; LIABILITY, PERSONAL EXPOSURES.

LIABILITY, ABSOLUTE *see* ABSOLUTE LIABILITY.

LIABILITY, BUSINESS EXPOSURES negligent acts or omissions which result in actual or imagined bodily injury and/or property damage to a third party, who brings suit against a business firm and its representatives.

LIABILITY, CIVIL alleged torts or breaches of contract, but not crimes. Action is brought by one individual against another at the litigant's own expense, within the statute of limitations. The losing party must pay any judgment plus court expenses. Casualty insurance provides coverage for an insured in a civil liability suit for alleged negligent acts or omissions, even if the suit is without foundation.

LIABILITY, CIVIL DAMAGES AWARDED three types of damages can be awarded to a plaintiff:

1. *Special Damages*—reimbursement for out-of-pocket expenses, including medical bills, legal charges, cost of repairing damaged or destroyed property, and loss of current and projected income.
2. *General Damages*—reimbursement for damages which do not readily lend themselves to quantitative measurement, commonly known as "pain and suffering."
3. *Punitive Damages*—reimbursement for damages due to gross negligence by a defendant.

LIABILITY CLAIM *see* CLAIMS MADE BASIS LIABILITY COVERAGE; CLAIMS OCCURRENCE BASIS LIABILITY COVERAGE.

LIABILITY, CONTINGENT *see* CONTINGENT LIABILITY (VICARIOUS LIABILITY).

LIABILITY, CONTRACTUAL *see* CONTRACTUAL LIABILITY.

LIABILITY, CRIMINAL wrong against the government or society as a whole. An individual representing the State (usually the district attorney) brings an action on behalf of the State against an individual(s) or entity who has broken a criminal (non-civil) law. Insurance is not designed to cover criminal liability; to do so would encourage criminal behavior.

LIABILITY INSURANCE coverage for all sums which the insured becomes legally obligated to pay because of bodily injury or property damage, and sometimes other wrongs to which an insurance policy applies. Personal liability policies include COMPREHENSIVE PERSONAL LIABILITY (CPL), HOMEOWNERS INSURANCE POLICY, PERSONAL AUTOMOBILE POLICY (PAP), *Personal Umbrella Liability*, and the *Uninsured Motorist Endorsement*. Business liability policies include BUSINESS AUTOMOBILE POLICY (BAP), BUSINESSOWNERS POLICY, *Completed Operations and Products Liability,* COMPREHENSIVE GENERAL LIABILITY INSURANCE (CGPL), *Employers Liability and Workers Compensation*, MANUFACTURERS AND CONTRACTORS LIABILITY (M&C), OWNERS, LANDLORDS AND TENANTS LIABILITY INSURANCE POLICY (OL&T), *Physicians, Surgeons and Dentists Professional Liability*, STOREKEEPERS LIABILITY INSURANCE, *Umbrella Liability Policy*, and the *Uninsured Motorists Coverage*.

LIABILITY, LEGAL obligations and responsibilities subject to evaluation, interpretation, and enforcement in a court of law. Casualty insurance provides coverage for an insured against a civil legal liability suit, not criminal legal liability, intentional torts, or liability for breach of contract. *See also* LIABILITY, CIVIL; LIABILITY, CIVIL DAMAGES AWARDED.

LIABILITY: LIMITATIONS ON INSURERS exceptions to coverage. There is no obligation for an insurance company to pay a claim if:
1. the loss is not covered by a policy or if a particular person is not included in the definition of the insured.
2. the loss takes place outside the territorial coverage of the policy. For example, there is no coverage under the PERSONAL AUTOMOBILE POLICY (PAP) outside the United States and Canada.
3. the loss takes place after the policy has expired.
4. the insured involved in the loss was in violation of public law, for example, an insured's car that is damaged as the result of his transporting drugs.
5. the insured is in violation of contract law.
6. the limit of coverage under the policy is not sufficient to cover a loss.

LIABILITY LIMITS maximum amount of coverage available under a liability insurance policy. *See also* AGGREGATE LIMIT; BASIC LIMITS OF LIABILITY; BUSINESS LIABILITY INSURANCE (Insuring Agreement section); LIABILITY: LIMITATIONS ON INSURERS; LOSS.

LIABILITY, NO-FAULT INSURANCE *see* NO-FAULT AUTOMOBILE INSURANCE.

LIABILITY, PERSONAL EXPOSURES acts or omissions which result in suits against an individual and/or residents of the individual's household for actual or imagined bodily injury and/or property damage to a third party. Exposures include:
1. ownership, use, and possession of property concerning: (a) trespass—the obligation is not to render property safe for a trespasser, but one cannot create a death trap or maintain an attractive nuisance, such as a swimming pool, without proper safeguards; (b) licensee—the obligation is not to render property safe for a licensee but to provide adequate warning of any hidden dangers such as quicksand at the side of an approach road; (c) invitation—the obligation is to render the property safe for an invitee's visit. For example, if someone trips on a throw rug, the owner or occupier of the premises can be held liable.
2. ownership, use, and possession of a motorized vehicle on or off premises.
3. involvement in sports.
4. actions of pets.

LIABILITY, PROFESSIONAL liability created when an individual who offers services to the general public claims expertise in a particular area greater than the ordinary layman. Today, suits are frequently brought alleging that a professional such as a physician, attorney, or CPA, has committed negligent acts or omissions in performing the purchased service. For some professions, such as medical specialties, it has become impossible to purchase professional liability insurance at a reasonable price. Premiums have become prohibitive because of the frequency and severity of both reasonable and unreasonable professional liability suits.

LIABILITY, PRO RATA *see* PRO RATA LIABILITY CLAUSE.

LIABILITY RISK *see* LIABILITY, BUSINESS EXPOSURES; LIABILITY, PERSONAL EXPOSURES.

LIABILITY, STRICT *see* STRICT LIABILITY.

LIABILITY, VICARIOUS *see* CONTINGENT LIABILITY (VICARIOUS LIABILITY).

LIABILITY WITHOUT REGARD TO FAULT *see* ABSOLUTE LIABILITY; STRICT LIABILITY.

LIBEL *see* TORT, INTENTIONAL.

LIBEL INSURANCE coverage for an insured in the event that he writes and publishes libelous statements and the injured party brings suit against the insured.

LIBERALIZATION CLAUSE in PROPERTY INSURANCE policy, clause which stipulates that, if legislative acts or acts of the insurance commissioner's office expand the coverage of an insurance policy or endorsement forms without requiring an additional premium, then all similar insurance policies and endorsement forms will automatically have such expanded coverage.

LICENSE in insurance, legal authority obtained by an insurance company, agent, broker, or consultant which permits them to do business in a particular state. The document issued by the state shows that the company or person is in compliance with the various governing laws and thus is authorized to conduct insurance business in that jurisdiction. A license, in and of itself, is not a guarantee that a consumer will be sold the best product to fit his needs or that an agent will have the proper technical expertise to evaluate the products on a consumer's behalf.

LICENSE BOND instrument that guarantees compliance with various city, county, and state laws that govern the issuance of a particular license to conduct business.

LICENSEE individual permitted to enter property with the permission of the owner or the person who controls the property. There is no mutual profit motive; the licensee comes onto the property for his sole benefit. For example, the owner of land gives an individual permission to hunt on the property but does not charge him a fee. The owner must warn the licensee of any hidden dangers on the property of which he is aware.

LICENSE FEE sum paid by an insurance company or other firms or individuals to designated types of business in a particular state or municipality.

LICENSING OF AGENTS AND BROKERS legal authority granting individuals the right to conduct insurance business in a particular state. In many states, agents and brokers must pass a written exam as a prerequisite to being licensed. In others, a professional designation such as the CLU or CPCU can be substituted for the examination requirement. The caliber of examinations varies from state to state. A license is usually issued for one or two year periods, and then must be renewed.

LIEN action brought by a worker or creditor for failure to receive payment for labor and material provided. Property insurance is available for individuals with an insurable interest in property against which they may bring a lien.

LIFE AND HEALTH, BUSINESS EXPOSURES loss of a key person due to death, disability, sickness, resignation, incarceration, or retirement. Because of the expertise of such an individual, there could be a loss of income, market share, research and development advantage, and line of credit by the firm. Also, there are extra expenses associated with training a replacement for a key person. Coverage for many of these exposures is available under key person life and health insurance. *See also* BUY AND SELL AGREEMENT.

LIFE AND HEALTH INSURANCE PARTNERSHIP *see* PARTNERSHIP, LIFE AND HEALTH INSURANCE

LIFE AND HEALTH INSURANCE, PERSONAL AND FAMILY EXPOSURES personal and family loss by death, disability, sickness, old-age, accident, and unemployment. All of these exposures are insurable, and coverages can be purchased under a variety of policies. In life insurance these include ADJUSTABLE LIFE, CURRENT ASSUMPTION, ENDOWMENT, FAMILY INCOME POLICIES, FAMILY MAINTENANCE POLICIES, FAMILY POLICY, LIMITED PAYMENT LIFE, TERM LIFE, UNIVERSAL LIFE, and VARIABLE LIFE. In annuities, both fixed and variable types are available in health insurance, medical expense and disability income coverages are available. In pensions, there are DEFINED BENEFIT and DEFINED CONTRIBUTION PENSION plans. The various Social Security benefits also provide considerable protection against personal and family exposures.

LIFE ANNUITY *see* ANNUITY.

LIFE ANNUITY CERTAIN ANNUITY guaranteeing a given number of income payments whether or not the annuitant is alive to receive them. If the annuitant is living after the guaranteed number of payments have been made, the income continues for life. If the annuitant dies within the guarantee period, the balance is paid to a beneficiary. For example, under one common contract, a life annuity certain for 10 years, income payments are guaranteed for a minimum of 10 years. If the annuitant dies after receiving two years of payments, the beneficiary would receive the remaining eight years of income. An annuitant who lives out the 10 years would receive income payments for life, but there would be none available to a beneficiary.

LIFE ANNUITY CERTAIN AND CONTINUOUS *see* LIFE ANNUITY CERTAIN.

LIFE ANNUITY DUE *see* ANNUITY DUE.

LIFE ESTATE *see* ESTATE PLANNING DISTRIBUTION.

LIFE EXPECTANCY probability of one's living to a specific age according to a particular MORTALITY TABLE. Life expectancy is the beginning point in calculating the pure cost of life insurance and annuities and is reflected in what is known as the BASIC PREMIUM. The probability of living longer has continued to increase in the U.S. and thus the pure cost of insurance continues to decrease. This is reflected in a declining premium rate. Increasing life expectancy is critical to the cash value projection in CURRENT ASSUMPTIONS life insurance products, such as universal life insurance and variable life insurance.

LIFE INCOME annuity payments that continue for the life of the annuitant. *See also* ANNUITY.

LIFE INCOME WITH PERIOD CERTAIN annuity payments that continue for the life of the annuitant; should the annuitant not survive a stated period, the payments are then made to a beneficiary until the stated period ends.

LIFE INSURANCE protection against the death of an individual in the form of payment to a beneficiary—usually a family member, business, or institution. In exchange for a series of premium payments or a single premium payment, upon the death of an insured, the face value (and any additional coverage attached to a policy), minus outstanding policy loans and interest, is paid to the beneficiary. *Living benefits* may be available for the insured in the form of surrender values or income payments. *See also* ADJUSTABLE LIFE INSURANCE; ENDOWMENT INSURANCE; FAMILY INCOME POLICY; FAMILY INCOME RIDER; FAMILY MAINTENANCE INSURANCE; LIMITED PAYMENT LIFE INSURANCE;

ORDINARY LIFE INSURANCE; TERM INSURANCE; UNIVERSAL LIFE INSURANCE; VARIABLE LIFE INSURANCE.

LIFE INSURANCE, ASSIGNMENT CLAUSE *see* ASSIGNMENT CLAUSE, LIFE INSURANCE.

LIFE INSURANCE, BUSINESS USES *see* BUSINESS LIFE AND HEALTH INSURANCE.

LIFE INSURANCE CONTRACT *see* INSURANCE CONTRACT, LIFE.

LIFE INSURANCE COST amount paid to an insurer. Determination of the actual cost (not the price paid) of a life insurance policy has been widely discussed for many years in life insurance and consumer circles. The *traditional* or *net cost* method (that adds a policy's premiums, and subtracts dividends, if any, and cash value) does not consider the TIME VALUE OF MONEY. The LINTON YIELD METHOD, a theoretical approach, attempted to remedy this by comparing a cash value policy with a combination of decreasing term insurance and the yield of a side fund of bonds and other investments. Other methods have been proposed. At present many states require prospective insureds to be given INTEREST-ADJUSTED COST figures that do take into consideration the time value of money. This method is not altogether practical for INTEREST SENSITIVE POLICIES, but it is generally felt that present work toward a new approach will eventually result in a useful means of comparing the costs of these policies.

LIFE INSURANCE, CREDITOR RIGHTS protection given to life insurance beneficiaries by state laws, under which the benefits of a life insurance policy usually cannot be attached by creditors of an insured and/or beneficiary. These laws are based on philosophical concerns— dating back to the founding of the U.S., and the Homestead Laws— that a widow and children should not be made to pay for the financial sins of the father.

LIFE INSURANCE, FAMILY PROTECTION *see* FAMILY INCOME POLICY; FAMILY INCOME RIDER; FAMILY MAINTENANCE POLICY; FAMILY POLICY.

LIFE INSURANCE IN FORCE aggregate of face amount of coverage paid up, or on which premiums are still being paid, as issued by a life insurance company. This is one measure used to rank life insurance companies by size.

LIFE INSURANCE: LIFE RISK *see* HUMAN LIFE VALUE APPROACH (EVOIL); NEEDS APPROACH.

LIFE INSURANCE LIMITS *see* FACE AMOUNT (FACE OF POLICY); RENEWABLE TERM LIFE INSURANCE.

LIFE INSURANCE, LIVING BENEFITS *see* LIVING BENEFITS OF LIFE INSURANCE.

LIFE INSURANCE MARKETING AND RESEARCH ASSOCIATION (LIMRA) organization that conducts research on distribution systems for the life and health insurance products on behalf of its member companies. Studies range from consumer attitudes towards the life insurance product to reasons for turnover of the agency field force. Headquarters in Hartford, Connecticut.

LIFE INSURANCE, ORDINARY *see* ORDINARY LIFE INSURANCE.

LIFE INSURANCE POLICIES PROVIDING FAMILY PROTECTION coverage giving income benefits to surviving family member(s) if one member should die. These include the FAMILY INCOME POLICY, FAMILY INCOME RIDER, FAMILY MAINTENANCE POLICY, and the FAMILY POLICY.

LIFE INSURANCE RENEWABILITY *see* RENEWABLE TERM LIFE INSURANCE.

LIFE INSURANCE RESERVES *see* FULL PRELIMINARY TERM RESERVE PLAN; PROSPECTIVE RESERVE; RETROSPECTIVE METHOD RESERVE COMPUTATION.

LIFE INSURANCE SETTLEMENT OPTIONS *see* OPTIONAL MODES OF SETTLEMENT.

LIFE INSURANCE, STRAIGHT *see* ORDINARY LIFE INSURANCE.

LIFE INSURANCE, TERM *see* TERM LIFE INSURANCE.

LIFE INSURANCE TRUST agreement establishing a trust for the named beneficiary under a life insurance policy. Upon the death of the insured, the trust has the legal obligation to pay the policy proceeds in the manner stipulated in the trust agreement.

LIFE INSURANCE, WHOLE LIFE *see* ORDINARY LIFE INSURANCE.

LIFE INSURERS CONFERENCE (LIC) organization of *home service debit* life insurance companies and combination companies. *See also* COMBINATION AGENT; DEBIT INSURANCE (HOME SERVICE INSURANCE, INDUSTRIAL INSURANCE).

LIFE MANAGEMENT INSTITUTE unit of the LIFE OFFICE MANAGEMENT ASSOCIATION (LOMA) which prepares and administers educational materials for the Fellow Life Management Institute (FLMI) Program. Upon successful completion of its examinations, the student receives the FLMI designation.

LIFE OFFICE MANAGEMENT ASSOCIATION (LOMA) organization which develops and administers educational materials and examinations for the life insurance industry. It awards the FELLOW, LIFE MANAGEMENT INSTITUTE (FLMI) designation to individuals who pass a series of 10 national life and health insurance examinations on insurance, accounting, marketing, information systems, finance, law, management, and computers.

LIFE PAID UP AT SPECIFIED AGE *see* LIMITED PAYMENT LIFE INSURANCE.

LIFE PLANNING *see* ESTATE PLANNING; ESTATE PLANNING DISTRIBUTION; HUMAN LIFE VALUE APPROACH (ECONOMIC VALUE OF AN INDIVIDUAL LIFE) (EVOIL).

LIFE REINSURANCE system whereby a life insurance company (the reinsured) reduces its possible maximum loss on either an individual life insurance policy (FACULTATIVE REINSURANCE) or on a large number of life insurance policies (AUTOMATIC REINSURANCE) by giving (ceding) a portion of its liability to another insurance company (the reinsurer). *See also* REINSURANCE.

LIFE RISK FACTORS information needed for underwriting a life insurance policy such as an applicant's age, weight, height, and build; personal and family health record; occupation, and personal habits. These factors decide into which rate classification to place the applicant since they determine to a significant degree the probability of an applicant's length of life.

LIFETIME DISABILITY BENEFIT provision in some disability income policies, which provides a monthly income benefit to a disabled insured for as long as he or she remains disabled according to the definition of disability in the policy. *See also* DISABILITY INCOME INSURANCE.

LIFETIME POLICY *see* LIFETIME DISABILITY BENEFIT.

LIFE UNDERWRITER life insurance agent.

LIFE UNDERWRITER POLITICAL ACTION COMMITTEE (LUPAC) affiliate of the NATIONAL ASSOCIATION OF LIFE UNDERWRITERS (NALU) that supports legislators in the interest of the insurance agents. One becomes a member of LUPCA through a monetary contribution.

LIFE UNDERWRITING TRAINING COUNCIL (LUTC) organization that develops and administers educational materials and examinations for life insurance agents. A significant objective of the courses is sales technique.

LIGHTNING discharge of electricity from the atmosphere, one of the perils covered in most fire insurance policies.

LIMIT, AGGREGATE *see* AGGREGATE LIMIT.

LIMIT, ANNUAL AGGREGATE *see* ANNUAL AGGREGATE LIMIT.

LIMITATIONS exceptions and limitations of coverage; that is, the maximum amount of insurance coverage available under a policy. *See also* COINSURANCE.

LIMITATIONS ON AMOUNT OF MONTHLY BENEFITS clause in some DISABILITY INCOME INSURANCE policies under which there is a maximum an insured can receive from all sources of disability income benefits. For example, the clause may stipulate that all sources of disability income cannot exceed 50% of the insured's gross earnings prior to the disability.

LIMITATIONS ON INSURERS LIABILITY *see* LIABILITY: LIMITATIONS ON INSURERS.

LIMIT, BASIC *see* BASIC LIMITS OF LIABILITY.

LIMIT, BLANKET *see* BLANKET LIMIT.

LIMIT, DIVIDED *see* SPLIT LIMIT.

LIMITED PAYMENT LIFE INSURANCE type of policy with premiums that are fully paid up within a stated period. For example, a 20-payment life insurance policy has 20 annual premium payments, with no further premiums to be paid.

LIMITED POLICY type of health insurance providing benefits for only a particular peril, such as cancer.

LIMITED POLLUTION LIABILITY COVERAGE FORM commercial liability insurance form providing coverage for an insured business in the event of a pollution liability suit. The insurance provides CLAIMS MADE BASIS LIABILITY COVERAGE. Excluded from coverage are clean-up costs.

LIMIT, EXCESS *see* EXCESS LIMIT.

LIMIT, LINE *see* LINE LIMIT.

LIMIT OF LIABILITY *see* LIABILITY: LIMITATIONS ON INSURERS.

LIMIT OF RECOVERY *see* COINSURANCE.

LIMIT, PER ACCIDENT *see* PER ACCIDENT LIMIT.

LIMIT, PER PERSON maximum amount under a liability policy that insurance company will pay for bodily injury incurred by any one person in any one accident.

LIMIT, POLICY *see* LIMITATIONS.

LIMITS *see* LIABILITY: LIMITATIONS ON INSURERS; COINSURANCE.

LIMIT, SCHEDULED *see* SCHEDULED LIMIT.

LIMIT, SINGLE *see* SINGLE LIMIT.

LIMIT, SPECIFIC *see* SPECIFIC LIMIT.

LIMIT, STANDARD *see* BASIC LIMITS OF LIABILITY.

LIMIT, VARIABLE *see* VARIABLE LIMIT.

LINE term used for a general class of insurance such as LIFE INSURANCE, PROPERTY INSURANCE, or WORKERS COMPENSATION INSURANCE.

LINE, GROSS *see* GROSS LINE.

LINE LIMIT maximum amount of a specified type of insurance coverage, according to underwriting guidelines, that an insurance company feels it can safely underwrite on a particular exposure without having to acquire REINSURANCE for that exposure. *See also* LINE; SURPLUS LINES; SURPLUS REINSURANCE.

LINE, NET *see* NET LINE.

LINE OF BUSINESS *see* LINE; LINES OF INSURANCE, MAJOR.

LINE OF CREDIT borrowing power that a business firm or an individual has with a lending institution such as a bank.

LINES *see* SURPLUS LINES.

LINE SHEET amount of insurance coverage that an insurance company is willing to write on a given category of business.

LINES OF INSURANCE, MAJOR five primary sectors of insurance coverage. Their purposes are:
1. LIFE INSURANCE—provides income to a beneficiary in the event of the death of the insured.
2. HEALTH INSURANCE—provides two types of coverage: (a) *Medical Expense*, which indemnifies an insured for hospital, physician and related expenses; (b) *Disability Income*, which provides a source of income for an insured in the event of partial or total disability. It is

generally felt that this source of income should approximate at least 50% of earnings prior to a disability.

3. ANNUITY—provides monthly income to an annuitant for life.

4. PROPERTY INSURANCE—indemnifies an insured for damages or destruction of property.

5. LIABILITY INSURANCE—covers damages on behalf of an insured who becomes legally obligated to pay because of actual (or alleged) negligent acts and omissions.

LINTON YIELD METHOD interest adjusted method that measures the cost of life insurance. Named for the late distinguished actuary, M. Albert Linton. This method compares a whole life policy with a combination of a decreasing term policy and a side fund. The rate of return of the side fund is called the Linton Yield, in that it brings the side fund up to an amount equal to the cash value of the whole life policy after a specified period of time.

LIQUIDATION AND REHABILITATION taking over of an insurance company's assets by the State Insurance Commissioner when examination of the annual report reveals that the company is in substantial financial difficulty. The State Insurance Commissioner will then operate the company in what is deemed to be the best interest of the policyowners, insureds, and creditors. If the State Insurance Commissioner believes it is possible to save the company, rehabilitation (reorganization of the company's structure) may be ordered; if salvage is deemed impossible, liquidation may be necessary.

LIQUIDATION CHARGE amount subtracted from an annuity or from mutual fund proceeds payable to an annuity owner or mutual fund owner to reflect expense fees described in the annuity contract or mutual fund prospectus. This charge may be viewed as a penalty for cashing in the annuity or mutual fund early. This fee is meant to discourage early withdrawal of funds and/or to enable the company to recoup its expenses associated with marketing, administering, and liquidating the product.

LIQUIDATION PERIOD time frame during which an annuitant receives income payments from the insurance company, usually on a monthly basis. The obligations of the company to the annuitant during the liquidation period depend on whether it is a *pure* or *refund* annuity. For the PURE ANNUITY, all payments cease upon the death of the annuitant. For the REFUND ANNUITY, a beneficiary is usually entitled to payments upon the death of the annuitant.

LIQUIDITY OF ASSETS financial holdings that can be converted into cash in a timely manner without the loss of principal, such as U.S. Treasury Bills. Liquidity of assets is one of the most important principles of investment strategies, especially the first layer of an investment portfolio. Life insurance is generally placed in this first layer because of its cash value. The owner has complete liquidity since it can be used as collateral for a loan at any time.

LIQUOR LIABILITY LAWS legislation that makes an establishment and/or individual selling liquor responsible for injuries caused by its customers to third parties. The best known law governing dispensation of liquor on premises is the DRAM SHOP LAW. For example, an individual is served liquor at an establishment and becomes intoxicated. On his way home he causes an accident, injuring another party. The injured third party can bring a liability suit against the establishment that dispensed the liquor for injuries suffered.

LIVE ANIMAL INSURANCE coverage under the *Commercial Property Floater* for loss under two forms: LIVESTOCK MORTALITY LIFE INSURANCE and LIVESTOCK FLOATER. This is really life insurance coverage for livestock.

LIVESTOCK FLOATER standard *Commercial Property Floater* form covering death or damage to livestock as the result of insured perils such as fire, lightning, explosion, smoke, wind, hail, aircraft, earthquake, theft, flood, collapse of bridges, collision, or overturn of a vehicle used in transporting the livestock from the point of destination. Some insurance companies also cover attacks by domestic or wild animals, drowning, and accidental shooting. Common exclusions include illegal acts, confiscation by the order of a government authority, loss due to quarantine, war, loss due to sleet or snow, and loss due to the acceptance by the owner of a check covered by insufficient funds.

LIVESTOCK INSURANCE coverage for designated horses and other farm animals if they are damaged or destroyed. The insurance includes registered cattle and herds, other farm livestock, and zoo animals. This type of insurance protects the farmer or rancher against the premature death of animals resulting from natural causes, fire, lightning, accidents, and acts of God, acts of individuals other than the owner or employees, and destruction for humane purposes.

LIVESTOCK MORTALITY (LIFE) INSURANCE coverage that provides a death benefit to the owner of a policy in the event of the death of insured livestock.

LIVESTOCK TRANSIT INSURANCE coverage in event of damage or destruction of animals that are being shipped.

LIVING still with life. This is a life insurance term used to describe the *living benefits* available under a life insurance policy such as a monthly retirement payment to an insured.

LIVING BENEFITS OF LIFE INSURANCE benefits provided to and obtained by those insured, while still alive. They include the ANNUITY, CASH SURRENDER VALUE, DISABILITY INCOME (DI), POLICY LOAN, and WAIVER OF PREMIUM (WP).

LIVING TRUST *see* ESTATE PLANNING DISTRIBUTION.

LIVING WILL legal document which permits the individual to declare his or her desires concerning the use of life-sustaining treatment to be made at the point in time when death is imminent and the individual no longer has control of his or her faculties. This type of will has the advantages of ensuring that the individual's wishes are followed to the conclusion and that a family member does not have the burden of making extremely agonizing decisions on behalf of the individual. It is the requirement of most state statutes that such a will be signed, dated, and witnessed (excluding anyone who has an interest in the estate of the individual affirming the will). Also required by most state statutes is that the will include both a statement of capacity and a statement of intent by the individual. The following states have statutes addressing the living will issue: Alabama, Arizona, Arkansas, California, Colorado, Connecticut, Delaware, Florida, Georgia, Idaho, Illinois, Indiana, Iowa, Kansas, Louisiana, Maine, Maryland, Mississippi, Missouri, Montana, Nevada, New Hampshire, New Mexico, North Carolina, Oklahoma, Oregon, South Carolina, Tennessee, Texas, Utah, Vermont, Virginia, Washington, West Virginia, Wisconsin, and Wyoming, as well as Washington, D.C. *See also* ESTATE PLANNING DISTRIBUTION.

LLOYD'S ASSOCIATION organization following the format of LLOYD'S OF LONDON.

LLOYD'S BROKER specialist whose task is to place insurance with the specialized syndicates that underwrite particular risks at LLOYD'S OF LONDON.

LLOYD'S OF LONDON insurance facility composed of many different syndicates, each specializing in a particular risk, for example, hull risks. Lloyd's provides coverage for primary jumbo risks as well as offering REINSURANCE and RETROCESSIONS. Membership in a syndicate is limited to individuals with a large personal net worth, and each member may belong to one or more syndicates depending upon his net worth. Although much of the publicity Lloyd's receives involves insuring exotic risks such as an actress' legs, this represents only a very small portion of its total business, most of which involves reinsurance and retrocessions.

LLOYD'S REGISTER OF SHIPPING classification of ships according to their construction material, age, physical condition, propulsion type, stress tests of structure, and owners. Marine insurance rates for a particular vessel are based on these demographics. Lloyd's register is used worldwide by government agencies and industry to track and identify vessels. In many instances the country of registration is of strategic importance if a vessel is exposed to attack, say in the Middle East and in danger points in the world.

LLOYD'S SYNDICATE group of underwriters with LLOYD'S OF LONDON who specialize in underwriting a particular risk such as hull insurance.

LLOYD'S UNDERWRITER individual member of one of the syndicates of LLOYD'S OF LONDON.

LOADING addition to the pure cost of insurance that reflects agent commissions, premium taxes, administrative costs associated with putting business on an insurance company's books, and contingencies.

LOAN money that is lent. In life insurance, a loan can be taken against the cash value of a life insurance policy at any time. The policyholder does not have to repay the loan until the policy matures or until the loan and any outstanding interest equals the cash value.

LOAN RECEIPT acknowledgment by the POLICYOWNER that he or she has received the POLICY LOAN requested.

LOAN VALUE amount that a policyowner can borrow from a cash value of a permanent life insurance policy.

LONGSHOREMEN AND HARBOR WORKERS ACT LIABILITY coverage under the Workers Compensation Act for all employees in the maritime industry who perform their function in navigable U.S. waters, including dry docks, wharves, piers, and other places for docking. Excluded are the master and crew of the ship, and any individual involved in loading, unloading, or repairing of a ship whose weight is less than 18 tons.

LONGSHOREMEN AND HARBOR WORKERS ENDORSEMENT extension of a Workers Compensation and Employers Liability Insurance policy to cover workers who go aboard ship to perform their jobs. *See also* WORKERS COMPENSATION BENEFITS; WORKERS COMPENSATION, COVERAGE B.

LONG-TAIL LIABILITY one where an injury or other harm takes time to become known and a claim may be separated from the circumstances that caused it by as many as 25 years or more. Some examples: exposure to asbestos, which sometimes results in a lung disease called asbestosis; exposure to coal dust, which might cause black lung disease; or use of certain drugs that may cause cancer or birth defects. These long-tail liabilities became very expensive for many corporations in the 1970s, and 1980s, also causing problems for insurers because it was unclear when the situation that gave rise to the claim happened and who should pay the claim. One theory, the MANIFESTATION/INJURY THEORY, states that the insurer is responsible whenever the disease is diagnosed. The other view, the OCCURRENCE/INJURY THEORY, states that the insurer must pay only when the person is injured.

LONG-TERM CARE (LTC) day-to-day care that a patient (generally older than 65) receives in a nursing facility or in his or her residence following an illness or injury, or in old age, such that the patient can no longer perform at least two of the five basic activities of daily living: walking, eating, dressing, using the bathroom, and mobility from one place to another. There are basically three types of LTC plans:

1. *Skilled nursing care* provided only by skilled medical professionals as ordered by a physician. MEDICARE will pay a limited amount of the associated cost.
2. *Intermediate care* provided only by skilled medical professionals as ordered by a physician. This care involves the occasional nursing and rehabilitative assistance required by a patient.
3. *Custodial care* provided only by skilled medical professionals as ordered by a physician. The patient requires personal assistance in order to conduct his or her basic daily living activities.

When selecting a LTC policy, some of the more important considerations include:

1. *Renewability*—policy should be a GUARANTEED RENEWABLE CONTRACT.
2. *Waiting period*—length of time before benefits are paid should not exceed 90 days.
3. *Age eligibility*—upper age limit should be at least 80.
4. *Length of time benefits are paid*—typically the range is 5 to 10 years. It would be preferable to have benefits paid for life.
5. *Inflation guard*—the benefit level should be automatically adjusted each year according to the increase in the costs charged by the long-term-care providers.
6. *Premium waiver*—after the patient has received benefits for at least 90 days, the patient is no longer required to make premium payments for as long as he or she is under long-term care.
7. No increase of premiums *with age*—premiums should be based on the age at the time of application and should never increase as a result of changes in age.
8. *No limitations for preexisting conditions*—there should be no PREEXISTING CONDITION limitations.

LONG-TERM DISABILITY INCOME INSURANCE coverage that provides monthly income payments for as long as an insured remains disabled. The insurance policy defines the nature of the disability it covers. Most policies discontinue income payments beyond age 65. *See also* DISABILITY INCOME INSURANCE.

LOSS damage through an insured's negligent acts and/or omissions resulting in bodily injury and/or property damage to a third party; damage to an insured's property; or amount an insurance company has a legal obligation to pay.
  1. a company is legally obligated to pay the least of the following amounts: (a) amount of the loss; (b) limits of coverage; (c) amount resulting from the application of the coinsurance formula, such that

$$\frac{\text{Insurance Carried}}{\text{Insurance Required}} \times \text{Amount of Loss} = \begin{array}{l}\text{Amount of}\\ \text{Payment to}\\ \text{Insured}\end{array}$$

where Insurance Required = Value of Property × Coinsurance
  For example, assume that the insured had a $200,000 home destroyed totally by fire; carried $150,000 in insurance coverage; and there was an 80% coinsurance requirement. Then, according to the formula

$$\frac{\$150,000}{\$200,000 \times 80\%} \times \$200,000 = \$187,500 = \begin{array}{l}\text{Amount}\\ \text{of Payment}\\ \text{to Insured}\end{array}$$

(d) amount according to the pro rata distribution clause. If there is more than one insurance policy covering the damaged or destroyed property, each policy will pay no more than its proportionate share of the loss. In the foregoing example if the insured had two separate $200,000 policies, each would pay no more than $100,000.
  2. questions regarding loss coverage include: Is the peril covered? Is the property covered? Is the person covered? Is the policy in force? Are the limits of coverage adequate? Is the location covered? Has the hazard been increased?
  3. steps an insured should take: (a) send written notice immediately to the insurance company or its agent; (b) do everything reasonable to protect the property from further damage; (c) separate damaged from undamaged property; (d) provide the insurance company with a written inventory of damaged or destroyed property; (e) submit within 60 days following the loss written proof of the loss; and (f) make the damaged or destroyed property available for examination by the insurance company.

LOSS ADJUSTMENT EXPENSE cost involved in an insurance company's adjustment of losses under a policy.

LOSS ASSUMPTION *see* RETENTION AND LIMITS CLAUSE; RISK MANAGEMENT; SELF INSURANCE.

LOSS AVOIDANCE *see* AVOIDANCE.

LOSS CLAUSE feature of property and casualty policy providing coverage without a reduction in the policy's limits after a loss is paid. For example, if the limit of coverage under a property policy is $100,000 and a loss of $50,000 is paid, the limit still remains $100,000. Thus, the total amount of coverage in force for future losses is $100,000. In the absence of a loss clause, the total limit of coverage is reduced after payment of a loss.

LOSS CONSTANT surcharge, in retrospective rating of property and liability insurance, added to the BASIC PREMIUM rate charged to reflect fixed cost of adjusting or settling losses.

LOSS CONTROL *see* ENGINEERING APPROACH; HUMAN APPROACH; RISK MANAGEMENT.

LOSS CONVERSION FACTOR measure used in the RESTROSPECTIVE RATING method for WORKERS COMPENSATION INSURANCE. A factor is applied to the INCURRED LOSSES during the rating period in question in order to generate a loss adjustment expense amount to be used in claim investigation and settlement.

LOSS DEVELOPMENT difference in the amount of losses between the beginning and end of a time period.

LOSS DEVELOPMENT FACTOR element used to adjust losses to reflect the INCURRED BUT NOT REPORTED CLAIM (IBNR) under the retrospective method of rating. *See also* RETROSPECTIVE RATING.

LOSSES reductions in the value of property due to physical damage or destruction.

LOSSES INCURRED important quantitative measure for an insurance company indicating the percentage of each premium dollar that is going to pay for losses. Based on losses incurred, appropriate reserves are established. Changes in incurred losses over several policy periods indicate the trend in the loss picture and the accuracy of the basic premium charged to reflect expected losses.

LOSSES OUTSTANDING losses representing claims not paid.

LOSSES PAID losses representing claims paid.

LOSS EVENT circumstance which produces the loss.

LOSS FREQUENCY *see* FREQUENCY; FREQUENCY AND DISTRIBUTION OF LOSSES.

LOSS FREQUENCY METHOD procedure used in projecting the number of future losses within a given time frame. This prediction of future losses forms the basic premium onto which loadings are made for an insurance company's expenses, profits, and contingencies.

LOSS OF INCOME INSURANCE coverage in property insurance for an employee's lost income if a peril such as fire damages or destroys the place of employment, causing the worker to become unemployed. For example, a fire destroys a manufacturing plant and as a result employees are placed on indefinite leave without pay. This coverage would then go into effect. In health insurance, loss of income benefits are paid when an insured becomes disabled and cannot work.

LOSS OF TIME INSURANCE *see* LOSS OF INCOME INSURANCE.

LOSS OF USE INSURANCE coverage in the event that property is damaged or destroyed so that an insured cannot use the property for its intended purpose. For example, loss of use of a drill press because of vandalism would be covered.

LOSS PAYABLE CLAUSE coverage for a mortgagee where real or personal property, used as security for a loan, is damaged or destroyed. For example, a bank (mortgagee) lends money to an individual (mortgagor) who pledges certain valuables as security. The valuables are stolen. If the individual defaults on the loan, the bank would be indemnified under the policy for an amount up to the outstanding loan.

LOSS PREVENTION *see* ENGINEERING APPROACH; LOSS PREVENTION AND REDUCTION.

LOSS PREVENTION AND REDUCTION risk management control procedure which emphasizes safety management. Its purpose is to reduce the frequency and severity of potential losses. Business firms apply this procedure by posting safety signs, holding safety meetings, and providing cash awards for employees with the best safety records. *See also* ENGINEERING APPROACH; HUMAN APPROACH.

LOSS RATE frequency of losses. *See also* LOSS FREQUENCY METHOD.

LOSS RATIO relationship of incurred losses plus loss adjustment expense to earned premiums.

LOSS RATIO METHOD modification of premium rates by a stipulated uniform percentage for closely related classes of property or liability insurance policies. The objective of such modification is to more directly align the combined actual loss ratio of the classes of policies under consideration with the expected loss ratio of these classes. The resultant alignment should show no significant STANDARD DEVIATION OR VARIATION of the actual loss ratio from the expected loss ratio.

LOSS RATIO RESERVE METHOD formula for a given line of insurance used by property and casualty insurance companies to compare losses and loss adjustment expense with premiums. This shows (1) the amount of each premium dollar generated which is used to pay losses and expenses, and (2) the reserves that must be maintained to pay for those losses and expenses.

LOSS REDUCTION *see* LOSS PREVENTION AND REDUCTION.

LOSS REPORT *see* CLAIM REPORT.

LOSS RESERVES provision for known claims due but not paid, known claims not yet due, and provision for INCURRED BUT NOT REPORTED (IBNR) claims. The critical problem facing a casualty insurance company is the amount of reserves necessary for the incurred but not reported losses (IBNR) because many of these claims and their resultant settlements may not manifest themselves until several years in the future. This is known as the *tail end distribution liability. See also* FULL PRELIMINARY TERM RESERVE PLAN; PROSPECTIVE RESERVE; RESERVE LIABILITIES REGULATION; RETROSPECTIVE METHOD RESERVE COMPUTATION.

LOSS RETENTION *see* RETENTION AND LIMITS CLAUSE; RISK MANAGEMENT; SELF INSURANCE.

LOSS RUN *see* LOSS DEVELOPMENT; LOSS FREQUENCY METHOD.

LOSS SETTLEMENT *see* LOSS SETTLEMENT AMOUNT.

LOSS SETTLEMENT AMOUNT in homeowners insurance, usually an 80% coinsurance requirement, which means the insured must carry insurance on the value of a home on a replacement cost basis of at least 80%. For example, a home is worth $200,000, and a fire does $50,000 damage. If there is $150,000 of insurance it may appear that the insured would be reimbursed for the total loss. But the homeowner would receive only $46,875 according to the following formula:

$$\frac{\text{Amount of Insurance Carried}}{\substack{\text{80\% Insurance to Value} \\ \text{(Replacement Cost Basis)}}} \times \text{Loss} \quad = \text{Insured Reimbursement}$$

$$\frac{\$150,000}{\$160,000} \times \$50,000 = \$46,875$$

If, however, the insured had carried an 80% insurance to value of $160,000, then the insured would have been reimbursed for the total loss of $50,000 according to the following formula:

$$\frac{\$160,000}{\$160,000} \times \$50,000 = \$50,000$$

See also COINSURANCE; SETTLEMENT OPTIONS, PROPERTY AND CASUALTY INSURANCE.

LOSS SEVERITY *see* SEVERITY RATE.

LOSS TRENDS projections of future accidental losses based on analyses of historical loss patterns. A projected loss picture is used to determine the pure cost of protection and the resultant basic premium, contingency reserves, and whether or not the company should continue selling a given line of business, or remain in a particular geographical area. However, loss trends based on historical data may not really represent likely loss outcomes in the future.

LOSS-YEAR STATISTICS *see* ACCIDENT-YEAR STATISTICS.

LOST-INSTRUMENT BOND indemnification bond under which a stock certificate holder who loses the original certificate will be issued a duplicate. The indemnity bond guarantees that if the original stock certificate is recovered, the holder will send it to the surety company.

LOST POLICY RECEIPT life insurance company form to be signed by a policyholder who wishes to surrender a policy that has been lost. The signed receipt then becomes evidence that the policy is no longer in force. This protects the insurance company if a policyholder claims that the policy was never surrendered.

LOST POLICY RELEASE *see* LOST POLICY RECEIPT.

LUMP SUM in life insurance, single payment instead of a series of installments. *See also* LUMP SUM DISTRIBUTION.

LUMP SUM DISTRIBUTION death benefit option in which a beneficiary of a life insurance policy receives the death benefit as a single sum payment instead of installments.

LUMP SUM REFUND ANNUITY *see* CASH REFUND ANNUITY (LUMP SUM REFUND ANNUITY).

M

MACHINERY MALFUNCTION (BREAKDOWN) INSURANCE *see* BOILER AND MACHINERY INSURANCE.

MAIL ORDER INSURANCE insurance marketed through advertising in such media as newspapers, magazines, television, and radio. The mail is used to collect the application and distribute the policy. An insurance agent is not involved in the process. *See also* DIRECT RESPONSE MARKETING (DIRECT SELLING SYSTEM).

MAINTAINING A NUISANCE *see* ATTRACTIVE NUISANCE.

MAINTENANCE BOND legal instrument posted by a contractor or craftsman to guarantee that completed work is free of flaws and will perform its intended function for a specified period of time.

MAJOR MEDICAL INSURANCE coverage in excess of that provided by a basic hospital medical insurance plan. After the limits of coverage have been exhausted under a basic plan, major medical then covers medical expenses relating to room and board; physician fess; miscellaneous expenses such as bandages, operating room expenses, drugs, X-ray, and fluoroscopy. There may be a lifetime limit. For example, if the lifetime limit is $500,000 and an insured uses $100,000 of coverage in a given year, the lifetime limit would be reduced to $400,000. *See also* GROUP HEALTH INSURANCE; HEALTH INSURANCE; HEALTH MAINTENANCE ORGANIZATION (HMO).

MALICIOUS MISCHIEF intentional damage or destruction of another person or business's property. Insurance can be purchased by the owner of the property to protect against this exposure. *See also* HOMEOWNERS INSURANCE POLICY; PERSONAL AUTOMOBILE POLICY (PAP); SPECIAL MULTIPERIL INSURANCE (SMP); VANDALISM AND MALICIOUS MISCHIEF INSURANCE.

MALINGERING effort by an individual to continue to receive disability income benefits by faking a continuing sickness or injury.

MALPRACTICE LIABILITY INSURANCE professional liability coverage for a practitioner in a given field of expertise. Coverage takes the form of defending the practitioner against liability suits whether or not with foundation, and paying on behalf of the insured, court awarded damages up to the limits of the policy. *See also* PROFESSIONAL LIABILITY INSURANCE.

MANAGED CARE plan to control employer's health care cost through the introduction of practice guidelines or protocols for health care providers, and to improve the methods used by employers and employees to select health care providers. The goal of the plan is to create a financial accounting system in order to manage the impact of medical treatment on the patient's clinical response and quality of life. Once such a system is created, the employer and the employee will be better able to judge which health provider is more effective and efficient.

MANAGER *see* AGENCY MANAGER.

MANAGING PHYSICIAN, HMO *see* HEALTH MAINTENANCE ORGA-NIZATION (HMO).

MANDATORY SECURITIES VALUATION RESERVE method established by the NATIONAL ASSOCIATION OF INSURANCE COMMISSIONERS (NAIC) for valuing stocks and bonds for reserve purposes. The method levels the fluctuations in stock and bond values due to market conditions through incremental increases in the reserve. Each incremental increase is related to capital gains earned by the stocks and bonds during the year. The objective is to eliminate surplus changes resulting from market fluctuations of owned stocks and bonds.

M&C *see* MANUFACTURERS AND CONTRACTORS LIABILITY INSURANCE.

MANIFESTATION INJURY THEORY approach that maintains injury or sickness begins when it is first detected by an obvious appearance. This argument is used in determining if liability insurance is afforded in a particular bodily injury case.

MANUAL publication stipulating underwriting rules applicable for a given line of insurance, classifications of exposures within that line of insurance, and premium rates per classification. For example, a life insurance manual shows the PREMIUM MODE factor, POLICY FEE, PRE-MIUMS, and values per $1,000 of coverage, to include CASH VALUE, PAID-UP INSURANCE and EXTENDED TERM INSURANCE, available at the end of each policy year. *See also* MANUAL RATE.

MANUAL RATE published cost per unit of insurance, usually the standard rate charged for a standard risk. For example, one company's manual yearly rate per $1000 of life insurance for a given policy for a male age 26 is $12.02. *See also* RATE MAKING.

MANUFACTURERS AND CONTRACTORS LIABILITY INSUR-ANCE coverage for liability exposures which result from manufacturing and/or contracting operations in process on a manufacturer's premises (all locations of ongoing operations) or, in the case of the contractor, off-premises operation at a construction site. Excluded are activities of independent contractors, damage to property by explosion, collapse, and underground property damage. Additional coverages apply to the acts of the insured's employees when constructing new structures, demolishing old structures, and changing the size and/or location of existing structures.

MANUFACTURERS OUTPUT INSURANCE coverage for personal property of a manufacturer on an ALL RISKS basis when that property is off the manufacturer's premises.

MANUFACTURING INSURANCE *see* BUSINESS INTERRUPTION INSURANCE.

MANUSCRIPT INSURANCE coverage tailored to the particular requirements of an insured, when a *standard policy* cannot be used to provide coverage for real or personal property. A manuscript policy is often written on site by an agent (most often representing a large *brokerage house*) to reflect the special conditions and provisions.

MAP diagram used in property insurance to locate the geographical area in which risks reside. Maps are also used to reveal areas of high concentration of insured risks and their potential impact on an insurance company should a catastrophe occur, such as a hurricane.

MARGIN fluctuation in claims arising from ADVERSE SELECTION.

MARGOLIN ACT legislation passed in California which establishes procedures applicable to any worker who incurs a job-related injury. This Act has far-reaching implications for WORKERS COMPENSATION INSURANCE in other states also. Under the Act, the employer must provide the Employee's Claim for Workers' Compensation Benefits form upon an employee's request or within 1 day of his or her injury. A series of penalties and fines is established in the event that claims rightfully due a claimant are inappropriately delayed. For example, one fine could result if indemnity payments do not begin within 14 days of the employer's knowledge of an employee's disability. Another fine could result if the entire compensability investigation is not completed within 90 days. Attorneys are required to provide prospective clients at the initial consultation with an Attorney Fee Disclosure Statement, which states attorneys' fees for handling the case, and also encourages the prospective client to use instead the Office of Benefit Assistance and Enforcement, which provides its service at no charge. It is a requirement that this form be signed by both the prospective client and the attorney.

MARINE INSURANCE coverage for goods in transit and the vehicles of transportation on waterways, land, and air. *See also* INLAND MARINE INSURANCE (TRANSPORTATION INSURANCE): BUSINESS RISKS; INSTRUMENTALITIES OF TRANSPORTATION INSURANCE; NATIONWIDE MARINE DEFINITION; OCEAN MARINE INSURANCE.

MARINE INSURANCE CERTIFICATE special policy blank issued by an insured for individual shipments or other purposes under an OPEN POLICY. The open policy allows an insured to buy protection for all marine business for an indefinite period. When required to show evidence of insurance for a particular shipment, or to protect the cargo or ship of a client, the insured may issue a certificate of insurance backed by his or her own overriding open policy.

MARINE INSURANCE OFFICERS PROTECTIVE *see* OFFICERS PROTECTIVE MARINE INSURANCE.

MARITAL DEDUCTION provision in the Federal Tax Code for favorable treatment of an estate. Under the UNLIMITED MARITAL DEDUCTION no Federal estate tax is imposed on qualified transfers between a husband and wife. Under the QUALIFIED TERMINABLE INTEREST PROPERTY (Q TIP) TRUST all income from assets in trust is paid at least annually for the life of the spouse. *See also* ESTATE PLANNING.

MARITAL TRUST TRUST that qualifies assets under the MARITAL DEDUCTION provision in the Federal Tax Code for favorable treatment of an estate. The surviving spouse has the full power to use the assets of the trust as well as to transfer assets to any heirs. Upon the death of the surviving spouse, any assets in the trust are subject to FEDERAL ESTATE TAX. See also BYPASS TRUST; ESTATE PLANNING DISTRIBUTION; GIFT IN TRUST.

MARKETING creation of a demand for a company's products, its distribution, and services for customers who purchase that product. Actuarial research and development, underwriting efficiency, and claim payment promptness is of little value if no one is willing to purchase insurance products. *Agency and marketing departments* are the focus of all sales activity within an insurance company, and touch every aspect of a company by generating (1) premium income for securities, real estate, and mortgage investments; (2) sales for review by the underwriting department and their issuance by policyholder services; (3) need for data storage and retrieval by the company's data processing center; (4) legal analysis and decisions by the law department; and (5) need for corporate planning.

MARKETING REPRESENTATIVE *see* SPECIAL AGENT.

MARKET TIMING investment strategy which advocates the transfer of amounts from one category of investment to another category according to a perception of how each of these categories of investments will perform relative to other categories of investments at a stipulated point in time. This strategy may be applied by purchasers of the VARIABLE DOLLAR ANNUITY or VARIABLE LIFE INSURANCE, both of which have provisions for the transfer of sums between stock, bond, and real estate accounts.

MARKET VALUE *see* MARKET VALUE V. ACTUAL CASH VALUE.

MARKET VALUE CLAUSE provision of property insurance which establishes the amount for which an insured must be reimbursed for damaged or destroyed property according to the price a willing buyer would pay for the property purchased from a willing seller, as opposed to the ACTUAL CASH VALUE of the damaged or destroyed property. *See also* MARKET VALUE V. ACTUAL CASH VALUE.

MARKET VALUE v. ACTUAL CASH VALUE value of property as established by the price a willing buyer would pay for property purchased from a willing seller, compared with the replacement cost of damaged or destroyed property minus depreciation and obsolescence. Usually, replacement cost basis is used in property insurance to indemnify an insured for damaged or destroyed property. *See also* MARKET VALUE CLAUSE.

MASS MARKETING *see* MASS MERCHANDISING.

MASS MERCHANDISING coverage for a group of individuals under one policy. Usually, members belong to a particular company, union, or trade association. In a *contributory plan* a lump sum premium is paid by the group to the insurance company using salary deductions.

MASS UNDERWRITING evaluation of the demographic characteristics of the entire group (such as age, sex, MORBIDITY, MORTALITY), as opposed to the evaluation of individuals in that group. *See also* MASS MERCHANDISING.

MASTER CONTRACT *see* MASTER POLICY.

MASTER POLICY single contract coverage on a group basis issued to an employer. Group members receive certificates as evidence of membership summarizing benefits provided. *See also* GROUP HEALTH INSURANCE; GROUP LIFE INSURANCE.

MASTER-SERVANT RULE assumption that an employer is liable for negligent acts or omissions of employees which result in bodily injury and/or property damage to third parties if those acts are in the course of employment.

MATCHED SET OR PAIR INSURANCE *see* SET CLAUSE (PAIR OR SET CLAUSE).

MATERIAL FACT *see* MATERIAL MISREPRESENTATION.

MATERIAL MISREPRESENTATION falsification of a material fact in such a manner that, had the insurance company known the truth, it would not have insured the risk. A material misrepresentation gives an insurance company grounds to rescind a contract. *See also* CONCEALMENT.

MATURED ENDOWMENT endowment period of time, in life insurance, at which the face amount of the policy is payable to the insured.

MATURITY DATE time at which life insurance death proceeds or endowments are paid, either at the death of an insured or at the end of the endowment period.

MATURITY VALUE specified amount received by an insured at the end of an endowment period (usually the face amount of the endowment policy), or by the owner of an ordinary life policy (usually the individual insured) who lives to a given age.

MAXIMUM total amount of insurance coverage available for an INSURED.

MAXIMUM BENEFIT *see* BENEFIT FORMULA; COINSURANCE.

MAXIMUM DEDUCTIBLE CONTRIBUTION limit allowed by law on employee salary reduction plans. Many pension plans, as well as the popular *401 (k) plan,* allow employees to set aside pre-tax dollars in a company-sponsored retirement account, often matched by a company contribution. But the amount contributed by the employee is regulated by law. For example, the maximum annual contribution for the 401 (k) plan, which was $30,000 per year in 1986, was reduced to $7000 by the TAX REFORM ACT OF 1986.

MAXIMUM FAMILY BENEFIT *see* COORDINATION OF BENEFITS; GROUP HEALTH INSURANCE.

MAXIMUM FORESEEABLE LOSS (MFL) worst case scenario under which an estimate is made of the maximum dollar amount that can be lost if a catastrophe occurs such as a hurricane or firestorm.

MAXIMUM POSSIBLE LOSS *see* MAXIMUM FORESEEABLE LOSS (MFL).

MAXIMUM PROBABLE LOSS (MPL) estimate of maximum dollar value which can be lost under realistic situations. For example, a fire or other peril occurs, but a sprinkler system works and a fire department responds in good order.

MAXI TAIL (FULL TAIL) extended reporting period, for an unlimited length of time, during which claims may be made after a CLAIMS MADE

BASIS LIABILITY COVERAGE policy has expired. *See also* INCURRED BUT NOT REPORTED LOSSES (IBNR); LONG-TAIL LIABILITY.

McCARRAN-FERGUSON ACT (PUBLIC LAW 15) 1945 Federal legislation in which the Congress declared that the states may continue to regulate the insurance industry. Nevertheless, in recent years Congress has expanded the Federal government's insurance activities into *flood insurance,* FEDERAL CROP INSURANCE, and *riot and civil commotion insurance*. *See also* SOUTH-EASTERN UNDERWRITERS ASSOCIATION (SEUA) CASE.

MEAN *see* EXPECTED LOSS.

MEASUREMENT *see* LOSS DEVELOPMENT; LOSS FREQUENCY METHOD; LOSS TRENDS.

MEDIAN statistical term indicating the central value of a frequency distribution, such that smaller and greater values than this central value occur at an equal rate. For example, given the numbers 1, 7, 10, 12, 14, 17, 19, 20, and, 22, the median is 14.

MEDICAID assistance program for the financially needy. Medicaid, also referred to as *Title XIX* of the Social Security Act, was enacted in 1965 at the same time as MEDICARE. It is a joint Federal-state program that provides medical assistance for the aged, blind, and disabled, and families with dependent children who cannot pay for such assistance themselves. Benefits vary widely among the states.

MEDICAID QUALIFYING TRUST IRREVOCABLE LIVING TRUST (rights to make any changes are forfeited by the GRANTOR permanently) in which the grantor forfeits control of all assets placed in the trust. However, the grantor retains the right to all income produced by the assets in the trust, and the assets can be distributed to beneficiaries at the grantor's death. The objective of this trust is to protect the assets of the grantor against depletion to pay the costs of LONG-TERM CARE or against dissipation by the grantor's heirs during the grantor's lifetime.

MEDICAL *see* MEDICAL EXAMINATION.

MEDICAL EXAMINATION physical checkup required of applicants for life and/or health insurance to ascertain if they meet a company's underwriting standards or should be classified as substandard or uninsurable. Physicals are administered by medical personnel selected by the insurance company at its expense. Physicals may also be used to determine extent of disability for insurance purposes. *See also* MEDICAL EXAMINER.

MEDICAL EXAMINER physician who conducts physicals of applicants for life and/or health insurance. This physician is selected by the insurance company at its expense. *See also* MEDICAL EXAMINATION.

MEDICAL EXPENSE INSURANCE *see* COORDINATION OF BENEFITS; GROUP HEALTH INSURANCE; HEALTH INSURANCE CONTRACT; HEALTH MAINTENANCE ORGANIZATION (HMO).

MEDICAL INFORMATION BUREAU (MIB) central computerized facility which keeps on file the health history of the applicants for life and health insurance with member MIB companies. For example, the health record of an applicant for insurance with a member MIB company in Atlanta, Georgia is available to another member MIB company in Shreveport, Louisiana. The MIB was organized to guard against fraud by applicants.

MEDICAL PAYMENTS INSURANCE provision of liability policies and the liability sections of *package insurance* policies, such as the PERSONAL AUTOMOBILE POLICY (PAP), which pay medical expenses without regard to fault. The insured does not admit liability for bodily injury to another party, nor does an injured party forfeit the right to sue the insured.

MEDICAL PAYMENTS TO OTHERS INSURANCE *see* HOMEOWNERS INSURANCE POLICY—SECTION II (LIABILITY COVERAGE).

MEDICARE program enacted in 1965 under Title XVIII of the Social Security Amendments of 1965 to provide medical benefits to those 65 and over. The program has two parts: *Part A, Hospital Insurance* and *Part B, Supplementary Medical Insurance*. Retired workers qualified to receive Social Security benefits, and their dependents, also qualify for the hospital insurance portion. The program is paid for by payroll taxes on employees and covered workers. The supplementary medical insurance provides additional coverage on a voluntary basis for physician services. Those enrolled in the program pay a monthly premium. Coverage is also available to persons under 65 who are disabled and have received Social Security disability benefits for 24 consecutive months.

MEDICARE CATASTROPHIC COVERAGE ACT Federal legislation passed in 1988 (repealed November 23, 1989) that significantly increased the benefit amounts provided under MEDICARE, both Part A and Part B, in the following manner:
1. *Doctors' bills*—effective January 1, 1990, Medicare patients under Part B would have had their out-of-pocket expenses for doctors' bills limited to $1,370. However, if the doctor charged more than Medicare approved, the patient would be liable for the difference. The patient would have paid the first $75 as a DEDUCTIBLE for the approved charges, and Medicare would have paid 80% of the remaining

approved charges up to $1,370 and 100% of the approved charges above $1,370. Any payments made by the patient's private insurance would be applied to the $1,370.

2. *Hospital bills*—effective January 1, 1990, Medicare patients would have paid a deductible of $564 per year for the first stay in the hospital. After this deductible was paid, Medicare would have paid 100% of all hospital bills regardless of the length of stay.

3. *Drugs*—effective January 1, 1990, Medicare would have begun paying for OUTPATIENT prescription drugs. After the patient paid a $550 deductible, Medicare would have paid 80% of the cost of intravenous drugs, to include antibiotics, and 50% of the cost of immunosuppressive drugs. Effective January 1, 1991, after the patient paid a $600 deductible and a 50% COPAYMENT, Medicare would have paid for most other prescription drugs and insulin. Effective January 1, 1992, after the patient paid a $652 deductible and a 40% copayment, most prescription drugs would have been covered by Medicare. Effective January 1, 1993 and beyond, after the patient paid a deductible yet to be determined and a 20% copayment, most prescription drugs would have been covered by Medicare.

4. *Skilled nursing facility*—effective January 1, 1989, after the patient paid a copayment of $22 per day for the first 8 days, Medicare would have paid for 150 days of skilled nursing facility care.

5. *Home health care*—effective January 1, 1990, patients who did not require daily care would have been eligible for up to 6 days a week of home health care for as long as the doctor prescribed.

6. *Hospice care*—effective January 1, 1989, terminal patients would have been entitled under Medicare to unlimited hospice care.

7. *Respite care*—effective January 1, 1990, an individual who was caring for a Medicare patient (provided the patient had met either the $1,370 Part B limit or the annual deductible for prescription drugs) at home who required daily care would have been entitled to 80 hours per year of home health aide and personal care services.

8. *Mammography*—effective January 1, 1990, a Medicare patient would have been covered up to $50 for X-ray expenses incurred to detect breast cancer.

The **costs** to Medicare participants would have been as follows:

1. Currently, all Medicare Part B beneficiaries must pay an extra $4 premium each month above the normal Medicare Part A premium. By 1993, the extra premium would have been $10.20 per month. All individuals who were entitled to Part A benefits for more than 6 months during a tax year and owed at least $150 in federal income taxes would also have paid a supplemental premium of 15% for each $150 for 1989, 25% for 1990, 26% for 1991, 27% for 1992, and 28% for 1993. For tax years starting after 1993, the annual limit would have been tied to increases in the costs of Medicare. The maximum supplemental premium would have been $800 per Medicare beneficiary, or $1,600 per couple enrolled in Medicare for tax

year 1989; $850 and $1,700, respectively, for tax year 1990; $900 and $1,800, respectively, for tax year 1991; $950 and $1,900, respectively, for tax year 1992; and $1,050 and $2,100, respectively, for tax year 1993.

MEDICARE GAP INSURANCE *see* MEDICARE; MEDIGAP INSURANCE.

MEDICARE SUPPLEMENTARY INSURANCE *see* MEDIGAP INSURANCE.

MEDIGAP INSURANCE (MEDICARE SUPPLEMENTARY INSURANCE) coverage for at least some portion of the expenses not paid for by MEDICARE. A good policy includes the following coverages:
1. Full payment of doctors' bills above the amount paid by Medicare.
2. Full payment of hospital bills above the amount paid by Medicare.
3. Immediate coverage of the patient for existing illness (no PREEXISTING CONDITION clause).
4. GUARANTEED RENEWABLE CONTRACT.
5. Full payment of nursing-home bills above the amount paid by Medicare (long-term custodial care will be excluded from this policy).
6. Coverage for illnesses incurred while in a foreign country.

MEMBER person covered by insurance under a BLUE CROSS or BLUE SHIELD plan.

MEMORANDUM CLAUSE provision in *ocean marine cargo* policies to limit an insurance company's liability for partial losses; the company has liability only for losses which exceed a stipulated percentage of the value of the cargo.

MERCANTILE OPEN-STOCK BURGLARY INSURANCE coverage for damage or destruction of property due to a crime, and property lost due to a burglary, whether successful or attempted. An endorsement provides coverage for robbery and theft of merchandise. Coverage is provided for merchandise, equipment, fixtures, furniture left in the open on the business premises. There is a coinsurance basis of 40 to 80%.

MERCANTILE ROBBERY INSURANCE coverage available under two forms for actual or attempted robbery of money, securities or other property. Under the *First Form* the policy covers if the robbery is committed on the premises of the business. The *Second Form* covers if the robbery is committed against a messenger of the business off its premises. An endorsement can provide coverage if employees have property of the business in their custody at home, and this property is lost through robbery or burglary.

MERCANTILE SAFE BURGLARY INSURANCE coverage in the event a safe of a business is forceably entered, either on or off the premises, and property is stolen from the safe. Also covered is damage to the premises during actual or attempted burglary. Premium rates can be reduced through precautions such as burglar alarms, guards, and other protective measures. There is no coinsurance or deductible requirement.

MERCHANT MARINE ACT *see* JONES ACT.

MERGER, CONSOLIDATION OR REORGANIZATION OF PLAN SPONSOR change in the nature of an employer or other organization that sponsors a *qualified pension plan*. A qualified plan must guarantee vested benefits due to participants in the event of a merger, acquisition, or change in employer status. For example, the value of benefits cannot be reduced as the result of a merger.

MERIT RATE *see* MERIT RATING.

MERIT RATING system of charges to an insured which fluctuates according to the loss experience of that insured. This is a form of EXPERIENCE RATING. *See also* PROSPECTIVE RATING; RETROSPECTIVE RATING.

MESSENGER INSURANCE *see* MESSENGER ROBBERY INSURANCE.

MESSENGER ROBBERY INSURANCE coverage for an insured who is authorized to convey property such as money, securities, and other valuables, away from a business's premises.

MEXICO INSURANCE coverage through an endorsement to the PERSONAL AUTOMOBILE POLICY (PAP) to extend its protection against accidents within a 25 mile radius of the U.S. border. This coverage is excess over liability insurance with a licensed Mexican insurance company. The purchase of Mexican liability insurance is prerequisite to the extended coverage of PAP.

MFL *see* MAXIMUM FORESEEABLE LOSS.

MIB *see* MEDICAL INFORMATION BUREAU (MIB).

MIDI TAIL automatically extended reporting period of 5 years, during which claims may be made after a CLAIMS MADE BASIS LIABILITY COVERAGE policy has expired, provided these claims are the result of an event that took place within 60 days of the termination of the policy. *See also* INCURRED BUT NOT REPORTED LOSSES (IBNR); LONG-TAIL LIABILITY.

MILITARY SERVICE EXCLUSION clause common to life and health insurance policies issued during wartime which exclude benefits for military service-connected perils of death, disability, illness, accident, or sickness. This clause is usually canceled with the declaration of peace.

MILLION DOLLAR ROUND TABLE (MDRT) association of life insurance agents who meet minimum life insurance sales standards predetermined each year by the organization. Membership is a primary goal of professional life insurance agents, as it denotes personal sales achievement.

MINIMUM AMOUNT POLICY *see* MINIMUM BENEFIT.

MINIMUM BENEFIT smallest face amount of life insurance that an insurance company will write on any one person.

MINIMUM CONTRIBUTION *see* MINIMUM PREMIUM PLAN.

MINIMUM DEPOSIT INSURANCE *see* FINAL INSURANCE (MINIMUM DEPOSIT INSURANCE).

MINIMUM DEPOSIT RESCUE technique designed to permit the exchange of a life insurance policy that has an outstanding loan charged against it for another life insurance policy on a tax-free basis. The procedure is for the insurer to issue a new policy subject to a loan in the amount equal to the outstanding loan on the old policy. If the new policy so issued is of the form of a FLEXIBLE PREMIUM policy such as UNIVERSAL LIFE, the loan from the old policy can be replaced by the new policy assuming the loan.

MINIMUM DEPOSIT WHOLE LIFE INSURANCE ORDINARY LIFE INSURANCE which generates a first year cash value from the payment of the first year premium. Using this cash value, loans could be made to finance premiums due in the future, with the interest deductible for tax purposes under specified IRS rules. However, the 1986 Tax Code revision appears to have canceled this arrangement.

MINIMUM GROUP smallest number of individuals for which an insurance company will issue a policy. A minimum number is required because the fixed expenses of placing a policy on the books exist regardless of the size of a group.

MINIMUM PREMIUM DEPOSIT PLAN *see* MINIMUM DEPOSIT WHOLE LIFE INSURANCE.

MINIMUM PREMIUM PLAN smallest acceptable premium for which an insurance company will write a policy. This minimum charge is necessary to cover fixed expenses in placing the policy on the books.

MINIMUM STANDARDS lowest acceptable criteria that a risk must meet in order to be insurable. For example, life insurance companies require an applicant for individual (nongroup) coverages to be free of terminal illness.

MINI TAIL automatically extended reporting period of 60 days, during which claims may be made after a CLAIMS MADE BASIS LIABILITY COVERAGE policy has expired. *See also* INCURRED BUT NOT REPORTED LOSSES (IBNR); LONG-TAIL LIABILITY.

MINOR'S TRUST (2503(c)) TRUST whereby asset management is provided until a child reaches the age of majority. Upon reaching majority, the child has full use and control over the assets. The GRANTOR of the trust cannot receive any income from the assets held in the trust. All undistributed income is taxed at trust rates, which are low. The grantor, through this type of trust, is able to control the time at which the minor has access to the assets given to him or her by the grantor (who wishes to take advantage of the annual GIFT TAX exclusion). *See also* ESTATE PLANNING DISTRIBUTION; GIFT IN TRUST.

MISCELLANEOUS EXPENSES hospital charges in addition to room and board. Miscellaneous expenses are covered under a *basic hospital plan,* with the limits of coverage expressed either as a multiple of the daily hospital benefit for room and board, or as a flat dollar amount. Expenses included in the coverage are X rays, drugs, bandages, operating room expenses, and ambulance services. *See also* GROUP HEALTH INSURANCE; HEALTH INSURANCE; HEALTH MAINTENANCE ORGANIZATION (HMO).

MISCELLANEOUS VEHICLES COVERAGE endorsement to the PERSONAL AUTOMOBILE POLICY (PAP) that insures other motorized vehicles such as golf carts and motorcycles owned by a policyholder.

MISREPRESENTATION (FALSE PRETENSE) intent to defraud. An insured is required to answer truthfully all questions on the application. The insurance company can void a contract if it would not have issued a policy had it known the true facts. For example, on a PERSONAL AUTOMOBILE POLICY application, if the insured answers that the car is used only for pleasure (when in fact it is used in stock car races), the insurance company can void the policy.

MISSTATEMENT OF AGE falsification of birth date by an applicant for a life or health insurance policy. If the company discovers that the wrong age was given, the coverage will be adjusted to reflect the correct age according to the premiums paid in.

MISSTATEMENT OF AGE OR SEX CLAUSE *see* MISSTATEMENT OF AGE.

MIXED INSURANCE COMPANY one that combines the two forms of ownership, stock and mutual. A STOCK INSURANCE COMPANY is owned by stockholders whereas a MUTUAL INSURANCE COMPANY is owned by its policyholders. A mixed company is owned in part by stockholders and in part by policyholders. Most mixed companies issue *participating* and *nonparticipating* policies.

MIXED PERILS several different types of perils covered under one policy. *See also* HOMEOWNERS INSURANCE POLICY; PERSONAL AUTOMOBILE POLICY (PAP); SPECIAL MULTIPERIL INSURANCE (SMP).

MOBILE EQUIPMENT INSURANCE *see* CONTRACTORS EQUIPMENT FLOATER.

MOBILE HOME INSURANCE coverage similar to a HOMEOWNERS INSURANCE POLICY in that Section I covers property exposure and Section II covers liability exposure.
1. *Section I (property)* Coverage A—structural coverage of the mobile home Coverage B—unscheduled personal property coverage Coverage C—additions to the structure of the mobile home to include equipment Coverage D—additional living expense.
2. *Section II (liability)* Coverage E—liability coverage for personal acts and/or omissions Coverage F—medical payments to others.

MODE frequency of premium payment, for example annually, semiannually, quarterly, or monthly.

MODEL INSURERS SUPERVISION, REHABILITATION, AND LIQUIDATION ACT OF 1977 model law endorsed by the NATIONAL ASSOCIATION OF INSURANCE COMMISSIONERS (NAIC) giving state regulators broad new powers to deal with financially troubled insurance companies. The act was intended to replace the model *Insurers Rehabilitation and Liquidation Act,* which the NAIC endorsed in 1969. The new model would make it easier for insurance commissioners to gain control of impaired insurers by listing new grounds for placing them in LIQUIDATION AND REHABILITATION. The act also sets liquidation standards for interstate cooperation among regulators.

MODE OF ENTRY
1. method of gaining illegal entry to perform a criminal act. If a policyholder makes a claim for loss of jewelry or rugs under a homeowners policy, or if a business owner makes a claim for damage caused by vandals, the insurer must establish how the vandal or burglar gained entry. The mode of entry is important both (a) to determine that someone did actually enter the premises and (b) to establish that the policyholder was not unduly negligent.
2. path by which a toxic substance enters the human body, such as by inhalation, injection, ingestion, or absorption.

MODIFICATION OF CONTRACT adaptation of a standard insurance contract for special needs. Standard forms do not cover all needs but they can be adapted by an underwriter, broker, or an insurance company at the request of an insured. Risk managers may request many modifications in property and casualty coverage to meet the needs they have diagnosed for their corporations. Some risk managers even write their own contracts. Many insurers write their own contracts as well rather than use forms designed by a RATING BUREAU.

MODIFICATION RATING (also known as MERIT RATING) method of setting property insurance rates by modifying or adjusting the MANUAL RATE for various classifications of risks. Modifications may be based on past or anticipated loss experience. The three types of modification rating are EXPERIENCE RATING, RETROSPECTIVE RATING, and SCHEDULE RATING.

MODIFIED CASH REFUND ANNUITY form of CASH REFUND ANNUITY used by contributory pension or employee benefit plans. When employee participants die before receiving all of their contributions in the form of retirement benefits, this type of annuity guarantees to repay the remainder of those contributions, with interest, to the beneficiaries.

MODIFIED LIFE INSURANCE ORDINARY LIFE INSURANCE under which premiums are calculated so that the first few years of premiums are less than normal, and subsequent premiums are higher than normal. *See also* GRADED PREMIUM, WHOLE LIFE INSURANCE.

MODIFIED PRIOR APPROVAL *see* RATING BUREAU.

MODIFIED PRIOR APPROVAL RATING form of state rating law that requires prior approval of property and casualty insurance premiums by the state insurance department for certain changes. Here, a state generally allows new rates to go into effect immediately after filing with the insurance department. However, changes in classification of risks or other substantial changes require prior insurance department approval. There are four methods of rate approval. In addition to modified prior approval, they are PRIOR APPROVAL RATING, *open competition*, and *file and use*.

MODIFIED RESERVE METHODS accounting procedures that defer the full funding of a life insurance NET LEVEL PREMIUM RESERVE to accommodate the policy ACQUISITION COST in the early years of a policy. First-year policy expenses, such as *agent commission*, MEDICAL EXAMINATION, and PREMIUM TAX, often result in little of the PREMIUM remaining for the premium reserve required under FULL VALUATION RESERVE standards. In such cases, the difference comes out of the insurer's SURPLUS ACCOUNT. To avoid this, two types of modified reserve methods are used: (1) the FULL PRELIMINARY TERM RESERVE VALUATION method and, (2) the modified preliminary term reserve valuation method, better known as the *commissioners' reserve valuation method*. The full preliminary term method does not require any TERMINAL RESERVE at the end of the first year and in effect accounts for reserves like *term insurance* during this period. This leaves more of the premium available to cover acquisition cost and first-year claims. In subsequent years, for reserve accounting purposes, the policy is considered to have been issued one year later than its actual date on an insured who was one year older than his actual age. This results in stepping up additions to the premium reserve, eventually making up for the first year's shortfall.

The commissioners' reserve valuation method limits first-year expenses and thus the amount of deferred funding of policy reserves. Policies whose premiums fall below a certain level can be accounted for under the full preliminary term method. For policies with premiums above that level, the full preliminary term method is modified by a limitation on the amount of expenses that can be used in figuring the schedule of deferred reserve funding.

MODIFIED RESERVE STANDARDS *see* MODIFIED RESERVE METHODS.

MONEY AND SECURITIES BROAD FORM POLICY coverage providing protection for a business against loss from a hazard under the *On-Premises Form,* which provides ALL RISK protection against the loss of money and securities; or the *Off-Premises Form,* ALL RISK protection against loss of money and securities while they are in possession of a messenger. There is no coinsurance deductible requirement.

MONEY DAMAGES payments awarded by a court in a liability suit. Money damages can be broken down into *compensatory* and *punitive*. Compensatory damages reimburse a plaintiff for expenses incurred for such things as disability, disfigurement, and pain and suffering. Punitive damages go beyond this to punish and make an example of a defendant. In recent years, punitive damages have become increasingly common and insurers claim that the frequency of multimillion dollar jury awards has made the business of underwriting so difficult.

MONEY MARKET INVESTMENTS short-term investments, to include the following: commercial paper, interest-bearing balances with banks, Federal funds sold and securities purchased under agreements to resell, trading account securities, and loans held for resale.

MONEY PURCHASE PLAN contributions to a pension plan on a fixed basis according to a formula, with variable benefits. Contributions can be made under an ALLOCATED FUNDING INSTRUMENT (paid to an insurance company that purchases an individual ANNUITY or a group DEFERRED ANNUITY), or under an UNALLOCATED FUNDING INSTRU-

MENT. Individual benefits will be determined by the person's age, sex, normal retirement age, and rate schedules in effect at the time the insurance company receives the contributions. These plans are appropriate for an organization that must know its premium outlay in the years ahead. *See also* DEFINED CONTRIBUTION PLAN.

MONOLINE POLICY insurance protection written in the form of a single line policy.

MONOPOLISTIC STATE FUND state operated insurance company used in WORKERS COMPENSATION INSURANCE in some states where the risks are so great that the commercial insurance companies cannot operate at affordable rates.

MONTHLY DEBIT ORDINARY INSURANCE (MDO) coverage in which premiums are collected monthly on an ordinary life insurance policy. *See also* DEBIT INSURANCE (HOME SERVICE INSURANCE, INDUSTRIAL INSURANCE).

MONTHLY REPORTING FORM type of INLAND MARINE insurance used to provide coverage for domesticated animals, including poultry, cattle, horses, sheep, and swine. *See also* LIVESTOCK INSURANCE; LIVESTOCK MORTALITY (LIFE) INSURANCE. For application to inventory and other fluctuating values, *see also* OPEN FORM (REPORTING FORM).

MOP *see* MANUFACTURERS OUTPUT INSURANCE.

MORALE HAZARD circumstance which increases the probability of loss because of the insured's indifferent attitude. For example, if an insured leaves the doors unlocked and the windows open when leaving home, a morale hazard is created.

MORAL HAZARD circumstance which increases the probability of loss because of an applicant's personal habits or morals, for example, if an applicant is a known criminal.

MORBIDITY frequency of illness, sickness, and diseases contracted.

MORBIDITY ASSUMPTION statistical projection of future illness, sickness, and disease.

MORBIDITY RATE relationship of the frequency of illness, sickness, and diseases contracted by individual members of a group to the entire group membership over a particular time period.

MORBIDITY TABLE number of individuals exposed to the risk of illness, sickness, and disease at each age, and the actual number of individuals who incurred an illness, sickness, and disease at each age.

MORTALITY frequency of death.

MORTALITY ADJUSTMENT additions or subtractions of a MORTALITY TABLE to reflect changing levels of mortality due to advancement in medicine, geriatrics, and sanitation. These adjustments make a mortality table more representative of probable future death experience.

MORTALITY ASSUMPTION statistical projection of future deaths.

MORTALITY CHARGES *see* MORTALITY ADJUSTMENT; MORTALITY RATE; MORTALITY TABLE.

MORTALITY RATE relationship of the frequency of deaths of individual members of a group to the entire group membership over a particular time period.

MORTALITY TABLE chart showing rate of death at each age in terms of number of deaths per thousand.

MORTGAGEE CLAUSE attachment to a property insurance policy to protect the interest of the mortgagee in the mortgaged property. If the property is damaged or destroyed, the mortgagee is indemnified up to his stated interest in the property.

MORTGAGEE INSURANCE *see* MORTGAGEE CLAUSE.

MORTGAGE GUARANTEE INSURANCE *see* MORTGAGE INSURANCE.

MORTGAGE INSURANCE life insurance that pays the balance of a mortgage if the mortgagor (insured) dies. Coverage is usually in the form of decreasing term insurance, with the amount of coverage decreasing as the debt decreases.

MORTGAGE PROTECTION INSURANCE *see* MORTGAGE INSURANCE.

MORTGAGE REDEMPTION INSURANCE *see* MORTGAGE INSURANCE.

MORTICIANS PROFESSIONAL LIABILITY INSURANCE coverage for malpractice suits resulting from professional acts and/or omissions of morticians. *See also* PROFESSIONAL LIABILITY INSURANCE.

MOTOR TRUCK CARGO INSURANCE protection required under the Motor Carrier Act of 1935. The policy covers the motor truck carrier if it is legally liable for the damage, destruction or other loss of the customer's property being shipped. This includes lost packages, broken contents, and stolen articles. Two types of policies are available: (1)

those that list the specific trucks to be covered in which the property may be damaged or destroyed; and (2) those that cover all of the insured's trucks, with no trucks listed specifically. This coverage is on the *Gross Receipts Form,* which in essence covers all operations of a motor carrier.

MOTOR TRUCK CARGO RADIOACTIVE CONTAMINATION INSURANCE coverage for a common carrier (the insured) for damage or destruction due to radioactive contamination from commercial radioisotopes of a property in the custody of the insured or that of a connecting carrier. Transport of nuclear waste is excluded.

MOTOR VEHICLES *see* MOTOR TRUCK CARGO INSURANCE.

MOVING AVERAGE RATING METHOD procedure, in insurance, used in time series analysis to smooth out irregularities in projections of loss expectations. Irregularities to be smoothed out include: (1) loss experience which is not homogeneous, (2) loss experience from early policy years not representative of current loss experience, (3) adverse selection by policyholders, (4) changes in loss experience due to changing social values, and (5) loss experience distortion due to misleading averages.

MOVING INSURANCE (FOR A MOVING COMPANY) INLAND MARINE policy to cover liability for goods that belong to clients while in a mover's possession.

MPL *see* MAXIMUM POSSIBLE LOSS; MAXIMUM PROBABLE LOSS.

MULTIEMPLOYER PLAN pension or other employee benefit to cover employees at two or more financially unrelated companies. The companies may employ workers from the same labor union or those in the same industry. Employer contributions go into a common pool from which benefits are paid. Employees may transfer between employers in the fund and still retain their benefits. Multiemployer plans have grown rapidly in recent years as smaller employers band together to provide pension benefits to employees. *See also* MULTIEMPLOYER TRUST.

MULTIEMPLOYER TRUST one that provides group health or pension benefits for a MULTIEMPLOYER PLAN. To lower the cost, small firms band together to take advantage of the economies of large group underwriting.

MULTIPLE EMPLOYER TRUST *see* MULTIEMPLOYER TRUST.

MULTIPLE INDEMNITY *see* ACCIDENTAL DEATH CLAUSE.

MULTIPLE LINE CONTRACT *see* MULTIPLE LINE INSURANCE.

MULTIPLE LINE INSURANCE combination of coverages from property and liability policies. *See also* HOMEOWNERS INSURANCE POLICY; PERSONAL AUTOMOBILE POLICY (PAP); SPECIAL MULTIPERIL INSURANCE (SMP).

MULTIPLE LINE LAW state legislation that allows insurers to offer both property and casualty insurance. At one time, U.S. insurers sold only one type of insurance, a practice that gradually became written into state law. Most significantly, New York State, where many insurers want to be licensed, allowed insurers to write only one line of insurance early in this century. But in 1949 New York passed a multiple line law and most other states followed.

MULTIPLE LOCATION FORMS type of coverage of property owned by one person at several locations, including merchandise, materials, fixtures, furniture, specified machinery, betterments, and improvements made by tenants.

MULTIPLE LOCATION POLICY *see* MULTIPLE LOCATION FORMS.

MULTIPLE LOCATION RISKS *see* MULTIPLE LOCATION FORMS.

MULTIPLE PERIL INSURANCE personal and business property insurance that combines in one policy several types of property insurance covering numerous *perils*. However, no liability insurance is provided.

MULTIPLE PROTECTION LIFE INSURANCE POLICY single LIFE INSURANCE policy combining TERM LIFE INSURANCE and ORDINARY LIFE INSURANCE. If the INSURED dies during the term period, a multiple of the FACE AMOUNT is paid to the BENEFICIARY. If the insured dies after the term period has expired, only the face amount is paid to the beneficiary. For example, if the insured dies during the first 10 years that the policy is in force, three times the face amount is paid to the beneficiary; after the 10 years expires, the single face amount is paid to the beneficiary. Thus, during the multiple protection period both term insurance and ordinary life insurance are in force; after the multiple protection period expires, only ordinary life insurance is in force.

MULTIPLE RETIREMENT AGES arrangement by which an employee can retire and receive full benefits without reduction, or reduced benefits subject to a penalty. These ages can be classified in the following manner:
1. *normal retirement*—earliest an employee can retire and receive full benefits, having reached a minimum age with a minimum number of years of service.
2. *early retirement*—earliest an employee can retire, having reached a minimum age and a minimum number of years of service, but with a penalty in the form of a reduction in benefits. The reduction is

usually a percentage of benefit subtracted for each month of retirement earlier than the normal retirement age.

3. *deferred retirement*—work beyond the normal retirement age. This may or may not result in an increase of benefits.

MUNICIPAL BOND INSURANCE coverage that guarantees bondholders against default by a municipality. This form of financial guarantee was introduced in the early 1970s and became a runaway success. Municipalities embraced it because their offerings took on the credit rating of the company that wrote the insurance, rather than their own ratings. It meant that most municipal bond offerings were elevated to Triple-A and municipalities could raise money at a lower rate of interest. For investors, it made municipal bonds less risky.

MUNICIPAL INSURANCE property and/or liability coverage for a municipality. Municipalities are responsible for maintenance of throughways as well as a myriad of public services. Liability insurance for municipalities became an issue in the insurance crunch of 1985–1986, when this coverage became difficult to find, or became overly expensive. The problem was aggravated by court decisions in negligence cases in which the doctrine of *joint and several liability* came into play. This doctrine provides that a judgment against several defendants could be collected from one if the others were unable to pay. A municipality found to have been 10% liable in a traffic accident because of the improper placement of a stop sign might end up paying 100% of the judgment if the driver who was 90% responsible had no assets. This resulted in sharply higher premiums for municipal insurance.

MUSICAL INSTRUMENTS INSURANCE coverage for musicians and other providers of musical services such as musical instrument dealers. Musical instruments, service equipment and sheet music are insured on an ALL RISKS basis at any location, subject to exclusions of wear and tear, war, and nuclear disaster. Each item must be specifically listed in the policy.

MUTUAL ASSENT offer and acceptance upon which an agreement is based. For a contract to be legal (and thus enforceable in a court of law), an offer must be made by one party to another party, who accepts the offer. If properly negotiated, the insurance contract is deemed to be a contract of mutual assent.

MUTUAL ATOMIC ENERGY REINSURANCE POOL group of mutual insurers that provides insurance for nuclear reactors which standard property and liability policies exclude. The Federal government provides supplementary coverage. *See also* NUCLEAR ENERGY LIABILITY INSURANCE.

MUTUAL BENEFIT ASSOCIATION *see* ASSESSMENT COMPANY; ASSESSMENT INSURANCE; ASSESSMENT PERIOD.

MUTUAL FUND combination of contributions of many investors whose money is used to buy stocks, bonds, commodities, options, and/or money market funds, or precious metals such as gold, or foreign securities. In theory, mutual funds offer investors professional money management and diversification into conservative investments, aggressive investments, or combinations of these. Mutual funds are sold either with a sales charge (load), no sales charge (no-load), or a moderate sales charge (low load). These funds charge a management fee as a percentage of assets under management, usually 1% per year on a downward sliding scale as the asset base increases. Many insurance companies sell mutual funds.

MUTUAL FUND INSURANCE financial guarantee policy that insures against loss of principal invested in a mutual fund.

MUTUAL INSURANCE COMPANY company owned by its *policyowners*; no stock is available for purchase on the stock exchanges. *See also* DIVIDEND OPTION, PARTICIPATING INSURANCE; STOCK INSURANCE COMPANY.

MUTUALIZATION transformation of a STOCK INSURANCE COMPANY into a MUTUAL INSURANCE COMPANY, in which the stock company buys up and retires its shares.

MUTUAL MORTGAGE INSURANCE FUND fund that insures mortgages on homes for one to four families; also insures property improvement loans and loans to repair homes after a disaster. It is one of three funds operated by the Federal Housing Administration, which oversees mortgage guarantee insurance.

MYSTERIOUS DISAPPEARANCE EXCLUSION policy clause that excludes coverage for loss of property if the cause of the loss cannot be identified. Mysterious disappearance is an exclusion in a standard INLAND MARINE insurance all-risks policy. Because some theft insurance policies do not contain this exclusion, they implicitly insure against mysterious disappearance and would cover the loss of a diamond necklace, for example, even if the owner did not recall how it had been lost.

N

NAIB *see* NATIONAL ASSOCIATION OF INSURANCE BROKERS (NAIB).

NAIC *see* NATIONAL ASSOCIATION OF INSURANCE COMMISSIONERS (NAIC).

NAIC: INFORMATION AND PRIVACY PROTECTION MODEL ACT NATIONAL ASSOCIATION OF INSURANCE COMMISSIONERS model state law designed to govern use of information collected from insurance applications. The law forbids any insurer or agent from impersonating someone else to gain information about an applicant, unless there is reasonable cause to suspect criminal activity. The law also provides that an insurer must give timely notice of renewal and other company policies. It also governs the method in which an insurer can gain information about a policyholder and the use that can be made of it. All applicants are allowed access to information that the insurer has collected about them, the right to correct it if wrong, and to learn the reason they were turned down for insurance.

NAIC: MODEL ASSET VALUATION ACT NATIONAL ASSOCIATION OF INSURANCE COMMISSIONERS model state law providing guidelines by regulators for valuation of securities on the books of insurance companies. The act has two sections: one for valuation of fixed-rate bonds and debt securities, and the other covering valuation of other securities such as common and preferred stocks as well as stock in an insurance company's subsidiaries. The model law provides that bonds be valued at cost, adjusted for any purchase discounts or premiums. Preferred and guaranteed stocks while paying dividends can be carried at par value, while other securities such as common stocks are carried at market or appraised value. Valuation of stock in subsidiaries is limited by the law to no more than the value of the subsidiary's ADMITTED ASSETS when valued as if they were on the books of the insurance company parent.

NAIC: MODEL GROUP LIFE INSURANCE DEFINITION AND GROUP LIFE INSURANCE STANDARD PROVISIONS MODEL ACT model state law of the NAIC setting general standards for group life insurance contracts. It specifies which types of organizations can sponsor group life insurance plans and outlines the authority of the state regulator, including the power to require reasonable premiums. It contains consumer protection provisions such as a 31-day GRACE PERIOD for late payment of premiums, a clause making the policy not *contestable* after two years except for nonpayment of premium, and a CONVERSION PRIVILEGE, allowing an insured to convert a group insurance policy to an individual policy, regardless of state of health.

**NAIC: MODEL LIFE INSURANCE SOLICITATION REGULA-
TION NATIONAL ASSOCIATION OF INSURANCE COMMIS-
SIONERS** model state regulation that governs method of selling life
insurance to prevent fraud or misrepresentation by agents or insurers.
A life insurance disclosure model regulation to help buyers understand
the basic policy features and evaluate costs of similar insurance plans
was adopted on an interim basis in 1973 and revised in 1976 and 1983.
Today, insurers must provide a *buyer's guide* and a *policy summary* to
prospective buyers. Insurers must keep files of authorized documents;
agents must identify themselves and the company they represent and
cannot represent themselves as financial planners or investment advisers
unless they in fact are. In addition, reference to a dividend or any
nonguaranteed item must be identified as such.

**NAIC: MODEL RATING LAWS NATIONAL ASSOCIATION OF
INSURANCE COMMISSIONERS** state laws based on a model law
of the NATIONAL ASSOCIATION OF INSURANCE COMMISSIONERS (NAIC)
that allow insurers to (1) set rates independently; or (2) adopt those
rates developed by a rating bureau that must first be approved by the
appropriate state regulator. Because state regulators believe that rate wars
can be disastrous to the financial health of insurers, insurance companies
are allowed to band together to set standard rates through rate making
bureaus. Model rating laws also allow independent insurers to set their
own rates, but prohibit the return of part of a premium to the insured
other than as a dividend. Legislation developed from this model bill is
called a *prior approval law* because the appropriate insurance commissioner must approve the rates involved. Other major types of rating laws
are FILE-AND-USE RATING LAWS and OPEN COMPETITION LAWS.

**NAIC: STANDARD NONFORFEITURE LAW NATIONAL ASSO-
CIATION OF INSURANCE COMMISSIONERS** model state statute
that governs terms for surrender of individual deferred annuities and
CASH VALUE LIFE INSURANCE. This model, adopted by most states in
the late 1970s and early 1980s, requires that annuity and whole-life
contracts have certain minimum values that are not forfeited by policyholders even if a policy is canceled. A formula is given for computing
the present value, cash surrender value, and paid-up annuity benefits.
The model requires insurers to state clearly if an annuity has limited or
no death benefits.

NAII *see* NATIONAL ASSOCIATION OF INDEPENDENT INSURERS (NAII).

NAMED INSURED person, business, or organization specified as the
insured(s) in a property or liability insurance policy. In some instances,
the policy provides broader coverage to persons other than those named
in the policy if they have the insured's permission to use the property
that is insured. For example, someone who drives a car with the per-

mission of the owner is protected by a PERSONAL AUTOMOBILE POLICY (PAP). In other cases, if the owner of a property is not named as an insured party, his interests may not be protected by the policy. For example, if two persons own a home and only one is named on the HOMEOWNERS INSURANCE POLICY, the interest of the other may not be covered. *See also* OTHER INSUREDS.

NAMED NONOWNER COVERAGE insurance under the PERSONAL AUTOMOBILE POLICY (PAP) through a *named nonowner coverage endorsement* offering protection for LIABILITY, *uninsured motorists,* and *medical payments* to a named insured who does not own an automobile.

NAMED PERIL POLICY insurance contract under which covered perils are listed. Benefits for a covered loss are paid to the *policyowner*. If an unlisted peril strikes, no benefits are paid. For example, under the *standard fire policy,* fire is a particular listed peril. If an insured's home burns, he will be indemnified. *See also* ALL RISKS.

NAME POSITION BOND FIDELITY BOND which covers a business if employees in listed positions commit dishonest acts, such as stealing money. *See also* BLANKET BOND; NAME SCHEDULE BOND.

NAME SCHEDULE BOND FIDELITY BOND under which an insured employer is reimbursed for loss caused by the dishonest act of two or more employees named or listed in a schedule attached to the bond. The specific amount of coverage is listed beside the name of each employee on the schedule. Coverage is the same as that found under the individual fidelity bond. *See also* INDIVIDUAL FIDELITY BOND.

NATIONAL ASSOCIATION OF INDEPENDENT INSURANCE ADJUSTERS (NAII) trade group of independent claims adjusters who settle claims for insurance companies on a fee basis. Some insurers use their own *staff adjusters* to settle a claim. Others use an INDEPENDENT ADJUSTER or, perhaps, both.

NATIONAL ASSOCIATION OF INDEPENDENT INSURERS (NAII) trade association of property and casualty insurance companies that do not have membership in a rating bureau. These companies do not follow standard rates and forms authored by a rating bureau.

NATIONAL ASSOCIATION OF INSURANCE BROKERS (NAIB) trade association of commercial insurance brokers whose objective is to further the interests of these brokers through education, lobbying, and adherence to professional ethics.

NATIONAL ASSOCIATION OF INSURANCE COMMISSIONERS (NAIC) membership organization of state *insurance commissioners*. One of its goals is to promote uniformity of state regulation and legislation as it concerns the insurance industry. The NAIC opposes Federal regulation of insurance. The organization has achieved considerable national uniformity through the adoption of a uniform blank for insurance companies' annual financial reports, a ZONE SYSTEM for the triennial examinations of insurance companies, a *standard valuation law for reserves,* standard *nonforfeiture benefits,* and model laws for valuation of the insurance company's securities.

NATIONAL ASSOCIATION OF INSURANCE WOMEN (NAIW) educational organization for insurance women whose objective is to further the interests of these women through education and adherence to professional ethics.

NATIONAL ASSOCIATION OF LIFE COMPANIES (NALC) membership organization primarily of medium and small life and health insurance companies. It represents the views and interests of smaller companies in various political forums.

NATIONAL ASSOCIATION OF LIFE UNDERWRITERS (NALU) organization of local life underwriter associations representing life and health insurance agents on practices of selling and servicing life and health insurance products. NALU sponsors public service programs nationally.

NATIONAL ASSOCIATION OF PROFESSIONAL INSURANCE AGENTS *see* PROFESSIONAL INSURANCE AGENTS (PIA).

NATIONAL ASSOCIATION OF PROFESSIONAL SURPLUS LINES OFFICES, LTD. (NAPSLO) trade association of SURPLUS LINES agents and INSURERS.

NATIONAL ASSOCIATION OF PUBLIC INSURANCE ADJUSTERS trade association whose objective is to further the interests of its membership, as well as to inform the public on the role of its members.

NATIONAL ASSOCIATION OF SECURITIES DEALERS (NASD) organization of brokers and securities dealers in the over-the-counter market operating under the auspices of the Securities and Exchange Commission (SEC). Its purpose is to enforce, on a self-regulating basis, the rules of the SEC, which are designed to protect investors against fraud and market manipulation of stocks. The NASD also publishes quotations of both national and regional stocks. Insurance agents selling VARIABLE LIFE INSURANCE, *variable annuities* and MUTUAL FUNDS are required to be licensed by the NASD.

NATIONAL AUTOMOBILE THEFT BUREAU (NATB) organization of property insurance companies whose goal is to prevent and uncover fraudulent automobile fire and theft claims.

NATIONAL BOARD OF FIRE UNDERWRITERS now-defunct bureau founded by fire insurance underwriters in 1866 to work for fire prevention and loss control. The board helped standardize the fire insurance policy. In the mid-1960s, the National Board of Fire Underwriters merged into the American Insurance Association. In 1971, 30 national and regional rating bureaus merged to form the INSURANCE SERVICES OFFICE (ISO).

NATIONAL BUILDING CODE set of standard safety guidelines adopted by many states to help provide uniformity in building construction and guard against fire hazards and other unsafe conditions in buildings.

NATIONAL COMMISSION ON STATE WORKERS COMPENSATION LAWS group appointed by President Nixon in 1971 to study workers compensation laws under the authorization of the OCCUPATIONAL SAFETY AND HEALTH ACT (OSHA). It issued sweeping recommendations to upgrade state workers compensation laws, including higher disability benefits, compulsory coverage, and unlimited medical care and rehabilitation benefits. Most states adopted the recommendations with a resulting increase in premiums for the new benefits.

NATIONAL CONFERENCE OF STATES ON BUILDING CODES AND STANDARDS group responsible for developing, updating, and publishing the NATIONAL BUILDING CODE.

NATIONAL COUNCIL ON COMPENSATION INSURANCE membership organization of insurance companies that write WORKERS COMPENSATION INSURANCE. The organization collects statistics on the FREQUENCY and *severity* of job-related injuries to establish a rate structure for member companies, files rate plans with insurance commissioners offices for member companies, and generates forms and policies for member companies.

NATIONAL FIRE PROTECTION ASSOCIATION (NFPA) private, not-for-profit group that develops and publishes safety codes and standards relating to protection of people and property against fire. The NFPA is financed by fees for technical manuals and other material. Most fire safety laws are developed from research done by this organization.

NATIONAL FLOOD INSURANCE PROGRAM coverage against flooding for personal and business property under the National Flood Act of 1968, which encourages participation by private insurers in the program through an industry flood insurance pool. Property insurance companies with assets of $1 million or more may become members, either as *risk bearers* (who may issue their own policies) or as *nonrisk bearers* (who are limited to act as fiscal agents for the pool, and hence must use a syndicate-type policy as dictated by the pool). National Flood Insurance makes reasonable coverage available to those who could not buy it through private insurers before the 1968 Act, and it encourages maximum participation extent by the private sector.

NATIONAL FLOOD INSURERS ASSOCIATION pool of private insurers that provide initial flood insurance in cooperation with the U.S. Department of Housing and Urban Development (HUD). In 1978, the association was superseded by the NATIONAL FLOOD INSURANCE PROGRAM administered by HUD.

NATIONAL HEALTH INSURANCE government health care program in several European countries that has been proposed in various forms for the U.S., to be administered by the Federal government.
  1. *Plan A*—would cover all U.S. residents. Comprehensive benefits, financed by a combination of payroll taxes and general revenues, would include physician services, impatient and outpatient hospital care, home health services, and supporting services such as optometry, podiatry, devices and appliances, and dental care.
  2. *Plan B*—would expand MEDICARE to cover the general population.
  3. *Plan C*—would pay premiums for the needy and allow income tax credits for others to purchase private health insurance. The entire U.S. population would be covered. Individuals with no Federal income tax liability would receive full payment of health insurance premiums.

NATIONAL INSTITUTE FOR OCCUPATIONAL SAFETY AND HEALTH Federal agency that researches injury and illness arising from workplace hazards and recommends standards for maximum exposures to hazardous substances.

NATIONAL INSURANCE DEVELOPMENT CORPORATION government group that provides reinsurance for private insurers that write RIOT AND CIVIL COMMOTION INSURANCE. Riot losses in major cities in the 1960s caused insurers to stop writing this coverage in certain urban areas, whereupon Congress created FEDERAL CRIME INSURANCE and the National Insurance Development Corporation.

NATIONAL INSURANCE PRODUCERS CONFERENCE organization of insurance broker and agent associations that includes the Independent Insurance Agents of America, National Association of Professional Insurance Agents, National Association of Insurance Brokers, National Association of Casualty and Surety Agents, and National Association of Surety Bond Producers.

NATIONAL SAFETY COUNCIL nonprofit organization of members of various industries nationwide that collects and publishes information and statistics on accidents. The council was established by Congress in 1913. Its statistics on injury in the workplace are an important source of information for loss prevention efforts. It also publishes and disseminates information on safety.

NATIONAL SERVICE LIFE INSURANCE (NSLI) *see* GOVERNMENT LIFE INSURANCE.

NATIONWIDE DEFINITION OF MARINE INSURANCE *see* NATIONWIDE MARINE DEFINITION.

NATIONWIDE MARINE DEFINITION statement of the types of exposures classified under *marine, inland marine* or *transportation insurance* by placing them in the following categories: imports, exports, domestic shipments (goods in transit), communication vehicles (tunnels, bridges, piers, and power transmission lines), personal property floaters (stamp collections, coin collections, fine arts, paintings, musical instruments, silverware, and furs), commercial property floaters (accounts receivable, valuable papers, valuable records, and physicians and surgeons instruments). The definition also makes use of the following differences in condition: electronic data, property in a bailee's custody, and property for sale by a dealer (such as musical instruments, cameras, fine arts, and jewelry).

NATURAL DEATH death from other than accidental means. *See also* ACCIDENTAL DEATH CLAUSE; RIDERS, LIFE POLICIES.

NATURAL LOSSES property damage, accident, or injury resulting from vagaries of nature, including tornadoes, hurricanes, and floods.

NATURAL PREMIUM *see* PURE PREMIUM RATING METHOD.

NAVIGATION RISK INSURANCE coverage during the operation of a ship for: (1) *Property of Ship* (ship's hull, tackle, passenger fittings, equipment, stores, boats), and ordnance; (2) *Property Damage Liability* (ship's owner and/or operator is protected if the ship collides with another, causing damage and loss of use). Excluded is liability to the owner and/or operator for damage to piers, wharves, bodily injury, or loss to the insured ship's hull and/or cargo (this coverage amount is in addition to the amount of coverage on the insured ship's hull and cargo); and (3) *Bodily Injury Liability Insurance.*

NCCI *see* NATIONAL COUNCIL ON COMPENSATION INSURANCE.

NEEDS APPROACH personal insurance method used to analyze the amount necessary to maintain a family in its customary life-style, should the primary wage earner die. This includes such considerations as:

1. immediate needs ("cleanup fund")—expenses associated with final medical treatments and burial, inheritance taxes, estate taxes, probate costs, outstanding debt;
2. continued income—while children are still in school and depend on family support;
3. continued income—for the surviving spouse after children no longer depend on family support;
4. continued income—to pay a mortgage, education expenses, emergency expenses, and miscellaneous expenses; and
5. retirement fund—for the surviving spouse.

From the sum of these expenses, subtract sources of income available to the surviving spouse (Social Security, investments, employee benefit plans such as group life insurance and pensions), to arrive at a final figure on which to base the amount of life insurance the wage earner should consider.

NEGLECT failure to exercise proper care. Many property insurance policies exclude losses that result from negligence. Neglect is also the basis for many liability suits. If an injury can be demonstrated to result from negligence on the part of a homeowner, a product manufacturer, or a municipality responsible for maintaining streets, an injured party can often collect damages.

NEGLIGENCE failure to act with the legally required degree of care for others, resulting in harm to them. *See also* TORT, UNINTENTIONAL.

NEGLIGENCE, COMPARATIVE *see* COMPARATIVE NEGLIGENCE.

NEGLIGENCE, CONTRIBUTORY *see* CONTRIBUTORY NEGLIGENCE.

NEGLIGENCE, GROSS *see* GROSS NEGLIGENCE.

NEGLIGENCE, PRESUMED *see* RES IPSA LOQUITOR.

NEGLIGENT MANUFACTURE charge against a business firm in a PRODUCT LIABILITY INSURANCE lawsuit. Manufacturers have been held responsible for their products. When consumers become injured while operating a lawnmower, flying in an airplane, driving a car, or any of hundreds of other ways, they have grounds to sue the manufacturer of these products for negligence. Product liability has become one of the most rapidly growing areas of liability exposure for businesses and one of the most difficult to insure against.

NEGOTIATED CONTRIBUTION PLAN defined contribution pension plan in which employer contributions are set under a collective bargaining agreement. It usually covers the employees of a number of firms and is administered by a board of trustees on which participating employers and unions are equally represented.

NEON AND ELECTRIC SIGNS FLOATER coverage on an ALL RISKS basis through an endorsement to a business PROPERTY INSURANCE policy in which each sign is specifically scheduled, subject to the exclusions of wear and tear, and damage caused by nuclear hazard, war, and electricity.

NEON AND FLUORESCENT SIGN INSURANCE coverage through an endorsement to the *glass insurance* policy on an ALL RISKS basis, subject to the exclusions of wear and tear, and damage caused by nuclear hazard, war, and electricity.

NET AMOUNT AT RISK in life insurance, difference between the face value of a life insurance policy and its cash value (also known as ''pure amount of protection'').

NET COST METHOD *see* LIFE INSURANCE COST.

NET INCREASE amount of the increase in the BOOK OF BUSINESS of an INSURANCE COMPANY over a specified time interval. This increase is calculated as follows:

> Net Increase = New Issued Policies + Renewed Policies
>   − Lapsed Policies − Cancelled Policies

NET INTEREST EARNED average interest earned by an insurer on its investments after investment expense, but before Federal income tax.

NET LEVEL *see* NET LEVEL PREMIUM; NET LEVEL PREMIUM RESERVE.

NET LEVEL PREMIUM life insurance payment that is constant from year to year. The premium may be paid throughout the life of an insured or may be limited to a maximum number, such as 30 annual premiums. The premium is based only on interest and a mortality assumption and does not consider an expense assumption. *See also* GROSS PREMIUM.

NET LEVEL PREMIUM RESERVE fund that comes into existence because premiums for ordinary life insurance policies in their early years are higher than necessary for the pure cost of protection. These excess premiums, plus the interest credited, create the net level reserve. When an insured dies, the reserve comprises part of the death benefit. The net premium is calculated according to this fundamental actuarial equation: *present value of future premiums = present value of future benefits.*

This relationship holds only at the point of issue of a life insurance policy. Thereafter, future benefits will exceed future premiums because fewer premiums are left to be paid and benefits are coming closer to being due. The reserve makes up the difference between the future benefits and future premiums at any point. This reserve can be calculated on either a *prospective* or *retrospective* basis, but it is important to note that the various state minimum reserve valuation laws are stated in terms of the prospective basis. *See also* FULL PRELIMINARY TERM RESERVE PLAN; PROSPECTIVE RESERVE; RETROSPECTIVE METHOD RESERVE COMPUTATION.

NET LINE *see* NET RETAINED LINES.

NET LINE LIMIT maximum amount of INSURANCE that an INSURANCE COMPANY will issue on a particular risk exposure. This limit is used by the insurance company to avoid having to pay for a loss on the exposure in excess of that which is acceptable to the company.

NET LOSS amount of the loss absorbed by an INSURANCE COMPANY after deducting any REINSURANCE applicable to the loss, as well as SUBROGATION and ABANDONMENT AND SALVAGE rights.

NET PAYMENT METHOD OF COMPARING COSTS *see* INTEREST ADJUSTED COST; LIFE INSURANCE COST.

NET PAYMENTS INDEX table charting relative costs of a group of CASH VALUE LIFE INSURANCE policies derived by using the *net cost method* of comparing costs *(traditional net cost method of comparing costs; net payment method)*. The net payments index contrasts with the interest adjusted SURRENDER COST INDEX and the INTEREST ADJUSTED COST index, which are derived by using the interest adjusted method of comparing policy costs.

NET PREMIUM *see* NET SINGLE PREMIUM.

NET PREMIUMS WRITTEN total premiums written by a CEDING COMPANY minus premiums ceded to its REINSURER.

NET RATE *see* NET SINGLE PREMIUM.

NET RETAINED LINES amount of insurance remaining on a CEDING COMPANY's books, net of the amount reinsured.

NET RETENTION *see* NET RETAINED LINES.

NET SINGLE PREMIUM *pure cost of protection,* or the premium covering the present value of future claims (not including loadings for the various expenses).

NET UNDERWRITING PROFIT (OR LOSS) statutory UNDERWRITING GAIN minus (or LOSS plus) POLICYHOLDER's dividends.

NET VALUATION PREMIUM *see* VALUATION PREMIUM.

NET WORTH total assets minus liabilities. It is used by underwriters to evaluate the financial standing of applicants for surety bonds.

NEW YORK INSURANCE CODE standard for insurance regulation in New York State and a model for insurance regulation elsewhere. For example, the *standard fire policy* was first adopted in New York State. Similarly, following the ARMSTRONG INVESTIGATION, the New York Insurance Code of 1906 became a model for cleaning up life insurance industry abuses. New York is widely viewed as the toughest state to get an insurance license, but because of the size of the insurance market there, many companies are willing to meet the stiff requirements.

NEW YORK INSURANCE EXCHANGE reinsurance marketplace modeled after LLOYD'S OF LONDON. Like Lloyd's, the New York Exchange is a market for hard-to-place risks and for the placement of excess or surplus lines. *See also* SURPLUS LINES (EXCESS SURPLUS LINES).

NEW YORK STANDARD FIRE POLICY contract first written in 1918 that provided the basis for modern day property insurance, both personal and commercial. *Forms* and *endorsements* must be added to complete the policy and tailor it to cover the particular insured property. This policy is also known as the ''165 Line'' policy, for the number of lines in its text that covers CONCEALMENT or MISREPRESENTATION (FALSE PRETENSE), property and perils excluded; OTHER INSURANCE; cancellation due to increase in hazards; obligations to a mortgagee; pro rata contribution of a company; requirements of an insured in case of loss; conditions when a company must pay a loss incurred by an insured; and SUBROGATION. The New York Standard Fire Policy has become largely obsolete since 1980, but its provisions have been incorporated into many other property insurance policies.

NFIA *see* NATIONAL FLOOD INSURERS ASSOCIATION.

NFPA *see* NATIONAL FIRE PROTECTION ASSOCIATION (NFPA).

NO-FAULT AUTOMOBILE INSURANCE type of coverage in which an insured's own policy provides indemnity for bodily injury and/or property damage without regard to fault. In many instances it is difficult if not impossible to determine the original cause—such as who is at fault in a chain car collision. In states with no-fault liability insurance, an insured cannot sue for general damages until special damages including medical expenses exceed a minimum amount. This is an effort to eliminate groundless suits for general damages.

NO FAULT LIABILITY INSURANCE *see* NO FAULT AUTOMOBILE INSURANCE.

NO LOAD INSURANCE *see* FLOW-THROUGH COST (NO LOAD INSURANCE).

NONADMITTED ASSETS assets, such as furniture and fixtures, which are not permitted by state law to be included in an insurance company's ANNUAL STATEMENT. *See also* ADMITTED ASSETS.

NONADMITTED INSURER company not licensed by a particular state to sell and service insurance policies within that state.

NONADMITTED REINSURANCE *see* SURPLUS LINES (EXCESS SURPLUS LINES).

NONASSESSABLE MUTUAL insurance company whose corporate charter and bylaws prevent assessment of its policyowners, regardless of how adverse its loss and expense experience may become. *See also* ASSESSMENT COMPANY.

NONASSESSABLE POLICY insurance contract under which a policyowner cannot be assessed for adverse loss and expense experience of the insurance company. *See also* ASSESSMENT INSURANCE.

NONASSIGNABLE POLICY insurance policy, particularly PROPERTY AND LIABILITY INSURANCE, which the owner cannot assign to a third party. *See also* ASSIGNMENT; ASSIGNMENT CLAUSE, LIFE INSURANCE.

NONCANCELLABLE GUARANTEED RENEWABLE POLICY health insurance that is not subject to alteration, termination, or increase in premium upon renewal.

NONCANCELLABLE HEALTH INSURANCE *see* COMMERCIAL HEALTH INSURANCE.

NONCONCURRENCY circumstance under which several insurance policies cover an insured's property against damage or destruction, but since the limits of coverage, kinds of property, and perils covered are not the same under all policies, the insured may not be fully covered in the event of a loss.

NONCONCURRENT APPORTIONMENT RULES standards used to determine claims payments in cases of overlapping property/liability insurance coverage. At one time, each type of insurance had its own rules to govern claims where more than one policy provided coverage. In 1963, several property/casualty industry groups agreed on a set of principles to be used in apportioning claims among insurers.

NONCONFINING SICKNESS sickness incurred by the insured which does not require restriction of activity to the indoors. *See also* HEALTH INSURANCE.

NONCONTRIBUTION MORTGAGE CLAUSE endorsement to *standard fire policy* to protect the interests of a mortgage lender without providing for APPORTIONMENT. A mortgage lender may choose to have his or her rights to the property protected by a MORTGAGE CLAUSE. Where an insured has more than one policy, claims are normally paid by assigning a portion of the loss among the insurance carriers under terms of the policy's PRO RATA LIABILITY CLAUSE. A *full contribution mortgage clause* provides that losses on the lender's interest would be apportioned in the same manner as the rest of the policy. But with a noncontribution mortgage clause, the lender's interest would be protected up to the policy limits with no apportionment.

NONCONTRIBUTORY EMPLOYEE BENEFIT INSURANCE PLAN under which an employer pays the entire direct cost of the plan; employees do not share in the cost, except perhaps through comparatively lower wages.

NONDEDUCTIBILITY OF EMPLOYER CONTRIBUTIONS law that payments by an employer to a NONQUALIFIED PLAN are not deductible as a business expense for Federal tax purposes.

NONDISABLING INJURY injury that does not qualify either for *partial* or *total disability income* under a disability income or Workers Compensation policy.

NONDUPLICATION OF BENEFITS *see* COORDINATION OF BENEFITS.

NONFORFEITABILITY
1. provision in a CASH VALUE INSURANCE policy that an insured will receive the equity in some form even if the insurance is canceled.
2. vested benefit to a retirement plan participant. It is enforceable against the plan.
   See also NONFORFEITURE BENEFIT (OPTION); NONFORFEITURE CASH SURRENDER BENEFIT; NONFORFEITURE EXTENDED TERM BENEFIT; NONFORFEITURE REDUCED PAID-UP BENEFIT.

NONFORFEITURE BENEFIT (OPTION) provision that the equity of an insured in a life insurance policy cannot be forfeited. There are four benefits a policyholder can select under the option: CASH SURRENDER VALUE, EXTENDED TERM INSURANCE, LOAN VALUE, and PAID-UP INSURANCE. If none is elected, a clause in the policy will stipulate the option that automatically goes into effect, usually extended term insurance.

NONFORFEITURE CASH SURRENDER BENEFIT amount in a cash value life insurance policy that a policyowner will receive upon surrender of the policy, minus any outstanding loan and accrued interest. A table in the policy shows the amount of cash surrender values. With some policies, the insurance company reserves the right to hold the cash surrender value for six months from time of notification, but this is rarely if ever applied today.

NONFORFEITURE EXTENDED TERM BENEFIT right of a policy-holder, in life insurance with cash values, to continue full coverage for a limited period, as shown in a table in the policy, with no further premiums payable.

NONFORFEITURE PROVISION value in life insurance policies that entitle the insured to these choices:

(1) to relinquish the policy for its CASH SURRENDER VALUE. (Note that in the beginning years the cash value may be minimal because of expenses such as agent's commission, premium tax, and the cost of putting the policy on the insurance company's books.)

(2) to take *reduced paid-up insurance* instead of the cash surrender value.

(3) To take EXTENDED TERM INSURANCE for the full face amount instead of the cash surrender value.

(4) to borrow from the company, using the cash value as collateral.

Each policy provides a table illustrating the first 20 years of its guaranteed cash values.

NONFORFEITURE REDUCED PAID-UP BENEFIT right of a policy-holder in life insurance with cash value to elect a smaller, fully paid up policy, without any further premiums to pay. The amount of the paid-up policy is determined by the insured's age and the cash surrender value.

NONFORFEITURE VALUES *see* NONFORFEITURE CASH SURRENDER BENEFIT; NONFORFEITURE EXTENDED TERM BENEFIT; NONFORFEITURE REDUCED PAID-UP BENEFIT.

NONINSURANCE RISK *see* UNINSURABLE RISK.

NONINSURANCE TRANSFER risk management technique for shifting a corporation's exposure from itself. A risk manager looks at many alternatives to insurance to limit the risks a business firm faces. One transfer method is by contract, such as HOLD-HARMLESS AGREEMENTS, or to insert in an existing contract an endorsement stating that the business firm will not be responsible for something that would normally fall within its responsiblity.

NONINSURED DRIVER operator with no liability insurance. If a non-insured driver hits another car, the victim sometimes has no recourse against the driver. For this reason, many motorists carry UNINSURED MOTORIST COVERAGE, an endorsement to the PERSONAL AUTOMOBILE POLICY (PAP) that covers them if they are involved in a collision with a driver without liability insurance. Some states also maintain an UNSAT-

ISFIED JUDGMENT FUND to pay claims to innocent victims of automobile accidents.

NONLEDGER ASSETS assets of an INSURER which are due and payable in the current year but have yet to be received by the insurer.

NONMEDICAL APPLICATION *see* NONMEDICAL LIFE INSURANCE.

NONMEDICAL LIFE INSURANCE coverage in which an applicant not required to take a medical examination, instead answers written questions to ascertain his current physical condition.

NONMEDICAL LIMIT dollar ceiling on a life insurance policy for applicants who are not given a medical examination. The insurer accepts a health questionnaire in the place of a physical examination. At one time, a medical examination was a requirement for anyone buying life insurance. In recent years, however, most companies write NONMEDICAL LIFE INSURANCE because the savings in expenses for the company have been found to offset the higher risk of underwriting insurance without the benefit of an examination. However, nonmedical policies are written only for a STANDARD RISK.

NONOCCUPATIONAL DISABILITY condition that results from injury or disease that is not job related. Workers compensation applies to employees disabled by on-the-job injuries or disease. In addition, five states require employers to pay income (not medical expense) benefits if a worker is disabled by illness or injury that did not occur at work: Rhode Island, California, New Jersey, New York, and Hawaii. Except for Rhode Island, employers may buy private coverage; in Rhode Island, they must get coverage from a state fund. Hawaii is the only state without an optional state fund.

NONOCCUPATIONAL HEALTH INSURANCE POLICY insurance coverage for accidents and sickness which are not job related.

NONOCCUPATIONAL POLICY health and medical insurance that excludes coverage for job-related injuries and illnesses. Most medical insurance policies do not provide benefits for job-related claims, which are covered by WORKERS COMPENSATION BENEFITS.

NONOWNERSHIP AIRCRAFT LIABILITY INSURANCE coverage in a separate policy or as an endorsement to the COMMERCIAL GENERAL LIABILITY (CGL) form, for insureds responsible for aircraft they do not own. If an aircraft is leased from another firm or owned by employees who operate it for a business owner, the insured's liability exposure is not covered by the CGL policy; a special endorsement is necessary.

NONOWNERSHIP AUTOMOBILE LIABILITY INSURANCE coverage in a separate policy or as an endorsement to the COMMERCIAL

GENERAL LIABILITY (CGL) form, for liability exposures for an employee who drives a leased car or his own automobile for business purposes.

NONOWNERSHIP LIABILITY INSURANCE coverage for an employer against liability for property damage or physical injury caused by an employee operating a personally owned vehicle for the business firm. Employers can be held liable if an employee has an accident while driving a leased automobile or operating a motorboat that the employee owns, if it is done for the benefit of the employer. *See also* NONOWNERSHIP AIRCRAFT LIABILITY INSURANCE; NONOWNERSHIP AUTOMOBILE LIABILITY INSURANCE.

NONPARTICIPATING INSURANCE policy not designed to pay the policyowner a dividend. *See also* CURRENT ASSUMPTION; PARTICIPATING INSURANCE.

NONPARTICIPATING LIFE INSURANCE *see* NONPARTICIPATING INSURANCE.

NONPARTICIPATING POLICY *see* NONPARTICIPATING INSURANCE.

NONPROFIT INSURER company formed and operated without the profit motive as its normal business objective; normally sells and services health insurance policies. *See also* BLUE CROSS; BLUE SHIELD.

NONPROPORTIONAL AUTOMATIC REINSURANCE obligatory reinsurance contract in which a reinsurer agrees to pay for all or a large portion of losses up to a limit, when these losses exceed the retention level of the cedent. The reinsurance premium paid by the cedent is calculated independently of the premium charged to the insured. It is not expected that every treaty will pay for itself or that every loss will be recouped by the reinsurer. When a cedent reinsures on a nonproportional basis, it retains substantially more of its profits than reinsuring on a proportional basis. Nonproportional differs from proportional reinsurance in that it does not involve the sharing of risks.

NONPROPORTIONAL FACULTATIVE REINSURANCE coverage in which an insurer is not bound to CEDE and a reinsurer is not bound to accept a risk. A separate reinsurance contract covers each cession. The contract is automatically renewed if the original insurance is renewed. Casualty facultative reinsurance is usually written on excess of loss basis, and the reinsurer shares only in losses which exceed retention level of the cedent.

NONPROPORTIONAL REINSURANCE arrangement in which a reinsurer makes payments to an insurer whose losses exceed a predetermined retention level. Nonproportional reinsurance is either *facultative* or *automatic. See also* CATASTROPHE LOSS; EXCESS OF LOSS REINSURANCE; STOP LOSS REINSURANCE.

NONQUALIFIED PLAN employee benefit plan which does not have the Federal tax advantages of a *qualified pension plan,* in which employers receive a Federal tax deduction for contributions paid into the plan on behalf of their employees. For an employer, not having a tax deduction can be a serious disadvantage, but a nonqualified plan has these advantages:
1. otherwise discriminatory coverage for some employees is allowed.
2. benefits can be allocated to certain employees whom the employer wishes to reward. The result could be that the total cost of the benefits for a particular group of employees may be less under a nonqualified plan than for all employees under a qualified plan.

NONRENEWAL CLAUSE provision in a policy that states the circumstances under which an insurer may elect not to renew the policy.

NONRESIDENT AGENT agent who is licensed and who markets and services insurance policies in a state in which he or she is not domiciled.

NONSMOKER health characteristic considered by an insurer underwriting an applicant for life or health insurance. Many insurance companies charge reduced premiums for nonsmokers.

NONTRADITIONAL REINSURANCE types of REINSURANCE instruments under which the amount of RISK transferred is more limited than under TRADITIONAL RISK REINSURANCE instruments. The limitations on risk transfer take the form of an aggregate dollar amount or loss ratio limits according to the reinsurance coverage in effect. Premiums for nontraditional reinsurance instruments are usually larger than those for traditional reinsurance instruments.

NORMAL ANNUITY FORM cost computation form that assumes retirement and commencement of annuity payments on the first day of the month nearest the birthday when a retiree reaches normal retirement age. Most employee pension plans provide for a normal retirement age of 65, with pension or annuity payments to begin at that time. But many also provide an *optional annuity form* for those who either wish to retire before, or continue working past, the normal retirement age. These employees receive reduced benefits, in the case of the early retirees, or possible enhanced benefits for those who work longer.

NORMAL LOSS particular type of loss which is expected by an organization and for which provision is usually made in the budgeting process of the organization. *See also* SELF INSURANCE; SELF-INSURED RETENTION (SIR).

NORMAL RETIREMENT AGE earliest age at which an employee can retire without a penalty reduction in pension benefits after having (1) reached a minimum age and (2) served a minimum number of years with an employer. Historically, this has been 65 years, but many private pension plans now envision earlier or later normal retirement ages.

NOTICE OF CANCELLATION CLAUSE provision in an insurance policy that permits an insured to cancel the policy and recoup the excess of the paid premiums above the customary *short rate* for the expired time. The clause also permits a company to cancel the policy at any time by sending the insured five days' written notice and repaying the excess of the paid premium above the *pro rata* premium for the expired time.

NOTICE TO COMPANY written notice, to be submitted by the CLAIMANT, required by the insurance company in the event of an INSURED PERIL. This notice is part of the standard PROPERTY AND CASUALTY INSURANCE PROVISIONS defining the insured's obligations after a loss.

NSC *see* NATIONAL SAFETY COUNCIL.

NUCLEAR ENERGY LIABILITY INSURANCE coverage for bodily injury and property damage liability resulting from the nuclear energy material (whether or not radioactive) on the insured business's premises or in transit. This insurance has become more significant since the Three Mile Island accident. In order to obtain a license for a nuclear facility, there must be evidence of financial responsibility such as insurance. Nuclear energy liability is excluded from nearly all other liability policies.

NUCLEAR REACTION EXCLUSION clause in most property insurance policies that excepts coverage for loss from a nuclear reaction or radiation, or radioactive contamination. (However, a fire resulting from one of these perils would be covered.) Because of this exclusion, insurer pools have been formed to write coverage for nuclear reactors. In addition, the NUCLEAR REGULATORY COMMISSION is authorized to provide coverage under the PRICE-ANDERSON ACT.

NUCLEAR REGULATORY COMMISSION U.S. government agency (formerly the Atomic Energy Commission) responsible for regulating the nuclear energy industry. The commission also provides supplemental insurance for nuclear facilities to augment coverage by private insurance pools.

NUISANCE product or service that does more harm than good to society, or endangers life or health. Society would probably be better off without such a product or service. *See also* ATTRACTIVE NUISANCE.

NUMERICAL RATING SYSTEM underwriting method used in classifying applicants for life insurance according to certain demographic factors and assigning weights to these factors. Factors include physical condition, build, family history, personal history, habits, and morals. For example, if an applicant is 5′8″ and weighs 250 pounds, his mortality expectation based on this height-weight ratio may be 160% of a standard risk who weighs 150 pounds at that height. In this instance a debit of 60 percentage points would be listed next to the weight factor on the applicant's underwriting sheet. If the applicant has an excellent family history (no hereditary diseases such as diabetes), his mortality expectation based on this factor is 90% of the standard risk. Here a credit of 10 percentage points would be listed next to the family history factor. Upon completion of the debiting/crediting process, debits and credits would be totaled for a final rate, which would classify the applicant as *standard, substandard,* or an *uninsurable risk.*

O

OASDHI *see* OLD AGE, SURVIVORS, DISABILITY, AND HEALTH INSURANCE (OASDHI).

OBLIGATORY REINSURANCE *see* AUTOMATIC REINSURANCE.

OBLIGEE *see* FIDELITY BOND; LIABILITY, BUSINESS EXPOSURES; SURETY BOND.

OBLIGOR individual or other entity who has promised to perform a certain act. For example, an insurance company promises to pay a death benefit if a life insurance policy is in force at the time of the death of an insured.

OBSOLESCENCE decrease in value of property as the result of technological advancement and/or changing social mores. This factor is used to measure the amount of depreciation in determining the ACTUAL CASH VALUE of damaged or destroyed property protected by PROPERTY INSURANCE COVERAGE.

OCCUPANCY AND FIRE RATES direct relationship between the use to which a building is put and the likelihood that it will catch on fire. Occupancy is one of the most important factors in setting fire insurance rates. For example, a building that houses an explosives manufacturer is at much greater risk than one occupied by a jewelry boutique. Other factors that influence the risk of fire are geographical location, construction, nature of the neighborhood, and the adequacy of protective devices.

OCCUPATION *see* OCCUPATIONAL HAZARD.

OCCUPATIONAL ACCIDENT work-related accident. Occupational accidents that injure employees are the responsibility of the employer and are covered by WORKERS COMPENSATION INSURANCE. In recent years, the term occupational accident has been expanded to include job-related long-term exposure to hazardous substances that result in occupational diseases, and such emotional injuries as nervous breakdowns and even heart attacks.

OCCUPATIONAL DISEASE illness contracted as the result of employment-related exposures and conditions. Coverage for such diseases is found under WORKERS COMPENSATION INSURANCE.

OCCUPATIONAL HAZARD condition surrounding a work environment which increases the probability of death, disability, or illness to a worker. This class of hazard is considered when writing WORKERS

COMPENSATION INSURANCE or determining which underwriting classification to place an applicant for life or health insurance.

OCCUPATIONAL INJURY *see* OCCUPATIONAL ACCIDENT; OCCUPATIONAL HAZARD; OCCUPATION RISK.

OCCUPATIONAL SAFETY AND HEALTH ACT (OSHA) 1970 legislation that set Federal standards for workplace safety and imposed fines for failure to meet them. A controversial law, it took much of the power from the states for regulating workplace safety. It authorized the U.S. Department of Labor to have Federal compliance officers make surprise inspections of business firms. It set up the NATIONAL COMMISSION OF STATE WORKERS COMPENSATION LAWS to recommend upgrade of worker protection, including higher disability benefits, compulsory coverage, and unlimited medical care and rehabilitation. Most states adopted the recommendations, which incidentally led to increases in workers compensation insurance premiums.

OCCUPATION, RISK relationship between occupation of an insured and degree of risk in such coverages as life, health, and workers compensation. Some occupations are more risky than others; for example, a high wire performer would have to pay more for life insurance than a banker. But the impact of occupation goes further. Claims resulting from exposure to toxic substances that result in occupational disease have been one of the most costly business insurance expenses of recent years. Life and health insurance underwriters also consider whether the occupation of a potential insured is likely to encourage a reckless lifestyle. For example, certain high-pressure occupations, like acting or Wall street trading, might be considered to lead to overconsumption of alcohol or drug abuse. Occupation is one of many factors weighed by the underwriter in RISK SELECTION.

OCCURRENCE BASIS coverage, in liability insurance, for harm suffered by others because of events occurring while a policy is in force, regardless of when a claim is actually made. *See also* CLAIMS MADE BASIS LIABILITY COVERAGE.

OCCURRENCE FORM *see* OCCURRENCE BASIS.

OCCURRENCE/INJURY THEORY viewpoint that an insurer whose liability policy is in force at the time of an accident or injury should pay a claim. *See also* LONG-TAIL LIABILITY; MANIFESTATION/INJURY THEORY.

OCCURRENCE LIMIT maximum amount that an insurance company is obligated to pay all injured parties seeking recourse as the result of the occurrence of an event covered under a LIABILITY INSURANCE policy.

In order for the coverage to apply, the policy must have been written on an OCCURRENCE BASIS.

OCEAN ACCIDENT AND GUARANTEE CORPORATION major credit insurer of the early 20th century that merged into the London Guarantee and Accident Co. in 1931.

OCEAN MARINE EXPOSURE possibility of loss associated with water transportation, including hull damage or destruction, cargo damage or destruction, liability to others for bodily injury, and property damage or destruction.

OCEAN MARINE INSURANCE coverage in the event of a marine loss. Marine loss is damage or destruction of a ship's hull and the ship's cargo (freight) as the result of the occurrence of an insured peril. Perils insured against include collision of the ship with another ship or object; the ship sinking, capsizing, or being stranded; fire; piracy; jettisoning (throwing overboard of property to save other property); barratry (fraud or other illegal act by a ship's master or crew, resulting in damage or destruction of the ship and/or cargo), and various other liability exposures. To be covered, an act cannot involve prior knowledge by the owner of the ship or its cargo. Excluded are wear and tear, dampness, decay, mold, and war. *See also* OCEAN MARINE INSURANCE, WAR RISKS.

OCEAN MARINE INSURANCE, WAR RISKS coverage on cargo in overseas ships for war-caused liability excluded under standard OCEAN MARINE INSURANCE. Not covered is cargo awaiting shipment on a wharf, or on ships after 15 days of arrival at a port. Confiscation of the cargo by a government is covered. Most policies have an automatic termination clause which goes into effect within 60 days of the declaration of war between countries specified in the policy.

OCEAN MARINE PROTECTION AND INDEMNITY INSURANCE coverage for bodily injury and property damage liability excluded under standard OCEAN MARINE INSURANCE. Coverage includes protection of wharfs, docks, and harbors; bodily injury; cost of removing the wreck if ship is sunk; and the cost of disinfecting and quarantining a ship.

ODDS probable number of times that a specified event is likely to occur. For example, if E is the event, then the odds *for* E occurring are X to Y according to the following relationship:

$$P(E) = \frac{X}{X + Y}$$

where P = probability. The odds *against* E occurring are Y to X. For example, if the probability of E occurring equals 0.6 [$P(E) = 0.6$], then

$$P(E) = \frac{6}{6 + 4} = \frac{6}{10}$$

Therefore, the odds for E occurring are 6 to 4. The odds against E occurring are 4 to 6.

OFFER application for a policy, in life insurance, accompanied by the first premium; in property and casualty insurance, the insurance application itself.

OFFEREE
1. in life insurance, receipt by a company of an insurance application accompanied by the first premium.
2. in property and casualty insurance, a company's receipt of an application.

OFFICE BURGLARY AND ROBBERY INSURANCE coverage for the office of a business, or an individual in a general office building or other structure. Includes burglary of a safe; damage caused by robbery and burglary, actual or attempted; theft of office furniture, equipment, supplies and fixtures within an office; robbery inside and outside an office; kidnapping so as to force managers of an office and/or their representatives to open the office from the outside; and theft of securities and monies from the home of a messenger of the office and/or from a night depository of a bank.

OFFICE CONTENTS FORM *see* OFFICE BURGLARY AND ROBBERY INSURANCE.

OFFICE PERSONAL PROPERTY FORM endorsement to many commercial property insurance policies that covers office equipment. Coverage includes all equipment, whether or not owned by an insured, improvements an insured has made to his office (if leased), and valuable documents such as manuscripts. This also applies to property that has been purchased for the office while in transit.

OFFICERS AND DIRECTORS LIABILITY INSURANCE *see* DIRECTORS AND OFFICERS LIABILITY INSURANCE.

OFFICERS PROTECTIVE MARINE INSURANCE type of insurance providing ALL RISKS coverage for personal property of the crew and passengers aboard a ship. Marine cargo insurance does not cover personal property of the crew and passengers, thus necessitating the purchase of an *Officers Protective Policy*.

OFFICIAL BONDS *see* PUBLIC EMPLOYEES BLANKET BOND; PUBLIC OFFICIAL BONDS.

OFF PREMISES location that is different from an insured's home or place of business. Under the standard HOMEOWNERS INSURANCE POLICY, the property of the insured is covered off premises; for example, if it is stolen from an airport. Likewise, an employer is liable for physical injury and property damage caused by an employee or by equipment, even if it does not occur at the place of business. If a truck spills chemicals on the highway or at another business site, or if a salesperson injures a client on a sales call, the employer is responsible. Business liability policies insure against such risks.

OFFSET APPROACH method of integrating an employee's Social Security or other retirement benefits with a qualified retirement plan. Some employers offset (reduce) retirement or disability income benefits from an employee's Social Security income, reasoning that since Social Security taxes are a business expense for them, they should reduce or offset employee pension benefits by a percentage of the Social Security money. An employer with a 100% offset would subtract the entire Social Security payment from the earned pension and pay only the difference as the employee pension. A 50% offset means the employer subtracts half of the Social Security benefit from the pension benefit and pays the difference.

OL&T *see* OWNERS, LANDLORDS, AND TENANTS LIABILITY POLICY.

OLD AGE, SURVIVORS, DISABILITY, AND HEALTH INSUR-ANCE (OASDHI) Federal social insurance program that provides monthly benefits to qualified retirees, their dependents, their survivors, and, in some cases, disabled workers. OASDHI was created by the Social Security Act of 1935. Federal taxes are withheld from the paychecks of all covered workers, which includes most workers with the exception of public employees and certain union employees. Self-employed persons are also required to pay the tax. Benefits are paid to retired workers after age 65, with a partial benefit for retirees at age 62. Dependents and survivors of qualified workers also qualify for benefits as do some categories of disabled workers and their dependents.

OLD LINE COMPANY imprecise term still occasionally used by commercial or PROPRIETARY INSURERS to differentiate them from *fraternal* insurers. "Old line" was apparently meant to make these companies sound more established and distinguished.

OLD LINE LEGAL RESERVE COMPANY commercial life insurers that operate on the LEGAL RESERVE system as opposed to FRATERNAL LIFE INSURANCE companies, many of which now operate on a legal reserve basis.

OMISSIONS wrongful inaction; failure to act; inactivity.

OMISSIONS CLAUSE provision of a *treaty reinsurance* contract stating that if an insurer fails to report a risk that would normally be covered, the reinsurer is still liable for the risk.

OMNIBUS BUDGET RECONCILIATION ACT OF 1987: IMPLICATIONS FOR ESTATE PLANNING legislation that provides for the inclusion in the estate of the decedent of lifetime transfers that involve a retained life interest in the following manner:
1. decedent sells or gives to a family member a remainder interest in a business.
2. decedent transfers more than 50% of appreciation interest into a general partnership but retains the limited partnership interest.
3. decedent sells or gives to a family member more than 50% of common stock interest in a corporation but retains the preferred stock interest in the corporation.

OMNIBUS CLAUSE provision in PERSONAL AUTOMOBILE POLICY (PAP) providing coverage to persons driving an automobile with permission of the NAMED INSURED.

OPEN CARGO FORM *see* SINGLE RISK CARGO INSURANCE.

OPEN CERTIFICATE *see* OPEN FORM (REPORTING FORM); OPEN POLICY.

OPEN COMPETITION LAW form of state rating legislation that allows each property/liability insurer to choose between using rates set by a bureau or its own rates. Individual states regulate insurers and approve their property insurance rates. There are three methods of rate approval in addition to open competition: PRIOR-APPROVAL RATING, MODIFIED PRIOR APPROVAL RATING and *file and use*. At one time the insurance industry operated like a cartel, with rates set by bureaus and filed with the insurance commissioners of each state. Experts believed that competition would result either in unfairly high rates or unreasonably low rates that would lead to mass insurance company insolvencies. But open competition became widespread after New York State adopted it in 1969.

OPEN COMPETITION STATE *see* RATING BUREAU.

OPEN DEBIT circumstance in which no agent is servicing a DEBIT. *See also* DEBIT INSURANCE (HOME SERVICE INSURANCE, INDUSTRIAL INSURANCE).

OPEN END POLICY *see* OPEN FORM (REPORTING FORM); OPEN POLICY.

OPEN FORM (REPORTING FORM) single policy covering all insurable property of specified type(s) at all locations of an insured business. The form is appropriate for the business that has several locations. There are several different types of reporting forms: (1) *Form ML.1* insures businesses with substantial risk exposures on a multiple location basis; (2) *Form ML.2* insures businesses with a distilled spirits risk exposure; and (3) *Form A* insures businesses with relatively small risk exposures, at either a single or multiple locations. *See also* BLANKET INSURANCE.

OPEN POLICY coverage normally used on an indefinite basis under OCEAN MARINE INSURANCE and INLAND MARINE INSURANCE (TRANSPORTATION INSURANCE): BUSINESS RISKS for the damage or destruction of a shipper's goods in transit. While the policy is in force, the shipper is required each month to submit to the insurance company reports on goods being shipped to be covered by the policy; premiums are also submitted at that time.

OPEN STOCK BURGLARY POLICY *see* MERCANTILE OPEN-STOCK BURGLARY INSURANCE.

OPERATIONS LIABILITY business liability for bodily injury or property damage resulting from operations of the business. Business firms can buy insurance for this risk with a variety of liability policies, including the COMPREHENSIVE GENERAL LIABILITY INSURANCE (CGL).

OPIC *see* OVERSEAS PRIVATE INVESTMENT CORPORATION (OPIC).

OPPORTUNITY COST value of a foregone opportunity, one rejected in favor of a presumably better opportunity. For example, investment of a sum into a MUTUAL FUND instead of a *variable annuity* with a comparable equities portfolio, thereby foregoing the tax deferred advantages of the investment build-up under the variable annuity.

OPTION *see* OPTIONAL MODES OF SETTLEMENT.

OPTIONAL ANNUITY FORM *see* ANNUITY.

OPTIONAL BENEFITS choice of a lump sum payment for an injury incurred instead of a series of periodic payments, available under a health insurance policy.

OPTIONALLY RENEWABLE CONTRACT health insurance contract that is renewable at the option of the insurer. On the anniversary date of the contract, the insurer has the right to decide whether or not to renew.

OPTIONALLY RENEWABLE HEALTH INSURANCE *see* HEALTH INSURANCE.

OPTIONAL MODES OF SETTLEMENT choice of one of the following available to a life insurance policyowner (or beneficiary, if entitled to receive a death benefit in a lump sum at the death of an insured):

1. INTEREST OPTION—death benefit left on deposit at interest with the insurance company with earnings paid to the beneficiary annually. The beneficiary can withdraw part or all of the principal of the death proceeds, subject to any restrictions the policyowner may have placed on this option.

2. *fixed amount option*—death benefit paid in a series of fixed amount installments until the proceeds and interest earned terminate.

3. *fixed period option*—death benefit left on deposit with the insurance company with the death benefit plus interest thereon paid out in equal payments for the period of time selected.

4. *life income option*—death benefit plus interest paid through a life ANNUITY. Income continues under a *straight life income option*, for as long as the beneficiary lives; or whether or not the beneficiary lives, under a *life income with period certain* option.

OPTIONAL PERIL ENDORSEMENT provision in many property insurance policies that allows an insured to pick coverage for selected perils. The choices are (1) explosion; (2) explosion, riot and civil commotion; (3) explosion, riot and civil commotion, and vandalism and malicious mischief; and (4) aircraft and vehicle damage to property.

ORDINARY AGENCY local life insurance office which sells and services *ordinary life insurance* as well as other forms of life insurance except DEBT INSURANCE.

ORDINARY LIFE INSURANCE policy that remains in full force and effect for the life of the insured, with premium payments being made for the same period. See also LIMITED PAYMENT LIFE INSURANCE; TERM LIFE INSURANCE.

ORDINARY PAYROLL *see* ORDINARY PAYROLL COVERAGE ENDORSEMENT.

ORDINARY PAYROLL COVERAGE ENDORSEMENT policy provision that provides coverage for continuing payroll expense of all employees of an insured business (except for officers and executives) for the first specified number of days of business interruption. Applies when the business's continuing operation is interrupted by damage or destruction by an insured peril.

ORDINARY PAYROLL EXCLUSION ENDORSEMENT provision in BUSINESS INTERRUPTION INSURANCE that excludes coverage for continuing the wages of rank and file employees. Business interruption insurance covers an employer for loss of earnings, including payroll expense, that occur when a business must be shut down as a result of a direct insurable loss, such as a fire. However, in order to save on the premium, an employer may not want payroll coverage for ordinary workers because, if the business were temporarily shut down, the workers could be replaced. In this case, the endorsement would be written to cover only officers and key employees.

ORDINARY REGISTER record of ordinary policies that a COMBINA-TION AGENT is responsible for servicing.

ORIGINAL AGE insured's age at the date a TERM LIFE INSURANCE policy is issued. An original age or *retroactive conversion* option permits the insured to convert the term policy to a cash value policy as of the original date of issue. Conversion is made without a physical examination, but a correction factor is charged to reflect the difference in premiums between the policies that would have been payable beginning at the original date of issue. This difference is accumulated at interest to reflect the time value of money. *See also* ATTAINED AGE.

ORIGINAL AGE CONVERSION *see* ORIGINAL AGE.

ORIGINAL COST actual price paid for property when it was acquired. The original cost might apply to a piece of jewelry, to a piece of equipment, or to a building. For insurance purposes, original cost is often different from *replacement cost* or ACTUAL CASH VALUE.

ORIGINAL COST LESS DEPRECIATION actual price paid for property when acquired, minus depreciation. Original cost less depreciation is used to compute ACTUAL CASH VALUE, which is often the insurable interest in a property.

OTHER INSURANCE presence of other contract(s) covering the same conditions. When more than one policy covers the exposure, each policy will pay an equal share of the loss.

OTHER INSURANCE CLAUSE provision in a property, liability, or health insurance policy stipulating the extent of coverage in the event that other insurance covers the same property. *See also* APPOR-TIONMENT; COORDINATION OF BENEFITS.

OTHER INSUREDS individuals or organizations covered by PROPERTY AND LIABILITY INSURANCE other than the named insured. For example, under the PERSONAL AUTOMOBILE POLICY (PAP), other insureds under Coverage A—Liability are the named insured's spouse, other relatives living with the insured, and any other person using the automobile with the permission of the insured or the insured's spouse. *See also* RIDERS, LIFE POLICIES.

OUTAGE INSURANCE *see* EXTRA EXPENSE INSURANCE.

OUTBOARD MOTOR BOAT INSURANCE coverage on an ALL RISKS basis for physical damage loss. Coverage applies to property damage to the insured boat or damage caused by the insured boat to a third party boat (property damage liability). Excluded perils are war damage, use of boat in a race or speed contest, nuclear loss, and so forth. Bodily injury liability coverage is excluded from this policy since the operator of the boat would be covered for this risk under a COMPREHENSIVE PERSONAL LIABILITY INSURANCE policy, HOMEOWNERS INSURANCE POLICY, or TENANTS INSURANCE.

OUT-OF-AREA EMERGENCY SERVICES *see* HEALTH MAINTENANCE ORGANIZATION (HMO).

OUTPATIENT individual receiving medical treatment who is not required to be hospitalized overnight.

OUTPATIENT HEALTH SERVICES AT HMO FACILITY *see* HEALTH MAINTENANCE ORGANIZATION (HMO).

OUTPATIENT HOSPITAL CARE, HMO *see* HEALTH MAINTENANCE ORGANIZATION (HMO).

OUTSTANDING PREMIUMS payments due to an insurance company but not yet paid.

OVERHEAD INSURANCE *see* BUSINESS INTERRUPTION INSURANCE.

OVERINSURANCE situation in which insurance benefits exceed the actual loss of an insured. Overinsurance can be a problem for the insurer because it may tempt the insured to make a false claim in order to profit financially. Various safeguards are designed to prevent overinsurance. For example, in group health insurance, companies break down benefits paid by the primary carrier and the secondary carrier through COORDINATION OF BENEFITS. Still, some types of coverage, particularly disability income insurance, are subject to overinsurance abuse.

OVERLAPPING INSURANCE coverage by at least two insurance policies providing the same coverage for the same risk. *See also* APPORTIONMENT; CONCURRENCY; COORDINATION OF BENEFITS; NONCONCURRENCY; PRIMARY INSURANCE.

OVER LINE coverage that exceeds the normal insurance capacity of an insurer or reinsurer.

OVERRIDING COMMISSION payment to a broker, master general agent, general agent, or agent on any particular line of insurance written by other agents within a particular geographical area.

OVERSEAS PRIVATE INVESTMENT CORPORATION (OPIC) Federal program to insure private U.S. investments in foreign countries, created by the Foreign Assistance Act of 1961. It is a joint government and private effort to encourage U.S. investments abroad by providing protection against three political risks: (1) inability to convert foreign currency; (2) expropriation of facilities by a foreign country; and (3) war or revolution. The program is guaranteed by the full faith and credit of the U.S. government.

OWNERS AND CONTRACTORS PROTECTIVE LIABILITY INSURANCE endorsement to OWNERS, LANDLORDS, AND TENANTS LIABILITY POLICY, MANUFACTURERS AND CONTRACTORS LIABILITY INSURANCE or other liability policies for business firms which provides liability coverage for an insured who is sued because of negligent acts or omissions of an independent contractor or subcontractor resulting in bodily injury and/or property damage to a third party.

OWNERSHIP OF EXPIRATIONS retention of all files of policies sold by the agent of record who, according to written agreement with the insurance company, has the exclusive rights to solicit renewals. *See also* INDEPENDENT AGENT; INDEPENDENT AGENCY SYSTEM.

OWNERSHIP OF LIFE INSURANCE *see* OWNERSHIP RIGHTS UNDER LIFE INSURANCE; POLICYHOLDER.

OWNERSHIP PROVISION *see* OWNERSHIP RIGHTS UNDER LIFE INSURANCE; POLICYHOLDER.

OWNERSHIP RIGHTS UNDER LIFE INSURANCE right of the *policyowner* as listed in a policy. An insured has the right to exercise all privileges and receive all benefits of the policy except when restricted by the right of an *irrevocable beneficiary* or an assignee of record. A policyowner can transfer ownership of the policy by making an *absolute assignment* (rights transferred to another individual without any conditions) or a COLLATERAL ASSIGNMENT (policy is security for a loan), transfer ownership by endorsement, change the plan of insurance (apply the cash value of present policy to purchase another type of policy with the original policy's date), *reinstate* the policy, select an OPTIONAL MODE OF SETTLEMENT, make a POLICY LOAN, select the DIVIDEND OPTION (if it is a *participating policy*), or select the NONFORFEITURE BENEFIT OPTION.

OWNERS, LANDLORDS, AND TENANTS LIABILITY POLICY coverage for bodily injury and property damage liability resulting from the ownership, use, and/or maintenance of an insured business's premises as well as operations by the business anywhere in the U.S. or Canada. Businesses that qualify for the Owners, Landlords, and Tenants Policy include mercantile establishments, apartment buildings, and office buildings. The only ineligible firms are those engaged in manufacturing. Excluded perils are: operation of an automobile, aircraft, contractual liability resulting from an agreement by the insured, war, nuclear disaster, and liquor liability.

P

PACKAGE INSURANCE *see* MULTIPLE LINE INSURANCE.

PACKAGE POLICY several basic property and/or liability policies combined to form a single policy. For example, the HOMEOWNERS INSURANCE POLICY is composed of such basic coverages as BROAD FORM PERSONAL THEFT INSURANCE, COMPREHENSIVE PERSONAL LIABILITY, and FIRE INSURANCE—STANDARD FIRE POLICY.

PAID BUSINESS life and health insurance business for which the prospective insured or insureds have signed the APPLICATION, completed the MEDICAL EXAMINATION, and paid the required PREMIUM.

PAID FOR insurance policy for which the required PREMIUM has been paid. *See also* PAID BUSINESS.

PAID-IN CAPITAL sum received by an insurance company at the sale of its stock. This capital represents the interest of the stockholders in the company.

PAID-IN SURPLUS excess of the value of an insurer's admitted assets over the total value of its liabilities and minimum capital requirements established by applicable statutes designed to assure the insurer's solvency.

PAID LOSSES actual amount of total losses paid by an insurance company during a specified time interval.

PAID-LOSS RETRO PLAN *see* RETROSPECTIVE RATING.

PAID-UP ADDITIONS option under a participating life insurance policy by which the policyowner can elect to have the dividends purchase paid-up increments of permanent insurance.

PAID-UP INSURANCE life insurance policy under which all premiums have already been paid, with no further premium payment due. *See also* LIMITED PAYMENT LIFE INSURANCE.

PAIR CLAUSE *see* SET CLAUSE (PAIR OR SET CLAUSE).

P&I *see* PROTECTION AND INDEMNITY INSURANCE (P&I).

PAR *see* PARTICIPATING INSURANCE.

PARAMEDICAL EXAMINATION medical check of an applicant for life or health insurance by a medical professional who is not a physician.

PARASOL POLICY *see* DIFFERENCE IN CONDITIONS INSURANCE.

PARCEL POST INSURANCE coverage for a shipper (owner/sender) for property damage or loss of goods in transit through the Post Office. A TRIP TRANSIT INSURANCE policy specifically excludes coverages on property sent through the Post Office since that agency is not a common carrier and does not incur the liability of a common carrier. This is why additional coverage must be purchased in the form of parcel post insurance, even if a business has a trip transit insurance policy. Parcel post insurance is sold by the Post Office in the form of a certificate, which covers property in its custody. It is issued on an ALL RISKS basis, subject to exclusions of spoilage, and financial instruments such as bills, currency, deeds, notes, and securities.

PARENT COMPANY insurer in a group of companies which act as subsidiaries. *See also* FLEET OF COMPANIES.

PARENT LIABILITY liability incurred by a parent by reason of a TORT committed by his or her minor child.

PAROL EVIDENCE RULE rule that prohibits the introduction into a court of law any oral or written agreement which contradicts the final written agreement. For example, an insurance contract containing clauses and provisions is in writing and as such this contract cannot be contradicted or modified by any oral statements or agreements that are inadmissible in a court of law.

PARTIAL DISABILITY *see* PERMANENT PARTIAL DISABILITY.

PARTIAL LOSS damage of property which is not total; average (in sense of partial) loss. *See also* SET CLAUSE.

PARTIAL PLAN TERMINATION scheme to recapture excess pension assets by splitting a qualified plan in two, and terminating one of them. In the mid-1980s, many pension plans became ''overfunded'' because their investments had performed so well. In order to recapture the ''extra'' money, some business firms split the pension plan into two plans, one for current employees and an overfunded one for retirees. The company buys annuities to pay the required benefits to retirees and reclaims the excess assets. The other plan is kept in place for current employees.

PARTICIPANT person covered under an EMPLOYEE BENEFIT INSURANCE PLAN.

PARTICIPATING *see* PARTICIPATING INSURANCE.

PARTICIPATING INSURANCE policy which pays a dividend to its owner. *See also* PARTICIPATING POLICY DIVIDEND.

PARTICIPATING POLICY DIVIDEND life insurance contract which pays its owner dividends, which can be: (1) taken as cash; (2) applied to reduce a premium; (3) applied to purchase an increment of PAID-UP INSURANCE; (4) left on deposit with the insurance company to accumulate at interest; and (5) applied to purchase *term insurance* for one year.

PARTICIPATING POLICY DIVIDEND OPTION *see* PARTICIPATING POLICY DIVIDEND.

PARTICIPATING REINSURANCE *see* PROPORTIONAL REINSURANCE; QUOTA SHARE REINSURANCE; SURPLUS REINSURANCE.

PARTICIPATION *see* PARTICIPATING INSURANCE.

PARTICULAR AVERAGE
1. expenses and damages incurred as the result of damage to a ship and its cargo, and/or of taking direct action to prevent initial or further damage to the ship and its cargo. These expenses and damages are paid by the owner of the part of the ship and cargo which actually suffers a loss. Contrast with GENERAL AVERAGE.
2. partial loss of property resulting from an OCEAN MARINE EXPOSURE for which the owner of that property must bear the entire loss. *See also* FREE OF PARTICULAR AVERAGE (FPA).

PARTNERSHIP LIFE AND HEALTH INSURANCE protection to maintain the value of a business in case of death or disability of a partner. Upon the death or long-term disability of a partner, insurance can provide for the transfer of a deceased or disabled partner's interest to the surviving partner according to a pre-determined formula. Funding can be achieved through either of two plans:
1. *Cross Purchase Plan*—each partner buys insurance on the lives of the other partners. The beneficiaries are the surviving partners who use the proceeds to buy out the deceased's interest. This plan can become complicated when there are more than two partners. For example, if there are four partners, partner A will buy insurance on the lives of partners B, C, and D. The procedure would be repeated with partners B, C, and D. Total policies would be 12.
2. *Entity Plan*—because of the number of policies required, the entity plan is most often used for buy-and-sell agreements by larger partnerships. The partnership owns, is beneficiary of, and pays the premiums on the life insurance of each partner. When one of the partners dies, the partnership as a whole purchases the deceased partner's interest. Premiums are not tax deductible as a business expense. If whole life insurance is used, the cash values are listed as assets on the balance sheet of the partnership and are available as collateral for loans.

Partners use insurance to fund other objectives. In personal service partnerships of doctors, lawyers, and accountants, when it is important to retain a deceased partner's name on the title of the firm, the heirs may agree to this for a share in subsequent partnership profits. An *income continuation insurance* plan funded through life insurance by the partnership, serves this purpose.

Disability of partner buy and sell insurance can be used by a partnership to provide income for the firm if a partner becomes disabled. The policy would pay a monthly income to the partnership for the duration of the partner's disability.

PARTY individual or entity who enters into a contract or other legal proceeding, such as a lawsuit.

PASSENGER BODILY INJURY LIABILITY INSURANCE coverage for automobile or aircraft operators if they are sued for negligently killing or injuring a passenger. The PERSONAL AUTOMOBILE POLICY (PAP) provides MEDICAL PAYMENTS INSURANCE for doctor and hospital bills for passengers of the insured, and BODILY INJURY liability insurance for anyone who is accidentally disabled, injured, or killed by the insured. Aviation policies split bodily injury liability into *general* and *passenger*. Passenger liability covers a passenger who is injured, killed, or disabled; general liability covers anyone else.

PASSIVE LOSS RULES rules passed as part of the TAX REFORM ACT OF 1986, that limit the amount of income investors can shelter from current tax. Losses can be deducted from passive activities only in the amount to which income results from passive activities. Furthermore, losses from one passive activity can be used only to offset the passive income earned from a similar passive activity. For example, losses from publicly traded partnerships can be applied only to offset passive income earned from publicly traded partnerships.

PASSIVE RETENTION practice in which no funds are set aside on a mathematical basis to pay for expected losses. This occurs when a risk manager is not aware of an exposure, when the cost of treating an exposure positively is prohibitive, or if the *severity* of a loss (should it occur) would be inconsequential. *See also* SELF INSURANCE.

PAST DUE ACCOUNTS funds receivable or payable that have not been paid in a timely manner. COMMERCIAL CREDIT INSURANCE protects an insured against declines in the value of receivables due to insolvency of a debtor. The insured may turn over to the insurer accounts that are up to 12 months past due or, by special endorsement, those that are 6 months overdue. For insurance purposes, these past due accounts will be treated as if they were accounts due from an insolvent company.

PAST SERVICE BENEFIT private pension plan credit given for an employee's past service with an employer prior to establishment of a pension plan. Usually, a lower percentage of compensation is credited for benefits for past service than for future service benefits.

PAST SERVICE CREDIT *see* PAST SERVICE BENEFIT.

PAST SERVICE LIABILITY employer's obligation to fund a pension plan for the time period when employees were qualified to participate but the plan was not yet established. For example, a pension plan is established at XYZ Co. in 1985. Because John Smith started at the firm in 1975, he would have a *past service credit* for his 10 years of service before the plan started. For funding purposes, annual contributions are broken down into FUTURE SERVICE BENEFITS and PAST SERVICE BENEFIT. Past service liability is not funded entirely in the initial year of a plan, primarily because it would be too expensive, and the IRS requires that deductions be spread over 10 years.

PAST SERVICE LIABILITY—INITIAL funding of an employee's benefits in a pension plan for his beginning past service of employment. This is a significant cost factor in pension planning and financing of future benefits.

PATENT AND COPYRIGHT INFRINGEMENT *see* UNFAIR TRADE PRACTICE.

PAUL v. VIRGINIA U.S. Supreme Court case in 1868 in which the decision (since overruled) was that an insurance policy was not an instrument of commerce, and thus did not involve interstate commerce transactions which would make it subject to Federal regulation. *See also* MCCARRAN-FERGUSON ACT (PUBLIC LAW 15); SOUTH-EASTERN UNDERWRITERS ASSOCIATION (SEUA) CASE.

PAY-AS-YOU-GO PLAN *see* CURRENT DISBURSEMENT.

PAYEE
1. recipient.
2. insurance company that receives a premium payment from a payer.
3. insured or beneficiary who receives a loss or benefit payment from an insurer.

PAYMASTER ROBBERY INSURANCE coverage for robbery of the payroll of a business. Coverage applies to money and checks from the time the payroll is withdrawn from the bank until it is distributed to the employees, whether inside or outside of the premises of the business. Employees are covered if robbed of their pay when the business itself is being robbed of the payroll. Excluded are manuscripts and records of accounts.

PAYMENT BOND bond guaranteeing that a contractor will pay fees owed for labor and materials necessary for construction of a project. If these fees are not paid, an owner who has paid the contractor might be confronted with subcontractor's or worker's liens filed against the completed project. If this happens, the owner could end up paying many times the value of the work done. *See also* PERFORMANCE BOND.

PAYMENT CERTAIN phrase used to describe a method of annuity payout that guarantees a specified number of years, regardless of whether an annuitant remains alive.

PAYMENT OF EXPOSURES INSURED BY COMPANY *see* CLAIM, OBLIGATION TO PAY; HOMEOWNERS INSURANCE POLICY; INTER-INSURANCE COMPANY CLAIMS; INTERPLEADER; PERSONAL AUTOMOBILE POLICY (PAP); PROPERTY AND CASUALTY INSURANCE PROVISIONS.

PAYMENT OF PREMIUMS ON BONDS act that seals a contract and is noncancellable. SURETY BONDS and FIDELITY BONDS resemble insurance contracts in many ways. However, the surety, which is often an insurance company, cannot cancel a bond once the premium has been paid.

PAYOR CLAUSE provision found in JUVENILE INSURANCE which waives the premiums due on the insured child's policy provided that the payor of the premiums becomes totally disabled or dies before the child reaches a stipulated age.

PAYOUT PHASE period when the accumulated assets in an ANNUITY are returned to the annuitant. An annuity may be purchased with either a single payment or with many payments over the life of the contract. At some point, usually upon retirement, the annuitant elects to have the payments, plus earnings, returned. The 1982 Federal Tax Code declared that any money received during the payout phase is considered earnings first and is taxable.

PAYROLL AUDIT insurance company's examination of an insured business's payroll records in order to determine the final premium due on a WORKERS COMPENSATION INSURANCE policy.

PAYROLL DEDUCTION INSURANCE plan under which an employee authorizes his employer to deduct from each paycheck premiums due on an insurance plan.

PAYROLL ENDORSEMENTS *see* ORDINARY PAYROLL EXCLUSION ENDORSEMENT.

PAYROLL STOCK OWNERSHIP PLANS (PAYSOP) EMPLOYEE STOCK OWNERSHIP PLAN (ESOP); TRUST (ESOP) under which an employer received tax credit instead of a tax deduction for contributions. Until passage of the TAX REFORM ACT OF 1986, the tax credit was limited to the lesser of the value of the stock contributed to the plan or .5% of the employer's payroll. The PAYSOP must have met all of the requirements of a qualified plan and all participants must have had 100% immediate VESTING. The Tax Reform Act of 1986 repealed PAYSOP.

PEAK SEASON ENDORSEMENT endorsement attached to PROPERTY INSURANCE COVERAGE which provides additional limits of protection on a merchant's inventories during specific time intervals. The time intervals generally are the periods during the year when shopping is most intense.

PEL *see* PERMISSIBLE EXPOSURE LIMIT.

PENALTY liability limit on a FIDELITY BOND or SURETY BOND. A fixed-penalty bond is one with a fixed liability limit that the surety company will pay in the event of nonperformance.

PENSION BENEFIT GUARANTY CORPORATION (PBGC) independent Federal government organization authorized by the EMPLOYEE RETIREMENT INCOME SECURITY ACT OF 1974 (ERISA) to administer the PENSION PLAN TERMINATION INSURANCE program. Its function is to ensure that *vested* benefits of employees, whose PENSION PLAN is being terminated, will be paid as they come due. The PBGC board of directors consists of the U.S. Secretaries of Labor, Commerce, and Treasury. Only qualified DEFINED BENEFIT PLANS are guaranteed; PROFIT SHARING PLANS, *stock bonus plans,* and MONEY PURCHASE PLANS are not. Plan termination insurance covers both voluntary termination and terminations ordered by the PBGC. Employers pay an annual premium rate per employee in their pension plans to the PBGC to finance the plan termination insurance program.

PENSION FUND *see* PENSION PLAN.

PENSION MAXIMIZATION plan under which life insurance is substituted for retirement income. Under the plan, a married individual selects a SINGLE LIFE ANNUITY payout from the pension plan, which will generate the maximum monthly income benefit while that individual is alive, with nothing being paid to the surviving spouse after the death of that individual. The higher income generated from the single life annuity, compared with that from a JOINT LIFE AND SURVIVORSHIP ANNUITY, is used to buy a life insurance policy on the married individual's life. If this individual dies first, the proceeds of the policy will be used to purchase an ANNUITY for the lifetime of the spouse. Should the spouse die first, the married individual still has the higher income benefit from the single life annuity.

PENSION PLAN retirement program to provide employees (and often, spouses) with a monthly income payment for the rest of their lives. To qualify, an employee must have met minimum age and service requirements. Benefit formulas can be either the DEFINED CONTRIBUTION PENSION (MONEY PURCHASE PLAN) or the DEFINED BENEFIT PLAN. The EMPLOYEE RETIREMENT INCOME SECURITY ACT OF 1974 (ERISA) requires a pension plan to provide an income for the rest of a retired employee's life, and at least 50% of that amount to the surviving spouse of a retired employee for the rest of her life, unless the spouse waives this right in writing. Death and disability benefits are also provided by most pension plans. THE TAX REFORM ACT OF 1986 has changed the VESTING requirements. Funds for these plans can be generated under numerous PENSION PLAN FUNDING INSTRUMENTS.

PENSION PLAN: FUND COLLEGE EDUCATION group of plans (to include SECTION 401(k) PLANS and SECTION 403(b) PLANS) which permit in-service withdrawals to fund a college education if a HARDSHIP exists.

PENSION PLAN FUNDING: GROUP DEPOSIT ADMINISTRA-TION ANNUITY pension plan funding instrument in which contributions paid by an employer are deposited to accumulate at interest. (These plans are usually NONCONTRIBUTORY.) Upon retirement, an *immediate annuity* is purchased for the employee. The benefit is determined by a formula and the investment earnings on funds left to accumulate at interest. Since the annuity is purchased at point of retirement, the deposit administration plan can be used with any benefit formula.

PENSION PLAN FUNDING: GROUP IMMEDIATE PARTICIPA-TION GUARANTEED (IPG) CONTRACT ANNUITY modification of the *group deposit administration annuity* under which an employer participates in the investment (which may prove to be adverse as well as favorable), mortality, and expense experience of the plan on an immediate basis. Under the IPG, contributions are paid into a fund to which interest is credited. At retirement, an IMMEDIATE ANNUITY is purchased for the employee. The size of the benefit will depend on the benefit formula used and the investment, mortality, and expense experience of the plan.

PENSION PLAN FUNDING: GROUP PERMANENT CONTRACT insurance policy under which the value equals the benefits to be paid to the plan participants (employees) at normal retirement age, assuming that (1) their rate of earnings remains the same until NORMAL RETIRE-MENT AGE, and (2) the contributions to the plan are sufficient to meet funding requirements for benefits under the plan. Adjustments to contributions are made as employee earnings increase. Retirement benefits depend on the benefit formula used, and the investment, mortality, and expense experience of the plan.

PENSION PLAN FUNDING: IMMEDIATE PARTICIPATION GUARANTEE CONTINGENT ANNUITY *see* PENSION PLAN FUNDING: GROUP IMMEDIATE PARTICIPATION GUARANTEED (IPG) CONTRACT ANNUITY.

PENSION PLAN FUNDING: INDIVIDUAL CONTRACT PENSION PLAN retirement plan for an individual based on a single contract with a benefit based on current earnings, as if they will remain static until NORMAL RETIREMENT AGE. As the earnings of the plan participant increase, additional contracts are purchased (with an increase in the contributions to the plan). The amount of retirement benefits depends on the benefit formula used and the investment experience of the company underwriting the plan.

PENSION PLAN FUNDING INSTRUMENTS means of paying the cost of benefits of pension plan participants including retirement, death, and disability. *See also* GROUP PERMANENT LIFE INSURANCE; PENSION PLAN; PENSION PLAN FUNDING: GROUP DEPOSIT ADMINISTRATION ANNUITY; PENSION PLAN FUNDING: GROUP IMMEDIATE PARTICIPATION GUARANTEED (IPG) CONTRACT ANNUITY.

PENSION PLAN FUNDING METHODS *see* PENSION PLAN FUNDING, GROUP DEPOSIT ADMINISTRATION ANNUITY; PENSION PLAN FUNDING, GROUP IMMEDIATE PARTICIPATION GUARANTEED (IPG) CONTRACT ANNUITY; PENSION PLAN FUNDING, GROUP PERMANENT CONTRACT; PENSION PLAN FUNDING, INDIVIDUAL CONTRACT PENSION PLAN.

PENSION PLAN INTEGRATION WITH SOCIAL SECURITY offset or subtraction of Social Security benefits from earned benefits in a qualified pension plan to reduce a pension benefit. Many business firms offset their pension payments by the amount of a retiree's Social Security benefit. For example, John Smith has earned a monthly pension benefit of $950. His monthly Social Security payment is $688. If his employer applies 100% integration, his pension is reduced by the entire Social Security benefit; he will receive $950 minus $688, or $262 monthly. More commonly, integration is based on a percentage of Social Security. With 50% integration, 50% of the Social Security benefit ($344) would be subtracted from the $950 pension for a monthly benefit of $606. Offsets were limited by the TAX REFORM ACT OF 1986.

PENSION PLANS: DISTRIBUTIONS prior to 1988, right to withdraw retirement assets before age $59\frac{1}{2}$ without having to pay a 10% penalty under the following circumstances:
1. medical expenses are incurred.
2. the plan participant becomes disabled.

With the passage of the TECHNICAL AND MISCELLANEOUS REVENUE ACT OF 1988 (TAMRA): EMPLOYEE BENEFITS a third option is available to the plan participant:

3. distribution must be a part of a scheduled series of substantially equal periodic payments. The distributions must be made in such a manner that they will continue for the lifetime of the plan participant or the joint lifetime of the plan participant and his or her beneficiary.

PENSION PLAN VALUATION FACTORS present value computation of the accrued or projected benefits of a retirement plan. This computation is known as the *actuarial valuation* because it is based on (1) probability (retirement event will take place); (2) demographic changes (increase or decrease in employee's earnings); (3) interest rate (discount rate used to derive present value of future benefits).

PENSION PLANS: WITHDRAWAL BENEFITS rights of employees who leave an employer with a qualified plan to withdraw their accumulated benefits. With a CONTRIBUTORY plan, employees have immediate rights to their own contributions, plus earnings. If they leave the employer, the accumulated money belongs to them. But they are not entitled to employer contributions, unless vested. VESTING depends on the terms of the plan, but maximum time limits are set by law. A vested employee who withdraws accumulated benefits upon separation may either pay tax on the amount contributed by the employer and spend it, or roll it over into an INDIVIDUAL RETIREMENT ACCOUNT (IRA).

PENSION PLAN TERMINATION INSURANCE coverage provided by the PENSION BENEFIT GUARANTY CORPORATION (PBGC) that guarantees participants a certain level of pension benefits even if the plan terminates without assets. The PBGC was authorized under the EMPLOYEE RETIREMENT INCOME SECURITY ACT OF 1974 (ERISA). The insurance, paid for by employers, protects *vested interest* only.

PENSION PORTABILITY employee's right to transfer pension benefit credits from a former employer to a current employer.

PENSIONS *see* PENSION PLAN.

PENSION TRUST provision that funds a tax-qualified plan. Trust funds are the oldest, and still the most common, method of funding pensions. All contributions made by employer and employees are deposited into a trust fund, with a trustee responsible for investing the money, administering the plan, and paying benefits.

PER ACCIDENT LIMIT maximum amount that an insurance company will pay under a liability insurance policy for claims resulting from a particular accident. This maximum amount applies regardless of the amount of property damage or the number of persons injured in that accident.

PER CAPITA distribution of a deceased beneficiary's share of an estate among all of his or her living heirs. Contrast with PER STIRPES.

PER CAUSE DEDUCTIBLE requirement that the deductible must be met for each separate illness or accident before benefits are payable under major medical insurance.

PERCENTAGE-OF-LOSS DEDUCTIBLE deductible, applied to every loss, expressed as a percentage of that loss. As the loss increases, the deductible amount increases.

PERCENTAGE PARTICIPATING DEDUCTIBLE (*stop loss*) amount over which a health insurance plan pays 100% of the costs in a PER-CENTAGE PARTICIPATION plan. Here, an insured shares costs with the insurer according to some predetermined ratio. For example, an insured may pay 20% of covered costs and the insurer 80%. However, most group medical plans pick up all covered expenses over a certain deductible amount or specified dollar limit. For example, once the insured has paid a $2000 deductible amount, the plan may pay 100% of covered expenses for the remainder of the policy year.

PERCENTAGE PARTICIPATION (COINSURANCE) plan where a portion of medical expenses are paid by an insured. Some health insurance policies provide that the insured shares expenses with the insurer according to a predetermined ratio. For example, many group health plans provide that, after paying a deductible amount, the insured pays a portion (usually 20–25%) of covered medical expenses. For some types of services, such as psychiatry or dentistry, the percentage participation, which the insured pays, may go as high as 50% of covered services.

PER DIEM BUSINESS INTERRUPTION POLICY type of BUSINESS INTERRUPTION INSURANCE policy which provides a specific daily dollar amount benefit to the business owner for each day the business is unable to resume normal business operations because of property damage or destruction resulting from an INSURED PERIL.

PERFORMANCE BOND bond guaranteeing that a contractor will perform under the contract in accordance with all specifications of the bid submitted.

PERIL *see* ALL RISKS.

PERIOD *see* POLICY PERIOD.

PERIOD CERTAIN *see* ANNUITY.

PERIODIC LEVEL *see* LEVEL.

PERMANENT DISABILITY *see* DISABILITY.

PERMANENT LIFE INSURANCE *see* ORDINARY LIFE INSURANCE.

PERMANENT PARTIAL DISABILITY disability in which a wage earner is forever prevented from working at full physical capability because of injury or illness. *See also* DISABILITY INCOME INSURANCE.

PERMANENT TOTAL DISABILITY disability in which a wage earner is forever prevented from working because of injury or illness suffered. *See also* DISABILITY INCOME INSURANCE.

PERMISSIBLE EXPOSURE LIMIT (PEL) standard set under the OCCUPATIONAL SAFETY AND HEALTH ACT that sets allowable levels of worker exposure to such toxic substances as asbestos, certain chemicals, and radiation. In many cases workers must wear devices to determine their exposure to toxic workplace substances and, when the maximum is reached, they must be transferred to another workplace. Business firms that violate the standard can be fined.

PERMISSIBLE LOSS RATIO *see* EXPECTED LOSS RATIO.

PERMISSION GRANTED CLAUSE provision in most property insurance policies on *real property* that permits a policyholder to use an insured place for normal purposes related to occupancy. This might include storing remodeling materials or hobby equipment. This clause is important because a policy may be voided for fraud, concealment, or misrepresentation. A policy may also be suspended for increased hazard by an insured. The permission granted clause provides a defense against a charge that a policyholder has increased the hazard of covered property if the materials in question are a part of the insured's everyday lifestyle.

PERMISSIVE LAW *see* FILE-AND-USE RATING LAWS.

PERMISSIVE USER person who uses personal property such as an automobile with permission of an owner. For example, for insurance purposes, someone who uses an automobile with the owner's permission would be covered by the latter's PERSONAL AUTOMOBILE POLICY (PAP). On the other hand, the owner of property may not be responsible for a TRESPASSER.

PERMIT BOND contract guaranteeing that a person licensed by a city, county, or state agency will perform activities for which the bond was granted, according to the regulations governing the license.

PER PERSON LIMIT maximum amount that an insurance company will pay under a liability insurance policy for bodily injury incurred by any single person as a result of any one accident.

PERPETUAL INSURANCE coverage on *real property* written to have no time limit. A single deposit premium pays for insurance for the life of the risk. The insurer earns enough investment income on the deposit to cover losses and costs. Upon cancellation, the insured is entitled to return of the initial deposit premium. Perpetual insurance, first issued in the U.S. in Philadelphia in 1752, is still used for fire and homeowner's insurance.

PERPETUAL MUTUAL INSURANCE COMPANY type of MUTUAL INSURANCE COMPANY that requires a substantial initial premium payment. After the initial premium payment is made, future premium payments required will be paid from the investment earnings of the initial premium payment. *See also* PERPETUAL INSURANCE.

PERSISTENCY percentage of life insurance or other insurance policies remaining in force; percentage of policies which have not *lapsed*. The higher the percentage the greater the persistency. Since it is an important measure of a company's retention of its life insurance business, most companies extend every effort to increase persistency. *See also* CONSERVATION.

PERSONAL ACCIDENT CATASTROPHE REINSURANCE *see* AUTOMATIC NONPROPORTIONAL REINSURANCE; AUTOMATIC PROPORTIONAL REINSURANCE; AUTOMATIC REINSURANCE; EXCESS OF LOSS REINSURANCE; FACULATIVE REINSURANCE; NONPROPORTIONAL REINSURANCE; PROPORTIONAL REINSURANCE; QUOTA SHARE REINSURANCE; STOP LOSS REINSURANCE; SURPLUS REINSURANCE.

PERSONAL ARTICLES INSURANCE coverage for all kinds of personal property whether inside or outside an insured's (home) to include jewelry, musical instruments, cameras, fine arts, and precious stones. The insurance policy can be issued separately as an INLAND MARINE INSURANCE policy or as an endorsement to the HOMEOWNERS INSURANCE POLICY. Protection is on an ALL RISKS basis subject to exclusions of wear and tear, war, and nuclear disaster. Each piece of jewelry and other expensive items must be specifically listed in the policy. *See also* PERSONAL EFFECTS INSURANCE.

PERSONAL AUTOMOBILE POLICY (PAP) replacement for the earlier *Family Automobile Policy (FAP)* with these nine basic coverages:
1. *Coverage A*—Liability. (a) the company pays damages for which an insured becomes legally obligated because negligent acts or omissions resulted in bodily injury and/or property damage to a third party; (b) the company defends the insured against liability suits for

damages caused to the third party, paying various expenses in this connection; and (c) vehicles covered include the insured's own cars, a newly acquired car, and a temporary substitute car.

2. *Coverage B*—Medical Payments. The company pays medical expenses for bodily injury incurred by the insured (including spouse and relatives) and any other person while they occupy the insured car.

3. *Coverage C*—Uninsured Motorist Coverage. The company pays damages which the insured is legally entitled to collect from the owner or driver of an uninsured motor vehicle.

4. *Coverage D*—Comprehensive. The company pays for loss to the insured's car for all damages, in excess of a deductible amount, except due to collision.

5. *Coverage E*—Collision. The company pays for loss to the insured's car for all damages in excess of a deductible amount caused by collision.

6. *Coverage F*—Car Rental Expense (optional). The company pays for car rental up to a daily dollar limit, when the insured's car cannot run due to a loss incurred.

7. *Coverage G*—Death, Dismemberment, and Loss of Sight (optional). The company pays the insured or beneficiary for death or loss caused by an accident to the insured.

8. *Coverage H*—Total Disability (optional). The company pays the insured a monthly disability income benefit because of bodily injury in an accident while occupying or being struck by a motor vehicle.

9. *Coverage I*—Loss of Earnings (optional). The company pays the insured a percentage of his loss of monthly earnings because of bodily injury as the result of an accident while occupying or being struck by a motor vehicle.

PERSONAL CATASTROPHE INSURANCE excess coverage over the first layer of medical insurance to provide for catastrophic medical payments. The first layer may be either group or individual medical insurance, or an individual may choose to pay for ordinary medical payments himself and buy insurance for those losses above a certain amount.

PERSONAL COMPREHENSIVE LIABILITY INSURANCE *see* COMPREHENSIVE PERSONAL LIABILITY INSURANCE.

PERSONAL CONTRACT agreement concerning an insured individual not the insured's property. A *property and casualty insurance contract* cannot be assigned, since it follows the insured, not the property. For example, a HOMEOWNERS INSURANCE POLICY cannot be transferred with the home upon its sale because the insured no longer has an insurable interest (expectation of monetary loss) in the home. But a LIFE INSURANCE contract can be assigned (for example, to secure a line of credit for a business). Banks use the *American Bankers Form* for the assignment of life insurance policies pledged as security for a loan.

PERSONAL EFFECTS INSURANCE coverage outside an insured's home for personal items usually carried or worn while traveling. Protection is for personal property (apparel and jewelry), not for real property or property not usually carried by the traveler (a piano, household furniture). Coverage applies anywhere in the world for the named insured and insured's spouse and unmarried children if residents of the household.

PERSONAL EXCESS LIABILITY INSURANCE *see* UMBRELLA LIABILITY INSURANCE.

PERSONAL FLOATER POLICY *see* PERSONAL ARTICLES INSURANCE; PERSONAL EFFECTS INSURANCE.

PERSONAL FURS INSURANCE *see* FURRIERS BLOCK INSURANCE; FURS INSURANCE.

PERSONAL HISTORY insurance applicant's life and health record, financial standing, driving record, general character, vocation, and habits. These factors are evaluated by a *home office underwriter* in classifying the applicant as insurable, preferred, extra-risk, or uninsurable. *See also* NUMERICAL RATING SYSTEM.

PERSONAL INJURY wrongful conduct causing false arrest, invasion of privacy, libel, slander, defamation of character and bodily injury. The injury is against the person in contrast to property damage or destruction. *See also* BUSINESS LIABILITY INSURANCE (Insuring Agreements Section).

PERSONAL INJURY PROTECTION (PIP) coverage to pay basic expenses for an insured and his family in states with NO FAULT AUTOMOBILE INSURANCE. No-fault laws generally require drivers to carry both LIABILITY INSURANCE and personal injury protection (PIP) coverage to pay for basic needs of the insured, such as medical expenses, in the event of an accident.

PERSONAL INSURANCE *see* ACCIDENTAL DEATH AND DISMEMBERMENT INSURANCE; ACCIDENT AND HEALTH INSURANCE; ADDITIONAL LIVING EXPENSE INSURANCE; ADJUSTABLE LIFE INSURANCE; ANNUITY; BROAD FORM PERSONAL THEFT INSURANCE; COMPREHENSIVE HEALTH INSURANCE; COMPREHENSIVE PERSONAL LIABILITY INSURANCE; DISABILITY INCOME INSURANCE; ENDOWMENT INSURANCE; FAMILY INCOME POLICY; FAMILY INCOME RIDER; FAMILY MAINTENANCE POLICY; FAMILY POLICY; FARMERS COMPREHENSIVE PERSONAL LIABILITY INSURANCE; HOMEOWNERS INSURANCE POLICY; LIFE INSURANCE;

MINIMUM DEPOSIT WHOLE LIFE INSURANCE; PAID-UP INSURANCE; PERSONAL AUTOMOBILE POLICY (PAP); PERSONAL INJURY PROTECTION (PIP); PLEASURE BOAT COVERAGE; PURE ENDOWMENT.

PERSONAL INSURANCE NEEDS *see* NEEDS APPROACH.

PERSONAL JEWELRY INSURANCE coverage on jewelry and precious stones on an ALL RISKS basis at any location subject to exclusions of wear and tear, war, and nuclear disaster. Each item must be specifically listed in the policy. This coverage is of importance to insureds with valuable jewelry since most property insurance policies such as the HOMEOWNERS INSURANCE POLICY have relatively low limits of coverage for jewelry and precious stones.

PERSONAL LEGAL EXPENSE LIABILITY INSURANCE coverage for routine personal legal expenses, including probate, criminal defense, and divorce.

PERSONAL LIABILITY CLAIM INSURANCE *see* COMPREHENSIVE PERSONAL LIABILITY INSURANCE; HOMEOWNERS INSURANCE POLICY; PERSONAL AUTOMOBILE POLICY (PAP).

PERSONAL LIABILITY EXPOSURES *see* LIABILITY, PERSONAL EXPOSURES.

PERSONAL LIABILITY INSURANCE *see* COVERAGE E POLICY SECTION II HOMEOWNERS INSURANCE POLICY—SECTION II (LIABILITY COVERAGE).

PERSONAL LINES insurance written on the personal and real property of an individual (or individuals) to include such policies as the HOMEOWNERS INSURANCE POLICY and PERSONAL AUTOMOBILE POLICY (PAP).

PERSONAL LOSS *see* PROPERTY INSURANCE COVERAGE.

PERSONAL PROPERTY *see* HOMEOWNERS INSURANCE POLICY; PERSONAL ARTICLES INSURANCE; PERSONAL EFFECTS INSURANCE; PERSONAL PROPERTY FLOATER.

PERSONAL PROPERTY FLOATER coverage for all personal property, regardless of location of an insured and household residents, including children away at school. Written on an ALL RISKS basis, subject to excluded perils such as war, wear and tear, mechanical breakdown, vermin, and nuclear disaster. "Personal property" includes clothing, television, musical instruments, cameras, jewelry, watches, furs, furniture, radios, and appliances. Coverage can be extended to damage of real property as the result of theft of personal property.

PERSONAL THEFT INSURANCE *see* BROAD FORM PERSONAL THEFT INSURANCE; HOMEOWNERS INSURANCE POLICY.

PER STIRPES distribution of a deceased beneficiary's share of an estate among that beneficiary's children. *Contrast with* PER CAPITA.

PET INSURANCE *see* LIVESTOCK FLOATER; LIVESTOCK INSURANCE; LIVESTOCK MORTALITY (LIFE) INSURANCE; LIVESTOCK TRANSIT INSURANCE.

PHYSICAL CONDITION *see* APPLICATION; DISABILITY INCOME INSURANCE; INSPECTION REPORT; PREEXISTING CONDITION; PREFERRED RISK; UNDERWRITING; UNIQUE IMPAIRMENT.

PHYSICAL DAMAGE INSURANCE property damage coverage for a vehicle under the COLLISION INSURANCE and COMPREHENSIVE INSURANCE sections of the BUSINESS AUTOMOBILE POLICY (BAP) and the PERSONAL AUTOMOBILE POLICY (PAP).

PHYSICAL DAMAGE TO PROPERTY OF OTHERS *see* HOMEOWNERS INSURANCE POLICY—SECTION II (LIABILITY COVERAGE); PERSONAL AUTOMOBILE POLICY (PAP); PROPERTY AND LIABILITY INSURANCE.

PHYSICAL EXAMINATION PROVISION *see* APPLICATION; DISABILITY INCOME INSURANCE; REINSTATEMENT.

PHYSICAL HARM *see* HOMEOWNERS INSURANCE POLICY—SECTION II (LIABILITY COVERAGE); LIABILITY; PERSONAL AUTOMOBILE POLICY (PAP); PROPERTY AND LIABILITY INSURANCE.

PHYSICAL HAZARD *see* HAZARD; INCREASED HAZARD.

PHYSICIANS AND SURGEONS EQUIPMENT INSURANCE coverage for equipment normally carried from location to location by a physician or surgeon; written on an ALL RISKS basis to include supplies and scientific books used in medical practice.

PHYSICIANS AND SURGEONS SERVICES IN HOSPITAL, HMO *see* HEALTH MAINTENANCE ORGANIZATION (HMO).

PHYSICIANS CARE *see* DISABILITY INCOME INSURANCE.

PHYSICIANS INSURANCE *see* PHYSICIANS AND SURGEONS EQUIPMENT INSURANCE; PHYSICIANS, SURGEONS, AND DENTISTS INSURANCE.

PHYSICIANS, SURGEONS, AND DENTISTS INSURANCE coverage for a practicing physician, surgeon, or dentist, when bodily injury, personal injury, and/or property damage is incurred by a patient and the patient sues for injuries and/or damages. The cost of defending the physician, surgeon, or dentist is in addition to the upper limits of the policy, and includes legal fees, court costs, and other general expenses. There is a crisis in this type of coverage, in that fewer companies are writing these policies. *See also* MALPRACTICE LIABILITY INSURANCE.

PIA *see* PRIMARY INSURANCE AMOUNT (PIA); PROFESSIONAL INSURANCE AGENTS (PIA).

PIERS, WHARVES, DOCKS, AND SLIPS INSURANCE coverage in the event of damage or destruction resulting from collision by a vessel or high waves. Excluded are fire, lightning, windstorm, earthquake, and explosion, since these perils are included under the *Standard Fire Policy* and the other business property policies. Piers, wharves, docks, and slips were the few properties that could be covered for flood damage under commercial insurance prior to passage of the Natural Disasters Act of 1968, of which the Federal Flood Insurance Program is a part.

PILFERAGE stealing small amounts of property. Insurance coverage is available under a number of policies. *See also* BLANKET CRIME POLICY; BROAD FORM PERSONAL THEFT INSURANCE; BURGLARY INSURANCE; BUSINESSOWNERS POLICY (BOP); DISHONESTY, DISAPPEARANCE, AND DESTRUCTION POLICY (''3-D'' POLICY), HOMEOWNERS INSURANCE POLICY; PERSONAL AUTOMOBILE POLICY (PAP); SPECIAL MULTIPERIL INSURANCE (SMP).

PIP *see* PERSONAL INJURY PROTECTION (PIP).

PIPELINE INSURANCE type of INLAND MARINE insurance that covers pipelines. Although pipelines are stationary, the coverage is written on inland marine forms because they are considered part of the transportation system.

PLAINTIFF party who asserts a claim against another party in a legal proceeding.

PLAINTIFF'S REPLEVIN BOND *see* JUDICIAL BOND.

PLAN ADMINISTRATION *see* ADMINISTERING AGENCY; ADMINISTRATIVE CHARGE; ADVISORY COMMITTEE.

PLAN DOCUMENT formal, written, legal statement listing the provisions of an EMPLOYEE BENEFIT INSURANCE PLAN.

PLAN PARTICIPANTS employees participating in and covered under an EMPLOYEE BENEFIT INSURANCE PLAN.

PLANS COVERED, INSURANCE *see* BUSINESS INSURANCE; GROUP INSURANCE; INDIVIDUAL INSURANCE.

PLAN SPONSOR employer, association, labor union, or other group offering a qualified employee benefit plan such as a pension or profit-sharing plan.

PLAN TERMINATION INSURANCE *see* PENSION PLAN TERMINATION INSURANCE.

PLATE GLASS INSURANCE *see* COMPREHENSIVE GLASS INSURANCE.

PLEASURE BOAT COVERAGE insurance for private pleasure boats. Coverage is not standard, but is generally broken down into insurance for (1) yachts, including sailboats; (2) boats with inboard motors under *marine* policies; and (3) outboard motor boats under INLAND MARINE policies.

Yacht insurance, which is written on an ALL RISKS or a *named peril* basis, is broken down into (1) hull insurance; (2) bodily injury and property damage liability insurance; (3) Federal compensation insurance for crew members; and (4) medical payments insurance. Outboard coverage insures a boat on land or in the water on an ALL RISKS or named peril basis.

PLUVIOUS INSURANCE *see* RAIN INSURANCE.

PML *see* MAXIMUM FORESEEABLE LOSS (MFL); MAXIMUM PROBABLE LOSS (MPL).

POLICY written agreement which puts insurance coverage into effect. *See also* HEALTH INSURANCE CONTRACT; INSURANCE CONTRACT, GENERAL; INSURANCE CONTRACT, LIFE; INSURANCE CONTRACT, PROPERTY AND CASUALTY.

POLICY ANNIVERSARY 12-month period from the date of issue of a policy as stated in its DECLARATIONS SECTION.

POLICY CONDITION *see* CONDITION.

POLICY DATE *see* EFFECTIVE DATE.

POLICY DECLARATION *see* DECLARATION.

POLICY DIVIDEND *see* PARTICIPATING POLICY DIVIDEND.

POLICY FACE *see* FACE AMOUNT (FACE OF POLICY).

POLICY FEE flat amount added to the basic premium rate to reflect the cost of issuing a policy, establishing the required records, sending premium notices, and other related expenses.

POLICYHOLDER individual or other entity who owns an insurance policy. Synonymous with *policyowner*.

POLICYHOLDER SURPLUS excess of an insurance company's assets above its legal obligations to meet the benefits (liabilities) payable to its policyholders. Also, the net worth in an insurance company adjusted for the overstatement of liabilities. *See also* SURPLUS ACCOUNT; SURPLUS LINES.

POLICY JACKET *see* JACKET.

POLICY LIMIT *see* BUSINESS LIABILITY INSURANCE (Insuring Agreement Section); COORDINATION OF BENEFITS.

POLICY LOAN amount that the owner of a life insurance policy can borrow at interest from the insurer, up to the cash surrender value. If interest is not paid when due, it is deducted from any remaining cash value. When the cash value is exhausted, the insurance ceases. If the insured dies, any outstanding policy loan and interest due are subtracted from the death benefit.

The policyowner may repay the loan in whole or in part at any time; or may continue the loan, as long as the interest plus the principal of the loan does not equal or exceed the cash value (in essence only the interest on the loan must be serviced) or until the policy matures. Insurance companies reserve the right to delay payment of a policy loan for up to six months to protect their solvency, but this has rarely been done since the Depression of the 1930s. *See also* AUTOMATIC PREMIUM LOAN PROVISION.

POLICYOWNER *see* OWNERSHIP RIGHTS UNDER LIFE INSURANCE; POLICYHOLDER.

POLICYOWNERS EQUITY portion of a life insurance policy cash value after the deduction of all the policyowner's indebtedness.

POLICY PERIOD time interval during which policy is in force. *See also* CLAIMS MADE BASIS LIABILITY COVERAGE; CLAIMS OCCURRENCE BASIS LIABILITY COVERAGE.

POLICY PROVISIONS words, sentences, and paragraphs in an insurance policy. *See also* ANALYSIS OF PROPERTY AND CASUALTY POLICY; HEALTH INSURANCE CONTRACT; HOMEOWNERS INSURANCE POLICY; INSURANCE CONTRACT, GENERAL; INSURANCE CONTRACT, LIFE; INSURANCE CONTRACT, PROPERTY AND CASUALTY; PERSONAL AUTOMOBILE POLICY (PAP).

POLICY PROVISIONS, LIFE stipulations of the rights and obligations of an *insured* and an *insurer* under a policy. *See also* ACCIDENTAL DEATH CLAUSE; ASSIGNMENT CLAUSE, LIFE INSURANCE; BENEFICIARY CLAUSE; DISABILITY INCOME RIDER; DIVIDEND OPTION; GRACE PERIOD; INCONTESTABLE CLAUSE; LIFE INSURANCE, CREDITOR RIGHTS; MISSTATE-

MENT OF AGE; NONFORFEITURE PROVISION; OPTIONAL MODES OF SETTL-
MENT; POLICY LOAN; REINSTATEMENT; SPENDTHRIFT TRUST CLAUSE;
SUICIDE CLAUSE; WAR EXCLUSION CLAUSE.

POLICY PURCHASE OPTION *see* GUARANTEED INSURABILITY.

POLICY REPLACEMENT *see* CONSERVATION; REPLACEMENT, LIFE INSURANCE.

POLICY RESERVE *see* FULL PRELIMINARY TERM RESERVE PLAN; PROS-
PECTIVE RESERVE; RETROSPECTIVE METHOD RESERVE COMPUTATION.

POLICY STRUCTURE general arrangement of a contract between an insurer and an insured. The policy defines the insured and the type of coverage, lays out what the insurer must do, lists exceptions and limitations, and states the conditions for coverage. In a standard property and liability contract, the provisions are grouped into these four categories: DECLARATION, INSURING AGREEMENT, EXCLUSIONS, and CONDITIONS FOR QUALIFICATION.

POLICY TERM *see* POLICY PERIOD.

POLICY YEAR *see* POLICY YEAR EXPERIENCE.

POLICY YEAR EXPERIENCE 12-month loss on a policy or line of business.

POLITICAL RISK INSURANCE coverage for business firms operating abroad to insure them against loss due to political unheavals including war, revolution, confiscation, incontrovertibility of currency, and other such losses. *See also* OVERSEAS PRIVATE INVESTMENT CORPORATION.

POLLUTION EXCLUSION liability insurance exception for pollution coverage that is not both sudden and accidental from the insured's standpoint. As a result of the damage suits from such incidents as the chemical pollution at Love Canal, insurance companies began to modify pollution coverage in their liability policies in the 1970s. First, companies changed coverage to apply only if pollution was "sudden and accidental," rather than "gradual." But some courts ruled that "sudden and accidental" could encompass several years of pollution problems. Consequently, the INSURANCE SERVICES OFFICE (ISO) introduced a new COMPREHENSIVE GENERAL LIABILITY INSURANCE (CGL) policy in 1985 (replaced today by the COMMERCIAL GENERAL LIABILITY form) that excluded coverage for nearly all types of pollution damage, leaving only limited liability coverage for pollution originating away from an insured's premises.

POOL syndicate or association of insurance companies or REINSURANCE companies organized to underwrite a particular risk, usually with high limits of exposure. Each member shares in premiums, losses, and expenses according to a predetermined agreement.

POOLING method by which each member of an insurance POOL shares in each and every risk written by the other members of the pool.

POOLING CHARGE amount that each member of a POOL contributes to that pool. *See also* POOLING.

POPULATION DECREMENTS reduction in a retirement plan's population resulting from the death, disability, and termination of its members.

POPULATION INCREMENTS additions of new entrants into an EMPLOYEE BENEFIT INSURANCE PLAN.

PORTABILITY *see* PENSION PORTABILITY.

PORTFOLIO insurance company's total investments in financial securities.

PORTFOLIO REINSURANCE coverage in which an insurance company's portfolio is *ceded* to a *reinsurer,* who reinsures a given percentage of a particular line of business.

PORTFOLIO RETURN process whereby a CEDING COMPANY resumes the insuring of a portfolio of insurance policies which it had previously CEDED to a REINSURER.

PORTFOLIO RUNOFF process of the continual REINSURANCE of a CEDING COMPANY'S portfolio of insurance policies. All premiums which have been CEDED become EARNED PREMIUMS.

PORT RISK INSURANCE coverage for ships in port for a lengthy stay and/or those which are under repair. Insures on an ALL RISKS basis to include the exposures associated with the ship moving from one dock to another.

POSITION SCHEDULE BOND *see* FIDELITY BOND.

POSSIBLE MAXIMUM LOSS *see* MAXIMUM FORESEEABLE LOSS (MFL).

POSTMORTEM DIVIDEND dividend in a *participating policy* paid after the death of an insured, representing dividends earned between the last dividend date and the insured's death.

POSTMORTEM PLANNING *see* ESTATE PLANNING; ESTATE PLANNING DISTRIBUTION; HUMAN LIFE VALUE APPROACH (ECONOMIC VALUE OF AN INDIVIDUAL LIFE (EVOIL); NEEDS APPROACH.

POSTRETIREMENT FUNDING method of funding a pension plan after a worker retires. An employer purchases an annuity or sets aside a sum when an employee retires that will pay monthly lifetime benefits. Postretirement funding is no longer permitted under the EMPLOYEE RETIREMENT INCOME SECURITY ACT OF 1974 (ERISA), which requires current funding of future pension liabilities.

POSTSELECTION OF INSURED underwriting practice involving regular review of insurance contracts in force with the intent of either cancelling a policy or not offering renewal for risks no longer deemed acceptable. *See also* CANCELLATION PROVISION CLAUSE; NONCANCELLABLE GUARANTEED RENEWABLE POLICY; NONRENEWAL CLAUSE; RENEWAL PROVISION.

POWER INTERRUPTION INSURANCE ENDORSEMENT addition to boiler and machinery insurance that covers loss to property or equipment caused by an interruption of power by a public utility. Coverage is available either on an hourly or daily basis for loss of use or for actual loss sustained.

POWER OF APPOINTMENT *see* ESTATE PLANNING DISTRIBUTION.

POWER OF ATTORNEY legal instrument whereby an individual is given the right to act on behalf of another individual. For example, the right to buy and sell stock and to sign all brokerage papers relating to buying and selling in a stockholder's account is given by the stockholder to another individual through power of attorney. Or, the right to decide which settlement option is to be used under a life insurance policy may be given by a policy owner to another individual. Experts often advise extreme care in assigning a power of attorney since that person becomes free to make financial decisions which can enhance—or ruin—an individual represented.

POWER PLANT INSURANCE
1. form of BOILER AND MACHINERY INSURANCE that covers power generating plants.
2. form of BUSINESS INTERRUPTION INSURANCE that covers a utility customer's losses resulting from interruption of power from a public utility.

PREAUTHORIZED CHECK PLAN plan for the automatic payment of premiums due through drafting by the insurer of the policyowner's preauthorized bank account. Usually, the insurer drafts this account on a monthly basis for the premium payment owed. Studies show that PERSISTENCY is highest when premium payments are made through bank draft plans.

PREAUTHORIZED CHECK SYSTEM (PAC) arrangement by which a policyowner authorizes an insurance company to draft his checking account for premiums due on an insurance policy. The drafting is usually monthly. PERSISTENCY of policies paid this way is substantially higher than when insureds pay them directly to an insurance company.

PREDICTABILITY *see* EXPECTED LOSS.

PREEXISTING CONDITION illnesses or disability for which the insured was treated or advised within a stipulated time period before making application for a life or health insurance policy. A preexisting condition can result in cancellation of the policy.

PREFERENCE BENEFICIARY CLAUSE *see* BENEFICIARY; BENEFICIARY CLAUSE.

PREFERRED BENEFICIARY *see* BENEFICIARY; BENEFICIARY CLAUSE.

PREFERRED PROVIDER ORGANIZATION (PPO) hospital, physician, or other provider of health care which an insurer recommends to insureds. A PPO allows insurance companies to negotiate directly with hospitals and physicians for health services at a lower price than would be normally charged. A PPO tries to combine the best elements of a fee-for-service and HEALTH MAINTENANCE ORGANIZATION (HMO) systems.

PREFERRED RISK insured, or an applicant for insurance, with lower expectation of incurring a loss than the *standard applicant*. For example, an applicant for life insurance who does not smoke can usually obtain a reduced premium rate to reflect his greater LIFE EXPECTANCY.

PRELIMINARY TERM life insurance accounting method that does not require any TERMINAL RESERVE for a policy at the end of the first year. First-year policy acquisition expenses, such as *agent commission*, MEDICAL EXAMINATION, and PREMIUM TAX, are often too large to leave enough of the end-of-the-year PREMIUM for addition to the premium reserve required under state FULL VALUATION RESERVE standards. In order to avoid taking the difference between the amount of the premium remaining and the required addition to reserves out of the insurance company's SURPLUS ACCOUNT, the FULL PRELIMINARY TERM RESERVE VALUATION method is sometimes used. This leaves more of the premium available to cover acquisition cost and first-year claims. *See also* MODIFIED RESERVE METHODS.

PREMISES AND OPERATIONS LIABILITY INSURANCE part of a business liability policy that covers an insured for bodily injury or property damage liability to members of the public while they are on his premises. This coverage is available in basic business policies that include COMPREHENSIVE GENERAL LIABILITY INSURANCE (CGL); MANUFACTURERS AND CONTRACTORS LIABILITY INSURANCE; OWNERS, LANDLORDS, AND TENANTS LIABILITY POLICY; STOREKEEPERS LIABILITY INSURANCE.

PREMISES LIABILITY   *see* LIABILITY, BUSINESS EXPOSURES; LIABILITY, PERSONAL EXPOSURES.

PREMISES MEDICAL PAYMENTS INSURANCE supplemental coverage written into or endorsed onto many business and personal liability policies. Covers medical costs and loss of income of persons injured on an insured's property, regardless of whether the insured was at fault in causing those injuries. This coverage enables the insured to volunteer to pay these medical costs and income losses when doing so serves the insured's business purposes or preserves personal relationships.

PREMISES SOLD EXCLUSION in a COMMERCIAL GENERAL LIABILITY (COMPREHENSIVE GENERAL LIABILITY) policy, exclusion of coverage for sold premises. The objective of this exclusion is to eliminate coverage for property damage and/or bodily injury due to inherently dangerous risks associated with property sold by the insured. For example, the insured may sell property that has defects which should have been repaired prior to the sale. These defects could then result in damage to the property, as well as bodily injury to a person or persons who came in contact with that property.

PREMIUM rate that an insured is charged, reflecting his/her expectation of loss or risk. The insurance company will assume the risks of the insured (length of life, state of health, property damage or destruction, or liability exposure) in exchange for a premium payment. Premiums are calculated by combining expectation of loss and expense and profit loadings. Usually, the periodic cost of insurance is computed by multiplying the premium rate per unit of insurance by the number of units purchased. The rate class in which the insured is placed includes large numbers of individuals with like characteristics who pose the same risk. Every individual in a given class will not incur the same loss; rather each has approximately the same *expectation* of loss (known as the *Principle of Equity*). *See also* EQUITY; GROSS PREMIUM; PURE PREMIUM RATING METHOD.

PREMIUM ADJUSTMENT ENDORSEMENT provision in an insurance policy allowing an INITIAL PREMIUM to be charged but subject to adjustment during the period of coverage or at the end of coverage depending on the actual loss experience of the insured risk.

PREMIUM ADJUSTMENT FORM   *see* PREMIUM ADJUSTMENT ENDORSEMENT.

PREMIUM ADVANCE *see* DEPOSIT PREMIUM.

PREMIUM, ANNUITY (consideration) cost of annuity based on expectation of life of the ANNUITANT and the expense and profit loadings of the insurance company. *See also* ANNUITY; CONSIDERATION.

PREMIUM BASE *see* BASE PREMIUM.

PREMIUM CHARGE *see* PREMIUM.

PREMIUM COMPUTATION *see* PREMIUM; PURE PREMIUM RATING METHOD.

PREMIUM DEFAULT *see* DISCONTINUANCE OF CONTRIBUTIONS; LAPSE.

PREMIUM DEFICIENCY RESERVE supplementary life insurance reserve required by state regulators when the GROSS PREMIUM is lower than the VALUATION PREMIUM. Some life insurers are able to charge policyholders a premium that is lower than required by the reserve valuation system they use. This may be because mortality tables are outdated and their own experience reflects different loss statistics. But if the insurer charges a premium lower than that dictated in the calculation of policy reserves, it must set up a deficiency reserve for the difference.

PREMIUM DEPOSIT *see* DEPOSIT PREMIUM.

PREMIUM DISCOUNT reduction in rate reflecting the present value of a premium due on an annuity one year hence.

PREMIUM DISCOUNT PLAN plan whereby adjustments are made in the premium, as the premium increases to reflect the nonproportionate increases in expenses. Generally, the expenses of acquisition costs, administrative costs of placing the policy on the insurer's books, taxes, and claims do not increase in proportion to the increase in the premium. Thus, the GROSS PREMIUM should not reflect a proportionate increase in expenses as the NET SINGLE PREMIUM increases.

PREMIUM, EARNED *see* EARNED PREMIUM.

PREMIUM, GROSS *see* GROSS PREMIUM.

PREMIUM LOAN amount borrowed against the cash value of a life insurance policy to pay the premium due. *See also* AUTOMATIC PREMIUM LOAN PROVISION.

PREMIUM, MINIMUM *see* MINIMUM PREMIUM PLAN.

PREMIUM MODE frequency of premium payment, monthly, quarterly, or annually.

PREMIUM, NET *see* NET LEVEL PREMIUM.

PREMIUM NOTICE message from an insurance company or insurance agency informing a policyowner that a premium is due by a specified date.

PREMIUM, PURE *see* PURE PREMIUM RATING METHOD.

PREMIUM RATE *see* PREMIUM.

PREMIUM RATE EQUITY *see* EQUITY.

PREMIUM RECEIPT written evidence given to a policyowner by an insurance company or insurance agency that it has received a premium.

PREMIUM REFUND in some life insurance policies, provision which permits the beneficiary, upon the death of the insured, to receive not only the DEATH BENEFIT payable under the policy but also all premiums paid into the policy.

PREMIUM RETURN *see* RETURN OF PREMIUM.

PREMIUMS WRITTEN *see* WRITTEN PREMIUMS.

PREMIUM TAX payment to a state or municipality by an insurance company based on premiums paid by residents.

PREMIUM, UNEARNED *see* UNEARNED PREMIUM RESERVE.

PREPAID GROUP PRACTICE PACKAGE health insurance plan where a group of physicians and dentists provide medical services to a group of individuals for a predetermined fee. It is a basic type of HEALTH MAINTENANCE ORGANIZATION (HMO).

PREPAID LEGAL INSURANCE *see* LEGAL EXPENSE INSURANCE.

PREPAYMENT *see* ADVANCE PAYMENTS.

PREPAYMENT OF PREMIUMS *see* ADVANCE PREMIUM.

PRESCRIPTION DRUG PLAN *see* COMMERCIAL HEALTH INSURANCE; COPAYMENT; COVERED EXPENSE; GROUP HEALTH INSURANCE; HEALTH MAINTENANCE ORGANIZATION (HMO).

PRESELECTION OF INSURED *see* INSPECTION REPORT; PREEXISTING CONDITION; PREFERRED RISK; UNDERWRITING; UNIQUE IMPAIRMENT.

PRESENT INTEREST (GIFT) *see* ESTATE PLANNING DISTRIBUTION; GIFT; GIFT TAX.

PRESENT VALUE *see* PRESENT VALUE FACTOR.

PRESENT VALUE FACTOR discount interest rate factor used to determine the present value of a sum in the future. The present value equation is:

$$P = R(1 + i)^{-N}$$

where:

P = present value of a sum in the future (discounted value of R)

R = sum of money in the future (accumulated value at the end of N periods)

N = number of periods a sum of money is to be discounted in the future

i = interest rate per period

For example, if one wished to determine a sum (P) which must be invested today in order for it to accumulate to $1000 ($R$) at the end of 20 years, (N) assuming an 8% interest rate (i), then the equation is:

$$P = \$1000 (1 + .08)^{-20}$$
$$= \$1000 (.2145482)$$
$$= \$214.55$$

PRESENT VALUE OF ANNUITY DUE *present value* of a series of payments such that the first payment is due immediately, the second payment one period from hence, the third payment two periods hence, and so forth. The continued payment is contingent upon the designated beneficiary (the ANNUITANT) continuing to live. *See also* PRESENT VALUE OF ANNUITY IMMEDIATE.

PRESENT VALUE OF ANNUITY IMMEDIATE *present value* of a series of payments such that the first payment is due one period hence, the second payment two periods hence, and so forth. The continued payment is contingent upon the designated beneficiary (the ANNUITANT) continuing to live. *See also* PRESENT VALUE OF ANNUITY DUE.

PRESENT VALUE OF FUTURE BENEFITS *see* PRESENT VALUE FACTOR.

PRESUMED NEGLIGENCE *see* RES IPSA LOQUITUR

PRESUMPTIVE DISABILITY assumption of total disability when an insured loses sight, hearing, speech, or a limb. When such a loss occurs to an insured with disability income insurance, the insurer often assumes that the individual is disabled, even if he or she later returns to work. Here insurers may pay a lump sum in addition to monthly disability payments for the maximum benefit period set by the policy.

PREVENTIVE CARE program of health care designed for the prevention and/or reduction of illnesses by providing such services as regular physical examinations. This care is in opposition to curative care, which goes into effect only after the occurrence of an illness. *See also* HEALTH MAINTENANCE ORGANIZATION (HMO).

PREVENTIVE HEALTH SERVICES *see* HEALTH MAINTENANCE ORGANIZATION (HMO).

PRICE-ANDERSON ACT 1957 Federal law setting a limit on the liability of operators of nuclear facilities. The law, an amendment to the Atomic Energy Act of 1954, authorized establishment of private insurance pools to provide liability insurance for nuclear facilities, giving the Atomic Energy Commission (now the NUCLEAR REGULATORY COMMISSION) authority to sell additional insurance in excess of the amount of pool coverage available. *See also* MUTUAL ATOMIC ENERGY REINSURANCE POOL; NUCLEAR ENERGY LIABILITY INSURANCE.

PRIESTLY v. FOWLER 1837 British case that established that an employer was not responsible for injury to an employee if the injury were caused by another employee. Prior to this, English common law provided that an employer took responsibility for his employees; *Priestly v. Fowler* was the first crack in that relationship. Later, other exceptions to employer responsibility were established until finally, the employee shouldered all responsibility for his own welfare because, it was argued, he had, after all, agreed to accept the job. Late in the 19th century in Great Britain, and early in the 20th century in the U.S., *workers compensation* laws were passed in which the employer accepts responsibility for on-the-job injuries and pays benefits according to an established schedule. In exchange, the employee accepts this as the exclusive remedy. However, in the past decade there have been many challenges to this system, including cases in which injured employees have been allowed to sue their employers.

PRIMA *see* PUBLIC RISK AND INSURANCE MANAGEMENT ASSOCIATION (PRIMA).

PRIMACY property, liability, or health coverage that takes precedence when more than one policy covers the same loss. In order to avoid OVERINSURANCE or paying an insured more than the actual loss, the covering policies accept responsibility for insurance in an established order. For example, if a husband and wife cover each other as dependents in group medical insurance, the injured person's own policy assumes primacy. Therefore, if the wife gave birth to a child, her policy would apply to obstetrical and hospital fees up to its limits. Only then would the husband's policy apply, covering the amount that had not been paid by his wife's policy up to the limits of his plan.

PRIMARY BENEFICIARY *see* BENEFICIARY.

PRIMARY INSURANCE property or liability coverage that provides benefits (usually after a deductible has been paid by an insured) up to the limits of a policy, regardless of other insurance polices in effect.

See also APPORTIONMENT; COORDINATION OF BENEFITS; EXCESS INSURANCE; GROUP HEALTH INSURANCE.

PRIMARY INSURANCE AMOUNT (PIA) monthly benefit payable to retired or disabled worker under Social Security. It is calculated by using the average monthly earnings of the covered person while working. Under this formula, lower-income workers receive a greater percent of the income they had earned while employed than do more highly paid workers. Benefits for spouse, other dependents, and survivors are figured as a percentage of the PIA. A worker who takes early retirement may receive a portion of the PIA at age 62. The PIA is used to calculate most other benefits.

PRIMARY INSURER *see* PRIMARY INSURANCE.

PRIMARY PLAN *see* COORDINATION OF BENEFITS.

PRINCIPAL *see* SURETY BOND.

PRINCIPAL SUM *accidental death benefit* option that can be added to a DISABILITY INCOME (DI) policy under which a lump sum is payable at the loss of life, dismemberment, or loss of sight.

PRINCIPLE OF INDEMNITY *see* INDEMNITY.

PRIOR ACTS COVERAGE liability insurance coverage for claims arising from acts that occurred before the beginning of the policy period. Policies written on a *claims made basis,* such as MALPRACTICE LIABILITY INSURANCE and ERRORS AND OMISSIONS LIABILITY INSURANCE, cover only claims during the policy period. Prior acts coverage is necessary for covering a claim made during a current policy period for an event that happened before a policy was in force.

PRIOR APPROVAL RATING requirement of state approval of property insurance rates and policy forms before they can be used. Individual states regulate insurers and approve their rates. There are three methods of rate approval, in addition to prior approval: *modified prior approval, open competition,* and *file and use.*

PRIOR-APPROVAL STATES those states requiring insurers to obtain PRIOR APPROVAL RATING of rates and policy forms before they use them. Although most states once fell into this category, many followed the lead of New York State in 1969 when it moved to a system of *open competition.*

PRIVATE INSURANCE *see* SOCIAL INSURANCE.

PRIVATE NONCOMMERCIAL HEALTH INSURANCE *see* HEALTH INSURANCE.

PRIVATE PENSION PLAN *see* PENSION PLAN; PENSION PLAN FUNDING, GROUP DEPOSIT ADMINISTRATION ANNUITY; PENSION PLAN FUNDING, GROUP IMMEDIATE PARTICIPATING GUARANTEED (IPG) CONTRACT ANNUITY; PENSION PLAN FUNDING, GROUP PERMANENT CONTRACT; PENSION PLAN FUNDING, INDIVIDUAL CONTRACT PENSION PLAN.

PROBABILITY chance that an event will occur. The foundation of insurance is probability and STATISTICS. By pooling a large number of *homogeneous exposures* an insurance company can predict with a given degree of accuracy the chance that a policyholder will incur a loss. The company reflects this expectation in the pure cost of insurance, known as the *pure premium*. The chance that an event will occur can be expressed as follows:

$$\frac{\text{Probability of}}{\text{Event Occurring}} = \frac{\text{Number of Successful Ways Event Can Occur}}{\text{Total Number of Ways Event Can Occur}}$$

For example, the probability of rolling a six on one die can be expressed as:

$$P(6) = \frac{1}{6}$$

PROBABILITY DISTRIBUTION outcomes of an experiment and their probabilities of occurrence. If the experiment were to be repeated any number of times the same probabilities should also repeat. For example, the probability distribution for the possible number of heads from two tosses of a fair coin having both a head and a tail would be as follows:

Number of Heads	Tosses	Probability of Event
0	(tail, tail)	.25
1	(head, tail) + (tail, head)	.50
2	(head, head)	.25

PROBABILITY OF LOSS *see* PROBABILITY.

PROBABLE MAXIMUM LOSS (PML) *see* MAXIMUM PROBABLE LOSS (MPL).

PROBATE legal proceeding whereby the will of a deceased is tested for validity.

PROBATE BOND *see* JUDICIAL BOND.

PROBATIONARY PERIOD time, in health insurance, from the first day of a disability, illness, or accident during which no benefits are payable. The longer the probationary period the lower the premium. *See also* ELIMINATION PERIOD.

PROCEEDS benefits payable under any insurance policy or annuity contract.

PRODUCER *see* AGENT.

PRODUCERS COOPERATIVE health plans established by associations of hospitals and physicians to provide hospital service and care, and medical and surgical care. *See also* BLUE CROSS; BLUE SHIELD.

PRODUCT DEVELOPMENT design, testing, packaging, and marketing of an insurance policy.

PRODUCT FAILURE EXCLUSION *see* BUSINESS RISK EXCLUSION.

PRODUCT LIABILITY CATASTROPHE REINSURANCE *see* AUTOMATIC NONPROPORTIONAL REINSURANCE; AUTOMATIC PROPORTIONAL REINSURANCE; AUTOMATIC REINSURANCE; EXCESS OF LOSS REINSURANCE; FACULTATIVE REINSURANCE; NONPROPORTIONAL REINSURANCE; PROPORTIONAL REINSURANCE; QUOTA SHARE REINSURANCE; STOP LOSS REINSURANCE; SURPLUS REINSURANCE.

PRODUCT LIABILITY INSURANCE coverage usually provided under the COMMERCIAL GENERAL LIABILITY INSURANCE (CGL); it can also be purchased separately. *See also* PRODUCTS AND COMPLETED OPERATIONS INSURANCE.

PRODUCT RECALL EXCLUSION exception in general liability policies for all expenses associated with product recall. In recent years, there have been increasing instances of Federal recalls. In addition, there have been many instances of deliberate tampering and of manufacturers issuing their own recalls. In either event, the cost of identifying the products, communicating with consumers, inspecting the returned products, and repairing or replacing them, can be enormous. These costs are excluded from general liability policies, but PRODUCT RECALL INSURANCE can be purchased for this purpose.

PRODUCT RECALL INSURANCE coverage for the expenses incurred by a business resulting from the recall of products, whether defective or not. *See also* PRODUCT LIABILITY INSURANCE; PRODUCT AND COMPLETED OPERATIONS INSURANCE; PRODUCT RECALL EXCLUSION.

PRODUCTS AND COMPLETED OPERATIONS INSURANCE coverage for an insured manufacturer for claims after a manufactured product has been sold and/or a claim results from an operation which the manufacturer has completed. *See also* COMPLETED OPERATIONS INSURANCE.

PRODUCT VARIABILITY uneven quality of a product made by the same manufacturer. A manufacturer is responsible for producing products of similar quality, and can be held liable for those that deviate materially from a model, sample, or standard.

PROFESSIONAL *see* PROFESSIONAL LIABILITY INSURANCE.

PROFESSIONAL INSURANCE AGENTS (PIA) (NATIONAL ASSOCIATION OF PROFESSIONAL INSURANCE AGENTS). Independent agent membership group, originally mutual agents but today open to both mutual and stock agents. Association views are presented both nationally and locally on insurance legislation. There is an extensive education program for members.

PROFESSIONAL LIABILITY *see* LIABILITY, PROFESSIONAL

PROFESSIONAL LIABILITY INSURANCE coverage for specialists in various professional fields. Since basic liability policies do not protect against situations arising out of business or professional pursuits, professional liability insurance is purchased by individuals who hold themselves out to the general public as having greater than average expertise in particular areas. *See also* ACCOUNTANTS PROFESSIONAL LIABILITY INSURANCE; DRUGGISTS LIABILITY INSURANCE; ERRORS AND OMISSIONS LIABILITY INSURANCE; INSURANCE AGENTS AND BROKERS LIABILITY INSURANCE; LAWYERS (ATTORNEYS PROFESSIONAL) LIABILITY INSURANCE; PHYSICIANS, SURGEONS, AND DENTISTS INSURANCE.

PROFESSIONAL REINSURER company formed to sell and service PROPORTIONAL REINSURANCE and NONPROPORTIONAL REINSURANCE with profit motive as the normal business objective.

PROFESSIONAL STANDARDS REVIEW ORGANIZATION (PSRO) group that monitors government health insurance programs. Authorized by the 1972 amendment to the Social Security Act, PSROs were set up to cut costs and minimize abuses by checking on the need of applicants for care and the cost and quality of care.

PROFITABILITY UNDERWRITING degree of UNDERWRITING profit that an insurance company's book of business shows. *See also* UNDERWRITING GAIN (LOSS).

PROFITS AND COMMISSIONS FORM coverage protecting future profits to be earned from a manufacturer's inventory. A manufacturer may lose all or part of an inventory of finished goods due to a peril such as fire and still be able to operate. But in the event that an inventory and other merchandise is destroyed by an insured peril, the insured is indemnified for the loss profit or commissions.

PROFITS AND COMMISSIONS INSURANCE *see* PROFITS AND COMMISSIONS FORM.

PROFIT SHARING PLAN arrangement by an employer in which employees share in profits of the business. To be a *qualified plan*, a predetermined formula must be used to determine contributions to the plan and benefits to be distributed, once a participant attains a specified age, becomes ill or disabled, severs employment, retires, or dies. When a profit sharing plan is first installed, employees with considerable past service usually do not receive such credit. An advantage to an employer is that in low or no profit years, the business does not have to contribute to the plan, since contributions are voluntary and the Internal Revenue Code does not require a minimum contribution, as with a *deferred benefit plan* or a MONEY PURCHASE PLAN.

PROGRESSIVE INCOME TAX structure under which tax rates increase with increases in income. One way to minimize such taxes is to purchase tax advantaged financial instruments. *See also* TAX DEFERRED ANNUITY; TAX BENEFITS OF LIFE INSURANCE.

PROGRESSIVELY DIMINISHING DEDUCTIBLE *see* DISAPPEARING DEDUCTIBLE.

PROHIBITED RISK uninsurable risk.

PROJECTION FACTORS expectations of investment return, mortality experience, and expenses used in projecting future cash values for life insurance and annuities. These projections cannot be part of the actual policy since they are not guaranteed. Rather, they take the form of separate computer printouts and are used in sales presentations.

PROOF OF INTEREST *see* INSURABLE INTEREST; INSURABLE INTEREST, LIFE INSURANCE; INSURABLE INTEREST, PROPERTY AND CASUALTY INSURANCE.

PROOF OF LOSS documentation of loss required of a policyowner by an insurance company. For example, in the event of an insured's death, a death certificate (or copy) must be submitted to the company for a life insurance death benefit to be paid to the beneficiary.

PROPERTY *real* (land and attachments) and *personal* (movable effects not attached to land). Both classifications of property give rise to an insurable interest. *See also* INSURABLE INTEREST; PROPERTY AND CASUALTY INSURANCE PROVISIONS.

PROPERTY AND CASUALTY INSURANCE CONTRACT *see* INSURANCE CONTRACT, PROPERTY AND CASUALTY.

PROPERTY AND CASUALTY INSURANCE PROVISIONS specifications dealing with exclusions, policy requirements, cancellations and related matters.

1. *Perils*—Most policies exclude enemy attack, invasions, insurrection, rebellion, revolution, civil war, unsurped power, neglect of an insured to reasonably preserve damaged property from further loss; and explosion or riot unless caused by fire. Other exclusions may be specified in a policy. Among them are concealment and fraud by the insured; increased hazard by an insured's actions; and vacancy in an insured building for at least 60 consecutive days.

2. *Requirements*—In the event of a loss the insured must give immediate written notice to the insurance company; protect the insured property from further damage; separate damaged from undamaged property; give the company a complete inventory of the damaged or destroyed property, with signed proof of loss within 60 days; and submit to the company's examination of damaged or destroyed property.

3. OTHER INSURANCE—If two or more separate policies over the same loss, each will pay no more than its pro rata share of the loss.

4. SUBROGATION—After the company pays the insured for a loss incurred as the result of actions of a third party, the company reserves the right to seek recovery for damages against that third party. (The insured has passed the right of suit against the third party to the insurance company.)

5. *Cancellation*—The insured and the insurance company can terminate the policy under specified circumstances. The insured can terminate the policy at any time, and will receive a return of part of the premium, less an amount for administrative expenses. The insurance company can cancel a property policy by sending the insured written notice at least 5 days before the intended date of cancellation. For a liability policy, after the policy has been renewed the first time, or has been in force for at least 60 days, the insurance company can cancel only for causes such as failure of an insured to pay a premium when due, if an insured is involved in illegal activities, drives while intoxicated, or is under the influence of drugs.

PROPERTY AND LIABILITY INSURANCE coverage for an insured whose property is damaged or destroyed by an insured peril, or whose negligent acts or omissions damage or destroy another party's property or cause bodily injury to another party. *See also* BUSINESS AUTOMOBILE POLICY (BAP); BUSINESS PROPERTY AND LIABILITY INSURANCE PACKAGE; BUSINESSOWNERS POLICY; CONDOMINIUM INSURANCE; HOMEOWNERS INSURANCE POLICY; PERSONAL AUTOMOBILE POLICY (PAP); SPECIAL MULTIPERIL INSURANCE (SMP); TENANTS INSURANCE.

PROPERTY AND LIABILITY INSURANCE PLANNING FOR BUSINESS *see* BUSINESS AUTOMOBILE POLICY (BAP); BUSINESS CRIME

INSURANCE; BUSINESS INSURANCE; BUSINESS INTERRUPTION INSURANCE; BUSINESS LIABILITY INSURANCE; BUSINESS PROPERTY AND LIABILITY INSURANCE PACKAGE; BUSINESSOWNERS POLICY.

PROPERTY AND LIABILITY INSURANCE PLANNING FOR INDIVIDUALS AND FAMILIES *see* COMPREHENSIVE PERSONAL LIABILITY INSURANCE; HOMEOWNERS INSURANCE POLICY; LIABILITY, PERSONAL EXPOSURES; LIABILITY, PROFESSIONAL; PERSONAL AUTOMOBILE POLICY (PAP); TENANTS INSURANCE.

PROPERTY CATASTROPHE *see* FIRE CATASTROPHE REINSURANCE INSURANCE; REINSURANCE, PROPERTY AND CASUALTY-CASUALTY CATASTROPHE.

PROPERTY DAMAGE *see* BUSINESS LIABILITY INSURANCE (Insuring Agreement Section); PERSONAL AUTOMOBILE POLICY (PAP).

PROPERTY DAMAGED OR DESTROYED *see* PROPERTY INSURANCE COVERAGE.

PROPERTY DAMAGE LIABILITY INSURANCE coverage in the event that the negligent acts or omissions of an insured result in damage or destruction to another's property. Coverage can be purchased with BODILY INJURY liability under various insurance policies. *See also* BUSINESS AUTOMOBILE POLICY (BAP); BUSINESS PROPERTY AND LIABILITY INSURANCE PACKAGE; HOMEOWNERS INSURANCE POLICY; PERSONAL AUTOMOBILE POLICY (PAP).

PROPERTY DEPRECIATION INSURANCE coverage that provides for replacement of damaged or destroyed property on a new replacement cost basis without any deduction for depreciation. This is equivalent to *replacement cost* property insurance.

PROPERTY INSURANCE indemnifies an insured whose property is stolen, damaged, or destroyed by a covered peril. The term property insurance encompasses numerous lines of available insurance.

PROPERTY INSURANCE COVERAGE coverage for direct or indirect property loss which can be analyzed under the following headings:
1. *Peril*—a particular peril may be included or excluded. For example, the *Standard Fire Policy* names specific perils such as fire and lighting; the ALL RISKS policy covers all entities unless specifically excluded.
2. Property—a policy may cover only specified or scheduled property such as an automobile; all of an insured's personal property up to a specified amount on each item regardless of its location (PERSONAL PROPERTY FLOATER); or all property of the insured with no specific limit (BLANKET POLICY).

3. Person—the person covered must be specifically identified as the *named insured* in a policy. Residents of that household also covered are the spouse, relatives of either, and anyone else below the age of 21 under the insured's care, custody, and control.

4. Duration—policies are usually written for one year; a personal automobile policy is usually for six months.

5. *Limits*—limits are stated as a face amount in a policy. The insurer will never pay more than the lesser of the following amounts: limits stated in a policy; actual cash value of destroyed or damaged property; or amount resulting from the coinsurance formula.

6. Location—a policy may cover perils which strike only the premises of the insured, or it may provide off-premises coverage subject to a geographic restriction. For example, the personal automobile policy covers only the U.S. and Canada.

7. HAZARD—the exclusions and suspension section states that if the insured increases a covered hazard the company can suspend or exclude the coverage. For example, the insured starts processing explosives at home.

8. LOSS—insurance contracts cover either direct or indirect (CONSEQUENTIAL) loss. For example, a homeowners policy covers damage due to the direct loss by fire, lightning, and other perils. It does not cover consequential losses such as loss of income by an insured who is unable to go to work because of fatigue.

PROPORTIONAL REINSURANCE system whereby the reinsurer shares losses in the same proportion as it shares premium and policy amounts. Proportional reinsurance may be divided into the two basic forms: AUTOMATIC PROPORTIONAL REINSURANCE and *facultative proportional reinsurance. See also* REINSURANCE.

PROPOSAL BOND *see* BID BOND.

PROPOSITION 103: CALIFORNIA legislation mandating that factors taken into account in the calculation of premium rates for automobile insurance include the insured's driving record, annual miles driven, and years of driving experience. Excluded from consideration is territorial rating. Also included in the provision is a required discount of 20% for being a good driver. The Proposition repeals previous laws which prohibited insurance brokers and agents from REBATING premiums or commissions as an inducement to prospective insureds to purchase insurance from them. Also repealed by the Proposition was the law which prohibited banks from becoming licensed to sell insurance. The Proposition requires California to be a prior-approval state for any rate changes concerning automobile insurance, as well as to submit certain specified rate-change requests to a public hearing.

PROPRIETARY INSURER for-profit insurance company, such as a mutual or stock company or LLOYD'S OF LONDON association. Proprietary insurers contrast with cooperative insurers, or Blue Cross/Blue Shield plans, or FRATERNAL LIFE INSURANCE organizations.

PRO RATA *see* PRO RATA CANCELLATION; PRO RATA DISTRIBUTION CLAUSE; PRO RATA LIABILITY CLAUSE; PRO RATA REINSURANCE.

PRO RATA CANCELLATION revocation of a policy by an insurance company, which returns to the policyholder the *unearned premium* (the portion of the premium for the remaining time period that the policy will not be in force). There is no reduction for expenses already paid by the insurer for that time period. *See also* SHORT RATE CANCELLATION.

PRO RATA DISTRIBUTION CLAUSE provision in many property insurance policies that automatically distributes coverage over insured property at various locations in proportion to their value. For example, if an insured buys a $100,000 policy to cover three properties worth $75,000, $30,000 and $20,000, the insurance (which would not be enough to cover a total loss) would be distributed in the same manner. If the $75,000 property were totally destroyed, the insured would receive 60% of the value of the insurance, or $60,000, because that property represents 60% of the covered property. If the insured buys adequate coverage, this clause is important because it can spread the insurance to different locations as inventories decrease or increase, rather than forcing the insured to constantly revise the coverage. *See also* DOUBLE RECOVERY.

PRO RATA LIABILITY CLAUSE provision in many property insurance policies that spreads the obligation to pay a claim among various insurers covering that claim in proportion to the insurance each has written on the property. For example, there are three different policies covering a $130,000 building. Co. A wrote a $60,000 policy, Co. B a $50,000 policy, and Co. C. a $20,000 policy. A fire results in $25,000 damage. The loss would be spread in the same ratio as the coverage: Co. A's share would be $11,750, or 47%; Co. B would pay $9,500, or 38%; and Co. C would pay $3,750, or 15%. One purpose of this clause is to prevent an insured from capitalizing on a loss. In the case cited, the insured could collect the full amount ($25,000) twice from the first two insurers, and $20,000 from the third, giving him $70,000 to cover a $25,000 loss.

PRO RATA RATE premium rate charged for a particular time interval which is less than the normal time interval. For example, if the time interval of coverage is 1 month, the premium due each month would be one-twelfth of the annual premium payment.

PRO RATA REINSURANCE *see* PROPORTIONAL REINSURANCE; QUOTA SHARE REINSURANCE; SURPLUS REINSURANCE.

PRORATION *see* PRO RATA CANCELLATION; PRO RATA LIABILITY CLAUSE.

PRORATION OF COVERAGE *see* OTHER INSURANCE CLAUSE.

PROSPECT individual or organization that is a potential purchaser of an insurance product.

PROSPECTING soliciting of customers for the purchasing of an insurance product. *See also* PROSPECT.

PROSPECTIVE COMPUTATION *see* PROSPECTIVE RATING.

PROSPECTIVE EXPERIENCE RATING *see* PROSPECTIVE RATING.

PROSPECTIVE RATING determination of (1) a future property or liability insurance or reinsurance rate or (2) a premium for a specified future period of time. It is based on the loss experience of a specified past period of time.

PROSPECTIVE RESERVE amount designated as a future liability for life or health insurance to meet the difference between future benefits and future premiums. NET LEVEL PREMIUM is determined so that this basic relationship holds: the present value of a future premium equals the present value of a future benefit. This relationship, incidentally, exists in fact only at the point of issuance of a life insurance policy. After that, the value of future premiums is less than the value of future benefits because fewer premiums are left to be paid. Thus, a reserve must be maintained at all times to make up this difference.

PROSPECTIVE VALUATION calculations involving the MORTALITY RATE of a company's insureds and the rate of return on the company's investments. It is used in calculating the PROSPECTIVE RESERVE.

PROTECTED RISK property to be insured, or that is insured, which is located within the specific geographical region falling under the auspices of the fire department.

PROTECTION *see* COVERAGE.

PROTECTION AND INDEMNITY INSURANCE (P&I) broad type of marine legal liability coverage. HULL MARINE INSURANCE is limited to an insured ship. With the addition of a RUNNING DOWN CLAUSE, a policy can be extended to cover liability in case of collision with another ship. But many shipowners desire the much broader coverage offered by protection and indemnity insurance since it covers the ship operator for liability to crew members and other people on board, damage to fixed objects like docks, and other miscellaneous claims.

PROTECTIVE LIABILITY INSURANCE *see* OWNERS AND CONTRACTORS PROTECTIVE LIABILITY INSURANCE.

PROVISIONAL PREMIUM (RATE) *see* DEPOSIT PREMIUM.

PROXIMATE CAUSE *see* DIRECT LOSS.

PRUDENT MAN RULE *see* TORT. UNINTENTIONAL.

PUBLIC ADJUSTER representative of an insurance claimant in situations only where an adjuster can act for an insurance company or an insured. *See also* ADJUSTER, STAFF.

PUBLIC EMPLOYEES BLANKET BOND fidelity bond provided under a BLANKET POSITION BOND (in which each position is covered on an individual basis) or a COMMERCIAL BLANKET BOND (in which a loss is covered on a blanket basis regardless of the number of employees causing the loss) for employees of public institutions and agencies.

PUBLIC LAW 15 *see* MCCARRAN-FERGUSON ACT (PUBLIC LAW 15).

PUBLIC LAW 87-311 1961 Federal legislation that allows the U.S. Export-Import Bank to set up insurance protection for U.S. exporters against credit risk and political risk in order to help make U.S. exports more competitive and bolster the U.S. trade balance. The *Foreign Credit Insurance Association* oversees the insurance program, which is written by private insurers.

PUBLIC LAW 91-156 1969 Federal legislation requiring states to treat national banks, including those whose principal offices are out of state, the same way for tax purposes as they treat their own state-chartered banks.

PUBLIC LAW 92-500 amendments to the WATER QUALITY IMPROVEMENT ACT OF 1970 that extends liability of shipowners to any hazardous substances discharged by their ships. The 1970 act made shipowners responsible for cleanup of oil spills. Public Law 92-500 (the Federal Water Pollution Control Act Amendments of 1972) extended responsibility to other hazardous substances.

PUBLIC LIABILITY INSURANCE very broad term for insurance covering liability exposures for individuals and business owners. It provides broad coverage, generally including all exposures for property damage and bodily injury, except exposures that relate to ownership of airplanes and automobiles, and to employees. Liability insurance may be written to cover specified hazards, as a COMPREHENSIVE GENERAL LIABILITY INSURANCE (CGL) policy, PACKAGE POLICY, or SCHEDULED POLICY.

PUBLIC OFFICIAL BOND type of SURETY BOND that guarantees the performance of public officials. Public officials are responsible for a broad range of property including fees that they collect, money they handle, and bank accounts that they oversee. They may also be held responsible for misdeeds that result in a loss of public funds by those they supervise. In some cases coverage is available for an entire group of employees under a PUBLIC EMPLOYEES BLANKET BOND.

PUBLIC RISK AND INSURANCE MANAGEMENT ASSOCIATION (PRIMA) organization based in Washington, D.C., which is composed of risk and insurance managers of various public entities, to include municipalities and school boards.

PUBLIC TRUCKMENS LEGAL LIABILITY FORM INLAND MARINE policy that covers truck drivers for loss or damage to merchandise they haul. The Interstate Commerce Commission requires this coverage for trucks engaged in interstate commerce.

PUNITIVE DAMAGES *see* LIABILITY, CIVIL DAMAGES AWARDED.

PUP COMPANY subsidiary, smaller company which is owned and controlled by a much larger company. In many instances pup companies are used to write SPECIAL RISK INSURANCE for which the larger company does not have UNDERWRITING facilities.

PURCHASE *see* OWNERSHIP RIGHTS UNDER LIFE INSURANCE; POLICYHOLDER.

PURCHASE PRICE cost of an ANNUITY. Annuities are often paid for in a lump sum rather than annual or other periodic payments. This sum, which guarantees an income, usually for life, is called the *purchase price* rather than the PREMIUM, which is generally associated with payments for insurance.

PURCHASING GROUP *see* GROUP HEALTH INSURANCE; GROUP LIFE INSURANCE; MASS MERCHANDISING; MASS UNDERWRITING; MASTER POLICY.

PURE *see* PURE ANNUITY; PURE ENDOWMENT; PURE PREMIUM RATING METHOD; PURE RISK.

PURE AMOUNT OF PROTECTION *see* NET AMOUNT AT RISK.

PURE ANNUITY contract sold by insurance companies that pays a monthly (quarterly, semiannual, or annual) income benefit for the life of a person (the ANNUITANT). The annuitant can never outlive the income from the annuity. Upon the death of the annuitant all income payments cease. There are no beneficiary benefits under this type of annuity. Contrast with REFUND ANNUITY.

PURE ASSIGNMENT MUTUAL INSURANCE COMPANY *see* ASSESSABLE MUTUAL.

PURE ENDOWMENT life insurance policy under which its face value is payable only if the insured survives to the end of the stated endowment period; no benefit is paid if the insured dies during the endowment period. Few if any of these policies are sold today. Contrast with ENDOWMENT INSURANCE.

PURE LOSS COST RATIO *see* BURNING COST RATIO.

PURE PREMIUM *see* PURE PREMIUM RATING METHOD.

PURE PREMIUM RATING METHOD approach that reflects losses expected. It is a calculation of the pure cost of property or liability insurance protection without loadings for the insurance company's expenses, premium taxes, contingencies, and profit margins. The pure premium is calculated according to the relationship:

$$\text{Pure Premium} = \frac{\text{Total Amount of Losses (and Loss Adjustment Expenses) Incurred per Year}}{\text{Number of Units of Exposure}}$$

PURE RISK situation involving a chance of a loss or no loss, but no chance of gain. For example, either one's home burns or it does not; this risk is insurable. *See also* STANDARD RISK.

PYRAMIDING situation in which several liability insurance policies are in force to cover the same risk thereby resulting in higher limits of coverage than is required to adequately insure the risk.

Q

Q SCHEDULE provision of the NEW YORK INSURANCE CODE and regulations under which (1) the life insurance company must file with the Insurance Commissioner all expenses associated with selling new life insurance policies; and (2) a limit is set on expenses to acquire new business.

The expense limitation serves to restrict agent commissions in New York State. This is one important reason why many national insurance companies do not sell life insurance in New York, or why some organize subsidiary companies for the sole purpose of conducting life insurance business only in New York. Many life insurance companies feel the expense limitation too restrictive to attract brokerage business.

QUADRUPLE INDEMNITY *see* ACCIDENTAL DEATH CLAUSE.

QUALIFIED IMPAIRMENT INSURANCE waiver of an impairment of an applicant for health insurance by attaching an ENDORSEMENT to the health insurance policy stating that the policy will pay no benefits in connection with the impairment. This waiver enables an applicant, who otherwise would not qualify, to be insured. *See also* SUBSTANDARD HEALTH INSURANCE (QUALIFIED IMPAIRMENT INSURANCE).

QUALIFIED JOINT AND SURVIVOR ANNUITY *see* ANNUITY, JOINT-LIFE AND SURVIVORSHIP ANNUITY; PENSION PLAN.

QUALIFIED PENSION PLAN *see* PENSION PLAN.

QUALIFIED TERMINABLE INTEREST PROPERTY (Q TIP) TRUST strategy which provides that all income from assets in trust be paid at least annually for the life of the surviving spouse. This trust, which prohibits transfer of any assets to anyone else, can provide for the surviving spouse to will the property to one or more individuals among a group previously designated by the deceased spouse. For example, a husband establishes a Q TIP trust that gives his widow income for life. At the death of the wife, the corpus of the Q TIP trust will go the children, even though the corpus is part of the wife's estate. Since the husband elects how much of the estate is to be treated as Q TIP property, the estate tax strategy is to have only that portion of Q TIP property necessary to achieve zero estate death tax. *See also* ESTATE PLANNING, ESTATE PLANNING DISTRIBUTION.

QUANTITY DISCOUNT *see* GROUP INSURANCE; MASS MERCHANDISING.

QUICK ASSETS liquid property that can be converted easily to cash. For example, a policyowner can borrow readily against the cash value of a life insurance policy. *See also* POLICY LOAN.

QUID PRO QUO exchange, in insurance, of an adequate *consideration* (premium paid by an insured) for the promise of an insurance company to pay benefits in the event the insured incurs a loss.

QUOTA SHARE REINSURANCE automatic reinsurance which requires the insurer to transfer and the reinsurer to accept a given percentage of every risk within a defined category of business written by the insurer. For example, in the case of a 20% quota share, the insurer transfers 20% of its liability and premiums on every risk to the reinsurer, who must pay 20% of any loss sustained, whether total or partial. The percentage is constant throughout and applies to premiums and losses alike. *See also* REINSURANCE.

R

RABBI TRUST TRUST named from a private-letter ruling by the IRS which involved a trust established by a Jewish congregation on behalf of its rabbi. The operation of the trust involves the employer's making contributions to the trust which are irrevocable. An independent trustee has control of the trust and must pay benefits from it if a stipulated event occurs, such as the death, disability, or retirement of the employee. If the employer becomes bankrupt or insolvent, the funds held in the trust are subject to the claims of the employer's creditors. The employer cannot take income tax deductions for its contributions to the trust until the funds in the trust are actually distributed to the employee.

RACKETEER INFLUENCED AND CORRUPT ORGANIZATIONS ACT OF 1970 (RICO) legislation that provides support for legal actions against individuals or organizations involved in systematic illegal activities. This act has been applied against insurance organizations when they were accused of bad-faith failure to pay claims or when there was a question of insolvency.

RADIOACTIVE CONTAMINATION INSURANCE form of INLAND MARINE INSURANCE under which an insured is indemnified for damage or destruction of his on-premises property if it is due to radioactive material stored or used within the premises. *See also* MOTOR TRUCK CARGO RADIOACTIVE CONTAMINATION INSURANCE; SHIPPERS RADIOACTIVE CONTAMINATION INSURANCE.

RADIO AND TELEVISION TRANSMITTING EQUIPMENT, TRANSMISSION LINES, PIPE LINES, TRAFFIC LIGHTS INSURANCE coverage if transmission equipment is damaged or destroyed on an ALL RISKS basis excluding the perils of war, wear and tear, inherent defect, and nuclear damage. CONSEQUENTIAL LOSS (indirect loss) may be added by endorsement to include such eventualities as lost revenue because of damage to a radio transmitting line. This endorsement can be of special importance to businesses, such as stock brokerages, which transmit buy and sell orders.

RADIUM FLOATER *see* RADIOACTIVE CONTAMINATION INSURANCE.

RAILROAD RETIREMENT ACT *see* RAILROAD RETIREMENT SYSTEM.

RAILROAD RETIREMENT SYSTEM insurance established under the Federal Railroad Retirement Act for railroad employees, covering death, retirement, disability, and unemployment. Benefits are adjusted for cost of living increases according to the formula used for Social Security.

RAILROAD ROLLING STOCK INSURANCE coverage for railroad equipment, liability of a railroad for damaging another railroad's equipment, or the damage to goods under its care, custody, and control. Coverage is provided on an ALL RISKS basis subject to perils specifically excluded in the policy.

RAILROAD SIDETRACK AGREEMENT *see* SIDETRACK AGREEMENT.

RAILROAD TRAVEL POLICY *see* TRAVEL ACCIDENT INSURANCE.

RAIN INSURANCE business interruption insurance in which the insured is indemnified for loss of earnings and payment of expenses resulting from adverse weather conditions. For example, the raining out of a fair, horse race, or boxing match can cause a substantial loss of money for a promoter who may have spent huge sums in advance of the event for rental, advertising, and site conditioning. However, the policy does not cover damage to property because of rain.

RANCHOWNERS INSURANCE *see* FARMOWNERS AND RANCHOWNERS INSURANCE.

RANDOM SAMPLE sample of *n* elements selected from a population of *N* elements in such a way that the sample has essentially the same characteristics as the population. The random sample serves as the foundation of all PROBABILITY theory as it relates to probability in sampling. In theory, all subsets drawn from the same sample have an equal chance of being drawn. Sampling is extremely important to the calculation of premium rates. For example, if the INSURER wants to predict the probability that a wood-frame house will burn, the sample must be drawn from the population of wood-frame houses, not brick-frame houses.

RANDOM INSURANCE coverage up to specific limits for payments demanded by kidnappers for the release of an insured held against his or her will. Most random insurance policies have a deductible and exclude abductions within certain geographical areas from coverage.

RATE *see* RATE MAKING; RATE MANUAL; RATING; RATING BUREAU.

RATE CREDIT OR DEFICIENCY annual contributions to a pension plan that exceed or are smaller than (1) the minimum required for future employee benefits currently being earned; and (2) any supplemental liability for past benefits earned but not previously funded.

RATED POLICY statement in which a life insurance applicant is charged a higher-than-standard premium to reflect a unique impairment, occupation, or hobby, such as a history of heart disease, a circus performer, or sky diver.

RATED UP *see* RATED POLICY.

RATE FACTORS *see* RATE MAKING.

RATE MAKING process of calculating a PREMIUM so that it is (1) *adequate*—sufficient to pay losses according to expected FREQUENCY and *severity* thereby safeguarding against the insurance company becoming insolvent; (2) *reasonable*—the insurance company should not be able to earn an excessive profit; and (3) *not unfairly discriminatory* or *inequitable*. Theoretically, it can be said that each insurance applicant should pay a personally unique premium to reflect a different expectation of loss, but this would be impractical. Instead, classifications are established for applicants to be grouped according to similar expectation of loss. Statistical studies of a large number of nearly homogeneous exposures in each underwriting classification enable the projection of losses after adjustments for future inflation and statistical irregularities. The adjusted statistics are used to calculate the *pure cost of protection* or *pure premium,* to which the insurance company adds on loads for agent commissions, premium taxes, administrative expenses, contingency reserves, other acquisition costs, and profit margin. The result is the GROSS PREMIUM to be charged to the insured.

RATE MANUAL publication which lists premiums charged for products sold by an insurance company. A manual also has underwriting guidelines for agents. A life insurance rate manual includes minimum guaranteed NONFORFEITURE values; and if a *participating* policy, *dividend* scales.

RATE OF RETURN METHOD OF COST COMPARISON approach advocated by the Federal Trade Commission (FTC) in its 1979 LIFE INSURANCE COST disclosure report. It calculates the rate of return earned by the savings element of a life insurance policy in these steps:
1. determine *pure cost of protection* (mortality expectation).
2. determine amount of dividends paid (if it is a *participating policy*).
3. subtract the pure cost of protection plus dividends from the GROSS PREMIUMS paid into the policy. This is the savings element.
4. the rate of return equals the interest rate at which the savings element must be accumulated in order to equal the cash value of the policy at some future specified time period. *See also* INTEREST ADJUSTED COST.

RATES cost per unit of insurance. *See also* RATE MAKING.

RATES AND SELECTION *see* RATE MAKING.

RATIFICATION BY AGENCY sanction or affirmation by an insurance company of acts of its agents which become the acts of the company, with all the legal obligations these acts entail.

RATING a valuation of risk of an individual or organization.

RATING BUREAU cooperative organization among insurers that rates and prepares new policy forms according to guidelines and regulations of the state INSURANCE DEPARTMENT. Loss experience, collected according to the line of business in specific geographical areas, is used to suggest rates for use by the rating bureau member companies. They may either use these rates or file their own *deviated rates* for approval by the state insurance department if it is a *prior approval state.* In an *open competition state,* a company does not need approval for a deviated rate. In a *file-and-use state,* a company can use a deviated rate without approval, after having filed it with the state insurance department. In a *modified prior approval state,* a company can use a deviated rate after filing it with the state insurance department provided it is a modest deviation and not a new rate classification.

RATING CLASS *see* CLASS RATE.

RATING CLAUSE *see* RATE MAKING.

RATING DOWN *see* AGE SETBACK.

RATING, EXPERIENCE *see* EXPERIENCE RATING.

RATING, MERIT *see* MERIT RATING.

RATING ORGANIZATION *see* RATING BUREAU.

RATING, RETROSPECTIVE *see* RETROSPECTIVE RATING.

RATING, SCHEDULE *see* SCHEDULE RATING.

READJUSTMENT INCOME *see* ADJUSTMENT INCOME.

REAL ESTATE land and attached structures. Interest in real estate can be protected through various insurance policies. *See also* BUSINESS PROPERTY AND LIABILITY INSURANCE PACKAGE; BUSINESSOWNERS POLICY; HOMEOWNERS INSURANCE POLICY.

REAL PROPERTY *see* REAL ESTATE.

REASONABLE AND CUSTOMARY CHARGE fee that is most consistent with that of physicians, hospitals, or other health providers for a given procedure; usual fee for a procedure charged by the majority of physicians with similar training and experience within the same geographical area.

REASONABLE EXPENSES *see* EXCLUSIONS, MEDICAL BENEFITS.

REASONABLE MAN TEST *see* TORT, UNINTENTIONAL.

REASONABLENESS OF PREMIUM RATE *see* RATE MAKING.

REASSURED *see* CEDING COMPANY.

REBATING *see* ANTI-REBATE LAW.

RECAPTURE practice of a CEDING COMPANY whereby insurance previously CEDED to a REINSURER is returned to that ceding company. *See also* RECAPTURE OF PLAN ASSETS BY EMPLOYER.

RECAPTURE OF PLAN ASSETS BY EMPLOYER return of employer contributions to a pension if that plan is (1) newly established and is determined by the IRS not to be tax qualified; or (2) long established but the IRS disallows a portion or all of the employer contribution.

RECIPIENT PROPERTY insurance against interruption of supply of goods and services. If firm A depends on firm B for its supply of goods and services, an interruption caused by damage or destruction to B can jeopardize A. CONTINGENT BUSINESS INTERRUPTION FORM can be used by A to protect against this possibility.

RECIPROCAL EXCHANGE unincorporated association with each insured insuring the other insureds within the association. (Thus, each participant in this pool is both an insurer and an insured.) An attorney-in-fact administers the exchange to include paying losses experienced by the exchange, investing premium inflow into the exchange, recruiting new members, underwriting the inflow of new business, underwriting renewal business, receiving premiums, and exchanging reinsurance contracts. Members share profits and losses in the same proportion as the amount of insurance purchased from the exchange by that member.

RECIPROCAL INSURANCE EXCHANGE *see* RECIPROCAL EXCHANGE.

RECIPROCAL INSURER *see* RECIPROCAL EXCHANGE.

RECIPROCAL LEGISLATION law under which one state gives favorable tax treatment to an insurance company *domiciled* in a different state that is admitted to do business, provided the second state does the same for companies domiciled in the first state. *See also* RETALIATION LAWS.

RECIPROCITY *see* RECIPROCAL EXCHANGE; RECIPROCAL LEGISLATION.

RECORDING AGENT *see* AGENT OF RECORD.

RECORDING METHOD *see* ACCIDENT-YEAR STATISTICS; CALENDAR YEAR EXPERIENCE.

RECORD KEEPING *see* DEBIT; DEBIT AGENT (HOME SERVICE AGENT); DEBIT INSURANCE (HOME SERVICE INSURANCE, INDUSTRIAL INSURANCE).

RECRUITING search, attraction, interview, and employment of insurance agents. This is a primary function of the GENERAL AGENT (GA) or AGENCY MANAGER.

RECURRENT DISABILITY *see* DISABILITY INCOME INSURANCE.

RECURRING CLAUSE time period in health insurance that must elapse between a previous illness and a current one, if the current one is to be considered a separate illness eligible for a new set of benefits.

REDLINING refusal by an insurance company to underwrite or to continue to underwrite questionable risks in a given geographical area. This is an important civil rights issue.

REDUCED PAID-UP INSURANCE *see* NONFORFEITURE REDUCED PAID-UP BENEFITS.

REDUCED RATE CONTRIBUTION CLAUSE *see* COINSURANCE; DOUBLE RECOVERY.

RE-ENTRY TERM LIFE INSURANCE *yearly renewable term (YRT)* life insurance under which an insured can usually re-apply for term insurance every fifth year at a lower premium than the guaranteed renewal rate. If the insured's health is good (as documented by evidence of insurability), the guaranteed renewable term premium can be reduced. If not, the guaranteed rate must be continued to be paid on renewal.

REFUND ANNUITY form of annuity returning premiums plus interest to a beneficiary if the annuitant dies during the accumulation period. A refund annuity costs more than a pure annuity. If the annuitant dies during the liquidation period, benefits paid to any beneficiary depend on whether the refund annuity is in the form of a LIFE ANNUITY CERTAIN, INSTALLMENT REFUND ANNUITY, or CASH REFUND ANNUITY.

REFUND LIFE INCOME OPTION *see* ANNUITY.

REGIONAL OFFICE BRANCH OFFICE of an insurance company's home office which markets, underwrites, and services the company's lines of business within a specified geographical area.

REGISTER record of debit or industrial insurance policies. *See also* DEBIT INSURANCE (HOME SERVICE INSURANCE, INDUSTRIAL INSURANCE).

REGISTERED MAIL AND EXPRESS MAIL INSURANCE coverage for damage or destruction of property with relatively high monetary value, such as stock brokerage house and bank shipments which involve the transfer of securities and monies to different locations and whose loss would result in great expense. Coverage is on an ALL RISKS basis excluding war, nuclear disaster, and illegal trade items.

REGISTERED MAIL INSURANCE *see* REGISTERED MAIL AND EXPRESS MAIL INSURANCE.

REGISTERED REPRESENTATIVE individual licensed to sell securities to the public. For example, to sell *variable annuities* and VARIABLE LIFE INSURANCE products and mutual funds, an insurance agent is required to pass examinations given by the National Association of Securities Dealers.

REGISTERED RETIREMENT SAVINGS PLAN (RRSP) Canadian retirement plan much like U.S. INDIVIDUAL RETIREMENT ACCOUNT (IRA). Here, an employee can contribute on a tax deductible basis C $3500 each year as a member of an employer pension plan. A nonmember employee can contribute C $5500 tax deductible. Earnings under this plan accumulate tax-deferred. RRSPs are issued by life insurance companies and trust companies.

REGULATION OF INSURANCE COMPANIES *see* STATE SUPERVISION AND REGULATION.

REGULATION OF LIFE INSURANCE *see* STATE SUPERVISION AND REGULATION.

REHABILITATION *see* REHABILITATION CLAUSE.

REHABILITATION CLAUSE provision in health insurance under which an insured disabled person is required to undertake (and is reimbursed) for expenses associated with vocational rehabilitation for retraining to perform another economic function.

REIMBURSEMENT OF INSURED payment of benefits by an insurance policy to a POLICYOWNER (usually the insured), if a loss occurs.

REINSTATEMENT restoration of a policy that has lapsed because of nonpayment of premiums after the grace period has expired. In life insurance the reinstatement time period is three years from the premium due date. The company usually requires the insured to show evidence of continued insurability (for example, by taking a medical examination); to pay all past premiums plus interest due; and to either reinstate or repay any loans that are still outstanding. Because the insured is now older and a new policy would require a higher premium it may be to the advantage of an insured to reinstate a policy.

REINSTATEMENT CLAUSE *see* REINSTATEMENT PROVISION.

REINSTATEMENT OF POLICY *see* REINSTATEMENT PROVISION.

REINSTATEMENT PREMIUM *see* REINSTATEMENT PROVISION.

REINSTATEMENT PROVISION *see* REINSTATEMENT.

REINSURANCE form of insurance that insurance companies buy for their own protection, "a sharing of insurance." An insurer *(the reinsured)* reduces its possible maximum loss on either an individual risk (FACULTATIVE REINSURANCE) or on a large number of risks (AUTOMATIC REINSURANCE) by giving *(ceding)* a portion of its liability to another insurance company *(the reinsurer)*.

Reinsurance enables an insurance company to (1) expand its capacity; (2) stabilize its underwriting results; (3) finance its expanding volume; (4) secure catastrophe protection against shock losses; (5) withdraw from a class or line of business, or a geographical area, within a relatively short time period; and (6) share large risks with other companies.

There are two broad forms of reinsurance; PROPORTIONAL REINSURANCE and NONPROPORTIONAL REINSURANCE.

REINSURANCE ASSOCIATION *see* REINSURANCE EXCHANGE.

REINSURANCE ASSUMED *see* CEDE.

REINSURANCE, AUTOMATIC *see* AUTOMATIC REINSURANCE.

REINSURANCE BROKER individual who represents a *ceding* insurance company in placing its business with a reinsurer. *See also* REINSURANCE.

REINSURANCE CAPACITY (1) largest amount of REINSURANCE available from a company or from the general market; (2) large amounts of reinsurance on one risk; or (3) maximum premium volume which can be written by a reinsurer.

REINSURANCE, CARPENTER PLAN *see* CARPENTER PLAN (SPREAD LOSS COVER, SPREAD LOSS REINSURANCE).

REINSURANCE CEDED *see* CEDE.

REINSURANCE CLAUSE provision that covers a business to be protected under a reinsurance treaty. The class can either appear at the beginning of the agreement or may be included in the RETENTION AND LIMITS CLAUSE at a later stage of the contract.

REINSURANCE CREDIT credit reflected on a CEDING COMPANY'S ANNUAL STATEMENT, showing REINSURANCE PREMIUMS CEDED and losses recoverable from the REINSURER.

REINSURANCE, EXCESS *see* EXCESS OF LOSS REINSURANCE.

REINSURANCE, EXCESS OF LOSS RATIO *see* STOP LOSS REINSURANCE.

REINSURANCE EXCHANGE group in which subscribing members agree to (1) regulations governing their behavior, and (2) the qualifications that REINSURANCE contracts *ceded* to them must meet in order to be acceptable. The exchange is run by a manager who has the power of attorney to represent each member and the exchange in the conduct of the reinsurance business. However, today these exchanges are no longer a factor in the reinsurance market.

REINSURANCE FACILITY
1. pool that contains various reinsurance companies with each sharing reinsurance contracts on a pro rata basis as they are submitted to the pool.
2. market that operates much like the New York Stock Exchange in that reinsurance contracts are bought and sold on a bid and asked basis. *See also* REINSURANCE.

REINSURANCE, FACULTATIVE *see* FACULTATIVE REINSURANCE.

REINSURANCE, LIFE *see* LIFE REINSURANCE.

REINSURANCE, POOLING *see* POOL; REINSURANCE FACILITY.

REINSURANCE PREMIUM *see* AUTOMATIC REINSURANCE; BURNING COST RATIO (PURE LOSS COST); CARPENTER PLAN (SPREAD LOSS COVER, SPREAD LOSS REINSURANCE); EXCESS OF LOSS REINSURANCE; FACULTATIVE REINSURANCE; NONPROPORTIONAL REINSURANCE; PROPORTIONAL REINSURANCE; QUOTA SHARE REINSURANCE; STOP LOSS REINSURANCE; SURPLUS REINSURANCE.

REINSURANCE, PROPERTY AND CASUALTY-CASUALTY CATASTROPHE *see* AUTOMATIC NONPROPORTIONAL REINSURANCE; AUTOMATIC PROPORTIONAL REINSURANCE; AUTOMATIC REINSURANCE; EXCESS OF LOSS REINSURANCE; FACULTATIVE REINSURANCE; NONPROPORTIONAL REINSURANCE; PROPORTIONAL REINSURANCE; QUOTA SHARE REINSURANCE; STOP LOSS REINSURANCE; SURPLUS REINSURANCE.

REINSURANCE, QUOTA SHARE *see* QUOTA SHARE REINSURANCE.

REINSURANCE RESERVE (UNEARNED PREMIUM RESERVE) fund in a segregated account to provide for the return of unearned premiums on policies which are cancelled. *See also* PRO RATA CANCELLATION; SHORT RATE CANCELLATION.

REINSURANCE, SPECIFIC EXCESS *see* SPECIFIC EXCESS REINSURANCE.

REINSURANCE, SPREAD LOSS *see* CARPENTER PLAN (SPREAD LOSS COVER, SPREAD LOSS REINSURANCE).

REINSURANCE, STOP LOSS *see* STOP LOSS REINSURANCE.

REINSURANCE, SURPLUS *see* SURPLUS REINSURANCE.

REINSURER insurance company which assumes all or part of an INSURANCE or REINSURANCE policy written by a primary insurance company (CEDING COMPANY). *See also* REINSURANCE; REINSURANCE BROKER; REINSURANCE EXCHANGE; REINSURANCE FACILITY.

REJECTION refusal by an insurance company to underwrite a risk. *See also* RISK CLASSIFICATION.

RELATIONSHIP BETWEEN RISK AND CHANCE *see* WAGERING V. INSURANCE.

RELATIVE VALUE SCHEDULE (RVS) list of the values of specific medical procedures in comparison with other medical procedures.

RELATIVE VALUE STUDY (RVS) SCHEDULE assignment of a unit value to each of various medical procedures for the purpose of cost comparisons.

REMOVAL insured peril in some property insurance policies that encompasses any accidental damage to insured property while being removed to safety from the immediate threat of damage by another peril covered by that policy. For example, if an insured removes a chair from his burning home, puts it on the lawn, and then rain damages the chair, the loss insured would be covered by fire insurance on the furnishings of the home.

REMOVAL BOND *see* JUDICIAL BOND.

RENEWABLE TERM HEALTH INSURANCE *see* COMMERCIAL HEALTH INSURANCE.

RENEWABLE TERM LIFE INSURANCE coverage that is renewable at the option of the insured, who is not required to take a medical examination. Regardless of physical condition, the insured must be allowed to renew the policy and the premium cannot be increased to reflect any adverse physical condition. However, the premium of each renewal increases to reflect the LIFE EXPECTANCY of the individual at that particular age.

RENEWAL automatic reestablishment of an insurance policy's in-force status, usually achieved through payment of the premium due. *See also* COMMERCIAL HEALTH INSURANCE RENEWAL CERTIFICATE; RENEWAL PREMIUM; RENEWAL PROVISION; RENEWABLE TERM LIFE INSURANCE.

RENEWAL CERTIFICATE form showing notification that an insurance policy has been renewed with the same provisions, clauses, and benefits of the previous policy.

RENEWAL COMMISSION commission paid to an AGENT after the FIRST YEAR COMMISSION has been paid to that agent. Renewal commissions generally form a substantial portion of an agent's income after 4 years in the business and serve as an important incentive for him or her to make every effort to keep the policies on an IN-FORCE BUSINESS status.

RENEWAL PREMIUM payment due on the renewal of an insurance policy. The premium may be adjusted up or down to reflect the loss experience of the UNDERWRITING classification to which the insured belongs. *See also* RENEWABLE TERM LIFE INSURANCE.

RENEWAL PROVISION clause in an insurance policy which permits an insured to renew without having to take a medical examination, regardless of his or her physical condition; the premium cannot be increased to reflect an adverse medical condition. *See also* RENEWABLE TERM LIFE INSURANCE.

RENEWALS *see* RENEWAL PREMIUM.

RENT *see* RENT INSURANCE.

RENTAL VALUE INSURANCE *see* RENT INSURANCE.

RENTERS INSURANCE *see* TENANTS INSURANCE.

RENT INSURANCE endorsement to an existing policy or a separate policy covering loss of rental income to the property owner, caused by the damage or destruction of a building, rendering it unrentable. The coverage applies whether or not the dwelling is rented at the time of loss. The insured can select a coinsurance requirement of either 50%, 80%, or 100%. The higher the coinsurance amount, the lower the premium.

REPARATIONS payment made by a party causing harm to the party incurring that harm.

REPLACEMENT COST *see* REPLACEMENT COST LESS PHYSICAL DEPRECIATION AND OBSOLESCENCE.

REPLACEMENT COST LESS PHYSICAL DEPRECIATION AND OBSOLESCENCE sum it takes to replace an insured's damaged or destroyed property with one of like kind and quality, equivalent to the actual cash value, minus physical depreciation (fair wear and tear) and obsolescence. The objective is to place the insured in the same financial position after a loss as prior to it; the insured should not profit or lose by incurring a loss.

REPLACEMENT, LIFE INSURANCE exchange of a new policy for one already in force. *See also* CONSERVATION.

REPLACEMENT RATIO measure showing how much life insurance an agent has lost through replacement. It is expressed as a percentage of number of policies, face amount, or premium volume.

REPLACEMENT, RECONSTRUCTION, AND REPRODUCTION COST option to an insurance company to replace, reconstruct (repair), or reproduce (rebuild) damaged or destroyed property covered by property insurance rather than indemnify an insured in cash. This is rarely done.

REPLEVIN BOND *see* JUDICIAL BOND.

REPORTABLE EVENT obligation of the insured to report losses from a covered peril to the insurance company or its representative as soon after its occurrence as possible.

REPORTING ENDORSEMENT *see* OPEN FORM (REPORTING FORM)

REPORTING FORM *see* OPEN FORM (REPORTING FORM)

REPORTING REQUIREMENTS *see* OPEN FORM (REPORTING FORM).

REPORT TO SOCIAL SECURITY ADMINISTRATION requirement of an employer to report annually to the U.S. Treasury Department the names of employees who terminated employment with vested benefits, and the amount of the benefits. The Treasury sends the Social Security Administration a copy, which is available to an employee on request. A statement on vested benefits is given by the Social Security Administration to an applicant for Social Security benefits.

REPRESENTATIONS statements by an insurance applicant concerning personal health history, family health history, occupation, and hobbies. These statements are required to be substantially correct; that is, applicants must answer questions to the best of their knowledge.

REPRESENTATIVE *see* AGENT; BROKER-AGENT; CAPTIVE AGENT; INDEPENDENT AGENT.

REPRESENTATIVE SAMPLE sample in which the relative sizes of the subpopulation samples are selected in such a manner as to be equal to the relative sizes of the subpopulations. For example, when measuring the viewing audience of a particular television show, the audience is stratified into several subpopulations: income groups, age groups, vocational groups, and so on. Then random samples are drawn from the various strata in proportion to the relative sizes of these strata.

REPRODUCTION VALUE *see* REPLACEMENT, RECONSTRUCTION, AND REPRODUCTION COST.

REQUIRED INSURANCE *see* COMPULSORY INSURANCE.

REQUIREMENTS *see* REQUIREMENTS OF INSURABLE RISK.

REQUIREMENTS OF INSURABLE RISK
1. a large number of homogeneous exposures (in order for the deviation of actual losses from expected losses to approach *zero*, and the creditability of the prediction to approach *one*).
2. loss must be definite in time and amount.
3. loss must be fortuitous. An insured cannot cause the loss to happen; it must be due to chance.
4. must not be an exposure to catastrophic loss; risks must be spread over a large geographical area to prevent their concentration. REINSURANCE often is used to spread potentially catastrophic risks.
5. premium must be reasonable in relation to the potential loss. In theory, one could even insure against a pencil point breaking, but the premium would be much greater than any possible loss.

RECISSION cancellation of a contract. Under the Federal Truth in Lending Act, a person who signs a contract can nullify it within three business days of having signed it without penalty; funds paid into the contract by the signer must be returned. Also, fraud or misrepresentation provides legal grounds for cancellation of a contract. For example, life insurance contracts with minors are voidable (by minors but not by insurers) since they are under legal age for making a contract.

RESERVE *see* RESERVES AND THEIR COMPUTATION.

RESERVE FACTORS *see* RESERVES AND THEIR COMPUTATION.

RESERVE, FULL PRELIMINARY TERM *see* FULL PRELIMINARY TERM RESERVE PLAN.

RESERVE, INCURRED BUT NOT REPORTED LOSSES *see* INCURRED BUT NOT REPORTED LOSSES (IBNR).

RESERVE LIABILITIES REGULATION

1. LIFE INSURANCE: specification by each state regarding (a) the minimum assumptions that must be used in reserve calculations as they pertain to the maximum interest rate that can be assumed; (b) the mortality table that can be used (the more conservative the table, the higher the death rates that will be shown which exceed the death rates actually expected); and (c) the reserve valuation that must be used (the minimum is established by the National Association of Insurance Commissioners *Standard Valuation Law*).

2. PROPERTY AND LIABILITY INSURANCE specification by each state regarding the minimum assumptions that must be used in reserve calculations as they pertain to unpaid loss reserves and *unearned premium reserves*.

RESERVE, LOSS *see* LOSS RESERVES.

RESERVE, PROSPECTIVE *see* PROSPECTIVE RESERVE.

RESERVE, RETROSPECTIVE *see* RETROSPECTIVE METHOD RESERVE COMPUTATION.

RESERVES AND THEIR COMPUTATION *see* FULL PRELIMINARY TERM RESERVE PLAN; PROSPECTIVE RESERVE; RETROSPECTIVE METHOD RESERVE COMPUTATION.

RESERVE, UNEARNED PREMIUM *see* UNEARNED PREMIUM RESERVE.

RESIDENT AGENT salesman who markets and services insurance policies in the state in which he is domiciled.

RESIDENTIAL CONSTRUCTION INSURANCE coverage in the event an insured's negligent acts and/or omissions involving the construction of a new one- or two-family residential structure result in bodily injury and/or property damage to a third party. The "insured" includes his employees and independent contractors. This coverage is normally part of the HOMEOWNERS INSURANCE POLICY and extends coverage on an automatic basis for this exposure at no extra premium.

RESIDENTIAL FORM *see* RESIDENTIAL CONSTRUCTION INSURANCE.

RESIDUAL AUTOMOBILE INSURANCE MARKET *see* BUSINESS AUTOMOBILE POLICY; PERSONAL AUTOMOBILE POLICY.

RESIDUAL DISABILITY inability to perform one or more important daily business duties, or inability to perform the usual daily business duties for the time period usually required for the performance of such duties. *See also* RESIDUAL DISABILITY INCOME INSURANCE.

RESIDUAL DISABILITY INCOME INSURANCE coverage for an individual with a residual disability. Benefits are usually payable for the unused portion of the total disability benefit period up to age 65. If an individual is at least age 55 at the time of disablement, and total disability lasts less than a year, residual benefits are payable for the unused portion of the benefit period for up to 18 months, but not beyond age 65. If there is at least a 25% loss in current earnings, the residual benefits will equal the percentage of loss times the monthly benefit for total disability. The residual disability monthly benefit can be expressed in this equation:

$$\frac{\text{Loss of Monthly Income}}{\text{Prior Monthly Income}} \times \text{Monthly Benefit for Total Disability}$$

See also RESIDUAL DISABILITY.

RESIDUAL MARKET *see* AUTOMOBILE ASSIGNED RISK INSURANCE PLAN; RESIDUAL DISABILITY; RESIDUAL DISABILITY INCOME INSURANCE.

RES IPSA LOQUITOR Latin phrase for "The facts speak for themselves." This is a rule of evidence under which an individual is deemed, under certain specific circumstances, to be negligent by the mere occurrence of an accident. These circumstances are defined when the law presumes that an accident could not have occurred had the individual not been negligent.

RESPONDEAT SUPERIOR Latin for "Let the superior reply." That is, an employer is liable for the torts of employees which result from their employment. For example, an insurance company (the master) acts through its agent (servant); because of this master-servant relationship, any wrongs the agent commits are deemed to have been committed by the insurance company, which must accept responsibility.

REST CURE care in a sanitarium, nursing home, or other facility designed to provide CUSTODIAL CARE on behalf of the mental and physical well being of the patient. The cost may or may not be provided by health insurance policies.

RESTORATION OF PLAN authority of the PENSION BENEFIT GUARANTY CORPORATION (PBGC) to stop the termination of a pension plan and restore it to its previous status by returning a portion or all of the plan's assets and liabilities. For example, such an action could be taken by the PBGC when a company whose pension plan is being terminated has experienced a reversal in the adverse conditions which originally caused the termination.

RESTORATION OF VESTED BENEFITS plan under the EMPLOYEE RETIREMENT INCOME SECURITY ACT OF 1974 (ERISA) for employees who are less than 50% *vested*. An employee must be permitted to buy back retirement benefits lost because of the withdrawal of his or her contributions. The employee pays back to the pension plan the withdrawal contributions, plus 5% interest compounded annually.

RESTORATION PREMIUM sum that an insurance company charges a business firm to restore a property or liability insurance policy, or a bond, to its initial face value after the insurance company has paid a claim either to the insured business or to a third party on behalf of the insured business.

RESUMPTION OF OPERATIONS CLAUSE in a BUSINESS INTERRUPTION INSURANCE policy, clause which stipulates that if, by resuming operations, the business can reduce a loss, the business is obligated to so do. If the business refuses to resume operations, it will incur a portion of the loss.

RETAIL CREDIT REPORT report developed by or supplied by a credit agency to an insurer dealing with the financial standing and character of an insurance applicant. These factors are carefully weighted by the company's *underwriter* in deciding the INSURABILITY of the applicant. *See also* NUMERICAL RATING SYSTEM.

RETAINED EARNINGS net profit of a business, less dividends. Reinvestment of retained earnings enables an insurance company to write more business from a stronger capital base. Contributions to retained earnings come from three sources: (1) excess interest from investment earnings; (2) loss savings (fewer and/or smaller losses than were loaded into premiums); and (3) expense savings (less expense costs than were loaded into premiums). *See also* SURPLUS ACCOUNT.

RETAINER CLAUSE provision in a *nonproportional reinsurance contract* that the reinsurance will protect only the business retained by the *cedent* for its own account. In this connection, losses must be assumed by the cedent if it cannot enforce payment for any loss falling under its other *surplus* or QUOTA SHARE REINSURANCE contract.

RETALIATION LAWS legislation by a state that taxes out-of-state insurance companies operating in its jurisdiction in the same way that the state's own insurance companies are taxed in the second state. For example, state #1 charges a tax of 4% on its *domiciled* insurers. But if these insurers are charged a higher tax when operating in state #2, then state #1 will charge the higher tax to insurers of state #2 who wish to do business in state #1.

RETALIATORY PREMIUM TAX *see* RETALIATION LAWS.

RETENTION *see* RETENTION AND LIMITS CLAUSE; RISK MANAGEMENT; SELF INSURANCE.

RETENTION AND LIMITS CLAUSE provision in almost all EXCESS OF LOSS REINSURANCE contracts under which payment is made by a reinsurer of each and every loss incurred by the *cedent* in excess of a specified sum, up to a fixed limit. Under this clause, there is no restriction on the number of claims that may be recovered by the cedent under the contract for any one event. The only stipulation is that each claim must arise as a result of the event in question.

RETENTION DEDUCTIBLE in UMBRELLA LIABILITY INSURANCE clause which stipulates that in the event of a loss where there are no underlying policies providing coverage, the DEDUCTIBLE will apply.

RETENTION OF LOSS *see* RETENTION AND LIMITS CLAUSE; RISK MANAGEMENT; SELF INSURANCE.

RETIREMENT AGE age at which a pension plan participant is entitled to receive retirement benefits; or point at which retirement benefits are payable: (1) NORMAL RETIREMENT AGE is the earliest age permitted to retire and receive full benefits; (2) EARLY RETIREMENT is earlier-than-normal age permitted to retire provided attained minimum age and service requirement are met, but there is a proportionate reduction in benefits; (3) DEFERRED RETIREMENT age beyond automatic retirement age permitted to retire, usually with no increase in benefits; (4) *Automatic retirement age* is age at which retirement is automatically effective.

RETIREMENT ANNUITY *see* ANNUITY; GROUP DEFERRED ANNUITY; PENSION PLAN FUNDING; GROUP DEPOSIT ADMINISTRATION ANNUITY; PENSION PLAN FUNDING; GROUP IMMEDIATE PARTICIPATION GUARANTEED (IPG) CONTRACT ANNUITY.

RETIREMENT BENEFITS *see* ALLOCATED FUNDING INSTRUMENT; DEFINED BENEFIT PLAN; DEFINED CONTRIBUTION PENSION (MONEY PURCHASE PLAN); PENSION PLAN FUNDING; GROUP DEPOSIT ADMINISTRATION ANNUITY; GROUP PERMANENT LIFE INSURANCE; PENSION PLAN FUNDING; GROUP IMMEDIATE PARTICIPATION GUARANTEED (IPG) CONTRACT ANNUITY; PENSION PLAN FUNDING; INDIVIDUAL CONTRACT PENSION PLAN; PENSION PLAN FUNDING INSTRUMENTS.

RETIREMENT INCOME ENDOWMENT POLICY type of ENDOWMENT INSURANCE which matures at a stipulated retirement age and whose purpose is to provide retirement income to the INSURED.

RETIREMENT INCOME PAYMENTS *see* RETIREMENT BENEFITS.

RETIREMENT INCOME POLICY form of DEFERRED ANNUITY; a life insurance policy which usually guarantees from 120 to 180 monthly income payments to the *annuitant* at retirement. If the annuitant dies during the deferral (or guaranteed) period, a beneficiary receives a death payment of the face amount or the cash value, whichever is larger. During the deferred period, the policyowner can withdraw part or all of the annuity's cash value (the latter terminating the annuity). *See also* ANNUITY.

RETIREMENT INSURANCE NEEDS *see* RETIREMENT ANNUITY; RETIREMENT BENEFITS; RETIREMENT INCOME POLICY; RETIREMENT PLANNING.

RETIREMENT PLAN *see* ALLOCATED FUNDING INSTRUMENT; DEFINED BENEFIT PLAN; DEFINED CONTRIBUTION PENSION (MONEY PURCHASE PLAN); PENSION PLAN FUNDING; GROUP DEPOSIT ADMINISTRATION ANNUITY; PENSION PLAN FUNDING INSTRUMENTS; RETIREMENT BENEFITS; RETIREMENT INCOME POLICY; RETIREMENT PLANNING; UNALLOCATED FUNDING INSTRUMENT.

RETIREMENT PLANNING formal process of setting aside funds on a mathematical basis to provide deferred income benefits. *See also* RETIREMENT PLAN.

RETIREMENT RATE ASSUMPTIONS *see* PENSION PLAN FUNDING INSTRUMENTS.

RETROACTIVE CONVERSION *see* ORIGINAL AGE.

RETROACTIVE INSURANCE *see* ORIGINAL AGE.

RETROACTIVE LIABILITY INSURANCE coverage which is purchased to provide protection for a loss that has already occurred. The severity of the loss, however, is uncertain.

RETROACTIVE PERIOD *see* ORIGINAL AGE.

RETROACTIVE RATE REDUCTION *see* RETROSPECTIVE RATING.

RETROCESSION REINSURANCE of a reinsurer. *See also* RETROCESSION CATASTROPHE COVER.

RETROCESSIONAIRE REINSURER of a reinsurer. *See also* RETROCESSION.

RETROCESSION CATASTROPHE COVER REINSURANCE of a *reinsurer* such that the reinsurer protects itself from a catastrophe occurrence. Just as an insurer must decide to CEDE to the reinsurer a portion of a risk it has underwritten, the reinsurer must make the same decision as to which risks it can sustain within its resources, and what portion of the risks it must retrocede. Retrocession may be either *proportional* or *nonproportional*. *See also* NONPROPORTIONAL REINSURANCE; PROPORTIONAL REINSURANCE.

RETRO-NOTE PLAN means of financing by which some large organizations pay their property or liability insurance premiums to reflect losses actually paid during the first year of coverage, plus claims expenses, administrative and servicing expenses, and a loading for the company's profit. The insured signs a promissory note to the company for the difference in the normal or standard premium that should have been charged.

RETROSPECTIVE COMPUTATION *see* RETROSPECTIVE PREMIUM.

RETROSPECTIVE METHOD RESERVE COMPUTATION accumulated value of assumed past net life insurance premiums, minus the accumulated value of past benefits (claims paid).

RETROSPECTIVE PREMIUM *see* RETROSPECTIVE RATING.

RETROSPECTIVE RATING method of establishing rates in which the current year's premium is calculated to reflect the actual current year's loss experience. An initial premium is charged and then adjusted at the end of the policy year to reflect the actual loss experience of the business.

RETURN COMMISSION return of a *pro rata* portion of an agent's commission for a policy that is cancelled prior to its expiration date. A commission is paid to an agent in the expectation that the premium will be earned over the life of a policy. If the policy is cancelled, a portion of the unearned premium (either pro rata or *short rate*) also must be returned to the policyowner.

RETURN OF CASH VALUE CLAUSE provision in a life insurance policy that if an insured dies within a given period of time, the beneficiary receives the *face value* of the policy plus its *cash value*. *See also* CASH SURRENDER VALUE.

RETURN OF PREMIUM *see* CANCELLATION PROVISION CLAUSE.

RETURN PREMIUM amount received by the POLICYHOLDER if the policy is cancelled, benefits are reduced, or the PREMIUM is reduced. *See also* PRO RATA CANCELLATION; SHORT RATE CANCELLATION.

REVENUE BULLETIN 1988–52 ruling issued in 1988 by the Internal Revenue Service which stipulates that, when computing the pension benefits of an employee still working after 1987, the years of service on the job after the employee reaches age 65 cannot be disregarded. The issuance of this revenue bulletin makes it mandatory that pension benefits reflect all years on the job, to include those years after age 65.

REVERSE-ANNUITY MORTGAGE (RAM) loan under which the owner of a home receives the equity in the form of a series of monthly income payments for life. Upon the owner's death, the lender institution (usually a bank) gains title to the home and is free to keep or sell it. The longer that monthly income payments are made the greater the reduction in the owner's equity in his home. This type of mortgage is of value to older individuals who own their homes free and clear. Their large equity enables them to continue to live there and to receive a monthly income benefit.

REVERSIONARY ANNUITY *see* SURVIVORSHIP ANNUITY.

REVERSIONARY INTEREST interest of a beneficiary in the proceeds of a SURVIVORSHIP ANNUITY. *See also* SURVIVORSHIP ANNUITY.

REVIVAL *see* REINSTATEMENT.

REVOCABLE *see* BENEFICIARY.

REVOCABLE BENEFICIARY *see* BENEFICIARY.

REVOCABLE LIVING TRUST TRUST in which rights to make any changes therein are retained by the GRANTOR. At the grantor's death all rights become irrevocable. This type of trust has several advantages: it can avoid PROBATE, it prevents public disclosure of the assets of the trust, it can easily be revised or terminated, and it promotes continuity for the transfer of the estate. However, since the grantor retains ownership rights under this trust, the trust loses all of the income and estate tax advantages available under an IRREVOCABLE LIVING TRUST.

RIDER endorsement to an insurance policy that modifies clauses and provisions of the policy, adding or excluding coverage.

RIDERS, LIFE POLICIES endorsements to life insurance policies that provide additional benefits or limit an insurance company's liability for payment of benefits under certain conditions. These include:
1. *Waiver of Premium for Disability.* An insured with total disability that lasts for a specified period no longer has to pay premiums for the duration of the disability. In effect, the company pays the premiums.
2. *Accidental Death Benefit.*
3. GUARANTEED INSURABILITY.
4. COST-OF-LIVING ADJUSTMENT (COLA).
5. *Other Insured.* Term life insurance is added on a person other than the primary insured, with the rate based on the other person's age, sex, underwriting classification, and amount of coverage.

6. *Children's Insurance.* Term insurance on each child is added, usually to the age of majority. Generally, a child cannot become insured before the age of 15 days or after his or her eighteenth birthday.

7. *Additional Insurance.* Term insurance can be added to *ordinary life* policies as an additional layer of coverage for some specified time interval.

8. *Transfer of Insureds.* In business situations, generally used to insure key persons with the cash value and the insurance coverage transferrable from the initial insured person to another person.

RIMS *see* RISK AND INSURANCE MANAGEMENT SOCIETY.

RIOT AND CIVIL COMMOTION INSURANCE coverage for damage to property resulting from riot or civil commotion. Riot is defined by most state laws as a violent disturbance involving three or more (in some states two or more) persons. Civil commotion is a more serious and prolonged disturbance or violent uprising. Losses from riots in major cities during the 1960s caused insurers to stop writing this type of coverage in certain urban areas. In response, Congress enacted legislation creating the FEDERAL CRIME INSURANCE program and providing riot reinsurance in states that established acceptable pooling plans. *See also* FAIR ACCESS TO INSURANCE REQUIREMENTS (FAIR) PLAN.

RIOT COVERAGE *see* RIOT AND CIVIL COMMOTION INSURANCE.

RIOT EXCLUSION clause in the *Standard Fire Policy* and many other property insurance policies that excepts coverage for losses caused by riot or civil commotion. Coverage for riot and civil commotion can be added with the EXTENDED COVERAGE ENDORSEMENT.

RISK uncertainty of financial loss; term used to designate an insured or a peril insured against.

RISK AND CHANGE *see* RISK CLASSIFICATION.

RISK AND NSURANCE MANAGEMENT SOCIETY (RIMS) society dedicated to the advancement of professional standards of RISK MANAGEMENT. Its membership is composed of risk and insurance managers of business organizations, public organizations, and service organizations. Both profit and nonprofit organizations are represented. The goal of RIMS is to upgrade the management of risk and employee benefit plans in order to preserve the assets of the organization in question. Included in the activities of RIMS are research, conferences and seminars, and sponsorship of the INSURANCE INSTITUTE OF AMERICA'S (IIA) ASSOCIATE IN RISK MANAGEMENT (ARM) program.

RISK AND OCCUPATION FREQUENCY and *severity* of accidents resulting from conditions and environment surrounding one's work place.

Occupation is an important underwriting factor when considering an applicant for insurance.

RISK APPRAISAL *see* RISK MANAGEMENT.

RISK ASSUMPTION *see* RETENTION AND LIMITS CLAUSE; RISK MANAGEMENT; SELF INSURANCE.

RISK AVOIDANCE *see* AVOIDANCE.

RISK BEARER *see* SELF INSURANCE.

RISK CLASSIFICATION analysis of uncertainty of financial loss. This classification can be according to whether a risk is FUNDAMENTAL, PARTICULAR, PURE, SPECULATIVE, DYNAMIC, or STATIC. In life insurance the process by which a company determines how much to charge for a policy according to an applicant's age, occupation, sex and health. *See also* UNDERWRITING.

RISK CONTROL *see* RISK MANAGEMENT.

RISK, DEGREE OF *see* DEGREE OF RISK.

RISK EQUIVALENT *see* ACTUARIAL EQUIVALENT.

RISK EXPERIENCE LOSS RATIO *see* EXPERIENCE RATING; FREQUENCY AND DISTRIBUTION OF LOSSES; LOSS RATIO.

RISK FINANCING utilization of source(s) of funds to pay for losses. Source(s) of funds can be classified as:
1. *internal*—a RETENTION program is established to use funds from within the organization to pay for losses.
2. *external*—a transfer program (generally through the purchase of INSURANCE) is established to use funds from without the organization to pay for losses.

   Usually, a RISK MANAGEMENT program combines retention and transfer to form a comprehensive program for loss protection.

RISK IDENTIFICATION *see* RISK MANAGEMENT.

RISK IDENTIFICATION IN LIABILITY EXPOSURES process of discovering sources of loss concerning the liability RISK faced by individuals and business firms. The first step in risk management is to identify the causes of a loss by analyzing possible negligent acts and/or omissions that could result in bodily injury and/or property damage. *See also* RISK MANAGEMENT.

RISK IDENTIFICATION IN PROPERTY EXPOSURES process of discovering sources of loss concerning the property RISK faced by individuals and business firms. The first step is to analyze possible *perils* that can damage or destroy both real and personal property. *See also* RISK MANAGEMENT.

RISK MANAGEMENT procedure to minimize the adverse effect of a possible financial loss by (1) identifying potential sources of loss; (2) measuring the financial consequences of a loss occurring; and (3) using controls to minimize actual losses or their financial consequences. *See also* BUSINESS PROPERTY AND LIABILITY INSURANCE PACKAGE; CONDOMINUM INSURANCE; DISABILITY INCOME INSURANCE; HEALTH INSURANCE; HOMEOWNERS INSURANCE POLICY; HUMAN LIFE VALUE APPROACH (EVOIL); LIFE INSURANCE; LOSS PREVENTION AND REDUCTION; PENSION PLAN; PERSONAL AUTOMOBILE POLICY (PAP); RISK IDENTIFICATION, LIABILITY EXPOSURE; RISK IDENTIFICATION, PROPERTY EXPOSURES; SELF INSURANCE; TENANTS INSURANCE.

RISK MANAGER *see* RETENTION AND LIMITS CLAUSE; RISK MANAGEMENT; SELF INSURANCE.

RISK MEASUREMENT *see* RISK MANAGEMENT.

RISK PHILOSOPHY personal view regarding how losses occur and the validity of loss prevention and reduction; also, whether an individual is a risk taker or a risk avoider. For example, if a driver takes the view that dying in a serious automobile accident is inevitable, then use of seat belts is unnecessary. On the other hand, a driver's philosophy may be that wearing a seat belt will minimize injury and reduce the chance of dying in an accident.

RISK PREMIUM INSURANCE *see* RENEWABLE TERM LIFE INSURANCE.

RISK RATING, INDIVIDUAL rating system under which a specific premium rate, rather than a manual or class rate, is assigned to each unit of exposure.

RISK REDUCTION *see* ENGINEERING APPROACH; HUMAN APPROACH; LOSS PREVENTION AND REDUCTION.

RISK RETENTION *see* SELF INSURANCE.

RISK RETENTION ACT OF 1986 Federal act composed of amendments to the Product Liability Risk Retention Act of 1981 and enacted to make the procedures more efficient for creating RISK RETENTION GROUPS (capitalized, member-owned INSURANCE COMPANY) and PURCHASING GROUPS (INSURANCE buyers' group formed to obtain coverage for homogeneous LIABILITY RISKS, in many instances hard to insure, from an insurance company).

RISK RETENTION GROUP *see* SELF INSURANCE.

RISK SELECTION methods by which a home office underwriter chooses applicants that an insurer will accept. The underwriter's job is to spread the costs equitably among members of the group to be insured. Therefore, the underwriter must determine which are normal, or *standard risks,* to be charged the standard rate; which are *substandard risks,* to be charged a higher rate; and which are *preferred risks,* to receive a discount. This process is made more difficult by SELF-SELECTION and ADVERSE SELECTION. The underwriter must screen applicants who are looking for insurance, specifically because they have a greater-than-normal chance of loss, and set the correct PREMIUM *rate* for them.

RISK SOURCES, PERSONAL *see* HUMAN LIFE VALUE APPROACH (ECONOMIC VALUE OF AN INDIVIDUAL LIFE—EVOIL); RISK MANAGEMENT.

RISK SPREAD *see* POOLING.

RISK, SUBJECTIVE *see* SUBJECTIVE PROBABILITY.

RISK, SYSTEMATIC *see* STATIC RISK.

RISK TRANSFER shifting a PURE RISK by means of a two party contract such as INSURANCE.

RISK, UNSYSTEMATIC *see* DYNAMIC.

ROBBERY use of the threat of violence, or actual violence, in taking property from someone else's possession. This peril is covered on a personal basis through the purchase of a HOMEOWNERS INSURANCE POLICY or *renter's insurance* or on a business basis through a SPECIAL MULTIPERIL INSURANCE (SMP) policy. Specialty items such as coin and stamp collections must be specifically scheduled on a property policy in order for the insured to receive full value for a loss.

ROLLOVER INDIVIDUAL RETIREMENT ACCOUNT individual retirement account (IRA) established to receive distribution of assets from a qualified pension or retirement plan. For example, if an employee resigns from his job and receives a lump sum distribution of $75,000, he may roll it over into an IRA without paying taxes. Rollover IRAs are governed by the same tax rules as other IRAs. They provide a way to maintain the tax-deferred status of distributions from pensions or other qualified plans until an age specified by law, when withdrawals must begin.

RUNNING DOWN CLAUSE coverage in liability insurance for a shipowner in the event of collision with another ship. A running down clause, when added to basic HULL MARINE INSURANCE, protects against liability for damage to the other vessel, its freight and cargo, and for lost income to the other vessel's owner during the time it cannot be used.

RUN-OFF liability of an insurance company for future claims that it expects to pay and for which a reserve has been established.

S

SAFE BURGLARY INSURANCE coverage against a loss resulting from the forcible entry of a safe. In order for this coverage to be applicable, there must be signs of forcible entry into the premises in which the safe is located. *See also* MERCANTILE SAFE BURGLARY INSURANCE.

SAFE DRIVER PLAN procedure for offering reduced auto insurance rates to drivers with good records, and imposing higher rates on bad drivers. Typically, premiums are weighted under a system that assigns points for traffic violations and accidents. The more points awarded during a certain rating period, the higher the premium. Most plans consider violations only during the past two or three years, giving bad drivers who improve their records a chance to reduce their premiums.

SAFETY important means of preventing accidents and injuries. Insurers take corporate safety programs into account when rating workers compensation and other business insurance policies. *See also* ENGINEERING APPROACH; HUMAN APPROACH; LOSS PREVENTION AND REDUCTION.

SAFETY OF ASSETS quality of investments of insurance companies. State insurance regulators establish rules for company investments. Authorized investments vary, depending on whether a company is a life insurer or property casualty company and, in some instances, on whether it is a mutual or stock company. Investments must meet standards for asset type, credit quality, and diversification. Generally, insurance company assets are limited to government securities, bonds, stocks, mortgages, and certain real estate holdings. *See also* ADMITTED ASSETS; LIQUIDITY OF ASSETS; SEPARATE ACCOUNT FUNDING.

SAFETY AUDIT study of an organization's operations, and real and personal property to discover existing and potential HAZARD and the actions needed to render these hazards harmless.

SAFETY RESPONSIBILITY LAW *see* FINANCIAL RESPONSIBILITY LAW.

SALARY CONTINUATION PLAN arrangement, often funded by life insurance, to continue an employee's salary in the form of payments to a beneficiary for a certain period after the employee's death. The employer itself may be the beneficiary, collecting the death benefit and making payments to the employee's beneficiary.

SALARY DEDUCTION GROUP INSURANCE *see* SECTION 401(K) PLAN (SALARY REDUCTION PLAN); PAYROLL DEDUCTION INSURANCE.

SALARY REDUCTION PLAN *see* SECTION 401(K) PLAN (SALARY REDUCTION PLAN).

SALARY SAVINGS INSURANCE (DEDUCTION OR ALLOTMENT) *see* SECTION 401(K) PLAN (SALARY REDUCTION PLAN).

SALARY SAVINGS PROGRAM *see* PAYROLL DEDUCTION INSURANCE.

SALARY SCALES system whereby benefits in an EMPLOYEE BENEFIT INSURANCE PLAN vary according to the employee's earnings. *See also* DEFINED BENEFIT PLAN; EMPLOYEE STOCK OWNERSHIP PLAN (ESOP), TRUST (ESOP); GROUP LIFE INSURANCE; PENSION PLAN.

SALESMAN'S SAMPLE FLOATER coverage for sample merchandise while in the custody of a salesperson.

SALES REPRESENTATIVE *see* AGENT, BROKER-AGENT; CAPTIVE AGENT; INDEPENDENT AGENT.

SALVAGE *see* ABANDONMENT AND SALVAGE.

SALVAGE CHARGES expense of recovering property by a salvor. Salvage charges are not provided for in insurance contracts. If the owner and the salvor cannot agree on salvage charges, a court makes a determination based on the value of the salvaged items and the salvor's expenses. Rules governing payment of salvage charges originated in marine insurance but are now used in other policies, such as personal automobile insurance.

SAMPLE item given or sold to a buyer that establishes a standard of quality by which later products will be judged. Since the UNIFORM COMMERCIAL CODE does not distinguish between a sample and a model, a sample may create an implied warranty that all goods will conform to this standard. If other goods shipped later do not meet this standard, the manufacturer may be held liable.

SAMPLE, RANDOM *see* RANDOM SAMPLE.

SAMPLE, REPRESENTATIVE *see* REPRESENTATIVE SAMPLE.

SAMPLING, STRATIFIED RANDOM *see* STRATIFIED RANDOM SAMPLING.

SAVINGS *see* SAVINGS ELEMENT, LIFE INSURANCE.

SAVINGS BANK LIFE INSURANCE (SBLI) low-cost life insurance sold by savings banks in the states of Connecticut, Massachusetts, and New York. SBLI is a popular source of life insurance in these states for two reasons: it is offered in bank lobbies, which makes it convenient;

and there are no commissions, as with commercial life insurance, which makes it cheaper. Although banks generally are barred from the insurance business, SBLI was allowed by these three states at the urging of consumer groups. Other states have refused to adopt similar legislation. Maximum policy amounts are limited by state law.

SAVINGS ELEMENT cash value of life insurance that accumulates according to a table in a policy. It reflects premiums in the early years that exceed the *pure cost of protection* during that period. If a policy is surrendered, the policyowner receives the cash surrender value and the insurance ends. This is why a cash value policy can be considered a savings or investment vehicle. Cash value is also the part of a life insurance product used as an investment for an INDIVIDUAL RETIREMENT ACCOUNT (IRA).

SAVINGS ELEMENT, LIFE INSURANCE buildup of policy cash value, as distinguished from the death benefit. A policyholder has a choice between surrendering the policy for its cash surrender value or keeping it in force for its death benefit. The rates of return on cash value policies, such as *whole life insurance, universal life,* or *variable life,* depend on schedules in the insurance contract or, in some types of policies, on prevailing interest rates or the performance of an investment portfolio. *See also* CASH SURRENDER VALUE.

SAVINGS, NEED FOR LIFE INSURANCE *see* SAVINGS ELEMENT, LIFE INSURANCE.

SCHEDULE BOND *see* NAME POSITION BOND; NAME SCHEDULE BOND.

SCHEDULED COVERAGE *see* SCHEDULED POLICY.

SCHEDULED LIMIT specified limit on the dollar amount of coverage for a given loss.

SCHEDULED PERSONAL PROPERTY ENDORSEMENT addition to a HOMEOWNERS INSURANCE POLICY, or other personal or business property policies, to provide extra coverage for listed articles. The standard policy has dollar limits on certain items, such as jewelry, furs, art, or guns. This endorsement allows a policyholder to purchase additional coverage for specific items of property, with each item or group of items, and the amount of coverage, listed.

SCHEDULED POLICY policy permitting an insured to choose desired coverages. These policies are important for items with relatively low limits of coverage under standard property insurance forms. For example, an insured would have to specifically schedule expensive jewelry, furs, and paintings in order to receive full value for a loss.

SCHEDULE OF BENEFITS *see* GROUP HEALTH INSURANCE (Schedule of Benefits).

SCHEDULE P RESERVE statutory reserve for automobile liability, representing specific dollar estimates for future claims. The NATIONAL ASSOCIATION OF INSURANCE COMMISSIONERS (NAIC) established formulas to project the amount that liability insurers must put aside for unpaid claims. These formulas are based on the assumption that future claims will approximate those paid out in recent years. The name comes from the NAIC convention ANNUAL STATEMENT blank, where it is designated as Schedule P.

SCHEDULE PROPERTY FLOATER *see* FLOATER; PERSONAL ARTICLES INSURANCE; PERSONAL PROPERTY FLOATER.

SCHEDULE Q *see* Q SCHEDULE.

SCHEDULE RATING method of pricing property and liability insurance. It uses charges and credits to modify a class rate based on the special characteristics of the risk. Insurers have been able to develop a schedule of rates because experience has shown a direct relationship between certain physical characteristics and the possibility of loss. For example, for fire insurance, the underwriter might make an additional charge above the standard rate for the class if a building contains a flammable liquid. A credit may be given if it has a sprinkler system. In automobile insurance, a credit might be given for driver education. In life insurance, credit is usually given for a nonsmoker. Schedule rating is commonly used for fire, automobile and workers compensation insurance. *See also* EXPERIENCE RATING; PREMIUM DISCOUNT; RETROSPECTIVE RATING.

SCLP *see* SIMPLIFIED COMMERCIAL LINES PORTFOLIO POLICY (SCLP).

SCREENS system established for checking claims to determine whether they should be paid immediately or checked further for validity.

SEASONAL RISK exposure present only at certain times of the year. For example, resort property faces a business interruption risk only from damage that cannot be repaired in time for the resort season.

SEAWORTHINESS ADMITTED CLAUSE part of a marine cargo policy that exempts the policyholder from vouching for the seaworthiness of the vessel. For example, while a purchaser of HULL MARINE INSURANCE warrants that a ship is in proper condition for a voyage, the purchaser of CARGO INSURANCE, who has no control over the ship's condition, is not expected to vouch for it.

SECONDARY BENEFICIARY *see* BENEFICIARY.

SECONDARY PLAN *see* COORDINATION OF BENEFITS.

SECOND DEATH INSURANCE life insurance policy with a death benefit that is paid only when the second of two insureds dies. No benefits are paid as long as both live or if just one lives.

SECOND INJURY FUND insurance fund set up by most states to encourage employers to hire handicapped workers. Where workers with existing handicaps suffer further work-related injuries or diseases that result in total disability, the employer is responsible for the *workers compensation* benefit only for the second injury or disease. The fund makes up the difference between the benefit for total disability and the benefit for the second injury. Second-injury funds are financed through general state revenues or assessments on workers compensation insurers.

SECOND MORTGAGE mortgage loan secured by real estate that already has a first mortgage. In case of default, the claim of the second mortgage holder is subordinate to that of the first mortgage holder. Generally, insurance companies are not permitted by state laws to offer or invest in second mortgages.

SECOND SURPLUS REINSURANCE amount of REINSURANCE accepted by a second REINSURER which is in excess of the original insurer's retention limit and the first reinsurer's first surplus treaty's limit. *See also* RETENTION AND LIMITS CLAUSE, SURPLUS REINSURANCE.

SECTION 79 PLAN group *whole life* insurance policy designed to reduce an employee's exposure to income tax on the value of life insurance provided by the employer. The policy separates the term element from the cash value element, and apportions part of the premium to each. The plan takes advantage of the tax exemption to employees on a specified amount of group term insurance plans and the special tax rate on the premium for the amount of insurance over that amount.

SECTION 401 (k) PLAN (SALARY REDUCTION PLAN) employer-sponsored retirement savings program named for the section of the Internal Revenue Code that permits it. These plans allow employees to invest pre-tax dollars that are often matched in some portion by employers. Because of their flexibility, 401 (k)s became a popular employee benefit during the 1980s. But the TAX REFORM ACT OF 1986 limited their use as short-term savings plans by imposing a 10 percent penalty on all money withdrawn before retirement. It also reduced the maximum annual contribution from $30,000 to $7000 and tightened nondiscrimination rules. Employees may still borrow the money, however, and pay themselves interest.

SECTION 403 (b) PLAN retirement plan offered by public employers and tax-exempt organizations. Under Section 403(b) of the Internal Revenue Code, certain tax-exempt organizations such as public school systems can make payments for retirement annuity policies for their employees and have the payments excluded from the employees' gross income for tax purposes, subject to certain limitations.

SECTION 408 (k) PLAN section of the Internal Revenue Code that provides for SIMPLIFIED EMPLOYEE PENSIONS (SEP).

SECTION 1035 EXCHANGE section of the Internal Revenue Code that provides for the taking of the proceeds from one LIFE INSURANCE policy or ANNUITY and the reinvesting of these proceeds immediately in another life insurance policy or annuity of the same type without being required to pay a tax on any gain. This exchange should be handled by the seller of the REPLACEMENT, LIFE INSURANCE policy or annuity.

SECULAR TRUST [402(b)] (NONEXEMPT TRUST) NONQUALIFIED PLAN of DEFERRED COMPENSATION whose goal is to compensate KEY EMPLOYEES without having to provide similar benefits to rank and file employees. The TRUST is irrevocable, and funds placed in it are protected against claims made by the company's creditors. Even though funds in this trust are not in the employee's possession, they are deemed by the Internal Revenue Service to have been constructively received by the employee. The company is allowed to take an income tax deduction for the funds it contributed to the trust, even though these funds have not been distributed to the employee while he or she has current taxable income. At the time funds from the trust are actually distributed, the employee is taxed only to the extent that these distributions are from earnings of the trust or from current trust income, which will allow the employee to pay taxes owed as the result of the company's contributions to the trust. The employer is not taxed on the trust income; the employee pays all taxes on this income. For example, assume that the company is in the 34% tax bracket and contributed $40,000 to the trust on behalf of John Employee, who is in the 28% tax bracket. The result is that John Employee will have an $11,200 tax liability ($40,000 × 28%) and the company will incur a $13,600 tax deduction ($40,000 × 34%). In order that John Employee will have the necessary funds to pay the taxes owed, the company usually will bonus him the $11,200 required, which of course is tax deductible as a business expense for the company.

SECURED CREDITOR creditor with a documented claim on a specific asset of a *debtor. See also* COLLATERAL BORROWER; COLLATERAL CREDITOR (ASSIGNEE).

SECURED LIEN *see* COLLATERAL BORROWER; COLLATERAL CREDITOR (ASSIGNEE); SECURED CREDITOR.

SECURITIES *see* SECURITIES AND EXCHANGE COMMISSION (SEC); SECURITIES BOND; SECURITIES INVESTOR PROTECTION CORPORATION (SIPC).

SECURITIES ACT OF 1933 landmark legislation passed by Congress providing the first regulation of the securities markets. The law, enforced by the SECURITIES AND EXCHANGE COMMISSION (SEC), requires registration of securities issues and disclosure of material information about the financial condition of the issuers. *Variable annuity* and VARIABLE LIFE INSURANCE policies have been determined to be securities under the terms of this law and thus are subject to regulation both by the SEC as well as by state insurance departments.

SECURITIES AND EXCHANGE COMMISSION (SEC) Federal agency that regulates the securities markets. The independent five-member commission was created under the Securities Exchange Act of 1934 to enforce the SECURITIES ACT OF 1933. Members are appointed by the President and serve five-year terms. The SEC has responsibility to regulate securities exchanges and markets, set disclosure and accounting rules for most issuers of corporate securities and to oversee securities firms, investment companies, and investment advisers.

SECURITIES BOND forgery insurance covering securities issues such as stocks and bonds. They protect the issuer of securities against forgery of the securities.

SECURITIES INVESTOR PROTECTION CORPORATION (SIPC) Federal insurance fund that protects assets in client accounts held by registered securities broker-dealers. The SIPC is a nonprofit corporation created by Congress in 1970 under the Securities Investor Protection Act. Membership in SIPC is mandatory for all broker-dealers registered with the SECURITIES AND EXCHANGE COMMISSION and with the national stock exchanges. When the SIPC is unsuccessful in finding a healthy firm to acquire a failed brokerage, it pays off account holders of the failed brokerage for losses up to the coverage limit. Maximum coverage for cash and securities in a customer's account is $500,000, with a limit of $100,000 on the amount of cash that is insured.

SECURITIES VALUATION RESERVE *see* VALUATION RESERVE (SECURITIES VALUATION RESERVE).

SECURITY VALUATION rules used by state regulators to value securities on the books of insurance companies. Bonds with acceptable credit quality are carried at *amortized value,* which is the face value, plus or minus the amount of any purchase discount or premium, as amortized over the life of the bond. Preferred stock is valued at cost and COMMON STOCK INVESTMENTS at year-end market price. Valuations for impaired securities such as bonds in default are determined by the Committee on Valuation of Securities of the NATIONAL ASSOCIATION OF INSURANCE

COMMISSIONERS (NAIC). *See also* MANDATORY SECURITIES VALUATION RESERVE.

SEGREGATION OF EXPOSURE UNITS risk management practice designed to control losses by physically separating assets or operations (on separating a single exposure unit into various parts) to reduce maximum potential loss. The objective of such a separation is to reduce the risk of loss to the whole exposure unit through dispersion. For example, two related chemical processing operations, both subject to loss from explosion or fire, would be built a sufficient distance apart—perhaps even on separate premises—so that the explosion of one would not damage the other.

SELECTION *see* SELECTION OF RISK.

SELECTION OF RISK *see* RISK SELECTION; UNDERWRITING.

SELECT MORTALITY TABLE MORTALITY TABLE that includes data only on people who have recently purchased life insurance. Experience shows that such people have a lower mortality rate in the years immediately following their purchase of insurance than those who have been insured for some time, probably because they have recently passed medical and other tests, and because they are younger. For example, a select mortality table would show the number of deaths per 1000 of individuals age 30 who have been insured for one year. An ULTIMATE MORTALITY TABLE shows the rate of the group, exclusive of the initial period after the purchase of insurance. An *aggregate mortality table* includes all data.

SELF-ADMINISTERED PLAN qualified pension or other employee benefit where responsibility rests with an employer rather than an insurer. A TRUST FUND plan, where assets are deposited with and invested by a trustee, is the most common self-administered plan. A TRUST AGREEMENT governs the plan administration and retirees are paid benefits from the trust or the *trustee* buys annuities for them. The self-administered, or trust fund plan, contrasts with the insured (insurance company) pension plan.

SELF FUNDING *see* SELF INSURANCE.

SELF-INFLICTED INJURY intentional injury a person causes to himself. For life and health insurance purposes, self-inflicted injury typically is not covered by accident policies, because it is intentional not an accident. This applies for WORKERS COMPENSATION INSURANCE purposes as well. However, for life insurance purposes, suicide is covered after the policy has been in force for two years.

SELF INSURANCE protecting against loss by setting aside one's own money. This can be done on a mathematical basis by establishing a separate fund into which funds are deposited on a periodic basis. Through self insurance it is possible to protect against high FREQUENCY low-*severity* losses. To do this through an insurance company would mean having to pay a premium that includes loadings for the company's general expenses, cost of putting the policy on the books, acquisition expenses, premium taxes, and contingencies.

SELF-INSURER *see* SELF INSURANCE; SELF-INSURED RETENTION (SIR).

SELF-INSURED RETENTION (SIR) portion of a property or liability loss retained by a policyholder. Most policyholders do not purchase insurance to cover their entire exposure. Rather, they elect to take a deductible, or portion that they will cover themselves. For example, a homeowner may purchase $150,000 worth of insurance with a $500 deductible for certain losses, such as roof damage by hail. The $500 deductible is one form of self insurance. It means the homeowner will cover all losses for that amount or less. *See also* SELF INSURANCE.

SELF-SELECTION effort of a poor risk to seek insurance coverage. The onset of a health problem such as heart disease, for example, may prompt a person to apply for life insurance before seeking medical treatment. Such applicants, if not screened out, would weight the insured pool toward bad risks. The UNDERWRITING process is intended to counter the natural tendency toward self-selection among insurance applicants, either by requiring higher rates for poorer risks or by denying them coverage. *See also* ADVERSE SELECTION.

SELLING AGENTS' COMMISSION INSURANCE coverage that provides for the indemnification of a salesperson for the amount of his or her lost commission on a product to be sold which cannot be produced because of damage incurred by the manufacturer or which, once produced, cannot be delivered by the manufacturer because of damage incurred. *See also* CONTINGENT BUSINESS INTERRUPTION FORM.

SELLING PRICE CLAUSE property insurance coverage available to businesses that pays the established market (sales) value of products that are damaged rather than simply their lower (production) cost. This fills the gap between ACTUAL CASH VALUE, which provides coverage only for the cost to the insured, and BUSINESS INTERRUPTION INSURANCE. For manufacturers, it covers the cost of all finished goods; for mercantile firms, it applies only to goods that have been sold but are not yet delivered.

SEPARATE ACCOUNT *see* SPLIT FUNDED PLAN.

SEPARATE ACCOUNT FUNDING *see* SPLIT FUNDED PLAN.

SERIES OF CATASTROPHES hazard covered under *catastrophe reinsurance*. This form of EXCESS OF LOSS REINSURANCE protects the CEDING COMPANY for loss above the *retention* limit caused by multiple catastrophic events. *See also* CATASTROPHE HAZARD; CATASTROPHE LOSS.

SERIOUS INJURY FREQUENCY RATE number of serious injuries per 1,000,000 employee-hours worked. *See also* FREQUENCY.

SERVICE ADJUSTMENT change in YEARS OF SERVICE credited to employee in calculating pension benefits and other employee benefits.

SERVICE INSURER AGREEMENT arrangement whereby an insurance company agrees to pay specified health care service vendors a predetermined sum for providing such services to the covered individuals. *See also* BLUE CROSS; BLUE SHIELD.

SERVICEMEN'S GROUP LIFE INSURANCE (SGLI) U.S. government group term life insurance for men and women members of the Federal uniformed forces on active duty, underwritten by private insurance companies. Premiums reflect peacetime mortality rates for this group, with any additional costs of military risks (such as wartime exposure) being borne by the Federal government. Upon discharge, SGLI policies can be converted either to five-year nonrenewable term VETERANS GROUP LIFE INSURANCE (VGLI) or to a permanent policy at the veteran's attained age (at higher cost) with one of the commercial insurance companies participating in the servicemen's plan.

SERVICE PLANS types of insurance coverage under which health care benefits are provided to the covered individuals instead of monetary reimbursement for health care expenses. *See also* BLUE CROSS; BLUE SHIELD.

SERVICES OFFERED POLICYHOLDERS range of administrative and risk management services that can be purchased by an insured. Increasingly, insurance can be purchased UNBUNDLED so that policyholders may pay for straight coverage without available services. However, some policyholders may want to purchase additional services such as loss control, claims adjustment, captive management, or other services from the insurer.

SETBACK *see* AGE SETBACK.

SET CLAUSE (PAIR OR SET CLAUSE) provision in many business and personal policies that loss or damage to one of a pair or set of individual items does not represent the loss of the pair or set. For example, the loss of one diamond earring would not entitle an insured to be reimbursed for a pair of earrings, but for only the resulting decrease in the overall pre-loss value of the pair.

SETTLEMENT disposition of a claim or policy benefit. Policies may specify time limits for payment of claims or benefits and designate various methods of settlement at the option of the insurer or the insured. *See also* OPTIONAL MODES OF SETTLEMENT; SETTLEMENT OPTIONS, PROPERTY AND CASUALTY INSURANCE.

SETTLEMENT AGREEMENT *see* OPTIONAL MODES OF SETTLEMENT; SETTLEMENT OPTIONS; PROPERTY AND CASUALTY INSURANCE.

SETTLEMENT ARRANGEMENT *see* OPTIONAL MODES OF SETTLE-MENT; LIFE INSURANCE; SETTLEMENT OPTIONS, PROPERTY AND CASUALTY INSURANCE.

SETTLEMENT OPTIONS, LIFE INSURANCE *see* OPTIONAL MODES OF SETTLEMENT.

SETTLEMENT OPTIONS, PROPERTY AND CASUALTY INSUR-ANCE methods for payment of the value of a policy. An insurance company can select one of three options in settlement of a loss: (1) make a cash payment; (2) take possession of damaged or destroyed property and replace it with property of like kind and quality; or (3) repair the property so that it is restored to its structural condition prior to the loss, and return the repaired property to the insured.

Usually insurance companies settle losses by a cash payment to the insured.

SEUA *see* SOUTH-EASTERN UNDERWRITERS ASSOCIATION (SEUA) CASE.

SEVERITY *see* SEVERITY RATE.

SEVERITY RATE size of the losses used as a factor in calculating *premium rates*. For example, the U.S. Bureau of Labor Statistics studies the number of days lost by injured employees per million man-hours worked. *See also* FREQUENCY AND DISTRIBUTION OF LOSSES.

SEX demographic designation used in life insurance to calculate *premium rates* for life and health insurance and annuity contracts. Since females have a longer LIFE EXPECTANCY than males of the same age, life insurance premiums for females are lower than for males the same age. Annuity income for females, by the same token, is lower than for males the same age. These differences are being contested.

SEX DISCRIMINATION classification of insured life and health risks based on the sex of the proposed insured. Gender has long been one of many factors in classifying, accepting, and rating risks. For example, because experience shows that women live longer than men, life insurance rates for women are lower. By the same token, annuity payments are lower for women because it is expected that they will be paid out for more years. On the other hand, women have sometimes paid lower rates for auto insurance. Insurance rating by sex became an issue in the early 1980s when many women charged that it was discriminatory. They demanded through UNISEX LEGISLATION to be rated no differently. Although insurers have resisted it, individual states have passed laws prohibiting the use of sex in risk classification. *See also* RISK CLASSIFICATION

SFP *see* FIRE INSURANCE—STANDARD FIRE POLICY.

SHARE REINSURANCE *see* PROPORTIONAL REINSURANCE; QUOTA SHARE REINSURANCE; SURPLUS REINSURANCE.

SHERMAN ANTITRUST ACT 1890 law prohibiting monopolies and restraint of trade in interstate commerce. The Sherman Act was strengthened in 1914 with amendments known as the Clayton Act that added further prohibitions against price-fixing conspiracies. These Federal antitrust laws at first were not applied to the insurance industry because of the 1869 Supreme Court ruling in PAUL V. VIRGINIA that insurance was not commerce and thus not subject to Federal regulation. After the SOUTH-EASTERN UNDERWRITERS ASSOCIATION (SEUA) CASE in 1944 and passage of the MCCARRAN-FERGUSON ACT (PUBLIC LAW 15) in 1945, Congress made it clear that states would retain the power to regulate insurance but price-fixing and restraint of trade not sanctioned by state laws and regulations would be subject to Federal antitrust prosecution.

SHIP INSURANCE, PLEASURE CRAFT AND COMMERCIAL *see* MARINE INSURANCE.

SHIPPERS RADIOACTIVE CONTAMINATION INSURANCE coverage for shippers of certain radioactive materials, such as medical or commercial isotopes, for direct loss or damage by radioactive contamination; does not cover transport of radioactive waste or nuclear reactor fuel. Coverage has two forms: one for transport on common carriers and the other for transport on vehicles operated by or for an insured. *See also* MOTOR TRUCK CARGO RADIOACTIVE CONTAMINATION INSURANCE; NUCLEAR ENERGY LIABILITY INSURANCE; RADIOACTIVE CONTAMINATION INSURANCE.

SHIPPING INSURANCE *see* INLAND MARINE INSURANCE (TRANSPORTATION INSURANCE): BUSINESS RISKS.

SHOCK LOSS loss so catastrophic in nature that the insurance company will experience a significant UNDERWRITING loss. Protection against such an event can be purchased through various REINSURANCE instruments. *See also* REINSURANCE, PROPERTY AND CASUALTY—CASUALTY CATASTROPHE.

SHORE CLAUSE provision in MARINE INSURANCE listing onshore perils covered. In the case of marine cargo, these may include such occurrences as damage from flooding, sprinklers, collapse of docks, and wharf or warehouse fires. It may also cover damage from accidents during ground transportation.

SHORT RATE CANCELLATION cancellation by the insured of a property or disability insurance policy for which the returned unearned premium is diminished by administration costs incurred when the insurance company placed the policy on its books.

SHORT RATE PREMIUM premium charge for a policy which is going to be in force for less than the normal period of time.

SHORT RATE, SHORT TERM INSURANCE coverage for less than one year. Insurers generally charge higher rates for short term policies than for longer term insurance, such as an ANNUAL POLICY, because of (1) the need to recoup relatively fixed administrative and processing costs over a shorter policy life; and (2) the likelihood of ADVERSE SELECTION, with buyers seeking insurance only at times of the year when they know they face greatest likelihood of loss.

SHORT RATE TABLE display of percentage of earned premiums as a function of the time in days for term property insurance policies originally written for one year or longer. These tables are used to compute the refund or the excess of the paid premium above the customary short rate for the expired term in the event the INSURED cancels the policy (makes a SHORT RATE CANCELLATION).

SHORT TERM DISABILITY INCOME INSURANCE *see* DISABILITY INCOME INSURANCE.

SHORT TERM POLICY *see* SHORT RATE, SHORT TERM INSURANCE.

SHORT TERM REVERSIONARY TRUST financial instrument established irrevocably for a minimum of 10 years, after which the principal reverts to the grantor upon termination of the trust. A key feature is that earnings from the principal traditionally have been taxed at the beneficiary's tax rate instead of the presumably higher tax rate of the grantor. An example is the CLIFFORD TRUST commonly used to save for a child's college expenses. Another example is the funded irrevocable LIFE INSURANCE TRUST. Under a typical arrangement, a grandparent might establish such a trust to fund premiums for permanent insurance on the life of a son or daughter, with the grandchildren as beneficiaries. At termination of the trust, the grandchildren would have a fully paid policy on their parent's life and the trust assets would revert to the grandparent. Congress curtailed the tax advantages of short-term reversionary trusts in the *Tax Reform Act of 1969* and again in the TAX REFORM ACT OF 1986.

SICKNESS COVERAGE *see* HEALTH INSURANCE.

SICKNESS INSURANCE *see* HEALTH INSURANCE.

SIDETRACK AGREEMENT type of *hold-harmless agreement* made by a property owner as a condition for being served by a railroad spur. If the owner wants a special sidetrack, the railroad requires the owner to assume responsibility for certain losses for property damage or injury arising from use of the track, even if the railroad is at fault. Most common in these agreements is responsibility for loss due to fire.

SIDETRACK INSURANCE *see* SIDETRACK AGREEMENT.

SIGN FLOATER INSURANCE endorsement to a business property floater policy that covers neon signs for all perils, both while they are being moved and once they are in place. Signs that are attached to a building can be covered under the underlying property insurance. The sign floater policy provides broader coverage for each sign that is listed on the policy.

SIMPLE PROBABILITY *see* PROBABILITY.

SIMPLIFIED COMMERCIAL LINES PORTFOLIO POLICY (SCLP) policy that provides coverage through four parts:
1. *Commercial property*—coverage is provided under the BUILDING AND PERSONAL PROPERTY COVERAGE FORM (BPPCF), divided into three major categories: owned buildings, owned business personal property, and nonowned business personal property.
2. *Crime*—coverage is provided under the commercial crime program, which includes the following coverages: forgery; theft, disappearance, and destruction; employee dishonesty; safe robbery and burglary; burglary of the premises; computer fraud; extortion; and liability for the property of guests.
3. *Boiler and machinery*—coverage is provided according to four items of classification: electrical, turbine, mechanical, and pressure and refrigeration. Property covered in these four groups is that which is owned by the insured or is under the care, custody, or control of the insured.
4. *Liability*—coverage is provided for general liability, products and completed operations liability, medical payments, advertising and personal liability, and fire legal liability. Each of these categories has a separate limit of liability which is applicable. However, an annual AGGREGATE LIMIT of liability is applicable to the total of these categories except for the products and completed operations liability, which has a separate annual aggregate limit.

SIMPLIFIED EARNINGS FORM addition to a business property insurance policy to cover loss of earnings, subject to a monthly limit, in the event that property of an insured is destroyed and a business cannot continue. The property insurance policy pays only in the event that property of an insured is destroyed and a business cannot continue. The property insurance policy pays only for DIRECT LOSS of income-producing property. A building destroyed by fire represents a direct loss. Lost income resulting from the shutdown of a manufacturing facility housed in the burned building represents an INDIRECT LOSS that would be covered by BUSINESS INTERRUPTION INSURANCE, which is written on a number of separate forms.

SIMPLIFIED EMPLOYEE PENSION (SEP) employee INDIVIDUAL RETIREMENT ACCOUNT funded by an employer or a self-employed person. (Also known as SEP-IRA.) Differs from a pension plan in that contributions are immediately vested and employees have control of the investment of the SEP-IRA. IRS rules require that SEP-IRA contributions be made according to a written allocation formula. The maximum contribution is 15% of compensation or $30,000, whichever is less. Employees may elect to take cash instead of their SEP-IRA contribution but must pay income taxes on it. The TAX REFORM ACT OF 1986 also allows a SEP-IRA to be used as an alternative to a SECTION 401 (K) PLAN (SALARY REDUCTION PLAN) for an employer with 25 or fewer employees. The maximum annual contribution limit per employee for such salary-reduction SEP-IRAs is $7000.

SINE QUA NON RULE Latin phrase meaning "without which not," signifying a legal rule in TORT and NEGLIGENCE cases. Under this rule, a plaintiff trying to prove that an injury was a direct result of a negligent act by the defendant would have to establish that the injury would not have occurred without the negligent act.

SINGLE ANNUITANT (SINGLE LIFE ANNUITY) ANNUITY that continues income payments as long as the annuitant lives, ceasing upon the individual's death.

SINGLE INTEREST POLICY property insurance coverage for only one of the parties having an INSURABLE INTEREST in that property.

SINGLE LIFE ANNUITY *see* SINGLE ANNUITANT (SINGLE LIFE ANNUITY).

SINGLE LIMIT *see* COMBINED SINGLE LIMIT.

SINGLE PREMIUM LIFE INSURANCE coverage in which one premium payment is made and the policy is fully paid up with no further premiums required. *See also* LIMITED PAYMENT LIFE INSURANCE.

SINGLE RISK CARGO INSURANCE marine cargo coverage for a single shipment of goods. Also known as SPECIAL RISK INSURANCE and *trip cargo insurance*. Contrasts with *open policy cargo insurance* that covers all of a shipper's goods in transit.

SINKING FUND money set aside to pay for losses. Rather than buy insurance coverage for all potential losses, some businesses and individuals choose this form of SELF INSURANCE to cover all or a portion of certain losses.

SIR *see* SELF-INSURED RETENTION (SIR).

SISTERSHIP CLAUSE *see* SISTERSHIP EXCLUSION.

SISTERSHIP EXCLUSION part of the BUSINESS RISK EXCLUSION in GENERAL LIABILITY INSURANCE that denies coverage for subsequent claims if a defective product is not recalled by an insured. For example, if a consumer filed a damage suit against XYZ Co. claiming that he or she became sick while eating a can of soup from a particular lot that was contaminated, the insurer would not pay later claims filed by other consumers if the XYZ Co. did not recall that lot of the soup. The general liability insurance policy for businesses also excludes costs associated with the withdrawal of a product from the market whether it is ordered by a government agency or by company management. A business that wants coverage for product recall would need to buy PRODUCT RECALL INSURANCE to include the extra wages and other costs of identifying the faulty product, notifying consumers, correcting or repairing the product, and redistributing it.

SIZE *see* FACE AMOUNT (FACE OF POLICY).

SLANDER *see* TORT, INTENTIONAL.

SLIDING SCALE COMMISSION percentage that has an inverse relationship to the loss experience on the business brought in. For example, if a CEDING COMPANY laid off better risks that resulted in better and more profitable business for the reinsurer, it would get a higher commission.

SMALL LOSS PRINCIPLE statement regarding an insured's retention of low severity risks because they are not catastrophic, and can be absorbed without having a dramatic effect on the financial structure of a business or individual. Insurance purchased for small-loss coverage is, in effect, swapping dollars with the insurance company, since the premium charged reflects the individual's expected losses plus loadings for the insurance company's expenses, profit margin and contingencies. *See also* LARGE LOSS PRINCIPLE.

SMOKE CLAUSE provision in the EXTENDED COVERAGE ENDORSEMENT stating that smoke damage is covered when it results from the sudden, unusual and faulty operation of an on-premises cooking or heating unit, provided that it has been connected to the chimney by means of a vent.

SMOKE DAMAGE *see* SMOKE CLAUSE.

SMP *see* SPECIAL MULTIPERIL INSURANCE (SMP).

SNOWMOBILE COVERAGE *see* SNOWMOBILE FLOATER.

SNOWMOBILE FLOATER endorsement to a HOMEOWNERS INSURANCE POLICY or a PERSONAL AUTOMOBILE POLICY (PAP) that covers physical damage to a snowmobile wherever it happens to be. Coverage can be on *named peril* or ALL RISKS basis.

SNOWMOBILE INSURANCE *see* SNOWMOBILE FLOATER.

SOCIAL INSURANCE compulsory employee benefit plan under which participants are entitled to a series of benefits as a matter of right. The plan is administered by a Federal or state government agency and has as its objective the provision of a minimum standard of living for those in lower and middle wage groups. *See also* SOCIAL SECURITY ACT OF 1935.

SOCIAL SECURITY ACT OF 1935 Federal legislation that established the OLD AGE SURVIVORS, DISABILITY, AND HEALTH INSURANCE (OASDHI).

SOCIAL SECURITY ACT, TITLE XIX 1965 Federal law that provides for medical assistance to those who cannot afford to pay for it. Four categories of the needy can qualify: aged, blind, disabled, and families with dependent children. The MEDICAID program was enacted at the same time as MEDICARE.

SOCIAL SECURITY ADJUSTMENT OPTION choice an employee can make of receiving higher private pension benefits prior to eligibility for Social Security, and lower pension benefits thereafter. For example, employees taking early retirement may wish to receive higher-than-normal benefits in the months or years before their Social Security benefits begin. In exchange, they would have to accept reduced pension benefits once the Social Security payments started.

SOCIAL SECURITY FREEZE maintenance of Social Security benefits at current dollar or percentage levels. Social Security benefits are indexed to the Consumer Price Index and rise in tandem with the Index. A benefit freeze is one solution that legislators and regulators have proposed to cope with a troubled Social Security system, but many powerful lobbying groups oppose such a remedy.

SOCIAL SECURITY OFFSET reduction of private pension benefits to avoid "duplication" of Social Security benefits, according to a formula. Many pension plans "offset" or reduce monthly pension benefits by a percentage of the employee's monthly Social Security benefit. *See also* PENSION PLAN INTEGRATION WITH SOCIAL SECURITY.

SOCIETY OF ACTUARIES (SA) membership organization of individuals especially trained in the application of ACTUARIAL mathematics, including compound interest, annuities, life contingencies, measurement of mortality, probability, and statistics. The organization holds a series of actuarial examinations for prospective members seeking the designation of Fellow or Associate of the Society of Actuaries (FSA, ASA).

SOCIETY OF CHARTERED PROPERTY AND CASUALTY UNDERWRITERS membership organization of individuals especially trained in the application of property and casualty insurance to personal and business situations. Membership is achieved by passing a series of examinations administered by the American Institute for Property and Liability Underwriters, plus three years of industry experience. Successful completion of the examinations results in the designation of Chartered Property Casualty Underwriter (CPCU).

SOCIETY OF INSURANCE RESEARCH organization formed to encourage research in insurance and to foster an exchange of ideas and research methodology among the society members.

SOLE PROPRIETOR LIFE AND HEALTH INSURANCE coverage for the owner of a business. When a proprietor dies, debts of the business become the debts of the estate since in this circumstance the law recognizes business and personal assets as one. The executor is required to dispose of the business as quickly as possible. Life insurance can fund the disposition in several ways:
1. If the business is transferred through a will, the life insurance's death benefit can be applied to the deceased proprietor's personal and business debts and estate taxes.
2. If the executor conducts a forced sale or liquidation, a death benefit can be used to reduce or eliminate any debts. The death benefit can also be used as a source of working capital for interim financing to operate the business in the short run.
3. If the business is to be transferred to a child or employee, the death benefit can provide funds to effect the transfer.
4. If the business is to be sold to a key employee(s) through a buy-and-sell agreement, the key employee(s) usually has previously bought a life insurance policy on the sole proprietor and made all premium payments. The buy-and-sell agreement stipulates the formula to be used in valuing the business as well as other conditions

of the sale. Upon the death of the proprietor and the sale of the business to the key employee(s), the proprietor's estate receives the cash amount according to the buy-and-sell agreement and the key employee(s) receives the deceased proprietor's business.

SOLICITING AGENT *see* SOLICITOR (SOLICITING AGENT).

SOLICITING OFFER *see* SOLICITOR (SOLICITING AGENT).

SOLICITOR (SOLICITING AGENT) insurance salesperson who contacts potential customers and handles clerical responsibilities but has no authority to make insurance contracts. *See also* BINDER; GENERAL AGENT (GA).

SOLVENCY minimum standard of financial health for an insurance company, where assets exceed liabilities. State laws require insurance regulators to step in when solvency of an insurer is threatened and proceed with *rehabilitation* or *liquidation*.

SONIC BOOM LOSSES property damage resulting from aircraft traveling faster than the speed of sound. Although the vibrations caused by such high speed can cause damage, it is excluded on most property forms.

SOUND EQUIPMENT INSURANCE special endorsement to PERSONAL AUTOMOBILE POLICY (PAP) covering loss of records, tapes, and other sound equipment caused by an insured peril in an insured automobile.

SOURCES OF INCOME in insurance, company revenues from underwriting and investment. Insurance companies make money firstly, by underwriting good risks so that their premium dollars cover claims losses and expenses (the money left over being called underwriting income); and secondly, by investing premium dollars until claims have to be paid (called investment income), sometimes many years later. In the late 1970s, for example, casualty insurers lost money on underwriting but made up for the loss with a gain in investment income.

SOURCES OF SURPLUS cash carried forward from the previous year, plus gains from operations for the current year, plus any capital gains.

SOUTH-EASTERN UNDERWRITERS ASSOCIATION (SEUA) CASE important 1944 U.S. Supreme Court ruling that the insurance business constituted interstate commerce and was thus subject to the SHERMAN ANTITRUST ACT. This decision came in *U.S.* v. *South-Eastern Underwriters Association,* a price-fixing case, brought against a fire insurance rate-making group by the U.S. Attorney General, at the urging of the state of Missouri. SEUA relied for its defense on the 1869 PAUL V. VIRGINIA decision by the Supreme Court that insurance activities were not commerce and the Sherman Act did not apply. The high court subsequently accepted the argument that the industry was subject to the antitrust law. In response, Congress passed the MCCARRAN-FERGUSON ACT (PUBLIC LAW 15) in 1945, in effect overruling the court by stating affirmatively that regulation of insurance was the job of the states, not the Federal government. The law exempted insurance from Federal antitrust rules if it was covered by state regulation.

SPECIAL ACCEPTANCE extension of a REINSURANCE treaty to include a risk that was not originally in its terms.

SPECIAL AGENT individual who sells and services life insurance in an exclusive territory; in property and casualty insurance, an individual who represents a property and casualty insurance company as a marketing representative.

SPECIAL BUILDING FORM endorsement to the SPECIAL MULTIPERIL INSURANCE (SMP) policy that provides ALL RISKS damage coverage for real property. This special form provides only minimum cover, leaving the option for adding forms to the policyholder. The policyholder has a choice of the general building form, which provides named peril coverage, or the special building form for the broader all-risks coverage.

SPECIAL CHARGE any fee imposed on insurance companies by a state. Insurers pay special taxes, including premium taxes and franchise taxes. In addition, various states have their own special charges to cover costs of such things as maintaining fire departments, licensing agents, or filing reports.

SPECIAL DAMAGES *see* LIABILITY, CIVIL DAMAGES AWARDED.

SPECIAL EXTENDED COVERAGE endorsement to a property insurance policy providing ALL RISKS coverage for insured property. Excluded properties include residences, farms, and manufacturing properties. This endorsement is generally used for property that does not qualify for a packaged form such as the standard multiperil policy.

SPECIAL FORM *see* SPECIAL PERSONAL PROPERTY FORM.

SPECIAL INSURANCE POLICIES *see* SPECIAL RISK INSURANCE.

SPECIAL MORTALITY TABLE one used to determine the life expectancy of ANNUITANTS. Annuity buyers are not representative of the population as a whole, or of life insurance buyers. Because annuities pay an income for life, only those in good health, and who expect to live a long time, will spend their money for an annuity contract. Recognizing this, life insurers, who sell annuity contracts, use special mortality tables, which chiefly consider age and sex, to predict their deaths. For example, if a 50-year-old applicant purchases an IMMEDIATE ANNUITY for life with $100,000, his income would be less than that for a 70-year-old. Likewise, because women have longer life expectancies, their monthly income payments would be lower than men the same age.

SPECIAL MULTIPERIL INSURANCE (SMP) coverage usually provided for large businesses in four areas:

1. *Section I (Property)*—The building(s) and contents are either covered against any peril (ALL RISKS basis), or only perils listed in Section I. It is to the advantage of the business to have coverage written on an ALL RISKS basis.

   Endorsements can be added for sprinkler leakage, business interruption, extra expense, water damage, rental loss, valuable records and papers, mercantile robbery and safe burglary, mercantile open stock burglary, glass and fine arts, or these items can be covered separately.

2. *Section II (Liability)*—The insured is covered for actions or nonactions which result in liability exposure arising out of ownership, use, possession and/or maintenance of the covered locations and structures. Also covered are the business's activities conducted by the insured whether at or from the covered locations and structures. Endorsements can be added to cover for medical payments, liability arising out of products and completed operations, and liability arising out of operation of a non-owned automobile. Additional endorsements can be added to this section to broaden liability coverage.

3. *Section III (Crime)*—Coverage for employee dishonesty, premises loss both inside and outside of the structure, forgery by depositions, paper currency which proves to be counterfeit, and money orders. The comprehensive DISHONESTY, DISAPPEARANCE, AND DESTRUCTION POLICY ("3-D" POLICY) and the BLANKET CRIME POLICY provide these coverages.

4. *Section IV (Boiler and Machinery)*—Coverage for explosion of a boiler, engine, turbines, and/or pipes owned or under the control of the insured. Endorsements can be added to cover indirect and consequential losses resulting from accidents associated with the boiler and machinery expenses.

SPECIAL PERSONAL PROPERTY FORM endorsement to the SPECIAL MULTIPERIL INSURANCE (SMP) policy that provides ALL RISKS damage coverage for personal property. There are special limitations on amounts of coverage for furs, jewelry, precious stones and metals, patterns and dies, and stamps, tickets and letters of credit. Certain electronic equipment and fragile materials are only covered for specific perils.

SPECIAL RISK INSURANCE transfer of highly individualized loss exposures that is not based on the usual pooling principles of insurance such as *risk identification* and *classification selection*. Rather than setting up an insurance pool of standard risks, the underwriter accepts responsibility for a unique or special risk. Some examples would be insurance by LLOYD'S OF LONDON underwriters for athletes, artists, and entertainers; insurance on Betty Grable's legs; or insurance for dangerous scientific experiments or moon travel.

SPECIFIC COVERAGE *see* SPECIFIC INSURANCE.

SPECIFIC EXCESS CONTRACT policy in which an insurer agrees to pay property or liability losses in excess of a specific amount per occurrence. For example, this type of coverage typically is used by an employer that self insures its workers compensation but wants to limit the loss per accident to, say, $40,000. Contrasts with *stop loss aggregate contract* that pays for total losses above a certain amount during the year.

SPECIFIC EXCESS REINSURANCE EXCESS OF LOSS REINSURANCE written on a FACULTATIVE REINSURANCE basis to provide cover for a particular PRIMARY INSURANCE policy.

SPECIFIC INSURANCE single insurance policy for only one kind of property at only one location of an insured. For example, property insurance on a rare piano in the insured's home would cover only that piano, not any other property of the insured.

SPECIFIC LIMIT maximum limit of LIABILITY of an insurance company for a particular claim or kind of loss which is applicable in general to all such claims or losses. This maximum limit of liability is usually less than the POLICY LIMIT of liability.

SPECIFIC RATE property insurance premium rate which is applicable to a single, particular piece of property.

SPECIFIC REINSURANCE *see* FACULTATIVE REINSURANCE.

SPECIFIED DISEASE POLICY *see* DREAD DISEASE INSURANCE.

SPECIFIED PERIL INSURANCE policy covering loss only for a named peril in the policy. For example, the *Standard Fire Policy* covers only the two named perils of fire and lightning. Other perils can be added by endorsement, such as theft, vandalism, malicious mischief, and burglary.

SPECULATIVE *see* SPECULATIVE RISK.

SPECULATIVE RISK uncertain prospect of financial gain or loss. A business investment that could either return a profit or sustain a loss, such as the purchase of a common stock, is an example of a speculative risk. In most instances, speculative risks are not insurable. *See also* PURE RISK; STANDARD RISK.

SPELL OF ILLNESS period of time, an insured is sick and entitled to receive health insurance benefits. *See also* DISABILITY INCOME INSURANCE, GROUP HEALTH INSURANCE.

SPENDTHRIFT TRUST *see* SPENDTHRIFT TRUST CLAUSE.

SPENDTHRIFT TRUST CLAUSE provision in a life insurance policy which protects its proceeds from the beneficiary's creditors. On payment, the beneficiary loses the protection of the spendthrift trust clause and the beneficiary's creditors can then bring suit to attach the proceeds.

SPLIT DEDUCTIBLE deductible applicable to each loss so that the amount of each loss retained by the insured varies according to the PERIL which caused the loss. For example, the split deductible in a policy may specify that the insured must retain the first $300 of any fire loss and $100 of any vandalism and malicious mischief loss.

SPLIT DOLLAR LIFE INSURANCE policy in which premiums, ownership rights, and death proceeds are split between an employer and an employee, or between a parent and a child. The employer pays the part of each year's premium that at least equals the increase in the *cash value*. The employee may pay the remainder of the premium, or the employer may pay the entire premium. When the increase in cash value equals or exceeds the yearly premium, the employer pays the entire premium. If the employee dies while in the service of the employer, a beneficiary chosen by the employee receives the difference between the face value and the amount paid to the employer (the cash value or the total of all premiums paid by the employer—whichever is greater). Thus, during employment, the employee's share of the death benefit decreases. If the employee leaves the employer, the latter has the option of surrendering the policy in exchange for return of all premiums, or selling the policy to the employee for the amount of its cash value. There are two types of split dollar life insurance policies: (1) *Endorsement*—the employer owns all policy privileges; the employee's only rights are to choose beneficiaries and to select the manner in which the death benefit is paid. (2) *Collateral*—the employee owns the policy. The employer's contributions toward the premiums are viewed as a series of interest-free loans, which equal the yearly increase in the cash value of the policy. The employee *assigns* the policy to the employer as collateral for these loans. When the employee dies, the loans are paid from the face value of the policy. Any remaining proceeds are paid to the beneficiary.

SPLIT FUNDED PLAN retirement arrangement in which contributions are divided between *allocated* (insured) and *unallocated funding instruments* (an uninsured plan). It seeks to combine the advantages of guarantees-of-income of the allocated funding instrument with the investment flexibility (and possible higher *yields*) of an unallocated funding instrument. For example, 60% of contributions could be placed in a RETIREMENT INCOME POLICY (or other permanent life insurance policy) and 40% in a DEPOSIT ADMINISTRATION PLAN (or other fund held and invested by a trustee).

SPLIT FUNDING *see* SPLIT FUNDED PLAN.

SPLIT LIMIT *see* SPLIT LIMITS COVERAGE.

SPLIT LIMITS COVERAGE technique for expressing limits of liability coverage under a particular insurance policy, stating separate limits for different types of claims growing out of a single event or combination of events. Coverage may be split (limited) per person, per occurrence, between bodily injury and property damage, or in other ways. Property damage liability is listed with a limit per accident. For example, a policy with split limits quoted as $100,000/$300,000/$25,000 would provide a maximum of $100,000 bodily injury coverage per person, $300,000 total bodily injury coverage per accident, and $25,000 total property damage liability coverage per accident.

SPOUSE'S BENEFIT insured sum paid regularly to a married partner (usually a wife but sometimes a husband) of a retired worker. There are several forms:
1. the Federal Retirement Equity Act mandates a spouse's benefit payable out of a husband's pension, unless cancelled under specified conditions.
2. under Social Security, a spouse receives a benefit upon reaching age 65, whether or not she has earned Social Security credits.
3. some business firms provide for a spouse's benefit at the death of a retired worker, usually a percentage of the deceased worker's last highest salary, funded out of his pension.
4. a joint and survivor annuity can provide a spouse's benefit. For example a joint and two-thirds annuity gives the couple an income for as long as both are alive, and when one dies the survivor receives two-thirds of the amount they had been getting.

SPREAD LOSS *see* CARPENTER PLAN (SPREAD LOSS COVER, SPREAD LOSS REINSURANCE).

SPREAD LOSS COVER *see* CARPENTER PLAN (SPREAD LOSS COVER, SPREAD LOSS REINSURANCE).

SPREAD LOSS REINSURANCE *see* CARPENTER PLAN (SPREAD LOSS COVER, SPREAD LOSS REINSURANCE).

SPREAD ON INTEREST-BEARING FUNDS difference between the yield on earning assets and the cost of interest-bearing liabilities.

SPREADSHEET risk management tool to determine risk exposure and to help spread the risk. A risk manager considers a business firm's individual exposures separately. As the number of exposures increases, the threat that all units will suffer loss decreases, and the manager is able to spread the risk.

SPRINKLER DAMAGE INSURANCE *see* SPRINKLER LEAKAGE INSURANCE; SPRINKLER LEAKAGE LEGAL LIABILITY INSURANCE.

SPRINKLER LEAKAGE INSURANCE coverage for property damage caused by untimely discharge from an automatic sprinkler system. This coverage, available through an endorsement to the *Standard Fire Policy,* typically excludes losses from fire, lightning, windstorm, earthquake, explosion, rupture of steam boiler, riot, civil commotion, and order of civil authority.

SPRINKLER LEAKAGE LEGAL LIABILITY INSURANCE coverage for liability for damage to property of others from untimely discharge of fire-fighting sprinkler systems. This coverage is available as an endorsement to broad-form COMPREHENSIVE GENERAL LIABILITY INSURANCE (CGL).

STACKING circumstance under which the insured maintains that, if an insurance policy covers at least two scheduled items of real or personal property, in the event of a loss applicable coverage should be twice the stated limit in the policy. In an effort to avoid the stacking issue, automobile policies include a stipulation that the limit of liability stated in the DECLARATIONS SECTION is the maximum amount the INSURER will pay for all damages resulting from one accident, regardless of the number of insureds, claims made, vehicles, or premiums stated in the declarations section, or vehicles involved in an accident.

STAFF ADJUSTER *see* ADJUSTER.

STAFF UNDERWRITER *see* UNDERWRITER, LAY.

STAMP AND COIN COLLECTIONS INSURANCE coverage on an ALL RISKS basis at any location for stamp and coin collections, excluding wear and tear, war, nuclear disaster, and mysterious disappearance. Usually each item is specifically listed and valued in the policy. This insurance is of particular importance for insureds with valuable stamp and coin collections. Standard property insurance policies such as the HOMEOWNERS INSURANCE POLICY have a relatively low limit of coverage of specialty items such as stamp and coin collections.

STAMP AND COIN DEALERS INSURANCE coverage on an ALL RISKS basis, subject to exclusions of war, wear and tear, loss resulting from delay, loss of market, infidelity of the insured's employee, loss due to rain, sleet, snow or flood, except while the stamps or coins are in transit. This is a special INLAND MARINE insurance coverage designed specifically for dealers.

STANDARD DEVIATION OR VARIATION statistic indicating the degree of dispersion in a set of outcomes, computed as the *arithmetic mean* of the differences between each outcome and the average of all outcomes in the set.

STANDARD FIRE POLICY *see* FIRE INSURANCE—STANDARD FIRE POLICY.

STANDARD FIRE POLICY ANALYSIS method of rating that compares property to be insured to a standard and adjusts the rate for deviations from the standard. A standard building is situated in a standard city of specific construction with specified fire protection. Other risks are compared to the standard and given credits or debits if they are a better or worse risk.

STANDARD FORM approved or accepted policy for a particular type of risk. The only type of risk covered by a standard form mandated by law is the fire policy. In 1886, New York adopted a standard fire form and that has since been revised and adopted by every other state. In other types of coverage, states may prescribe mandatory or optional minimums or may forbid certain provisions. Therefore, while life and health benefits may vary widely, for example, policyholders are given certain uniform rights like grace periods for paying premiums. In other areas, insurers have voluntarily adopted standard forms. One example is the standard automobile policy. Other types of coverage are offered on standard forms developed by rating bureaus such as the INSURANCE SERVICES OFFICE (ISO). Although insurers may use these forms, they are not obligated to do so, and many develop their own forms.

STANDARD GROUP *see* STANDARD RISK.

STANDARD INSURANCE CONTRACT PROVISION *see* STANDARD PROVISIONS, LIFE INSURANCE; STANDARD PROVISIONS, PROPERTY AND CASUALTY INSURANCE.

STANDARD LIMIT *see* BASIC LIMITS OF LIABILITY.

STANDARD MORTGAGE CLAUSE *see* MORTGAGEE CLAUSE.

STANDARD POLICY *see* STANDARD FORM; STANDARD PROVISIONS, LIFE INSURANCE; STANDARD PROVISIONS, PROPERTY AND CASUALTY INSURANCE.

STANDARD PREMIUM *see* BASIC PREMIUM.

STANDARD PROVISIONS, LIFE INSURANCE elements common to all life insurance policies. While state insurance laws do not prescribe the exact words which must be in a life insurance policy, certain standard provisions must be included to provide specified basic benefits for an insured, who cannot be charged extra for them. Additional benefits can be provided, if the insurance company desires. Standard provisions include the BENEFICIARY; GRACE PERIOD; INCONTESTABLE CLAUSE; NONFORFEITURE (CASH SURRENDER BENEFIT, REDUCED PAID-UP BENEFIT, EXTENDED TERM BENEFIT); POLICY LOAN; REINSTATEMENT; SUICIDE CLAUSE; WAR EXCLUSION CLAUSE.

STANDARD PROVISIONS, PROPERTY AND CASUALTY INSURANCE sections with standard wording common to all property and casualty insurance contracts: CONDITIONS, DECLARATIONS, EXCLUSIONS, INSURING AGREEMENT. *See also* PROPERTY AND CASUALTY INSURANCE PROVISIONS.

STANDARD RISK one that is regarded by underwriters as normal and insurable at standard rates. Other classifications of risks are given credits or debits based on their deviation from the standard.

STANDARD WORKERS COMPENSATION INSURANCE *see* WORKERS COMPENSATION INSURANCE.

STANDING TIMBER INSURANCE coverage against only two perils, fire and lightning. The amount of coverage is per acre of standing timber for either merchantable trees (living trees with no decay, and minimum diameter), or for trees used in reforestation. This coverage is commonly purchased by tree farmers and investors. Historically, because of tax write-offs, investing in tree farms has been particularly popular among certain investors. With the passage of the TAX REFORM ACT OF 1986 such a tax shelter is no longer possible, but the reason for purchasing timber insurance for protection remains unchanged.

STARE DECISIS Latin phrase meaning "to stand by the decisions." This legal doctrine under common law requires courts to rely on precedents, or previous decisions, when deciding disputes unless there is a compelling reason to reject those precedents. In most instances, this doctrine means that courts will decide disputes over insurance contracts the same way they have decided cases with similar facts and legal issues in the past.

STATE AGENT insurance salesperson who markets and services policies in one or more states and holds a supervisory position. *See also* SPECIAL AGENT.

STATE ASSOCIATIONS OF INSURANCE AGENTS *see* INDE-PENDENT INSURANCE AGENTS OF AMERICA (IIAA); NATIONAL ASSOCIA-TION OF LIFE UNDERWRITERS (NALU); PROFESSIONAL INSURANCE AGENTS (PIA).

STATED AMOUNT ENDORSEMENT addition to a property policy providing coverage for a specified amount. This endorsement is typically used for an unusual or valuable piece of property that does not fit standard descriptions and, instead of declining, retains its value. For example, a classic Austin Healey 3000 Mark IV might be covered by this type of endorsement to a PERSONAL AUTOMOBILE POLICY (PAP).

STATE DISABILITY PLAN account established and administered by a state agency to finance a mandatory state insurance program for job-related injuries or to finance a nonjob related injuries insurance program on a state-wide basis. *See also* WORKERS COMPENSATION INSURANCE.

STATE EXEMPTION STATUTE laws in most cases protecting life insurance policies from an insured's creditors. These laws typically exempt death benefit proceeds and policy cash values from attachment by creditors, particularly if the beneficiary is a spouse or child of the insured. Many exemption laws have limits, with all insurance proceeds over a certain amount, say $20,000, available to the insured's creditors. In some states, *endowment* and ANNUITY policies are granted less protection from creditors than ORDINARY LIFE INSURANCE because such policies are often used as investment vehicles. *See also* LIFE INSURANCE, CREDITOR RIGHTS.

STATE FUND account established and administered by a state agency to finance a mandatory insurance program, for example, WORKERS COMPENSATION INSURANCE.

STATE GOVERNMENT INSURANCE health insurance coverage offered by some states for medical expenses and loss of income from nonoccupational disability. The merits of Federal health insurance have been debated for some time. In the meantime, several states have passed plans that may be used as a testing ground for a more comprehensive plan. For example, Rhode Island pays for out-of-pocket expenses that total more than $5000 or a certain percentage of income. Other states have passed similar laws, including Georgia, Maine, Minnesota, and Connecticut.

STATE INSURANCE DEPARTMENT *see* INSURANCE DEPARTMENT.

STATE LIFE FUND *see* WISCONSIN STATE LIFE FUND.

STATEMENT BLANK *see* ANNUAL STATEMENT.

STATEMENT (INSURANCE COMPANY TO INSURED) annual report to policyholders of certain CASH VALUE LIFE INSURANCE products and annuities to inform them of the value of the investment portion of their contracts. Buyers of whole life insurance can be said to purchase both an insurance product and a tax-deferred savings vehicle. If the insurance is terminated, the policyholder is entitled to the cash value buildup. In addition, newer forms of these policies, such as UNIVERSAL LIFE INSURANCE, *variable annuities* and VARIABLE LIFE INSURANCE offer policyholders a choice of investments rather than a guaranteed return. A statement informs the insured of the annual cash buildup and the performance of the investment portion.

STATEMENT OF OPINION (ACCOUNTANTS REPORT, AUDITORS REPORT) statement by an auditor or certified public accountant indicating if a company's financial statements fairly present its true financial condition. A statement of opinion may be unqualified, qualified, or adverse. An unqualified or ''clean'' opinion indicates no exceptions or qualifications were found by the auditor. A qualified report means the statement makes a fair presentation of a firm's financial condition except for some important uncertainties with effects that cannot be determined by the auditor. In the case of an insurance company, an example of an important uncertainty that might lead to a qualified opinion would be the outcome of litigation over a major disputed claim. An adverse opinion means the auditor is unwilling to vouch for the financial statements presented by the company.

STATE MUTUAL assessment mutual company that operates on a statewide basis or in more than one state. *See also* ASSESSABLE MUTUAL.

STATE RATE standard property/casualty insurance premium set by a state rating bureau. States have responsibility for regulating insurers and making certain that rates are reasonable. To this end, experience information is gathered by rating bureaus and standard, or advisory, rates are set for various lines of insurance in that state. The rates are simply for guidance and individual companies may charge more or less as long as their rates are approved by the state commissioner. The bureau may represent the companies that write a particular line of insurance in that state, such as *workers compensation,* and may request rate increases from the state commissioner on behalf of its members.

STATE RATE SHEET *see* STATE RATE.

STATE SAVINGS GUARANTEE CORPORATION state-sponsored insurance fund that was intended to guarantee deposits at state-chartered savings institutions. A handful of these funds existed in the early 1980s, but after a string of savings and loan failures in Maryland and Ohio in 1985, these funds were phased out and the member savings institutions converted to Federal Deposit Insurance.

STATE SUPERVISION AND REGULATION primary responsibility for overseeing the insurance industry that has rested with individual states since 1945, after Congress passed the MCCARRAN-FERGUSON ACT (PUBLIC LAW 15). In addition to supervision and regulation, states receive taxes and fees paid by the industry that amount to several billion dollars a year. State insurance laws are administered by state insurance departments that are responsible for making certain that (1) rates are adequate, not unfairly discriminatory, and not unreasonably high, and (2) insurance companies in the state are financially sound and able to pay future claims.

To this end, states set requirements for company reserves, require annual financial statements, and examine company books. Each state has an insurance commissioner or superintendent who is either elected or appointed by the governor, with responsibility for investigating company practices, approving rates and policy forms and ordering liquidation of insolvent insurers. The NATIONAL ASSOCIATION OF INSURANCE COMMISSIONERS (NAIC) has drafted model legislation and worked for policy uniformity, but regulations vary widely from state to state.

Whether insurers should be regulated by the states or the Federal government remains at issue, but so far insurers and the NAIC lobbying have been effective in resisting Federal regulation. Nevertheless, the Federal government has a profound effect in the insurance industry through its taxes and a variety of regulations. *See also* STATE TAXATION OF INSURANCE.

STATE TAXATION OF INSURANCE authority of states to tax the insurance companies they regulate. States levy income taxes, real and personal property taxes, and special levies, the most important of which is a premium tax—in effect, a sales tax on premiums. Although it is generally 2% of premiums, some states tax as much as 4%. Insurers also pay franchise taxes, licensing fees, and SPECIAL CHARGES. Insurance taxes are an important source of revenue for the states, amounting to several billion dollars a year. *See also* FEDERAL TAXATION.

STATIC RISK damage or destruction of property and/or property that is illegally transferred as the result of misconduct of individuals. The risk is insurable.

STATISTICS collection of numbers to record and analyze data such as occurrences of events and particular characteristics. Statistics are absolutely vital to all elements of insurance. In life and health insurance, they are used to tabulate age, sex, disability, cause of death, occupation, and other data needed to construct a MORBIDITY TABLE and MORTALITY TABLE, which in turn figure importantly in calculating premiums. Similarly, in property and casualty insurance statistics are used to record losses and injuries to help predict their future occurrence in order to calculate premiums.

STATUTE OF LIMITATIONS period, set by law, after which a damage claim cannot be made. Limits are set by individual states and usually range from one to seven years.

STATUTORY ACCOUNTING rules that insurance companies must follow in filing an annual financial statement known as the *convention blank,* with state insurance departments. The reported financial condition of an insurance company can differ markedly depending on whether statutory accounting rules or GENERALLY ACCEPTED ACCOUNTING PRINCIPLES (GAAP) are used in preparing financial statements. In general, statutory accounting is more conservative than GAAP because it tends to overstate expenses and liabilities while understating income and assets.

STATUTORY BONDS any of a number of types of SURETY BONDS that the law requires of government contractors, licensed businesses, litigants, fiduciaries, government officials, and others whose performance of some duty or obligation must be assured in the public interest. *See also* APPEAL BOND; BAIL BOND; BID BOND; COMPLETION BOND; CONTRACT BOND; FEDERAL OFFICIALS BOND; JUDICIAL BOND; LICENSE BOND; LOST INSTRUMENT BOND; PERFORMANCE BOND; PERMIT BOND; SECURITIES BOND; TRUSTEE ROLE; PENSION PLANS.

STATUTORY EARNINGS revenue based on conservative reserve requirements of various states. Statutory earnings do not meet GENERALLY ACCEPTED ACCOUNTING PRINCIPLES (GAAP). A role of state regulation is to make certain that insurers have enough money set aside in STATUTORY RESERVES to pay all future claims and that the company will remain solvent. For this reason, regulators take a conservative approach to setting reserve requirements. But because an increase in reserves translates into lower earnings for a stock insurer, investors and securities analysts argue that they are not helpful in gauging the health of a company for investment purposes. Therefore, insurers calculate statutory earnings for regulators and another set of earnings, based on natural reserves, for investors.

STATUTORY LAW *see* STATUTORY LIABILITY.

STATUTORY LIABILITY *see* ANNUAL STATEMENT; FULL PRELIMINARY TERM RESERVE PLAN; LIABILITIES: LIFE INSURANCE COMPANIES; PROSPECTIVE RESERVE; RETROSPECTIVE METHOD RESERVE COMPUTATION; STATUTORY ACCOUNTING; STATUTORY REQUIREMENTS; STATUTORY RESERVES.

STATUTORY PROVISIONS *see* STANDARD PROVISIONS, PROPERTY AND CASUALTY INSURANCE.

STATUTORY REQUIREMENTS standards set by the various state regulatory authorities that determine how financial statements must be prepared for regulators. The states are responsible for making certain that insurers will remain solvent and have enough set aside in reserves to pay future claims. To this end, they have devised STATUTORY ACCOUNTING principles that govern insurance company reporting. These requirements differ from GENERALLY ACCEPTED ACCOUNTING PRINCIPLES (GAAP). Among other things, statutory requirements include the setting of STATUTORY RESERVES, and the immediate expensing of the cost of acquiring new business, rather than allowing insurers to spread the exposure over the life of the policy. *See also* STATE SUPERVISION AND REGULATION.

STATUTORY RESERVES reserves required by state regulators. Because regulators must assure that an insurance company remains solvent and that it can pay future claims, they set conservative standards for insurer reserves. Regulators have various formulas for valuing reserves, such as the LOSS FREQUENCY METHOD and the *Commissioners Reserve Valuation Method.*

STATUTORY RESTRICTION limitation imposed on insurance companies by state law. States oversee the insurance industry, among other things, being responsible for making certain that the rates are fair, reasonable, and adequate, and that the companies that write insurance in the state are financially sound and able to pay future claims. To this end, the states restrict the types of investments insurance companies can make with their premium dollars and they control insurers' relationships with insureds by guaranteeing certain minimum rights to insureds.

STATUTORY UNDERWRITING PROFIT OR LOSS difference between the EARNED PREMIUMS and the losses and expenses of an insurance company. *See also* STATUTORY EARNINGS; STATUTORY REQUIREMENTS; STATUTORY RESERVES.

STEVEDORES LEGAL LIABILITY INSURANCE liability coverage for dockworkers for damage to property in transit while in their care.

STIPULATED PREMIUM COMPANY *see* STIPULATED PREMIUM INSURANCE.

STIPULATED PREMIUM INSURANCE a form of ASSESSMENT INSURANCE for which a regular premium is charged. In addition to paying the regular stipulated premium, an insured and other members of a mutual ASSESSMENT COMPANY may be subject to an additional assessment premium to make up for underwriting losses.

STOCK *see* STOCK INSURANCE COMPANY.

STOCK COMPANY INSURANCE insurance sold by a stock insurance company which is usually in the form of NONPARTICIPATING INSURANCE.

STOCKING A MUTUAL *see* DEMUTUALIZATION (STOCKING A MUTUAL).

STOCK INSURANCE COMPANY business owned by stockholders, as contrasted to a MUTUAL INSURANCE COMPANY that is owned by its policyholders. Many major life insurers are mutual companies whereas some leading *property/casualty* and *multiline* insurers are stock insurance companies. *See also* DEMUTUALIZATION (STOCKING A MUTUAL).

STOCK INSURER *see* STOCK INSURANCE COMPANY.

STOCK PROCESSING INSURANCE coverage in the event that stock sent to others for processing is damaged or destroyed en route or at their premises except those perils specifically excluded. For example, this coverage can be used when processing milk into cheese since the farmer would lose everything if the milk were damaged or destroyed en route or at the processor's premises.

STOCK REDEMPTION PLAN *see* CLOSE CORPORATION PLAN.

STOP LOSS *see* STOP LOSS REINSURANCE.

STOP LOSS AGGREGATE CONTRACT *see* STOP LOSS REINSURANCE.

STOP LOSS PROVISION *see* STOP LOSS REINSURANCE.

STOP LOSS REINSURANCE protects a *cedent* against an aggregate amount of claims over a period, in excess of a specified percentage of the earned premium income. Stop loss reinsurance does not cover individual claims. The *reinsurer's* liability is limited to a stipulated percentage of the loss and/or a maximum dollar amount. The stop loss method protects the cedent against the possibility that the aggregate value of an accumulation of small losses will exceed a specified percentage of earned premium income of a particular class. Stop loss reinsurance is the exact opposite of the QUOTA SHARE REINSURANCE and SURPLUS REINSURANCE, and differs considerably from other forms of EXCESS OF LOSS REINSURANCE. For example, a reinsurer can provide a cedent with 50% of the amount by which aggregate incurred losses of the cedent in any year exceed 70% of the cedent's earned premium income during that year.

STOREKEEPERS BURGLARY AND ROBBERY INSURANCE coverage for small mercantile establishments on a package basis. Combines six layers of protection: burglary of a safe; damage caused by robbery and burglary, whether actual or attempted; robbery of a guard and burglary of the business's merchandise; robbery inside or outside the premises of the business; kidnapping to physically force a businessowner and/or his/her representative(s) to open the premises of the business from the outside; and theft of securities and monies either from the home of a messenger of the business and/or from a night depository of a bank.

STOREKEEPERS LIABILITY INSURANCE coverage for bodily injury and property damage liability resulting from ownership, use, and/or maintenance of the insured business's premises, completed operations and products. Covers medical payment expenses associated with bodily inury to another party when an accident causes hazardous conditions on the business's premises or within the business's operation. Also covers costs in defending the insured against liability suits, even if the suits are without foundation.

STORM INSURANCE (WINDSTORM INSURANCE) additional coverage to a property policy. Windstorms are not one of the standard covered perils. If an insured desires coverage for windstorms and hail, it requires an endorsement.

STRAIGHT DEDUCTIBLE CLAUSE section of a policy that specifies the dollar amount or percentage of any loss that the insurance does not pay. Most property and medical policies specify that the first portion of any loss is absorbed by the insured. A straight deductible clause, which is common in auto and homeowners insurance, might provide for a deductible stated in a dollar amount, such as $500. For example, the Smiths have a homeowners policy with a $500 straight deductible clause. Fire damage to the home amounts to $1500. Under the terms of the policy, the Smiths would pay the first $500 and the insurance company would reimburse them for $1000. Some straight deductibles are expressed as a specific percentage of value rather than a dollar amount. For example, the insured might absorb the loss for 5% of the value of property that is totally destroyed. *See also* DISAPPEARING DEDUCTIBLE.

STRAIGHT LIFE ANNUITY *see* ANNUITY; ANNUITY DUE; LIFE ANNUITY; CERTAIN; PURE ANNUITY; REFUND ANNUITY.

STRAIGHT LIFE INSURANCE *see* ORDINARY LIFE INSURANCE.

STRAIGHT LINE RULE method of depreciating an asset in which its useful life is divided into an appropriate number of years (or other periods), the final salvage value is deducted, and the asset is written off in an equal portion for each period. Depreciation is a business expense for tax purposes. Straight line depreciation is the simplest method, but is not as advantageous to an owner as ACCELERATED DEPRECIATION, which allows a company to recover its costs more quickly.

STRATIFICATION OF LOSSES technique of breaking down the various losses as a whole into useful components called *subsets (strata)* so that no subset is overrepresented. The result is the classification of losses according to dollar amount in order to predict the probabilities of various degrees of loss severity so that the organization can adopt the proper RISK MANAGEMENT techniques. *See also* RATE MAKING.

STRATIFIED RANDOM SAMPLING selection of restricted random samples in order to obtain a more accurate estimate of the EXPECTED LOSS (mean) than could be obtained by the selection of completely RANDOM SAMPLES. For example, assume it is the desire to obtain an accurate estimate of the average number of automobile accidents experienced by juniors in the Louisiana State University System. By selecting proper size random samples among the various colleges within the system, a more accurate estimate of the number of automobile accidents experienced by juniors system-wide can be obtained than by selecting the same total random sample from the system as a whole.

STREET CLOCK FLOATER endorsement to a *scheduled property floater* that provides ALL RISKS protection for street clocks. Clocks and signs attached to business property can be covered under the *Standard Fire Policy*. But a street clock floater provides broader coverage and protects the owner of the clock both in transit and wherever it is located. Each clock and its value must be listed on the schedule.

STRICT LIABILITY tort liability, which is defined by law, requiring an injured party to prove only that he or she was harmed in a specified way in order to collect damages. For example, the law provides that an employer is responsible if a worker is injured on the job. All the worker must do to collect WORKERS COMPENSATION BENEFITS is to prove that the injury took place at work. *See also* ABSOLUTE LIABILITY.

STRIKE INSURANCE coverage to protect employers from losses due to labor disruptions. The *ocean marine policy* exempts losses caused by strikes, riots, and civil commotion. Special coverage is necessary.

STRIKES, RIOTS, AND CIVIL COMMOTION CLAUSE exemption in *ocean marine policy* for losses caused by strikes, riots, and civil commotion. *See also* RIOT AND CIVIL COMMOTION INSURANCE; RIOT EXCLUSION; STRIKE INSURANCE.

STRIKE-THROUGH CLAUSE (CUT-THROUGH CLAUSE) provision that holds a reinsurer liable for its share of losses even if the CEDING

COMPANY becomes insolvent before paying these losses. For example, XYZ Insurance Co. writes a fire policy for Acme Manufacturing and then reinsures 80% of the risk with ABC Reinsurance. XYZ is declared insolvent. Then Acme Manufacturing burns to the ground. ABC Reinsurance would be responsible for the 80% of the risk it reinsured and would pay the claim directly to Acme.

STRUCTURED SETTLEMENT periodic payments to an injured person or survivor for a determinable number of years or for life typically in settlement of a claim under a liability policy. Terms may include immediate reimbursement for medical and legal expenses and rehabilitation, and long-term payments for loss of income or as compensation for other injuries. A structured settlement can be expected to be less costly to the insurance carrier than a LUMP SUM settlement, especially if it enables costly litigation to be avoided.

SUBJECTIVE PROBABILITY projections of losses based on qualitative (emotional) rather than quantitative reasoning.

SUBJECTIVE RISK *see* SUBJECTIVE PROBABILITY.

SUBJECT PREMIUM *see* BASE PREMIUM.

SUBLIMITS *see* BROAD FORM PERSONAL THEFT INSURANCE; HOMEOWNERS INSURANCE POLICY—SECTION I (PROPERTY COVERAGE).

SUBMITTED BUSINESS applications for insurance coverage that have been forwarded to an insurer but not yet processed.

SUBROGATION *see* SUBROGATION CLAUSE.

SUBROGATION CLAUSE section of PROPERTY INSURANCE and LIABILITY INSURANCE policies giving an insurer the right to take legal action against a third party responsible for a loss to an insured for which a claim has been paid. For example, an insurance company pays a claim for $40,000 in damages to an insured storekeeper for losses caused by a negligent contractor working next door. The policy's subrogation clause gives the insurer the right to be subrogated to, or take on as its own, the storekeeper's claim and to sue the contractor for damages.

SUBROGATION PRINCIPLE surrender of rights by an insured against the third party to an insurance company that has paid a claim.

SUBROGATION, PROPERTY AND CASUALTY INSURANCE circumstance where an insurance company takes the place of an insured in bringing a liability suit against a third party who caused injury to the insured. For example, if a third party, through negligence, damages an insured's car and the insured's insurance company pays to restore the car, the insurance company has recourse against the third party for the costs involved. The insured cannot sue the third party for damage, since if successful, the insured could collect twice for the same damage.

SUBROGATION RELEASE *see* SUBROGATION CLAUSE.

SUBROGATION, WAIVER OF *see* WAIVER OF SUBROGATION RIGHTS CLAUSE.

SUBROSEE insurance company which becomes subrogated to the rights of another party. *See also* SUBROGATION CLAUSE; SUBROGATION PRINCIPLE; SUBROGATION, PROPERTY AND CASUALTY INSURANCE.

SUBROSOR insured whose rights against a third party are transferred to an insurance company (the SUBROSEE) according to the process required by the SUBROGATION CLAUSE in the policy.

SUBSCRIBER, BLUE CROSS, BLUE SHIELD person insured under a BLUE CROSS hospitalization or BLUE SHIELD medical health insurance plan.

SUBSEQUENT NEGLIGENCE *see* LAST CLEAR CHANCE.

SUBSIDIZATION difference between the ACTUARIAL EQUIVALENT (rate) and the often lower rate actually charged to insure a risk.

SUBSTANDARD *see* SUBSTANDARD HEALTH INSURANCE (QUALIFIED IMPAIRMENT INSURANCE); SUBSTANDARD LIFE INSURANCE.

SUBSTANDARD GROUP *see* SUBSTANDARD HEALTH INSURANCE (QUALIFIED IMPAIRMENT INSURANCE); SUBSTANDARD LIFE INSURANCE.

SUBSTANDARD HEALTH INSURANCE (QUALIFIED IMPAIRMENT INSURANCE) coverage for persons whose medical history includes serious illness such as heart disease or whose physical condition is such that they are rated below standard. A policy may specifically deny coverage for recurrence of a particular illness or medical condition through an *impairment exemption rider,* or may provide only partial benefits. *See also* RATED POLICY.

SUBSTANDARD LIFE INSURANCE coverage for risks deemed uninsurable at standard rates by normal standards (persons whose medical histories include serious illness such as heart disease or whose physical conditions are such that they are rated below standard.) A policy may specifically deny benefits for death caused by a specific illness or medical condition or may provide only partial benefits. Many risks that would have been rejected as uninsurable under earlier underwriting standards, either because of their hazardous occupations or physical impairment, now can be insured under an extra-risk policy at an extra premium; even applicants who have survived cancer may be acceptable.

The premium may include an extra flat fee of so much per thousand dollars of coverage, or is one that would normally be charged to an older person. *See also* RATED POLICY.

SUBSTANDARD RISK *see* IMPAIRED RISK (SUBSTANDARD RISK); SUBSTANDARD HEALTH INSURANCE (QUALIFIED IMPAIRMENT INSURANCE); SUBSTANDARD LIFE INSURANCE.

SUBSTANTIAL EMPLOYER *see* SUBSTANTIAL OWNER BENEFIT LIMITATION.

SUBSTANTIAL OWNER effective proprietor of a business. Under the TAX REFORM ACT OF 1986, a uniform accrual rule prevents a qualified PENSION PLAN from being weighted in favor of the substantial owner of the business. The owner can select the accrual method to be applied provided the same method is used for all qualified employees of the business.

SUBSTANTIAL OWNER BENEFIT LIMITATION restriction on the benefit that owners and other highly compensated individuals may receive from a qualified pension or other employee benefits. The U.S. Tax Code requires that benefits under a qualified plan, and some other benefits, do not unduly favor a business firm's top hierarchy. The TAX REFORM ACT OF 1986 provides a uniform definition of "highly compensated" as an employee who either owned more than 5% interest in the business, received more than $75,000 in compensation, received more than $50,000 in compensation and was in the top 20% of employees as ranked by salary, or was an officer and received compensation greater than 150% of Section 415 defined contribution dollar amount. *See also* SUBSTANTIAL OWNER.

SUCCESSION BENEFICIARY CLAUSE section of a LIFE INSURANCE policy setting the procedure for revoking a current beneficiary and designating a successor beneficiary. Insurers require written notice of a beneficiary change, usually on a form designated for that purpose. Some may require return of the policy for the beneficiary change to be added. *See also* BENEFICIARY; BENEFICIARY CLAUSE.

SUCCESSOR BENEFICIARY *see* SUCCESSION BENEFICIARY CLAUSE.

SUCCESSOR PAYEE *see* SUCCESSION BENEFICIARY CLAUSE.

SUE AND LABOR CLAUSE section of *ocean marine policy* making it an obligation of the insured to take specific measures to limit losses to ship or cargo when a mishap occurs. Expenses incurred to limit physical damages, or to take legal action to protect the ship and its cargo, are reimbursed by the insurer to the extent they reduce the loss otherwise payable by the insurer, according to policy terms.

SUE, LABOR, AND TRAVEL CLAUSE *see* SUE AND LABOR CLAUSE.

SUICIDE CLAUSE limitation in all life insurance policies to the effect that no death payment will be made if an insured commits suicide within the first two years that the policy is in force. This clause protects the company against ADVERSE SELECTION—that is, purchase of a policy in contemplation of planned death in order for a beneficiary to collect the proceeds.

SUPERGRIT type of GRANTOR-RETAINED INCOME TRUST (GRIT) in which the grantor retains the right to the assets of the trust should he or she die before the term of the trust expires.

SUPERINTENDENT OF INSURANCE *see* COMMISSIONER OF INSURANCE (INSURANCE COMMISSIONER, SUPERINTENDENT OF INSURANCE).

SUPERSEDED SURETYSHIP RIDER endorsement to a FIDELITY BOND or SURETY BOND to cover losses that occurred after lapse of the DISCOVERY PERIOD of the previous bond. Coverage is limited to the amount provided by the previous bond.

SUPPLEMENTAL ACCIDENT EXPENSE *see* GROUP HEALTH INSURANCE.

SUPPLEMENTAL BENEFIT FORMULA procedure in Social Security that sets the benefit level for a dependent of a retired or disabled person who is receiving Social Security benefits. For example, if a retired or disabled worker has a spouse over age 65, the spouse is entitled to a benefit that is 50% of that paid to the primary recipient. This benefit is also available to dependent children. Further, the spouse can elect to take a reduced benefit if he or she is between age 62 and 65.

SUPPLEMENTAL CONTRACT *see* SUPPLEMENTARY CONTRACT.

SUPPLEMENTAL EXTENDED REPORTING PERIOD period of time after the expiration of a CLAIMS MADE BASIS LIABILITY COVERAGE policy during which claims may be made. *See also* MAXI TAIL (FULL TAIL); MIDI TAIL; MINI TAIL.

SUPPLEMENTAL LIABILITY INSURANCE broad excess protection for liability over the level of primary coverage or self insurance. Umbrella policies are written for both business and personal liability. For example, a personal umbrella policy might add $1 million in liability coverage for an insured's negligent use of a car, boat, and all other property, over and above his regular coverage. For a business, its applications would be even broader, including workers compensation, general liability, and all other coverage. Policyholders must have a certain minimum level of primary insurance before they can buy this supplemental coverage. For a personal policy the minimum might be $100,000 in homeowner's liability insurance and $500,000 per accident for bodily injury in an auto policy. *See also* UMBRELLA LIABILITY INSURANCE.

SUPPLEMENTAL MAJOR MEDICAL INSURANCE *see* SUPPLEMENTARY MEDICAL INSURANCE.

SUPPLEMENTAL MEDICAL INSURANCE *see* SUPPLEMENTARY MEDICAL INSURANCE.

SUPPLEMENTAL SECURITY INCOME (SSI) income supplement program under Social Security to provide a minimum monthly income to aged, blind, and disabled persons. The SSI payments, which were introduced in January 1974, make up the difference between family income and a guaranteed minimum amount for families who have only a specified amount of other resources such as savings accounts.

SUPPLEMENTARY CONTRACT terms of a settlement of a life insurance or annuity contract under which monies are currently payable or used at least in part by the beneficiary to fund a new insurance policy. Supplementary contracts are a balance sheet liability for a life company. They represent money held for policyholders that will eventually be paid out. But because the contract no longer involves insurance on a life, it is not included in the company's policy reserves.

SUPPLEMENTARY COVERAGE in property insurance, percentages of basic coverages which may be applied to provide coverage for other real and personal property. For example, under the HOMEOWNERS INSURANCE POLICY—SECTION I (PROPERTY COVERAGE) *Coverage B,* structures not attached to or part of the home (garage or appurtenant private structures) can be covered up to 10% of the basic home structure as found under *Coverage A.*

SUPPLEMENTARY MEDICAL INSURANCE part of the Federal Medicare program for additional coverage on a voluntary basis. The Medicare program is divided into two parts: (1) *Hospital Insurance* provides hospital benefits to persons over 65 who qualify for Social Security, and to disabled persons who have been receiving Social Security benefits for at least two years; and (2) SUPPLEMENTARY MEDICAL INSURANCE provides physician services to those over 65, and their dependents, who have enrolled in the program. Those enrolled in the program pay half the cost and the U.S. government pays the other half.

SUPPLEMENTARY PAYMENTS in a LIABILITY INSURANCE policy, provision for the payment of the insured's expenses as stated in the policy in three areas above the policy limit of liability: legal fees resulting from defending the insured, expenses incurred by the insured as the result of legal actions taken against him or her as the result of requests by the insurance company, and premium payments for bonds required by the insured.

SUPPLIES AND TRANSPORTERS FORMS *see* INLAND MARINE INSURANCE (TRANSPORTATION INSURANCE): BUSINESS RISKS.

SURETY *see* FIDELITY BOND; LIABILITY, BUSINESS EXPOSURES; OBLIGOR; SURETY BOND.

SURETY ASSOCIATION OF AMERICA (SAA) association whose membership is composed of surety bonding companies. The association's primary purpose is to act as a rating bureau for member companies by collecting statistics and developing rating tables.

SURETY BOND contract by which one party agrees to make good the default or debt of another. Actually, three parties are involved: the *principal*, who has primary responsibility to perform the obligation (after which the bond becomes void); the *surety*, the individual with the secondary responsibility of performing the obligation if the principal fails to perform. (After the surety performs, recourse is against the principal for reimbursement of expenses incurred by the surety in the performance of the obligation, known as *surety's right of exoneration*); and the *obligee,* to whom the right of performance *(obligation)* is owed.

SURETY BOND GUARANTEE PROGRAM program instituted by the Small Business Administration (SBA) that guarantees a construction contract bond in the event the issuing surety company suffers a loss. This is an effort by the SBA to encourage the awarding of more construction bids to minority contractors. *See also* SURETY BOND.

SURETYSHIP *see* FIDELITY BOND; SURETY BOND.

SURETY'S RIGHT OF EXONERATION *see* SURETY BOND.

SURGICAL EXPENSE INSURANCE policy providing benefits to pay for surgery.

SURGICAL INSURANCE BENEFITS *see* SURGICAL EXPENSE INSURANCE.

SURGICAL SCHEDULE list of cash allowances for various types of surgeries. *See also see* SURGICAL EXPENSE INSURANCE.

SURPLUS *see* SURPLUS ACCOUNT; SURPLUS LINES.

SURPLUS ACCOUNT assets minus liabilities of the insurance company. *See also* STATUTORY LIABILITY.

SURPLUS LINES

Reinsurance: SURPLUS REINSURANCE contracts under which the agreement between an insurer and a reinsurer is based on the *ceding* company's line guide, such that the amount reinsured is expressed in terms of the multiples of the retention and is referred to as a number of lines. *See also* SURPLUS REINSURANCE.

Regular market: insurance coverage not available from an ADMITTED COMPANY in the regular market; thus a surplus lines broker/agent representing an applicant seeks coverage in the surplus lines market from a NONADMITTED INSURER according to the insurance regulations of a particular state.

SURPLUS LINES BROKER *see* EXCESS LINE BROKER (SURPLUS LINE BROKER).

SURPLUS LINES (EXCESS-SURPLUS LINES) specialized property or liability coverage provided by a NONADMITTED INSURER in instances where it is unavailable from insurers licensed by the state. Examples of surplus lines are coverage for some environmental impairment liability risks, or liability coverage for directors and officers of certain companies. *See also* EXCESS LINE BROKER (SURPLUS LINE BROKER).

SURPLUS RATIO percentage of total assets set aside by an insurance company to provide for unexpected losses. In general, a minimum of a 5% surplus ratio (5 cents in reserve for each $1 of assets) is advocated for determining whether the company has an adequate reserve against unexpected losses.

SURPLUS REINSURANCE automatic REINSURANCE which requires an insurer to transfer (CEDE) and the reinsurer to accept the part of every risk which exceeds the insurer's predetermined retention limit. The reinsurer shares in premiums and losses in the same proportion as it shares in the total policy limits of the risk. The *surplus method* permits the insurer to keep for its own account small policies, and to transfer the amount of risk on large policies above its retention limit.

For example, assume an insurer issues a policy for $20,000. The insurer keeps $5,000 (¼) and transfers the remaining $15,000 (¾) to its reinsurer. This is called a *three line surplus* because the amount transferred equals three times the retained line of the insurer. The insurer keeps ¼ and transfers ¾ of the premium to the reinsurer. In the event of total loss, the settlements between the insurer and the reinsurer would be effected on the identical ¼-¾ basis. The same principal applies if there is a partial loss, in that the reinsurer must reimburse the insurer in the same proportion as the reinsurance premium received.

SURPLUS RELEASE method of using REINSURANCE to counteract the unexpected impact of business on the POLICYHOLDER SURPLUS. *See also* PORTFOLIO REINSURANCE; REINSURANCE.

SURPLUS SHARE *see* SURPLUS REINSURANCE.

SURPLUS TO POLICYHOLDERS *see* POLICYHOLDER SURPLUS.

SURPLUS TREATY REINSURANCE *see* SURPLUS REINSURANCE.

SURRENDER CHARGE fee charged to a policyowner when a life insurance policy or annuity is surrendered for its cash value. This fee reflects insurance company expenses incurred by placing the policy on its books, and subsequent administrative expenses. *See also* BACK LOAD.

SURRENDER COST INDEX method of comparing the costs of a set of CASH VALUE LIFE INSURANCE policies that takes into account the TIME VALUE OF MONEY. The true costs of alternative cash value policies with the same death benefit depend on a number of factors—amount and timing of premiums paid, amount and timing of dividends (in the case of *participating* policies), time period involved, and the CASH SURRENDER VALUE. In evaluating a particular group of policies, a surrender cost index can be calculated using INTEREST ADJUSTED COST comparison. The index ranks the policies for the same period of time, say the first 20 years of the policy life, by cost per \$1000 of FACE AMOUNT, showing the cheapest through the most expensive. In effect, the index illustrates the relative cost of acquiring a dollar's worth of each policy's cash surrender value after 20 years. Contrast with the NET PAYMENTS INDEX, a ranking of policy costs using the traditional *net cost method* of comparison, that ignores the time value of money and thus gives a less accurate picture of relative policy costs.

SURRENDER COST METHOD *see* SURRENDER COST INDEX.

SURRENDER, LIFE INSURANCE action by the owner of a cash value policy to relinquish it for its CASH SURRENDER VALUE. Since the Depression of the 1930s, companies have reserved the right to delay payment of a cash surrender value up to six months; however, payments have been prompt.

SURRENDER VALUE *see* SURRENDER, LIFE POLICY.

SURVEY *see* SURVEY APPROACH.

SURVEY APPROACH study of buying habits of consumers to determine their insurance needs.

SURVIVAL STATUTE *see* UNIFORM SIMULTANEOUS DEATH ACT.

SURVIVOR PURCHASE OPTION provision applied as a RIDER attached to an ORDINARY LIFE INSURANCE POLICY for the purpose of meeting ESTATE PLANNING requirements. When the INSURED dies, the BENEFICIARY is entitled to receive the DEATH BENEFIT in cash or to use the death benefit to purchase a new ordinary life insurance policy. This new policy is not subject to additional underwriting requirements and has, as the date of issue, the same time as the original policy. The initial premium due is automatically subtracted from the original policy's death benefit.

SURVIVORSHIP ANNUITY agreement under which an annuitant receives a predetermined monthly income benefit for life upon the death of the insured. Should the annuitant predecease the insured, the contract is terminated and no benefits are ever paid. The life expectancy of both the insured and annuitant must be taken into consideration in determining the premium, and such, the annuitant cannot be changed once selected. This is also called a *revisionary annuity* (a life insurance policy combined with an annuity agreement).

SURVIVORSHIP BENEFIT retirement income benefit of a survivor (or survivors) of an insured individual, according to a particular formula. For example, if a retired worker dies, all or a portion of his monthly pension (perhaps half or two-thirds) may continue to go to his wife, if he has elected the JOINT AND SURVIVOR OPTION. Survivors of a person entitled to Social Security benefits also may be entitled to receive a survivorship benefit. For example, the widow may get as much as 100% of the husband's benefits, if claimed at age 65 or over.

SURVIVORSHIP CLAUSE *see* COMMON DISASTER CLAUSE (SURVIVORSHIP CLAUSE).

SURVIVORSHIP INCOME PAYMENTS *see* SURVIVORSHIP BENEFIT.

SURVIVORSHIP LIFE INSURANCE coverage on more than one person that pays a benefit after all of the insureds die. This type of *joint life policy* is significantly cheaper than a regular policy. Survivorship life insurance might be used to help fund estate taxes after the deaths of a husband and wife or as a form of *business continuation insurance*. *See also* TONTINE.

SURVIVORS RIGHT TO SUE legal recourse available to survivors of a person who suffers a wrongful death. Under COMMON LAW, only an injured person had the right to sue for damages. If a wrongfully injured person died of those injuries, there was no one with a legal right to sue to recover damages for the death. State laws now provide for the survivors' right to sue, not just for the wrongful death but for loss of income and other losses.

SUSPENSION OF COVERAGE interruption of insurance provided for in most property insurance policies under circumstances where a substantial increase in hazard has arisen with the knowledge or control of the insured. The policy's WORK AND MATERIALS CLAUSE gives the insured the right to use materials and processes needed in his or her business without facing suspension from increased hazard. But major changes in the characteristics of the risk will trigger suspension of coverage. For example, a building used to warehouse dry goods when fire insurance first is written on it, may be converted by the insured to store paint. The substantial increase in hazard results in suspension of coverage. Vacancy for more than 60 days and riot or explosion also result in suspension. Coverage is reinstated automatically for the remainder of the policy term when the condition that triggered suspension is corrected.

SUSPENSION PROVISION *see* SUSPENSION OF COVERAGE.

SYNDICATE group of insurers or reinsurers involved in joint underwriting. Members typically take predetermined shares of premiums, losses, expenses, and profits. Syndicates, more common in REINSURANCE than in PRIMARY INSURANCE, are formed to cover major risks that are beyond the CAPACITY of a single underwriter. *See also* POOL; POOLING.

SYSTEM SAFETY method of accident prevention whose objective is to detect system-component deficiencies which have the potential for causing accidents.

SYSTEMS SAFETY ENGINEERING risk management technique for identifying risks and taking steps to minimize losses.

T

TABLE OF MORBIDITY *see* MORBIDITY TABLE.

TABLE OF MORTALITY *see* MORTALITY TABLE.

TABULAR COST OF INSURANCE *see* TABULAR PLANS.

TABULAR INTEREST RATE *see* TABULAR PLANS.

TABULAR MORTALITY *see* TABULAR PLANS.

TABULAR PLANS RETROSPECTIVE RATING system with basic, minimum, and maximum premium rates listed in manual tables. Calculation of an individual premium involves adjusting the basic premium for appropriate discounts, losses, and a tax multiplier. The rate is then set between the minimum and the maximum, based on the loss experience, the size of the risk, and the underwriter's judgment.

TABULAR-VALUE RESERVE METHOD means of setting life insurance reserves based on expected mortality rates as reflected in a MORTALITY TABLE. *See also* RETROSPECTIVE METHOD RESERVE COMPUTATION.

TAFT-HARTLEY ACT provision of Federal legislation that prohibits an employer from making contributions (premium payments) directly to a union for the purchase of employee benefits; instead the contributions can be paid into a trust fund established for these purposes.

TAIL COVERAGE liability insurance that extends beyond the end of the policy period of a liability insurance policy written on a *claims-made* basis. Liability claims are often made long after the accident or event that caused the injury. Many liability policies are written on a claims made basis, which means the insurer pays only claims that are received during the policy period. In that case, an insured needs tail coverage to protect against claims he did not know about at the end of the policy period. For example, a doctor retires, allows his insurance policy to lapse, and a claim comes in six months later. In order to protect himself, the doctor purchases tail coverage.

TAPES INSURANCE *see* DATA PROCESSING INSURANCE.

TARGET BENEFIT PLAN type of pension in which benefits may vary depending on the investment performance of the pension plan assets. Contributions are made to fund a target benefit, such as 35% of compensation, using acceptable mortality and interest rate assumptions. Funds are invested wholly or partially in such vehicles as variable annuities or mutual funds, and benefits may exceed or fall below target levels depending on investment performance. Target plans are subject to the same annual contribution limits for individual participants as a MONEY PURCHASE PLAN. *See also* VARIABLE DOLLAR ANNUITY.

TARGET RISK
1. prospective buyers of insurance classified according to various demographics such as age, sex, and insurance.
2. risk so hazardous that it is difficult to obtain insurance coverage.

TARIFF *see* TARIFF RATE.

TARIFF RATE standard property-liability insurance premium set by a rating bureau for a particular class of risk.

TAXABLE-EQUIVALENT YIELD tax-free yield ÷ (1 − individual's combined Federal and state income tax bracket). The calculation is made according to the following steps:
1. Determine individual's effective state tax rate (percentage that individual pays in state taxes after deduction of these state taxes from his or her Federal tax).

where: effective state tax rate = (state tax rate + local tax rate) × (1 − Federal income tax rate).

Assume that the individual's taxable income is \$60,000. The individual is in the 33% Federal marginal income tax bracket, and his or her state tax rate on dividend income is 7.9%. Then the effective state tax rate = 0.079(1 − 0.33) = 0.05293.
2. Determine individual's combined Federal and state income tax bracket (Federal marginal tax rate + effective state tax rate). For the above example, this relationship equals 0.33 + 0.05293 = 0.38293.
3. Determine taxable-equivalent yield. Assume, for the above example, that an individual is considering an investment that has a tax-free yield of 8%. Then

tax-equivalent yield = tax-free yield ÷ (1 − individual's combined Federal and state income tax bracket)

$$= \frac{0.08}{0.61707} = 12.96\%$$

TAXABLE INCOME earned and unearned income on which current taxes must be paid. Tax avoidance is one of the goals of investment and various tax-free or tax-deferred investments have been devised for this purpose. In the past, real estate and oil and gas limited parnerships have been a method of avoiding tax on current income, but changing tax legislation frequently alters the nature of taxable income and the taxes that must be paid on it. For example, the TAX REFORM ACT OF 1986 eliminated contributions to INDIVIDUAL RETIREMENT ACCOUNTS as a deduction for many taxpayers.

Insurance products have long enjoyed special tax benefits because of the belief in the importance of protecting one's family. For example, the interest buildup in annuities is allowed to accumulate tax deferred. Taxes are paid on the earnings only when the money is withdrawn. Because the 1986 Federal tax law eliminated so many other forms of tax shelters, insurance products became even more attractive for these properties.

TAX ADVANTAGES OF QUALIFIED PLAN see PENSION PLAN.

TAX-APPRAISED VALUE estimate of an asset that is used to determine tax obligations. It is usually in the interest of the owner to have a low value put on a piece of property for tax purposes. However, the owner sometimes wants the same property to carry a higher appraisal value for insurance purposes so that losses can be easily recovered if the property is lost or damaged.

TAXATION, INSURANCE COMPANIES see TAX EQUITY AND FINANCIAL RESPONSIBILITY ACTS OF 1982 AND 1983 (TEFRA); TAX REFORM ACT OF 1984.

TAXATION, INTEREST ON DIVIDENDS interest earned on dividends from a *participating life insurance policy* left on deposit with the insurance company and subject to taxation.

TAXATION, LIFE INSURANCE COMPANIES see TAX EQUITY AND FINANCIAL RESPONSIBILITY ACTS OF 1982 AND 1983 (TEFRA); TAX REFORM ACT OF 1984.

TAXATION, PARTICIPATING DIVIDENDS dividends of a *participating life insurance policy* deemed by the Internal Revenue Service to be a return of a portion of premiums and thus not subject to taxation.

TAXATION, PROCEEDS see AUTHORITY TO TERMINATE PLAN; GIFT TAX; TAXABLE INCOME; TAXATION, INTEREST ON DIVIDENDS; TAXATION, PARTICIPATING DIVIDENDS; TAX DEFERRAL; TAX DEFERRED ANNUITY (TDA); TAX EQUITY AND FINANCIAL RESPONSIBILITY ACTS OF 1982 AND 1983 (TEFRA); TAX FREE ROLLOVER; TAX PLANNING; TAX REFORM ACT OF 1984; TAX REFORM ACT OF 1986.

TAX BENEFITS OF ANNUITY see ANNUITY.

TAX BENEFITS OF LIFE INSURANCE tax advantages of investing in life insurance fall into two main areas: (1) TAX DEFERRAL on untaxed buildup of earnings in such *cash value* policies as whole life insurance and annuities, and (2) exclusion from Federal income tax of the proceeds of a death benefit of an insurance policy. *See also* TAX REFORM ACT OF 1986.

TAX BRACKET SHIFTING arrangement of financial affairs such that a family member who is in a lower income tax bracket receives income that another family member would otherwise have received (thereby reducing the taxes paid by the family unit).

TAX DEFERRAL postponement of taxes on investment or other earnings until the investor begins to consume them and anticipates being in a lower tax bracket. One example of a tax-deferred investment is an INDIVIDUAL RETIREMENT ACCOUNT (IRA). Earnings accumulate tax free until the account holder retires after age 59½. At that time, taxes must be paid on the earnings as money is withdrawn from the account. Other examples of tax deferred investments are insurance products such as *annuities* and various types of *whole life insurance* such as VARIABLE LIFE and UNIVERSAL LIFE. The TAX REFORM ACT OF 1986 limited the use of IRAs, making insurance products one of the few tax-deferred investments still available.

TAX DEFERRED ANNUITY (TDA) retirement vehicle permitted under SECTION 403 (b) PLAN of the U.S. Internal Revenue Code for emloyees of a public school system or a qualified charitable organization. Under such an agreement, the maximum annual contribution is $9500. Cash values and dividends accrue but are not taxed until the annuitant actually receives benefits. At that time, the annuitant is taxed only on the amount that exceeds the investment in the annuity. Should the annuitant receive a monthly benefit under one of the various *annuities,* the percentage of each payment that would not be subject to taxation is determined by the *exclusion ratio*:

$$\text{Exclusion Ratio} = \frac{\text{Amount Invested in Annuity}}{\text{Expected Return under Annuity}}$$

where the expected return under the annuity equals the life expectancy of the annuitant $\times$ the annual income payment.

For example, if an annuitant invested $40,000 in an annuity, and at age 60 has a 14 year life expectancy, and receives an annual income of $5000, then 57.14% of each income payment would not be subject to taxation.

TAX EQUITY AND FINANCIAL RESPONSIBILITY ACTS OF 1982 AND 1983 (TEFRA) legislation that redefined life insurance and raised taxes on life insurance companies. Among the provisions were new rules for some life insurance products, including a definition of FLEXIBLE PREMIUM LIFE INSURANCE, and an increase in life insurance company taxes. Congress was concerned that a policyholder could take a substantial amount, say $1 million, and, after putting a few dollars toward a life insurance premium, put the remainder into a tax-free investment vehicle. One of two tests had to be satisfied for a policy to qualify as life insurance: (1) the cash surrender value policy could not exceed a net single premium, and (2) the death benefit had to represent a certain percentage of the cash value, which declined as the policyholder got older. For example, at age 40, the death benefit must be 140% of cash value. The second rule closed a loophole on tax-free withdrawals from annuities. Prior to 1982 an annuity holder could withdraw his initial premium tax free at any time. The 1982 code decreed that any money withdrawn from an annuity would be considered income first and would therefore be taxable.

The older 1959 tax code devised a shorthand formula for determining taxes paid by insurers. The formula worked when interest rates were low, but as they soared, insurers found ways to reduce the increased tax bite. The 1982 code introduced a stopgap measure designed to raise taxes on life insurers by $3 billion.

TAX-EQUIVALENT INCOME tax-exempt income which, for comparative purposes, has been increased by an amount equal to the taxes that would be paid if this income were fully taxable at statutory rates. *See also* TAXABLE-EQUIVALENT YIELD.

TAX (FEDERAL), INCOME OF PENSION PLAN *see* PENSION PLAN.

TAX-FREE EXCHANGE OF INSURANCE PRODUCTS under Section 1035 of the Internal Revenue Code, stipulation that the exchange of one life insurance policy for another life insurance policy will generally not result in a recognized gain for the purpose of federal income tax purposes to the policyowner who exchanges the policy. The insured must be the same person under both policies. If the policyowner should surrender the second policy in a taxable transaction, the untaxed gain is then recognized. The types of policy exchanges which can be made on a tax-free basis are as follows: a life insurance policy for another life insurance policy, a life insurance policy for an annuity contract, and an annuity contract for another annuity contract (an annuity contract cannot be exchanged on a tax-free basis for a life insurance policy. The ANNUITANT must be the same person under both annuity contracts in order to maintain the tax-free basis.) *See also* MINIMUM DEPOSIT RESCUE.

TAX-FREE INCOME *see* TAXATION, PARTICIPATING DIVIDENDS; TAX BENEFITS OF LIFE INSURANCE; TAX DEFERRAL; TAX DEFERRED ANNUITY (TDA); TAX FREE ROLLOVER; TAX PLANNING.

TAX-FREE ROLLOVER
1. transfer of money from or into an employer-sponsored pension or other qualified plan into an INDIVIDUAL RETIREMENT ACCOUNT (IRA) without paying tax on the distribution.

2. transfer of money from one individual retirement account to another without paying tax.

In both cases, the law allows the account holder 60 days to place the money in a new IRA account. Transfer from one account to another can be accomplished either by withholding the money from one account and depositing it in another within 60 days or by instructing one institution to transfer it to a second. As long as the new deposit is made within 60 days, there is no current tax liability.

TAX LIEN claim against property for payment of taxes. Life insurance proceeds and annuity benefits are protected against certain creditors of the insured, but the Federal government is not one of them. Thus life insurance and annuity benefits can be held liable if the Federal government has a tax lien against the insured.

TAX MULTIPLIER factor applied in RETROSPECTIVE RATING in order to increase the BASIC PREMIUM to cover state premium taxes for liability and workers compensation insurance. For example, if a state premium tax is 2%, the tax multiplier used in the formula to determine the *retrospective premium* would be 1.02.

TAX PLANNING arrangement of discretionary income, expenses, and investments in a way that enhances after-tax wealth. Insurance policies can be used to increase after-tax income through the tax-deferral features of CASH VALUE LIFE INSURANCE and to reduce estate taxes through the preferential tax treatment of the life insurance DEATH BENEFIT. *See also* ESTATE PLANNING.

TAX REFORM ACT OF 1976 legislation that provided temporary rules for implementing the EMPLOYEE RETIREMENT INCOME SECURITY ACT OF 1974 (ERISA).

TAX REFORM ACT OF 1984 legislation that raised taxes on life insurers and further defined life insurance. Because the TAX EQUITY AND FINANCIAL RESPONSIBILITY ACT OF 1982 AND 1983 (TEFRA) failed to raise the amount of revenue the U.S. Treasury wanted, the 1984 Act again raised the corporate tax on life insurance companies. It also expanded the definition of life insurance to all life insurance contracts, rather than just those with flexible premiums that had been addressed in the *Tax Reform Act of 1982*. For FLEXIBLE PREMIUM contracts, the 1982 Act established the death benefits had to represent a certain percentage of the cash value, which declined as the policyholder got older. The 1984 Act raised that ratio. For example, at age 40, the death benefit must be at least 250% of cash value for the product to qualify as life insurance. This act also attempted to redistribute the tax burden between mutual and stock life insurance companies. It also replaced a three-tier structure for taxing life insurance companies with a single-phase structure.

TAX REFORM ACT OF 1986 legislation to eliminate most tax shelters and writeoffs in exchange for lower rates for both corporation and individuals. It was intended to be revenue neutral; that is, to bring in the same amount of revenue as the previous law.

1. for individuals, it eliminated deductions for most tax shelters such as tax-advantaged limited partnerships; it eliminated special treatment for capital gains by taxing them at the same rate as ordinary income.

2. deductions for an INDIVIDUAL RETIREMENT ACCOUNT (IRA) no longer applied to those with incomes above $35,000 and couples above $50,000 unless they had no company pension plan. Individuals with incomes between $25,000 and $35,000 and couples between $40,000 and $50,000 got a partial deduction.

3. for company-sponsored 401 (k) salary reduction plans, the maximum annual limit was reduced from $30,000 to $7000; antidiscrimination rules were tightened; and a 10% penalty was imposed for withdrawals before age 59½.

4. other administrative changes made it more expensive for companies to start or maintain a company pension plan.

5. CASH VALUE LIFE INSURANCE was one of the few retirement vehicles to retain its tax-deferred status.

6. top individual tax rates were reduced from a series of rates going up to 50% to two rates: 15% and 28%, although the top marginal rate was 33%.

7. the top corporate rate down from 46% to 34%.

8. the investment tax credit was eliminated and depreciation schedules were lengthened.

9. many industries lost special advantages they held under the old code.

10. the alternative minimum tax was stiffened for individuals and one was added for corporations.

TAX-SHELTERED ANNUITY (TSA) *see* TAX DEFERRED ANNUITY (TDA).

TEACHERS INSURANCE AND ANNUITY ASSOCIATION—COLLEGE RETIREMENT EQUITIES FUND (TIAA-CREF) life insurance company that sells life insurance and annuities to the faculty and staff of colleges and universities. Its TIAA-CREF Tax-Sheltered Annuity (TSA) uses a traditional FIXED DOLLAR ANNUITY, the TIAA portion, and a VARIABLE DOLLAR ANNUITY, the CREF portion. Most participants have a SPLIT FUNDED PLAN with 50% of the premium going to each, but this proportion can be changed as often as a participant desires. *See also* TAX DEFERRED ANNUITY (TDA).

TECHNICAL AND MISCELLANEOUS REVENUE ACT OF 1988 (TAMRA): CHILDREN'S EDUCATION determination that investments by parents in their children's education through the purchase of Series EE Savings Bonds which generate interest income are tax-exempt if the proceeds are applied to qualified education expenses. To qualify for this tax exemption, the following criteria must be met:

1. In order for education expenses to qualify, they must be incurred in the year of redemption of the bonds. Such expenses include tuition and required fees. In a year in which the proceeds from the redeemed bonds are greater than the qualifying expenses, a prorated percentage of the redeemed bonds' earnings becomes taxable income for that year.

2. In order for the education expenses to qualify, they must be the expenses of the bond's purchaser or those of the purchaser's dependent in the year of redemption of the bonds.

3. In order for the education expenses to qualify, the purchaser of the bonds must be at least 24 years of age and the bonds must be in the name of the purchaser or in the joint names of the purchaser and his or her spouse. Also, married individuals must file joint tax returns.

4. Bonds purchased must have been issued after December 31, 1987.

TECHNICAL AND MISCELLANEOUS REVENUE ACT OF 1988 (TAMRA): EMPLOYEE BENEFITS determination that group plans offering legal services are limited to an annual tax-free benefit of $70 per employee; group plans may offer employer-provided educational assistance plans on a tax-exclusion basis to employees, with the exception of graduate school expenses; if an employer elects to treat highly compensated employees as those earning in excess of $50,000, then the employer must have significant business operations in at least two geographically separate locations; and each plan must be tested for discrimination on a date to be chosen by the employer in 1990, and the same date must be used each year in the future unless a date change is approved in advance by the Secretary of the Treasury.

TECHNICAL AND MISCELLANEOUS REVENUE ACT OF 1988 (TAMRA): INCOME TAXATION OF CASH VALUE LIFE INSURANCE determination that policies entered into on or after June 21, 1988, that fail the 7-pay test (aggregate premiums paid at any time during the first 7 years of the contract exceed the annual net level premium of a 7-pay policy multiplied by the number of years the policy has been in force) are considered by the Internal Revenue Service (IRS) to be modified endowment contracts (MECS). If the policy is determined to be a MEC, it may be subject to income taxes as well as penalty taxes. Any policy loans, dividends, or partial withdrawals of funds are treated by the IRS for income tax purposes on a last-in, first-out basis.

TELEGRAM PROPOSAL OF INSURANCE binding contract for insurance completed by telegraph. The law has recognized the date an insurance agreement is made as the date that coverage commences, rather than the date stated on the insurance policy. Acceptance of a proposal by telegram, like a letter or an oral agreement, represents a binding contract.

TEMPERATURE EXTREMES EXCLUSION provision in an ALL RISKS INLAND MARINE policy that denies coverage for exposure to dampness and extremes of temperature. Some property, like living plants, might be particularly vulnerable to extremes of temperature and is not considered as insurable risk.

TEMPORARY DISABILITY BENEFITS income paid to a worker who is temporarily disabled by an injury or sickness that is not work related. Compare with WORKERS COMPENSATION BENEFITS, which are available only to workers injured on the job. And unemployment benefits are available only to those who are able to work. Temporary disability benefits fill in for those who cannot work because of illness and who were not injured on the job. After a waiting period that is typically about a week, the disabled worker is paid a weekly income. Temporary disability benefits may come from a group benefit plan, from a union medical plan or, in some cases, from a state insurance fund. Five states have temporary disability plans: California, Hawaii, New Jersey, New York, and Rhode Island.

TEMPORARY LIFE ANNUITY annuity payment for a limited period of time. *See also* ANNUITY.

TEMPORARY LIFE ANNUITY DUE limited number of payments, the first of which is due immediately and payments thereafter are contingent upon the designated beneficiary (the ANNUITANT) continuing to live. After the limit has been reached all payments cease even if the annuitant is still alive.

TEMPORARY LIFE INSURANCE *see* TERM LIFE INSURANCE.

TEMPORARY NONOCCUPATIONAL DISABILITY PLAN social insurance that provides benefits to temporarily disabled workers in a few states. Five states require employers to pay cash benefits if workers are disabled. They are Rhode Island, California, New Jersey, New York, and Hawaii.

TEMPORARY PARTIAL, TOTAL DISABILITY *see* DISABILITY INCOME INSURANCE; TEMPORARY DISABILITY BENEFITS.

TENANCY *see* ESTATE PLANNING DISTRIBUTION; JOINT TENANTS; TENANCY BY THE ENTIRETY.

TENANCY BY THE ENTIRETY ownership of property by a husband and wife together; the law views the couple as one person. This can have a bearing on insurance claims. For example, if the wife willfully destroys property, her husband's claim may be denied by an insurer on the grounds that he is not separate from his wife for insurance purposes, and this constitutes destruction by the insured. Contrasts with TENANTS IN COMMON.

TENANTS IMPROVEMENTS AND BETTERMENTS improvements or renovations to a leased business or residential property made by a tenant to meet its particular needs. Loss of use of these improvements as a result of damage is covered by an endorsement to the *Standard Fire Policy.*

TENANTS IN COMMON ownership of property by two or more persons who do not have rights of survivorship. If one tenant dies, his property passes to his heirs and not to the other tenants. Because insurance is a personal contract, all parties with an interest in the property must be listed. When filing an insurance claim, the policyholder must prove there was a loss and that the property damaged belonged to him. For example, four tenants in common own a resort condominium. Only one is listed on the insurance policy. A fire destroys the condo. The insurer probably could argue successfully that the interests of the other three are not covered.

TENANTS INSURANCE coverage for the contents of a renter's home or apartment and for liability. Tenant policies are similar to homeowners insurance, except that they do not cover the structure. They do, however, cover changes made to the inside structure, such as carpeting, kitchen appliances, and built-in bookshelves.

TENDER OFFER DEFENSE EXPENSE INSURANCE coverage for defense costs incurred in defending a company from an unfriendly takeover attempt. Hostile takeovers have been one of the hottest business topics of the 1980s. Vulnerable companies have responded in a variety of ways including changing the corporate bylaws, selling off their most attractive assets and, in the last resort, voting themselves huge severance packages or "golden parachutes." When a company or individual makes a tender offer for the stock of its takeover target, the latter company usually hires legal experts and mounts a costly defense. This insurance is an example of a specialized coverage that grew to meet a specific need.

TENDER OF UNEARNED PREMIUM return of a pro rata portion of premium after a policy is cancelled by the insurer. Under most property and liability insurance policies, the insurer can cancel at any time but must return the portion of the premium that has not been used to the insured. Although some courts have held that a policy has not been cancelled until the insurer returns the unearned premium, others allow the insurer to cancel the policy and inform the insured that the unearned premium will be refunded on demand.

TEN YEAR AVERAGING accounting method used to reduce income taxes on distributions from qualified pension or retirement plans. Ten-year averaging was repealed by the TAX REFORM ACT OF 1986 but is still available to persons who reached age 50 before January 1, 1986. They are allowed at any future date to make a one-time use of 10-year averaging at 1986 income tax and capital gains rates. Everyone else is limited to *5-year forward averaging*. For those still eligible, 10-year averaging provides the opportunity to pay tax on a lump sum distribution as if it were the only income received over a 10-year period. For example, a lump sum distribution of $50,000 would be taxed at $5,874. This amount is calculated as shown on page 419.

TEN-YEAR VESTING (CLIFF VESTING) method of vesting under the EMPLOYEE RETIREMENT INCOME SECURITY ACT OF 1974 (ERISA) that requires an employee to have 10 years of service with an employer to be vested. An employee who leaves an employer prior to that time does not receive retirement benefits from that job. Under the TAX REFORM ACT OF 1986, after December 31, 1988 the 10-year vesting rule is reduced to 5 years. *See also* VESTING.

TERM period of time of insurance coverage. If a loss occurs during this time, insurance benefits are paid. If a loss occurs after this time period has expired, no insurance benefits are paid.

TERMINAL DIVIDEND additional policy dividend paid to a life insurance policyholder when a policy terminates. A MUTUAL INSURANCE COMPANY is owned by its policyholders and writes participating policies, which pay annual policy dividends to policyholders. (Some *stock insurance* companies pay dividends on some policies as well.) In addition to the annual dividend, many policies pay a terminal dividend when the policy terminates after a minimum period in force—usually 10 to 20 years. This represents a return to the policyholder of an equitable portion of the overall increase in the insurer's surplus over this period. Some companies pay this dividend no matter how a policy is terminated; others pay it only under certain conditions.

TERMINAL FUNDING former method of funding a pension plan. When employees retire, the employer sets aside a lump sum that will pay them lifetime monthly benefits. When determining the amount, these factors are considered: life expectancy, the promised monthly benefit, and expected earnings on the sum set aside. The lump sum can either be placed in a trust fund or used to buy an annuity. Terminal funding, along with the current disbursement method, are no longer permitted for qualified pension plans under the EMPLOYEE RETIREMENT INCOME SECURITY ACT

Form 4972 (1989)   Page 2

Part IV — Complete this part to choose the 10-year averaging method. (See Instructions.)

1	Ordinary income part from Form 1099-R, Box 2 minus Box 3. If you did not make the Schedule D election or complete Part II, enter the amount from Box 2 of Form 1099-R (taxable amount). (See Instructions.)	1	$50,000 00
2	Death benefit exclusion. (See Instructions.)	2	–0–
3	Subtract line 2 from line 1 (total taxable amount)	3	$50,000 00
4	Current actuarial value of annuity, if applicable (from Form 1099-R, Box 8)	4	–0–
5	Add lines 3 and 4 (adjusted total taxable amount). If this amount is $70,000 or more, skip lines 6 through 9, and enter this amount on line 10	5	$50,000 00
6	Multiply line 5 by 50% (.50), but do not enter more than $10,000 .... **6** $10,000 00		
7	Subtract $20,000 from line 5. Enter difference. If line 5 is $20,000 or less, enter zero **7** $30,000 00		
8	Multiply line 7 by 20% (.20) ...... **8** $ 6,000 00		
9	Subtract line 8 from line 6 (minimum distribution allowance)	9	$ 4,000 00
10	Subtract line 9 from line 5	10	$46,000 00
11	Federal estate tax attributable to lump-sum distribution. Do not deduct on Form 1040 or Form 1041 the amount attributable to the ordinary income entered on line 1. (See Instructions.)	11	–0–
12	Subtract line 11 from line 10	12	$46,000 00
13	Enter $2,480 plus 10% (.10) of line 12	13	$ 7,080 00
14	Tax on amount on line 13. Use Tax Rate Schedule in the Instructions for Form 4972	14	$ 587 40
15	Multiply line 14 by 10. If no entry on line 4, skip lines 16 through 21, and enter this amount on line 22	15	$ 5,874 00
16	Divide line 4 by line 5 and enter the result as a decimal. (See Instructions.)	16	N/A
17	Multiply line 9 by the decimal amount on line 16	17	N/A
18	Subtract line 17 from line 4	18	N/A
19	Enter $2,480 plus 10% (.10) of line 18	19	N/A
20	Tax on amount on line 19. Use Tax Rate Schedule in the Instructions for Form 4972	20	N/A
21	Multiply line 20 by 10	21	N/A
22	Subtract line 21 from line 15. (Multiple recipients, see Instructions.)	22	$ 5,874 00
23	Tax on lump-sum distribution (add Part II, line 2, and Part IV, line 22). Enter on Form 1040, line 39, or Form 1041, Schedule G, line 1b ▶	23	$ 5,874 00

OF 1974 (ERISA). ERISA requires current funding of future pension liabilities.

TERMINAL RESERVE life insurance reserve at the end of any policy year. Insurers are required by state regulatory authorities to set up reserves to pay for future claims. The *initial reserve* is the reserve at the beginning of the policy year; the *mean reserve* is the average of the initial reserve and the terminal reserve for that year. The terminal reserve is used for dividend distributions and to set *nonforfeiture* values for CASH VALUE LIFE INSURANCE. The terminal reserve for one policy year is the initial reserve for the next policy year.

TERMINATION cancellation of a policy by an insurance company. *See also* PENSION BENEFIT GUARANTY CORPORATION (PBGC); TERMINATION INSURANCE.

TERMINATION DATE *see* EXPIRATION; EXPIRATION NOTICE.

TERMINATION INSURANCE *see* PENSION PLAN TERMINATION INSURANCE.

TERMINATION RATE measure of the rate at which policies are cancelled or allowed to lapse. The termination rate is a factor in setting premiums for group life and health policies.

TERM INSURANCE *see* TERM LIFE INSURANCE.

TERM INSURANCE COST low-cost life insurance providing coverage only for a limited time, such as one year, five years, or to age 65. Term insurance costs less at younger ages than a comparable amount of CASH VALUE LIFE INSURANCE, or permanent insurance, which covers an insured for the rest of his life. Term insurance has become increasingly popular; it costs less because there is less likelihood that an insured will die during the term, whereas with cash value insurance, a policy must pay off whenever a policyholder dies. However, the premium for term insurance increases dramatically as an insured grows older, but the premium for permanent insurance usually remains level throughout an insured's lifetime.

TERM LIFE INSURANCE life insurance which stays in effect for only a specified, limited period. If an insured dies within that period, the BENEFICIARY receives the death payments. If the insured survives, the policy ends and the beneficiary receives nothing. For example, if an insured with a five year term policy dies within that period, the beneficiary receives the face amount of the policy. If the insured survives the five year period, the policy ends, with no benefit payable. *See also* ORDINARY LIFE INSURANCE; RENEWABLE TERM LIFE INSURANCE.

TERRITORIAL GROUPING OF RISKS method of classifying risks to establish equitable rates. In many property and liability insurance lines, the location of an insured has a significant impact on the loss experience. For example, in automobile insurance the chance of a policyholder sustaining a loss is much greater in New York City than in rural Iowa. In lines like workers compensation, insurers may consider the attitude of the state courts and its impact on the cost of claims in that state. The insurer's task is to define a territorial grouping that has an exposure that is either smaller or greater than the standard, yet the group must be large enough to provide significant loss experience for rate making.

TERRITORIAL LIMITS condition for INLAND MARINE liability insurance coverage that states a loss or claim must occur in the policy territory. Policy territory for a liability policy includes the U.S., its territories, and Canada; international water or air space (except for when the injured person is traveling to another country); and injuries sustained anywhere in the world if a product is produced in the U.S. and the suit is brought in the U.S.

TERRITORIAL LIMITS LIABILITY INSURANCE *see* TERRITORIAL LIMITS.

TERTIARY BENEFICIARY third-in-line BENEFICIARY to receive benefits from an insurance policy should the primary and secondary beneficiaries not survive.

TESTAMENTARY TRUST *see* ESTATE PLANNING DISTRIBUTION; TESTAMENTARY DISPOSITION.

TESTAMENTARY DISPOSITION disposition or transfer of property at time of death. Although the law provides that property may be transferred at death only by means of a will that meets the requirements of state statutes, life insurance proceeds are exempt from this requirement. They pass to the stated beneficiary without regard to the state requirements for wills.

TESTATE DISTRIBUTION *see* ESTATE PLANNING DISTRIBUTION.

THEATRICAL FLOATER endorsement to a *scheduled property floater* that provides named perils coverages for props, costumes, and other materials that might be used by a theatrical company. Coverage is provided for these perils: fire, lightning, windstorm, explosion, collapse of bridges, flood, theft, smoke, and transportation perils.

THEFT act of stealing. Coverage can be purchased under most property insurance policies such as the HOMEOWNERS INSURANCE POLICY.

THEFT, CHARACTERISTICS *see* BURGLARY INSURANCE; HOME-OWNERS INSURANCE POLICY; PERSONAL AUTOMOBILE POLICY (PAP); SPECIAL MULTIPERIL INSURANCE (SMP).

THEFT, EXCLUSION *see* BURGLARY INSURANCE; HOMEOWNERS INSURANCE POLICY; PERSONAL AUTOMOBILE POLICY (PAP); SPECIAL MULTIPERIL INSURANCE (SMP).

THEFT, HOMEOWNERS INSURANCE POLICY *see* HOMEOWNERS INSURANCE POLICY.

THEORY OF PROBABILITY *see* LAW OF LARGE NUMBERS; PROBABILITY; PROBABILITY DISTRIBUTION.

THIEF *see* BURGLARY INSURANCE; HOMEOWNERS INSURANCE POLICY; PERSONAL AUTOMOBILE POLICY (PAP); SPECIAL MULTIPERIL INSURANCE (SMP).

THIRD PARTY individual other than the insured or insurer who has incurred a loss or is entitled to receive a benefit payment as the result of the acts or omissions of the insured.

THIRD PARTY: ADMINISTRATION performance of managerial and clerical functions related to an EMPLOYEE BENEFIT INSURANCE PLAN by an individual or committee that is not an original party to the benefit plan. *See also* ADMINISTERING AGENCY; ADMINISTRATIVE CHARGE; ADVISORY COMMITTEE.

THIRD PARTY: BENEFICIARY individual who has a legally enforceable right to receive all benefits allocated to him or her under the insurance policy or employee benefit plan even though this person was not an original party to the insurance policy contract or employee benefit contract.

THIRD PARTY: INSURANCE liability insurance purchased by the insured (first party) from an insurance company (second party) for protection against possible suits brought by another (third party). *See also* LIABILITY INSURANCE.

"3-D" POLICY *see* DISHONESTY, DISAPPEARANCE, AND DESTRUCTION POLICY ("3-D" policy).

THREE-FOURTHS LOSS CLAUSE provision requiring insurance company to pay no more than three-fourths of the actual cash value of the damaged or destroyed property. Historically, this clause was found in property insurance policies and marine insurance policies. Today, this clause is no longer used.

THREE-FOURTHS VALUE CLAUSE *see* THREE-FOURTHS LOSS CLAUSE.

THREE STEPS INVOLVED *see* RISK MANAGEMENT.

THRESHOLD LEVEL minimum degree of injury or loss for which an injured party can sue, even though covered by NO FAULT AUTOMOBILE INSURANCE. Traditionally, an accident victim had to prove the other driver was at fault in order to collect damages from that driver's insurance company. Today, more than 20 states have some type of automobile no fault law designed to eliminate long and costly legal action, and to assure quick payment for medical and hospital costs, loss of income, and other unavoidable costs stemming from automobile accidents. An injured person can collect from his or her insurance company up to the threshold level, or specified limit, no matter who is at fault. For expenses above these limits, the injured person is still allowed to sue. There are three types of thresholds: a *specific dollar amount,* a *specific period of disability,* or *specified injuries* such as loss of a leg.

TICKET POLICY *see* TRANSPORTATION TICKET INSURANCE.

TIME ELEMENT (TIME POLICY) COVERAGE insurance that covers an INDIRECT LOSS stemming from a DIRECT LOSS by a covered peril to income-producing property. A building destroyed by fire represents a direct loss. Lost income resulting from the shutdown of a manufacturing facility housed in the burned building represents an indirect time element loss and would be covered by BUSINESS INTERRUPTION INSURANCE, a form of time element insurance.

TIME FOR NOTIFICATION OF LOSS period allowed an insured to notify an insurer of loss. Many policies require immediate written notice, or notice as soon as practicable. Different types of policies have their own time periods. For example, health insurance policies require notice within 20 days, windstorm insurance policies within 10 days, and hail insurance policies within 48 hours. The purpose of a time period is to allow the insurer to investigate the loss and protect the property from further damage.

TIME LIMIT
    1. part of the *Model Uniform Life and Health Insurance Policy Provisions Law* giving an insurer a time limit on contesting coverage for preexisting conditions or misrepresentation. This law, developed in 1950 as model legislation by the NATIONAL ASSOCIATION OF INSURANCE COMMISSIONERS (NAIC), has been adopted by all states. While the model law gave insurers three years for certain defenses, such as misrepresentation of facts by an insured or nondisclosure of a preexisting condition, many states have lowered it to two years.

2. period of time that proof of loss or claim must be filed with an insurance company.

TIME LIMITS period of time during which notice of claim and proof of loss must be submitted by the INSURED or his or her legal representatives.

TIME POLICY *see* TIME ELEMENT (TIME POLICY) COVERAGE; VOYAGE POLICY.

TIME VALUE OF MONEY relationship determined by the mathematics of COMPOUND INTEREST between the value of a sum of money at one point in time, and its value at another point in time. Time value of money can be illustrated by the fact that a dollar received today is worth more than a dollar received a year from now because today's dollar can be invested and earn interest as the year elapses. Implicit in any consideration of time value of money are the rate of interest and the period of compounding. For example, the *present value* of $1 million received 10 years from now is only $386,000 today, assuming a 10% rate of interest and annual compounding. Insurance companies make use of time value of money by earning investment income on premiums between the time of receipt and the time of payment of claims or benefits. *See also* STRUCTURED SETTLEMENT.

TITLE INSURANCE coverage for losses if a land title is not free and clear of defects that were unknown when the title insurance was written. Title insurance protects a purchaser if there is a defect in the title, such as a lien against the property, that is not discovered when he buys the property. Although a title search is a routine part of a property transaction, it is possible that a search may overlook some encumbrance. Title insurance is written by title insurance companies that generally operate in a specific geographic area because of the need to examine local records. The TORRENS SYSTEM is a form of title insurance used in some states.

TITLE XIX INSURANCE *see* MEDICAID.

TLO *see* TOTAL LOSS ONLY (TLO) INSURANCE.

TONTINE early life insurance that provided benefits only to survivors who lived to the end of a certain period of time. In the mid-17th century, Lorenzo Tonti, an Italian, devised a scheme to raise money for the French government of Louis XIV. It involved a state lottery in which the oldest survivor would collect the pot. One woman, age 96, hit the jackpot shortly before her death. Tontine policies were introduced in the U.S. in the 1860s, but condemned in the ARMSTRONG INVESTIGATION in 1905 in New York State and subsequently outlawed everywhere 45 years later.

TOP-HEAVY PLAN pension or other employee benefit plan that favors highly compensated employees or top executives or owners of a company. Prior to the TAX REFORM ACT OF 1986, there was no uniform definition of a "highly compensated" employee, but that law provides a specific definition that is used for *qualified pension plans, 401 (k) plans,* and some other employee benefits. An employee is considered highly compensated if he or she: (1) directly or indirectly owns more than a 5% interest in the company, (2) receives compensation from the company of more than $75,000, (3) is paid more than $50,000 *and* was among the top 20% of employees ranked by compensation, or (4) is at any time an officer and receives compensation that was more than 150% of the Section 415 defined-contribution dollar amount.

TORRENS SYSTEM means of land title registration used in some states that, in effect, provides a government sponsored form of TITLE INSURANCE. Under this system, a government official, such as county recorder or county clerk, maintains Torrens system deed records and guarantees clear title when property is transferred. Fees charged for registration and transfer of title are used in part to finance a Torrens insurance fund in each jurisdiction to compensate claimants for damages resulting from errors.

TORT in general, a civil wrong, other than breach of contract, for which a court will provide a remedy in the form of a suit for damages. Torts include negligent acts or omissions on the part of a defendant. Liability insurance is designed to cover an insured (defendant) for *unintentional tort acts. See also* NEGLIGENCE.

TORT, DEFENSE AGAINST UNINTENTIONAL excuses raised by a defendant in a negligent suit (unintentional tort). There are three basic defenses to unintentional torts or negligence.
1. ASSUMPTION OF RISK—an individual (plaintiff), by not objecting to the negligent conduct of another, acknowledges that he is aware and consents to the present danger.
2. CONTRIBUTORY NEGLIGENCE—both individuals have contributed an injury or property damage sustained by one or both individuals. Under this circumstance neither should be allowed to collect from the other.
3. COMPARATIVE NEGLIGENCE—where both plaintiff and defendant contributed to plaintiff's injury, the apportionment of some fault to the plaintiff reduces the liability of the defendant.

TORT FEASOR person who commits a TORT, a type of wrongful act, that causes injury or damage.

TORT, INTENTIONAL deliberate act or omission. These torts include *trespass*—an individual enters property owned or in the possession of another without permission; *conversion*—an individual exerts control and subverts another's property to his own benefit; *assault*—an individual's conduct causes another to fear for his life or the damage to his property; *battery*—an individual physically strikes another without permission; *false imprisonment*—an individual confines another illegally; *libel*—dissemination of written injurious and false information about another's character; and *slander*—oral dissemination of injurious and false information about another's character.

TORT LAW legislation governing wrongful acts, other than breaches of contract by one person against another or his property, for which civil action can be brought. Tort law and contract law define civil liability exposures. The four areas of torts are negligence, intentional interference, absolute liability, and strict liability. For example, the owner of a decrepit boat dock that collapses while people are standing on it might be liable under negligence. Assault and battery are an example of intentional interference. The owner of a poisonous snake that bit someone could be liable for injury under absolute liability, even if he did not intend to harm anyone. The maker of a defective product that harms the buyer might be held liable under strict liability. *See also* TORT LIABILITY.

TORT LIABILITY *see* TORT; TORT, DEFENSE AGAINST UNINTENTIONAL; TORT, INTENTIONAL; TORT; UNINTENTIONAL.

TORT, UNINTENTIONAL individual action or failure to act as a reasonably prudent person would under similar circumstances, resulting in harm to another. Also called NEGLIGENCE. A reasonably prudent person is defined by the standards of the profession he follows, and the level of expertise expected of a person with like training. An example is a CPA who fails to complete tax returns on behalf of a client according to GENERALLY ACCEPTED ACCOUNTING PRINCIPLES.

TOTAL DISABILITY *see* DISABILITY.

TOTAL LOSS condition of real or personal property when it is damaged or destroyed to such an extent that it cannot be rebuilt or repaired to equal its condition prior to the loss.

TOTAL LOSS ONLY (TLO) INSURANCE ocean marine policy that pays an insured only if a ship or cargo is a total loss. Because total loss is rare, these policies are much less expensive than regular hull insurance. Therefore, it is used by shipowners who cannot afford more complete coverage or who cannot get it for some other reason.

TOURIST BAGGAGE INSURANCE coverage for personal effects of a tourist, including apparel, books, toilet articles, watches, jewelry, luggage, portable typewriters, photographs and photography equipment and supplies. This is a SPECIFIED PERIL INSURANCE policy that specifically includes fire, lightning, damage due to automobile accident, theft of items in the care, custody, and control of a common carrier, and theft of items from the hotel room in which the insured tourist is registered. Excluded are baggage theft from checkrooms, baggage theft from hotel lobbies unless checked, items at the permanent premises of the insured tourist, and items that cannot be found but have not been stolen.

TOWING INSURANCE endorsement to an automobile policy that pays specified amount for towing and related labor costs.

TOWNHOUSE MULTIPLE LINE INSURANCE homeowners policy to cover the owner of a townhouse. *See also* HOMEOWNERS INSURANCE POLICY.

TRADITIONAL NET COST METHOD OF COMPARING COSTS *see* INTEREST ADJUSTED COST; LIFE INSURANCE COST.

TRADITIONAL RISK REINSURANCE application of conventional terms and conditions to the REINSURANCE of a RISK. Contrast with NONTRADITIONAL REINSURANCE.

TRAILER INSURANCE liability and physical damage coverage for trailers under business or personal auto policies. Most *automobile insurance* policies offer liability coverage for common types of trailers owned by an insured, including house trailers, boat trailers, and campers. For *collision insurance* coverage, personally owned trailers must be scheduled on a personal policy. The BUSINESS AUTOMOBILE POLICY (BAP) offers only limited insurance without scheduled coverage for both liability and collision.

TRANSACTING INSURANCE *see* NAIC: MODEL LIFE INSURANCE SOLICITATION REGULATION; NATIONAL ASSOCIATION OF INSURANCE COMMISSIONERS (NAIC).

TRANSFERABILITY *see* ASSIGNMENT; ASSIGNMENT CLAUSE, LIFE INSURANCE; COLLATERAL ASSIGNMENT.

TRANSFER ABSOLUTE *see* LIFE INSURANCE, ASSIGNMENT CLAUSE.

TRANSFER BY ASSIGNMENT *see* ASSIGNMENT CLAUSE, LIFE INSURANCE.

TRANSFER BY ENDORSEMENT *see* ASSIGNMENT; COLLATERAL ASSIGNMENT; LIFE INSURANCE, ASSIGNMENT CLAUSE.

TRANSFER OF INSUREDS provision in corporate life insurance policies that allows coverage to be transferred to a new individual with proof of insurability, for a premium appropriate to the age of the new individual. These policies are designed to cover key executives of a corporation and to provide continuous insurance in force without the necessity of obtaining a new policy. For example, if a corporation buys insurance to cover the chief executive officer and he retires, the policy could be transferred to the new CEO. *See also* RIDERS, LIFE INSURANCE.

TRANSFER OF RISK *see* RISK TRANSFER.

TRANSIT INSURANCE INLAND MARINE policy that protects an insured against loss for property that is shipped. One policy may be written for a single shipment, as for a family moving household goods, or it may be an open policy written for a manufacturer who continuously ships products. The basic inland transit policy is written on one of two policy forms, the ANNUAL POLICY or the OPEN POLICY. TRIP TRANSIT INSURANCE is available for single shipments.

TRANSPORTATION INSURANCE *see* INLAND MARINE INSURANCE (TRANSPORTATION INSURANCE): BUSINESS RISKS.

TRANSPORTATION INSURANCE RATING BUREAU (TIRB) one of two bureaus that writes forms and files standard rates for inland marine insurance. The other is the INLAND MARINE INSURANCE BUREAU.

TRANSPORTATION TICKET INSURANCE accident policy that covers a traveler for a single trip on an airplane or other common carrier. The name comes from its origin as part of the ticket or ticket stub, but these policies are no longer sold with the ticket. They are commonly sold in airports, often from vending machines.

TRAUMATIC INJURY bodily or emotional injury resulting from physical or mental wound or shock. A traumatic injury is caused by something outside the person's body as opposed to a sickness or a disease. An example would be injury to a hand that is smashed in a machine or a nervous breakdown caused by stress on the job.

TRAVEL ACCIDENT INSURANCE special-purpose health insurance policy that covers an insured for accidents while traveling. The policy may cover the insured for one specific trip or one particular type of travel, or it may cover all trips taken in a year. This type of insurance can be purchased in airport vending machines or from an agent.

TREATMENT OF DEATH BENEFITS *see* TAX BENEFITS OF LIFE INSURANCE; TAX PLANNING; ESTATE PLANNING; ESTATE PLANNING DISTRIBUTION; GROUP LIFE INSURANCE; PENSION PLAN.

TREATMENT OF EMPLOYEE WITHDRAWALS *see* PENSION PLANS: WITHDRAWAL BENEFITS.

TREATMENT OF GAINS AND LOSSES *see* TAX REFORM ACT OF 1986.

TREATY REINSURANCE *see* AUTOMATIC NONPROPORTIONAL REINSURANCE; AUTOMATIC PROPORTIONAL REINSURANCE; AUTOMATIC REINSURANCE.

TRESPASS *see* TRESPASSER, TORT, INTENTIONAL.

TRESPASSER person who enters property without the right to do so. For liability purposes, it has been held that property owners are not responsible for trespassers as long as they do not intentionally trap or injure them. On the other hand, a property owner can be liable for injury to a person who has been invited onto his property, including messengers, delivery people, and service people, as well as guests. However, trespassers are very narrowly defined. No one in a public place is considered a trespasser. Likewise owners of an ATTRACTIVE NUISANCE have been held liable for injuries to trespassing children. Further, recent interpretations by the courts have sometimes made owners liable for injury to trespassers if the owner was negligent.

TRIP CARGO INSURANCE *see* CARGO INSURANCE.

TRIPLE INDEMNITY *see* ACCIDENTAL DEATH CLAUSE.

TRIPLE PROTECTION combination life insurance policy consisting of ORDINARY LIFE and double the amount of TERM LIFE. Should the insured die within a stipulated time period, the double term amount and ordinary life amount are paid to the beneficiary. If the insured dies beyond the stipulated time period, only the ordinary amount is paid to the beneficiary. This policy may be applicable in situations where the family is young and extra amounts of protection are required until the children reach the age of majority.

TRIP TRANSIT INSURANCE coverage on a single shipment of property while in temporary storage or in transit. This policy is most commonly used in moving of household goods, which are covered from the time they are picked up, put in temporary storage, shipped to another location and put in temporary storage, and then delivered to the insured's new address. Protection is on an ALL RISKS basis subject to exclusions such as war, wear and tear, and nuclear disaster.

TRUCKERS INSURANCE limited special purposes policy that provides liability and physical damage insurance for owners and operators of trucks while engaged in business. This insurance is often purchased by a business that employs owner-operators.

TRUE GROUP PLAN insurance arrangement in which all employees of a given business firm are accepted into a plan regardless of their physical condition. The employee cannot be required to take a physical examination in order to qualify. The employees are covered under a *Master Contract*. *See also* GROUP HEALTH INSURANCE; GROUP LIFE INSURANCE.

TRUE NO-FAULT AUTOMOBILE INSURANCE *see* NO-FAULT AUTOMOBILE INSURANCE.

TRUST legal entity that provides for ownership of property by one person for the benefit of another. The TRUSTEE receives title to the property, but does not have the right to benefit personally from that property. The trustee has a legal obligation to manage the property and invest its assets solely for the BENEFICIARY OF TRUST. Since the trustee is required to manage the property and its assets in a prudent manner, if he or she fails to perform in accordance with the PRUDENT MAN RULE the trustee becomes personally responsible for any lost funds or profits incurred by the trust. There are basically two types of trusts: LIVING TRUST (established during the life of the GRANTOR) and TESTAMENTARY TRUST. For example, a trust may be established by a parent to hold assets for the benefit of a child. *See also* BENEFICIARY OF TRUST; ESTATE PLANNING DISTRIBUTION.

TRUST AGREEMENT legal document setting out the rules to be followed by a TRUSTEE in administering assets of a TRUST. The trust agreement may limit investment of trust assets to specified types of securities, for example, or provide for distribution of the trust principal or earnings to a BENEFICIARY OF TRUST only under certain circumstances.

TRUSTEE *see* ESTATE PLANNING DISTRIBUTION.

TRUSTEE, BOND *see* TRUSTEE ROLE, PENSION PLANS.

TRUSTEE LIABILITY INSURANCE coverage provided for the fiduciaries of a retirement plan as well as for the plan itself in the event negligence of the fiduciaries results in losses to the plan and/or liability suits filed against the plan and/or the fiduciaries.

TRUSTEE, NEGLIGENCE *see* TRUSTEE LIABILITY INSURANCE.

TRUSTEE ROLE, PENSION PLANS *see* PENSION PLAN; PENSION PLAN FUNDING INSTRUMENTS; PENSION PLAN FUNDING, GROUP DEPOSIT ADMINISTRATION ANNUITY; PENSION PLAN FUNDING, GROUP IMMEDIATE PARTICIPATION GUARANTEED (IPG) CONTRACT ANNUITY; PENSION PLAN FUNDING, GROUP PERMANENT CONTRACT; PENSION PLAN FUNDING, INDIVIDUAL CONTRACT PENSION PLAN.

TRUSTEE, TERMINATED PLAN one named under provisions of the EMPLOYEE RETIREMENT INCOME SECURITY ACT OF 1974 (ERISA) for a terminated pension plan with an unfunded liability for its benefits.

TRUST FUND PLAN one of two basic types of funding instruments for pensions or employee benefits, in which responsibility for plan assets is vested in a trustee. The other type is known as an *insured plan,* whose assets are held by a life insurance company, typically under a group annuity contract that guarantees payment of benefits. A COMBINATION PLAN makes use of both approaches, with some contributions going to a trustee and the remainder to an insurance company. *See also* SELF-ADMINISTERED PLAN.

TRUST FUND PLAN ANALYSIS *see* TRUST FUND PLAN.

TRUST INDENTURE document setting out the responsibilities of a borrower, such as a corporation issuing bonds, and the powers of a trustee who will be looking after the interests of the bondholders.

TRUSTOR *see* ESTATE PLANNING DISTRIBUTION.

TUITION FEES INSURANCE indemnification of a school for the loss of tuition, and room and board fees when it is forced to suspend classes because of the occurrence of a peril. *See also* TUITION FORM.

TUITION FORM coverage in the event a school, summer camp, or similar operation suffers loss of tuition because a peril destroys a building. The tuition form reimburses the institution for loss of tuition and rental income from room and board. *See also* TUITION FEES INSURANCE.

TUNNEL INSURANCE coverage in the event a tunnel is damaged or destroyed. Written on an ALL RISKS basis, excluding perils of war, wear and tear, inherent defect, and nuclear damage. For example, this coverage would be important to businesses which have underground tunnels connecting different locations.

TURNKEY INSURANCE Contractor's and Architect's Errors and Omissions Insurance, which also serves as a general liability policy for these professionals.

TURNOVER RATE frequency with which employees resign, are fired, or retire from a company, usually computed as the percentage of an organization's employees at the beginning of a calendar year. The turnover rate is one of the factors affecting the cost of a pension plan. Employees who leave a company before they have a *vested interest* in the plan represent a cost saving to plan administrators, because they will not receive benefits when they retire. For this reason, most actuaries make assumptions about the turnover rate of a particular company when calculating how much money must be contributed to a retirement plan to pay future benefits.

TWISTING UNFAIR TRADE PRACTICE, in insurance, whereby an agent or broker attempts to persuade a life insurance policyholder through misrepresentation to cancel one policy and buy a new one. Some states have laws requiring full disclosure of relevant comparative information about existing and proposed policies by an agent trying to convince a customer to switch policies. These laws may provide for notification of the insurance company that issued the existing policy to give it an opportunity to respond to the agent's proposal.

U

U&O *see* USE AND OCCUPANCY INSURANCE.

UBERRIMAE FIDEI CONTRACT agreement "of utmost good faith." Under law, it is assumed that insurance contracts are entered into by all parties in good faith, meaning that they have disclosed all relevant facts and intend to carry out their obligations. Where lack of good faith can be proved, such as in a fraudulent application to obtain insurance, the contract may be nullified.

UJF *see* UNSATISFIED JUDGMENT FUND.

UL *see* UNDERWRITERS LABORATORIES, INC. (UL).

ULTIMATE MORTALITY TABLE presentation of data that excludes the first 5 to 10 years of experience of those who purchase life insurance. A MORTALITY TABLE shows the number of deaths per 1000 of a group of people. Experience shows that people have a lower mortality rate in the first years after they have purchased insurance, probably because they have recently passed a medical and other tests. A SELECT MORTALITY TABLE includes data only on people who have recently purchased insurance. An *aggregate mortality table* includes all data.

ULTIMATE NET LOSS insurer's total payments resulting from a claim, including all related expenses, less any recoveries from salvage, reinsurance, and the exercise of *subrogation* rights or other rights against third parties. *See also* LOSS DEVELOPMENT.

ULTRA VIRES Latin phrase meaning "beyond power or authority" describing an act by a corporation that exceeds its legal powers. For example, corporations do not have the authority to engage in the insurance business without a charter. A corporation offering insurance without authority would be acting ultra vires. Similarly, an insurance company chartered to engage in a single line of business would be operating ultra vires by offering some other line.

UMBRELLA LIABILITY INSURANCE excess liability coverage above the limits of a basic business liability insurance policy such as the OWNERS, LANDLORDS AND TENANTS LIABILITY POLICY. For example, if a basic policy has a limit of $500,000, and it is exhausted by claims, the umbrella will pay the excess above $500,000 up to the limit of the umbrella policy, which may be as high as $10,000,000, $25,000,000 or more. The umbrella policy also fills gaps in coverage under basic liability policies.

UMBRELLA REINSURANCE protection for all classes of business including automobile, fire, general liability, homeowners, multiple peril, burglary, and glass, by combining the contracts for these classes of business into one reinsurance contract. This enables the *cedant* to obtain reinsurance more cheaply, with greater capacity and with greater spread of risk. An umbrella reinsurance contract is offered to one set of reinsurers who all take a fixed percentage of every treaty in the contract. One reinsurer may take 5% across the board, another may take 10%, and so on until the umbrella contract is totally placed. All the treaties that compose the umbrella contract are written as one block of business; hence, the reinsurers are prohibited from choosing which treaty they want to reinsure. By combining all the reinsurance treaties into one contract, if a catastrophe loss results, each reinsurer will assume only a percentage of the loss instead of assuming the entire loss by itself.

UMPIRE arbitrator who settles disputes over the amount of loss when an insurer and an insured do not agree.

UNALLOCATED BENEFIT *see* UNALLOCATED FUNDING INSTRUMENT.

UNALLOCATED FUNDING INSTRUMENT pension funding agreement under which funds paid into a retirement plan are not currently allocated to purchase retirement benefits. The funds of one plan cannot be commingled with funds of another plan and the plan trustee guarantees neither principal nor interest of the funds deposited. At retirement the trustee can either purchase an *immediate retirement annuity* for the retiring employee or pay the benefits directly from the fund as they become due. *See also* PENSION PLAN FUNDING: GROUP DEPOSIT ADMINISTRATION ANNUITY; PENSION PLAN FUNDING; GROUP IMMEDIATE PARTICIPATION GUARANTEED (IPG) CONTRACT ANNUITY; PENSION PLAN FUNDING INSTRUMENTS; TRUST FUND PLAN.

UNAUTHORIZED INSURER *see* NONADMITTED INSURER

UNAUTHORIZED PRACTICE OF LAW act of practicing law or providing legal advice without a license.

UNBUNDLED term that describes commercial insurance with no administrative services attached, or alternatively, administrative services from an insurer without insurance coverage. Years ago, insureds bought a package that included coverage for exposures as well as claims paying, loss control, and other risk management services. With the increasing sophistication of risk management in the past decade, and to reduce their costs, many corporations elect to perform some of these duties themselves and to purchase insurance and other services on an unbundled basis.

UNBUNDLED LIFE INSURANCE POLICY coverage in which the investment features, mortality element, and cost factors of a LIFE INSURANCE policy are separated, permitting each part to be independently analyzed. The SAVINGS ELEMENT of the policy then becomes interest-sensitive (rate of return paid to the POLICYHOLDER is more consistent with the rate of returns earned by the life insurance company over a period of time than is the rate of return paid to the holder of a traditional life insurance policy). *See also* UNIVERSAL LIFE INSURANCE.

UNDERINSURANCE
   1. failure to maintain adequate coverage for a specific loss or damage.
   2. failure to meet a COINSURANCE requirement.

UNDERINSURED MOTORIST ENDORSEMENT addition to a PERSONAL AUTOMOBILE POLICY (PAP) that covers an insured who is involved in a collision with a driver who does not have sufficient liability insurance to pay for the damages. *See also* UNINSURED MOTORIST INSURANCE.

UNDERLYING MORTALITY ASSUMPTION *see* MORTALITY ASSUMPTION.

UNDERLYING RETENTION *see* RETENTION AND LIMITS CLAUSE; RISK MANAGEMENT; SELF INSURANCE.

UNDERWRITER, LAY individual who works in the home office of an insurance company and performs the function of UNDERWRITING to determine if an applicant is insurable at standard rates, substandard rates, insurable at preferred rates, or is uninsurable.

UNDERWRITER, LIFE *see* AGENT.

UNDERWRITERS ASSOCIATION *see* POOL; PRODUCERS COOPERATIVE.

UNDERWRITERS LABORATORIES, INC. (UL) independent agency supported by the insurance industry that tests a variety of materials, products, and devices, such as appliances and electrical equipment, to assure that they meet safety standards.

UNDERWRITER SYNDICATE *see* LLOYD'S OF LONDON.

UNDERWRITING process of examining, accepting, or rejecting insurance risks, and classifying those selected, in order to charge the proper premium for each. The purpose of underwriting is to spread the risk among a pool of insureds in a manner that is equitable for the insureds and profitable for the insurer. *See also* RISK MANAGEMENT; RISK SELECTION.

UNDERWRITING CYCLE tendency of property and liability insurance premiums, insurers' profits, and availability of coverage to rise and fall with some regularity over time. A cycle can be said to begin when insurers tighten their underwriting standards and sharply raise premiums after a period of severe underwriting losses. Stricter standards and higher premium rates often bring dramatic increases in profits, attracting more capital to the insurance industry and raising underwriting capacity. On the other hand, as insurers strive to write more premiums at higher levels of profitability, premium rates may be driven down and underwriting standards relaxed in the competition for new business. Profits may erode and then turn into losses if more lax underwriting standards generate mounting claims. The stage would then be set for the cycle to begin again.

UNDERWRITING GAIN (LOSS) profit (deficit) that remains after paying claims and expenses. Insurers generate profits from underwriting and from investment income. Their chief business is insuring against risks for a profit, and one measure of success is whether there is money left after paying claims and expenses. This amount, if any, is their underwriting gain. *See also* COMBINED RATIO.

UNDERWRITING PROFIT (LOSS) *see* UNDERWRITING GAIN (LOSS).

UNEARNED PREMIUM *see* UNEARNED PREMIUM INSURANCE; UNEARNED PREMIUM RESERVE; UNEARNED REINSURANCE PREMIUM.

UNEARNED PREMIUM INSURANCE coverage for loss of unearned premium if insured property is destroyed before the end of a policy period. The policyholder pays in advance for insurance, but the insurer does not earn the premium until coverage is provided. For example, if a policy period is one year, one-twelfth of the premium is earned each month. After six months, one-half of the premium is still unearned and belongs to the policyholder if the policy is cancelled. If the property is destroyed in the second month and the insurer pays the claim, the policyholder would have nothing left to insure. Unearned premium insurance reimburses the insured for the part of the premium paid up front that is no longer needed for insurance coverage.

UNEARNED PREMIUM RESERVE fund that contains the portion of the premium that has been paid in advance for insurance that has not yet been provided. For example, if a business pays an annual premium of $1000 on January 1, the money is not earned by the insurer until the insurance coverage has been provided. On July 1, $500 would have been earned and $500 would remain as unearned premium, belonging to the policyholder. If either party cancels the contract, the insurer must have the unearned premium ready to refund. For this reason, insurance regulators require that insurers maintain an unearned premium reserve so that, in the event an insurer must be liquidated, there is enough money to pay claims and refund the unearned premium. Because computations for individual policies would be cumbersome, regulators have devised formulas for figuring unearned premium reserves. *See also* REINSURANCE RESERVE (UNEARNED PREMIUM RESERVE).

UNEARNED REINSURANCE PREMIUM portion of reinsurance premium received by the reinsurer which relates to the unexpired part of the reinsured policy. *See also* AUTOMATIC PROPORTIONAL REINSURANCE; FACULTATIVE REINSURANCE; NONPROPORTIONAL REINSURANCE; PROPORTIONAL REINSURANCE; REINSURANCE.

UNEMPLOYMENT COMPENSATION money paid through state and Federal programs to workers who are temporarily unemployed. The program, which was created by the SOCIAL SECURITY ACT OF 1935, is managed by the individual states, which decide the level of benefits that will be paid and assess a payroll tax on employers to pay for the program. Employers may pay more or less tax depending on the stability of their workforces. Weekly benefits vary widely among the states.

UNFAIR CLAIMS PRACTICE abuse by an insurer in an effort to avoid paying a claim filed by an insured, or to reduce the size of the payment. The NATIONAL ASSOCIATION OF INSURANCE COMMISSIONERS (NAIC) has developed model legislation requiring that claims be handled fairly and that there be free communication between policyholder and insurer. Many states have adopted unfair claims practice laws.

UNFAIR TRADE PRACTICE in insurance, fraudulent or unethical practice that is illegal under state law. States may fine or revoke the licenses of agents and brokers for unfair trade practices, including misrepresentation, false advertising, misappropriation of policyholder's money, and TWISTING. Many states have adopted the NAIC model *Unfair Trade Practices Act.*

UNFRIENDLY FIRE *see* HOSTILE FIRE.

UNFUNDED *see* UNALLOCATED FUNDING INSTRUMENT.

UNIFORM COMMERCIAL CODE standardized set of business laws that has been adopted by most states. The Uniform Commercial Code governs a wide range of transactions including borrowing, contracts, and many other everyday business practices. It is useful because it standardizes practices from state to state.

UNIFORM FORMS widely accepted standard policy forms that have been developed by various RATING BUREAUS or insurance companies. Some forms are required by state law, and some are used by custom. In some cases provisions are mandated but a form is not. Even so, many companies use the same forms, which become widely recognized as the standard for certain types of risk.

UNIFORM INDIVIDUAL ACCIDENT AND SICKNESS POLICY PROVISIONS ACT regulations of the NATIONAL ASSOCIATION OF INSURANCE COMMISSIONERS (NAIC) that dictate provisions which all individual health insurance policies must contain. All states now require these provisions, which include the circumstances under which changes can be made to the policy; how the BENEFICIARY can be changed; submission of PROOF OF LOSS; REINSTATEMENT of the policy; and GRACE PERIOD.

UNIFORM POLICY PROVISIONS, HEALTH INSURANCE basic contract language in individual health and accident insurance policies. These provisions are required under a model state law known as the UNIFORM INDIVIDUAL ACCIDENT AND SICKNESS POLICY PROVISIONS ACT. The uniform provisions, some mandatory and some optional under the model act, deal with such questions as proof of loss, medical examination, claims notice, claims forms, policy renewal, and premium grace period. The act does not require companies to adopt exact wording in their policies but to substantially follow the provision guidelines.

UNIFORM PROVISIONS language adopted by the NATIONAL ASSOCIATION OF INSURANCE COMMISSIONERS (NAIC) and recommended or required by state law. While they rarely dictate the language of policies, states often prescribe mandatory or optional policy minimums, or may forbid certain provisions. Therefore, while life and health benefits may vary widely, for example, policyholders are given certain uniform rights, like grace periods for paying premiums and loan and surrender values.

UNIFORM RECIPROCAL LICENSING ACT law by which many states attempt to regulate insurers who are unlicensed in those states. With a few notable exceptions, such as reinsurers, insurance companies must be licensed in the states where they do business. If a U.S. insurer sells insurance in a state where it is unauthorized, the insurer's home state may revoke its license under the Uniform Reciprocal Licensing Act.

UNIFORM SIMULTANEOUS DEATH ACT statute in most states under which, if no evidence exists in a *common disaster* (when an insured and beneficiary die within a short time of each other in an accident for which determination cannot be made as to who died first), the presumption is that the insured survived the beneficiary and the life insurance proceeds will either be paid to a secondary beneficiary (if named in a policy) or if not named, then to the insured's estate.

UNILATERAL CONTRACT legal agreement in which only one of the two parties makes legally enforceable promises. An insurance contract is a unilateral contract because only the insurer has made a promise of future performance and only the insurer can be charged with breach of contract. In contrast, in a bilateral contract, both parties promise future performance.

UNINSURABLE PROPERTY *see* UNINSURABLE RISK.

UNINSURABLE RISK risk that substantially fails to meet the REQUIREMENTS OF INSURABLE RISK.

UNINSURED MOTORIST COVERAGE endorsement to PERSONAL AUTOMOBILE POLICY (PAP) that covers an insured involved in a collision with a driver who does not have liability insurance. *See also* UNDERINSURED MOTORIST ENDORSEMENT.

UNINTENTIONAL TORT *see* NEGLIGENCE; TORT, UNINTENTIONAL.

UNIQUE IMPAIRMENT physical, moral, or financial circumstance of a life insurance applicant that sets him apart from a physically, morally, and financially sound standard applicant. The underwriting weight attached to this impairment (such as a history of bankruptcy or a serious health condition) could result in the applicant being classified as substandard or uninsurable.

UNISEX LEGISLATION regulations affecting the right of insurance companies to use sex as one of the factors in the actuarial determination of premium rates. The precedent case for such legislation is Arizona Governing Committee v. Norris in which the decision was that a municipal retirement plan could not provide retirement benefits based on sex.

UNIT BENEFIT *see* DEFINED BENEFIT PLAN; UNIT BENEFIT PLAN.

UNIT BENEFIT APPROACH *see* DEFINED BENEFIT PLAN.

UNIT BENEFIT PLAN retirement plan under which a discrete increment of periodic retirement income is credited to an employee for each year of service with an employer. This increment is either a flat dollar amount or, more often, a percentage of compensation. If percentage of compensation is credited, it generally is 1¼-2½%. At retirement, years of service are multiplied by percentage of compensation. The resulting percentage is applied to the employee's final average or career average of earnings. For example, if an employee has 30 years of service, a final average earnings of $100,000, and the percentage of compensation is 1½%, the employee's annual retirement benefit would be $45,000 ($30 × $100,000 × .015). *See also* DEFINED BENEFIT PLAN.

UNITED STATES AIRCRAFT INSURANCE GROUP one of the major underwriting organizations for insurance company .pools insuring commercial aircraft liability exposure.

UNITED STATES GOVERNMENT LIFE INSURANCE (USGLI) *see* GOVERNMENT LIFE INSURANCE.

UNITED STATES LONGSHOREMEN AND HARBOR WORKERS ACT OF 1927 *see* LONGSHOREMEN AND HARBOR WORKERS ACT LIABILITY.

UNITED STATES v. THE SOUTH-EASTERN UNDERWRITERS ASSOCIATION *see* SOUTH-EASTERN UNDERWRITERS ASSOCIATION (SEUA) CASE.

UNIVERSAL LIFE II *see* UNIVERSAL VARIABLE LIFE INSURANCE.

UNIVERSAL LIFE INSURANCE ADJUSTABLE LIFE INSURANCE under which (1) premiums are flexible, not fixed; (2) protection is adjustable, not fixed; and (3) insurance company expenses and other charges are specifically disclosed to a purchaser. This policy is referred to as *unbundled life insurance* because its three basic elements (investment earnings, *pure cost of protection*, and company expenses) are separately identified both in the policy and in an annual report to the policyowner. After the first premium, additional premiums can be paid at any time. (There usually are limits on the dollar amount of each additional payment.) A specified percentage expense charge is deducted from each premium before the balance is credited to the cash value, along with interest. The pure cost of protection is subtracted from the cash value monthly. As selected by the insured, the death benefit can be a specified amount plus the cash value or the specified amount which includes the cash value. After payment of the minimal initial premium required, there are no contractually scheduled premium payments (provided the cash value account balance is sufficient to pay the pure cost of protection each month and any other expenses and charges. Expenses and charges may take the form of a flat dollar amount for the first policy year, a sales charge for each premium received, and a monthly expense charge for each policy year). An annual report is provided the policyowner which shows the status of the policy (death benefit option selected, specified amount of insurance in force, cash value, surrender value, and the transactions made each month under the policy during the year—premiums received, expenses charged, guaranteed and excess interest credited to the cash value account, pure cost of insurance deducted, and cash value balance). *See also* UNIVERSAL VARIABLE LIFE INSURANCE.

UNIVERSAL VARIABLE *see* UNIVERSAL VARIABLE LIFE INSURANCE.

UNIVERSAL VARIABLE LIFE INSURANCE policy combining features of UNIVERSAL LIFE INSURANCE and VARIABLE LIFE INSURANCE in that excess interest credited to the cash value account depends on investment results of separate accounts (equities, bonds, real estate, etc.). The policyowner selects the accounts into which the premium payments are to be made. However, since this is an EQUITY product, filing with the SECURITIES AND EXCHANGE COMMISSION (SEC), an annual prospectus, an audit of separate accounts, and agent registration with the NATIONAL ASSOCIATION OF SECURITIES DEALERS (NASD) are required. This policy can be considered a replacement for universal life insurance when interest rates of U.S. Treasury issues and other money market instruments are low. *Contrast with* UNIVERSAL LIFE INSURANCE.

UNLIMITED MARITAL DEDUCTION deduction allowed for gifts and bequests to a spouse for Federal estate and gift tax purposes. Under the Economic Recovery Tax Act of 1981 (ERTA), the deduction became unlimited. Prior to this, there was a dollar and percentage limitation for the marital deduction.

UNOCCUPANCY absence of people for at least 60 consecutive days from a given property. Many property insurance policies suspend coverage after a structure has been unoccupied for 60 consecutive days because the probability of loss increases dramatically from such perils as vandalism and malicious mischief. Premiums for these policies were based on statements of an insured that the structure would be occupied. Unoccupancy results in an increase in hazards within the control of an insured, which gives the insurance company the right to suspend the policy. *See also* VACANCY.

UNREPORTED CLAIMS *see* INCURRED BUT NOT REPORTED LOSSES (IBNR).

UNSATISFIED JUDGMENT FUND money set aside in some states to pay otherwise uncompensated bodily injury claims to innocent victims of automobile accidents. The claimant must prove that he was not at fault and that he cannot collect damages from the driver who hit him. The responsible driver then loses his license until he reimburses the fund.

UNSCHEDULED PROPERTY FLOATER insurance that offers blanket coverage up to a certain dollar amount on all property of the classification covered by the policy. Floater policies, which cover property wherever it happens to be and while it is in transit, can also be purchased as a SCHEDULED POLICY where each individual item is listed.

UNSOLICITED APPLICATION request for life insurance coverage by an individual, not through an agent or broker. It is given extra scrutiny by an insurance company because of the possibility of SELF-SELECTION, which is the likelihood that poorer risks will seek insurance on their own initiative. *See also* ADVERSE SELECTION; RISK SELECTION.

UNVALUED MARINE POLICY coverage that does not put a dollar value on a hull or cargo that is insured. A *valued marine policy* puts a specific value on the insured property. With unvalued property, the value is determined at the time of loss.

URBAN DEVELOPMENT ACT OF 1970 law that provided for Federal crime insurance. Because private insurance is not available for business owners and residents of certain high-crime areas, the act provides that the FEDERAL INSURANCE ADMINISTRATION write the coverage. Private insurers service the program.

USE AND OCCUPANCY INSURANCE type of BUSINESS INTERRUPTION INSURANCE that provides indirect loss coverage by endorsement to BOILER AND MACHINERY INSURANCE. The latter, sometimes called POWER PLANT INSURANCE, provides for both direct and indirect loss coverage. Direct loss would indemnify an insured for damage to property. Use and occupancy insurance covers an insured for loss of use of the equipment due to damage from a named peril.

USGLI *see* GOVERNMENT LIFE INSURANCE.

USUAL AND CUSTOMARY CHARGE
1. fee that is the most consistently charged by the physician for a particular procedure.
2. fee that is usual for a particular procedure charged by the majority of physicians with similar training and experience within the same geographic area.

USUAL, CUSTOMARY AND REASONABLE CHARGES (UCR) limits on reimbursement by an insurance company. Health insurance plans pay a doctor's full charge for service if it does not exceed the usual charge; that is, if it does not exceed the charge for the same service by other physicians in the area or if it is reasonable.

UTILIZATION measurement of the use of health insurance by employees of an insured employer, stated in terms of the average number of claims per employee.

UTILITY quality of being useful. Risk diminishes maximum utility in society because resources gravitate to activities, businesses, and investments that are least risky. By absorbing or protecting against some risks, insurance increases utility. When individuals know they will have some cushion against loss, their assets can be spread out over a greater range of activities and enterprises.

UTMOST GOOD FAITH *see* UBERRIMAE FIDEI CONTRACT.

V

VACANCY circumstance where no people or contents occupy or are kept in a building for at least 60 consecutive days. The same stipulations apply to property coverages as found in unoccupancy. *See also* UNOCCUPANCY.

VALIDATION PERIOD length of time required to amortize the excess expenses of acquiring a given group of life insurance policies. In acquiring a policy, a life insurance company may incur expenses (such as the costs of sales commissions, paperwork, and medical examinations) that are greater than the amount allocated for LOADING in the first year's premium. In effect, this means new policies are acquired at a loss, forcing insurers to dip into *surplus* to add the new business. After the first year, because expenses are lower, premiums and their invested earnings begin to generate a contribution to surplus, gradually making up for the excess expense of the first year. The length of the validation period depends on many factors, including the levels of GROSS PREMIUMS and expenses, but in some companies validation periods can extend for 10 years or more.

VALID CONTRACT agreement signed by both parties that meets the requirements of state law and is therefore in force.

VALUABLE PAPERS (RECORDS) INSURANCE coverage in the event that papers of intrinsic value are damaged or destroyed. Coverage is on an ALL RISKS basis. Limits of coverage can be quite high; but the insurance company will not pay an amount in excess of the actual cash value of the loss, or the amount necessary to repair or replace the damaged or destroyed papers. Also, the papers must be kept under lock and key.

VALUATION
1. method of determining the worth of property to be insured, or of property that has been lost or damaged.
2. method of setting insurance company reserves to pay future claims.

VALUATION FACTORS, PENSION PLANS *see* PENSION PLAN VALUATION FACTORS.

VALUATION METHOD means of determining that a loss has occurred and setting an economic value on it so that a claim can be paid. When an insured suffers a loss, an adjuster must determine that it actually occurred, that it was covered by insurance, and the value of the lost or damaged property. The adjuster, with the help of the insured, determines the cost to repair or replace the covered property. The adjuster computes actual cash value, or replacement cost, minus depreciation. For indirect losses, such as *business interruption*, the adjuster must make rough estimates, and then must consider COINSURANCE and adjust claims payments for it.

VALUATION OF ASSETS rules by state insurance regulators for valuing ADMITTED ASSETS on the books of insurance companies. Part of the STATE SUPERVISION AND REGULATION of insurers is the determination of which assets—"admitted assets"—are allowed to back STATUTORY RESERVES. Admitted assets include real estate, mortgages, securities, cash, and bank deposits. Mortgage loans, cash, and bank deposits are recognized at face value. Real estate is allowed at book value. Securities are carried according to SECURITY VALUATION rules. *Bonds* with acceptable credit quality are carried at *amortized value*, which is the face value plus or minus the amount of any purchase discount or premium, as amortized over the life of the bond. Preferred stock is valued at cost and COMMON STOCK INVESTMENTS at year-end market price. Valuations for impaired securities such as bonds in default are determined by the Committee on Valuation of Securities of the NATIONAL ASSOCIATION OF INSURANCE COMMISSIONERS (NAIC). *See also* MANDATORY SECURITIES VALUATION RESERVE.

VALUATION OF LOSS method of setting a dollar value on loss suffered by an insured. In some cases, a loss is straightforward, such as the cost of gall bladder surgery. But with burglary of a home or a traffic accident that damages a car, the amount of loss is open to interpretation. In many cases, the insured needs receipts, appraisal documents or other evidence of value. In other cases, a claim adjuster values the loss and determines how much the insurer will pay.

VALUATION OF POTENTIAL PROPERTY LOSS risk management technique that evaluates property exposures preparatory to managing the risk. Although risk managers consider the ORIGINAL COST, DEPRECIATION, *market value*, and TAX-APPRAISED VALUE of property, *replacement cost* is the most helpful in determining the value of the property, giving the truest indication of the degree of the exposure to be insured or otherwise financed.

VALUATION PREMIUM life insurance rate determined by the valuation of company policy reserves. State regulators set strict standards for policy reserves to make certain that life insurers will have enough assets to make good on their policies. Once the reserves are valued, the company works backward to set a valuation premium that will cover all of its liabilities. However, some companies determine that they can justify setting a GROSS PREMIUM that is lower than the valuation premium because their experience, based on updated mortality tables, is better than that used to determine the valuation premium. If they do charge a premium that is lower, they are required to deposit the difference in a DEFICIENCY RESERVE.

VALUATION RESERVE (SECURITIES VALUATION RESERVE) amount set up as a cushion against fluctuations in securities prices. *See also* MANDATORY VALUATION SECURITIES RESERVE.

VALUE *see* ACTUAL CASH VALUE; MARKET VALUE V. ACTUAL CASH VALUE; MARKET VALUE CLAUSE; REPLACEMENT COST LESS PHYSICAL DEPRECIATION AND OBSOLESCENCE.

VALUED agreement by an insurance company to pay a predetermined amount, as indicated in an insurance policy, should a loss occur.

VALUED CLAUSE provision in an insurance policy that states the monetary value of each piece of property to be insured.

VALUED CONTRACT *see* VALUED POLICY.

VALUED FORM *see* VALUED POLICY.

VALUED MARINE POLICY *see* VALUED POLICY.

VALUED POLICY policy that pays a specified sum not related in any way to the extent of the loss. The term applies to a life insurance policy rather than to a contract of indemnity because the former does not purport to restore an insured (or beneficiary) to the same financial position after a loss as prior to the loss. The sum of money that a life insurance policy pays as a death benefit is a definite amount which may or may not have any relation to the quantitative value of the death. Thus, the life insurance policy is deemed to be a valued policy.

VALUED POLICY LAW legislation in a number of states requiring insurers to pay the FACE AMOUNT of a fire insurance policy in case of total loss to a dwelling (or sometimes another specified type of building), rather than the ACTUAL CASH VALUE of the loss. Such laws in effect override the principle of INDEMNITY that normally governs property and liability insurance contracts.

VALUE REPORTING FORM form that provides coverage for a business whose inventory has fluctuating values during the year. The amount of insurance coverage is adjusted monthly, quarterly, or annually to reflect the changing monetary value of the inventory. The use of this FORM should eliminate the problem of overinsurance as well as under-insurance.

VALUES *see* NONFORFEITABILITY; NONFORFEITURE BENEFIT (OPTION); NONFORFEITURE PROVISION.

VANDALISM AND MALICIOUS MISCHIEF INSURANCE coverage usually written as an endorsement to property policies such as the *Standard Fire Policy*. A loss must be by the intentional acts of vandals. This peril is of particular importance to owners of structures which are not occupied during particular periods during the day, such as schools and churches. Vandals have little risk of being caught during these periods, when they are most likely to strike. Because of high frequency, a high deductible is usually required when insuring churches and schools.

VANDALISM ENDORSEMENT *see* VANDALISM AND MALICIOUS MISCHIEF INSURANCE.

VANISHING PREMIUM (PREMIUM OFFSET) life insurance policy under which there is rapid build-up of cash values due to high initial premiums such that after a given point in time no further premium payments are required (future premium payments are borrowed from the cash value).

VARIABLE ANNUITIES *see* VARIABLE DOLLAR ANNUITY.

VARIABLE BENEFIT PLAN *see* VARIABLE DOLLAR ANNUITY; VARIABLE LIFE INSURANCE.

VARIABLE DOLLAR ANNUITY annuity in which premium payments are used to purchase *accumulation units*, their number depending on the value of each unit. The value of a unit is determined by the value of the portfolio of stocks in which the insurance company invests the premiums.

At the time of the payment of benefits to the annuitant, the accumulation units are converted to a monthly fixed number of units. The variable element is the dollar value of each unit. For example, assume that the annuitant pays a monthly premium of $100. If the accumulation unit value during one month is $50, two units are purchased. In another month, if the value of the accumulation unit is $25, four units are purchased. In a third month, the value of the unit is $10, resulting in the purchase of 10 units. This allows the market use of the investment strategy of dollar cost averaging. Accumulation units are credited to the annuitant's account, a procedure that is similar to purchasing shares in a mutual fund.

When income benefits are scheduled to begin, total accumulation units are converted to assume 100 income benefit units per month. The value of the income unit will vary according to the company's stock investments; in one month the annuitant's income might be $1000, in another month $500, in another month $1200. Changes in the investment experience by the insurance company are passed on to the annuitant but the company absorbs fluctuations in expenses and mortality experience. *See also* ANNUITY.

VARIABLE LIFE INSURANCE investment-oriented *whole life insurance* policy that provides a return linked to an underlying portfolio of securities. The portfolio typically is a group of mutual funds established by the insurer as a *separate account*, with the policyholder given some investment discretion in choosing the mix of assets among, say, a common stock fund, a bond fund, and a money market fund. Variable life insurance offers fixed premiums and a minimum death benefit. The better the total return on the investment portfolio, the higher the death benefit or surrender value of the variable life policy. *See also* INDEXED LIFE INSURANCE.

VARIABLE LIMIT in property insurance coverages, provision whereby the limit of the policy automatically increases at each policy anniversary date, subject to the insured's rejection of such an increase. The objective of the variable limit is to increase the amount of coverage in tandem with the annual increase in the inflation rate so as to prevent less than adequate coverage in the event of a loss. *See also* UNDERINSURANCE.

VARIABLE PAY LIFE INSURANCE *see* VARIABLE PREMIUM LIFE INSURANCE.

VARIABLE PREMIUM LIFE INSURANCE policy that allows premium payments to vary, within certain limits, at the option of the policyholder. In return, the death benefit and rate of cash value accumulation vary with the premium payments. UNIVERSAL LIFE INSURANCE is the most common type of policy offering variable premiums. *See also* FLEXIBLE PREMIUM LIFE INSURANCE.

VARIABLE UNIVERSAL LIFE *see* UNIVERSAL VARIABLE LIFE INSURANCE.

VARIANCE *see* STANDARD DEVIATION OR VARIATION.

VARIANCE FROM PRESCRIBED STANDARDS *see* STANDARD DEVIATION OR VARIATION.

VEHICLE COVERAGE *see* BUSINESS AUTOMOBILE POLICY (BAP); INLAND MARINE INSURANCE (TRANSPORTATION INSURANCE): BUSINESS RISKS; INSTRUMENTALITIES OF TRANSPORTATION INSURANCE; OCEAN MARINE INSURANCE; PERSONAL AUTOMOBILE POLICY (PAP).

VENDING MACHINE MARKETING sale of life insurance policies through vending machines. This method of distribution is generally limited to TRAVEL ACCIDENT INSURANCE, supplemental health or disability policies, or life insurance policies with a small face amount.

VERMIN EXCLUSION section of some INLAND MARINE insurance (*transportation insurance*) and many other property insurance policies excluding coverage for damage to shipped goods by vermin such as rats. *See also* INSECT EXCLUSION.

VESSEL *see* HULL MARINE INSURANCE.

VESTED ACCOUNT *see* VESTING.

VESTED INTEREST *see* VESTING.

VESTING entitlement of a pension plan participant (employee) to receive full benefits at NORMAL RETIREMENT AGE, or a reduced benefit upon EARLY RETIREMENT, whether or not the participant still works for the same employer. The EMPLOYEE RETIREMENT INCOME SECURITY ACT OF 1974 (ERISA) mandates vesting under one of these rules:
1. FORTY-FIVE YEAR RULE
2. FIVE TO FIFTEEN YEAR RULE
3. TEN YEAR RULE
On January 1, 1989, under the TAX REFORM ACT OF 1986, the above vesting requirements will be replaced with the following:
1. full vesting (100%) after a participant completes 5 years of service with an employer; or
2. vesting of 20% after completion of 3 years of service with an employer, increasing by 20% for each year of service thereafter, until 100% vesting is achieved at the end of 7 years of service.

VESTING, CONDITIONAL limitation under a contributory pension plan of an employee's right to receive vested benefits. The employee can withdraw contributions to the pension plan only according to stated conditions. *See also* VESTING.

VESTING, DEFERRED specified requirements of minimum age and years of service to be met by an employee before the individual's benefits are vested. For example, under the TEN YEAR VESTING rule, an employee must work 10 years for the particular employer before benefits vest. *See also* VESTING, IMMEDIATE.

VESTING, FULL *see* FULL VESTING.

VESTING, IMMEDIATE employee's full entitlement, with no waiting period, to benefits under a pension or retirement plan. In the case of a CONTRIBUTORY plan, there is immediate vesting of the employee's own contributions, plus the earnings attributable to those contributions. As to employer contributions in contributory and NONCONTRIBUTORY plans, VESTING depends on the terms of the plans, although maximum time limits for full vesting are set by law. Some plans provide immediate vesting of employer contributions in the case of death or disability. SIMPLIFIED EMPLOYEE PENSION (SEP) plans require immediate vesting of employer contributions. *See also* TAX REFORM ACT OF 1986; VESTING.

VETERANS ADMINISTRATION (VA) U.S. government agency that administers life insurance, health insurance, welfare, mortgage loans, education, pension benefits, and other programs for veterans of the U.S. armed forces.

VETERANS GROUP LIFE INSURANCE (VGLI) five-year nonrenewable TERM LIFE INSURANCE policy for veterans who were covered by SERVICEMENS GROUP LIFE INSURANCE (SEGLI) while on active duty in the U.S. uniformed forces. At the end of the five-year term, the insured may convert the policy to individual *permanent life insurance* with any company that participates in the VGLI program.

VICARIOUS LIABILITY *see* CONTINGENT LIABILITY (VICARIOUS LIABILITY).

VICTIM COMPENSATION payment under a state-sponsored program for victims of crimes. *See also* FEDERAL CRIME INSURANCE.

VISION CARE INSURANCE health insurance coverage for eye examinations and eyeglass or contact lens prescriptions.

VIS MAJOR Latin phrase meaning "overpowering force"; an unavoidable accident or calamity; an accident for which no one is responsible; an ACT OF GOD.

VOIDABLE CONTRACT VALID CONTRACT that can be canceled for cause by one or more parties to the contract. An insurance contract can be voided by the insurer if the insured has used fraudulent means to obtain it or has intentionally concealed information or misrepresented the risk.

VOID CONTRACT apparent agreement that is not a valid contract.

VOLUNTARY COMPENSATION ENDORSEMENT addition to a WORKERS COMPENSATION INSURANCE policy to cover payments to injured employees who are not covered by a state's workers compensation law. This endorsement provides employees who are not covered by the state law a choice of receiving WORKERS COMPENSATION BENEFITS or suing the employer. Under workers compensation laws, employers agree to supply, according to a formula, income lost by workers accidentally injured on the job, as well as medical and rehabilitation benefits and death and survivor benefits. In exchange, these benefits are to be the final obligation of the employer to compensate workers, or the exclusive remedy. However, there has been considerable erosion of the exclusive remedy concept since the early 1970s. Workers have been allowed to sue their employers for various types of on-the-job injuries. Each state has its own workers compensation law.

VOLUNTARY DEDUCTIBLE EMPLOYEE· CONTRIBUTION PLAN pension plan that allows an employee to contribute by electing to have money deducted from each paycheck. Some qualified plans such as 401 (k) allow employees to contribute pre-tax dollars, while others require employees to put in after-tax dollars.

VOLUNTARY GOVERNMENT INSURANCE *see* SOCIAL INSURANCE.

VOLUNTARY INSURANCE *see* SOCIAL INSURANCE.

VOLUNTARY PLAN TERMINATION ending a pension plan at the election of an employer or sponsor. The employer has the unilateral right to change or terminate a pension plan at any time. However, the termination must meet requirements set out by the EMPLOYEE RETIRE-MENT INCOME SECURITY ACT OF 1974 (ERISA). Assets must be distributed to participants according to Federal guidelines.

VOLUNTARY RESERVE amount established by an insurance company, but not required by state law, for any of a number of reasons, such as a reserve for payment of future dividends. A voluntary reserve is likely to appear as a LIABILITY on the company's balance sheet. Contrasts with STATUTORY RESERVES. *See also* BALANCE SHEET RE-SERVES; POLICY RESERVE.

VOYAGE POLICY OCEAN MARINE INSURANCE covering one trip. Ocean marine insurance is written either for a specific time period or per trip. A voyage policy is usually written for cargo, whereas a *time policy* covers a ship.

W

WAGE INDEX table used, among other purposes, to determine monthly Social Security benefit for a retired or disabled worker and his or her dependents. The AVERAGE MONTHLY WAGE (AMW) of the worker is computed, disregarding certain periods of low earnings. The AMW is used to determine the PRIMARY INSURANCE AMOUNT (PIA). Then, benefits are figured from the table depending on how old the worker is upon retirement, whether there are dependents or survivors and when they wil! retire.

WAGERING v. INSURANCE common misunderstanding about insurance. In gambling a RISK is created that did not exist prior to placing a bet. Under insurance, a risk exists whether or not an insurance policy is purchased. For example, the uncertainty of one's home burning exists independent of the purchase of insurance; the purchase of insurance should not affect the probability of loss.

WAITING PERIOD *see* DISABILITY INCOME INSURANCE (ELIMINATION PERIOD).

WAIVE *see* WAIVER; WAIVER OF INVENTORY CLAUSE; WAIVER OF PREMIUM (WP); WAIVER OF PREMIUM FOR PAYER BENEFIT; WAIVER OF RESTORATION PREMIUM; WAIVER OF SUBROGATION RIGHTS CLAUSE.

WAIVER relinquishment of a legal right to act. For example, an insured relies on statements of an agent of an insurance company concerning coverages under an insurance policy. The agent by his actions may have waived certain provisions the insurance company has written in the insurance policy, with the company's authority. Another example would be the provision in the HOMEOWNERS INSURANCE POLICY which suspends coverage if a hazard is increased by the actions of an insured. An insured who stores explosives near his home notifies the insurance company; the company gives him permission to do so, thereby waiving its defense of the increase in hazard clause.

WAIVER OF INVENTORY CLAUSE provision in property insurance that waives, under specified circumstances, the requirement for an inventory of undamaged property when a damage claim is filed. A COINSURANCE clause in a fire insurance policy typically requires such an inventory or appraisal at the time of a claim. The waiver avoids the expense of an inventory when the claim is small. Under one common formula, the inventory requirement is waived when the claim is for less than $10,000 and is also for less than 5% of the limit of all insurance coverage applicable to the property.

WAIVER OF PREMIUM FOR DISABILITY *see* RIDERS, LIFE POLICIES.

WAIVER OF PREMIUM FOR PAYER BENEFIT clause added to an insurance policy providing WAIVER OF PREMIUM (WP) if the premium payer dies or becomes disabled. For example, this option is available on insurance policies on a child's life where the premium is paid by an adult, or on life and health policies for adults..

WAIVER OF PREMIUM RIDER *see* WAIVER OF PREMIUM (WP).

WAIVER OF PREMIUM (WP) in life insurance, action by an insurance company canceling premium payments by an insured who has been disabled for at least six months. The policy remains in force and continues to build cash values and pay dividends (if it is a participating policy), just as if the insured was still making premium payments. Experts suggest that this clause should be considered in a life insurance policy since the probability of becoming disabled is 7 to 10 times greater than death at younger and middle ages.

WAIVER OF RESTORATION PREMIUM clause in a SURETY BOND contract providing for restoration of coverage after a loss without requirement of a RESTORATION PREMIUM.

WAIVER OF SUBROGATION RIGHTS CLAUSE endorsement to a property liability policy whereby an insurer gives up the right to take action against a third party for a loss suffered by an insured. Typically, under terms of the SUBROGATION CLAUSE, the insurer, having paid an insured for a loss, takes over any rights possessed by the insured who has suffered the loss. For example, an insured, John Smith, is hit by another car while he is driving. His insurance company pays his claim and then may sue or attempt to recover damages from the other driver. In certain instances, the insured might want to get a waiver of subrogation rights from the insurer. For example, if a landlord assured a tenant that he was not responsible for damage to his property, the landlord could make good on his promise only by getting the insurer to waive its subrogation rights. Otherwise, if the landlord's property was damaged by the tenant, the insurer would have to pay the claim and could then try to collect damages from the tenant.

WANTON DISREGARD legal phrase used in NEGLIGENCE cases to describe one person's overwhelming lack of care for the rights or well-being of another. Wanton disregard of another's rights is evidence of GROSS NEGLIGENCE..

WAR DAMAGE INSURANCE CORPORATION government reinsurance program that provided coverage for U.S. properties during World War II. Private insurers shared the first layer of coverage, with the government providing catastrophic loss coverage. This is one of several government insurance programs for exposures that private insurers cannot cover because techniques of spreading the risk do not apply.

WAREHOUSE BOND type of surety bond that guarantees that goods stored in a warehouse will be delivered upon presentation of a re~eipt.

WAREHOUSERS LIABILITY FORM special insurance that covers warehousers liability to customers whose property is damaged by an insured peril while in the custody of an insured warehouser. Policy deductibles may range from $50 to $10,000. Typical exclusions are war risks, money, securities, and spoilage of perishable goods.

WAREHOUSE-TO-WAREHOUSE CLAUSE part of an *ocean marine* policy that provides coverage of goods through all of the stages of a journey. Coverage begins when goods leave the warehouse of a shipper, and continues until they reach the customer's warehouse.

WAR EXCLUSION CLAUSE provision in a life insurance policy that death benefits will not be paid in the event an insured dies from war related causes; or in lieu of a death benefit there is a return of premiums plus interest, or a refund equal to the reserve portion (cash value) of the policy. For example, during the Vietnam War, if a whole life policy with a war exclusion clause had a face amount of $10,000 and an insured died as the result of war related injuries, the beneficiary would receive the cash value of the policy. This clause cannot be added to a policy that had none originally. If it is included in a policy bought in time of war, it is typically removed by life insurance companies at the war's end, and once removed, can never be restored.

WARN *see* WORKER ADJUSTMENT AND RETRAINING NOTIFICATION ACT (WARN).

WAR PERIL *see* WAR RISK INSURANCE.

WARRANTY pledge by an insured in writing and a part of the actual contract, that a particular condition exists or does not exist. For example, an insured warrants that a sprinkler system works. In exchange, the insurance company charges a reduced premium for fire coverage. Statements by an insured in an application for property insurance are deemed to be warranties, not representations as is generally the case in life insurance policy applications. *See also* REPRESENTATIONS.

WAR RISKS exposures usually excluded from life and health insurance, or subject to a maximum limit if covered. For property coverage, *see* WAR RISK INSURANCE.

WAR RISK INSURANCE coverage for damage due to peril of war, usually written as part of an OCEAN MARINE INSURANCE policy.

WATERCRAFT ENDORSEMENT addition to the HOMEOWNERS INSURANCE POLICY and SPECIAL MULTIPERIL INSURANCE (SMP) policy that provides liability and medical coverage for damages resulting from the operation of motor boats too large to qualify for insurance under homeowners and SMP policies.

WATERCRAFT NONOWNED INSURANCE endorsement to COMMERCIAL GENERAL LIABILITY INSURANCE (CGL) for a business responsible for boats it does not own. Whether the boats are leased from another firm or owned by employees who operate them for the benefit of the business owner, a business has a liability exposure that is not covered by a CGL policy; the special endorsement is needed for this coverage.

WATER DAMAGE INSURANCE protection in the event of accidental discharge, leakage, or overflow of water from plumbing systems, heating, air conditioning, and refrigerating systems, and rain or snow through broken doors, open doors, windows, and skylights resulting in damage or destruction of the property scheduled in the policy. This type of water damage coverage can also be acquired through an endorsement of a standard property insurance policy.

WATER DAMAGE LEGAL LIABILITY INSURANCE coverage for an insured's liability for damage to another's property from leakage or overflow of water. Some liability policies specifically exclude water damage, including that caused by rain or snow. Therefore, a special policy was necessary to cover this exposure. However, most liability policies today have dropped this exclusion, and coverage for water damage liability is part of the regular liability policy.

WATER EXCLUSION CLAUSE provision in many property insurance policies that excludes coverage for floods and backup from sewers or drains and underground water. Because floods and hurricanes are generally confined to certain areas, only policyholders in those areas need flood insurance. Therefore, it is impossible for underwriters to spread the risk, which is the basis of underwriting. But because homeowners in the endangered areas need insurance, the U.S. government developed a special FEDERAL FLOOD INSURANCE program.

WATER POLLUTION LIABILITY obligations of shipowners for water polluted by spills from their ships. If a ship discharges oil or other polluting or hazardous substances into the water, the ship owner is responsible either for removing them, paying for their removal, or, if the substances cannot be removed, paying a fine. Following passage of the WATER QUALITY IMPROVEMENT ACT OF 1970 establishing the liability of shipowners, marine underwriters formed the WATER QUALITY INSURANCE SYNDICATE to provide insurance.

WATER QUALITY IMPROVEMENT ACT OF 1970 Federal law that requires shipowners to clean up or pay for the cleanup of waters polluted by discharges from their ships. Shipowners may be refused navigation privileges if they cannot demonstrate that they have the financial resources to pay for cleanups.

WATER QUALITY INSURANCE SYNDICATE group of marine underwriters formed in 1971 to provide coverage for shipowners for WATER POLLUTION LIABILITY. The Federal WATER QUALITY IMPROVEMENT ACT OF 1970 made shipowners responsible for hazardous substances discharged by their ships into the water. This led to the Water Quality Insurance Syndicate. Coverage extends to liabilities imposed by states. The syndicate vouches for the financial responsibility of those it insures.

WEAR AND TEAR EXCLUSION denial of coverage for damage, in INLAND MARINE insurance, stemming from routine use of the property. Property can be expected to deteriorate somewhat over time from normal use. This is not considered an insurable loss.

WEDDING PRESENTS FLOATER personal property insurance that provides ALL-RISKS coverage for wedding presents, wherever they may be in the world, until they are permanently located. Because the new owners of wedding presents may not yet have a home or a HOMEOWNERS INSURANCE POLICY, and because their gifts may be moved from place to place until they are settled, this policy fills a gap in coverage, but it can be purchased only for as long as 90 days following the wedding.

WEEKLY PREMIUM INSURANCE *see* DEBIT INSURANCE (HOME SERVICE INSURANCE, INDUSTRIAL INSURANCE).

WEIGHT OF ICE, SNOW, OR SLEET INSURANCE coverage for damage to a building or its contents due to the weight of these elements. Outdoor property such as patios, swimming pools, and sidewalks, are usually excluded.

WELFARE AND PENSION PLANS DISCLOSURE ACT Federal law that requires administrators of pension plans with more than 25 participants to file a plan description with the U.S. Department of Labor. A plan description includes schedules of benefits, type of administration, and copies of the plan. If the plan has more than 100 participants, the administrator must also file an annual financial report. This information must be made available to plan participants upon request and the person responsible for handling the funds must be bonded.

WELLNESS PROGRAM employee benefit program which emphasizes the pursuit of a lifestyle that minimizes the occurrence of sickness through an organized program of preventive medicine. Such a program includes screening for high blood pressure, obesity, breast cancer, and stress; a smoke-free workplace; a systematized exercise and fitness approach for general health; and training and education programs for employees concerning proper nutrition, stress management, weight control, cardiopulmonary resuscitation, and prenatal care.

WHITE COLLAR CRIME *see* BLANKET POSITION BOND; BOND; FIDELITY BOND; JUDICIAL BOND; SURETY BOND.

WHOLE LIFE ANNUITY *see* ANNUITY; ANNUITY DUE; LIFE ANNUITY CERTAIN; PURE ANNUITY; REFUND ANNUITY.

WHOLE LIFE ANNUITY DUE *see* ANNUITY DUE.

WHOLE LIFE INSURANCE *see* ORDINARY LIFE INSURANCE.

WHOLESALE INSURANCE *see* FRANCHISE INSURANCE (WHOLESALE INSURANCE).

WHOLESALE LIFE INSURANCE variation of GROUP LIFE INSURANCE that covers a small group of persons who work for the same employer. With group life insurance, the employer owns the policy; with wholesale insurance, each employee applies for and owns his own policy. However, the employer must agree to pay at least part of wholesale life insurance premiums for the group to qualify for wholesale insurance. Wholesale insurance was devised for groups as small as 10 persons when group insurance was limited by law to a minimum of 50 members. Today, group insurance is sold to smaller groups and wholesale insurance is written for groups as small as five persons. *See also* FRANCHISE INSURANCE (WHOLESALE INSURANCE).

WINDSTORM HAZARD *see* STORM INSURANCE; (WINDSTORM INSURANCE).

WINDSTORM INSURANCE additional coverage available on most property insurance policies through the EXTENDED COVERAGE ENDORSEMENT. Windstorms, including hurricanes, cyclones, and high winds, are not among the covered perils under most property insurance policies. *See also* STORM INSURANCE (WINDSTORM INSURANCE).

WISCONSIN STATE LIFE FUND life insurance distribution system under which the state underwrites and sells life insurance to any resident of Wisconsin who makes application.

WINTER RANGE FORM type of livestock insurance that covers for cattle and sheep on the range from October 1 to May 1 in the Western states. Perils insured against are the weather, including freezing; most natural disasters; riot and civil commotion; collision with vehicles; and theft.

WITH BENEFIT OF SURVIVORSHIP phrase describing a form of joint tenancy ownership where property passes to the survivors when one party dies.

WITHDRAWAL BENEFITS, PENSION PLAN *see* PENSION PLANS: WITHDRAWAL BENEFITS.

WITHDRAWAL CREDITS, PENSION PLAN *see* PENSION PLANS: WITHDRAWAL BENEFITS.

WOMEN LEADERS ROUND TABLE group of women life insurance agents who sell sufficient insurance to qualify for membership. The round table is sponsored by the NATIONAL ASSOCIATION OF LIFE UNDER-WRITERS (NALU).

WOOL GROWERS FLOATER INLAND MARINE policy addition that provides coverage to owners of sheep, and to warehousemen who store wool, as well as wool in transit.

WORK AND MATERIALS CLAUSE provision in most property insurance policies that permits a policyholder to use the insured premises to store materials and handle them in the manner needed to pursue his or her line of business. Without this clause, a policy may be voided for fraud, concealment, or misrepresentation of an undisclosed INCREASED HAZARD. The clause provides a defense for a policyholder against a charge of increasing the hazard of a workplace if the materials in question are necessary to the business.

WORKER ADJUSTMENT AND RETRAINING NOTIFICATION ACT (WARN) Federal law, effective February 4, 1989, that requires company notification of employees prior to laying them off or closing a plant or an office. Workers covered under WARN are to include office workers, field representatives, agents, managers, and any other employees of insurance companies. To be affected by WARN, the company must employ at least 100 full-time employees. Part-time employees are not included in the 100 full-time employees count unless the total hours worked per week by all employees is at least 4,000 hours. WARN requires the company to notify its employees of impending lay-offs when one or more of the following circumstances occur:
1. at least 500 employees are terminated or laid off during a 30-day period.
2. at least 50 employees are terminated or laid off, comprising at least 33% of the total employment force during a 30-day period.
3. a plant or an office is closed, whether on a temporary or permanent basis.

WORKERS COMPENSATION *see* WORKERS COMPENSATION INSURANCE.

WORKERS COMPENSATION BENEFITS income, medical, rehabilitation, death, and survivor payments to workers injured on the job. State workers compensation laws, which date from early in the twentieth century, provide that employers take responsibility for on-the-job injuries. Each state defines the benefit level for employers in that state. Although these benefits were designed to be the final obligation of an employer to his employees, there has been considerable erosion of this concept since the early 1970s; workers have been allowed by the courts to sue employers for various on-the-job injuries in addition to workers compensation benefits. Because workers compensation benefits are a routine and fairly predictable risk, many employers use SELF INSURANCE. Some states mandate that employers buy workers compensation insurance from a state fund, but some offer a choice of a state fund, self insurance, or commercial insurance.

WORKERS COMPENSATION CATASTROPHE COVER excess coverage for employers who use SELF INSURANCE for routine workers compensation risks. Many employers consider workers compensation exposure to be routine and predictable and set up a fund to pay these losses themselves rather than trade premium and claims dollars with an insurance company. To supplement a self-insurance program, an employer may buy insurance for catastrophic loss above a certain limit. A *stop loss aggregate contract* will pay all losses in one year over a specified dollar limit. A SPECIFIC EXCESS CONTRACT pays losses over a stated limit per accident.

WORKERS COMPENSATION, COVERAGE A agreement under which an insurance company promises to pay all compensation and all benefits required of an insured employer under the workers compensation act of the state or states listed in the policy.

WORKERS COMPENSATION, COVERAGE B coverage under a commercial *Workers Compensation Policy* for situations in which an employee not covered under Workers Compensation laws could sue for injuries suffered under common law liability.

WORKERS COMPENSATION INSURANCE coverage providing four types of benefits (medical care, death, disability, rehabilitation) for employee job-related injuries or diseases as a matter of right (without regard to fault). This insurance is usually purchased by the employer from an insurance company although in a few states there are monopolistic state funds through which the insurance must be purchased. The premium rate is based on a percentage of the employer's payroll and varies according to the employee's occupation. *See also* WORKERS COMPENSATION BENEFITS.

WORLD INSURANCE *see* WORLDWIDE COVERAGE.

WORLDWIDE COVERAGE endorsement to the COMMERCIAL GENERAL LIABILITY INSURANCE (CGL) policy that provides liability coverage to an insured business for damages anywhere in the world. Policies typically have territorial limits for liability coverage, but this endorsement extends coverage worldwide, so long as a damage suit is brought in the U.S. or Canada.

WORRY state of anxiety and distress. One goal of adequate insurance is to eliminate, or alleviate, worry on the part of a policyholder. Many people, for example, are concerned that they would not be able to handle the financial burden if they became ill, or that their spouse would be impoverished if they died. Insurance is designed to eliminate these concerns by assuring that benefits will be provided.

WRAP-UP INSURANCE liability policy that covers all liability exposures for a large group that has something in common. For example, wrap-up insurance can be written for all the various businesses working together on a special project, to provide coverage for losses arising out of that work only.

WRIGHT, ELIZUR Massachusetts Commissioner of Insurance responsible for the passage of legislation (1861) which guaranteed policyowners of that state equity in the cash value of their life insurance. The nonforfeiture legislation stipulated that four-fifths of the cash value of a life insurance policy be applied to the purchase of extended term life insurance.

WRITE to sell a specific amount of insurance.

WRITTEN BUSINESS insurance for which (1) an application has been filed but the first premium has not yet been paid or (2) a life insurance policy that has not yet been delivered to an insured.

WRITTEN PREMIUMS total premiums generated from all policies written by an insurance company within a given period of time. *See also* EARNED PREMIUM.

WRONGFUL ACT error, misstatement, or breach of duty by an officer or director of a company that results in a lawsuit against the company. DIRECTORS AND OFFICERS LIABILITY INSURANCE covers claims arising from wrongful acts by directors or officers of a company while in that capacity. Wrongful acts specifically exclude dishonesty, theft, libel, and slander. During the liability insurance crisis of the 1980s, this type of coverage became unavailable in many industries as wrongful acts received an increasingly liberal interpretation by the courts and many expensive lawsuits were filed against business firms. *See also* TORT; TORT, DEFENSE AGAINST UNINTENTIONAL; TORT, INTENTIONAL; TORT, UNINTENTIONAL.

WRONGFUL DEATH death caused by a person without legal justification. Wrongful death may be the result of negligence, such as when a drunken driver hits and kills someone; or it may be intentional, as when someone kills another person with a gun. In most states, suits can be filed for damages caused by wrongful death. Much work has been done in an attempt to put a value on human life and, therefore, to determine the compensation allowable to the family of an individual who has been killed. *See also* HUMAN LIFE VALUE APPROACH (ECONOMIC VALUE OF AN INDIVIDUAL LIFE (EVOIL).

WRONGFUL TERMINATION CLAIM under a general liability policy, a claim by an employer arising when an employee terminated by a supervisor without authority or just cause brings suit against the employer. Such a claim is covered under most general liability policies provided that the following elements are in evidence:
1. the insurance policy is in force on the date of loss.
2. there has been no willful misinterpretation of any material facts.
3. the POLICYHOLDER did not have a willful (preconceived) intent to harm or injure the employee who was terminated.

X Y Z

XCU *see* EXPLOSION, COLLAPSE, AND UNDERGROUND EXCLUSION.

YACHT INSURANCE coverage for fire and explosion, against fire and any damage caused by explosion whether or not fire ensues, and whether or not an explosion occurs on or off board; sinking from floating debris, sunken hulks, and reefs; stranding against sand bars and filled channels resulting in salvage costs, material and labor expenses to refloat and repair a yacht; collision causing legal liability for damage to another vessel; assailing thieves (theft by forcible entry); and jettison and barratry of mariners or masters. Coverage for liability for bodily injury and loss of life is available through OCEAN MARINE PROTECTION AND INDEMNITY INSURANCE.

YEARLY RENEWABLE TERM (YRT) *see* RENEWABLE TERM LIFE INSURANCE.

YEARS CERTAIN ANNUITY *see* LIFE ANNUITY CERTAIN.

YEARS OF SERVICE length of employment as measured to determine eligibility, VESTING, and benefit levels for employee participants in tax *qualified pension* plans. There is often a requirement that years of service be continuous (without unexcused breaks).

YIELD OF ASSETS *see* YIELD ON ASSETS.

YIELD ON ASSETS annual or other periodic rate of return on investments. Because life insurance companies act as custodians of premiums for many years, until money must be paid out in death benefits or other types of claims, they invest it to achieve a yield adequate to meet these obligations. Yield is also important to the policyowner of life policies that include a specific investment element. For example, some *annuities* and CASH VALUE LIFE INSURANCE policies pay a yield that approximates the market rate the policyholder could get elsewhere. While other contracts, such as a *variable annuity* and VARIABLE LIFE INSURANCE do not guarantee a specified yield, they pay one based on the performance of the underlying investments.

YIELD RATE *see* YIELD ON ASSETS.

YORK ANTWERP RULES treaty adopted by most major countries to determine adjustment for *general average* in OCEAN MARINE INSURANCE.

YRT *see* YEARLY RENEWABLE TERM (YRT).

ZONE SYSTEM method for triennial examination of insurance companies as established by the NATIONAL ASSOCIATION OF INSURANCE COMMISSIONERS (NAIC). Teams are composed of representatives from several state insurance commissioners offices. Their findings are acceptable by all the states in which the examined insurance companies are licensed to conduct business.

ABBREVIATIONS AND ACRONYMS

A

AAI Alliance of American Insurers

AIA American Insurance Association

AIME Average Indexed Monthly Earnings

AMW Average Monthly Wage

ASO Administrative Services Only

B

BAP Business Automobile Policy

BOP Businessowners Policy

C

CAS Casualty Actuarial Society

CEBS Certified Employee Benefit Specialist

CFP Certified Financial Planner

CGL Comprehensive General Liability Insurance

ChFC Chartered Financial Consultant

CLU Chartered Life Underwriter

COLA Cost of Living Adjustment

CPCU Chartered Property and Casualty Underwriter

CSI Commissioners Standard Industrial Mortality Table

CSO Commissioners Standard Ordinary Mortality Table

D

DB&C Dwelling, Buildings, and Contents Insurance

DI Disability Income

DOC Drive Other Car Insurance

DWI Driving While Intoxicated

E

EEL Emergency Exposure Limit

ERISA Employee Retirement Income Security Act of 1974

ESOP Employee Stock Ownership Plan

EVOIL Economic Value of an Individual Life

F

FAIR Fair Access to Insurance Requirements Plan

FCAS Fellow, Casualty Actuarial Society

FDIC Federal Deposit Insurance Corporation

FEGLI Federal Employee Group Life Insurance

FELA Federal Employers Liability Act

FLMI Fellow, Life Management Institute

FPA Free of Particular Average

FSA Fellow, Society of Actuaries

FSLIC Federal Savings and Loan Insurance Corporation

FTC Federal Trade Commission

G

GA General Agent

GAAP Generally Accepted Accounting Principles

GAB General Adjustment Bureau

GAMC General Agents and Managers Conference

GIC Guaranteed Investment Contract

H

HIAA Health Insurance Association of America

HMO Health Maintenance Organization

HOLUA Home Office Life Underwriters Association

I

IBNR Incurred But Not Reported Losses

ICC Interstate Commerce Commission

IIA Insurance Institute of America

IIAA Independent Insurance Agents of America

IPG Immediate Participation Guarantee Plan

IRA Individual Retirement Account

IRIS Insurance Regulatory Information System

ISO Insurance Services Office

L

LIC Life Insurers Conference

LIMRA Life Insurance Marketing and Research Association

LOMA Life Office Management Association

LUPAC Life Underwriter Political Action Committee

LUTC Life Underwriting Training Council

M

MDO Monthly Debit Ordinary Insurance

MDRT Million Dollar Round Table

MLF Maximum Forseeable Loss

MIB Medical Information Bureau

MPL Maximum Probable Loss

N

NAIC National Association of Insurance Commissioners

NAII National Association of Independent Insurance Adjusters

NALC National Association of Life Companies

NALU National Association of Life Underwriting

NASD National Association of Securities Dealers

NATB National Automobile Theft Bureau

NFPA National Fire Protection Association

NSLI National Service Life Insurance

O

OASDHI Old Age, Survivors, Disability, and Health Insurance

OPIC Overseas Private Investment Corporation

OSHA Occupational Safety and Health Act

P

PAC Preauthorized Check System

P&I Protection and Indemnity Insurance

PAP Personal Automobile Policy

PAYSOP Payroll Stock Ownership Plans

PBGC Pension Benefit Guaranty Corporation

PEL Permissible Exposure Limit

PIA Primary Insurance Amount

PIA Professional Insurance Agents

PIP Personal Injury Protection

PML Probable Maximum Loss

PPO Preferred Provider Organization

PSRO Professional Standards Review Organization

Q

QTIP Qualified Terminable Interest Property Trust

R

RAM Reverse-Annuity Mortgage

RRSP Registered Retirement Savings Plan

S

SA Society of Actuaries

SAA Surety Association of America

SBLI Savings Bank Life Insurance

SEC Securities and Exchange Commission

SEP Simplified Employee Pension

SEUA South-Eastern Underwriters Association Case

SGLI Servicemen's Group Life Insurance

SIPC Securities Investor Protection Corporation

SIR Self-Insured Retention

SMP Special Multiperil Insurance

SSI Supplemental Security Income

T

TDA Tax Deferred Annuity

TEFRA Tax Equity and Financial Responsibility Acts of 1982 and 1983

TIAA-CREF Teachers Insurance and Annuity Association—College Retirement Equities Fund

TIRB Transportation Insurance Rating Bureau

TLO Total Loss Only Insurance

TSA Tax-Sheltered Annuity

U

UL Underwriters Laboratories Inc.

V

VA Verterans Administration

VGLI Veterans Group Life Insurance

W

WP Waiver of Premium

Y

YRT Yearly Renewable Term

More selected BARRON'S titles:

DICTIONARY OF COMPUTER TERMS, 2nd EDITION
Douglas Downing and Michael Covington
Nearly 1,000 computer terms are clearly explained, and sample programs included. Paperback, $8.95, Canada $11.95/ISBN 4152-6, 288 pages

DICTIONARY OF FINANCE AND INVESTMENT TERMS,
3rd EDITION, *John Downs and Jordan Goodman*
Defines and explains over 3000 Wall Street terms for professionals, business students, and average investors.
Paperback $9.95, Canada $13.95/ISBN 4631-5, 544 pages

DICTIONARY OF INSURANCE TERMS, 2nd EDITION
Harvey W. Rubin
Approximately 3000 insurance terms are defined as they relate to property, casualty, life, health, and other types of insurance.
Paperback, $9.95, Canada $13.95/ISBN 4632-3, 416 pages

DICTIONARY OF REAL ESTATE TERMS, 2nd EDITION
Jack P. Friedman, Jack C. Harris, and Bruce Lindeman
Defines over 1200 terms, with examples and illustrations. A key reference for everyone in real estate. Comprehensive and current.
Paperback $9.95, Canada $13.95/ISBN 3898-3, 224 pages

ACCOUNTING HANDBOOK, *Joel G. Siegel and Jae K. Shim*
Provides accounting rules, guidelines, formulas and techniques etc. to help students and business professionals work out accounting problems.
Hardcover: $24.95, Canada $33.95/ISBN 6176-4, 832 pages

REAL ESTATE HANDBOOK, 2nd EDITION
Jack P. Friedman and Jack C. Harris
A dictionary/reference for everyone in real estate. Defines over 1500 legal, financial, and architectural terms.
Hardcover, $21.95, Canada $29.95/ISBN 5758-9, 700 pages

HOW TO PREPARE FOR REAL ESTATE LICENSING
EXAMINATIONS-SALESPERSON AND BROKER, 4th EDITION
Bruce Lindeman and Jack P. Friedman
Reviews current exam topics and features updated model exams and supplemental exams, all with explained answers.
Paperback, $10.95, Canada $14.95/ISBN 4355-3, 340 pages

BARRON'S FINANCE AND INVESTMENT HANDBOOK,
3rd EDITION, *John Downes and Jordan Goodman*
This hard-working handbook of essential information defines more than 3000 key terms, and explores 30 basic investment opportunities. The investment information is thoroughly up-to-date. Hardcover $26.95, Canada $36.95/ISBN 6188-8, approx. 1152 pages

FINANCIAL TABLES FOR MONEY MANAGEMENT
Stephen S. Solomon, Dr. Clifford Marshall, Martin Pepper,
Jack P. Friedman and Jack C. Harris
Pocket-sized handbooks of interest and investment rates tables used easily by average investors and mortgage holders. Paperback
Savings and Loans, $6.95, Canada $9.95/ISBN 2745-0, 272 pages
Real Estate Loans, $6.95, Canada $9.95/ISBN 2744-2, 336 pages
Mortgage Payments, $5.95, Canada $8.50/ISBN 2728-0, 304 pages
Stocks and Bonds, $5.50, Canada $7.95/ISBN 2727-2, 256 pages
Comprehensive Annuities, $5.50, Canada $7.95/ISBN 2726-4, 160 pages
Canadian Mortgage Payments, Canada $9.95/ISBN 3939-4, 336 pages
Adjustable Rate Mortgages, $5.95, Canada $8.50/ISBN 3764-2, 288 pages

All prices are in U.S. and Canadian dollars and subject to change without notice. At your bookseller, or order direct adding 10% postage (minimum charge $1.75, Canada $2.00), N.Y. residents add sales tax.   ISBN PREFIX: 0-8120

Barron's Educational Series, Inc.
250 Wireless Boulevard, Hauppauge, NY 11788
Call toll-free: 1-800-645-3476, in NY 1-800-257-5729
In Canada: Georgetown Book Warehouse
34 Armstrong Ave., Georgetown, Ontario L7G 4R9
Call toll-free: 1-800-247-7160

More selected BARRON'S titles:

DICTIONARY OF ACCOUNTING TERMS
Siegel and Shim
Nearly 2500 terms related to accounting are defined.
Paperback, $9.95, Can. $13.95 (3766-9)

DICTIONARY OF ADVERTISING AND DIRECT MAIL TERMS
Imber and Toffler
Nearly 3000 terms used in the ad industry are defined.
Paperback, $9.95, Can. $13.95 (3765-0)

DICTIONARY OF BANKING TERMS
Fitch
Nearly 3000 terms related to banking, finance and money
management.
Paperback, $9.95, Can. $13.95 (3946-7)

DICTIONARY OF BUSINESS TERMS
Friedman, general editor
Over 6000 entries define business terms.
Paperback, $9.95, Can. $13.95 (3775-8)

BARRON'S BUSINESS REVIEW SERIES
These guides explain topics covered in a college-level business
course.
Each book: paperback
ACCOUNTING, 2nd EDITION. *Eisen.* $11.95, Can. $15.95 (4375-8)
BUSINESS LAW, *Hardwicke and Emerson.* $11.95, Can. $15.95 (3495-3)
BUSINESS STATISTICS, *Downing and Clark.* $11.95, Can. $15.95 (3576-3)
ECONOMICS, *Wessels.* $10.95, Can. $14.95 (3560-7)
FINANCE, 2nd EDITION. *Groppelli and Nikbakht.* $11.95,
Can. $15.95 (4373-1)
MANAGEMENT, *Montana and Charnov.* $10.95, Can. $14.95 (3559-3)
MARKETING, *Sandhusen.* $11.95, Can. $15.95 (3494-5)
QUANTITATIVE METHODS, *Downing and Clark.* $10.95,
Can. $14.95 (3947-5)

TALKING BUSINESS SERIES: BILINGUAL DICTIONARIES
Five bilingual dictionaries translate about 3000 terms not found in
most foreign phrasebooks.
Each book: paperback
TALKING BUSINESS IN FRENCH, *Le Gal.* $9.95, Can. $13.95
(3745-6)
TALKING BUSINESS IN GERMAN, *Strutz.* $8.95, Can. $11.95
(3747-2)
TALKING BUSINESS IN ITALIAN, *Rakus.* $6.95, Can. $9.95
(3754-5)
TALKING BUSINESS IN JAPANESE, *C. Akiyama and N. Akiyama.*
$8.95, Can. $11.95 (3848-7)
TALKING BUSINESS IN KOREAN, *Cheong.* $8.95, Can. $11.95
(3992-0)
TALKING BUSINESS IN SPANISH, *Fryer and Faria.* $9.95,
Can. $13.95 (3769-3)

Barron's Educational Series, Inc.
250 Wireless Boulevard, Hauppauge, NY 11788
Call toll-free: 1-800-645-3476, in NY 1-800-257-5729
In Canada: Georgetown Book Warehouse
34 Armstrong Ave., Georgetown, Ontario L7G 4R9
Call toll-free: 1-800-247-7160